Arctic Ocean

80°N

NORWAY

SWEDEN

FINLAND

ESTONIA

RUSSIA

ARCTIC CIRCLE

60°N

DENMARK

LATVIA

LITHUANIA

NETH.

Spy ● Neander Valley

POLAND BELARUS

BEL.

LUX. CZECH REP. SLOVAKIA UKRAINE

Heidelberg (Mauer)

FRANCE

AUS. HUNG. ROMANIA

KAZAKHSTAN

MONGOLIA

60°N

Krapina

SWITZERLAND

1

SLOVENIA MOLDOVA

2

UZBEKISTAN

Jinniushan

NORTH KOREA

Arago

3

BULGARIA

Dmanisi

Teshik Tash

KYRGYZSTAN

Zhoukoudian

JAPAN

40°N

Ceprano ●

Petralona ●

5

GEORGIA

ARMENIA AZERBAIJAN

TAJIKISTAN

SOUTH KOREA

Tighenif ●

4

GREECE

TURKEY

TURKMENISTAN

Lantian

Dali

CHINA

TUNISIA

CYPRUS

SYRIA

IRAN

AFGHANISTAN

Hexian

Amud ●

LEBANON ISRAEL

IRAQ

Shanidar

Skhul/Tabun

JORDAN

KUWAIT

PAKISTAN

NEPAL

BHUTAN

Maba

TAIWAN

ALGERIA

LIBYA

EGYPT

SAUDI ARABIA

BAHRAIN QATAR

U.A.E.

BANGLADESH

HONG KONG (U.K.)

TROPIC OF CANCER

20°N

OMAN

INDIA

MYANMAR (BURMA)

LAOS

MACAU (Port.)

Pacific Ocean

NIGER

Toros-Menalla ●

CHAD

SUDAN

ERITREA

YEMEN

THAILAND

VIETNAM

PHILIPPINES

NORTHERN MARIANA ISLANDS (U.S.)

REPUBLIC OF THE MARSHALL ISLANDS

NIGERIA

DJIBOUTI

Hadar ●

CAMBODIA

Middle Awash (Aramis; Bouri)

CENTRAL AFRICAN REP.

Bodo ●

ETHIOPIA

SRI LANKA

Omo ●

BRUNEI

FEDERATED STATES OF MICRONESIA

CAMEROON

SOMALIA

East and West Turkana

MALDIVES

MALAYSIA

TOGO

UGANDA

Tugen Hills ● Kanapoi

Borneo

EQUATOR

0°

GUINEA

GABON

RWANDA

KENYA

Singapore SINGAPORE

SAO TOME PRINCIPE

CONGO

BURUNDI

Olduvai/Laetoli

Sumatra

INDONESIA

Ngandong

SOLOMON ISLANDS

CABINDA (Angola)

DEMOCRATIC REPUBLIC OF THE CONGO

TANZANIA

SEYCHELLES

Sangiran

Trinil

PAPUA NEW GUINEA

TUVALU

COMOROS IS.

Indian Ocean

ANGOLA

ZAMBIA

MALAWI

VANUATU

FIJI

Broken Hill ●

MADAGASCAR

MAURITIUS

NEW CALEDONIA (Fr.)

20°S

NAMIBIA

BOTSWANA

ZIMBABWE

MOZAMBIQUE

TROPIC OF CAPRICORN

WALVIS BAY (Status to be determined)

Taung ●

Sterkfontein/Swartkrans/Drimolen

AUSTRALIA

Florisbad ●

SWAZILAND

LESOTHO

SOUTH AFRICA

Border Cave

Lake Mungo ●

Klasies River Mouth

Kow Swamp ●

NEW ZEALAND

40°S

1. SLOVENIA
2. CROATIA
3. BOSNIA AND HERZEGOVINA
4. ALBANIA
5. MACEDONIA

60°S

ANTARCTIC CIRCLE

ANTARCTICA

80°S

20°E   40°E   60°E   80°E   100°E   120°E   140°E   160°E   180°

www.wadsworth.com

www.wadsworth.com is the World Wide Web site for Thomson Wadsworth and is your direct source to dozens of online resources.

At *www.wadsworth.com* you can find out about supplements, demonstration software, and student resources. You can also send email to many of our authors and preview new publications and exciting new technologies.

www.wadsworth.com
Changing the way the world learns®

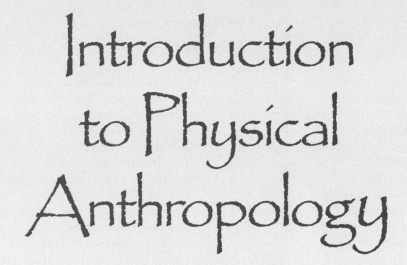

Introduction to Physical Anthropology

TENTH EDITION

Robert Jurmain
San Jose State University

Lynn Kilgore
Colorado State University

Wenda Trevathan
New Mexico State University

THOMSON™

WADSWORTH

Australia • Canada • Mexico • Singapore • Spain
United Kingdom • United States

THOMSON

WADSWORTH

Senior Acquisitions Editor: *Lin Marshall*
Development Editor: *Sherry Symington*
Assistant Editor: *Nicole Root*
Editorial Assistant: *Kelly McMahon*
Technology Project Manager: *Dee Dee Zobian*
Marketing Manager: *Matthew Wright*
Marketing Assistant: *Tara Pierson*
Senior Advertising Project Manager: *Linda Yip*
Project Manager, Editorial Production: *Catherine Morris*
Art Director: *Rob Hugel*
Print/Media Buyer: *Barbara Britton*
Permissions Editor: *Sarah Harkrader*
Production Service: *Hespenheide Design*
Text Designer: *Ellen Pettengell*

Art Editor: *Hespenheide Design*
Photo Researcher: *Hespenheide Design*
Copy Editor: *Janet Greenblatt*
Illustrators: *Alexander Productions, Joanne Bales, Randy Miyake, Paragon 3, Sue Sellars, Cyndie Wooley*
Cover Designer: *Rob Hugel*
Cover Image: *Left to right:* © *W. McIntyre/Photo Researchers, Inc. (DNA),* © *Robert Jurmain (student in lab),* © *Manoj Shah/Getty Images (chimpanzees),* © *Mission Paléoanthropologique Franco-Tchadienne (skull)*
Compositor: *Hespenheide Design*
Text and Cover Printer: *Transcontinental Printing/Interglobe*

Printed in Canada
1 2 3 4 5 6 7 08 07 06 05 04

For more information about our products, contact us at:
Thomson Learning Academic Resource Center
1-800-423-0563

For permission to use material from this text or product, submit a request online at **http://www.thomsonrights.com**.
Any additional questions about permissions can be submitted by email to **thomsonrights@thomson.com**.

Library of Congress Control Number: 2004106776

Student Edition: ISBN 0-534-63902-X

Instructor's Edition: ISBN 0-534-63903-8

Thomson Wadsworth
10 Davis Drive
Belmont, CA 94002-3098
USA

Asia
Thomson Learning
5 Shenton Way #01-01
UIC Building
Singapore 068808

Australia/New Zealand
Thomson Learning
102 Dodds Street
Southbank, Victoria 3006
Australia

Canada
Nelson
1120 Birchmount Road
Toronto, Ontario M1K 5G4
Canada

Europe/Middle East/Africa
Thomson Learning
High Holborn House
50/51 Bedford Row
London WC1R 4LR
United Kingdom

Latin America
Thomson Learning
Seneca, 53
Colonia Polanco
11560 Mexico D.F.
Mexico

Spain/Portugal
Paraninfo
Calle Magallanes, 25
28015 Madrid, Spain

Brief Contents

PART 4 Contemporary Human Evolution

Contents

PART 1 Heredity and Evolution

© Bettmann/CORBIS

David Haring, Duke University Primate Zoo

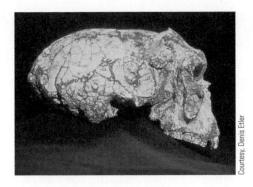

Courtesy, Denis Etler

CHAPTER TWELVE
Premodern Humans 329

CHAPTER THIRTEEN
The Origin and Dispersal of Modern Humans 365

PART 4 Contemporary Human Evolution

Preface

In the preface for the previous edition of this text, we emphasized how rapidly scientific knowledge accumulates. We wondered, in fact, whether the pace of new discoveries in physical anthropology would continue and perhaps even speed up beyond that in recent years and suggested that "if history is any teacher, we can anticipate there will be even *greater* changes accumulating ever more rapidly."

We made that prediction a mere two years ago, and changes in our field since then have been nothing short of breathtaking. In fact, just as the ninth edition was published in July 2002, a startling seven-million-year-old fossil find from Central Africa was announced. Many anthropologists consider this new find as perhaps the most significant one for human origins studies in the last 80 years. And that was not all. Two months later the announcement of an additional skull from an almost two-million-year-old site in the Republic of Georgia (in easternmost Europe) significantly shook up our previous views of this somewhat later phase of human (hominid) evolution. Then, in June 2003, a dramatic fossil find bearing on the origins of modern humans from East Africa was published.

Any of these discoveries would have required a rewriting of a major portion of the text concerning hominid evolution. The combined ramifications of the three finds have necessitated that this entire section of the text (Chapters 10–13) be reorganized and reinterpreted.

Moreover, the tremendous advances of molecular biology in all phases of physical anthropology have also accelerated rapidly in the last two years. And, again, significant portions of several chapters have been expanded and updated.

From the recognition that the content of a scientific discipline can change so rapidly, come both challenges and lessons. For you, as introductory students in a course about human evolution, it is most advantageous to learn basic principles—rather than memorizing mountains of individual facts (many of which in the near future will most likely be revised or reinterpreted). It is thus better to master these fundamental principles and learn to apply basic tools including: the biological principles pertaining to all life; the key concepts of evolutionary theory; an understanding of the place of the human species in the biological world; and perhaps most basic of all, the ability to apply critical thinking to all intellectual aspects of your life.

As our perspectives are widened, we come to know and appreciate more completely the human condition. You will see that these perspectives have recently been extended ever farther back in time to the dawn of the most remote ancestors of the human family. At the same time, genetic technologies have extended our knowledge within—indeed, to the very chemical basis of what makes us alive, what makes us an animal, even what makes us human. Beyond our intellectual perspectives are personal and emotional viewpoints, which can also be transformed—sometimes unexpectedly so. From this textbook you will learn about aspects of DNA identification of individuals as well as other forensic anthropological techniques for identifying human physical remains. In the aftermath of September 11, 2001, can any of us ever think about these topics in quite the same way as before?

It's difficult to imagine where and how fast scientific investigation will take us in the next few years, to say nothing of actually attempting to make predictions. Where do you think scientific research in human biology will lead us in the next five years? In the next ten years? Such prognostications are stimulating and good fun, but they must remain largely conjectural. There is, however, a more pertinent question: Whatever comes, will you be ready?

What's New in the Tenth Edition?

As we have mentioned, the two most obvious areas of new research influencing physical/biological anthropology are in molecular (DNA-based) applications and new discoveries of fossil hominids. The wide impact of new DNA-based knowledge has been extraordinary, influencing every aspect of the discipline (and the ramifications are addressed in virtually every chapter of the text).

In addition, to provide further insights into fascinating and innovative molecular applications, we have added four new major boxed features discussing "New Frontiers in Research" specifically discussing aspects of molecular anthropology. We have also slightly reorganized the order of chapters. Materials on vertebrate and mammalian evolutions as well as general principles of macroevolution now are introduced in Chapter 5. Our reasoning, and our response to reviewers' suggestions, is to place these topics *prior* to our coverage of nonhuman primates (Chapters 6, 7, 8) rather than after this material.

Another feature you will see throughout the text is a series of linked questions. "Key Questions" begin each chapter, focusing on central topics for that chapter. Moreover, at the end of each chapter, questions "For Further Thought" ask students to think critically about their new knowledge and to expand on it.

Throughout the book these questions are linked around a central theme in human evolution: How do humans fit into the overall pattern of life? In other words, how does an evolutionary perspective help explain *who* and *what* we are—and *how* we come to be this way?

We have also worked to improve the pedagogical aids for students, especially to make them more visually accessible. In every chapter, you will find concise "At a Glance" boxes that very briefly summarize complex and/or controversial material. Further, at the end of each chapter, along with the written summary, there is now also a Visual Summary. Again, the pedagogical goal is to provide an accessible visual learning aid.

As we mentioned above, a central intention of our text is to stimulate critical thinking; thus, the Questions for Review at the end of each chapter have been thoroughly revised to emphasize a more critical and intellectually creative approach to incorporating *and* applying knowledge.

FEATURES

Issues are major boxed features, which are found at the end of every other chapter. Issues focus on current controversial topics discussed and debated within physical anthropology. A second type of major boxed feature follows four other chapters. These **New Frontiers in Research** boxes discuss recent innovative work by molecular anthropologists. They cover four major research areas of biological anthropology:

- New Frontiers in Research: Molecular Applications in Forensic Anthropology (following Chapter 4).
- New Frontiers in Research: Molecular Applications in Primatology (following Chapter 8).
- New Frontiers in Research: Ancient DNA (following Chapter 12).
- New Frontiers in Research: Molecular Applications in Modern Human Biology (following Chapter 14).

Boxed highlights titled **"A Closer Look"** are high-interest features found throughout the book. They expand on the topic under discussion in the chapter by providing a more in-depth overview.

IN-CHAPTER LEARNING AIDS

- **Chapter outlines**, at the beginning of each chapter list all major topics covered.
- **Key Questions** at the beginning of each chapter focus on the central topic of that chapter.
- A **running glossary** in the margins provides definitions of terms immediately adjacent to the text when the term is first introduced. A **full glossary** is provided in the back of the book.
- **At a Glance** boxes briefly summarize complex or controversial material in a visually simple fashion.
- **Figures**, including numerous photographs, line drawings, maps, most in full color, are carefully selected to clarify text materials and are placed to directly support discussion in the text.
- **Visual Summaries** are found with the written summary at the end of each chapter and provide a simple and visually appealing aid for students.
- **For Further Thought** questions linked to the Key Questions posed at the beginning of the chapter, inspire students to expand upon their new knowledge.
- **Questions for Review** at the end of each chapter reinforce key concepts and encourage students to think critically about what they have read.
- **Suggested Further Reading** features, also found at the end of each chapter, are carefully selected to direct interested students toward recent accessible and interesting sources for further reading.
- **Full bibliographic citations** throughout the entire book provide sources from which the materials are drawn. This type of documentation guides students to published source materials and illustrates for students the proper use of referencing; all cited sources are listed in the comprehensive bibliography at the back of the book.
- **Resources on the Internet** is a learning aid found at the end of each chapter. Students are directed here to the *Wadsworth Anthropology Resource Center*.
- Icons are strategically placed throughout the text to integrate text materials with those found in the *Virtual Laboratories for Physical Anthropology* CD-ROM, Third Edition, prepared by John Kappelman of the University of Texas at Austin. The icons are found in the margins adjacent to related materials in the text:

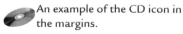
An example of the CD icon in the margins.

Acknowledgments

Over the years many friends and colleagues have assisted us with our books. For this edition we are especially grateful to the reviewers who so carefully commented on the manuscript and made such helpful suggestions: Donald Tyler, University of Idaho; Debra L. Martin, Hampshire College; Leila Porter, University of Washington; Elizabeth Peters, Florida State University; Lois Lippold, San Diego State University; Leonard Lieberman, Central Michigan University; Sang-Hee Lee, University of California at Riverside; and Robert Quinlan, Ball State University.

We also wish to thank at Wadsworth Publishing Lin Marshall, Anthropology Editor, Sherry Symington, Development Editor, Nicole Root, Assistant Editor, Kelly McMahon, Editorial Assistant, Dee Dee Zobian, Technology Product Manager, Matthew Wright, Executive Marketing Manager, Catherine Morris, Project Editor, Eve Howard, Editor-in-Chief, and Susan Badger, President and CEO. Moreover, for their unflagging expertise and patience we are grateful to our copy editor, Janet Greenblatt, our production service, Hespenheide Design: Patti Zeman, production coordinator and Bridget Neumayr, proofreader/editor.

To the many friends and colleagues who have generously provided photographs we are greatly appreciative: C.K. Brain, Günter Bräuer, Desmond Clark, Ron Clarke, Raymond Dart, Jean deRousseau, Denis Etler, Diane France, David Frayer, Kathleen Galvin, David Haring, Ellen Ingmanson, Fred Jacobs, Peter Jones, Leslie Knapp, Arlene Kruse, Richard Leakey, Carol Lofton, Margaret Maples, Lorna Moore, John Oates, Bonnie Pedersen, Lorna Pierce, David Pilbeam, Willaim Pratt, Judith Regensteiner, Sastrohamijoyo Sartono, Wayne Savage, Eugenie Scott, Rose Sevick, Elwyn Simons, Meredith Small, Fred Smith, Judy Suchey, Heather Thew, Li Tianyuan, Philip Tobias, Alan Walker, Milford Wolpoff, and Xinzhi Wu.

Robert Jurmain
Lynn Kilgore
Wenda Trevathan

Supplements

SUPPLEMENTS FOR INSTRUCTORS

Instructor's Manual with Test Bank This comprehensive manual offers chapter outlines, learning objectives, key terms and concepts, lecture suggestions and enrichment topics as well as 40–60 test questions per chapter. Concise user guides for InfoTrac College Edition and WebTutor are included as appendices. Included with the manual is the book-specific Multimedia Manager Instructor Resource CD-ROM, which contains digital media and Microsoft® PowerPoint® presentations for the text, placing images, lectures, and video clips at your fingertips. The extensive Test Bank is also available in computerized form.

Exam View® **Computerized Testing** Create, deliver, and customize tests and study guides (both print and online) in minutes with this easy-to-use assessment and tutorial system. *Exam View* offers both a Quick Test Wizard and an Online Test Wizard that guide you step-by-step through the process of creating tests, while the unique "WYSIWYG" capability allows you to see the test you are creating on the screen exactly as it will print or display online. You can build tests of up to 250 questions, using up to 12 question types. Using *Exam View's* complete word processing capabilities, you can enter an unlimited number of new questions or edit existing questions.

Primate Evolution Module This 48-page free-standing module is actually a complete text chapter featuring the same quality of pedagogy and illustrations that are contained in this book—offering you an excellent opportunity to incorporate the basics of primate evolution into your course. Jurmain examines primate evolution as it has developed over the last 60 million years, helping students understand the ecological adaptations and evolutionary relationships of fossil forms to each other and to contemporary primates. Also available to view in full color online.

Forensic Anthropology Module This 48-page free-standing module is actually a complete text chapter featuring the same quality of pedagogy and illustrations that are contained in the text—offering you an excellent opportunity to incorporate the basics of forensic anthropology into your course. The author, Diane France, introduces students to the essentials of forensic anthropology as it is practiced in the United States and Canada, exploring the field's myths and realities, what it is, how it is applied, and what careers are available within the field. Edited by Robert Jurmain and Lynn Kilgore, the module is consistent with chapters in the physical anthropology text. Also available to view in full color online.

CLASSROOM PRESENTATION TOOLS FOR INSTRUCTORS

Wadsworth's Physical Anthropology Transparency Acetates 2005 This set of four-color acetates features images from Wadsworth's 2005 physical anthropology texts to help prepare lecture presentations.

Wadsworth Anthropology Video Library Qualified adopters may select full-length videos from an extensive library of offerings drawn from excellent educational video sources such as *Films for the Humanities and Sciences.*

CNN Today Physical Anthropology **Video Series, Volumes 1–6** The *CNN Today Physical Anthropology* Video Series is an exclusive series jointly created by Wadsworth and CNN for the physical anthropology course. Each video in the series consists of approximately 45 minutes of footage originally broadcast on CNN within the last several years. The videos are broken into short two- to seven-minute segments, which are perfect for classroom use as lecture launchers, or to illustrate key anthropological concepts. An annotated table of contents accompanies each video with descriptions of the segments and suggestions for their possible use within the course.

SUPPLEMENTS FOR STUDENTS

Study Guide This useful guide enables students to fully comprehend and appreciate what the text has to offer. Each chapter of the study guide features learning objectives, chapter outlines, key terms, concept applications, and practice tests consisting of 30–40 multiple-choice questions and 5–10 true/false questions with answers and page references, in addition to several short answer and essay questions.

Virtual Laboratories for Physical Anthropology CD-ROM, Third Edition By John Kappelman, University of Texas at Austin. The new edition of this interactive CD-ROM provides students with a hands-on computer component for doing lab assignments at school or at home. It encourages students to participate actively in their physical anthropology lab or course through the taking of measurements and the plotting of data, as well as giving them a format for testing their knowledge of important concepts. Contains full-color images, video clips, 3-D animations, sound, and more. New to this edition is a special quizzing section where students can take online tutorial quizzes based on the 12 laboratories and have their answers scored and e-mailed to their instructor!

Lab Manual and Workbook for Physical Anthropology, **Fifth Edition** Written by Diane France, this lab manual emphasizes human osteology, forensic anthropology, anthropometry, primates, human evolution, and genetics, and provides students with hands-on lab assignments to help clarify difficult concepts in physical anthropology. The extensively revised and reorganized Fifth Edition is more problem-oriented as chapters are organized around new opening critical thinking questions and the techniques used to answer the questions. Each chapter concludes with a new "Reexamining the Issues" feature that addresses the answers to the initial chapter questions. Chapter exercises have been increased in number and offer a wider variety of question types and levels of difficulty. The Fifth Edition features increased coverage of evolution and genetics, new skeletal comparisons of quadrupeds, brachiators, and bipeds, a new fossil summary chart, and many more enhancements.

Researching Anthropology on the Internet, **Second Edition** Written by David Carlson, this useful guide is designed to assist anthropology students in all of their needs when doing research on the Internet. Part One contains general information necessary to get started and answers questions about security, the type of material available on the Internet, the information that is reliable and the sites that are not, the best ways to find research, and the best links to take students where they want to go. Part Two looks at each main discipline in anthropology and refers students to sites where the most enlightening research can be obtained.

WEB RESOURCES AND SUPPLEMENTS FOR INSTRUCTORS AND STUDENTS

Anthropology Online: Wadsworth's Anthropology Resource Center The Wadsworth Anthropology Resource Center contains a wealth of information and useful tools for both instructors and students. After logging on to the Wadsworth home page at http:// anthropology.wadsworth.com, click on Course Materials, Physical Anthropology, and the Jurmain book cover. Proceed to the Student Resources section by clicking "For Students." There, students will find many exciting chapter specific resources such as CNN video clips, crossword puzzles, Internet Exercises, InfoTrac Exercises, practice quizzes that calculate results which can then be e-mailed to instructors, and much more. Instructors, too, will find a wealth of materials such as an online Instructor's Manual and PowerPoint Lecture slides.

A Virtual Tour of Applying Anthropology This special section of the Web site serves as an online resource center for the anthropology student. Students will find Applied Anthropologists at Work, Graduate Studies info, Job boards, Internships and Field Work, and an Essay on Careers with video.

InfoTrac College Edition Ignite discussions or augment lectures with the latest developments in physical anthropology. InfoTrac College Edition (available as a free option with newly purchased texts) gives instructors and students 4 months free access to an easy-to-use online database of reliable, full-length articles (not abstracts) from hundreds of top academic journals and popular sources. Among the journals which are available 24-hours a day, seven days a week, are *American Anthropologist, Current Anthropology, Journal of Contemporary Ethnography, Canadian Review of Sociology and Anthropology,* and thousands more. Contact your Wadsworth/Thomson Learning representative for more information.

WebTutor Advantage™ on WebCT and Blackboard For students, **WebTutor Advantage** offers real-time access to a full array of study tools, including chapter summaries, flashcards (with audio), practice quizzes, interactive maps and timelines, online tutorials, and Web links. Professors can use **WebTutor Advantage** to provide virtual office hours, post syllabi, set up threaded discussions, track student progress with quizzing material, and more. **WebTutor Advantage** provides rich communication tools, including a course calendar, asynchronous discussion, "real-time" chat, a whiteboard, and an integrated e-mail system. New to WebTutor Advantage is seamless access to the power of **InfoTrac College Edition.** Also new to **WebTutor Advantage** is access to *NewsEdge,* an online news service that delivers the latest news to your **WebTutor Advantage** site daily.

Introduction

A human chromosome

© Biophoto Associates / Photo Researchers, Inc.

Key Questions

What do physical anthropologists do?

Why is physical anthropology a scientific discipline, and what is its importance to the general public?

See the following sections of the CD-ROM for topics covered in this chapter: Virtual Lab I, sections I and II, and Virtual Lab 2.*

Hominidae The taxonomic family to which humans belong; also includes other, now extinct, bipedal relatives.

hominids Members of the family Hominidae.

bipedally On two feet. Walking habitually on two legs is the single most distinctive feature of the family Hominidae.

FIGURE 1–1 Early hominid footprints at Laetoli, Tanzania. The tracks to the left were made by one individual, while those to the right appear to have been formed by two individuals, the second stepping in the tracks of the first.

*This CD-ROM icon indicates additional material that can be found on the Virtual Laboratories for Physical Anthropology CD-ROM, which is further described in the preface to this book.

Introduction

One day, perhaps at the beginning of the rainy season some 3.7 million years ago, two or three individuals walked across a grassland savanna in what is now northern Tanzania in East Africa. These individuals were early members of the taxonomic family **Hominidae**, the family that also includes ourselves, modern *Homo sapiens*. Fortunately for us, a record of their passage on that long-forgotten day remains in the form of fossilized footprints, preserved in hardened volcanic deposits.

As chance would have it, shortly after heels and toes were pressed into the dampened soil, a volcano about 12 miles away erupted. The ensuing ashfall blanketed everything on the ground surface, including the footprints of the **hominids** as well as those of numerous other species. In time, the ash layer hardened into a deposit, which preserved a remarkable assortment of tracks and other materials that lay beneath it (Fig. 1–1).

These now-famous prints indicate that two hominids, one smaller than the other, perhaps walked side by side, leaving parallel sets of tracks. But because the prints of the larger individual are obscured, possibly by those of a third, it is unclear how many actually made that journey so long ago. What is clear from the prints is that they were left by an animal that habitually walked **bipedally** (on two feet). It is this critical feature that led scientists to consider these ancient passersby as hominids.

Courtesy, Peter Jones

In addition to the footprints, scientists at this site, called Laetoli, and at other locations have discovered numerous fossilized skeletal remains of what we now call *Australopithecus afarensis*. These fossils and prints have a great deal to say about the beings they represent, provided we can learn to interpret them.

From the footprints and fossilized fragmentary skeletons, we know that these hominids walked upright. Thus, they were, in a great many respects, anatomically similar to ourselves, but their brains were only about one-third the size of ours. Although they may have used stones and sticks as tools, there is no current evidence to suggest they manufactured stone tools. In short, these early hominids were very much at the mercy of nature's whims. They certainly could not outrun most predators, and their lack of large canine teeth rendered them relatively defenseless.

We could ask hundreds of questions about the Laetoli hominids, but we will never be able to answer them all. They walked down a path into what became their future, and their immediate journey has long since ended. It remains for us to sort out what little we can know about them and the **species** they represent. In this sense, their greater journey continues.

On July 20, 1969, a television audience numbering in the hundreds of millions watched as two human beings stepped out of a spacecraft and onto the surface of the moon. To anyone born after that date, this event is taken or granted. But the significance of that first moonwalk can't be overstated, because it represents humankind's presumed mastery over the natural forces that govern our presence on earth. For the first time ever, people actually walked upon the surface of a celestial body that has never given birth to biological life.

As the astronauts gathered geological specimens and frolicked in near weightlessness, they left traces of their fleeting presence in the form of footprints in the lunar dust (Fig. 1–2). On the atmosphereless surface of the moon, where no rain falls and no wind blows, the footprints remain undisturbed to this day. They survive as mute testimony to a brief visit by a medium-sized, big-brained creature who presumed to challenge the very forces that created it.

You may be wondering why anyone would care about early hominid footprints and how they can possibly have any relevance to your life. And even though you know that a moon landing occurred in the late 1960s, you may not have spent much time actually thinking about it. Furthermore, why would a textbook about physical anthropology begin with a discussion of two such seemingly unrelated phenomena?

Physical, or biological, anthropology is a scientific discipline concerned with the biological and behavioral characteristics of human beings; our closest relatives, the nonhuman **primates** (apes, monkeys, and promisians); and their ancestors. It is through such study that we can attempt to explain what it means to be human. This may be an ambitious and not fully attainable goal, but it is certainly worth pursuing. We are the only species to ponder our own existence and wonder how we fit into the spectrum of life on earth. Most people view humanity as separate from the rest of the animal kingdom. But at the same time, some are curious about the similarities we share with other species. Maybe, as a child, you looked at your dog and tried to figure out how his front legs might correspond to your arms. Perhaps, while at the zoo, you marveled at the similarities between a chimpanzee's hands or facial expressions and your own. While considering the many physical similarities between chimpanzees and humans, you may have wondered if they also shared our thoughts and feelings. If you have ever had such thoughts, then you have indeed been curious about humankind's place in nature.

In 1978, biological anthropologists and archaeologists uncovered the Laetoli footprints, and they continue to raise questions about the animal who made them. Perhaps one day, creatures as yet unimagined will ponder the essence of the being that made the lunar footprints. What do you suppose they will think?

species A group of organisms that can interbreed to produce fertile offspring. Members of one species are reproductively isolated from members of all other species (i.e., they cannot mate with them to produce fertile offspring).

FIGURE 1–2 Human footprints left on the lunar surface during the *Apollo* mission.

primates Members of the order of mammals *Primates* (pronounced "pry-may´-tees"), which includes prosimians, monkeys, apes, and humans.

We humans, who can barely comprehend a century, can only grasp at the enormity of 3.7 million years. We want to know more about those creatures who traveled that day across the savanna. We want to know how an insignificant but clever bipedal primate such as *Australopithecus africanus,* or perhaps a close relative, gave rise to a species that would eventually walk on the surface of a moon some 230,000 miles from earth.

How did *Homo sapiens,* a result of the same evolutionary forces that produced all other life on this planet, gain the power to control the flow of rivers and alter the very climate in which we live? As tropical animals, how were we able to leave the tropics and eventually occupy most of the earth's land surfaces? How did we adjust to different local environmental conditions as we dispersed? How could our species, which numbered fewer than 1 billion individuals until the mid-nineteenth century, come to number more than 6 billion worldwide today and, as we now do, add another billion people every 11 years?

evolution A change in the genetic structure of a population. The term is also frequently used to refer to the appearance of a new species.

These are some of the many questions that physical anthropologists attempt to answer, and these questions are largely the focus of the study of human **evolution**, variation, and adaptation. These issues, and many others, are the topics covered directly or indirectly in this textbook, because physical anthropology is, in part, human biology seen from an evolutionary perspective.

As biological organisms, humans are subject to the same evolutionary forces as all other species. On hearing the term *evolution,* most people think of the appearance of new species. Certainly, new species formation is one consequence of evolution; however, biologists see evolution as an ongoing biological process with a precise genetic meaning. Quite simply, evolution is a change in the genetic makeup of a population from one generation to the next, and the accumulation of such changes, over considerable periods of time, can result in the appearance of a new species. Therefore, evolution can be defined and studied at two different levels. At one level there are genetic alterations *within* populations. Although this type of change may not lead to the development of new species, it often results in variation between populations with regard to the frequency of certain traits. Evolution at this level is referred to as *microevolution*. At the other level is genetic change sufficient to result in the appearance of a new species, a process termed *macroevolution* or speciation. Evolution as it occurs at both these levels will be addressed in this book.

See Virtual Lab 2 for several examples of evolution and human adaptation.

culture All aspects of human adaptation, including technology, traditions, language, religion, marriage patterns, and social roles. Culture is a set of *learned* behaviors that is transmitted from one generation to the next by nonbiological (i.e., nongenetic) means.

But physical anthropologists are not involved solely in the study of physiological systems and biological phenomena. When such topics are placed within the broader context of human evolution, another factor must also be considered: the role of **culture**. Culture is an extremely important concept, not only as it pertains to modern human beings, but also in terms of its critical role in human evolution. It has been said that there are as many definitions of culture as there are people who attempt to define it. Quite simply, and in a very broad sense, culture can be said to be the strategy by which humans adapt to the natural environment. In this sense, culture includes technologies that range from stone tools to computers; subsistence patterns ranging from hunting and gathering to agribusiness on a global scale; housing types, from thatched huts to skyscrapers; and clothing, from animal skins to high-tech synthetic fibers (Fig. 1–3). Because religion, values, social organization, language, kinship, marriage rules, gender roles, inheritance of property, and so on, are all aspects of culture, each culture shapes people's perceptions of the external environment, or **world view**, in particular ways that distinguish that culture from all others.

world view General cultural orientation or perspective shared by members of a society.

One fundamental point to remember is that culture is passed from one generation to the next independently of biological factors (i.e., genes). In other words, culture is *learned,* and the process of learning one's culture begins, quite literally, at birth. All humans are products of the culture in which they are raised, and since most of human behavior is learned, it follows that most behaviors, perceptions, and reactions are shaped by culture.

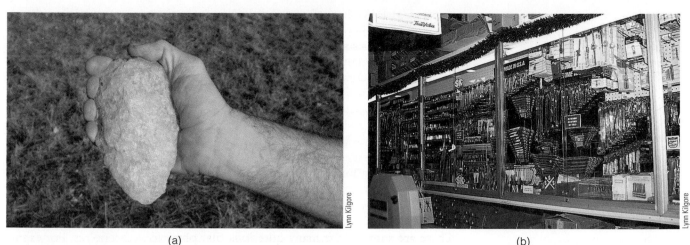

(a)   (b)

(c)   (d)

It is important to emphasize, however, that even though culture is not genetically determined, the human *predisposition to assimilate culture and function within it is influenced by biological factors.* As you will see, many nonhuman animals, especially primates, rely heavily on learned behavior, and chimpanzees, in particular, exhibit numerous aspects of culture. The predisposition for culture is perhaps the most critical component of human evolutionary history, and it was inherited from early hominid or prehominid ancestors. It may well have existed in the common ancestor we share with chimpanzees. But in the course of human evolution, the role of culture increasingly assumed an added importance. Over time, culture and biology interacted in such a way that humans are said to be the result of **biocultural evolution**. In this respect, humans are unique among biological organisms.

Biocultural interactions have resulted in such anatomical, biological, and behavioral changes as increased brain size, reorganization of neurological structures, decreased tooth size, and development of language in humans, to list a few, and they even continue to be critical in changing disease patterns as well. As a contemporary example, rapid culture change (particularly in Africa) and changing social and sexual mores may have influenced evolutionary rates of HIV, the virus that causes AIDS. Certainly, these cultural factors influenced

FIGURE 1–3 (a) An early stone tool from East Africa. This artifact represents one of the oldest types of stone tools found anywhere. (b) Assortment of implements available today in a modern hardware store. (c) A Samburu woman building a simple, traditional dwelling of stems, plant fibers, and mud. (d) A modern high-rise apartment complex, typical of industrialized cities.

biocultural evolution The mutual, interactive evolution of human biology and culture; the concept that biology makes culture possible and that developing culture further influences the direction of biological evolution; a basic concept in understanding the unique components of human evolution.

adaptation Functional response of organisms or populations to the environment. Adaptation results from evolutionary change (specifically, as a result of natural selection).

anthropology The field of inquiry that studies human culture and evolutionary aspects of human biology; includes cultural anthropology, archaeology, linguistics, and physical, or biological, anthropology.

See Virtual Lab I, section I, for a discussion of physical anthropology as a subdiscipline of anthropology.

ethnographies Detailed descriptive studies of human societies. In cultural anthropology, an ethnography is traditionally the study of a non-Western society.

the spread of HIV throughout populations in both the developed and developing worlds.

Human biologists also study many biological aspects of humankind, including **adaptation** and evolution. However, particularly in the United States, when such research also considers the role of cultural factors, it is placed within the discipline of **anthropology**.

What Is Anthropology?

Stated ambitiously but simply, anthropology is the study of humankind. (The term *anthropology* is derived from the Greek words *anthropos,* meaning "human," and *logos,* meaning "word" or "study of.") Anthropologists aren't the only scientists who study humans, and the goals of anthropology are shared by other disciplines within the social, behavioral, and biological sciences. For example, psychologists and psychiatrists investigate various aspects of human motivation and behavior while developing theories that have clinical significance. Historians focus on recorded events in the past, but since their research concerns documented occurrences, it is limited to, at most, a few thousand years. The main difference between anthropology and such related fields is that anthropology integrates the findings of many disciplines, including sociology, economics, history, psychology, and biology.

In the United States, anthropology comprises three main subfields: cultural, or social, anthropology; archaeology; and physical, or biological, anthropology. Additionally, some universities include linguistic anthropology as a fourth area. Each of these subdisciplines, in turn, is divided into several specialized areas of interest. Following is a brief discussion of the main subdisciplines of anthropology.

Cultural Anthropology

Cultural anthropology is the study of all aspects of human behavior. The beginnings of cultural anthropology are found in the nineteenth century, when Europeans became increasingly aware of what they termed "primitive" societies in Africa and Asia. Likewise, in the New World, there was much interest in the vanishing cultures of Native Americans.

The interest in traditional societies led numerous early anthropologists to study and record lifeways that unfortunately are now mostly extinct. These studies produced many descriptive **ethnographies** that became the basis for subsequent comparisons between groups. Early ethnographies emphasized various phenomena, such as religion, ritual, myth, use of symbols, subsistence strategies, technology, gender roles, child-rearing practices, dietary preferences, taboos, medical practices, and how kinship was reckoned.

Ethnographic accounts, in turn, formed the basis for comparative studies of numerous cultures. Such *cross-cultural* studies, called *ethnologies,* broadened the context within which cultural anthropologists studied human behavior. By examining the similarities and differences between diverse cultures, anthropologists have been able to formulate many theories about the fundamental aspects of human behavior.

The focus of cultural anthropology shifted over the course of the twentieth century. For example, in recent decades, ethnographic techniques have been applied to the study of diverse subcultures and their interactions with one another in contemporary metropolitan areas. The subfield of cultural anthropology that deals with issues of inner cities is appropriately called *urban anthropology.* Another relevant area for cultural anthropologists today is in the resettlement of refugees in many parts of the world. To develop plans that properly accommodate the needs of displaced peoples, governments may find the special talents of cultural anthropologists of considerable benefit.

Medical anthropology is the subfield of cultural anthropology that explores the relationship between various cultural attributes and health and disease. One area of interest is how different groups view disease processes and how these views affect treatment or the willingness to accept treatment. When a medical anthropologist focuses on the social dimensions of disease, physicians and physical anthropologists may also collaborate. In fact, many medical anthropologists have received much of their training in physical anthropology.

Many of the subfields of cultural anthropology (e.g., medical anthropology) have practical applications and are pursued by anthropologists working outside the university setting. This approach is called *applied anthropology*. While most applied anthropologists regard themselves as cultural anthropologists, the designation is also sometimes used to describe the pursuits of archaeologists and physical anthropologists. Indeed, the various fields of anthropology, as practiced in the United States, overlap to a considerable degree, which, after all, was the rationale for combining them under the umbrella of anthropology in the first place.

Archaeology

Archaeology is the study of earlier cultures and lifeways by anthropologists who specialize in the scientific recovery, analysis, and interpretation of the material remains of past societies. Although archaeology often deals with cultures that existed before the invention of writing (the period commonly known as *prehistory*), *historic archaeologists* examine the evidence of later, complex civilizations that produced written records.

Archaeologists are concerned with culture, but they differ from cultural anthropologists in that their sources of information aren't living people but rather the **artifacts** and other **material culture** left behind by earlier societies. Obviously, no one has ever excavated such aspects of culture as religious belief, spoken language, or a political system. However, archaeologists assume that the surviving evidence of human occupation reflects some of those important but less tangible features of the culture that created them. Therefore, the material remains of a given ancient society may serve to inform us about the nature of that society.

Today, the main goal of archaeology is to answer specific questions pertaining to human behavior. Sites are not excavated simply because they exist or for the artifacts they may contain; rather, they are excavated to gain information about human behavior. Patterns of behavior are reflected in the dispersal of human settlements across a landscape and in the distribution of cultural remains within them. Through the identification of these patterns, archaeologists can identify the commonalities shared by many or all populations as well as those features that differ between groups. Research questions may focus on specific localities or peoples and attempt to identify, for example, various aspects of social organization, subsistence techniques, or the factors that led to the collapse of a civilization. Alternatively, inquiry may reflect an interest in broader issues relating to human culture in general, such as the development of agriculture or the rise of cities. But the design of most archaeological projects centers around a number of questions that address a wide range of interests.

In the United States, the greatest expansion in archaeology in recent years has been in the important area of *cultural resource management (CRM)*. This applied approach arose from environmental legislation requiring the archaeological evaluation and even excavation of sites that may be threatened by construction and other forms of development. Many contract archaeologists (so called

artifacts Objects or materials made or modified for use by hominids. The earliest artifacts tend to be tools made of stone or, occasionally, bone.

material culture The physical manifestations of human activities; includes tools, campsites, art, and structures. As the most durable aspects of culture, material remains make up the majority of archaeological evidence of past societies.

because their services are contracted out to developers or government agencies) are affiliated with private archaeological consulting firms, state or federal agencies, or educational institutions. In fact, an estimated 40 percent of all archaeologists in the United States now fill such positions.

Archaeological techniques are used to identify and excavate not only remains of human cities and settlements, but also paleontological sites containing remains of extinct species, including everything from dinosaurs to early hominids. Together, prehistoric archaeology and physical anthropology form the core of a joint science called *paleoanthropology,* described below.

Linguistic Anthropology

Linguistic anthropology is the study of human speech and language, including the origins of language in general as well as specific languages. By examining similarities between contemporary languages, linguists have been able to trace historical ties between languages and groups of languages, thus facilitating the identification of language families and perhaps past relationships between human populations. There is also much interest in the relationship between language and culture: how language reflects the way members of a society perceive phenomena and how the use of language shapes perceptions in different cultures.

Because the spontaneous acquisition and use of language is a uniquely human characteristic, it is a topic that holds considerable interest for linguistic anthropologists, who, along with specialists in other fields, study the process of language acquisition in infants. Since insights into the process may well have implications for the development of language skills in human evolution, as well as in growing children, it is also an important subject to physical anthropologists.

Physical Anthropology

As we have already said, *physical anthropology* is the study of human biology within the framework of evolution and with an emphasis on the interaction between biology and culture. This subdiscipline is also referred to as *biological anthropology,* and you will find the terms used interchangeably. *Physical anthropology* is the original term, and it reflects the initial interests anthropologists had in describing human physical variation. The American Association of Physical Anthropologists, its journal, many college courses, and numerous publications retain this term. The designation *biological anthropology* reflects the shift in emphasis to more biologically oriented topics, such as genetics, evolutionary biology, nutrition, physiological adaptation, and growth and development. This shift occurred largely as a result of advances in the field of genetics since the late 1950s. Although we have continued to use the traditional term in the title of this textbook, you will find that all the major topics pertain to biological matters.

The origins of physical anthropology are to be found in two principal areas of interest among nineteenth-century scholars. First, there was increasing concern among many scientists (at the time called *natural historians*) regarding the mechanisms by which modern species had come to be. In other words, increasing numbers of scholars were beginning to doubt the literal, biblical interpretation of creation. This doesn't mean that all natural historians had completely abandoned religious explanations of natural occurrences. But scientific explanations emphasizing natural, rather than supernatural, phenomena were becoming increasingly popular in scientific and intellectual circles. Although few scientists were actually prepared to believe that humans had evolved from earlier forms, discoveries of several Neandertal fossils in the 1800s began to raise questions regarding the origins and antiquity of the human species.

FIGURE 1-4 Paleoanthropologists excavating at the Drimolen site, South Africa.

The sparks of interest in biological change over time were fueled into flames by the publication of Charles Darwin's *On the Origin of Species* in 1859. Today, **paleoanthropology**, or the study of human evolution, particularly as evidenced in the fossil record, is one of the major subfields of physical anthropology (Fig. 1-4). There are now thousands of specimens of human ancestors housed in research collections. Taken together, these fossils cover a span of at least 4 million years of human prehistory, and although incomplete, they provide us with significantly more knowledge than was available just ten years ago. It is the ultimate goal of paleoanthropological research to identify the various early hominid species, establish a chronological sequence of relationships among them, and gain insights into their adaptation and behavior. Only then will there emerge a clear picture of how and when humankind came into being.

Observable physical variation, particularly as seen in skin color, was a second nineteenth-century interest that had direct relevance to anthropology. Enormous effort was aimed at describing and explaining the biological differences between various human populations. Although some endeavors were misguided and even racist, they gave birth to literally thousands of body measurements that could be used to compare people. Physical anthropologists use many of the techniques of **anthropometry** today, not only to study living groups, but also to study skeletal remains from archaeological sites (Fig. 1-5). Moreover, anthropometric techniques have considerable application in the design of everything from airplane cockpits to office furniture.

Anthropologists today are concerned with human variation because of its possible *adaptive significance* and also because they want to identify the genetic and other related evolutionary factors that have acted to produce variation. In other words, many traits that typify certain populations are seen as having evolved as biological adaptations, or adjustments, to local environmental conditions, including infectious disease. Other characteristics may be the results of geographical isolation or the descent of populations from small founding groups. Examining biological variation between populations of any species provides valuable information as to the mechanisms of genetic change in groups over time, which is really what the evolutionary process is all about.

paleoanthropology The interdisciplinary approach to the study of earlier hominids—their chronology, physical structure, archaeological remains, habitats, etc.

anthropometry Measurement of human body parts. When osteologists measure skeletal elements, the term *osteometry* is often used.

FIGURE 1-5 Anthropology student using spreading calipers to measure cranial length.

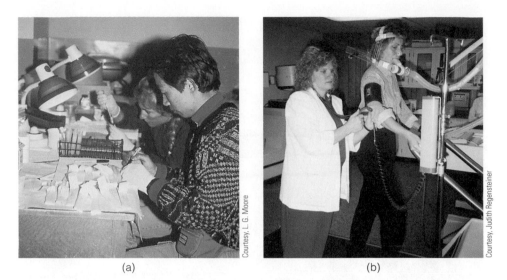

Courtesy, L. G. Moore

Courtesy, Judith Regensteiner

(a)   (b)

FIGURE 1–6 (a) Dr. Jianguo Zhuang (foreground) and Dr. Stacy Zamudio (rear) are separating white blood cells from whole blood samples taken from Tibetan research subjects. The white blood cells provide DNA used to investigate genetic variation in populations residing at high altitude. (b) This researcher is using a treadmill test to assess a subject's heart rate, blood pressure, and oxygen consumption.

Modern population studies also examine other important aspects of human variation, including how various groups respond physiologically to different kinds of environmentally induced stress (Fig. 1–6). Such stresses may include high altitude, cold, or heat.

Other physical anthropologists conduct nutritional studies, investigating the relationships between various dietary components, cultural practices, physiology, and certain aspects of health and disease (Fig. 1–7). Investigations of human fertility, growth, and development closely related to the topic of nutrition. These fields of inquiry are fundamental to studies of adaptation in mod-

FIGURE 1–7 Dr. Kathleen Galvin measures upper arm circumference in a young Maasai boy in Tanzania. Data derived from various body measurements, including height and weight, were used in a health and nutrition study of groups of Maasai cattle herders.

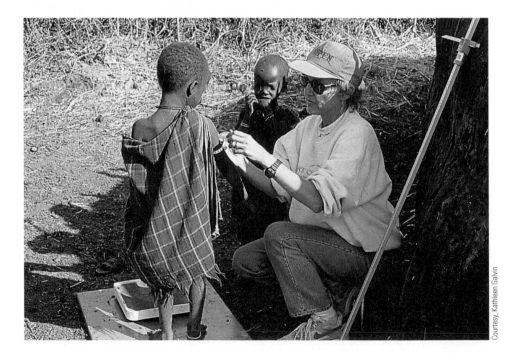

Courtesy, Kathleen Galvin

Robert Jurmain

FIGURE 1–8 Cloning and sequencing methods are frequently used to identify genes in humans and nonhuman primates. This graduate student identifies a genetically modified bacterial clone.

ern human populations, and they can provide insights into hominid evolution as well.

It would be impossible to study evolutionary processes without a knowledge of genetic principles. For this reason and others, **genetics** is a crucial field for physical anthropologists. Modern physical anthropology would not exist as an evolutionary science were it not for advances in the understanding of genetic mechanisms.

In this exciting time of rapid advances in genetic research, *molecular anthropologists* use cutting-edge technologies to investigate evolutionary relationships between human populations and also between humans and nonhuman primates. To do this, they examine similarities and differences in DNA sequences between individuals, populations, and species. In addition, by extracting DNA from certain fossils, they have contributed to our understanding of relationships between extinct and living species. As genetic technologies continue to be developed, molecular anthropologists will play a key role in explaining human evolution, adaptation, and our biological relationships with other species (Fig. 1–8).

Primatology, the study of nonhuman primates, has become increasingly important since the late 1950s (Fig. 1–9). Behavioral studies, especially those conducted on groups in natural environments, have implications for numerous scientific disciplines. Because nonhuman primates are our closest living relatives, the identification of underlying factors related to social behavior, communication, infant care, reproductive behavior, and so on, helps us develop a better understanding of the natural forces that have shaped so many aspects of modern human behavior.

Moreover, nonhuman primates are important to study in their own right. This is particularly true today because the majority of primate species are threatened or seriously endangered. Only through study will scientists be able to recommend policies that can better ensure the survival of many nonhuman primates and thousands of other species as well.

Primate paleontology, the study of the primate fossil record, has implications not only for nonhuman primates but also for hominids. Virtually every year,

genetics The study of gene structure and action and the patterns of inheritance of traits from parent to offspring. Genetic mechanisms are the underlying foundation for evolutionary change.

primatology The study of the biology and behavior of nonhuman primates (prosimians, monkeys, and apes).

Courtesy, Bonnie Pedersen/Arlene Kruse

FIGURE 1–9 Yahaya Alamasi, a member of the senior field staff at Gombe National Park, Tanzania. Alamasi is recording behaviors in free-ranging chimpanzees.

fossil-bearing beds in North America, Africa, Asia, and Europe yield important new discoveries. By studying fossil primates and comparing them with anatomically similar living species, primate paleontologists are able to learn much about factors such as diet or locomotion in earlier forms. They can also make certain assumptions about behavior in some extinct primates and attempt to clarify what we know about evolutionary relationships between extinct and modern species, including ourselves.

osteology The study of skeletal material. Human osteology focuses on the interpretation of the skeletal remains of past groups. Some of the same techniques are used in paleoanthropology to study early hominids.

Osteology, the study of the skeleton, is central to physical anthropology. In fact, it is so important that when many people think of biological anthropology, the first thing that comes to mind is bones (although frequently they ask about dinosaurs). The emphasis on osteology exists partly because of the concern with the analysis of fossils, and a thorough knowledge of the structure and function of the skeleton is critical to the interpretation of fossil material.

Bone biology and physiology are of major importance to many other aspects of physical anthropology, in addition to paleontology. Many osteologists specialize in studies that emphasize various measurements of skeletal elements. This type of research is essential, for example, to the identification of stature and growth patterns in archaeological populations.

paleopathology The branch of osteology that studies the evidence of disease and injury in human skeletal (or, occasionally, mummified) remains.

One subdiscipline of osteology is the study of disease and trauma in archaeologically derived skeletal populations. **Paleopathology** is a prominent subfield that investigates the incidence of trauma, certain infectious diseases (including syphilis and tuberculosis), nutritional deficiencies, and numerous other conditions that may leave evidence in bone (Fig. 1–10). This research tells us a great deal about the lives of individuals and populations from the past. Paleopathology also provides information pertaining to the history of certain disease processes and for this reason it is of interest to scientists in biomedical fields.

forensic anthropology An applied anthropological approach dealing with legal matters. Physical anthropologists work with coroners and others in the identification and analysis of human remains.

Forensic anthropology is directly related to osteology and paleopathology. Technically, this approach is the application of anthropological (usually osteological and sometimes archaeological) techniques to legal issues (Fig. 1–11). Forensic anthropologists are commonly called on to help identify skeletal remains in cases of disaster or other situations where a human body has been found.

Forensic anthropologists have been involved in numerous cases having important legal, historical, and human consequences. They were prominent in the identification of the skeletons of most of the Russian imperial family, executed in 1918. They also participated in the identification of missing American soldiers in Southeast Asia. And recently, many forensic anthropologists participated in the

FIGURE 1–10 (a) A partially healed fracture of the femur (thigh bone) from a child's skeleton (estimated age at death is 6 years). Cause of death was probably an infection resulting from this injury. (b) Cranial lesions, probably resulting from metastasized cancer.

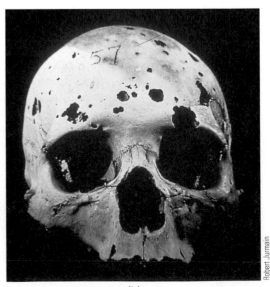

(a)   (b)

(a)

Courtesy, Lorna Pierce/Judy Suchey

FIGURE 1-11 (a) Physical anthropologists Lorna Pierce (left) and Judy Suchey (center) working as forensic consultants. The dog has just located a concealed human cranium during a training session. (b) Forensic anthropologists at the location on Staten Island where all materials from the World Trade Center were taken for investigation after September 11, 2001. They are wearing HAZMAT (hazardous materials) suits for protection.

(b)

Provided by D. France

overwhelming task of trying to identify the remains of victims of the September 11, 2001, terrorist attacks in the United States (Fig.1–11b).

Anatomical studies constitute another important area of interest for physical anthropologists. In the living organism, bone and teeth are intimately linked to the soft tissues that surround and act on them. Consequently, a thorough knowledge of soft tissue anatomy is essential to the understanding of biomechanical relationships involved in movement. Such relationships are important to the accurate assessment of the structure and function of limbs and other components in fossilized remains. For these reasons and others, many physical anthropologists specialize in anatomical studies. In fact, several physical anthropologists hold professorships in anatomy departments at universities and medical schools (Fig.1–12).

Applied approaches in biological anthropology are numerous. And while *applied anthropology* is aimed at the practical application of anthropological

FIGURE 1–12 Dr. Linda Levitch teaching a human anatomy class at the University of North Carolina School of Medicine.

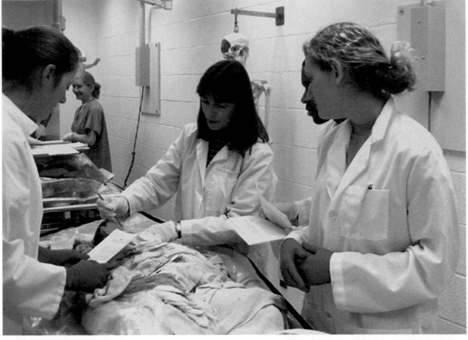

Courtesy, Linda Levitch

theories and methods outside the academic setting, applied and academic anthropology are not mutually exclusive approaches. In fact, applied anthropology relies on the research and theories of academic anthropologists and at the same time has much to contribute to theory and techniques. Probably the majority of applied anthropologists are trained as cultural anthropologists, and perhaps the best-known example is provided by archaeologists working in cultural resource management (see p. 7). Within biological anthropology, forensic anthropologists provide a good example of the applied approach. But the practical application of the techniques of physical anthropology is not new. During World War II, for example, physical anthropologists, were extensively involved in the design of gun turrets and airplane cockpits. Since that time, many physical anthropologists have pursued careers in genetic and biomedical research, public health, evolutionary medicine, medical anthropology, and conservation of non-human primates, and many hold positions in museums and zoos. In fact, a background in physical anthropology is excellent preparation for almost any career in the medical and biological fields.

From this brief overview, it can be seen that physical anthropology is the subdiscipline of anthropology that focuses on many varied aspects of the biological and behavioral nature of human beings. Humans are a product of the same forces that produced all life on earth. As such, we represent one contemporary component of a vast biological **continuum** at one point in time, and in this regard, we are not particularly unique. Stating that humans are part of a continuum does not imply that we are at the peak of development on that continuum. Depending on which criteria one uses, humans can be seen to exist at one end of the continuum or the other or somewhere in between. But humans don't necessarily occupy a position of inherent superiority over other species.

There is, however, one dimension in which human beings are truly unique, and that is intellect. After all, humans are the only species, born of earth, to stir the lunar dust. Humans are the only species to develop language and complex culture as a means of buffering the challenges posed by nature and by so doing eventually gain the power to shape the very destiny of the planet.

continuum A set of relationships in which all components fall along a single integrated spectrum. All life reflects a single biological continuum.

Physical Anthropology and the Scientific Method

Science is a process of understanding phenomena through observation, generalization, and verification. By this we mean that there is an **empirical** approach to gaining information through the use of systematic and explicit techniques. Because biological anthropologists are engaged in scientific pursuits, they adhere to the principles of the **scientific method**, whereby a research problem is identified and information is then gathered in order to solve it.

The gathering of information is referred to as **data** collection, and when scientists use a rigorously controlled approach, they are able to describe precisely their techniques and results in a manner that facilitates comparisons with the work of others. For example, when scientists collect data on tooth size in hominid fossils, they must specify which teeth are being measured, how they are being measured, and what the results of the measurements are (expressed numerically, or **quantitatively**). Then it is up to the investigators to draw conclusions as to the meaning and significance of their measurements. This body of information then becomes the basis of future studies, perhaps by other researchers, who can compare their own results with those already obtained. The eventual outcome of this type of inquiry may be the acceptance or rejection of certain stated facts and explanations.

Once facts have been established, scientists try to explain them. First, a **hypothesis**, a provisional explanation of a phenomenon, is developed. But before a hypothesis can be accepted, it must be tested by means of data collection and analysis. Indeed, the testing of hypotheses with the possibility of proving them false is the very basis of the scientific method.

Scientific testing of hypotheses may take several years (or longer) and may involve researchers who were not involved with the original work. In subsequent studies, other investigators may attempt to obtain the original results, but that may not happen. For example, repeated failures to duplicate the results of highly publicized cold fusion experiments led most scientists to question and ultimately reject the claims made in the original research. While it is easier to duplicate original studies conducted in laboratory settings, it is equally important to verify data collected outside tightly controlled situations. In the latter circumstance, results are tested relative to other, often larger, samples. The predicted patterns will either be confirmed through such further research or be viewed as limited or even incorrect.

If a hypothesis cannot be falsified, it is accepted as a **theory**. There is a popular misconception that theories are nothing more than hunches or unfounded beliefs. But in scientific terms, a theory is much more than mere speculation because it has been repeatedly tested and scientists have not been able to disprove it. As such, theories not only help organize current knowledge, but also predict how new facts may fit into the established pattern.

Use of the scientific method not only allows for the development and testing of hypotheses, but also permits various types of *bias* to be addressed and controlled. It's important to realize that bias occurs in all studies. Sources of bias include how the investigator was trained and by whom; what particular questions interest the researcher; what specific skills and talents he or she possesses; what earlier results (if any) have been established in this realm of study and by whom (e.g., the researcher, close colleagues, or those with rival approaches or even rival personalities); and what sources of data are available (e.g., accessible countries or museums) and thus what samples can be collected.

science A body of knowledge gained through observation and experimentation; from the Latin *scientia*, meaning "knowledge."

empirical Relying on experiment or observation; from the Latin *empiricus*, meaning "experienced."

scientific method A research method whereby a problem is identified, a hypothesis (or hypothetical explanation) is stated, and that hypothesis is tested through the collection and analysis of data. If the hypothesis is verified, it becomes a theory.

data (*sing.*, datum) Facts from which conclusions can be drawn; scientific information.

quantitatively In a manner involving measurements of quantity and including such properties as size, number, and capacity. When data are quantified, they are expressed numerically and are capable of being tested statistically.

hypothesis (*pl.*, hypotheses) A provisional explanation of a phenomenon. Hypotheses require verification or falsification through testing.

scientific testing The precise repetition of an experiment or expansion of observed data to provide verification; the procedure by which hypotheses and theories are verified, modified, or discarded.

theory A broad statement of scientific relationships or underlying principles that has been at least partially verified.

See Virtual Lab 3, section III, for a discussion of the scientific method.

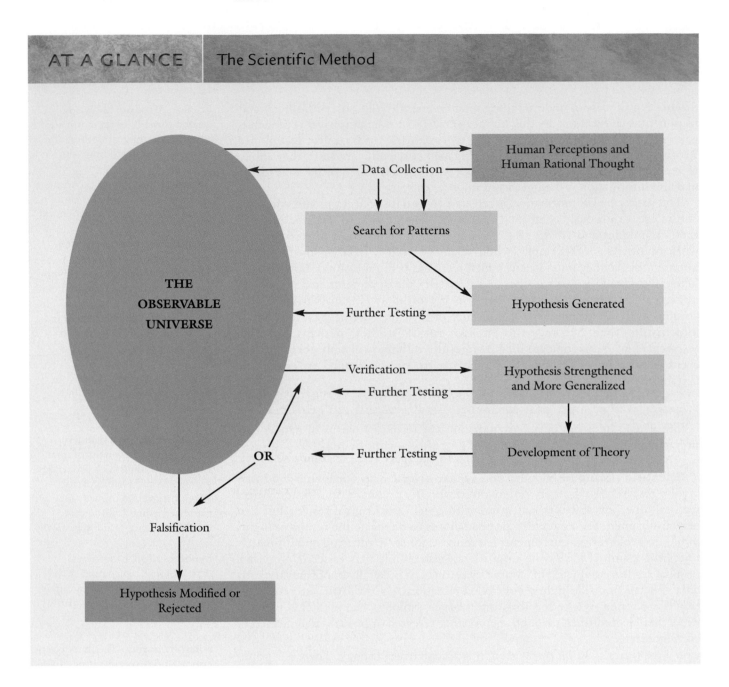

AT A GLANCE   The Scientific Method

Application of the scientific method thus requires constant vigilance by all those who practice it. The goal is not to establish "truth" in any absolute sense, but rather to generate ever more accurate and consistent explanations of phenomena in our universe. At its very heart, scientific methodology is an exercise in rational thought and critical thinking (see Issue, pp. 20–21).

The Anthropological Perspective

Perhaps the most important benefit you will receive from this textbook—and this course—is a wider appreciation of the human experience. To understand human beings and how our species came to be, it is necessary to broaden our viewpoint, both through time and over space. All branches of anthropology fundamentally seek to do this in what we call the *anthropological perspective*.

Physical anthropologists, for example, are keenly interested in how humans differ from and are similar to other animals, especially nonhuman primates. For example, we have defined *hominids* as bipedal primates, but what are the major components of bipedal locomotion, and how do they differ from, say, those in a quadrupedal ape? To answer these questions, we would need to study human locomotion and compare it with the locomotion seen in various nonhuman primates.

Through a broadened perspective, we can begin to grasp the diversity of the human experience within the context of biological and behavioral continuity with other species. In this way, we may better understand the limits and potentials of humankind. And by extending the breadth of our knowledge to include cultures other than our own we may hope to avoid the **ethnocentric** pitfalls inherent in a more limited view of humanity.

Before the term *ethnocentric* came into use, Mark Twain, wrote that "Travel is fatal to prejudice, bigotry, and narrowmindedness, and many of our people need it sorely on these accounts." (*Innocents Abroad*, 1869). What he meant was that when we become familiar with other cultures, stereotypes break down and we realize that we cannot—and should not—use our own culture as the gold standard by which to judge others. This **relativistic** view of culture is perhaps more important now than ever before because it allows us to understand other people's concerns and to view our own culture from a different perspective. Likewise, by examining our species as part of a broad spectrum of life, we realize that we cannot judge other species using human criteria. Each species is unique, with needs and a behavioral repertoire not exactly like that of any other. By recognizing that we share many similarities (both biological and behavioral) with other animals, perhaps we may come to recognize that they have a place in nature just as surely as we ourselves do.

In addition to broadening perspectives over space (i.e., encompassing many cultures and ecological circumstances as well as nonhuman species), an anthropological perspective also extends our horizons *through time*. For example, in Chapter 16 we will discuss human nutrition. However, the vast majority of the foods people eat today (coming from domesticated plants and animals) were unavailable prior to 10,000 years ago. Human physiological mechanisms for chewing and digesting foods nevertheless were already well established long before that date. These adaptive complexes go back millions of years. In addition to the obviously different diets prior to the development of agriculture (approximately 10,000 years ago), earlier hominids might well have differed from humans today in average body size, **metabolism,** and activity patterns. How, then, does the basic evolutionary "equipment" (i.e., physiology) inherited from our hominid forebears accommodate our modern diets? Clearly, the way to understand such processes is not just by looking at contemporary human responses, but also by placing them in the perspective of evolutionary development through time.

Indeed, most of the topics covered in this book are addressed by using a broad application of the anthropological perspective. For physical anthropologists, such an approach usually means extending the perspective over space as well as through considerable periods of time.

We hope that the following pages will help you develop an increased understanding of the similarities we share with other biological organisms and also of the processes that have shaped the traits that make us unique. We live in what may well be the most crucial period for our planet in the last 65 million years. We are members of the one species that, through the very agency of culture, has wrought such devastating changes in ecological systems that we must now alter our technologies or face potentially unspeakable consequences. In such a time, it is vital that we attempt to gain the best possible understanding of what it means to be human. We believe that the study of physical anthropology is one endeavor that aids in this attempt, and that is indeed the goal of this text.

ethnocentric Viewing other cultures from the inherently biased perspective of one's own culture. Ethnocentrism often results in other cultures being seen as inferior to one's own.

relativistic Pertaining to relativism. Viewing entities as they relate to something else. Cultural relativism is the view that cultures have merits within their own historical and environmental contexts and that they should not be judged through comparisons with one's own culture.

metabolism The chemical processes within cells that break down nutrients and release energy for the body to use. (When nutrients are broken down into their component parts, such as amino acids, energy is released and made available for the cell to use.)

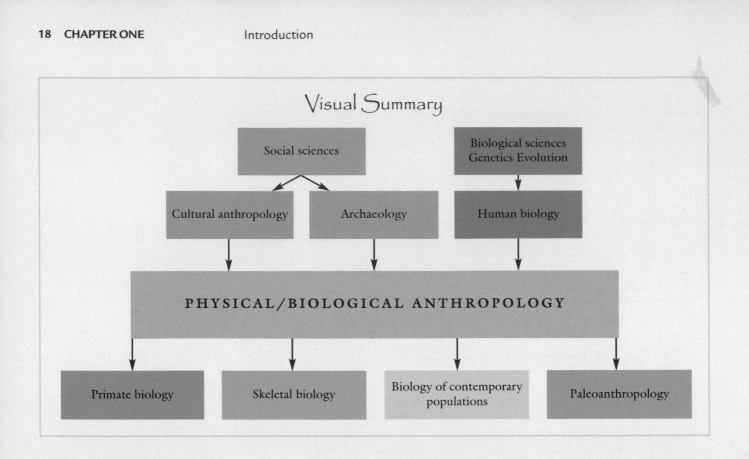

Visual Summary

Social sciences

Biological sciences
Genetics Evolution

Cultural anthropology   Archaeology   Human biology

PHYSICAL/BIOLOGICAL ANTHROPOLOGY

Primate biology   Skeletal biology   Biology of contemporary populations   Paleoanthropology

Summary

In this chapter, we have introduced you to the field of physical, or biological, anthropology, placing it within the overall context of anthropological studies. As a major academic discipline within the social sciences, anthropology also includes archaeology, cultural anthropology, and linguistic anthropology as its other major subfields.

Physical anthropology is the study of many aspects of human biology, including genetics, genetic variation, adaptations to environmental factors, nutrition, and anatomy. These topics are discussed within an evolutionary framework because all human characteristics are either directly or indirectly the results of biological evolution, which in turn is driven by genetic change. Hence, biological anthropologists also study our closest relatives, the nonhuman primates, primate evolution, and the genetic and fossil evidence for human evolution.

Because biological anthropology is a scientific discipline, the role of the scientific method in research was also discussed. We presented the importance of objectivity, observation, data collection and analysis, and the formation and testing of hypotheses to explain natural phenomena. We also emphasized that this approach is an empirical one and does not rely on supernatural explanations.

Because evolution is the core of physical anthropology, in the next chapter we present a brief historical overview of changes in Western scientific thought that led to the discovery of the basic principles of biological evolution. As you are probably aware, evolution is a highly controversial subject (much more so in the United States than in other countries). The next chapter will address some of the reasons for this controversy as well as explain the evidence for evolution as the single thread that unites all the biological sciences.

Questions for Review

1. Given that you have only just been introduced to the field of physical anthropology, why do you think subjects such as anatomy, genetics, nonhuman primate behavior, and human evolution are integrated into a discussion of what it means to be human?

2. Is it important to you, personally, to know about human evolution? Why or why not?

3. Do you see a connection between hominid footprints that are almost 4 million years old and human footprints left on the moon in 1969? If so, do you think this relationship is important? What does the fact that there are human footprints on the moon say about human adaptation? (You may wish to refer to both biological and cultural adaptation.)

4. Explain how physical anthropology relates to the other subfields of anthropology.

For Further Thought

1. What is meant by the term "biological continuum"? How do humans fit into it?

2. In 50 years, what kinds of research do you think physical anthropologists will be doing? What types of technologies do you think they will use?

Go to the book website at **http://www.anthropology.wadsworth.com** for resources to help you explore these questions further. Click on "For Further Thought" for this chapter.

Suggested Further Reading

Angeloni, Elvio (ed.). 2003. Annual Editions: Physical Anthropology. Guildford, CT: Dushkin Publishing Group (a division of McGraw-Hill).

Boaz, Noel and Linda D. Wolfe. 1995. *Biological Anthropology: the State of the Science*. Bend, OR: International Institute for Human Evolution.

Strum, S., D. G. Lundburg, and D. Hamburg. 1999. *The New Physical Anthropology: Science, Humanism, and Cultural Reflection*. Upper Saddle River, NJ: Prentice Hall.

Online Anthropology Resource Center

Go to the Anthropology Resource Center at **http://www.anthropology.wadsworth.com** for a wealth of online resources, including a companion website for your text that provides study aids such as self-quizzes for each chapter and a practice final exam, as well as links to anthropology websites and information on the latest theories and discoveries in the field. Also, check out InfoTrac College Edition®, your online library that offers full-length articles from thousands of scholarly and popular publications. Just click on the InfoTrac button at the companion website and use the passcode that came with your book.

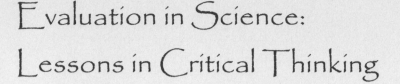

Evaluation in Science: Lessons in Critical Thinking

At the end of various chapters throughout this book, you will find a brief discussion of a contemporary topic. Some of these subjects are not usually covered in anthropology textbooks. However, we think it's important to address such issues because scientists shouldn't simply dismiss those views or ideas of which they are skeptical. Similarly, you should be reluctant to *accept* a view based solely on its personal appeal. Accepting or rejecting an idea based on personal feelings is as good a definition of "bias" as one could devise. Science is an approach—indeed, a *tool*—used to eliminate (or at least minimize) bias.

Scientific approaches of evaluation are, in fact, a part of a broader framework of intellectual rigor called *critical thinking*. The development of critical thinking skills is an important and lasting benefit of a college education. Such skills enable people to evaluate, compare, analyze, critique, and synthesize information so they won't accept all they hear and read at face value but will instead be able to reach their own conclusions. Critical thinkers are able to assess the evidence supporting their own beliefs (in a sense, to step outside themselves) and to identify the weaknesses in their own positions. They recognize that knowledge is not merely a collection of facts but an ongoing process of examining information to expand our understanding of the world.

In scientific inquiry, individual "facts" (or better put, *observations*) must be presented clearly, with appropriate documentation. That is the purpose of bibliographical citation, as exemplified throughout this textbook. Once "facts" are established, scientists attempt to develop explanations concerning their relationships. In this way, initial hypotheses can be broadened into more general and better-supported theories.

A crucial aspect of scientific statements is that they are *falsifiable;* that is, there must be a means of evaluating the validity of hypotheses and theories to demonstrate that the statements may be incorrect. In this way, scientific conclusions are constantly *tested*. Statements such as "Heaven exists" may well be "true" (i.e., describe some actual state), but there is no rational, *empirical* means (based on experience or experiment) by which to test it. Acceptance of such a view is thus based on faith rather than on scientific verification.

We should emphasize that perceived phenomena understood through faith don't necessarily conflict with empirical demonstration. In fact, precisely because there may be areas of knowledge beyond the reach of scientific inquiry, faith-based beliefs provide a powerful influence for many people. Furthermore, these beliefs need not (and for many individuals, scientist and nonscientist alike, don't) conflict with the demonstrable values of scientific thought.

One of the most appealing aspects of perspectives based in faith is that such beliefs are widely and comfortably accepted as true. In science, statements can be tested and falsified (indeed, this is a central component of the scientific method), but they can never completely be proved "true." Theories can simply be better substantiated and are thus more fully established. However, new evidence can also require modification of hypotheses and theories; and some theories might prove so inadequate as to be rejected altogether. Thus, Newton's theory of gravitation was substantially altered by Einstein's theory of relativity. The old theory of a "missing link" (a kind of halfway compromise between modern humans and modern apes) preceded modern evolutionary thinking and is now seen as simplistic, misleading, and, at a practical level, of no value.

This inherent aspect of scientific inquiry in which theories are always subject to ongoing evaluation is widely misunderstood, frequently with disturbing consequences. For example, as we will note in Chapter 2, claims are often made that evolution is "just a theory." Pronouncements like these, as related to the teaching of evolution in public schools, have found their way into court decisions in California and policy statements by the Alabama State Board of Education. In science, knowledge is always proposed, organized, and tested in the form of hypotheses and, more generally, as theories. Our understanding of the action of gravity is just a theory, and so is the sun-centered depiction of the solar system. These two theories have, of course, been supported by an overwhelming amount of highly consistent evidence—but *so has evolutionary theory*. The constraint that science can never establish absolute "truth" shouldn't be confused with an inability to understand the world around us. The human brain is one product of 4 billion years of evolution on this planet, and by using this neurological structure, *Homo sapiens* has the ability to apply rational thought. In the last few hundred years, the scientific method has developed into the most powerful tool invented by our species to utilize these rational capabilities and, in so doing, to come to grips with the universe and how we fit into it.

Throughout this book, you will be presented with the results of numerous studies that utilize numerical data. For example, it might be stated that female chimpanzees eat more insects than male chimpanzees or that Neandertal males were bigger than females or that the gene for cystic fibrosis is more common in European populations than in other groups. First of all, you should always be cautious of generalizations. What is the specific nature of the argument? What data support it? Can these data be quantified? If so, how is this information presented? (*Note:* Always read the tables in textbooks or articles.)

Regardless of the discipline you ultimately study, at some point in your academic career you should take a course in statistics. Many universities now make statistics a general education requirement (sometimes under the category "quantitative reasoning"). Whether you are required to take such a course or choose to do so, we strongly encourage it. Statistics often seems a very dry subject, and many students are intimidated by the math it requires. Nevertheless, perhaps more than any other skill you will acquire in your college years, quantitative critical reasoning is a tool you will be able to use every day of your life.

The topics chosen for the chapter-closing issues are those that intrigue the authors, and we hope that you also will find them stimulating. Some subjects are of historical interest. In addition, we address several topics that relate to recent advances in science, as exemplified by newly developed genetic technologies. Here, in addition to challenging you to grasp the basic scientific principles involved, we also ask you to consider the *social implications* of scientific/technological advances.

A responsibility of an educated society is to be both informed and vigilant. The knowledge we possess and attempt to build on is neither "good" nor "bad"; however, the uses to which knowledge may be put have highly charged moral and ethical implications. Thus, a goal of the chapter-closing issues is to stimulate your interest and provide you with a basis to reach your own conclusions. Here are some useful questions to ask in making critical evaluations about these issues or any other controversial scientific topic:

1. What data are presented?
2. What conclusions are presented, and how are they organized (as tentative hypotheses or as more dogmatic assertions)?
3. Are these views simply the opinions of the authors, or are they supported by a larger body of research?
4. What are the research findings? Are they adequately documented?
5. Is the information consistent with information that you already possess? If not, can the inconsistencies be explained?
6. Are the conclusions (hypotheses) testable? How might one go about testing the various hypotheses that are presented?
7. If presentation of new research findings is at odds with previous hypotheses (or theories), must these hypotheses now be modified (or completely rejected)?
8. How do your own personal views bias you in interpreting the results?
9. Once you have identified your own biases, are you able to set them aside in order to evaluate the information objectively?
10. Are you able to discuss both the pros and cons of a scientific topic in an evenhanded manner?

The Development of Evolutionary Theory

A human chromosome
© Biophoto Associates / Photo Researchers, Inc.

Introduction

Has anyone ever asked you, "If humans evolved from monkeys, then why do we still have monkeys?" Or maybe you have encountered this one: "If evolution happens, then why don't we ever see new species?" Such questions are often asked by people who have no understanding of evolutionary processes and who may not even believe that such processes exist. The fact that anyone today, given the overwhelming evidence for biological evolution, would ask such questions is a depressing reflection of the poor quality of biological education in the United States. And because the topic is frequently avoided in high school classes, evolution is one of the most misunderstood of all natural phenomena. Indeed, if you are not an anthropology or biology major and you are taking a class in biological anthropology mainly to fill a science requirement, it is likely that this is the only class in which you will ever study evolution.

By the end of this course, you will know the answers to the two questions posed in the previous paragraph. In brief, no one who studies evolution would ever say that humans evolved from monkeys—because they didn't. The earliest human ancestors evolved from a species that lived some 5 to 8 million years ago (m.y.a.). This ancestral species also gave rise to the lineage now represented by chimpanzees and gorillas. The lineage that led to the apes and ourselves separated from a monkey-like ancestor some 20 m.y.a. Monkeys are still around because as lineages diverged from a common ancestor, each group went its separate way. Over time, these groups evolved into the species that exist today. Each species is the current product of processes that go back millions of years, processes that ultimately produce diversity as populations adapt to local conditions. Because evolution takes time, and lots of it, we rarely witness the appearance of new species (although microorganisms are a different matter). However, as you will learn later in this chapter, we do see *microevolutionary* changes in living species.

The subject of evolution is controversial, particularly in the United States, because some religious views hold that evolutionary statements run counter to biblical teachings. Indeed, as you are probably aware, there continues to be much opposition to the teaching of evolution in public schools.

Those who wish to denigrate evolution frequently insist that it is "only a theory" in an attempt to reduce its status to supposition. Actually, to refer to a concept as "theory" is to lend it support. As we noted in Chapter 1, theories are general hypotheses that have been tested and subjected to verification through accumulated evidence. Evolution *is* a theory, one that has increasingly been supported by a mounting body of genetic evidence. It is a theory that has stood the test of time, and today it stands as the most fundamental unifying force in biological science.

See the following sections of the CD-ROM for topics covered in this chapter: Virtual Lab 1, section III and Virtual Lab 2, sections I and VII.

Because physical anthropology is concerned with all aspects of how humans came to be and how we adapt physiologically to the external environment, the details of the evolutionary process are crucial to the field. Moreover, given the central importance of evolution to physical anthropology, it is valuable to know how the mechanics of the process came to be discovered. Additionally, to appreciate the nature of the controversy that continues to surround the issue today, it is important to examine the discovery of basic evolutionary principles within the social and political context in which the theory emerged.

A Brief History of Evolutionary Thought

The discovery of evolutionary principles occurred in western Europe and was made possible by advances in scientific thinking that began in the sixteenth century. Having said this, it must at the same time be recognized that Western science borrowed many of its ideas from other cultures, especially the Arabs, Indians, and Chinese. Intellectuals in these three cultures and in ancient Greece, had notions of biological evolution (Teresi, 2002) but they never formulated their ideas into a cohesive theory.

The individual most responsible for the elucidation of the evolutionary process was Charles Darwin. But while Darwin was formulating his theory of **natural selection,** his ideas were being duplicated by another British naturalist, Alfred Russel Wallace. That natural selection, the single most important mechanism of evolutionary change, should be proposed at more or less the same time by two British men in the mid-nineteenth century may seem unlikely. But actually, it is not all that surprising. Indeed, if Darwin and Wallace had not made their simultaneous discoveries, someone else would have. That is to say, the groundwork had already been laid, and many within the scientific community were prepared to accept explanations of biological change that would have been unacceptable even 25 years before.

Like other human endeavors, scientific knowledge is usually gained through a series of small steps rather than giant leaps. Just as technological innovation is based on past achievements, scientific knowledge builds on previously developed theories. Given the stepwise progression of scientific discovery, it is informative to examine the development of ideas that led Darwin and Wallace independently to develop the theory of evolution by natural selection.

Throughout the Middle Ages, one predominant component of the European world view was that all aspects of nature, including all forms of life and their relationships to one another, were fixed and unchanging. This view of natural phenomena was shaped in part by a feudal society that was very much a hierarchical arrangement supporting a rigid class system that had changed little for several centuries.

The world view of Europeans during the Middle Ages was also shaped by a powerful religious system. The teachings of Christianity were taken quite literally, and it was generally accepted that all life on earth had been created by God exactly as it existed in the present. This belief that life forms could not change eventually came to be known in European intellectual circles as **fixity of species.**

Accompanying the notion of fixity of species was the belief that all God's creations were arranged in a hierarchy that progressed from the simplest organisms to the most complex. At the top of this linear sequence were humans. This concept of a ranked order of living things, called the *Great Chain of Being,* was first proposed in the fourth century B.C. by the Greek philosopher Aristotle. Although position within the chain was based on physical similarities between species, evolutionary and biological relationships were not implied. And since all of nature and the Great Chain of Being were created by God in a fixed state,

natural selection The mechanism of evolutionary change first articulated by Charles Darwin; refers to genetic change or changes in the frequencies of certain traits in populations due to differential reproductive success between individuals.

fixity of species The notion that species, once created, can never change; an idea diametrically opposed to theories of biological evolution.

change was inconceivable. Thus, questioning the assumptions of fixity was ultimately seen as a challenge to God's perfection and could be considered heresy, a crime punishable by a very nasty and potentially fiery death.

The plan of the entire universe was seen as the Grand Design—that is, God's design. In what is called the "argument from design," anatomical structures were viewed as planned to meet the purpose for which they were required. Wings, arms, eyes—all these structures were interpreted as fitting the functions they performed, and nature was considered to be a deliberate plan of the Grand Designer.

The date the Grand Designer had completed his works was relatively recent. According to Archbishop James Ussher (1581–1656), an Irish scholar who worked out the date of creation by analyzing the "begat" chapter of Genesis, the earth was created in 4004 B.C. Archbishop Ussher was not the first person to propose a recent origin of the earth, but he was responsible for providing a precise date for it.

The prevailing notion of the earth's brief existence, together with fixity of species, provided a formidable obstacle to the development of evolutionary theory because evolution requires time. And scientists also needed a theory of immense geological time in order to formulate evolutionary principles. In fact, until the concepts of fixity and time were fundamentally altered, it was impossible to conceive of evolution by means of natural selection.

See Virtual Lab 7, section I, for a discussion of several geological methods of determining the age of the earth.

THE SCIENTIFIC REVOLUTION

What, then, upset the medieval belief in a rigid universe of planets, stars, plants, and animals? How did the scientific method as we know it today develop and, with the help of Newton and Galileo in the seventeenth century, demonstrate a moving, not static, universe? Actually, we would be justified in asking why it took so long for Europe to break from traditional belief systems when Arab and Indian scholars had developed theories of planetary motion centuries earlier.

For Europeans, the discovery of the New World and circumnavigation of the globe in the fifteenth century overturned some very fundamental ideas about the planet. For one thing, the earth could no longer be viewed as flat. Also, as Europeans began to explore the New World, their awareness of biological diversity was greatly expanded through exposure to plants and animals previously unknown to them.

There were other attacks on the complacency of traditional beliefs. In 1514, a Polish mathematician named Copernicus challenged Aristotle's long-believed assertion that the earth, circled by the sun, moon, and stars, was the center of the universe. In fact, in India, scholars had figured this out long before Copernicus. But Copernicus is generally credited with removing the earth as the center of all things by proposing a sun-centered solar system.

Copernicus' theory did not attract much attention at the time, but in the early 1600s, it was restated and further substantiated by an Italian mathematics professor, Galileo Galilei. Galileo came into direct confrontation with the Catholic Church over his publications, to the extent that he spent the last nine years of his life under house arrest. Even so, in intellectual circles, the universe had changed from one of fixity to one of motion, although most people still believed that change was impossible for living forms.

European scholars of the sixteenth and seventeenth centuries developed methods and theories that revolutionized scientific thought. The seventeenth century, in particular, was a beehive of scientific activity and saw the discoveries of the laws of physics, motion, and gravity. Other achievements included the discovery of the true function of the heart and the circulatory system, and the development of numerous scientific instruments, including the telescope, barometer, and microscope. These technological advances permitted investigations of natural phenomena and opened up entire worlds for discoveries such as had never before been imagined.

Scientific achievement increasingly came to direct as well as reflect the changing views of Europeans. Investigations of stars, planets, animals, and plants came to be conducted without significant reference to the supernatural. In other words, nature was seen as a mechanism, functioning according to certain universal physical laws, and it was these laws that scientists were seeking. Yet, most scientists still insisted that a First Cause initiated the entire system. The argument from design was still defended, and support for it continued well into the nineteenth century and strongly persists even today (see p. 40).

PRECURSORS TO THE THEORY OF EVOLUTION

Before early naturalists could begin to understand the forms of organic life, it was necessary to list and describe those forms. As attempts in this direction were made, scholars became increasingly impressed with the amount of biological diversity that confronted them.

John Ray   By the sixteenth century, a keen interest in nature's variation had developed, and by the mid-1500s, there were a few descriptive works on plants, birds, fish, and mammals. But it was not until the seventeenth century that the concept of species was clearly defined by Englishman John Ray (1627–1705), an ordained minister trained at Cambridge University.

Ray was the first to recognize that groups of plants and animals could be distinguished from other groups by their ability to reproduce with one another and produce offspring. Such groups of reproductively isolated organisms were placed into a single category he called *species* (*pl.,* species). Thus, by the late 1600s, the biological criterion of reproduction was used to define species much as it is today (Young, 1992).

Ray also recognized that species frequently shared similarities with other species, and these he grouped together in a second level of classification he called the *genus* (*pl.,* genera). Ray was the first to use the labels *genus* and *species* in this manner, and they are the terms still in use today. But Ray was very much an adherent of fixity of species. His 1691 publication, *The Wisdom of God Manifested in the Works of Creation*, was intended to demonstrate God's plan in nature, and in this work Ray stressed that nature was a deliberate outcome of a Grand Design.

Carolus Linnaeus   Carolus Linnaeus (1707–1778), of Sweden (Fig. 2–1) was one of the leading naturalists of the eighteenth century. He is best known for developing a classification of plants and animals, the *Systema Naturae* (Systems of Nature), first published in 1735. (His highly ambitious goal was to categorize *all* known species.)

Linnaeus standardized Ray's more sporadic use of two names (genus and species) for organisms and established the use of **binomial nomenclature.** Moreover, he added two more categories: class and order. Linnaeus' four-level system of classification became the basis for **taxonomy,** the system of classification still used today.

Another of Linnaeus' innovations was to include humans in his classification of animals, placing them in the genus *Homo* and species *sapiens.* Including humans in this scheme was controversial because it defied contemporary thought that humans, made in God's image, should be considered unique and not part of the animal kingdom.

Linnaeus also believed in fixity of species, although in later years, faced with mounting evidence to the contrary, he came to question this long-held assumption. Indeed, fixity of species was being challenged on many fronts, especially in France, where voices were being raised in favor of a universe based

---

See Virtual Lab, section II, for a discussion of the species concept.

binomial nomenclature (*binomial,* meaning "two names") In taxonomy, the convention established by Carolus Linnaeus whereby genus and species names are used to refer to species. For example, *Homo sapiens* refers to human beings.

taxonomy The branch of science concerned with the rules of classifying organisms on the basis of evolutionary relationships.

Courtesy, Dept. of Library Services, American Museum of Natural History

FIGURE 2–1 Linnaeus developed a classification system for plants and animals.

on change and, more to the point, in favor of the relationship between similar forms based on descent from a common ancestor.

Comte de Buffon Georges-Louis Leclerc (1707–1788), who was a count under the name Buffon, was Keeper of the King's Gardens in Paris (Fig. 2–2). He believed neither in the perfection of nature nor in the idea that nature had a purpose, as declared by the argument from design, but he did recognize the dynamic relationship between the external environment and living forms. In his *Natural History,* first published in 1749, he repeatedly stressed the importance of change in the universe, and he underlined the changing nature of species.

Buffon believed that when groups of organisms migrated to new areas of the world, each group would subsequently be influenced by local climatic conditions and would gradually change as a result of adaptation to the environment. Buffon's recognition of the external environment as an agent of change in species was an important innovation. However, he rejected the idea that one species could give rise to another.

Erasmus Darwin Today, Erasmus Darwin (1731–1802) is best known as Charles Darwin's grandfather (Fig. 2–3). This is somewhat unfortunate, because Erasmus Darwin was a physician, inventor, naturalist, philosopher, poet, and leading member of a well-known intellectual community in Lichfield, England. Living in the English midlands, birthplace of the industrial revolution, which was in full swing, Darwin counted among his friends some of the leading figures of this crucial time of rapid technological and social change. Among his many friends were James Watt, inventor of the steam engine; Josiah Wedgwood, founder of the Wedgwood pottery factory, where many new techniques of mass production were developed; and an American inventor, writer, and statesman named Benjamin Franklin.

Darwin achieved considerable fame during his lifetime as a poet. His most famous work was *Zoonomia,* a medical book of over 500,000 words written entirely in verse and published in 1794. In this book (which, admittedly, few of us would read today), he publicly expressed his views that life had originated in the seas and that all species had descended from a common ancestor. But his best poem, *The Temple of Nature,* published posthumously in 1803, is an account of the development of all life from microscopic organisms in the seas. In these two publications, Erasmus Darwin introduced many of the ideas that would again be proposed 56 years later by his grandson. These concepts include vast expanses of time for life to evolve, competition for resources, and the importance of the environment in evolutionary processes. From letters and other sources, it is known that Charles Darwin had read and was fond of his grandfather's writings. But the degree to which the grandson's theories were influenced by the grandfather is not known.

Jean-Baptiste Lamarck Neither Buffon nor Erasmus Darwin attempted to *explain* the evolutionary process. The first European scientist to do so was Jean-Baptiste Pierre Antoine de Monet Chevalier de Lamarck (1744–1829) of France. (Thankfully, most references to Lamarck use only his surname.)

Expanding beyond the views of Buffon, Lamarck (Fig. 2–4) did attempt to explain how species could change. He proposed a dynamic interaction between organic forms and the environment, such that organic forms could become altered in the face of changing environmental circumstances. Thus, as the environment changed, an animal's activity patterns would also change, resulting in increased or decreased use of certain body parts. As a result of this use or disuse, body parts became altered.

Physical alteration occurred as a function of perceived bodily "needs." If a particular part of the body felt a certain need, "fluids and forces" would be

FIGURE 2–2 Buffon recognized the influence of the environment on life forms.

FIGURE 2–3 Erasmus Darwin, grandfather of Charles Darwin, believed in species change.

See Virtual Lab 1, section II, for a discussion of the Linnaean system of classifying plants and animals.

FIGURE 2–4 Lamarck believed that species change was influenced by environmental change. He is best known for his theory of the inheritance of acquired characteristics.

directed toward that point and the structure would be modified to satisfy the need. Because the modification would render the animal better suited to its habitat, the new trait would be passed on to offspring. This theory is known as the *inheritance of acquired characteristics,* or the *use-disuse* theory.

One of the most frequently given examples of Lamarck's theory is the giraffe, who, having stripped all the leaves from the lower branches of a tree (environmental change), strives to reach those leaves on upper branches. As vital forces progress to tissues of the neck, the neck increases slightly in length, enabling the giraffe to obtain more food. The longer neck is subsequently transmitted to offspring, with the eventual result that all giraffes have longer necks than did their predecessors (Fig. 2–5a). Thus, according to this theory, *a trait acquired by an animal during its lifetime can be passed on to offspring.* Today we know this explanation is inaccurate, since only those traits coded for by genetic information contained within sex cells (eggs and sperm) can be inherited (see Chapters 3 and 4).

Because Lamarck's explanation of species change was not genetically correct, his theories are frequently derided. But actually Lamarck deserves much credit, because he was the first to stress the importance of interactions between organisms and the environment in the evolutionary process. Moreover, Lamarck was one of the first to acknowledge the need for a distinct branch of science that dealt solely with living things (i.e., separate from geology). For this new science, Lamarck coined the term *biology,* and a central feature of this new science was the notion of evolutionary change.

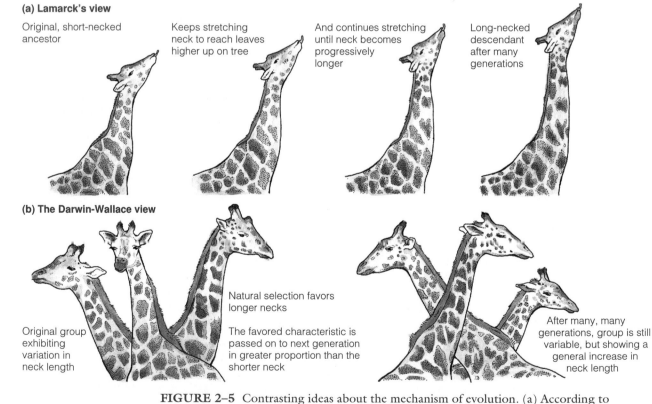

(a) Lamarck's view

Original, short-necked ancestor

Keeps stretching neck to reach leaves higher up on tree

And continues stretching until neck becomes progressively longer

Long-necked descendant after many generations

(b) The Darwin-Wallace view

Original group exhibiting variation in neck length

Natural selection favors longer necks

The favored characteristic is passed on to next generation in greater proportion than the shorter neck

After many, many generations, group is still variable, but showing a general increase in neck length

FIGURE 2–5 Contrasting ideas about the mechanism of evolution. (a) According to Lamarck's theory, acquired characteristics can be passed to subsequent generations. Thus, short-necked giraffes stretched their necks to reach higher into trees for food, and, according to Lamarck, this acquired trait was passed on to offspring, who were born with longer necks. (b) According to the Darwin-Wallace theory of natural selection, among giraffes there is variation in neck length. If having a longer neck provides an advantage for feeding, this trait will be passed on to a greater number of offspring, leading to an overall increase in the length of giraffe necks over many generations.

Georges Cuvier The most vehement opponent of Lamarck was a young colleague, Georges Cuvier (1769–1832). Cuvier (Fig. 2–6) specialized in vertebrate paleontology, and he introduced the concept of extinction to explain the disappearance of animals represented by fossils. Although a brilliant anatomist, Cuvier never grasped the dynamic concept of nature, and he adamantly insisted on the fixity of species. Just as the abundance of fossils in geological strata was becoming increasingly apparent, it also became more important to explain what they were. But rather than assume that similarities between certain fossil forms and living species indicated evolutionary relationships, Cuvier proposed a variation of a theory known as **catastrophism.**

Catastrophism held that the earth's geological features were the results of sudden, worldwide cataclysmic events, such as the Noah flood. Cuvier's version of catastrophism also postulated a series of regional disasters that destroyed most or all of the local plant and animal life. These areas of destruction were subsequently restocked with new forms that migrated in from neighboring, unaffected regions.

To be consistent with the fossil evidence, Cuvier also proposed that destroyed regions were repopulated by new organisms of a more modern appearance and that these forms were the results of more recent creation events. (The last of these creations is the one depicted in Genesis.) Thus, Cuvier's explanation of increased complexity over time avoided any notion of evolution while still being able to account for the evidence of change as preserved in the fossil record.

Thomas Malthus In 1798, Thomas Robert Malthus (1766–1834), an English clergyman and economist, wrote *An Essay on the Principle of Population,* which inspired both Charles Darwin and Alfred Wallace in their separate discoveries of the principle of natural selection (Fig. 2–7). In his essay, Malthus pointed out that if not kept in check by limited food supplies, human populations could double in size every 25 years. That is, population size increases exponentially while food supplies remain relatively stable.

Malthus focused on humans because the ability to increase food supplies artificially reduces constraints on population growth, and he was arguing for population control. However, the same logic could be applied to nonhuman organisms. In nature, the tendency for populations to increase is continuously checked by resource availability. Thus, there is constant competition for food and other resources. In time, the extension of Malthus' principles to all organisms would be made by both Darwin and Wallace.

Charles Lyell Charles Lyell (1797–1875), the son of Scottish landowners, is considered the founder of modern geology (Fig. 2–8). He was a barrister by training, a geologist by avocation, and for many years Charles Darwin's friend and mentor. Before he met Darwin in 1836, Lyell had earned wide popular acclaim as well as acceptance in Europe's most prestigious scientific circles, thanks to his highly praised *Principles of Geology,* first published during the years 1830–1833.

In this immensely important work, Lyell argued that the geological processes observed in the present are the same as those that occurred in the past. This theory, which has come to be known as **uniformitarianism,** did not originate entirely with Lyell, but had been proposed by James Hutton in the late 1700s. Nevertheless, it was Lyell who demonstrated that such forces as wind, water erosion, local flooding, frost, the decomposition of vegetable matter, volcanoes, earthquakes, and glacial movements all had contributed in the past to produce the geological landscape that exists in the present. Moreover, the fact that these processes could still be observed in operation indicated that geological change continued to occur and that the forces that drove such change were consistent, or *uniform,* over time. In other words, although various aspects of the earth's

FIGURE 2–6 Cuvier explained the fossil record as the result of a succession of catastrophes followed by new creation events.

catastrophism The view that the earth's geological landscape is the result of violent cataclysmic events. This view was promoted by Cuvier, especially in opposition to Lamarck.

FIGURE 2–7 Thomas Malthus' *Essay on the Principle of Population* led both Darwin and Wallace to the principle of natural selection.

uniformitarianism The theory that the earth's features are the result of long-term processes that continue to operate in the present as they did in the past. Elaborated on by Lyell, this theory opposed catastrophism and provided for immense geological time.

FIGURE 2–8 Lyell, the father of geology, stated the theory of uniformitarianism in his *Principles of Geology.*

Courtesy, Dept. of Library Services, American Museum of Natural History

FIGURE 2–9 Portrait of Mary Anning

The Natural History Museum, London

surface (e.g., climate, plants, animals, and land surfaces) are variable through time, the *underlying processes* that influence them are constant.

The theory of uniformitarianism flew in the face of Cuvier's catastrophism and did not go unopposed. Additionally, and every bit as controversially, Lyell emphasized the obvious: namely, that for such slow-acting forces to produce momentous change, the earth must indeed be far older than anyone had previously suspected.

By providing an immense time scale and thereby altering perceptions of earth's history from a few thousand to many millions of years, Lyell changed the framework within which scientists viewed the geological past. Thus, the concept of "deep time" (Gould, 1987) remains one of Lyell's most significant contributions to the discovery of evolutionary principles. The immensity of geological time permitted the necessary time depth for the inherently slow process of evolutionary change.

Mary Anning The roots of evolutionary theory are deeply embedded in the late eighteenth and early nineteenth centuries, when the fields of geology and paleontology were emerging. People had become interested in collecting fossils, many of which were believed to be the remains of creatures killed in the biblical flood. Because of this interest, Mary Anning (1799–1847), living in the town of Lyme Regis on the south coast of England, became an important but largely unknown contributor to the developing scientific discipline of paleontology (Fig. 2–9).

Anning's father died when she was 11, leaving the family in dire poverty. But because her father had taught her to recognize fossils embedded in the cliffs near the town, Mary began collecting and selling them to support her family. After her discovery of the first complete fossil of *Ichthyosaurus*, a large, fishlike marine reptile, and the first *Plesiosaurus* fossil (another ocean-dwelling reptile), the Anning home was visited by some of the most famous scientists in England. Over the years Anning supplied researchers, museums, and wealthy private collectors with hundreds of fossils. Often excavating in perilous conditions, she became known as one of the world's leading "fossilists." However, since she was a woman and because of her lowly social position, she was not acknowledged in scientific publications. Fortunately, she has now achieved recognition and her portrait hangs prominently in the British Museum (Natural History) in London near one of her famous *Ichthyosaurus* fossils.

THE DISCOVERY OF NATURAL SELECTION

Charles Darwin Having already been introduced to Erasmus Darwin, you should not be surprised that his grandson Charles grew up in an educated family with ties to intellectual circles. Charles Darwin (1809–1882) was one of six children of Dr. Robert and Susanna Darwin (Fig. 2–10). Being the grandson of Erasmus Darwin and of Erasmus' friend, the wealthy Josiah Wedgwood, Charles grew up enjoying the lifestyle of the landed gentry in rural England.

As a boy, he displayed a keen interest in nature and spent his days fishing and collecting shells, birds' eggs, and rocks. However, this developing interest in natural history did not dispel the generally held view of family and friends that he was not in any way remarkable. In fact, his performance at school was no more than ordinary.

After the death of his mother when he was eight, Darwin's upbringing was guided by his father and his older sisters. Because he showed little interest in, or aptitude for, anything except hunting, shooting, and perhaps science, his father, fearing Charles would sink into dissipation, sent him to Edinburgh University to study medicine. It was in Edinburgh that Darwin first became acquainted with the evolutionary theories of Lamarck and others.

During this time (the 1820s), notions of evolution were becoming much feared in England and elsewhere. Certainly, anything identifiable with post-revolutionary France was viewed with grave suspicion by the established order in England. Lamarck, especially, was vilified by most English academicians, the majority of whom were also members of the Anglican clergy.

This was also a time of growing political unrest in Britain. The Reform Movement, which sought to undo many of the wrongs of the class system, was under way, and as with most social movements, this one contained a radical faction. Because many of the radicals were atheists and socialists who also supported Lamarck's evolutionary theory, evolution came to be associated, in the minds of many, with atheism and political subversion. Such was the growing fear of evolutionary ideas that many people believed that if they were generally accepted "the Church would crash, the moral fabric of society would be torn apart, and civilized man would return to savagery" (Desmond and Moore, 1991, p. 34). It is unfortunate that some of the most outspoken early proponents of **transmutation** were so vehemently anti-Christian, because their rhetoric helped establish the entrenched suspicion and misunderstanding of evolutionary theory that persists today.

While at Edinburgh, young Darwin spent endless hours studying with professors who were outspoken supporters of Lamarck. Darwin's second year in Edinburgh saw him examining museum collections and attending natural history lectures. Therefore, although he hated medicine and left Edinburgh after two years, his experience there was a formative period in his intellectual development.

Subsequently, Darwin took up residence at Christ's College, Cambridge, to study theology, although he was rather indifferent to religion. It was during his Cambridge years that Darwin seriously cultivated his interests in natural science, and he often joined the field excursions of botany classes. He was also immersed in geology and was a frequent and serious participant in geological expeditions.

It was no wonder that following his graduation in 1831 at age 22, he was invited to accompany a scientific expedition that would circle the globe. And so it was that Darwin set sail aboard the HMS *Beagle* on December 17, 1831 (Fig. 2–11). The famous voyage of the *Beagle* was to last for almost five years and

FIGURE 2–10 Charles Darwin, photographed 5 years before the publication of *Origin of Species*.

transmutation The change of one species to another. The term *evolution* did not assume its current meaning until the late nineteenth century.

FIGURE 2–11 The route of the HMS *Beagle*.

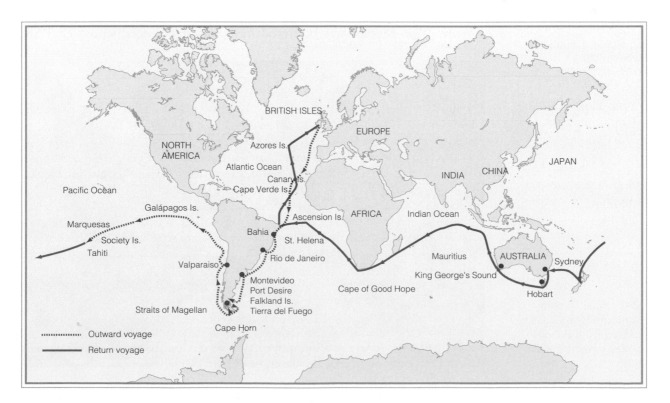

(a) Ground finch
Main food: seeds
Beak: heavy

(b) Tree finch
Main food: leaves, buds,
blossoms, fruits
Beak: thick, short

(c) Tree finch (called
woodpecker finch)
Main food: insects
Beak: stout, straight

(d) Ground finch (known as
warbler finch)
Main food: insects
Beak: slender

FIGURE 2–12 Beak variation in Darwin's Galápagos finches.

See Virtual Lab 2, section I, for an example of Darwin's finches.

FIGURE 2–13 The Darwin home, Down House, in the village of Down, as seen from the rear garden. *On the Origin of Species* was written here.

would forever change not only the course of Darwin's life, but also the history of biological science.

Darwin went aboard the *Beagle* believing in fixity of species. But during the voyage, he privately began to have doubts. As early as 1832, for example, he noted in his diary that a snake with rudimentary hind limbs marked "the passage by which Nature joins the lizards to the snakes." He came across fossils of ancient giant animals that, except for size, looked very much like living species in the same vicinity, and he wondered whether the fossils were the ancestors of those living forms.

During the famous stopover at the Galápagos Islands (see Fig. 2–11), Darwin noted that the vegetation and animals (especially birds) of South America showed striking similarities to those of the Galápagos. But, there were also some intriguing differences. Even more surprising, the inhabitants of the various islands differed slightly from one another.

For example, Darwin collected 13 different varieties of Galápagos finches. These varieties shared many structural similarities, and clearly they represented a closely affiliated group. But at the same time, they differed with regard to certain physical traits, particularly in the shape and size of their beaks (Fig. 2–12). Darwin also collected finches from the South American mainland, and these appeared to represent only one group, or species.

The insight that Darwin gained from the finches is legendary. He recognized that the various Galápagos finches had all descended from a common, mainland ancestor and had become modified in response to the varying island habitats and to altered dietary preferences. But actually, it was not until *after* he had returned to England that Darwin recognized the significance of the variation in beak structure. In fact, during the voyage, Darwin had paid little attention to the finches. It was only in retrospect that he considered the factors that could lead to the modification of 1 species into 13 (Gould, 1985; Desmond and Moore, 1991).

Darwin returned to England in October 1836 and almost immediately was accepted into the most eminent scientific circles. He married his cousin Emma Wedgwood and moved to the village of Down, near London, where he spent the rest of his life writing on topics ranging from fossils to orchids (Fig. 2–13). But his overriding concern was the question of species change.

At Down, Darwin began developing his views on what he called *natural selection*. This concept was borrowed from animal breeders, who "select" as

Lynn Kilgore

Wolf: John Giustina/Getty Images   Dogs surrounding wolf: Lynn Kilgore and Lin Marshall

breeding stock those animals that exhibit specific traits they hope to emphasize in offspring. Animals with undesirable traits are "selected against," or prevented from breeding.

Darwin was keenly interested in domestic animals—pigeons, in particular—and how breeders could develop distinctive varieties in just a few generations. (The variations seen in domestic dog breeds may be the best example of the effects of selective breeding. See Fig. 2–14.) He applied his knowledge of domesticated species to naturally occurring ones, recognizing that in undomesticated organisms, the selective agent was nature, not humans.

By the late 1830s, Darwin recognized that biological variation within a species was critically important. Furthermore, he acknowledged the importance of sexual reproduction in increasing variation. Then, in 1838, Darwin read Malthus' essay, and in it he found the answer to his question of how new species came to be. He accepted from Malthus that populations increase at a faster rate than do resources, and he recognized that in nonhuman animals, increase in population size is continuously checked by limited food supplies. He also accepted Lyell's observation that in nature there is a constant "struggle for existence." The idea that in each generation more offspring are born than survive to adulthood coupled with the notions of competition for resources and biological diversity were all Darwin needed to develop his theory of natural selection. He wrote: "It at once struck me that under these circumstances favourable variations would tend to be preserved, and unfavourable ones to be destroyed. The result of this would be the formation of a new species" (F. Darwin, 1950, pp. 53–54). Basically, this quotation summarizes the whole of natural selection theory.

Darwin wrote a short summary of his views on natural selection in 1842 and revised it in 1844. The 1844 sketch is similar to the argument he presented

FIGURE 2–14 All domestic dog breeds share a common ancestor, the wolf. The extreme variation that dog breeds exhibit today has been achieved in a relatively short period of time through artificial selection. In this situation, humans allow only certain dogs to breed because they possess specific characteristics that humans want to emphasize. (We should note that not all traits deemed desirable by human breeders are advantageous to the dogs themselves.)

See Virtual Lab 2, section I, for an example of artificial selection.

15 years later in *On the Origin of Species,* but in 1844 he didn't believe he had sufficient data to support his views, so he continued his research without publishing.

Darwin had other reasons for not publishing what he knew would be, to say the least, a highly controversial work. He was troubled by the fact that his wife Emma saw his ideas as running counter to her strong religious convictions (Keynes, 2001). Also, as a member of the established order, he knew that many of his friends and associates were concerned with threats to the status quo, and evolutionary theory was viewed as a serious threat indeed. In addition, Darwin was a man to whom reputation was of paramount importance, and he was tormented by fears of bringing dishonor and public criticism to those he loved. So he hesitated.

FIGURE 2–15 Alfred Russel Wallace independently discovered the key to the evolutionary process.

Alfred Russel Wallace Unlike Darwin, Alfred Russel Wallace (1823–1913) was born into a family of modest means (Fig. 2–15). He went to work at the age of 14, and without any special talent and little formal education, he moved from one job to the next. He became interested in collecting plants and animals, and in 1848 he joined an expedition to the Amazon, where he acquired firsthand knowledge of many natural phenomena. Then, in 1854, he sailed for Southeast Asia and the Malay Peninsula to continue his study and to collect bird and insect specimens.

In 1855, Wallace published a paper suggesting that species were descended from other species and that the appearance of new species was influenced by environmental factors (Trinkaus and Shipman, 1992). The Wallace paper spurred Lyell and others to urge Darwin to publish, but still he hesitated. Wallace and Darwin even corresponded briefly.

Then, in 1858, Wallace sent Darwin another paper titled "On the Tendency of Varieties to Depart Indefinitely from the Original Type." In this paper, Wallace described evolution as a process driven by competition and natural selection. When he received Wallace's paper, Darwin despaired. He feared that Wallace might be credited for a theory (natural selection) that he himself had formulated. He quickly wrote a paper presenting his ideas, and both the paper by Darwin and the one by Wallace were read before the Linnean Society of London in 1858. Neither author was present. Wallace was not in the country, and Darwin was mourning the very recent death of his young son.

The papers received little notice at the time, but at the urging of Lyell and others, Darwin completed and published his greatest work, *On the Origin of Species,** in December 1859. Upon publication, the storm broke, and it has not abated even to this day. While there was much praise for the book, public opinion was negative. But scientific opinion gradually came to Darwin's support, assisted by his able friend, Thomas Huxley, who for years wrote and spoke in favor of natural selection. The riddle of species was now explained: Species were mutable, not fixed; and they evolved from other species through the mechanism of natural selection.

NATURAL SELECTION

See Virtual Lab 2, section I, for a discussion of natural selection.

Early in his research, Darwin had realized that selection was the key to evolution. With the help of Malthus' ideas, he saw *how* selection in nature could be explained. In the struggle for existence, those *individuals* with favorable variations would survive and reproduce; those with unfavorable variations would not.

---

*The full title is *On the Origin of Species by Means of Natural Selection, or the Preservation of Favoured Races in the Struggle for Life.*

For Darwin, the explanation of evolution was simple. The basic processes, as he understood them, are as follows:

1. All species are capable of producing offspring at a faster rate than food supplies increase.
2. There is biological variation within all species; except for identical twins, no two individuals are genetically the same.
3. Because in each generation more individuals are produced than can survive, and owing to limited resources, there is competition between individuals. (*Note:* This statement does not imply that there is constant fierce fighting.)
4. Those individuals who possess favorable variations or traits (e.g., speed, disease resistance, protective coloration) have an advantage over individuals that do not possess them. By virtue of the favorable trait, these individuals are more likely to survive and produce offspring than are others.
5. The environmental context determines whether or not a trait is beneficial. That is, what is favorable in one setting may be a liability in another. In this way, which traits become most advantageous is the result of a natural process.
6. Traits are inherited and are passed on to the next generation. Because individuals who possess favorable traits contribute more offspring to the next generation than do others, over time, such traits become more common in the population; less favorable traits are not passed on as frequently, and they become less common. Those individuals who produce more offspring, compared to others, are said to have greater **reproductive success.**
7. Over long periods of geological time, successful variations accumulate in a population, so that later generations may be distinct from ancestral ones. Thus, in time, a new species may appear.
8. Geographical isolation may also lead to the formation of new species. As populations of a species become geographically isolated from one another, for whatever reasons, they begin to adapt to different environments. Over time, as populations continue to respond to different **selective pressures** (i.e., different ecological circumstances), they may become distinct species, descended from a common ancestor. The 13 species of Galápagos finches, presumably all descended from a common ancestor on the South American mainland, provide an example of the role of geographical isolation.

reproductive success The number of offspring an individual produces and rears to reproductive age; an individual's genetic contribution to the next generation.

selective pressures Forces in the environment that influence reproductive success in individuals.

Before Darwin, scientists thought of species as entities that could not change. Because individuals within the species did not appear to be significant, they were not the object of study; therefore, it was difficult for many scientists to imagine how change could occur. Darwin, as we have pointed out, saw that variation among individuals could explain how selection occurred. Favorable variations were selected for survival by nature; unfavorable ones were eliminated.

This emphasis on the uniqueness of the individual led Darwin to natural selection as the mechanism that made evolution work. *Natural selection operates on individuals,* favorably or unfavorably, but *it is the population that evolves.* The unit of natural selection is the individual; the unit of evolution is the population.

Natural Selection in Action

The most frequently cited example of natural selection concerns changes in coloration in a species of moth. In recent years, the moth story has come under some criticism, but since the basic premise remains valid, we use it to begin our discussion of natural selection.

Before the nineteenth century, the most common variety of the peppered moth was a mottled gray color. During the day, as the moths rested on lichen-covered tree branches and trunks, this light, mottled coloration provided effective camouflage (Fig. 2–16). Also present, but less common, was a dark variety

FIGURE 2–16 Variation in the peppered moth. (a) The dark form is more visible on the light, lichen-covered tree. (b) On trees darkened by pollution, the lighter form is more visible.

(a)   (b)

of the same species. But these dark, uncamouflaged moths resting on a light lichen background were more visible to birds that prey on moths, and so they were eaten more frequently. (In this example, the birds are the *selective agent,* and they apply *selective pressures* on moth populations.) Therefore, the dark moths produced fewer offspring than the camouflaged moths. Yet, by the end of the nineteenth century, the common gray form had been almost completely replaced by the darker variety.

What brought about this rapid change? The answer traditionally cited is air pollution. Coal dust, ubiquitous in industrial areas of Britain during the industrial revolution, killed the lichen and coated the trees, turning them dark gray. With this environmental change, the lighter moths became increasingly conspicuous and began to be preyed on more frequently. Consequently, they contributed fewer genes to the next generation than the darker moths, and the proportion of lighter moths decreased while the dark moths became more numerous.

In the 1950s, a series of experiments, conducted under somewhat artificial conditions, seemed to confirm that the color shift was due to the absence of lichen (Kettelwell, 1956). However, some aspects of the study were questionable. Furthermore, the same shift in coloration had occurred in North America, where lichen wasn't present on trees. And finally, evidence that birds can see ultraviolet (UV) light suggests that a resemblance to lichen may have played no part in protecting the moths, since in the UV spectrum, moths and lichen would be perceived differently (Weiss, 2003). And yet, the color shift occurred in both regions during periods of increased air pollution. As clean air acts in both Britain and the United States have reduced the amount of air pollution (at least from coal), the predominant color of the peppered moth is once again the light mottled gray. And even though the explanation for the observed changes in moth color is probably more complex than originally believed and may involve factors in addition to bird predation, this phenomenon still serves as a very good example of microevolution in a contemporary population.

The substance that produces coloration is a pigment called *melanin* (see p. 424), and the evolutionary shift in the peppered moth, as well as in many other moth species, is termed *industrial melanism*. This kind of evolutionary shift in response to environmental change is called *adaptation*.

Another example of natural selection is provided by the medium ground finch of the Galápagos Islands. In 1977, drought conditions eliminated many of the plants that produced smaller, softer seeds, compelling a study population on the island of Daphne Major to feed on larger, harder seeds. The population already exhibited some variation in beak size, and during the drought, mortality rates were higher in birds with smaller beaks because they were less able to process the larger seeds. Consequently, although population size was dramatically reduced, average beak thickness in the survivors and their offspring was seen to increase, simply because thicker-beaked individuals were contributing more offspring to the next generation (i.e., they had greater reproductive success). But during the rains of the 1982–1983 El Niño event, smaller seeds became more plentiful again and the pattern in beak size reversed itself, thus providing a beautiful illustration of how reproductive success is related to environmental conditions (Grant, 1975, 1986; Ridley, 1993).

But that isn't the end of the story. The medium ground finch was being observed as part of an ongoing, 30-year study that revealed numerous fluctuations in average body size and beak size and shape in this species and also in another bird the cactus finch (Grant and Grant, 2002). In some instances, change in beak structure in one species occurred in one direction for two or three years, while in the other species there was a less discernable pattern. Generally, average body size and beak size in the medium ground finch followed a pattern of increase, rapid decrease, then slower increase again. The larger cactus finch experienced a more uniform shift toward smaller body size and more pointed beaks. Ultimately, these alterations accompanied climatic changes that affected the availability of food sources. But after 30 years and numerous shifts, neither species had the same average body size and beak structure as at the beginning of the study, demonstrating that the effects of natural selection are not always predictable. This study of Darwin's finches clearly demonstrates the necessity of long-term studies of naturally occurring populations if we are truly to understand the many complexities and subtleties involved in natural selection.

The best illustration of natural selection, and certainly the one with potentially grave consequences for humans, is the increase in resistant strains of disease-causing microorganisms. When antibiotic therapy was introduced in the 1940s, it was hailed as the end of bacterial disease, but this notion failed to take into account the fact that bacteria, like other organisms, possess genetic variability. Consequently, while exposure to an antibiotic will kill most bacteria in an infected individual, those pathogens with an inherited resistance to that particular therapy will survive and pass on their resistance to the next generation. Moreover, because bacteria produce new generations every few hours,

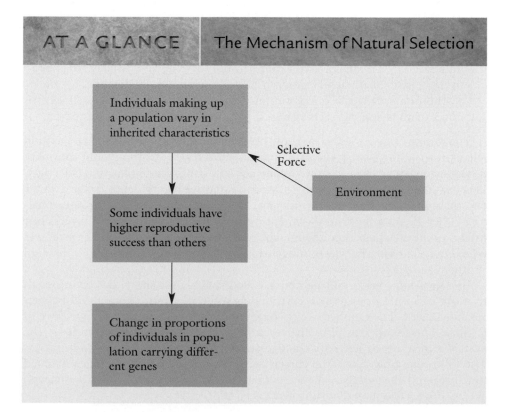

AT A GLANCE   The Mechanism of Natural Selection

Individuals making up a population vary in inherited characteristics

Selective Force

Environment

Some individuals have higher reproductive success than others

Change in proportions of individuals in population carrying different genes antibiotic-resistant strains are continuously being produced. As a result, many types of infection no longer respond to treatment. For example, tuberculosis was once thought to be well controlled, but it has seen a resurgence in recent years because the bacterium that causes it no longer responds to some antibiotic therapies. Similarly, the organism that is transmitted by mosquitoes and causes malaria has become resistant to the traditional preventive medication, chloraquin. And if that weren't enough, many populations of mosquitoes have become resistant to the insecticide DDT, which is still used in many parts of the world to control the spread of malaria.

These examples provide numerous insights into the mechanisms of evolutionary change produced by natural selection:

1. *A trait must be inherited if natural selection is to act on it.* A characteristic that is not hereditary (such as a temporary change in hair color produced by the hairdresser) won't be passed on to succeeding generations. In moths, pigmentation is a demonstrated hereditary trait.

2. *Natural selection cannot occur without population variation in inherited characteristics.* If, for example, all the peppered moths had initially been gray (you will recall that some dark forms were always present) and the trees had become darker, the survival and reproduction of all moths could have been so low that the population might have become extinct. Such an event isn't unusual and without variation would nearly always occur. *Selection can work only with variation that already exists.*

3. **Fitness** *is a relative measure that changes as the environment changes.* Fitness is simply differential reproductive success. In the initial stage, the lighter moths were the more fit variety because they produced more offspring. But as the environment changed, the dark gray moths became more fit, and a further change reversed the adaptive pattern. It should be obvious that statements regarding the "most fit" life form mean nothing without reference to specific environments.

4. *Natural selection can only act on traits that affect reproduction.* If a characteristic is not usually expressed until later in life, after organisms have reproduced, then natural selection has no opportunity to influence it. This is because those components of the trait that are inherited have already been passed on to offspring. Many forms of cancer and cardiovascular disease are influenced by hereditary factors, but because these diseases usually affect people later in life, natural selection can't act against them. By the same token, if a condition usually kills or compromises the individual before he or she reproduces, natural selection acts against it because the trait won't be passed on.

The examples discussed so far show how different death rates influence natural selection (e.g., moths that die early tend to leave fewer offspring). But mortality is not the entire picture. Another important aspect of natural selection is fertility, since an animal that gives birth to more young passes its genes on at a faster rate than one that bears fewer offspring. However, fertility is not the entire picture either, because the crucial element is the number of young raised successfully to the point at which they themselves reproduce. We call this *differential net reproductive success.* The way this mechanism works can be demonstrated through another example.

In a common variety of small birds called swifts, data show that giving birth to more offspring does not necessarily guarantee that more young will be successfully raised. The number of eggs hatched in a breeding season is a measure of fertility. The number of birds that mature and are eventually able to leave the nest is a measure of net reproductive success, or offspring successfully raised. The following table shows the correlation between the number of eggs hatched (fertility) and the number of young that leave the nest (reproductive success) averaged over four breeding seasons (Lack, 1966):

fitness Pertaining to natural selection, a measure of *relative* reproductive success of individuals. Fitness can be measured by an individual's genetic contribution to the next generation compared to that of other individuals. The terms *genetic fitness, reproductive fitness,* and *differential reproductive success* are also used.

Number of eggs hatched (fertility)	2 eggs	3 eggs	4 eggs
Average number of young raised (reproductive success)	1.92	2.54	1.76
Sample size (number of nests)	72	20	16

As you can see, the most efficient fertility number is three eggs, since that number yields the highest reproductive success. Raising two is less beneficial to the parents, since the end result isn't as successful as with three eggs. Trying to raise more than three young is actually detrimental, since the parents may not be able to provide adequate nourishment for any of the offspring. An offspring that dies before reaching reproductive age is, in evolutionary terms, equivalent to never having been born in the first place. Actually, such a result may be an evolutionary minus to the parents, because this offspring will drain their resources and may inhibit their ability to raise other offspring, thereby lowering their reproductive success even further. Selection will favor those genetic traits that yield the maximum net reproductive success. If the number of eggs laid* is a genetic trait in birds (and it seems to be), natural selection in swifts should act to favor the laying of three eggs as opposed to two or four.

Constraints on Nineteenth-Century Evolutionary Theory

Darwin argued for the notion of evolution in general and the role of natural selection in particular, but he didn't entirely comprehend the exact mechanisms of evolutionary change.

As we have seen, natural selection acts on *variation* within species. Neither Darwin nor anyone else in the nineteenth century understood the source of all this variation. Consequently, Darwin speculated about variation arising from "use"—an idea similar to Lamarck's. Darwin, however, wasn't as dogmatic in his views as Lamarck and most emphatically argued against inner "needs" or "effort." Darwin had to confess that when it came to explaining variation, he simply did not know.

In addition to his inability to explain the origins of variation, Darwin also didn't completely understand the mechanism by which parents transmit traits to offspring. Almost without exception, nineteenth-century scholars were confused about the laws of heredity, and the popular view was that inheritance was *blending* by nature. In other words, offspring were expected to express intermediate traits as a result of a blending of their parents' contributions. Given this notion, we can see why the actual nature of genes was unimaginable. Without any viable alternatives, Darwin accepted this popular misconception. As it turned out, a contemporary of Darwin's had systematically worked out the rules of heredity. However, the work of this Augustinian monk, Gregor Mendel (whom you will meet in Chapter 4), was not recognized until the beginning of the twentieth century.

The first three decades of the twentieth century saw the merger of Mendel's discoveries and natural selection. This was a crucial development because until then, scientists thought they were unrelated phenomena. Then, in 1953, the structure of **deoxyribonucleic acid (DNA)** was discovered. This landmark achievement has been followed by even more amazing advances in the field of genetics, including the recent sequencing of the human **genome.** We may finally be on the threshold of revealing the remaining secrets of the evolutionary process. If only Darwin could know.

deoxyribonucleic acid (DNA) The double-stranded molecule that contains the genetic code.

genome The entire genetic makeup of an individual or species.

---

*The number of eggs hatched is directly related to the number of eggs laid.

Opposition to Evolution

The publication of *On the Origin of Species* fanned the flames of controversy over evolution into an inferno, but the question had already been debated in intellectual circles for some years, with most people vehemently opposed to evolutionary theory. The very idea that species could give rise to other species was particularly offensive to many Christians because it appeared to be in direct conflict to the special creation event depicted in Genesis. People were horrified at the notion that humans might be biologically related to other animals and especially that they might share a common ancestor with apes. Even to make such a claim was degrading, for it denied humanity its unique and exalted place in the universe; in the minds of many, it denied the very existence of God.

The debate has not ended even now, almost 150 years later. For the majority of scientists today, evolution is indisputable. The genetic evidence for it is solid and accumulates daily. Anyone who appreciates and understands genetic mechanisms cannot avoid the conclusion that populations and species evolve. Moreover, the majority of Christians don't believe that biblical depictions are to be taken literally. But at the same time, surveys show that almost half of all Americans believe that evolution does not occur. There are a number of reasons for this.

The mechanisms of evolution are complex and don't lend themselves to simple explanations. To understand these mechanisms requires some familiarity with genetics and biology, a familiarity that most people don't have. Moreover, many people who haven't been exposed to scientific training want definitive answers to complicated questions. But as you learned in Chapter 1, science doesn't prove truths, and it frequently doesn't provide definitive answers.

Another fact to consider is that while all religions offer explanations for natural phenomena, and some even feature the transformation of individuals from one form to another, none really proposes biological change over time. Most people, regardless of their culture, are raised in belief systems that do not emphasize biological continuity between species or offer scientific explanations for natural phenomena.

The relationship between science and religion has never been easy. While both serve, in their own ways, to explain phenomena, scientific explanations are based in data analysis and interpretation. Religion, meanwhile, is a system of beliefs not amenable to scientific testing and falsification; it is based in faith. Religion and science concern different aspects of the human experience, and although they use different approaches in areas where they overlap, they are not inherently mutually exclusive. In fact, many people see them as two sides of the same coin. Moreover, evolutionary theories aren't considered anathema by all religions (or by all forms of Christianity). Some years ago, the Vatican hosted an international conference on human evolution, and in 1996, Pope John Paul II issued a statement to the Pontifical Academy of Sciences acknowledging that "fresh knowledge leads to recognition of the theory of evolution as more than just a hypothesis." Today, the official position of the Catholic Church is that evolutionary processes do occur but that the human soul is of divine creation and not subject to evolutionary processes. Likewise, mainstream Protestants do not generally see a conflict. Unfortunately, those who believe in a literal interpretation of the Bible (termed fundamentalists) do not accept any form of compromise.

Reacting to rapid cultural changes after World War I, conservative Christians in the United States sought a revival of what they considered traditional values. In their view, one way to do this was to prevent any mention of Darwinism in public schools. The Butler Act, passed in Tennessee in 1925, was one result of this effort, and it banned the teaching of evolution in public schools in that state. To test the validity of the law, the American Civil Liberties Union persuaded John Scopes, a high school teacher, to be arrested and ultimately tried for teaching evolution.

The subsequent trial was the famous Scopes Monkey Trial, in which the well-known orator William Jennings Bryan was the prosecuting attorney. The lawyer for the defense was Clarence Darrow, a nationally known labor and criminal lawyer. The trial ended with the conviction of Scopes, who was fined $100. The case was appealed to the Tennessee Supreme Court, which upheld the law, and the teaching of evolution remained illegal in Tennessee. Eventually, several other states, mostly in the South, passed similar laws, and it wasn't until 1967 that the last two states (Tennessee and Arkansas) ceased to prohibit the teaching of evolution.

But the story doesn't end there. In the more than 75 years since the Scopes trial, religious fundamentalists have persisted in their attempts to remove evolution from public school curricula. Known as creationists because they explain the existence of the universe as a result of a sudden creation, they are determined either to eliminate the teaching of evolution or to introduce antievolutionary material into public school classes. In the past 20 years, creationists have insisted that "creation science" is just as valid a scientific endeavor as is the study of evolution. They argue that in the interest of fairness, a balanced view should be offered: If evolution is taught as science, then creationism should also be taught as science. But "creation science" is, by definition, not science at all. Creationists assert that their view is absolute and infallible. Consequently, creationism is not a hypothesis that can be tested, nor is it amenable to falsification. Because such testing is the basis of all science, creationism, by its very nature, cannot be considered science. It is religion.

Still, creationists have been active in state legislatures, promoting the passage of laws mandating the inclusion of creationism in school curricula. To this effect, the Arkansas state legislature passed Act 590 in 1981. But this law was challenged and overturned in 1982. Judge William Ray Overton, in his ruling against the state, found that "a theory that is by its own terms dogmatic, absolutist and never subject to revision is not a scientific theory." And he added: "Since creation is not science, the conclusion is inescapable that the only real effect of Act 590 is the advancement of religion." In 1987, the United States Supreme Court struck down a similar law in Louisiana.

So far, these and similar laws have been overturned because they violate the principle of separation of church and state provided in the First Amendment to the Constitution. But this has not stopped the creationists, who have encouraged teachers to claim "academic freedom" to teach creationism. Also, they have dropped the term *creationism* in favor of less religious sounding terms, such as *intelligent design theory*. And as recently as August 1999, the Kansas state legislature adopted a policy that, had it not been overturned, could have eliminated evolution from standardized public school curricula. Moreover, antievolution feeling remains strong among politicians. In 1999, one very prominent U.S. congressman went so far as to say that the teaching of evolution is one of the factors behind violence in America today!

Although the courts have consistently ruled against the creationists, religious fundamentalists have nevertheless had an impact on the teaching of evolution. Many public school teachers, attempting to avoid controversy, simply don't cover evolution, or they refer to it as "just a theory" (see p. 20). As a result, students may not be exposed to theories of evolution until they go to college—and only then if they take related courses. This consequence is ultimately to the detriment of the biological sciences (and education in general) in the United States.

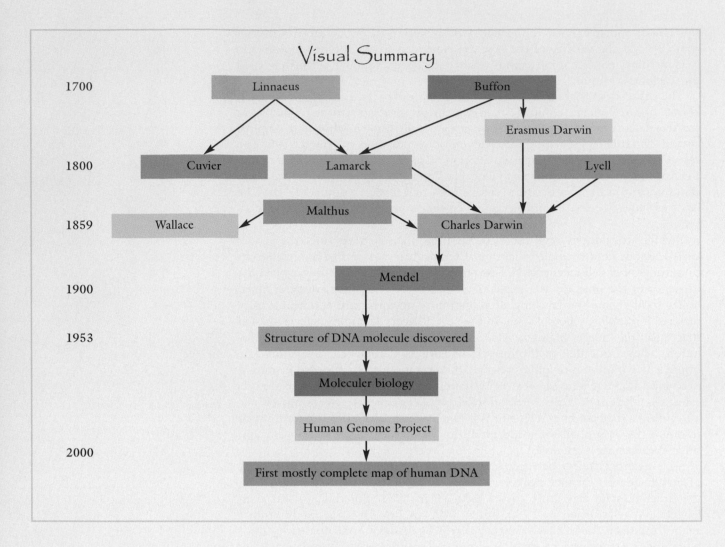

Visual Summary

| 1700 | Linnaeus | | Buffon |

Erasmus Darwin

| 1800 | Cuvier | Lamarck | Lyell |

| 1859 | Wallace | Malthus | Charles Darwin |

| 1900 | | Mendel |

| 1953 | | Structure of DNA molecule discovered |

Moleculer biology

Human Genome Project

| 2000 | | First mostly complete map of human DNA |

Summary

Our current understanding of evolutionary processes is directly traceable to developments in intellectual thought in western Europe over the last 300 years. Many people contributed to this shift in perspective, and we have named only a very few. Linnaeus placed humans in the same taxonomic scheme as all other animals. Importantly, Lamarck and Buffon both recognized that species could change in response to environmental circumstances, but Lamarck attempted to explain *how* the changes occurred. He proposed the idea of *inheritance of acquired characteristics,* which has long since been discredited. Lyell, through his theory of uniformitarianism, provided the necessary expanse of time for evolution to occur, and Malthus dis-

cussed how population size is kept in check by the availability of resources. Darwin and Wallace, influenced by their predecessors, independently recognized that because of competition for resources, individuals with favorable characteristics would tend to survive to pass those traits on to offspring. Those lacking beneficial traits would produce fewer offspring, if they survived to reproductive age at all. That is, they would have lower reproductive success and reduced fitness. Thus, over time, advantageous characteristics accumulate in a population (i.e., they are selected for) while disadvantageous ones are eliminated (or selected against). This, in a nutshell, is the theory of evolution by means of natural selection.

For Further Thought

1. In your own words, summarize how natural selection works.

2. Do you personally see a conflict between evolutionary and religious explanations of how species came to be?

Go to the book website at **http://www.anthropology.wadsworth.com** for resources to help you explore these questions further. Click on "For Further Thought" for this chapter.

Questions for Review

1. Describe the theory of natural selection. What are its basic premises? Can you think of some examples that weren't discussed in this chapter?
2. How does Lamarck's theory differ from Darwin and Wallace's? What main feature do they have in common?
3. After having read this chapter, how would you respond to the following questions?

   - Why are there monkeys if humans evolved from monkeys?
   - Why don't we see the appearance of new species?

4. Do you, personally, object to the idea that humans are closely related to chimpanzees? (By closely related, we mean that the two species are extremely similar genetically.) Explain your answer.
5. What are selective agents? Can you think of some examples we didn't discuss? Why did Darwin look at domesticated species as models for natural selection, and what is the selective agent in artificial selection? List some examples of artificial selection.
6. Darwin approached the subject of species change by emphasizing the importance of *individuals* within populations. Why was this significant to the development of the theory of natural selection?

Suggested Further Reading

Cadbury, D. 2001. *Terrible Lizard: The First Dinosaur Hunters and the Birth of a New Science.* New York: Holt.

Desmond, Adrian, and James Moore. 1991. *Darwin.* New York: Warner Books.

Gould, Stephen Jay. 1987. *Time's Arrow, Time's Cycle.* Cambridge, MA: Harvard University Press.

Grant, P. R. 1991. "Natural Selection in Darwin's finches." *Scientific American* 265(4): 82–87.

Keynes, Randal. 2002. *Darwin, His Daughter, and Human Evolution.* New York: Riverhead Books.

Mayr, Ernst. 2000. "Darwin's Influence on Modern Thought." *Scientific American* 283(1): 78–83.

Ridley, Mark. 1993. *Evolution.* Boston: Blackwell Scientific Publications.

Scott, Eugenie C. 1997. "Antievolutionism and Creationism in the United States." *Annual Review of Anthropology* 2: 263–289.

Young, David. 1992. *The Discovery of Evolution.* London: Natural History Museum Publications, Cambridge University Press.

Online Anthropology Resource Center

Go to the Anthropology Resource Center at **http://www.anthropology.wadsworth.com** for a wealth of online resources, including a companion website for your text that provides study aids such as self-quizzes for each chapter and a practice final exam, as well as links to anthropology websites and information on the latest theories and discoveries in the field. Also, check out InfoTrac College Edition, your online library that offers full-length articles from thousands of scholarly and popular publications. Just click on the InfoTrac button at the companion website and use the passcode that came with your book.

3 The Biological Basis of Life

A human chromosome

Key Questions

What is the molecular basis for life? Does it vary from species to species?

How do human beings fit into a biological continuum?

Introduction

Envision yourself, tired after a rotten day, watching the evening news on TV. The first story, following an endless string of commercials, is about genetically modified foods, a newly cloned species, or the controversy over human cloning. What do you do? Do you change the channel? Leave the room? Go to sleep? Or do you follow the story? And if you do follow it, do you understand it? Do you think it's important or relevant to you personally? Well, the fact is, you live in an age when genetic discoveries and genetically based technologies are advancing daily, and they will have a profound effect on your life.

At some point, you or someone you love will probably require lifesaving medical treatment, perhaps for cancer, and this treatment will be based on genetic research. Like it or not, you already eat genetically modified foods. You may take advantage of developing reproductive technologies, and sadly, you may see the development of biological weapons based on genetically altered bacteria and viruses. But fortunately, you will also probably live to see many of the secrets of evolution revealed through genetic research. So even if you haven't been particularly interested in genetic issues, you should be aware that your life is affected by them on a daily basis.

As you already know, this book is about human evolution and adaptation, both of which are intimately linked to life processes that involve cells, the replication and decoding of genetic information, and the transmission of this information between generations. Thus, to present human evolution and adaptation in the broad sense, we need to examine how life is organized at the cellular and molecular levels. This, in turn, necessitates a discussion of the fundamental principles of genetics.

Genetics is the study of how traits are transmitted from one generation to the next. Because physical anthropologists are concerned with human evolution, adaptation, and variation, they must have a thorough understanding of the factors that lie at the very root of these phenomena. In fact, although many physical anthropologists do not actually specialize in genetics, it is genetics that ultimately links the various subdisciplines of biological anthropology.

See the following section of the CD-ROM for topics covered in this chapter: Virtual Lab 2, section II.

The Cell

To discuss genetic and evolutionary principles, we must first have a fundamental understanding of cell function. Cells are the basic units of life in all living organisms. In some forms, such as bacteria, a single cell constitutes the entire organism. However, more complex *multicellular* forms, such as plants, insects, birds, and mammals, are composed of billions of cells. Indeed, an adult human is made up of perhaps as many as 1,000 billion (1,000,000,000,000) cells, all functioning in complex ways that ultimately promote the survival of the individual.

Life on earth can be traced back at least 3.7 billion years, in the form of *prokaryotic* cells. Prokaryotes are single-celled organisms, represented today by

FIGURE 3–1 Structure of a generalized eukaryotic cell, illustrating the cell's three-dimensional nature. Although various organelles are shown, for the sake of simplicity only those we discuss are labeled.

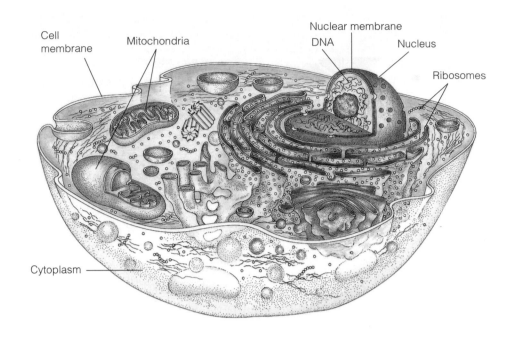

organelles Structures contained within cells, surrounded by a membrane. There are many different types, and each performs specific functions.

nucleus A structure (organelle) found in all eukaryotic cells. The nucleus contains chromosomes (nuclear DNA).

molecules Structures made up of two or more atoms. Molecules can combine with other molecules to form more complex structures.

deoxyribonucleic acid (DNA) The double-stranded molecule that contains the genetic code. DNA is a main component of chromosomes.

ribonucleic acid (RNA) A single-stranded molecule, similar in structure to DNA. Three forms of RNA are essential to protein synthesis. They are messenger RNA (mRNA), transfer RNA (tRNA), and ribosomal RNA (rRNA).

cytoplasm The portion of the cell contained within the cell membrane, excluding the nucleus. The cytoplasm consists of a semifluid material and contains numerous structures involved with cell function.

proteins Three-dimensional molecules that serve a wide variety of functions through their ability to bind to other molecules.

protein synthesis The assembly of chains of amino acids into functional protein molecules. The process is directed by DNA.

mitochondria (*sing.,* mitochondrion) Structures contained within the cytoplasm of eukaryotic cells that convert energy, derived from nutrients, into a form that is used by the cell.

bacteria and blue-green algae. Structurally more complex cells appeared approximately 1.2 billion years ago, and these are referred to as *eukaryotic* cells. Because eukaryotic cells are found in all multicellular organisms, they are the focus of the remainder of this discussion. In spite of the numerous differences between various life forms and the cells that constitute them, it is important to understand that the cells of all living organisms share many similarities as a result of their common evolutionary past.

In general, a eukaryotic cell is a three-dimensional entity composed of *carbohydrates, lipids (fats), nucleic acids,* and *proteins.* It contains a variety of structures called **organelles** within the *cell membrane* (Fig. 3–1). One of these organelles is the **nucleus** (*pl.,* nuclei), a discrete unit surrounded by a thin nuclear membrane. Within the nucleus are two nucleic acids that contain the genetic information that controls the cell's functions. These two critically important **molecules** are **deoxyribonucleic acid (DNA)** and **ribonucleic acid (RNA).** (In prokaryotic cells, genetic information is not contained within a walled nucleus.) Surrounding the nucleus is the **cytoplasm,** which contains numerous other types of organelles involved in various activities, such as breaking down nutrients and converting them to other substances (*metabolism*), storing and releasing energy, eliminating waste, and manufacturing **proteins (protein synthesis).**

Two of these organelles—**mitochondria** and **ribosomes**—require further mention. The mitochondria (*sing.,* mitochondrion) are responsible for energy production in the cell; hence they are the "engines" that drive the cell. Mitochondria are round or oval structures enclosed within a folded membrane, and they contain their own distinct DNA, called **mitochondrial DNA (mtDNA),** which directs mitochondrial activities. Mitochondrial DNA has the same molecular structure and function as nuclear DNA (i.e., DNA found in the nucleus), but it is organized somewhat differently. In recent years, mtDNA has attracted much attention because of particular traits it influences and because it has significance for studies of certain evolutionary processes. For these reasons, mitochondrial inheritance will be discussed in more detail in Chapters 4 and 13. Ribosomes are roughly spherical in shape and are the most common type of cytoplasmic organelle. They are made up partly of RNA and are essential to the synthesis of proteins (see p. 52).

There are basically two types of cells: **somatic cells** and **gametes.** Somatic cells are the cellular components of body tissues, such as muscle, bone, skin, nerve, heart, and brain. Gametes, or sex cells, are specifically involved in reproduction and are not important as structural components of the body. There are two types of gametes: egg cells, produced in the ovaries in females, and *sperm* cells, which develop in male testes. The sole function of a sex cell is to unite with a gamete from another individual to form a **zygote,** which has the potential of developing into a new individual. In this way, gametes transmit genetic information from parent to offspring.

DNA Structure

Cellular functions are directed by DNA. Therefore, if we are to understand these functions and how characteristics are inherited, we need to know something about the structure and function of DNA.

The exact physical and chemical properties of DNA were unknown until 1953, when at Cambridge University, in England, an American researcher named James Watson and three British scientists, Francis Crick, Maurice Wilkins, and Rosalind Franklin, developed a structural and functional model (Fig. 3–2) of DNA (Watson and Crick, 1953a, 1953b). It would be difficult to overstate the importance of their achievement because it completely revolutionized the fields of biology and medicine and forever altered our understanding of biological and evolutionary mechanisms (see A Closer Look, p. 50).

The DNA molecule is composed of two chains of even smaller molecules called **nucleotides.** A nucleotide, in turn, is made up of three components: a sugar molecule (deoxyribose), a phosphate unit, and one of four nitrogenous bases (Fig. 3–3). In DNA, nucleotides are stacked upon one another to form a chain that is bonded along its bases to another **complementary** nucleotide chain. Together the two twist to form a spiral, or helical, shape. The resulting DNA molecule, then, is two-stranded and is described as forming a *double helix* that resembles a twisted ladder. If we follow the twisted ladder analogy, the sugars and phosphates represent the two sides, while the bases and the bonds that join them form the rungs.

ribosomes Structures composed of a form of RNA called ribosomal RNA (rRNA) and protein. Ribosomes are found in the cell's cytoplasm and are essential to the manufacture of proteins.

mitochondrial DNA (mtDNA) DNA found in the mitochondria; mtDNA is inherited only from the mother.

somatic cells Basically, all the cells in the body except those involved with reproduction.

gametes Reproductive cells (eggs and sperm in animals) developed from precursor cells in ovaries and testes.

zygote A cell formed by the union of an egg and a sperm cell. It contains the full complement of chromosomes (in humans, 46) and has the potential of developing into an entire organism.

nucleotides Basic units of the DNA molecule, composed of a sugar, a phosphate, and one of four DNA bases.

complementary Referring to the fact that DNA bases form base pairs in a precise manner. For example, adenine can bond only to thymine. These two bases are said to be *complementary* because one requires the other to form a complete DNA base pair.

A. Barrington Brown / Photo Researchers, Inc.

FIGURE 3–2 James Watson (left) and Francis Crick in 1953 with their model of the structure of the DNA molecule.

FIGURE 3–3 Part of a DNA molecule. The illustration shows the two DNA strands with the sugar and phosphate backbone and the bases extending toward the center.

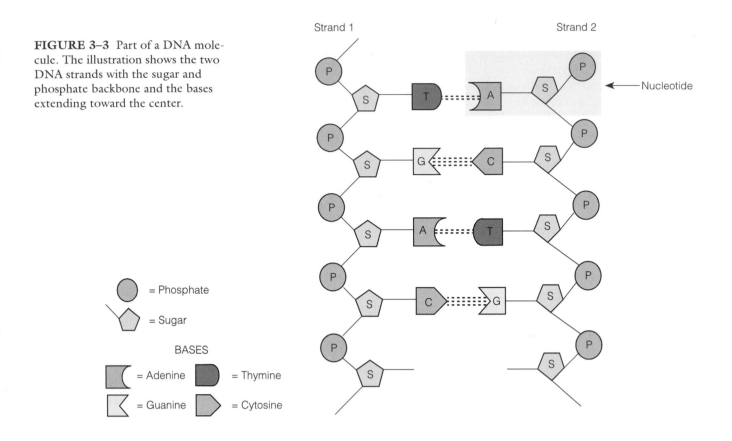

The secret of how DNA functions lies within the four bases. These bases are *adenine, guanine, thymine,* and *cytosine,* and they are usually referred to by their initial letters, A, G, T, and C. In the formation of the double helix, it is possible for one type of base to pair, or bond, with only one other type. Base pairs can form *only* between adenine and thymine and between guanine and cytosine (see Fig. 3–3). This specificity is essential to the DNA molecule's ability to **replicate,** or make an exact copy of itself.

replicate To duplicate. The DNA molecule is able to make copies of itself.

DNA Replication

Growth and development of organisms and tissue repair following injury or disease are among the crucial processes made possible by cell division. Cells multiply by dividing in such a way that each new cell receives a full set of genetic material. This is important because a cell can't function properly without the appropriate amount of DNA. For new cells to receive the essential amount of DNA, it is first necessary for the DNA to replicate.

enzymes Specialized proteins that initiate and direct chemical reactions in the body.

Prior to cell division, specific **enzymes** break the bonds between bases simultaneously at numerous locations in the DNA molecule, leaving the two previously joined strands of nucleotides with their bases exposed (Fig. 3–4). The exposed bases then attract unattached DNA nucleotides, which are continuously produced and present in the cell nucleus. Because one base can be joined to only one other, the attraction between bases occurs in a complementary fashion. Thus, the two previously joined parental nucleotide chains serve as models for the formation of new strands of nucleotides. As each new strand is formed, its bases are joined to the bases of an original strand. When the process is completed, there are two double-stranded DNA molecules exactly like the original one, and each newly formed molecule consists of one original nucleotide chain joined to a newly formed chain (see Fig. 3–4).

See Virtual Lab 2, section II, for discussions of DNA structure and replication.

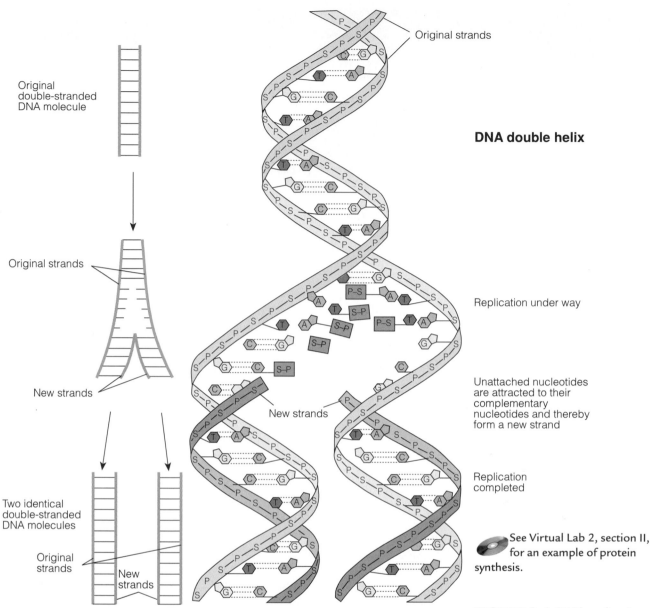

Original double-stranded DNA molecule

Original strands

New strands

Two identical double-stranded DNA molecules

Original strands

New strands

Original strands

DNA double helix

Replication under way

Unattached nucleotides are attracted to their complementary nucleotides and thereby form a new strand

Replication completed

See Virtual Lab 2, section II, for an example of protein synthesis.

FIGURE 3–4 DNA replication. During DNA replication, the two strands of the DNA molecule are separated, and each strand serves as a template for the formation of a new strand. When replication is complete, there are two DNA molecules. Each molecule consists of one new and one original DNA strand.

hemoglobin A protein molecule that occurs in red blood cells and binds to oxygen molecules.

hormones Substances (usually proteins) that are produced by specialized cells and that travel to other parts of the body, where they influence chemical reactions and regulate various cellular functions.

Protein Synthesis

One of the most important functions of DNA is to direct protein synthesis within the cell. Proteins are complex, three-dimensional molecules that function through their ability to bind to other molecules. For example, the protein **hemoglobin,** found in red blood cells, is able to bind to oxygen and serves to transport oxygen to cells throughout the body.

Proteins function in countless ways. Some are structural components of tissues. Collagen, for example, is the most common protein in the body and is a major component of all connective tissues. Aside from minerals, collagen is the most abundant structural material in bone. Other proteins bind directly to DNA to regulate genetic functions. Enzymes are also proteins, and their function is to initiate and enhance chemical reactions. An example of a digestive enzyme is *lactase,* which breaks down *lactose,* or milk sugar, into two simpler sugars. Another class of proteins includes many types of **hormones.** Specialized cells produce and release hormones into the bloodstream to circulate to other areas of the body,

A CLOSER LOOK

Rosalind Franklin: The Fourth (but Invisible) Member of the Double Helix Team

In 1962, three men—James Watson, Francis Crick, and Maurice Wilkins—won the Nobel Prize for medicine and physiology. They earned this most prestigious of scientific honors for their discovery of the structure of the DNA molecule, on which they had published in 1953. But due credit was not given to a fourth, equally deserving person, Rosalind Franklin, who had died of ovarian cancer in 1958. Even if she had been acknowledged in 1962, she still would not have been a Nobel recipient because the Nobel Prize is not awarded posthumously.

Franklin, a physical chemist, arrived at Cambridge University in 1951. She had been invited there to study the structure of DNA using a technique called X-ray diffraction that she had been working with in Paris. (X-ray diffraction is a process that reveals the positions of atoms in crystalline structures.) What Franklin didn't know was that a colleague in her lab, Maurice Wilkins, was working on the same project. And he, having been uninformed of her position, thought she had been hired as his assistant. This was hardly a good way to begin a working relationship, and apparently there were some tense moments.

Franklin soon produced some excellent X-ray diffraction images of wet DNA fibers that had been provided by Wilkins. The images clearly showed that the structure was helical, and she worked out that there were two strands. Wilkins innocently (but without Franklin's knowledge)

FIGURE 1
Rosalind Franklin

showed the images to Watson and Crick, who were working in another laboratory, also at Cambridge. Within two weeks, Watson and Crick developed their now famous model of a double-stranded helix.

Desperately unhappy at Cambridge, Franklin took a position at King's College, London, in 1953. In April of that year, she and a student published an article in the journal *Nature* that dealt indirectly with the helical structure of DNA. In the same issue were the Watson and Crick article and another by Wilkins and two colleagues.

During her life, Franklin did gain recognition for her work in carbons, coals, and viruses, topics on which she published many articles, and she was happy with the reputation she achieved. After her death, Watson made many rather nasty comments about Rosalind Franklin, several in print. Nevertheless, it appears they remained on friendly terms until she died at age 37, and she also remained friendly with Crick. But she never knew that their revolutionary discovery was made possible in part by her photographic images.

where they produce specific effects in tissues and organs. A good example of this type of protein is *insulin,* produced by cells in the pancreas. Insulin causes cells in the liver and certain types of muscle tissue to absorb essential energy-producing glucose (sugar) from the blood. (Enzymes and hormones will be discussed in more detail in Chapter 16.)

As you can see, proteins make us what we are. Not only are they the major constituents of all body tissues, but they also direct and perform physiological and cellular functions. It is therefore critical that protein synthesis occur accurately, because if it doesn't, physiological development and activities can be disrupted or even prevented.

amino acids Small molecules that are the components of proteins.

Proteins are composed of chains of smaller molecules called **amino acids.** In all, there are 20 amino acids, 8 of which must be obtained from dietary sources (see Chapter 16). The remaining 12 are produced in cells. These 20 amino acids are combined in different amounts and sequences to produce potentially millions of proteins. What makes proteins different from one another is the number of amino acids involved and the *sequence* in which they are arranged. For a protein to function properly, its amino acids must be arranged in the proper sequence.

DNA serves as a recipe for making a protein, since it's the sequence of DNA bases that ultimately determines the order of amino acids in a protein molecule. In the DNA instructions, a *triplet,* or group of three bases, specifies a particular amino acid. For example, if a triplet consists of the base sequence cytosine, guanine, and adenine (CGA), it specifies the amino acid *alanine.* If the next triplet in the chain consists of the sequence guanine, thymine, and cytosine (GTC), it refers to another amino acid—*glutamine.* Therefore, a DNA recipe might look like this: AGA CGA ACA ACC TAC TTT TTC CTT AAG GTC, and so on (Table 3–1 and A Closer Look on p. 52).

Protein synthesis is a little more complicated than the preceding few sentences would imply. For one thing, protein synthesis occurs outside the nucleus at specialized structures in the cytoplasm called *ribosomes* (see p. 46). A logistics problem arises because the DNA molecule can't leave the cell's nucleus. So the first step in protein synthesis is to copy the DNA message into a form that can pass through the nuclear membrane into the cytoplasm. This is accomplished through the formation of a molecule similar to DNA called ribonucleic acid, or RNA. RNA is different from DNA in three important ways:

1. It is single-stranded.
2. It contains a different type of sugar.
3. It contains the base uracil as a substitute for the DNA base thymine. (Uracil is attracted to adenine, just as thymine is.)

The RNA molecule forms on the DNA template in much the same manner as new DNA molecules are assembled. As in DNA replication, the two DNA strands separate, but only partially, and one of these strands attracts free-floating RNA nucleotides (also produced in the cell), which are joined together on the

TABLE 3–1 The Genetic Code

AMINO ACID SYMBOL	AMINO ACID	DNA TRIPLET	mRNA CODON
Ala	Alanine	CGA, CGG, CGT, CGC	GCU, GCC, GCA, GCG
Arg	Arginine	GCA, GCG, GCT, GCC, TCT, TCC	CGU, CGC, CGA, CGG, AGA, AGG
Asn	Asparagine	TTA, TTG	AAU, AAC
Asp	Aspartic acid	CTA, CTG	GAU, GAC
Cys	Cysteine	ACA, ACG	UGU, UGC
Gln	Glutamine	GTT, GTC	CAA, CAG
Glu	Glutamic acid	CTT, CTC	GAA, GAG
Gly	Glycine	CCA, CCG, CCT, CCC	GGU, GGC, GGA, GGG
His	Histidine	GTA, GTG	CAU, CAC
Ile	Isoleucine	TAA, TAG, TAT	AUU, AUC, AUA
Leu	Leucine	AAT, AAC, GAA, GAG, GAT, GAC	UUA, UUG, CUU, CUC, CUA, CUG
Lys	Lysine	TTT, TTC	AAA, AAG
Met	Methionine	TAC	AUG
Phe	Phenylalanine	AAA, AAG	UUU, UUC
Pro	Proline	GGA, GGG, GGT, GGC	CCU, CCC, CCA, CCG
Ser	Serine	AGA, AGG, AGT, AGC, TCA, TCG	UCU, UCC, UCA, UCG, AGU, AGC
Thr	Threonine	TGA, TGG, TGT, TGC	ACU, ACC, ACA, ACG
Trp	Tryptophan	ACC	UGG
Tyr	Tyrosine	ATA, ATG	UAU, UAC
Val	Valine	CAA, CAG, CAT, CAC	GUU, GUC, GUA, GUG
Terminating triplets		ATT, ATC, ACT	UAA, UAG, UGA

A CLOSER LOOK

Characteristics of the DNA Code

1. **The Code is universal.** In other words, the same basic messages apply to all life forms on the planet, from bacteria to oak trees to humans. The same triplet code, specifying each amino acid, thus applies to all life on earth. This commonality is the basis for the methods used in recombinant DNA technology.

2. **The Code is triplet.** Each amino acid is specified by a sequence of three bases in the mRNA (the codon), which in turn is coded for by three bases in the DNA.

3. **The Code is continuous—without pauses.** There are no pauses separating one codon from another. Thus, if a base should be deleted, the entire frame would be moved, drastically altering the message downstream for successive codons. Such a gross alteration is termed a *frame-shift mutation*. Note that although the code lacks "commas," it does contain "periods"; that is, three specific codons act to stop translation.

4. **The Code is redundant.** While there are 20 amino acids, there are 4 DNA bases and 64 possible triplets or mRNA codons. Even considering the three "stop" messages, that still leaves 61 codons specifying the 20 amino acids. Thus, many amino acids are specified by more than one codon (see Table 3–1). For example, leucine and serine are each coded for by six different codons. In fact, only two amino acids (methionine and tryptophan) are coded for by a single codon. Redundancy is useful. For one thing, it serves as a safety net of sorts by helping to reduce the likelihood of severe consequences if there is a change, or *mutation,* in a DNA base. For example, four different DNA triplets—CGA, CGG, CGT, and CGC—code for the amino acid alanine. If, in the codon CGA, A mutates to G, the resulting triplet, CGG, will still specify alanine; thus, there will be no functional change.

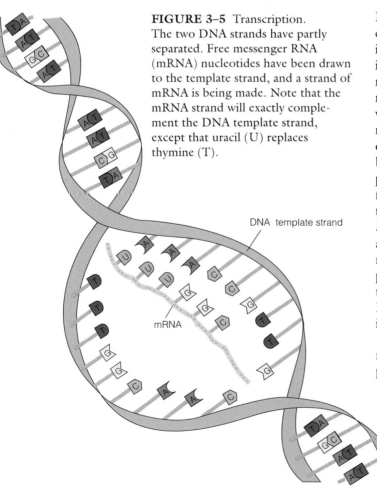

FIGURE 3–5 Transcription. The two DNA strands have partly separated. Free messenger RNA (mRNA) nucleotides have been drawn to the template strand, and a strand of mRNA is being made. Note that the mRNA strand will exactly complement the DNA template strand, except that uracil (U) replaces thymine (T).

DNA template strand

mRNA

DNA template. This new RNA nucleotide chain is called **messenger RNA (mRNA),** and its formation is called *transcription* because, in fact, it is transcribing, or copying, the DNA code (Fig. 3–5). But the resulting mRNA segment is actually a complement, rather than an identical copy, of the DNA strand on which it is formed. If, for example, the DNA triplet reads CTA, then the corresponding mRNA triplet, or **codon,** will be GAU. (Remember that in RNA, the base uracil replaces thymine; see Table 3–1.) The process continues until a section of DNA called a terminator region (composed of one of three DNA triplets) is reached and transcription stops (see Table 3–1). At this point, the mRNA strand, comprising anywhere from 5,000 to perhaps as many as 200,000 nucleotides, peels away from the DNA model, and a portion of it travels through the nuclear membrane to the ribosome. Meanwhile, the bonds between the DNA bases are reestablished, and the DNA molecule is once more intact.

As the mRNA strand arrives at the ribosome, the message it contains is translated. (This stage of the process is called *translation* because at this point, the genetic instructions are actually being decoded and implemented.) Just as each DNA triplet specifies one amino acid, mRNA codons also serve this function. Therefore, the mRNA strand is "read" in codons, or groups of three bases taken together (see Table 3–1).

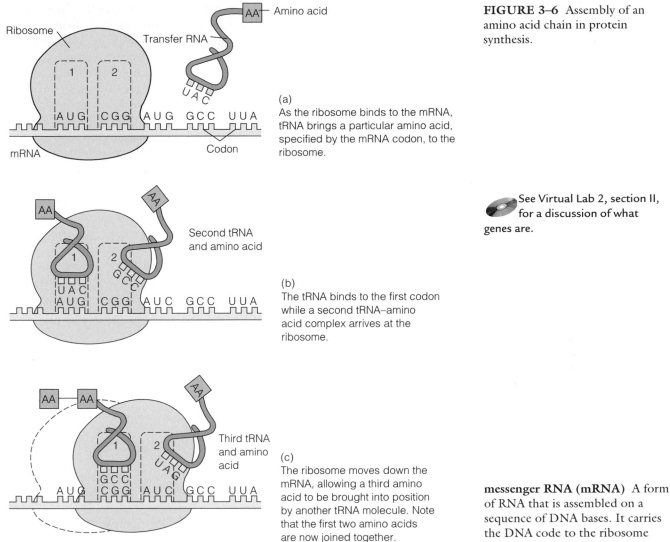

FIGURE 3–6 Assembly of an amino acid chain in protein synthesis.

(a) As the ribosome binds to the mRNA, tRNA brings a particular amino acid, specified by the mRNA codon, to the ribosome.

(b) The tRNA binds to the first codon while a second tRNA–amino acid complex arrives at the ribosome.

(c) The ribosome moves down the mRNA, allowing a third amino acid to be brought into position by another tRNA molecule. Note that the first two amino acids are now joined together.

See Virtual Lab 2, section II, for a discussion of what genes are.

Another form of RNA, **transfer RNA (tRNA),** is essential to the actual assembly of a protein. Each molecule of tRNA has the ability to bind to one specific amino acid. A particular tRNA molecule carrying the amino acid matching the mRNA codon being translated arrives at the ribosome and deposits its amino acid (Fig. 3–6). As a second amino acid is deposited, the two are joined in the order dictated by the sequence of mRNA codons. In this way, series of amino acids are linked together to form a structure that will eventually function as a protein.

What Is a Gene?

The entire sequence of DNA bases responsible for the synthesis of a protein or, in some cases, a portion of a protein is referred to as a **gene.** Or, put another way, a gene is a segment of DNA that specifies the sequence of amino acids in a particular protein. Even more precisely, a gene codes for the production of a **polypeptide chain.** Those proteins composed of only a single polypeptide chain are produced through the action of a single gene. However, some proteins (collagen and hemoglobin, for example) are made up of two or more polypeptide chains, each of which results from the action of a different gene. Thus, while some proteins result from the action of only one gene, others are produced by two or more.

messenger RNA (mRNA) A form of RNA that is assembled on a sequence of DNA bases. It carries the DNA code to the ribosome during protein synthesis.

codon A triplet of messenger RNA bases that refers to a specific amino acid during protein synthesis.

transfer RNA (tRNA) The type of RNA that binds to specific amino acids and transports them to the ribosome during protein synthesis.

gene A sequence of DNA bases that specifies the order of amino acids in an entire protein, a portion of a protein, or any functional product. A gene may be made up of hundreds or thousands of DNA bases organized into coding and noncoding segments.

polypeptide chain A sequence of amino acids that may act alone or in combination with others as a functional protein.

mutation A change in DNA. *Mutation* refers to changes in DNA bases (specifically called point mutations) and also to changes in chromosome number and/or structure.

A gene may comprise only a few hundred bases, or it may be composed of thousands. If the sequence of DNA bases is altered through **mutation** (a change in the DNA), the manufacture of some proteins may not occur, and the cell (or indeed the organism) may not function properly (if it functions at all).

This definition of a gene is a functional one and is technically correct. But over the years, the definition of a gene has changed to keep up with genetic research. The notion of *one gene–one polypeptide*, although not 100 percent incorrect, has been greatly modified, partly in recognition of the fact that DNA also codes for RNA and DNA nucleotides (see A Closer Look, this page). One new and more inclusive definition simply states that a gene is "a complete chromosomal segment responsible for making a functional product" (Snyder and Gerstein, 2003).

It is important to understand that gene action is an incredibly complex phenomenon that is still only partly understood. For example, the DNA segments that are transcribed into mRNA and therefore code for specific amino acids are termed *exons*. But the vast majority of nucleotide sequences in a gene are not expressed during protein synthesis. In fact, some sequences, called *introns,* are initially transcribed but subsequently eliminated (see A Closer Look, this page). Thus, introns aren't represented in the newly formed mature mRNA segment, and they aren't translated into amino acid sequences. But while introns aren't instrumental in protein synthesis, they are indeed a part of the DNA molecule,

A CLOSER LOOK

Genetic Junk and Jumping Genes

In all fields of inquiry, important discoveries always raise new questions that eventually lead to further revelations. Probably, there is no statement that could be more aptly applied to the field of genetics. For example, in 1977, geneticists recognized that during protein synthesis (see p. 49), the initially formed mRNA molecule contained many more nucleotides than were represented in the subsequently produced proteins. This finding led to the discovery of *introns* (see next page), portions of genes that don't code for, or specify, proteins. What happens is that once the mRNA molecule peels away from the DNA template, but before it leaves the nucleus, enzymes snip out the introns. The original mRNA molecule is sometimes called *pre-mRNA,* but once the introns have been deleted, the remainder is mature mRNA (Fig. 1). It is the mature mRNA that leaves the cell nucleus carrying its code for protein production.

In the 1980s, geneticists learned that only about 2 percent of the roughly 3 billion DNA bases in the human genome is contained within *exons,* the segments that actually provide the code for protein synthesis. This means that while an estimated 28 percent of human DNA is composed of genes (including introns and exons), only 5 percent of the DNA within these genes is actually composed of coding sequences (Baltimore, 2001). And we also know that a human gene can specify the production of as many as three different proteins by using different combinations of the exons interspersed within it (Pennisi, 2001). So the notion that one gene specifies only one protein has fallen by the wayside.

With only 2 percent of the human genome directing protein synthesis, humans have more noncoding DNA than any other species so far studied (Vogel, 2001). Invertebrates and some vertebrates have only small amounts of noncoding sequences, and yet they are fully functional organisms. So just what does all this noncoding DNA (originally called "junk DNA") do in humans? Scientists are beginning to answer that question.

It appears that repeated segments near the ends of chromosomes contain genes that may be involved in many of the activities of the telomeres, crucial structures at the very ends of chromosomes. Among other things, telomeres (composed of the same repeated sequence of apparently noncoding DNA) influence cellular aging and the regulation of cell cycles (Reithman et al., 2001).

Almost half of all human DNA consists of noncoding segments that are repeated over and over and over. Depending on their length, these segments are referred to as tandem repeats, satellites, or microsatellites. Microsatellites have an extremely high mutation rate and can gain or lose repeated segments and then return to their former length. But this tendency to mutate means that the number of repeats in a given microsatellite varies between individuals. And this tremendous variation has been the

and it is the combination of introns and exons, interspersed along a strand of DNA, that comprises the unit we call a gene.

Although we usually think of genes as coding for the production of structural proteins, some genes function primarily to control the expression of other genes. Basically, these *regulatory genes* produce enzymes and other proteins that either switch on or turn off other segments of DNA. Consequently, this mechanism is critical for individual organisms and also has important evolutionary implications.

All somatic cells contain the same genetic information, but in any given cell, only a fraction of the DNA contained within exons is actually involved in protein synthesis. For example, bone cells carry the same DNA that codes for the production of digestive enzymes, as do the cells of the stomach lining. But bone cells don't produce digestive enzymes. Instead, they manufacture collagen, the major organic component of bone. Bone cells produce collagen and not digestive enzymes because of the differentiation of cell lines early in embryonic development. During this process, cells undergo changes in form, their functions become specialized, and most of their DNA is permanently deactivated through the action of regulatory genes. In other words, they become specific types of cells. (See Issue, pp. 72–73.)

Gene regulation also means that some genes are expressed only at certain times during the life cycle. A good example of gene regulation is the production of

basis for DNA fingerprinting, a technique commonly used to provide evidence in criminal cases (see p. 68). Actually, microsatellite variation is now being used by anthropologists for all kinds of research, from tracing movements of peoples to paternity testing in chimpanzees (see p. 224).

Some of the variations in microsatellite composition are associated with neurological disorders, so one can't help but wonder why we have them. One possible answer is that some noncoding regions may switch functioning genes on and off. Or they may modulate the activities of genes in other ways. Also, by losing or adding material, they can alter the sequences of bases in genes, thus becoming a source of mutation in functional genes. Moreover, these mutations and the enormous abundance of noncoding sequences combine to provide a source of variation for natural selection to act on.

Lastly, there are transposable elements (TEs), the so-called *jumping genes*. These are DNA sequences that are able to change position within the genome. They mainly code for proteins that enable them to move about, and because they can land right in the middle of coding sequences, they can change the function of genes. So TEs are also a cause of mutations, since they change the DNA sequence. Frequently, these alterations are harmful, and TEs have been associated with numerous disease conditions, including a form of breast cancer (Deragon and Capy, 2000). But if the changes are neutral or even beneficial, then TEs are generating variations that may prove to be advantageous in certain environmental conditions, i.e., more fuel for natural selection.

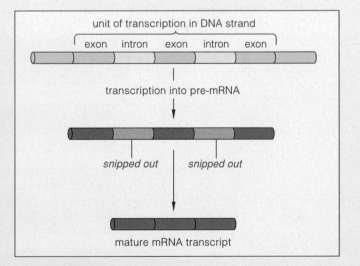

FIGURE 1 Diagram of a DNA sequence being transcribed. The introns are deleted from the pre-mRNA before it leaves the cell nucleus. The remaining mature mRNA contains only exons.

hemoglobin in human development. As we mentioned, hemoglobin is the protein molecule contained in red blood cells that is responsible for carrying oxygen molecules to body cells and tissues. But humans produce three different varieties of hemoglobin at different developmental stages, due to variation in the availability of oxygen. Consequently, the hemoglobin produced in an early embryo differs from that in a 6-month fetus, which is again different from the hemoglobin of a 6-month-old infant. The existence of embryonic, fetal, and post-natal hemoglobin results from genes being turned off and on at various developmental stages by regulatory genes.

Probably the most important regulatory genes are the **homeotic genes.** These genes are expressed only during embryonic development, and they interact in complex ways with other genes and cells to direct the development of the body plan (i.e., front to back, head to tail; how many limbs and where they will be located; how many vertebrae; etc.) They also direct early segmentation of embryonic tissues including those that give rise to the spine, nerves, and muscles. Homeotic genes contain a region called the *homeobox,* and so they are also referred to as homeobox or *Hox* genes.

Homeotic genes are highly conserved, meaning they have been maintained pretty much throughout all of evolutionary history. They are present in all insects and vertebrates and don't vary greatly from species to species. Counterparts of human homeotic genes are present in fruit flies, for example, where they perform similar functions. This type of conservation means that they are vitally important and that they evolved from genes that ultimately were present in some of the earliest forms of life. Also, alterations in the behavior of homeotic genes are probably responsible for some of the physical differences between closely related species. For example, some of the anatomical differences between humans and chimpanzees are almost certainly the results of evolutionary changes in regulatory genes in both lineages. For these reasons, homeotic genes are now a critical area of research in evolutionary and developmental biology.

homeotic genes An evolutionarily ancient family of regulatory genes that directs the development of the overall body plan and the segmentation of body tissues; also called homeobox or *Hox* genes.

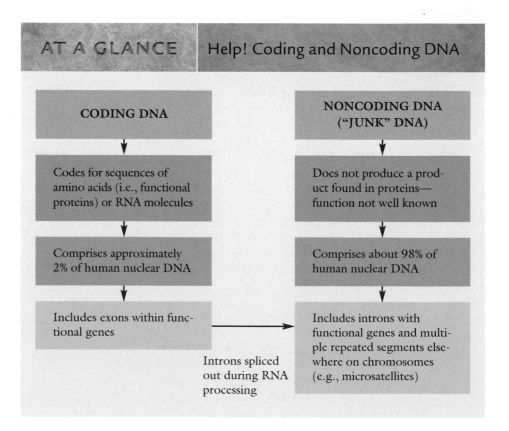

AT A GLANCE Help! Coding and Noncoding DNA

CODING DNA	**NONCODING DNA ("JUNK" DNA)**
Codes for sequences of amino acids (i.e., functional proteins) or RNA molecules	Does not produce a product found in proteins—function not well known
Comprises approximately 2% of human nuclear DNA	Comprises about 98% of human nuclear DNA
Includes exons within functional genes	Includes introns with functional genes and multiple repeated segments elsewhere on chromosomes (e.g., microsatellites)

Introns spliced out during RNA processing

Mutation: When a Gene Changes

The best way to envision how genetic material is organized and functions is to see what happens when it changes, or mutates. The first clearly elucidated example of a molecular mutation in humans concerns a portion of the hemoglobin molecule. Normal adult hemoglobin is made up of four polypeptide chains (two *alpha* chains and two *beta* chains) that are direct products of gene action. Each beta chain is in turn composed of 146 amino acids.

There are several hemoglobin disorders with genetic origins, and perhaps the best known of these is **sickle-cell anemia,** which results from a defect in the beta chain. Individuals with sickle-cell anemia inherit a variant of a gene from *both* parents that contains the substitution of one amino acid (*valine*) for the normally occurring *glutamic acid*. This single amino acid substitution on the beta chain results in the production of an altered and less efficient form of hemoglobin called hemoglobin S (Hb^S). The normal form is called hemoglobin A (Hb^A). In situations where the availability of oxygen is reduced, such as high altitude, or when oxygen requirements are increased through exercise, red cells bearing Hb^S collapse, roughly assuming a sickle shape (Fig. 3–7). What follows is a cascade of events, all of which result in severe anemia and its consequences (Fig. 3–8). Briefly, these events include impaired circulation from blocked capillaries, red blood cell destruction, oxygen deprivation to vital organs (including the brain), and, without treatment, death.

Individuals who inherit the altered form of the gene from only one parent have what is termed *sickle-cell trait;* because only about 40 percent of their hemoglobin is abnormal, they are much less severely affected and usually have a normal life span.

The cause of all the serious problems associated with sickle-cell anemia is a change in the Hb gene. Remember that both normal hemoglobin and the sickle-cell variety have 146 amino acids, 145 of which are identical. Moreover, to emphasize the importance of a seemingly minimal alteration, consider that triplets of DNA bases are required to specify amino acids. Therefore, it takes 438 bases (146 × 3) to produce the chain of 146 amino acids forming the adult hemoglobin beta chain. But a change in only one of these 438 bases produces the life-threatening complications seen in sickle-cell anemia.

sickle-cell anemia A severe inherited hemoglobin disorder that results from inheriting two copies of a mutant allele. This allele results from a single base substitution in the DNA.

(a)

(b)

FIGURE 3–7 (a) Scanning electron micrograph of a normal, fully oxygenated red blood cell. (b) Scanning electron micrograph of a collapsed, sickle-shaped red blood cell that contains Hb^S.

© Dr. Stanley Flegler / Visuals Unlimited

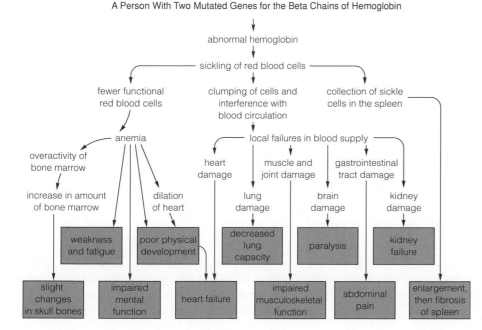

FIGURE 3–8 Diagram showing the cascade of symptoms that can occur in people with sickle-cell anemia.

FIGURE 3–9 Substitution of one base at position #6 produces sickling hemoglobin.

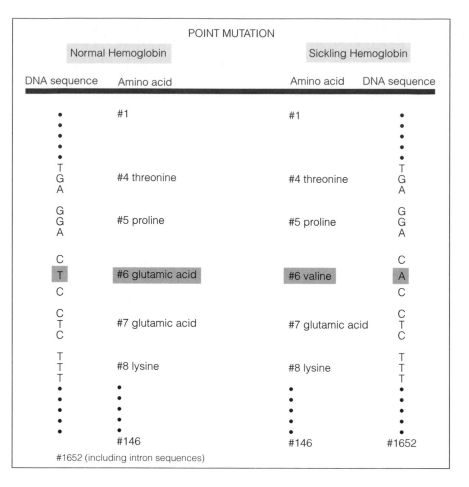

Figure 3–9 shows a DNA base sequence and the resulting amino acid products for both normal and sickling hemoglobin. As can be seen, a single base substitution (from CTC to CAC) can result in an altered amino acid sequence, from

> . . . proline—*glutamic acid*—glutamic acid . . .

to

> . . . proline—*valine*—glutamic acid . . .

point mutation A chemical change in a single base of a DNA sequence.

Such a change in the genetic code is referred to as a **point mutation,** and in evolution, it is a common and important source of new genetic variation in populations. Point mutations, like that for the Hb gene, probably occur relatively frequently. But a new mutation can have evolutionary significance only if it is passed on to offspring through the gametes. Once such a mutation has occurred, its fate in the population will depend on the other evolutionary forces, especially natural selection. In fact, sickle-cell anemia is the best-demonstrated example of natural selection acting on human beings, a point that will be considered in more detail in Chapter 4.

Chromosomes

interphase The portion of a cell's cycle during which metabolic processes and other cellular activities occur. Chromosomes are not visible as discrete structures at this time. DNA replication occurs during interphase.

chromatin The loose, diffuse form of DNA seen during interphase. When it condenses, chromatin forms into chromosomes.

Much of a cell's existence is spent in **interphase,** the portion of its life cycle during which the cell is involved with metabolic processes and other activities. During interphase, the cell's DNA exists as an uncoiled, granular substance called **chromatin.** (Incredibly, there are an estimated 6 feet of DNA in the nucleus of

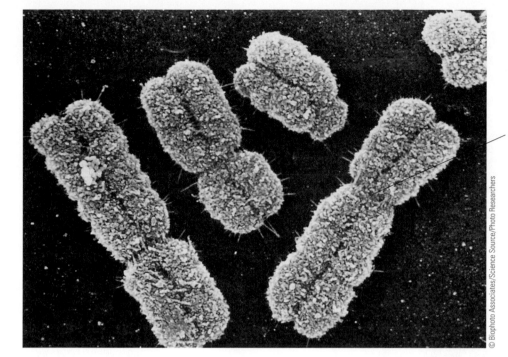

— Centromere

FIGURE 3–10 Scanning electron micrograph of human chromosomes during cell division. Note that these chromosomes are composed of two strands, or two DNA molecules.

every one of your somatic cells!) However, at various times in the life of most types of cells, interphase is interrupted, and the cell divides.

Cell division results in the production of new cells, and it's during this process that the chromatin becomes tightly coiled and is visible under a microscope as a set of discrete structures called **chromosomes** (Fig. 3–10). A chromosome is composed of a DNA molecule and associated proteins (Fig. 3–11). During normal cell function, if chromosomes were visible, they would appear as single-stranded structures. However, during the early stages of cell division, they are made up of two strands, or two DNA molecules, joined together at a constricted area called the **centromere.** There are two strands because the DNA molecules have *replicated* during interphase, and one strand of a chromosome is an exact copy of the other.

Every species is characterized by a specific number of chromosomes in somatic cells (Table 3–2). In humans, there are 46. Chimpanzees and gorillas have 48. This difference doesn't mean that humans have less DNA than chimpanzees and gorillas. The DNA is simply packaged differently in the three species.

Chromosomes occur in pairs, so human somatic cells contain 23 pairs. One member of each pair is inherited from the father (paternal), while the other member is inherited from the mother (maternal). Members of chromosomal pairs are said to be **homologous** because they are alike in size and position of the centromere and they carry genetic information influencing the same *traits*. This is not to say that homologous chromosomes are genetically identical. It simply means that the characteristics they govern are the same. For example, on both of a person's ninth chromosomes, there is a **locus,** or gene position, that determines which of the four ABO blood types (A, B, AB, or O) he or she will have. However, these two ninth chromosomes might not have identical DNA segments at the ABO locus. In other words, at numerous genetic loci, there may be more than one possible form of a gene, and these different forms are called **alleles.** Alleles are alternate forms of a gene that can direct the cell to produce slightly different forms of the same protein and, ultimately, different expressions of traits as in the hemoglobin S (Hb^S) example presented on page 57. At the ABO locus, there are three possible alleles: *A, B,* and *O.* However, since individuals only possess two ninth

chromosomes Discrete structures composed of DNA and protein found only in the nuclei of cells. Chromosomes are only visible under magnification during certain phases of cell division.

centromere The constricted portion of a chromosome. After replication, the two strands of a double-stranded chromosome are joined at the centromere.

homologous Referring to members of chromosome pairs. Homologous chromosomes carry loci that govern the same traits. During meiosis, homologous chromosomes pair and exchange segments of DNA. They are alike with regard to size, position of centromere, and banding patterns.

locus (*pl.,* loci) (lo´-kus, lo-sigh´) The position on a chromosome where a given gene occurs. The term is sometimes used interchangeably with *gene,* but this usage is technically incorrect.

alleles Alternate forms of a gene. Alleles occur at the same locus on homologous chromosomes and thus govern the same trait. However, because they are different, their action may result in different expressions of that trait. The term is sometimes used synonymously with *gene.*

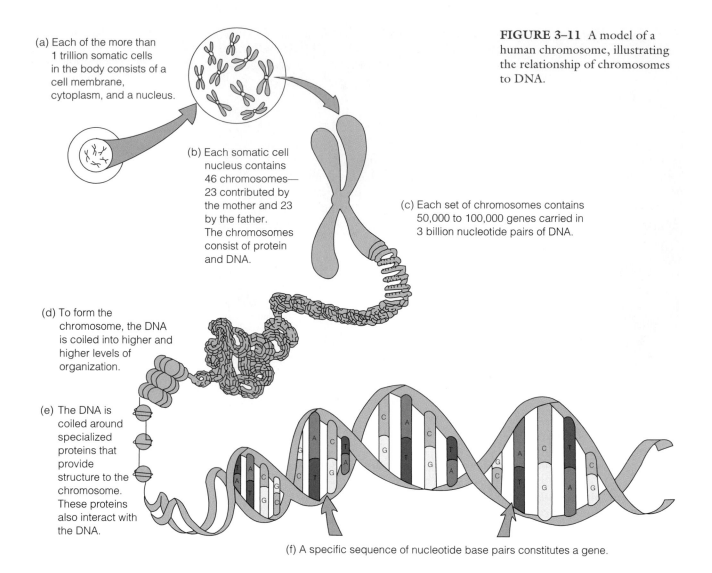

(a) Each of the more than 1 trillion somatic cells in the body consists of a cell membrane, cytoplasm, and a nucleus.

FIGURE 3–11 A model of a human chromosome, illustrating the relationship of chromosomes to DNA.

(b) Each somatic cell nucleus contains 46 chromosomes— 23 contributed by the mother and 23 by the father. The chromosomes consist of protein and DNA.

(c) Each set of chromosomes contains 50,000 to 100,000 genes carried in 3 billion nucleotide pairs of DNA.

(d) To form the chromosome, the DNA is coiled into higher and higher levels of organization.

(e) The DNA is coiled around specialized proteins that provide structure to the chromosome. These proteins also interact with the DNA.

(f) A specific sequence of nucleotide base pairs constitutes a gene.

TABLE 3–2 Standard Chromosomal Complement in Various Organisms

ORGANISM	CHROMOSOME NUMBER IN SOMATIC CELLS	CHROMOSOME NUMBER IN GAMETES
Human (*Homo sapiens*)	46	23
Chimpanzee (*Pan troglodytes*)	48	24
Gorilla (*Gorilla gorilla*)	48	24
Dog (*Canis familiaris*)	78	39
Chicken (*Gallus domesticus*)	78	39
Frog (*Rana pipiens*)	26	13
Housefly (*Musca domestica*)	12	6
Onion (*Allium cepa*)	16	8
Corn (*Zea mays*)	20	10
Tobacco (*Nicotiana tabacum*)	48	24

Source: Cummings, 1991, p. 16.

chromosomes, only two alleles are present in any one person. It is the allelic variation at the ABO locus that is responsible for the variation among humans in ABO blood type. Moreover, the potential variation that exists at specific loci in homologous chromosomes (as illustrated by the ABO example) explains how members of a chromosome pair may influence the same traits and yet not be genetically identical. (This point is covered in more detail in Chapter 4.)

There are two basic types of chromosomes: **autosomes** and **sex chromosomes.** Autosomes carry genetic information that governs all physical characteristics except primary sex determination. The two sex chromosomes are the X and Y chromosomes. In mammals, the Y chromosome carries genetic information directly involved with determining maleness. The X chromosome is larger than the Y. Although called a "sex chromosome," it functions more like an autosome in that it is not actually involved in primary sex determination but does influence a number of other traits.

Among mammals, all genetically normal females have two X chromosomes (XX); they are female simply because there is no Y chromosome. All genetically normal males have one X and one Y chromosome (XY). In other classes of animals, such as birds or insects, primary sex determination is governed by differing chromosomal mechanisms.

It's important to remember that *all* autosomes occur in pairs. Normal human somatic cells have 22 pairs of autosomes and one pair of sex chromosomes. Abnormal numbers of autosomes, with few exceptions, are fatal to the individual, usually soon after conception. Although abnormal numbers of sex chromosomes are not usually fatal, they may result in sterility and frequently have other consequences as well (see p. 67 for further discussion). Therefore, to function normally, it is essential for a human cell to possess both members of each chromosomal pair, or a total of 46 chromosomes.

autosomes All chromosomes except the sex chromosomes.

sex chromosomes In mammals, the X and Y chromosomes.

karyotype The chromosomal complement of an individual or that which is typical for a species. Usually displayed in a photomicrograph, the chromosomes are arranged in pairs and according to size and position of the centromere.

KARYOTYPING CHROMOSOMES

One method frequently used to examine chromosomes in an individual is to produce what is called a **karyotype.** (An example of a human karyotype is shown in Fig. 3–12.) Chromosomes used in karyotypes are obtained from dividing cells. (You will remember that chromosomes are visible as discrete entities only during cell division.) For example, white blood cells, because they are easily obtained, may be cultured, chemically treated, and microscopically examined to identify those that are dividing. These cells are then photographed through a microscope to produce *photomicrographs* of intact, double-stranded chromosomes. Homologous chromosomes are then matched up, and the entire set is arranged in descending order by size so that the largest (number 1) appears first.

In addition to overall size, position of the centromere also helps to identify individual chromosomes, since the position of the centromere is characteristic of each chromosome. Moreover, with the development of special techniques to highlight DNA segments that differentially take up various colored stains, it is now possible to identify every chromosome on the basis of specific *banding patterns.*

Karyotyping has numerous practical applications. Physicians and genetic counselors routinely use karyotypes to help them diagnose

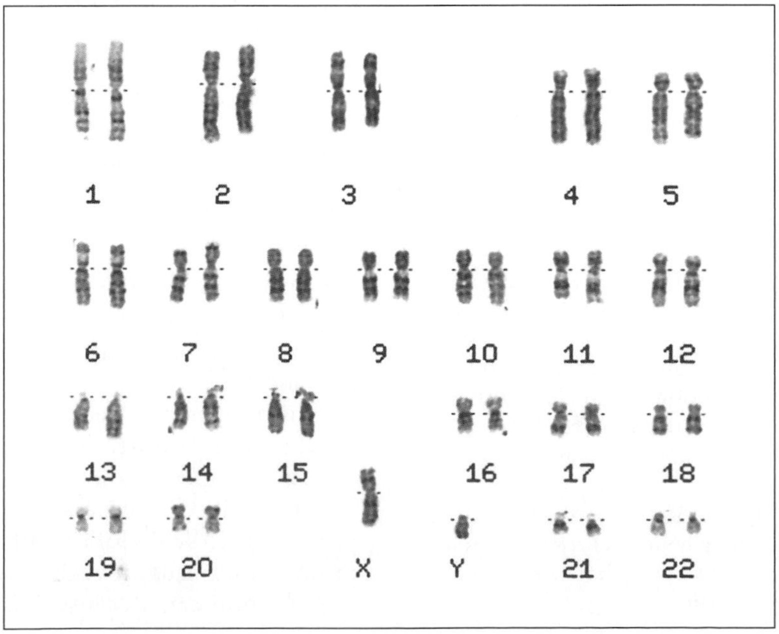

FIGURE 3–12 A karyotype of a male, with the chromosomes arranged by size and position of the centromere, as well as by the banding patterns.

chromosomal disorders in patients. Moreover, karyotypes are often employed in the prenatal diagnosis of chromosomal abnormalities in developing fetuses.

Karyotypes have also been extremely useful in comparing the chromosomes of different species. Indeed, karyotype analysis has revealed many chromosomal similarities shared by different primate species, including humans. The similarities in overall karyotype, as well as the biochemical and DNA similarities indicated by banding patterns (discussed in Chapter 6), point to close *genetic* relationships especially between humans and the African great apes (chimpanzees and gorillas).

Cell Division

MITOSIS

mitosis Simple cell division; the process by which somatic cells divide to produce two identical daughter cells.

Cell division in somatic cells is called **mitosis** which occurs during growth. It also enables injured tissues to heal and replaces older cells with newer ones. In short, it is the way somatic cells reproduce.

In the early stages of mitosis, a human somatic cell possesses 46 double-stranded chromosomes. As the cell begins to divide, the chromosomes line up in random order along the center of the cell (Fig. 3–13). The chromosomes then split apart at the centromere, so that the strands are separated. Once the two strands are apart, they pull away from each other and move to opposite ends of the dividing cell. Each strand is now a distinct chromosome, *composed of one DNA molecule*. Following the separation of chromosome strands, the cell membrane pinches in and becomes sealed, so that two new cells are formed, each with a full complement of DNA, or 46 chromosomes.

Mitosis is referred to as "simple cell division" because a somatic cell divides one time to produce two daughter cells that are genetically identical to each other and to the original cell. In mitosis, the original cell possesses 46 chromosomes, and each new daughter cell inherits an exact copy of all 46. This arrangement is made possible by the ability of the DNA molecule to replicate. Thus, it is DNA replication that ensures that the quantity and quality of the genetic material remain constant from one generation of cells to the next.

We should mention that not all somatic cells undergo mitosis. Red blood cells are produced continuously by specialized cells in bone marrow but they can't divide since they possess no nucleus and no nuclear DNA. Once the brain and nervous system are fully developed brain and nerve cells (neurons) don't divide, although some debate currently surrounds this issue. Liver cells also don't divide after growth has ceased unless this vital organ is damaged through injury or disease. However, with these three exceptions (red blood cells, mature neurons, and liver cells), somatic cells are regularly duplicated through the process of mitosis.

MEIOSIS

meiosis Cell division in specialized cells in ovaries and testes. Meiosis involves two divisions and results in four daughter cells, each containing only half the original number of chromosomes. These cells can develop into gametes.

diploid Referring to the full complement of chromosomes in a somatic cell—both members of each pair.

While mitosis produces new cells, **meiosis** may lead to the development of new individuals, since it produces reproductive cells, or gametes. Although meiosis is another form of cell division and is in some ways similar to mitosis, it is a more complicated process.

During meiosis, specialized cells in male testes and female ovaries divide and develop, eventually to become sperm and egg cells. Initially, these cells contain the full complement of chromosomes (46 in humans) and are referred to as **diploid** cells. (The number of chromosomes forming a complete set in a somatic cell is called the diploid number.) Meiosis is characterized by two divisions that result in four daughter cells, each of which contains 23 chromosomes, or half the original number. Because each of these newly formed cells receives only one

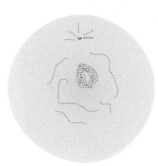

(a) The cell is involved in metabolic activities. DNA replication occurs, but chromosomes are not visible.

(b) The nuclear membrane disappears, and double-stranded chromosomes are visible.

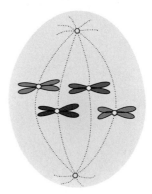

(c) The chromosomes align themselves at the center of the cell.

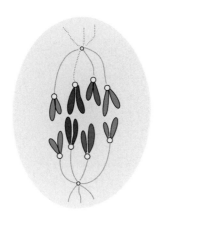

(d) The chromosomes split at the centromere, and the strands separate and move to opposite ends of the dividing cell.

(e) The cell membrane pinches in as the cell continues to divide. The chromosomes begin to uncoil (not shown here).

(f) After mitosis is complete, there are two identical daughter cells. The nuclear membrane is present, and chromosomes are no longer visible.

member of each chromosomal pair, they are said to be **haploid** cells, containing a haploid number of chromosomes.

Reduction of chromosome number is a critical feature of meiosis, because the resulting gamete, with its 23 chromosomes, may ultimately unite with another gamete, which also carries 23 chromosomes. Consequently, the product of this union, the *zygote*, or fertilized egg, has the diploid number of chromosomes (46). In other words, the zygote inherits the full complement of DNA it needs (half from each parent) to develop and function normally. If it were not for *reduction division* (the first division) in meiosis, it wouldn't be possible to maintain the correct number of chromosomes from one generation to the next.

During the first meiotic division, partner chromosomes come together, forming pairs of double-stranded chromosomes. In this way, pairs of chromosomes line up along the cell's center (Fig. 3–14). Pairing of homologous chromosomes

FIGURE 3–13 Mitosis.

haploid Referring to a half set of chromosomes, one member of each pair. Haploid sets are found in gametes.

 See Virtual Lab 2, section II, for a discussion of meiosis.

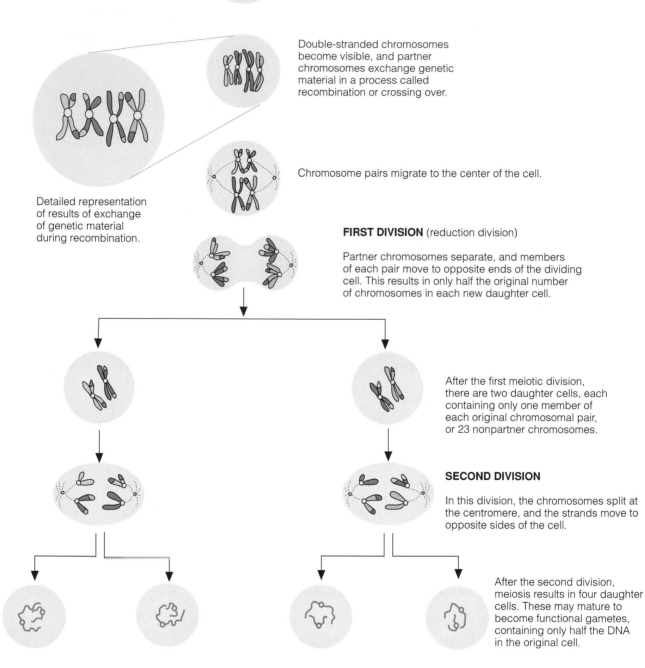

Chromosomes are not visible as DNA replication occurs in a cell preparing to divide.

Double-stranded chromosomes become visible, and partner chromosomes exchange genetic material in a process called recombination or crossing over.

Detailed representation of results of exchange of genetic material during recombination.

Chromosome pairs migrate to the center of the cell.

FIRST DIVISION (reduction division)

Partner chromosomes separate, and members of each pair move to opposite ends of the dividing cell. This results in only half the original number of chromosomes in each new daughter cell.

After the first meiotic division, there are two daughter cells, each containing only one member of each original chromosomal pair, or 23 nonpartner chromosomes.

SECOND DIVISION

In this division, the chromosomes split at the centromere, and the strands move to opposite sides of the cell.

After the second division, meiosis results in four daughter cells. These may mature to become functional gametes, containing only half the DNA in the original cell.

FIGURE 3–14 Meiosis.

Recombination (crossing over)
The exchange of genetic material between homologous chromosomes during meiosis.

is significant, because while they are together, members of pairs exchange genetic information in a process called **recombination,** or crossing over. Pairing is also important because it ensures that each new daughter cell will receive only one member of each pair.

As the cell begins to divide, the chromosomes themselves remain intact (i.e., double-stranded), but *members of pairs* separate and migrate to opposite ends of the cell. After the first division, there are two new daughter cells, but they are not identical to each other or to the parental cell because each contains only one member of each chromosome pair and therefore only 23 chromosomes, each of which

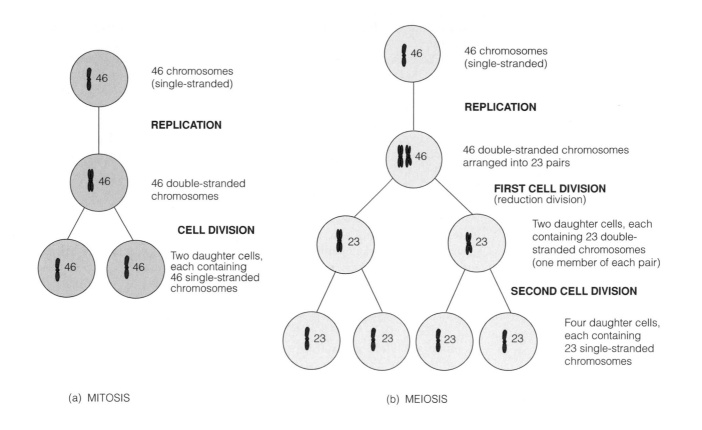

(a) MITOSIS   (b) MEIOSIS

still has two strands (see Fig. 3–14). Moreover, because of crossing over, each chromosome now contains some genetic variations it didn't have previously.

The second meiotic division proceeds in much the same way as in mitosis (Fig. 3–14). In the two newly formed cells, the 23 double-stranded chromosomes align themselves at the cell's center and, as in mitosis, the strands of each chromosome separate at the centromere and move apart. Once this second division is completed, there are four daughter cells, each with 23 single-stranded chromosomes, or 23 DNA molecules (Fig. 3–15).

THE EVOLUTIONARY SIGNIFICANCE OF MEIOSIS

Meiosis occurs in all sexually reproducing organisms, and it is an extremely important evolutionary innovation, because it increases genetic variation in populations at a faster rate than mutation alone could do. Individual members of sexually reproducing species are not genetically identical clones of other individuals. Rather, they result from the contribution of genetic information from two parents. In human matings an enormous number of genetic combinations can result in the possible offspring of two parents. From just the random arrangements of chromosome pairs lining up along the center of the cell during the first division of meiosis, each parent can produce 8 million genetically different gametes. And given the joint probability accounting for both parents, the total number of possible genetic combinations for any human mating is about 70 trillion. It should be noted that this staggering number is the result solely of the paired arrangements (called **random assortment**) and does not even take into account the many more combinations resulting from crossing over.

Genetic diversity is therefore considerably enhanced by meiosis. As was mentioned in Chapter 2, natural selection acts on genetic variation in populations. In all species, *mutation* is the only source of *new* genetic variation. But in sexually reproducing species, recombination produces new *arrangements* of genetic

FIGURE 3–15 Mitosis and meiosis compared. In mitosis, one division produces two daughter cells, each of which contains 46 chromosomes. Meiosis is characterized by two divisions. After the first, there are two cells, each containing only 23 chromosomes (one member of each original chromosome pair). Each daughter cell divides again, so that the final result is four cells, each with only half the original number of chromosomes.

random assortment The chance distribution of chromosomes to daughter cells during meiosis; along with recombination, the source of variation resulting from meiosis.

information, which potentially provide additional material for natural selection to act on.

Genetic variation is essential if species are to adapt to changing selective pressures. If all individuals were genetically identical, natural selection would have nothing to act on and evolution could not occur. It has been argued that this influence on variation is the principal adaptive advantage of sexual reproduction. Therefore, although reproduction has been strictly asexual for most of the time life has existed on this planet, sexual reproduction and meiosis are of major evolutionary importance because they contribute to the role of natural selection in populations.

PROBLEMS WITH MEIOSIS

For meiosis to ensure a reasonably good opportunity for normal fetal development, the process must be exact. The two-stage division must produce a viable gamete with only one member of each chromosome pair present. Superficially, it appears that the process works quite well, since more than 98 percent of newborns have the correct number of chromosomes. However, this statistic is misleading. It has been estimated that as many as half of all pregnancies naturally terminate early as spontaneous abortions (miscarriages). An estimated 70 percent of these miscarriages are caused by an improper number of chromosomes (Cummings, 2000). Thus, it appears that there are frequent errors during meiosis and they can have serious consequences.

nondisjunction The failure of homologous chromosomes or chromosome strands to separate during cell division.

If chromosomes or chromosome strands fail to separate during either of the two meiotic divisions, serious problems can arise. This failure to separate is called **nondisjunction.** The result of nondisjunction is that one of the daughter cells receives two copies of the affected chromosome, while the other daughter cell receives none. If such an affected gamete unites with a normal gamete containing 23 chromosomes, the resulting zygote will have either 45 or 47 chromosomes. Having only one member of a chromosome pair is referred to as *monosomy*. The term *trisomy* refers to the presence of three copies of a particular chromosome.

The far-reaching effects of an abnormal number of chromosomes can be appreciated only by remembering that the zygote will reproduce itself through mitosis. Consequently, every cell in the developing body will also have the abnormal chromosome number. Most situations of this type involving autosomes are lethal, and the embryo is spontaneously aborted, frequently before the pregnancy is even recognized.

One example of an abnormal number of autosomes is trisomy 21, formerly called Down syndrome, where there are three copies of the twenty-first chromosome. This is the only example of an abnormal number of autosomes being compatible with life beyond the first few months after birth. Trisomy 21, which occurs in approximately 1 out of every 1,000 live births, is associated with a number of developmental and health problems. These problems include congenital heart defects (seen in about 40 percent of affected newborns), increased susceptibility to respiratory infections, and leukemia. However, the most widely recognized effect of trisomy 21 is mental impairment, which is variably expressed and ranges from mild to severe.

Trisomy 21 is partly associated with advanced maternal age. For example, the risk of a 20-year-old woman giving birth to an affected infant is just 0.05 percent (5 in 10,000). However, 3 percent of babies born to mothers 45 and older are affected (a 60-fold increase). Actually, most affected infants are born to women under the age of 35, but this statistic is due to the fact that the majority of babies are born to women in this age category. The increase in incidence with maternal age is thought to be related to the early initiation of meiosis in females and presumed age-related changes in the gametes, resulting in increased risk of nondisjunction. Indeed, a number of conditions related to nondisjunction of chromosomes are thought to be influenced, in part, by increased maternal age.

TABLE 3-3 Examples of Nondisjunction in Sex Chromosomes

CHROMOSOMAL COMPLEMENT	CONDITION	ESTIMATED INCIDENCE	MANIFESTATIONS
XXX	Trisomy X	1 per 1,000 female births	Affected women are usually clinically normal, but there is a slight increase in sterility and mental impairment compared to the general population. In cases with more than three X chromosomes, mental retardation can be severe.
XYY	XYY syndrome	1 per 1,000 male births	Affected males are fertile and tend to be taller than average.
XO	Turner syndrome	1 per 10,000 female births	Affected females are short-statured, have broad chests and webbed necks, and are sterile. There is usually no mental impairment, but concepts relating to spatial relationships, including mathematics, can pose difficulties. Between 95 and 99 percent of affected fetuses die before birth.
XXY	Klinefelter syndrome	1 per 1,000 male births	Symptoms are noticeable by puberty: reduced testicular development, reduced facial and body hair, some breast development in about half of all cases, and reduced fertility or sterility. Some individuals exhibit lowered intelligence. Additional X chromosomes (XXXY) are associated with mental impairment.

Nondisjunction may also occur in sex chromosomes, producing individuals who, for example, are XXY (47 chromosomes), XO (45 chromosomes), XXX (47 chromosomes), or XYY (47 chromosomes). While these conditions don't always result in death or cognitive disability, some are associated with impaired mental function and/or sterility (Table 3–3). Moreover, still greater numbers of X chromosomes, such as XXXX or XXXY, result in marked mental deficiency. And some nondisjunctions of sex chromosomes are lethal. While it is possible to survive without a Y chromosome (roughly half of all humans do), it is not possible to live without an X chromosome. Indeed, the evidence suggests that embryos that possess only a Y chromosome are spontaneously aborted before the woman is aware she is pregnant.

Clearly, the importance of accuracy during meiosis can't be overstated. If normal development is to occur, the correct number of both autosomes and sex chromosomes must be present.

New Frontiers

Since the discovery of DNA structure and function in the 1950s, the field of genetics has revolutionized biological science and reshaped our understanding of inheritance, genetic disease, and evolutionary processes. For example, a technique developed in 1986 called **polymerase chain reaction (PCR)** enables scientists to produce multiple copies of DNA, making it possible to analyze segments of DNA as small as one molecule. This ability is critically important because samples of DNA, such as those obtained at crime scenes or from fossils, are frequently too small to permit reliable analysis of nucleotide sequences.

In PCR, the two strands of a DNA sample are separated, and an enzyme synthesizes complementary strands on the exposed bases, as in DNA replication. Because this process can be repeated many times, it's possible to produce over a million copies of the original DNA material! Thus, scientists have been able to identify nucleotide sequences in, for example, fossils (including Neandertals) and Egyptian mummies. As you can imagine, PCR has limitless potential for many disciplines, including forensic science, medicine, and evolutionary biology.

polymerase chain reaction (PCR) A method of producing thousands of copies of a DNA segment using the enzyme DNA polymerase.

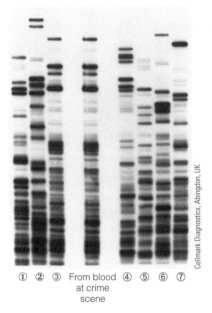

① ② ③ From blood ④ ⑤ ⑥ ⑦
at crime
scene

Cellmark Diagnostics, Abingdon, UK

FIGURE 3–16 Eight DNA fingerprints, one of which is from a blood sample left at an actual crime scene. The other seven are from suspects. By comparing the banding patterns, it is easy to identify the guilty party.

recombinant DNA technology
A process in which genes from the cell of one species are transferred to somatic cells or gametes of another species.

clone An organism that is genetically identical to another organism. The term may also be used to refer to genetically identical DNA segments, molecules, and cells.

By examining multiplied DNA samples provided by PCR, scientists can identify *DNA fingerprints,* so called because they appear as patterns of repeated DNA sequences that are unique to each individual. For example, one person might have a segment of six bases such as ATTCTA repeated 3 times and another might have the same sequence repeated 10 times.

DNA fingerprints are produced by forcing the DNA through an electrically charged gel. This process breaks up the DNA into fragments, which in turn separate into bands that vary in thickness. Each person has a unique banding pattern, and it is these patterns that comprise the DNA fingerprint (Fig. 3–16).

DNA fingerprinting is perhaps the most powerful tool available for human identification. Scientists have used it to identify scores of unidentified remains including members of the Russian royal family murdered in 1918 and victims of the terrorist attack on the World Trade Center in 2001. The technique has also been used to exonerate innocent people convicted and imprisoned for crimes committed years previously.

Over the last two decades, using the techniques of **recombinant DNA technology,** scientists have been able to transfer genes from the cells of one species into those of another. The most common method has been to insert human genes that direct the production of various proteins into bacterial cells, which causes the altered bacteria to produce human gene products. There are numerous commercial applications for this technology, many of which are aimed at treating genetic disease in humans. For example, until the early 1980s, diabetic patients relied on insulin derived from nonhuman animals. However, this insulin was not plentiful, and some patients developed allergies to it. But since 1982, abundant supplies of human insulin, produced by bacteria, have been available; and bacteria-derived insulin does not cause allergic reactions in patients.

Human genes may also be inserted into the fertilized eggs of nonhuman animals. The eggs are then implanted into the uteri of females who subsequently give birth to genetically altered offspring. These offspring serve as a source of various substances needed in medical practice. For example, genetically altered female sheep can carry a human gene that causes them to produce an enzyme that is present in most people and which prevents a serious form of emphysema. This enzyme is produced in the sheep's milk, and once extracted and purified, it can be administered to people who don't normally produce it.

In recent years, genetic manipulation has become increasingly controversial owing to questions related to product safety, environmental concerns, and animal welfare, among others. For example, the insertion of bacterial DNA into certain crops has made them toxic to leaf-eating insects, thus reducing the need for pesticide use. And cattle and pigs are commonly treated with antibiotics and genetically engineered growth hormone to increase growth rates. Although there is no current evidence that humans are susceptible to the insect-repelling bacterial DNA or adversely affected by the consumption of meat and dairy products from animals treated with growth hormone, there are serious concerns over the unknown effects of such long-term exposure. In fact, tremendous opposition to genetically modified foods has resulted in greatly increased demand for organically grown produce and hormone-free meats, especially in Europe and Africa.

Regardless of how contentious these new techniques may be, nothing has generated as much controversy as cloning. The controversy escalated with the birth of Dolly (Fig. 3–17), a **clone** of a female sheep, in

Roslind Institute/PA Photos Limited

FIGURE 3–17 The cloned sheep Dolly with one of her lambs, which was produced the old-fashioned way.

1997 (Wilmut et al., 1997). Actually, cloning is not as new as you might think. Anyone who has ever taken a cutting from a plant and rooted it to grow a new plant has produced a clone. In the 1960s, an African toad became the first animal to be cloned. Since then, cloning has become almost commonplace. As of this writing, the most recent newly cloned species is a horse, born in May 2003. The foal is a clone of her mother (a first in cloning history). Her chromosomes were extracted from cells in a tissue sample taken from her mother using a process called nuclear transfer (Fig. 3–18). The nucleus (containing the chromosomes) was inserted into an egg derived from the ovary of another mare. The fused egg was then inserted into the uterus of the foal's mother, where it developed into a live foal (Galli et al., 2003).

The list of cloned mammals now includes mice, rats, rabbits, cats, sheep, cattle, a horse, and recently a mule (Woods et al., 2003). But all the harangue among politicians about the ethics of human cloning, whether for reproductive purposes or not, may be in vain, at least for now (see Issue, p. 72). Apparently, it's going to be more difficult to clone a human than scientists originally thought, because so far, all attempts to clone nonhuman primates have failed (Simerly et al., 2003).

How successful cloning will be is yet to be determined. Dolly, who had developed health problems, was euthanized in February 2003 at the age of 6 years (Giles and Knight, 2003). Long-term studies have yet to show whether cloned animals live out their normal life span, but some evidence in mice suggests that they don't. Also, only about 3 percent of cell nuclei inserted into donor eggs result in a live birth (Giles and Knight, 2003).

As exciting as these innovations are, probably the single most important advance in genetics has been the progress made by the **Human Genome Project.** The goal of this international effort, begun in 1990, was to sequence the entire human **genome,** which consists of some 3 billion bases comprising approximately 30,000 genes. In February 2001, two research teams announced they had revealed a virtually complete sequence of human DNA. Then in 2003, the remainder of the project was completed. As phenomenal as this achievement is, scientists are still several years away from sorting out which DNA segments operate as functional genes and which do not. It will also be years before the identity and function of many of the proteins produced by these genes are explained. It is one thing to know a gene's chemical makeup, but quite another to know what the gene does. Nevertheless, the magnitude and importance of the achievement cannot be overstated, because it will ultimately transform biomedical and pharmaceutical research and will change forever how many human diseases are diagnosed and treated.

Moreover, at the same time scientists were sequencing human genes, the genomes of other organisms were also being studied. As of September 2000, the genomes of over 600 species (mostly microorganisms) had been either partially or completely identified. In December 2002, the mouse genome had been completely sequenced (Waterstone et al., 2002). Then, in December 2003, a rough draft of the chimpanzee genome was announced. Already scientists have begun to compare human and chimpanzee DNA for evidence as to how our lineage became distinct from that of chimpanzees (Clark et al., 2003). This research has enormous implications not only for biomedical research but also for studies of evolutionary relationships among species. We already know that humans share many genes with other organisms, but just how many and which ones will partly be clarified by upcoming projects aimed at sequencing nonhuman primate genomes. Eventually, comparative genome analysis should provide a thorough assessment of genetic similarities and differences, and thus the evolutionary relationships, between humans and other primates. Indeed, it would not be an exaggeration to say that this is the most exciting time in the history of evolutionary biology since Darwin published *On the Origin of Species.*

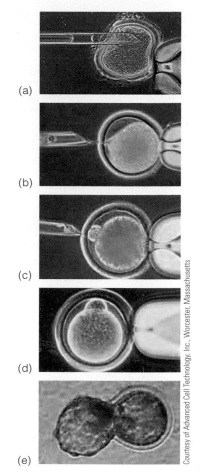

(a)

(b)

(c)

(d)

(e)

Courtesy of Advanced Cell Technology, Inc., Worcester, Massachusetts

FIGURE 3–18 A series of photomicrographs showing a nuclear transfer process. (a) The nucleus of an egg cell (from a donor) is drawn into a hollow needle. (b) The enucleated egg with only the cytoplasm remaining. (c) The nucleus of a skin cell from the individual being cloned is injected into the enucleated egg. (d) Electric shock causes the nucleus of the skin cell to fuse with the egg's cytoplasm. (e) The egg begins to divide, and a few days later the cloned embryo will be transferred into the uterus of a host animal.

Human Genome Project An international effort aimed at sequencing and mapping the entire human genome.

genome The entire genetic makeup of an individual or species. In humans, it is estimated that each individual possesses approximately 3 billion DNA nucleotides.

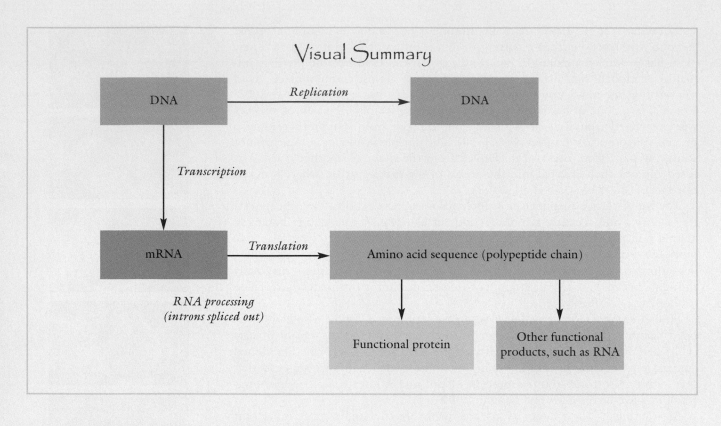

Summary

The topics covered in this chapter relate almost entirely to discoveries made after Darwin and Wallace described the fundamentals of natural selection. But all the issues presented here are basic to an understanding of biological evolution, adaptation, and human variation.

It has been shown that cells are the fundamental units of life and that there are basically two types of cells. Somatic cells make up body tissues, while gametes (eggs and sperm) are reproductive cells that transmit genetic information from parent to offspring.

Genetic information is contained in the DNA molecule, found in the nuclei of cells. The DNA molecule is capable of replication, or making copies of itself. Replication makes it possible for daughter cells to receive a full complement of DNA (contained in chromosomes).

DNA also controls protein synthesis by directing the cell to arrange amino acids in the proper sequence for each particular type of protein. Also involved in the process of protein synthesis is another, similar molecule called RNA.

There are many genes that regulate the function of other genes. Homeotic genes are expressed only in embryonic development, and they direct the development of the body plan. Other regulatory genes turn genes on and off. In some cases, this results in the production of different forms of a protein, such as hemoglobin, during different stages of life.

There are also many segments of DNA that don't code for protein production, and much of their function is unknown. We do know that genes contain noncoding segments called introns that are initially transcribed into mRNA but are then deleted before the mRNA leaves the cell nucleus. Also, there are microsatellites, or tandem repeats, that don't specify proteins but probably serve some function. They are highly mutable and are useful in DNA fingerprinting and in evolutionary studies.

Cells multiply by dividing, and during cell division, DNA is visible under a microscope in the form of chromosomes. In humans, there are 46 chromosomes (23 pairs). If the complement is not precisely distributed to succeeding generations of cells, severe consequences may follow.

Somatic cells divide during growth or tissue repair or to replace old, worn-out cells. Somatic cell division is called mitosis. A cell divides one time to produce two daughter cells, each possessing a full and identical (diploid) set of chromosomes.

Sex cells are produced when specialized cells in the ovaries and testes divide during meiosis. Unlike mitosis, meiosis is characterized by two divisions that produce four nonidentical daughter cells, each containing only half (haploid) the amount of DNA (23 chromosomes) as that carried by the original cell.

For Further Thought

1. We only briefly touched on the topic of recombinant DNA technologies. From what we said and from things you have heard elsewhere, what is your view on this important topic? Are you generally in favor of most of the goals of recombinant DNA research? What are your objections?

2. Before you read this chapter, were you aware that the DNA in your body is structurally the same as in all other organisms? How do you see this fact as having potential to clarify some of the many questions we still have regarding biological evolution?

Go to the book website at **http://www.anthropology.wadsworth.com** for resources to help you explore these questions further. Click on "For Further Thought" for this chapter.

Questions for Review

1. Knowing what you now know about the various types of noncoding sequences in DNA, how do you think they could cause mutations in genes?
2. In your own words, summarize the process of DNA replication. Why is it important?
3. What are genes, and what do they do?
4. In your own words, summarize the process of protein synthesis.
5. Explain the differences between mitosis and meiosis. What is the outcome of each process? Why is meiosis important to the evolutionary process?
6. There are many kinds of mutations, including the type we discussed most, point mutations. What are point mutations? Can you think of examples other than the one we discussed? Maybe you know someone who has a condition caused by a point mutation. If so, what is it?

Suggested Further Reading

Brown, Kathryn. 2001. "Seeds of Concern." *Scientific American* 284(4): 52–57.

Collins, Francis S., and Karin G. Jegalian. 1999. "Deciphering the Code of Life." *Scientific American* 281(6): 86–91.

Cummings, Michael R. 2000. *Human Heredity.* 4th ed. Belmont, CA: Brooks/Cole.

Hopkin, Karen. 2001. "The Risks on the Table." *Scientific American* 284(4): 60–61.

Moxon, E. Richard and Christopher Wills, 1999. "DNA Microsatellites: Agents of Evolution?" *Scientific American* 280(1): 94–99.

Pedersen, Roger A. 2001. "Embryonic Stem Cells for Medicine." *Scientific American* 280(4): 68–73.

Ridley, Matt. 2000. *Genome. The Autobiography of a Species in 23 Chapters.* New York: Perennial.

Wallace, Douglas C. 1997. "Mitochondrial DNA in Aging and Disease." *Scientific American* 277(2): 40–47.

Online Anthropology Resource Center

Go to the Anthropology Resource Center at **http://www.anthropology.wadsworth.com** for a wealth of online resources, including a companion website for your text that provides study aids such as self-quizzes for each chapter and a practice final exam, as well as links to anthropology websites and information on the latest theories and discoveries in the field. Also, check out InfoTrac College Edition®, your online library that offers full-length articles from thousands of scholarly and popular publications. Just click on the InfoTrac button at the companion website and use the passcode that came with your book.

Stem Cell Research: Promise and Controversy

Stem cells are undifferentiated, or unspecialized, cells that can divide and replicate indefinitely, and depending on their origins (and given the right circumstances), they can give rise to many, if not all, the specialized cells that make up an organism.

Adult stem cells are found in specialized tissues, such as bone marrow, skin, and the gastrointestinal tract. They are able to replicate themselves throughout the life of the organism and can also give rise to all the specialized types of cells *that make up the tissue in which they are found*. For example, stem cells in bone marrow give rise to all the cells that comprise blood, including oxygen-transporting red cells and all the white cells involved in the immune response. In short, adult stem cells replace certain types of cells that have lived out their life span or have been lost through disease or trauma.

For years, one type of adult stem cell, hematopoietic (blood-producing) stem cells (HSCs) have been transplanted into patients with immune disorders and various forms of cancer, especially leukemias. These procedures, called bone marrow transplants, require the painful extraction of bone marrow cells from a donor (usually from the pelvis) and then their transplantation into a recipient. Nowadays, bone marrow transplants are beginning to be replaced by injections of hematopoietic stem cells extracted directly from the donor's circulating blood. Stem cell transfer, as the procedure is now called, is dangerous, particularly in the treatment of cancer, because the patient's cancerous blood-producing cells and immune system are virtually destroyed by chemotherapy or radiation prior to the stem cell transfer; thus, there is a risk of death due to infection or graft-versus-host immune reactions. But success rates are increasing, and in many cases, the stem cells give rise to healthy white and red blood cells in a patient whose cancer has been eradicated or at least put into remission.

By the late 1980s, researchers recognized that HSCs are also present in the approximately 3 ounces of blood contained in umbilical cords. Since 1988, HSCs derived from cord blood have been used to treat thousands of children with various forms of leukemia. In one highly publicized case, the parents of a daughter with a type of leukemia conceived a second child, in part to provide HSCs derived from the cord blood of a close relative. In this case, several embryos were produced through *in vitro* fertilization (i.e., in a test tube or culture dish). The embryos were checked for compatability and the closest match was implanted into the mother's uterus. In the press, considerable outrage was expressed over the notion that parents would deliberately conceive a child to provide donor cells to treat their daughter. However, a team of bioethicists had ruled that this course of action was indeed ethical, since the resulting infant would in no way be harmed by the procedure and, importantly, the parents wanted another child. Subsequently, a son was born and the daughter received a transplant of normal HSCs from her new brother's umbilical cord blood, and she is currently in remission.

Human embryonic stem cells are, as the name implies, derived from 5-day-old embryos consisting of 200 to 250 cells. Most of these embryos are the unused products of *in vitro* fertilization of eggs at fertility clinics and are donated by patients. In some cases, embryos resulting from therapeutic abortions have also been used but, contrary to the claims of some, the mothers were not financially compensated. At this stage, the embryo consists of two portions: one that becomes the placenta and the other, an inner cell mass consisting of about 40 cells, that develops into the fetus. Those cells comprising the inner cell mass are the undifferentiated embryonic stem cells that have the potential of giving rise to the more than 200 types of cells found in mammals. It's this potential that makes embryonic stem cells so attractive to researchers, because it isn't yet fully known if adult stem cells have this same capacity.

Work with embryonic stem cells is still in the early stages, but when such cells are exposed to certain chemicals, they give rise to specialized cells that produce substances (proteins) potentially capable of curing symptoms related to disease or trauma. For example, exposing mouse embryonic stem cells to a derivative of vitamin A stimulates genes that cause the cells to produce nerve cells (neurons). Furthermore, embryonic stem cells transplanted into mouse brains have given rise to neurons that produce an enzyme necessary for the synthesis of dopamine, the neurochemical lacking in patients with Parkinson disease. These findings have led researchers to consider the possibility that, in the future, embryonic stem cells can be implanted into patients with Alzheimer disease or those with brain and spinal cord injuries to replace damaged or destroyed neurons. It is also hoped that nonfunctioning pancreatic cells in diabetic patients can be replaced with stem cells that will produce healthy, insulin-producing cells. Or perhaps it will be possible to replace damaged cardiac muscle cells in patients with heart disease—and even skin cells in burn victims.

But there are many ethical objections to the use of embryonic stem cells and many technical problems to overcome. The strongest objections are raised by abortion opponents and those who believe that any fertilized egg, with the potential to develop into a human being if implanted into a woman's uterus, should not be destroyed. It is this objection that has led, in the United States, to a presidential executive order that limits federal funding for embryonic stem cell research to the approximately 60 cell lines already established by the summer of 2001. Privately funded research remains unaffected by this decision, and Harvard and Stanford Universities continue privately funded programs that use embryonic stem cells. There is also a funding ban on all projects that create embryos solely for research.

Although in general agreement with the guidelines at first, the scientific community questioned the suitability of some of the existing cell lines for certain types of research. Since that time, however, the scientific community has become increasingly concerned over efforts of the federal government to limit or ban all stem cell research involving the use of human embryos. For one thing, in reality there are only about 20 cell lines available for study (Check, 2004). And the scientific community has argued that, in the course of fertility treatments, it's necessary to create more embryos than will actually be used, so that fertility clinics destroy thousands of surplus embryos every year. It's these surplus embryos that have been used in research, and scientists argue that it's better to use them for the benefits they may provide than to destroy them. At the same time, many abortion opponents were unhappy with the executive order because they believe that although the existing cell lines no longer possess the potential for human life, *any* use of human embryos in research is wrong. And there are concerns that the ruling may leave the door open for future use of embryos. Consequently, neither side of the debate has been completely happy with the current state of affairs.

Funding limitations similar to those in the United States exist in some other countries, including Germany. But in Britain, public funds are available for embryonic stem cell studies, even those that include nonreproductive cloning and the creation of embryos for research purposes.

In addition to funding constraints, there are other concerns the scientific community must address. First, the potential of stem cells to produce malignant (i.e., constantly replicating) cell lines is not known. Second, there is the problem of tissue rejection in patients receiving stem cell transplants that are recognized as foreign by their own immune systems. These two problems alone will require years of investigation to solve.

This discussion illustrates the conflicts between technology, ethical standards, and the legal system. The questions raised by developing technologies challenge traditionally held views about fundamental aspects of life. In the past, people with hereditary disorders frequently died. They still do. But now there are treatments, however costly, for some conditions. How we come to view these new discoveries and how we come to terms with the ethical and legal issues surrounding our new technologies will increasingly become social, religious, and ultimately political concerns. Solutions will not come easily, and they will not please everyone.

Critical Thinking Questions

1. What do you see as the most disturbing aspect of stem cell research? What do you think is the most positive? Explain your answers.
2. Do you approve of the nonreproductive cloning of human embryos for stem cell research? Why or why not?
3. Do you approve of the decision of the parents to conceive a second child partly to provide donor cells for their daughter? Why or why not? What would you do in their position?

Sources

Check, E. "Bush Pressured as Nancy Reagan Pleads for Stem-Cell Research." *Nature,* 429:116.

Kline, Ronald M. "Whose Blood Is It, Anyway?" *Scientific American* 284(4): 42–49.

Stem Cells: Scientific Progress and Future Research Directions. Report from the National Institutes of Health to Secretary of Health and Human Services, Tommy G. Thompson, February 2001. Internet version obtained from the NIH website: **www.nih.gov/ news/stemcell/scireport/htm.**

4

Heredity and Evolution

A human chromosome

© Biophoto Associates / Photo Researchers, Inc.

Key Questions

Why is it important to know the basic mechanisms of inheritance to understand the processes of evolution?

How do the patterns of human inheritance compare with those of other organisms?

Introduction

Have you ever had a cat with five, six, or even seven toes? Even if you haven't you may have seen one, because it's fairly common in cats. Maybe you've known someone with an extra finger or toe, because it's not unheard of in people. Anne Boleyn, mother of England's Queen Elizabeth 1 and the first of Henry VIII's wives to lose her head, apparently had an extra little finger. (Of course, this had nothing to do with her early demise, but that's another story.)

The condition of having extra digits is called polydactyly, and it's fairly certain that one of Anne Boleyn's parents was also polydactylous. It is also probable that any polydactylous cat has a parent with extra toes. But how do we know this? Actually, it's fairly simple. We know this because polydactyly is a Mendelian characteristic, meaning that its pattern of inheritance is one of those discovered almost 150 years ago by a monk named Gregor Mendel.

In this chapter, we shift from the structure and function of DNA to how traits are passed from parent to offspring. These principles form much of the basis of modern genetics, and we cover them in some detail because of their relevance to the evolutionary process. Later in the chapter, we integrate the basics of DNA function and Mendelian patterns of inheritance into a comprehensive theory of the forces that guide biological evolution.

For at least 10,000 years, beginning with the domestication of plants and animals, people have attempted to explain how offspring inherit characteristics from their parents. Although the explanations were inaccurate, farmers have known for millennia that they could enhance the frequency and expression of desirable attributes through selective breeding. But they didn't know why.

From the time ancient Greek philosophers considered the problem until well into the nineteenth century, one predominant belief was that characteristics of offspring resulted from the *blending* of parental traits. Blending supposedly occurred because of certain particles found in every part of the body. These particles contained miniatures of the body part (limbs, organs, etc.) from which they came, and they traveled through the blood to the reproductive organs and blended with particles of another individual during reproduction. There were variations on this theme, and numerous scholars, including Charles Darwin, adhered to some aspects of the theory.

See the following sections of the CD-ROM for topics covered in this chapter: Virtual Lab 2, sections I, II, III, and IV.

The Genetic Principles Discovered by Mendel

It was not until Gregor Mendel (1822–1884) addressed the question of heredity that it began to be resolved (Fig. 4–1). Mendel was living in an abbey at Brno in what is now the Czech Republic. At the time he began his research, he had already acquired scientific expertise in botany, physics, and mathematics at the University of Vienna, and he had conducted various experiments in the

FIGURE 4–1 Portrait of Gregor Mendel.

Raychel Ciemma and Precision Graphics

FIGURE 4–2 The traits Mendel studied in peas.

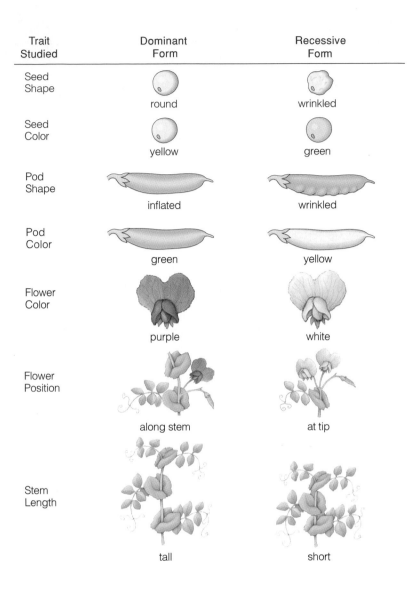

hybrids Offspring of individuals that differ with regard to certain traits or certain aspects of genetic makeup; heterozygotes.

monastery gardens. These experiments led him to explore the ways that physical traits, such as color or height, could be expressed in plant **hybrids.** He hoped that by making crosses between two strains of *purebred* plants and examining their offspring, he could determine (and predict) how many different forms of hybrids there were, arrange the forms according to generation, and evaluate the proportion of each type in each generation.

Mendel worked with garden peas, concentrating on seven different traits, each of which could be expressed two ways (Fig. 4–2). Because the genetic principles Mendel discovered apply to humans as well as to peas (and all other biological organisms), we discuss his work to illustrate the basic rules of inheritance.

SEGREGATION

The plants Mendel used in the first cross were called the P (parental) generation, and all were either tall or short. The hybrid offspring of the P generation were designated the F_1 generation. As they matured, they weren't intermediate in height, as blending theories of inheritance would have predicted. To the contrary, they were all tall (Fig. 4–3).

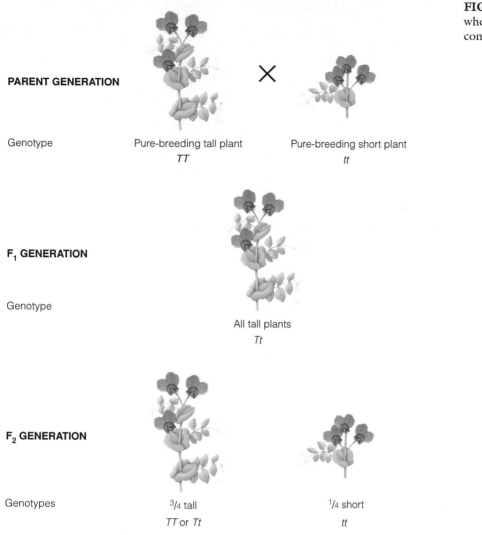

FIGURE 4–3 Results of crosses when only one trait at a time is considered.

PARENT GENERATION

Genotype

Pure-breeding tall plant
TT

Pure-breeding short plant
tt

F₁ GENERATION

Genotype

All tall plants
Tt

F₂ GENERATION

Genotypes

³/₄ tall
TT or *Tt*

¹/₄ short
tt

Next, Mendel allowed the F₁ plants to self-fertilize and produce a second generation of plants (the F₂ generation). But this time, only approximately ³/₄ of the offspring were tall, and the remaining ¹/₄ were short. One expression of the trait had completely disappeared in the F₁ generation and then reappeared in the F₂ generation. Moreover, the expression that was present in the F₁ generation was more common in the F₂ plants, occurring in a ratio of approximately 3:1.

These results suggested that different expressions of a trait were controlled by discrete *units,* which occurred in pairs, and that offspring inherited one unit from each parent. Mendel realized that the members of a pair of units controlling a trait somehow separated into different sex cells and were again united with another member during fertilization of the egg. This is Mendel's *first principle of inheritance,* known as the **principle of segregation.**

Today we know that meiosis explains Mendel's principle of segregation. You will remember that during meiosis, paired chromosomes, and the genes they carry, separate from one another and are distributed to different gametes. However, in the zygote, the full complement of chromosomes is restored, and both members of each chromosome pair are present in the offspring.

principle of segregation Genes (alleles) occur in pairs (because chromosomes occur in pairs). During gamete production, the members of each gene pair separate, so that each gamete contains one member of each pair. During fertilization, the full number of chromosomes is restored, and members of gene or allele pairs are reunited.

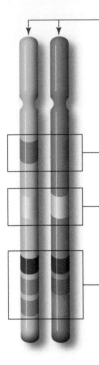

Pair of homologous chromosomes, one from a male parent and its partner from a female parent

Gene locus, the location for a specific gene on a specific type of chromosome

Pair of alleles. Although they influence the same characteristic, their DNA varies slightly, so they produce somewhat different expressions

Three pairs of alleles (at three loci on this pair of homologous chromosomes). Note that at two loci the alleles are identical (homozygous), and at one locus they are different

FIGURE 4–4 As this diagram illustrates, alleles are located at the same locus on paired chromosomes, but they aren't always identical. For the sake of simplicity, they are shown here as single-stranded chromosomes.

recessive Describing a trait that is not expressed in heterozygotes; also refers to the allele that governs the trait. For a recessive allele to be expressed, there must be two copies of the allele (i.e., the individual must be homozygous).

dominant Describing a trait governed by an allele that can be expressed in the presence of another, different allele (i.e., in heterozygotes). Dominant alleles prevent the expression of recessive alleles in heterozygotes. (This is the definition of *complete* dominance.)

homozygous Having the same allele at the same locus on both members of a chromosome pair.

heterozygous Having different alleles at the same locus on members of a chromosome pair.

DOMINANCE AND RECESSIVENESS

Mendel also realized that the expression that was absent in the F_1 plants hadn't actually disappeared at all. It had remained present, but somehow it was masked and could not be expressed. To describe the trait that seemed to be lost, Mendel used the term **recessive;** the trait that was expressed was said to be **dominant.** Thus, the important principles of *dominance* and *recessiveness* were formulated, and they remain today as important concepts in the field of genetics.

As you already know, one definition of *gene* is a segment of DNA that directs the production of a specific protein, part of a protein, or a functional product. Furthermore, the location of a gene on a chromosome is its *locus (pl., loci)*. At numerous genetic loci, however, there is more than one possible form of the gene, and these variations of genes at specific loci are called *alleles* (Fig. 4–4). Therefore, alleles are alternate forms of a gene that can direct the cell to produce slightly different forms of the same protein and, ultimately, different expressions of traits.

As it turns out, plant height in garden peas is controlled by two different alleles at one genetic locus. The allele that determines that a plant will be tall is dominant to the allele for short. (It is worth mentioning that height is not controlled this way in all plants.)

In Mendel's experiments, all the parent (P) plants had two copies of the same allele, either dominant or recessive, depending on whether they were tall or short. When two copies of the same allele are present, the individual is said to be **homozygous.** Thus, all the tall P plants were homozygous for the dominant allele, and all the short P plants were homozygous for the recessive allele. (This homozygosity explains why tall plants crossed with tall plants produced only tall offspring, and short plants crossed with short plants produced all short offspring; i.e., they were "pure lines" and lacked genetic variation at this locus.) However, all the F_1 plants (hybrids) had inherited one allele from each parent plant; therefore, they all possessed two different alleles at specific loci. Individuals that possess two different alleles at a locus are **heterozygous.**

Figure 4–3 (previous page) illustrates the crosses that Mendel initially performed. Geneticists use standard symbols to refer to alleles. Uppercase letters refer to dominant alleles (or dominant traits), and lowercase letters refer to recessive alleles (or recessive traits). Therefore,

T = the allele for tallness
t = the allele for shortness

The same symbols are combined to describe an individual's actual genetic makeup, or **genotype.** The term *genotype* can be used to refer to an organism's entire genetic makeup or to the alleles at a specific genetic locus. Thus, the genotypes of the plants in Mendel's experiments were

TT = homozygous tall plants
Tt = heterozygous tall plants
tt = homozygous short plants

Figure 4–5 is a *Punnett square.* It represents the different ways the alleles can be combined when the F_1 plants are self-fertilized to produce an F_2 generation. In this way, the figure shows the *genotypes* that are possible in the F_2 generation, and it also demonstrates that approximately ¼ of the F_2 plants are homozygous dominant (TT); ½ are heterozygous (Tt); and the remaining ¼ are homozygous recessive (tt).

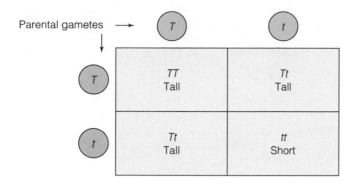

Parental gametes →

	T	t
T	TT Tall	Tt Tall
t	Tt Tall	tt Short

FIGURE 4–5 Punnett square representing possible genotypes and phenotypes and their proportions in the F_2 generation. The circles across the top and at the left of the Punnett square represent the gametes of the F_1 parents. The four squares illustrate that ¼ of the F_2 plants can be expected to be homozygous tall (TT); another ½ also can be expected to be tall but will be heterozygous (Tt); and the remaining ¼ can be expected to be short (tt). Thus, ¾ can be expected to be tall and ¼ to be short.

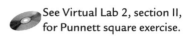 See Virtual Lab 2, section II, for Punnett square exercise.

genotype The genetic makeup of an individual. Genotype can refer to an organism's entire genetic makeup or to the alleles at a particular locus.

phenotypes The observable or detectable physical characteristics of an organism; the detectable expressions of genotypes.

phenotypic ratio The proportion of one phenotype to other phenotypes in a group of organisms. For example, Mendel observed that there were approximately three tall plants for every short plant in the F_2 generation. This is expressed as a phenotypic ratio of 3:1.

Mendelian traits Characteristics that are influenced by alleles at only one genetic locus. Examples include many blood types, such as ABO. Many genetic disorders, including sickle-cell anemia and Tay-Sachs disease, are also Mendelian traits.

principle of independent assortment The distribution of one pair of alleles into gametes does not influence the distribution of another pair. The genes controlling different traits are inherited independently of one another.

linked Describing genetic loci or genes located on the same chromosome.

The Punnett square can also be used to show (and predict) the proportions of F_2 **phenotypes,** or the observed physical manifestations of genes. Moreover, the Punnett square illustrates why Mendel observed three tall plants for every short plant in the F_2 generation. By examining the Punnett square, you can see that ¼ of the F_2 plants are tall because they have the TT genotype. Furthermore, an additional ½, which are heterozygous (Tt), will also be tall because T is dominant to t and will therefore be expressed in the phenotype. The remaining ¼ are homozygous recessive (tt), and they will be short because no dominant allele is present. It is important to note that the *only* way a recessive allele can be expressed is if it occurs with another recessive allele, that is, if the individual is homozygous recessive at the particular locus in question.

In conclusion, ¾ of the F_2 generation will express the dominant phenotype, and ¼ will show the recessive phenotype. This relationship is expressed as a **phenotypic ratio** of 3:1 and typifies all **Mendelian traits** (characteristics governed by only one genetic locus) when only two alleles are involved, one of which is completely dominant to the other.

INDEPENDENT ASSORTMENT

Mendel also made crosses in which two traits were considered simultaneously to see if they tended to be inherited together. Figure 4–6 illustrates that the recessive traits disappeared in the F_1 generation and reappeared in the F_2 plants, but the combinations of characteristics occurred in different proportions because plant height and seed color are independent of each other. In other words, there is nothing to dictate that a tall plant must have yellow (or green) seeds, because the allele for tallness has a 50-50 chance of ending up with the allele for either green or yellow seeds.

Mendel stated this relationship as the **principle of independent assortment,** which says that the genes that code for different traits assort independently of each other during gamete formation. Today we know that this occurs because the genes that control these two characteristics are located on different chromosomes, and during meiosis, the chromosomes travel to newly forming cells independently of one another. But if Mendel had used just *any* two traits, his results might have been quite different. For example, if the two traits in question had been influenced by **linked** genes (i.e., genes located on the same chromosome), Mendel's results would have been considerably altered. Because linked genes usually remain together during meiosis, they are not independent of one another; therefore, the traits they influence do not conform to the ratios predicted by independent assortment. While Mendel didn't know about linkage, he was certainly aware that all characteristics did not sort out independently of one another in the F_2 generation. He therefore reported only on those traits that did in fact illustrate independent assortment.

In 1866, Mendel's results were published, but the methodology and statistical nature of the research were beyond the thinking of the time, and their significance

FIGURE 4–6 Results of crosses when two traits are considered simultaneously. Stem length and seed color are independent of each other. Also shown are the genotypes associated with each phenotype. Note that the ratio of tall plants to short plants is $\frac{3}{4}$ to $\frac{1}{4}$, or 3:1, the same as in Figure 4–3. The ratio of yellow to green seeds is also 3:1. Note that the phenotypic ratios in the F_2 generation are 9:3:3:1.

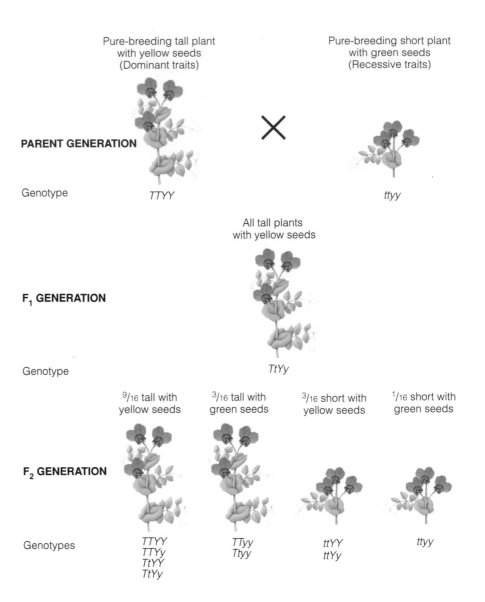

was overlooked and unappreciated. However, by the end of the nineteenth century, several investigators had made important contributions to the understanding of chromosomes and cell division. These discoveries paved the way for the acceptance of Mendel's work by 1900, when three different groups of scientists, conducting similar breeding experiments, came across his paper. Regrettably, Mendel had died 16 years earlier and never saw his work vindicated.

Mendelian Inheritance in Humans

Mendelian traits, also called *discrete traits* or *traits of simple inheritance,* are characteristics controlled by alleles at only one genetic locus (or, in some cases, two or more very closely linked loci). The most comprehensive listing of Mendelian traits in humans is V. A. McKusick's (1998) *Mendelian Inheritance in Man,* first published in 1965 and now in its twelfth edition. This volume, as well as its continuously updated Internet version, *Online Mendelian Inheritance in Man* (www.ncbi.nlm.nih.gov/omim/), currently lists over 15,000 human characteristics shown to be inherited according to Mendelian principles.

Although there are some Mendelian characteristics that have readily visible phenotypic expressions, the majority don't. Most Mendelian traits are biochemical in nature, and many genetic disorders (some of which do produce visible phenotypic abnormalities) result from harmful alleles inherited in Mendelian fashion (Table 4–1). Thus, if it seems like textbooks overly emphasize genetic disease in discussions of Mendelian traits, it's because many of the known Mendelian characteristics are the results of harmful alleles.

TABLE 4–1 Some Mendelian Traits in Humans

DOMINANT TRAITS		RECESSIVE TRAITS	
Condition	**Manifestations**	**Condition**	**Manifestations**
Achondroplasia	Dwarfism due to growth defects involving the long bones of the arms and legs; trunk and head size usually normal.	Cystic fibrosis	Among the most common genetic (Mendelian) disorders among European Americans; abnormal secretions of the exocrine glands, with pronounced involvement of the pancreas; most patients develop obstructive lung disease. Until the recent development of new treatments, only about half of all patients survived to early adulthood.
Brachydactyly	Shortened fingers and toes.		
Familial hyper-cholesterolemia	Elevated cholesterol levels and cholesterol plaque deposition; a leading cause of heart disease, with death frequently occurring by middle age.		
Neurofibromatosis	Symptoms range from the appearance of abnormal skin pigmentation to large tumors resulting in gross deformities; can, in extreme cases, lead to paralysis, blindness, and death.	Tay-Sachs disease	Most common among Ashkenazi Jews; degeneration of the nervous system beginning at about 6 months of age; lethal by age 2 or 3 years.
Marfan syndrome	The eyes and cardiovascular and skeletal systems are affected; symptoms include greater than average height, long arms and legs, eye problems, and enlargement of the aorta; death due to rupture of the aorta is common. (Abraham Lincoln may have had Marfan syndrome.)	Phenylketonuria (PKU)	Inability to metabolize the amino acid phenylalanine; results in mental retardation if left untreated during childhood; treatment involves strict dietary management and some supplementation.
Huntington disease	Progressive degeneration of the nervous system accompanied by dementia and seizures; age of onset variable but commonly between 30 and 40 years.	Albinism	Inability to produce normal amounts of the pigment melanin; results in very fair, untannable skin, light blond hair, and light eyes; may also be associated with vision problems. (There is more than one form of albinism.)
Camptodactyly	Malformation of the hands whereby the fingers, usually the little finger, is permanently contracted.	Sickle-cell anemia	Abnormal form of hemoglobin (HbS) that results in collapsed red blood cells, blockage of capillaries, reduced blood flow to organs, and, without treatment, death.
Hypodontia of upper lateral incisors	Upper lateral incisors are absent or only partially formed (peg-shaped). Pegged incisors are a partial expression of the allele.	Thalassemia	A group of disorders characterized by reduced or absent alpha or beta chains in the hemoglobin molecule; results in severe anemia and, in some forms, death.
Cleft chin	Dimple or depression in the middle of the chin; less prominent in females than males.		
PTC tasting	The ability to taste the bitter substance phenylthiocarbamide (PTC). Tasting thresholds vary, suggesting that alleles at another locus may also exert an influence.	Absence of permanent dentition	Failure of the permanent dentition to erupt. The primary dentition is not affected.

TABLE 4–2 ABO Genotypes and Associated Phenotypes

GENOTYPE	ANTIGENS ON RED BLOOD CELLS	ABO BLOOD TYPE (PHENOTYPE)
AA, AO	A	A
BB, BO	B	B
AB	A and B	AB
OO	None	O

See Virtual Lab 2, section II, for an example of human blood groups.

antigens Large molecules found on the surface of cells. Several different loci govern various antigens on red and white blood cells. (Foreign antigens provoke an immune response.)

codominance The expression of two alleles in heterozygotes. In this situation, neither allele is dominant or recessive; thus, both influence the phenotype.

A number of genetic disorders are inherited as dominant traits (see Table 4–1). This means that if a person inherits only one copy of a harmful, dominant allele, the condition it causes will be present, regardless of the existence of a different, recessive allele on the corresponding chromosome.

Recessive conditions are commonly associated with the lack of a substance, usually an enzyme (see Table 4–1). For a person actually to have a recessive disorder, he or she must have *two* copies of the recessive allele that causes it. Heterozygotes who have only one copy of a harmful recessive allele are unaffected. Such individuals are frequently called *carriers.* Although carriers do not actually have the recessive condition they carry, they can pass the allele that causes it to their children. (Remember, half their gametes will carry the recessive allele.) If their mate is also a carrier, then it is possible for them to have a child who will be homozygous for the allele, and that child will be affected. In fact, in a mating between two carriers, the risk of having an affected child is 25 percent (refer back to Fig. 4–5).

Among the best examples of Mendelian traits in humans are the blood groups, such as the ABO system. The ABO system is governed by three alleles, *A, B,* and *O,* found at the ABO locus on the ninth chromosome. These alleles determine which ABO blood type an individual has by coding for the production of substances called **antigens** on the surface of red blood cells. If only antigen A is present, the blood type (phenotype) is A; if only B is present, the blood type is B; if both are present, the blood type is AB; and when neither is present, the blood type is O.

Dominance and recessiveness are clearly illustrated by the ABO system. The *O* allele is recessive to both *A* and *B;* therefore, if a person has type O blood, he or she must be homozygous for (have two copies of) the *O* allele. However, since both *A* and *B* are dominant to *O,* an individual with blood type A can actually have one of two genotypes: *AA* or *AO.* The same is true of type B, which results from the genotypes *BB* and *BO* (Table 4–2). However, type AB presents a slightly different situation and is an example of **codominance.**

Codominance is seen when two different alleles occur in heterozygous condition, but instead of one having the ability to mask the expression of the other, the products of *both* are expressed in the phenotype. Therefore, when both *A* and *B* alleles are present, both A and B antigens can be detected on the surface of red blood cells.

MISCONCEPTIONS REGARDING DOMINANCE AND RECESSIVENESS

Traditional methods of teaching genetics have led to some misunderstanding of dominance and recessiveness. Perhaps the most glaring misunderstanding of this type is one that is still perpetuated in some high school biology textbooks, namely that eye color is a Mendelian characteristic and that brown eyes are dominant to blue eyes. However, eye color is not a Mendelian trait. In fact, it is influenced by alleles occurring at two or perhaps three loci. Interestingly, however, it does appear that at one of these loci, the allele for blue is recessive to that for brown; and at another locus, the allele for blue is recessive to that for green.

Virtually all introductory students (and most people in general) also have the impression that dominance and recessiveness are all-or-nothing situations. This misconception especially pertains to recessive alleles, and the general view is that when these alleles occur in heterozygotes (i.e., carriers), they have absolutely no effect on the phenotype—that is, they are completely inactivated by the presence of another (dominant) allele. Certainly, this is how it appeared to Gregor Mendel and, until the last three decades or so, to most geneticists.

However, various biochemical techniques, unavailable in the past but in wide use today, have demonstrated that some recessive alleles *do* exert some influence on phenotype, although these effects are not usually detectable through simple observation. Indeed, it is now clear that our *perception* of recessive alleles greatly depends on one important factor: whether we examine them at the directly observable phenotypic level or the biochemical level.

Consider Tay-Sachs disease, a lethal condition that results from the inability to produce an enzyme called hexosaminidase A (see Table 4–1). This inability, seen in people who are homozygous for a recessive allele (*ts*) on chromosome 15, invariably results in death by early childhood. Carriers do not have the disease, and practically speaking, they are unaffected. However, in 1979, it was shown that Tay-Sachs carriers, although functionally normal, have only about 40 to 60 percent of the amount of the enzyme seen in normal people. In fact, there are now voluntary tests to screen carriers in populations at risk for Tay-Sachs disease.

Similar misconceptions also relate to dominant alleles. The majority of people see dominant alleles as somehow "stronger" or "better," and there is always the mistaken notion that dominant alleles are more common in populations because natural selection favors them. These misconceptions undoubtedly stem partly from the label "dominant" and the connotations that the term carries. But in genetic usage, those connotations are somewhat misleading. Just think about it. If dominant alleles were always more common, then a majority of people would be affected by such conditions as achondroplasia and Marfan syndrome (see Table 4–1).

As you can see, the relationships between recessive and dominant alleles and their functions are more complicated than they would appear to be at first glance. Previously held views of dominance and recessiveness were guided by available technologies; as genetic technologies continue to change, new theories emerge, and our perceptions will be further altered. In fact, it's possible that one day the concepts of dominance and recessiveness, as traditionally taught, will be obsolete.

PATTERNS OF INHERITANCE

It is of obvious importance to be able to establish the pattern of inheritance of genetic traits, especially those that result in serious disease. Equally important, particularly in families with a history of inherited disorders, is the ability to determine an individual's risk of inheriting harmful alleles or expressing symptoms. But because humans can't be used in experimental breeding programs, a more indirect approach must be used to demonstrate patterns of inheritance. The principal technique traditionally used in human genetic studies has been the construction of a **pedigree chart,** a diagram of matings and offspring in a family over the span of a few generations.

Pedigree analysis helps determine if a trait is indeed Mendelian in nature. It also helps establish the mode of inheritance. From considerations of whether the locus that influences a particular trait is located on an autosome or sex chromosome and whether it is dominant or recessive, six different modes of Mendelian inheritance have been recognized in humans: *autosomal dominant, autosomal recessive, X-linked recessive, X-linked dominant, Y-linked,* and *mitochondrial.* We discuss the first three of these in some detail.

pedigree chart A diagram showing family relationships in order to trace the hereditary pattern of particular genetic (usually Mendelian) traits.

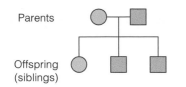

FIGURE 4–7 Typical symbols used in pedigree charts.

Standardized symbols are used in pedigree charts. Squares and circles represent males and females, respectively. Horizontal lines connecting individuals indicate matings, and offspring are connected to horizontal mating lines by vertical lines. Siblings are joined to one another by a horizontal line to which they are connected by vertical lines (Fig. 4–7).

Autosomal Dominant Traits   As the term implies, autosomal dominant traits are governed by loci on autosomes (i.e., any chromosomes except X or Y). One example of an autosomal dominant trait is brachydactyly, a condition characterized by malformed hands and shortened fingers (see Table 4–1).

Because brachydactyly is caused by a dominant allele, anyone who inherits just one copy will express the trait. (For purposes of this discussion, we will use the symbol *B* to refer to the dominant allele that causes the condition and *b* for the recessive, normal allele.) Since the allele is rare, virtually everyone who has brachydactyly is a heterozygote (*Bb*). Unaffected individuals are homozygous recessive (*bb*).

Figure 4–8 is a partial pedigree for brachydactyly. It is apparent from this pedigree that all affected members have at least one affected parent; thus, the abnormality does not skip generations. This pattern is true of all autosomal dominant traits. Another characteristic of autosomal dominant traits is that there is no sex bias, and males and females are more or less equally affected.

One other fact illustrated by Figure 4–8 is that approximately half the offspring of affected parents are also affected. This proportion is what we would predict for an autosomal dominant trait where only one parent is affected, and it is explained by events in meiosis as well as by Mendel's principle of segregation (Fig. 4–9).

FIGURE 4–8 Inheritance of an autosomal dominant trait: a human pedigree for brachydactyly. How can individuals 5, 11, 14, 15, and 17 be unaffected? What is the genotype of all affected individuals?

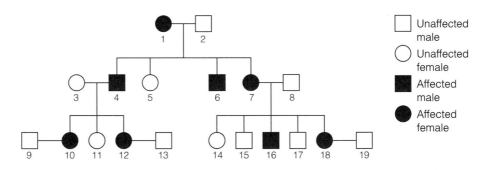

Autosomal Recessive Traits   Autosomal recessive traits are also influenced by loci on autosomes but show a different pattern of inheritance. A good example is shown in Figure 4–10, a pedigree for albinism, a metabolic disorder causing deficient production of a skin pigment called melanin (see Chapter 15). This disorder is phenotypically expressed as very light skin, hair, and eyes.

Actually, albinism is a group of genetic disorders, each influenced by different loci. Some forms affect only the eyes, while others also involve skin and hair. The most widely known variety influences eye, skin, and hair pigmentation and is caused by an autosomal recessive allele. The frequency of this particular form of albinism varies widely among populations, with an incidence of about 1 in 37,000 in people of European ancestry but a much higher frequency, approaching 1 in 200, among Hopi Indians. How populations have come to be so different in the frequencies of various alleles (such as those for albinism) will be a major focus of Chapter 14.

Pedigrees for autosomal recessive traits show obvious differences from those for autosomal dominant characteristics. For one thing, recessive traits often appear to skip generations, so that an affected offspring is produced by two

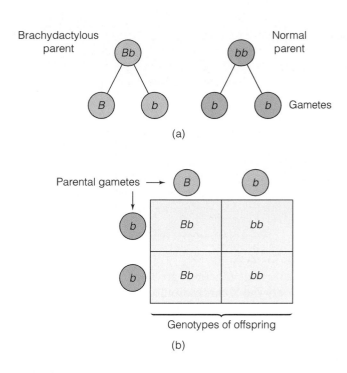

(a)

(b)

FIGURE 4–9 The pattern of inheritance of autosomal dominant traits is the direct result of the distribution of chromosomes, and the alleles they carry, into gametes during meiosis. (a) Diagrammatic representation of possible gametes produced by two parents, one with brachydactyly and another with normal hands and fingers. The brachydactylous individual can produce two types of gametes: half with the dominant allele (*B*) and half with the recessive allele (*b*). All the gametes produced by the normal parent will carry the recessive allele. (*b*) A Punnett square depicting the possible genotypes in the offspring of one parent with brachydactyly (*Bb*) and one with normal hands and fingers (*bb*). Statistically speaking, half the offspring would be expected to have the *Bb* genotype and thus brachydactyly. The other half would be homozygous recessive (*bb*) and would be normal.

phenotypically normal parents. In fact, most affected individuals have unaffected parents. In addition, the proportion of affected offspring from most matings is less than half. However, when both parents have the trait, all the offspring will be affected. As in the pattern for autosomal dominant traits, males and females are equally affected.

As Figure 4–11 illustrates, the Mendelian principle of segregation explains the pattern of inheritance of autosomal recessive traits. In fact, this pattern is the very one first described by Mendel in his pea experiments (refer back to Fig. 4–3). Unaffected parents who produce an albino child *must* both be carriers, and their child is homozygous for the recessive allele that causes the abnormality. The Punnett square in Figure 4–11 shows how such a mating produces both unaffected and affected offspring in predictable proportions—the typical phenotypic ratio of 3:1.

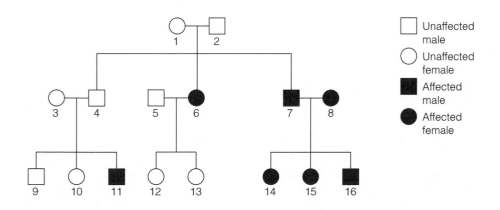

Unaffected male

Unaffected female

Affected male

Affected female

FIGURE 4–10 Partial pedigree for albinism, an autosomal recessive trait. Why are some of the offspring of affected individuals unaffected? Individuals 6 and 7, children of unaffected parents, are affected. Why? Four individuals are *definitely* unaffected carriers. Which ones are they? Does the pattern of inheritance in this chart conform to the *expected* ratios shown in Figure 4–11?

Sex-Linked Traits   Sex-linked traits are controlled by genes located on the X and Y chromosomes. Almost all of the more than 880 sex-linked traits listed in OMIM (see p. 80) are influenced by genes on the X chromosome (Table 4–3). Most of the coding sequences (i.e., those segments that actually specify a protein) on the Y chromosome are involved in determining maleness and testis function. Although some Y-linked genes are expressed in areas other than the testes

FIGURE 4–11 A cross between two phenotypically normal parents, both of whom are carriers of the albinism allele. From a mating such as this between two carriers, we would expect the following possible proportions of genotypes and phenotypes in the offspring: homozygous dominants (*AA*) with normal phenotype, 25 percent; heterozygotes, or carriers (*Aa*), with normal phenotype, 50 percent; and homozygous recessives (*aa*) with albinism, 25 percent. This yields the phenotypic ratio of three normal to one albino.

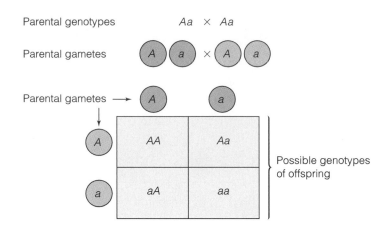

(Skaletsky et al., 2003), their functions are not well known. For this reason, our discussion concerns only the X chromosome.

The best known of the X-linked traits is hemophilia, caused by a recessive allele at a locus on the X chromosome. Consequently, this type of condition is said to be an *X-linked recessive*. Hemophilia results from the lack of a clotting factor in the blood, and affected individuals suffer bleeding episodes and may hemorrhage to death from incidents that most of us would consider trivial.

The most famous pedigree that illustrates this condition is that of Queen Victoria and her descendants (Fig. 4–12). The most striking feature shown by this pattern of inheritance is that usually only males are affected. To understand this pattern, we need to refer to the principle of segregation, but with one additional stipulation: We are now dealing with *sex chromosomes*.

Because they possess two X chromosomes, females show the same pattern of expression of X-linked traits as for autosomal traits. That is, the only way an X-linked recessive allele can be phenotypically expressed in a female is when she is homozygous for it. And heterozygous females are unaffected unless it is dominant.

TABLE 4–3 Some Mendelian Disorders Inherited as X-Linked Recessive Traits in Humans

CONDITION	MANIFESTATIONS
G-6-PD (glucose-6-phosphate dehydrogenase) deficiency	Lack of an enzyme (G-6-PD) in red blood cells; produces severe, sometimes fatal anemia in the presence of certain foods (e.g., fava beans) and/or drugs (e.g., the antimalarial drug primaquin).
Muscular dystrophy	One form; other forms can be inherited as autosomal recessives; progressive weakness and atrophy of muscles beginning in early childhood; continues to progress throughout life; some female carriers may develop heart problems.
Red-green color blindness	Actually, there are two separate forms, one involving the perception of red and the other affecting only the perception of green. About 8 percent of European males have an impaired ability to distinguish green.
Lesch-Nyhan disease	Impaired motor development noticeable by 5 months; progressive motor impairment, diminished kidney function, self-mutilation, and early death.
Hemophilia	There are three forms; two (hemophilia A and B) are X-linked. In hemophilia A, a clotting factor is missing; hemophilia B is caused by a defective clotting factor. Both produce abnormal internal and external bleeding from minor injuries; severe pain is a frequent accompaniment; without treatment, death usually occurs before adulthood.
Ichthyosis	There are several forms; one is X-linked. A skin condition due to lack of an enzyme; characterized by scaly, brown lesions on the extremities and trunk. In the past, people with this condition sometimes were exhibited in circuses and sideshows as "the alligator man."

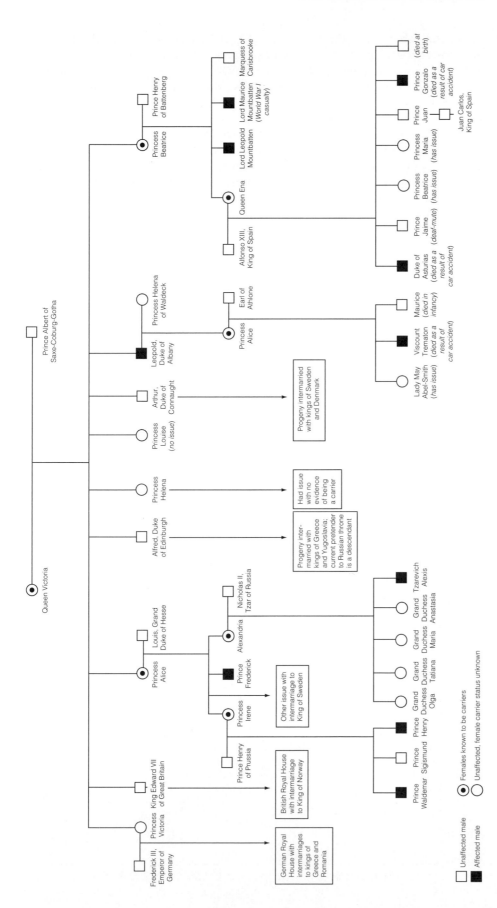

FIGURE 4–12 Pedigree for Queen Victoria and some of her descendants, showing inheritance of hemophilia, an X-linked recessive trait in humans.

hemizygous (*hemi,* meaning "half") Having only one member of a pair of alleles. Because males have only one X chromosome, all their X-linked alleles are hemizygous. All recessive alleles on a male's X chromosome are expressed in the phenotype.

polygenic Referring to traits that are influenced by genes at two or more loci. Examples of such traits are stature, skin color, and eye color. Many polygenic traits are also influenced by environmental factors.

FIGURE 4–13 (a) This histogram shows the discontinuous distribution of a Mendelian trait (ABO blood type) in a hypothetical population. The expression of the trait is described in terms of frequencies. (b) This histogram represents the continuous expression of a polygenic trait (height) in a large group of people. Note that the percentage of extremely short or tall individuals is low; the majority of people are closer to the mean, or average, height, represented by the vertical line at the center of the distribution. (c) (on next page) A group of male students arranged according to height. Note that the most common height is 70 inches, which is the mean, or average, for this group.

On the other hand, since males are XY and have only one X chromosome, they possess only one copy of an X-linked gene. With only one X chromosome, males can never be homozygous or heterozygous for X-linked loci, and they are referred to as **hemizygous.** Moreover, males don't exhibit dominance or recessiveness for X-linked traits because *any* allele located on their X chromosome, even a recessive one, will be expressed.

The difference between males and females in number of X chromosomes is directly related to the incidence of hemophilia seen in Figure 4–12. Females who have one copy of the hemophilia allele are carriers for the trait. Although they may have some tendency toward bleeding, they are not severely affected. On the other hand, males who have the allele on their *only* X chromosome are severely afflicted, and prior to the availability of treatment, they faced short and painful lives.

Non-Mendelian Patterns of Inheritance

POLYGENIC INHERITANCE

Mendelian traits are said to be *discrete,* or *discontinuous,* because their phenotypic expressions don't overlap; instead, they fall into clearly defined categories (Fig. 4–13a). For example, Mendel's pea plants were either short or tall, but none was intermediate in height. In the ABO system, the four phenotypes are completely distinct from one another; that is, there is no intermediate form between type A and type B to represent a gradation between the two. In other words, Mendelian traits do not show *continuous* variation.

However, many traits do have a wide range of phenotypic expressions that form a graded series. These are called **polygenic,** or *continuous,* traits (Fig. 4–13b and c). While Mendelian traits are governed by only one genetic locus, polygenic characteristics are influenced by alleles at two or more loci, with each locus making a contribution to the phenotype. For example, one of the most frequently cited instances of polygenic inheritance in humans is skin color. The single most important factor influencing skin color is the amount of the pigment melanin present.

Melanin production is believed to be influenced by between three and six genetic loci, with each locus having at least two alleles, neither of which is dominant. Individuals having only alleles for more melanin production (i.e., they are

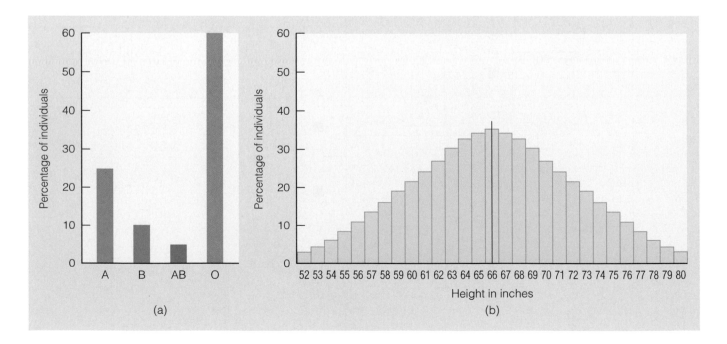

(a)

(b)

FIGURE 4–13 (continued)

5'3" 5'4" 5'5" 5'6" 5'7" 5'8" 5'9" 5'10" 5'11" 6'0" 6'1" 6'2" 6'3" 6'4" 6'5"
Height (feet/inches)

(c)

Courtesy, Ray Carson, University of Florida News and Public Affairs

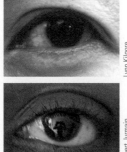

See Virtual Lab 2, section IV, for a discussion of human skin color.

homozygous at all loci) have the darkest skin. Those having only alleles that code for reduced melanin production have very fair skin.

As there are perhaps six loci and at least 12 alleles, there are numerous ways in which these alleles can combine in individuals. If an individual inherits 11 alleles coding for maximum pigmentation and only one for reduced melanin production, skin color will be very dark. A person who inherits a higher proportion of reduced pigmentation alleles will have lighter skin color. This is because in this system, as in some other polygenic systems, there is an *additive effect*. This means that each allele that codes for melanin production makes a contribution to increased melanization (although for some characteristics the contributions of the alleles are not all equal). Likewise, each allele coding for reduced melanin production contributes to reduced pigmentation. Therefore, the effect of multiple alleles at several loci, each making a contribution to individual phenotypes, is to produce continuous variation from very dark to very fair skin within the species. (Skin color is also discussed in Chapter 15.)

Polygenic traits actually account for most of the readily observable phenotypic variation seen in humans, and they have traditionally served as a basis for racial classification (see Chapter 14). In addition to skin color, polygenic inheritance in humans is seen in hair color, weight, stature, eye color (Fig. 4–14), shape of face, shape of nose, and fingerprint pattern. Because they exhibit continuous variation, most polygenic traits can be measured on a scale composed of equal increments. For example, height (stature) can be measured in feet and inches (or meters and centimeters). If one were to measure height in a large number of individuals, the distribution of measurements would continue uninterrupted from the shortest extreme to the tallest. That is what is meant by *continuous traits*.

Because polygenic traits usually lend themselves to metric analysis, biologists, geneticists, and physical anthropologists treat them statistically. Although statistical analysis can be complicated, the use of simple summary statistics, such as the *mean* (average) or *standard deviation* (a measure of variation within a group), permits basic descriptions of, and comparisons between, populations. For example, one might be interested in average height in two different populations and whether or not differences between the two are significant, and if so, why. Or a researcher might determine that in the same geographical area, one group shows significantly more variation in skin color than another, and it would be useful to

FIGURE 4–14 Examples of the continuous variation seen in human eye color.

explain this variability. (Incidentally, you should also note that *all* physical traits measured and statistically treated in fossils are polygenic in nature.)

These particular statistical manipulations are not possible with Mendelian traits simply because those traits can't be measured in the same manner. They are either present or they aren't; they are expressed one way, or another, and can be described in terms of frequencies. But just because Mendelian traits aren't amenable to the same types of statistical tests as polygenic traits doesn't mean that Mendelian traits are less worthy of study or less informative of genetic processes. It just means that scientists approach the study of these two types of inheritance from somewhat different perspectives.

Mendelian characteristics can be described in terms of frequency within populations, yielding comparisons between groups regarding incidence. Moreover, these characteristics can also be analyzed for mode of inheritance (dominant or recessive) from pedigree data. Finally, for many Mendelian traits, the approximate or exact positions of genetic loci are known, and this makes it possible to examine the mechanisms and patterns of inheritance at these loci. This type of study is not possible yet for polygenic traits because polygenic characters are influenced by several genes and they cannot be traced to specific loci on specific chromosomes.

GENETIC AND ENVIRONMENTAL FACTORS

From the preceding discussion, it might appear that the phenotype is solely the expression of the genotype, but this isn't true. (Here the terms *genotype* and *phenotype* are used in a broader sense to refer to an individual's *entire* genetic makeup and *all* observable or detectable characteristics.) The genotype sets limits and potentials for development, but it also interacts with the environment, and many aspects of the phenotype are influenced by this genetic-environmental interaction. For many traits, scientists have developed statistical methods for calculating what proportion of phenotypic variation is due to genetic or environmental factors. However, it usually isn't possible to identify the *specific* environmental components that influence the phenotype.

Many polygenic traits are quite obviously influenced by environmental conditions. Adult stature is strongly affected by the individual's nutritional status during growth and development (see 454). One study showed that children of Japanese immigrants to Hawaii were, on average, 3 to 4 inches taller than their parents. This dramatic difference, seen in one generation, was attributed to environmental alteration—specifically to a change in diet (Froelich, 1970).

Other important environmental factors include exposure to sunlight, altitude, temperature, and, unfortunately, increasing levels of exposure to toxic waste and airborne pollutants. These and many more factors contribute in complex ways to the continuous phenotypic variation seen in characteristics governed by multiple loci.

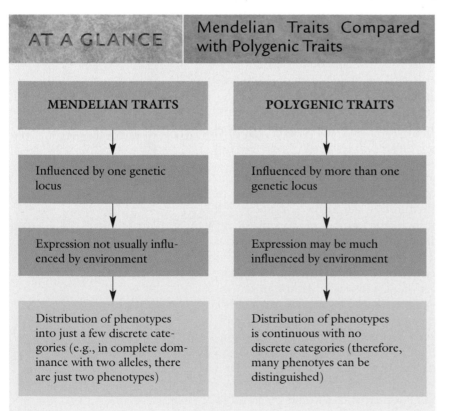

AT A GLANCE — Mendelian Traits Compared with Polygenic Traits

MENDELIAN TRAITS	POLYGENIC TRAITS
Influenced by one genetic locus	Influenced by more than one genetic locus
Expression not usually influenced by environment	Expression may be much influenced by environment
Distribution of phenotypes into just a few discrete categories (e.g., in complete dominance with two alleles, there are just two phenotypes)	Distribution of phenotypes is continuous with no discrete categories (therefore, many phenotyes can be distinguished)

Mendelian traits are less likely to be influenced by environmental factors. For example, ABO blood type is determined at fertilization and remains fixed throughout the individual's lifetime, regardless of diet, exposure to ultraviolet radiation, temperature, and so forth.

Mendelian and polygenic inheritance produce different kinds of phenotypic variation. In the former, variation occurs in discrete categories, while in the latter, it is continuous. However, it's important to understand that even for polygenic characteristics, Mendelian principles still apply at individual loci. In other words, if a trait is influenced by seven loci, each one of those loci may have two or more alleles, with some perhaps being dominant to others or with the alleles being codominant. It's the combined action of the alleles at all seven loci, interacting with the environment, that results in observable phenotypic expression.

PLEIOTROPY

Whereas polygenic traits are governed by the actions of several genes, **pleiotropy** is a situation where a single gene influences more than one phenotypic expression. Although this might seem unusual, pleiotropic effects are probably the rule rather than the exception.

pleiotropy A situation whereby several seemingly unrelated phenotypic effects are influenced by the action of a single gene.

The autosomal recessive disorder phenylketonuria (PKU) provides one example of pleiotropy (see Table 4–1). Individuals who are homozygous for the PKU allele do not produce phenylketonurase, the enzyme involved in the initial conversion of the amino acid phenylalanine to another amino acid, tyrosine. Because of this block in the metabolic pathway, phenylalanine breaks down into substances that accumulate in the central nervous system, and without dietary management, they lead to mental deficiencies. And there are several other consequences. Because tyrosine is ultimately converted into several other substances, including the pigment melanin, numerous other systems can also be affected. Consequently, one additional manifestation of PKU, owing to a diminished ability to produce melanin, is that affected people usually have blue eyes, fair skin, and light hair.

There are many known examples of pleiotropic genes, including the allele that causes sickle-cell anemia (see Fig. 3–8, p. 57). Although it isn't necessary to include a detailed discussion here, it is clear that gene action may exert an influence over a number of seemingly unrelated phenotypic expressions.

Mitochondrial Inheritance

There is another component of inheritance that has gained much attention in recent years, and it involves organelles called *mitochondria* (see p. 46). All cells contain several hundred of these oval-shaped structures that convert energy (derived from the breakdown of nutrients) into a form that can be used by the cell.

Each mitochondrion contains several copies of a ring-shaped DNA molecule, or chromosome. While *mitochondrial DNA (mtDNA)* is distinct from the DNA found within cell nuclei, its molecular structure and functions are the same. The entire molecule has been sequenced and is known to contain around 40 genes that direct the conversion of energy within the cell.

Mitochondrial DNA is subject to mutations just like nuclear DNA, and such mutations can lead to certain genetic disorders, some of which have been traced to specific loci. In general, these disorders result from impaired energy conversion and can produce a wide range of symptoms. Importantly, mitochondrial DNA is transmitted to offspring only from the mother; therefore, it's the mother who transmits all mitochondrial traits to her offspring of both sexes. This is so because mitochondria occur in cellular cytoplasm, and while egg cells retain their cytoplasm, sperm cells lose theirs prior to fertilization.

Mitochondrial mutation rates have been used as a basis for constructing evolutionary relationships between species. They have also been used to trace ancestral relationships within the human lineage and to study genetic variability between individuals and/or populations. While these techniques are still being refined, it is clear that we have much to learn from mitochondrial DNA.

Modern Evolutionary Theory

By the beginning of the twentieth century, the foundations for evolutionary theory had already been developed. Darwin and Wallace had articulated the key principle of natural selection 40 years earlier, and the rediscovery of Mendelian genetics in 1900 contributed the other major component—a mechanism for inheritance. We might expect that these two basic contributions would have been combined into a consistent theory of evolution. But that didn't happen immediately. For the first 30 years of the twentieth century, rival explanations emphasized mutation *or* natural selection as the prime mover of evolutionary change. A *synthesis* of these two views was not achieved until the mid-1930s, and we owe much of our current view of the evolutionary process to this intellectual development (see A Closer Look).

THE MODERN SYNTHESIS

Biologists working on mathematical models of evolutionary change in the late 1920s and early 1930s came to realize that mutational and selective processes were not opposing themes, but that both were actually needed to provide a comprehensive explanation of organic evolution. Small new changes in the genetic material transmitted from parent to offspring are, in fact, the fuel for natural selection. The two major foundations of the biological sciences had thus been brought together in what Julian Huxley called the Modern Synthesis.

From such a "modern" (i.e., the middle of the twentieth century onward) perspective, we define evolution as a two-stage process. These two stages are:

variation (genetic) Inherited differences between individuals; the basis of all evolutionary change.

1. The production and redistribution of **variation** (inherited differences between individuals)

2. *Natural selection* acting on this variation, whereby inherited differences, or variation, among individuals differentially affect their ability to successfully reproduce.

Definition of Evolution

As discussed in Chapter 2, Darwin saw evolution as the gradual unfolding of new varieties of life from previous forms over long periods of time. This depiction is what most of us think of as evolution, and it is indeed the end result of the evolutionary process. But these long-term effects can come about only by the accumulation of many small genetic changes occurring over the generations. To understand how the process of evolution works, we must study these short-term events. Today, we look at evolutionary changes occurring between generations in various organisms (including humans) and are able to demonstrate how evolution works. From such a modern genetic perspective, we define **evolution** as *a change in **allele frequency** from one generation to the next*.

evolution (modern genetic definition) A change in the frequency of alleles from one generation to the next.

allele frequency In a population, the percentage of all the alleles at a locus accounted for by one specific allele.

population Within a species, a community of individuals where mates are usually found.

Allele frequencies are indicators of the genetic makeup of an interbreeding group of individuals known as a **population.** (We'll return to this topic in more detail in Chapter 4.) Let us illustrate the way allele frequencies change (i.e., how evolution occurs) through a simplified example. First of all, we need to look at a

A CLOSER LOOK

Development of Modern Evolutionary Theory

Our understanding of the evolutionary process came about through contributions of biologists in the United States, Great Britain, and Russia.

While "mutationists" were arguing with "selectionists" about the single primary mechanism in evolution, several population geneticists began to realize that small genetic changes and natural selection were both necessary ingredients in the evolutionary formula.

These population geneticists were largely concerned with mathematical reconstructions of evolution—in particular, measuring those small accumulations of genetic changes in populations over just a few generations. Central figures in these early theoretical developments included Ronald Fisher and J.B.S. Haldane in Great Britain, Sewall Wright in the United States, and Sergei Chetverikov in Russia.

While the work of these scientists often produced brilliant insights (see particularly Fisher's *The Genetical Theory of Natural Selection,* 1930), their conclusions were largely unknown to most evolutionary biologists, especially in North America. It remained, therefore, for someone to transcend these two worlds: the mathematical jargon of the population geneticists and the general constructs of theoretical evolutionary biologists. The scientist who performed this task (and who is credited as the first true synthesizer) was Theodosius Dobzhansky (Fig. 1). In his *Genetics and the Origin of Species* (1937), Dobzhansky skillfully integrated the mathematics of population genetics with overall evolutionary theory. His insights then became the basis for a period of tremendous activity in evolutionary thinking that directly led to major contributions by George Gaylord Simpson (who brought paleontology into the synthesis), Ernst Mayr, and others. In fact, the Modern Synthesis produced by these scientists stood basically unchallenged for an entire generation as *the* explanation of the evolutionary process. In recent years, however, some aspects of this theory have been brought under serious question (see Chapter 5).

FIGURE 1
Theodosius Dobzhansky

Reprinted, with permission, from the *Annual Review of Genetics,* Volume 10 ©1976 by Annual Reviews   www.annualreviews.org

physical trait that is inherited—again, human blood types. The best known of the human blood types is ABO (see p. 82). There are, however, many similar blood type systems controlled by different loci that determine genetically transmitted properties of the red blood cells.

Let's assume that your present class of students represents a population, an interbreeding group of individuals, and that we have determined the ABO blood type of each member. (To be considered a population, individuals must choose mates more often from *within* the group than from outside it. Of course, the individuals in your class will not meet this requirement, but for the sake of our example, we will overlook this stipulation.) The proportions of the *A, B,* and *O* alleles are the allele frequencies for this trait. For example, suppose 50 percent of all the ABO alleles in your class are *A,* 40 percent are *B,* and 10 percent are *O.* Then the frequencies of these alleles are $A = .50$, $B = .40$, and $O = .10$.*

Since the frequencies for these alleles represent only proportions of a total, it's obvious that allele frequencies can refer only to groups of individuals—that

---

*This is a simplified example. Because the ABO system is governed by three alleles, calculating allele frequencies is more complicated than for a two-allele system. The way allele frequencies are calculated for a simple two-allele locus will be shown in Chapter 14.

is, populations. Individuals do not have an allele frequency; they have either *A*, *B*, or *O* in any combination of two. Nor can individuals change alleles. From conception onward, the genetic composition of an individual is fixed. If you start out with blood type A, you will remain type A. Therefore, an individual cannot evolve: Only a group of individuals—a population—can evolve over time.

What happens when a population evolves? Assume that 25 years from now, we calculate the frequencies of the ABO alleles for the children (offspring) of our classroom population and find the following: *A* = .30, *B* = .40, and *O* = .30. We can see that the relative proportions have changed: *A* has decreased, *O* has increased, and *B* has remained the same. Such a simple, apparently minor change is what we call evolution. Over the short span of just a few generations, such changes in inherited traits may be only very small, but if further continued and elaborated, the results can and do produce spectacular kinds of adaptation and whole new varieties of life.

Whether we are talking about the short-term effects (as in our classroom population) from one generation to the next, which is sometimes called **microevolution**, or the long-term effects through time (speciation), sometimes called **macroevolution**, the basic evolutionary mechanisms are similar. As we will discuss in Chapter 5, however, they aren't identical.

The question may be asked, How do allele frequencies change? Or, to put it another way, what causes evolution? The modern theory of evolution isolates general factors that can produce changes in allele frequencies. As we have noted, evolution is a two-stage process. Genetic variation must first be produced and distributed before it can be acted on by natural selection.

microevolution Small changes occurring within species, such as a change in allele frequencies.

macroevolution Changes produced only after many generations, such as the appearance of a new species.

Factors That Produce and Redistribute Variation

MUTATION

You have already learned that a molecular alteration in genetic material is one type of mutation. A gene may occur in one of several alternative forms, which we have defined as alleles (*A, B,* or *O* for example). If one allele changes to another—that is, if the gene itself is altered—a mutation has occurred. In fact, alleles are the results of mutation. For such changes to have evolutionary significance, they must occur in the sex cells, which are passed between generations. Evolution is a change in allele frequencies *between* generations. If mutations do not occur in gametes (either the egg or sperm), they will not be transmitted to the next generation, and no evolutionary change will result. If, however, a genetic change occurs in the sperm or egg of one of the individuals in our classroom (*A* mutates to *B*, for instance), the offspring's blood type will also be altered, causing a minute shift in allele frequencies of the next generation. In Chapter 3, we showed how a change in a single DNA base, a *point mutation*, could cause a change in hemoglobin structure (from normal to sickle-cell). Also in Chapter 3, we discussed how transposable elements and microsatellites can change the structure of a gene. Other mutations (as discussed in this chapter) can result in albinism, brachydactyly, or Tay-Sachs disease.

Actually, it would be rare to see evolution occurring by mutation alone, except in microorganisms. Mutation rates for any given trait are quite low; thus, mutations would rarely be seen in such a small population as our class. In larger populations, mutations might be observed (1 individual in 10,000, say), but would by themselves have very little impact on allele frequencies. However, when mutation is coupled with natural selection, evolutionary changes not only can occur, but they can occur more rapidly.

It's important to remember that mutation is the basic creative force in evolution because it's the *only* way to produce *new* genetic variation. Its key role in the production of variation represents the first stage of the evolutionary process. Darwin, who recognized the importance of variation, wasn't aware of the nature of mutation. Only in the last 50 years or so , with the development of molecular biology, have the secrets of genetic structure been revealed.

GENE FLOW

The exchange of genes between populations is called **gene flow.** The term *migration* is frequently used instead, but strictly speaking, migration means movement of people, whereas gene flow refers to the exchange of *genes* between groups, and this can occur only if the migrants interbreed. Moreover, it should be remembered that even if individuals move temporarily and mate in the new population (thus leaving a genetic contribution), they need not remain as part of the population. For example, the offspring of U.S. soldiers and Vietnamese women represent gene flow, even though the fathers may have returned to their native population.

gene flow Exchange of genes between populations.

In humans, social rules more than any other factor determine mating patterns, and cultural anthropologists can work closely with physical anthropologists to isolate and measure this aspect of evolutionary change. Population movements (particularly in the last 500 years) have reached enormous proportions, and few breeding isolates remain. It should not, however, be assumed that significant population movements didn't occur prior to modern times. Migration between populations has been a consistent feature of hominid evolution since the first dispersal of our genus, and gene flow between populations (even though sometimes limited) helps explain why, in the last million years, speciation has been rare. Of course, migration patterns are a manifestation of human cultural behavior, once again emphasizing the essential biocultural nature of human evolution.

See Virtual Lab 2, section III, for examples of mutation, gene flow, genetic drift, and recombination.

An interesting example of how gene flow influences microevolutionary changes in modern human populations is seen in African Americans. African Americans in the United States are largely of West African descent, but there has also been considerable genetic admixture with European Americans. By measuring allele frequencies for specific genetic loci (e.g., Rh and HLA, discussed in Chapter 14), we can estimate the amount of migration of European alleles into the African American gene pool. Data from northern and western U.S. cities (including New York, Detroit, and Oakland) have shown the migration rate (i.e., the proportion of *non*-African genes in the African American gene pool) at 20 to 25 percent (Cummings, 2000). However, more restricted data from the southern United States (Charleston and rural Georgia) have suggested a lower degree of gene flow (4 to 11 percent). The most consistent of these studies employ new genetic techniques, especially those involving direct DNA comparisons.

It would be a misconception to think that gene flow can occur only through large-scale movements of entire groups. In fact, significant changes in allele frequencies can come about through long-term patterns of mate selection whereby members of a group obtain mates from one or more other groups. If exchange of mates consistently moves in one direction over a long period of time, allele frequencies will ultimately be altered.

Transportation plays a crucial role in determining the potential radius for finding mates. Today, modern transportation makes the potential radius of mate choice worldwide, but actual patterns are obviously somewhat more restricted. For example, data from Ann Arbor, Michigan, indicate a mean marital distance (the average distance between birthplaces of partners) of about 160 miles, which obviously includes a tremendous number of potential marriage partners.

GENETIC DRIFT

genetic drift Evolutionary changes—that is, changes in allele frequencies—produced by random factors. Genetic drift is a result of small population size.

Genetic drift is the random factor in evolution, and it's directly tied to population size. Genetic drift occurs when, because of small population size, some individuals contribute a disproportionate share of genes to succeeding generations. This situation can be a function of social status in some small societies where, for example, high-ranking males have numerous mates while others don't. This effect may also be seen in nonhuman species in which low-ranking individuals may have fewer mating opportunities. In such a situation, one individual who carries a rare deleterious allele may pass it on to a high proportion of his or her descendants, and the frequency of the allele consequently increases in succeeding generations. Drift may also occur solely because the population is small; just by chance, alleles with low frequencies may simply not be passed on to offspring, eventually disappearing from the population.

founder effect A type of genetic drift in which allele frequencies are altered in small populations that are taken from, or are remnants of, larger populations.

The results of the particular kind of genetic drift called **founder effect** are seen in many modern populations. Founder effect can occur when a small migrant band of "founders" colonizes a new region away from its parent group. Over time, a new population will be established, and as long as mates are chosen only from within this population, all of its members will be descended from the founders. In effect, all of the genes in the expanding group will have been contributed by the original colonists. In such a case, an allele that was rare in the founders' parent population but that is present in even one individual in the founding group can eventually become common in that group's descendants.

Colonization is not the only way founder effect can happen. Small founding groups may also consist of a small number of survivors when famine, war, disease, or other disasters ravage large populations. The small founder population (the survivors) possesses only a sample of all the alleles that were present in the original group. Just by chance alone, some alleles may be completely removed from the **gene pool;** other alleles may become "fixed," or established, at a locus where originally there may have been two or more. The outcome is a reduction of genetic diversity, and the allele frequencies of succeeding generations may perhaps be substantially different from those of the original large population. The loss of genetic diversity in this type of situation is called a *genetic bottleneck,* and the effects can be very detrimental to a species.

gene pool The total complement of genes shared by the reproductive members of a population.

There are many known examples (both human and nonhuman) of species or populations that have passed through genetic bottlenecks. Genetically, cheetahs are an extremely uniform species, and it's believed that at some point in the past, these magnificent cats suffered a catastrophic decline in numbers. For reasons not well understood but related to the species-wide loss of numerous alleles, male cheetahs produce a high percentage of defective sperm compared to other cat species. Decreased reproductive potential, greatly reduced genetic diversity, and other factors have combined to jeopardize the continued existence of this species. Other examples include California elephant seals, sea otters, and condors. Indeed, our own species is genetically uniform, compared to chimpanzees, and it now appears that all modern human populations are the descendants of a few small groups (see Chapter 13).

Many specific examples of founder effect in human populations have been documented in small, usually isolated populations (e.g., island groups or small agricultural villages in New Guinea or South America). Even larger populations that are descended from fairly small groups of founders can show the effects of genetic drift many generations later. French Canadians are one such example. While currently numbering close to 6 million, the French Canadian population of Quebec derives from only about 8,500 founders who migrated during the sixteenth and seventeenth centuries. Because the genes carried by the initial founders represented only a sample of the gene pool from which they were derived, by chance a number of alleles occurred in frequencies that differed from those in the original French population. Among these genetic disparities are the increased prevalence of several harmful alleles, including those that cause some of the diseases listed in Table 4–1), such as cystic fibrosis, a variety of Tay-Sachs, thalassemia, and PKU (Scriver, 2001). Moreover, internal migrations within Quebec during the last 300 years have produced additional clusters of genes, again largely the result of drift acting on small populations (Heyer, 1999).

One other example of genetic drift is provided by a recently discovered fatal recessive condition called Amish microcephaly, in which a defect in DNA production results in abnormally small brains and heads in fetuses. The disorder is found only in the Old Order Amish community of Lancaster County, Pennsylvania, where it occurs in approximately 1 in 500 births (Kelley et al., 2002; Rosenberg et al., 2002). Genealogical research revealed that affected families have all been traced back nine generations to a single couple. One member of this couple carried the deleterious recessive allele, which, because of customs that promote marriage within a small group, has greatly increased in frequency with very serious consequences. Indeed, much insight concerning the evolutionary factors that have acted in the past can be gained by understanding how such mechanisms continue to operate on human populations today. In small populations, drift plays a major evolutionary role because fairly sudden fluctuations in allele frequency can and do occur owing entirely to small population size. Likewise, throughout a good deal of human evolution (at least the last 4–5 m.y.*), hominids probably lived in small groups, and drift would have had significant impact.

While drift has been a factor producing evolutionary change in certain circumstances, the effects have been irregular and nondirectional (for drift is *random* in nature). Certainly, the pace of evolutionary change could have been accelerated if many small populations were isolated and thus subject to drift. By modifying such populations, drift can provide significantly greater opportunities for the truly directional force in evolution—natural selection.

It's important to emphasize that natural selection is not the *only* driving force behind evolutionary change. As we've already seen, both gene flow and genetic drift can produce some evolutionary changes by themselves. However, these changes are usually *microevolutionary* ones; that is, they produce changes within species over the short term. To yield the kind of evolutionary changes that ultimately result in entire new groups (e.g., the diversification of the first primates or the appearance of the hominids), natural selection most likely would play the major role. But natural selection does not and cannot operate independently of the other evolutionary factors—mutation, gene flow, and genetic drift. All four factors (sometimes called the "four forces of evolution") work interactively.

Additional insight concerning the relative influences of the different evolutionary factors has emerged in recent studies of the early dispersal of modern *Homo sapiens* (discussed in Chapter 13). New evidence suggests that in the last 100,000 to 200,000 years, our species experienced a genetic bottleneck, which considerably influenced the pattern of genetic variation seen in all human populations today. In this sense, modern humans can be seen as the fairly recent product of a form of genetic drift (founder effect) acting on a somewhat grand scale. Such evolutionary changes could be potentially significant over tens of thousands of years and could cause substantial genetic shifts within species.

RECOMBINATION

Since in any sexually reproducing species both parents contribute genes to offspring, the genetic information is reshuffled every generation. Such recombination does not in itself change allele frequencies (i.e., cause evolution). However, it does produce the whole array of genetic combinations, which natural selection can then act upon. In fact, we've shown how the reshuffling of chromosomes during meiosis can produce literally trillions of gene combinations, making every human being genetically unique (see p. 65).

---

*The abbreviation m.y. stands for "million years."

Natural Selection Acts on Variation

See Virtual Lab 2, section I, for an example of how selection operates variation within populations.

The evolutionary factors just discussed—mutation, gene flow, genetic drift, and recombination—interact to produce variation and to distribute genes within and between populations. But there is no long-term *direction* to any of these factors. How, then, do populations adapt? The answer is natural selection. Natural selection provides directional change in allele frequency relative to *specific environmental factors*. If the environment changes, then the selection pressures change as well. Such a functional shift in allele frequencies is what we mean by *adaptation*. If there are long-term environmental changes in a consistent direction, then allele frequencies should also shift gradually each generation. If sustained for many generations, the results can be dramatic.

In Chapter 2, we discussed the general principles underlying natural selection and gave some nonhuman examples. Physical anthropology is, of course, centrally concerned with human evolution, and therefore it's more relevant to show how natural selection operates in *human* populations. The best documented example of natural selection in humans involves hemoglobin S, an altered form of hemoglobin that results from a point mutation in the gene that produces the hemoglobin beta chain (see p. 58). As you've already learned, if an individual inherits this allele (Hb^S) from both parents, he or she will suffer the severe manifestations of sickle-cell anemia. Even with aggressive medical treatment, life expectancy in the United States today is less than 45 years for patients with sickle-cell anemia. Worldwide, sickle-cell anemia causes an estimated 100,000 deaths each year, and in the United States, approximately 40,000 to 50,000 individuals, mostly of African descent, suffer from this disease.

Apparently, Hb^S is a mutation that occurs occasionally in all human populations, but the allele usually remains relatively rare. In some populations, however, Hb^S is more common, and this is especially true in western and central Africa, where its frequency approaches 20 percent. The frequency of the allele is also moderately high in parts of Greece and India (Fig. 4–15). Given the devastating effects of Hb^S in homozygotes, how do we explain its higher prevalence in some populations? The answer to this question lies in malaria, a serious infectious disease that has exerted enormous selective pressures in the past and continues to do so today. Malaria currently kills an estimated 1 to 3 million people worldwide annually. It is caused by one of several protozoan parasites belonging to the genus *Plasmodium*. These parasites are in turn transmitted to humans by mosquitoes.

Very briefly, after an infected mosquito bite, plasmodial parasites invade red blood cells, where they obtain the oxygen they need for reproduction (Fig. 4–16). The consequences of this infection to the human host include fever, chills, headache, nausea, vomiting, and, frequently, death. In parts of western and central Africa, where malaria is always present, the burden of the disease is borne by children, with as many as 50 to 75 percent of 2- to 9-year-olds being afflicted.

See Virtual Lab 2, section III, for a presentation of the relationship between malaria and sickle cell anemia.

The geographical correlation between malaria and the distribution of the sickle-cell allele is indirect evidence of a biological relationship (Figs. 4–15 and 4–17). Further confirmation was provided by British biologist A. C. Allison in the 1950s. Allison's study showed that individuals with one Hb^S allele (i.e., those with sickle-cell trait) and thus some hemoglobin S had greater resistance to malaria than the homozygous "normals." It was subsequently demonstrated that heterozygotes resist infection because their red blood cells provide a less conducive environment for the parasite to reproduce. Thus, in environments where the prevalence of malaria is always high, individuals with sickle-cell trait have higher reproductive success than those with normal hemoglobin. Those with sickle-cell anemia, of course, have the lowest reproductive success, since without treatment, most die before reaching adulthood.

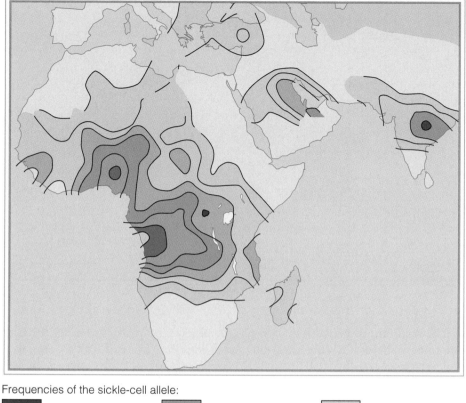

FIGURE 4–15 A frequency map of the sickle-cell distribution in the Old World.

Frequencies of the sickle-cell allele:

■ Greater than .14	■ .08–.10	■ .02–.04
■ .12–.14	■ .06–.08	□ .00–.02
■ .10–.12	■ .04–.06	

FIGURE 4–16 The life cycle of the parasite that causes malaria.

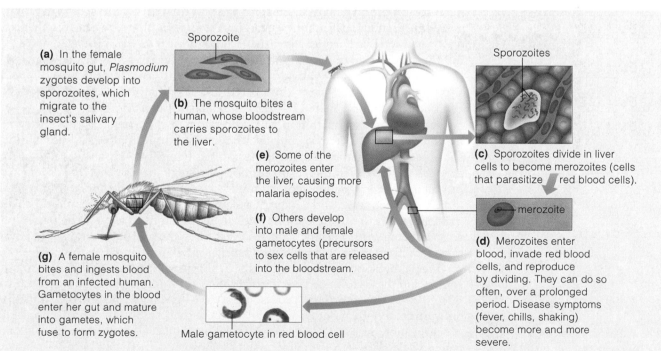

(a) In the female mosquito gut, *Plasmodium* zygotes develop into sporozoites, which migrate to the insect's salivary gland.

Sporozoite

(b) The mosquito bites a human, whose bloodstream carries sporozoites to the liver.

Sporozoites

(c) Sporozoites divide in liver cells to become merozoites (cells that parasitize red blood cells).

(e) Some of the merozoites enter the liver, causing more malaria episodes.

(f) Others develop into male and female gametocytes (precursors to sex cells that are released into the bloodstream.

merozoite

(d) Merozoites enter blood, invade red blood cells, and reproduce by dividing. They can do so often, over a prolonged period. Disease symptoms (fever, chills, shaking) become more and more severe.

(g) A female mosquito bites and ingests blood from an infected human. Gametocytes in the blood enter her gut and mature into gametes, which fuse to form zygotes.

Male gametocyte in red blood cell

FIGURE 4–17 Malaria distribution in the Old World.

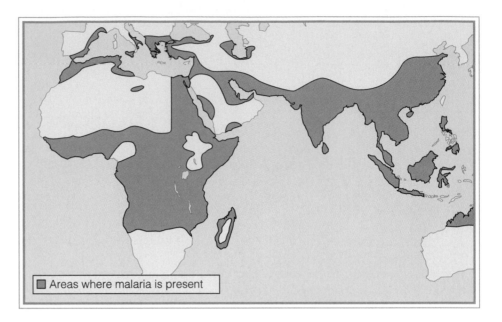

☐ Areas where malaria is present

The relationship between malaria and hemoglobin S provides one of the best examples we have of natural selection in contemporary humans. In this case, natural selection has favored the heterozygous phenotype, thus increasing the frequency of *Hb^S*, an allele that in homozygotes causes severe disease and early death.

Review of Genetics and Evolutionary Factors

Beginning in Chapter 3 with a discussion of the molecular and cellular bases of heredity, we proceeded in this chapter to show how such genetic information is passed from individuals in one generation to those in the next. In this chapter, we've also reviewed evolutionary theory and its current applications, emphasizing the crucial role of natural selection. These different levels—molecular, cellular, individual, and populational—are different aspects of evolution, and they're all related and highly integrated in a way that can eventually produce evolutionary change. A step-by-step example will make this clear.

We begin with a situation in which everyone in the population has the same hemoglobin type; therefore, initially no variation for this trait exists, and without some source of new variation, evolution isn't possible. How does this gene change? We have seen that a substitution of a single base in the DNA sequence can alter the code significantly enough to alter the protein product and ultimately the phenotype of the individual. Consider that in each generation such an incident occurs in one or a few individuals. For a mutated allele to be passed on to succeeding offspring, the gametes must carry the alteration. Any new mutation, therefore, must be transmitted during sex cell formation.

Once a mutation has occurred in the DNA, it will be packaged into chromosomes, and these chromosomes in turn will assort during meiosis to be passed to offspring. The results of this process are seen by looking at phenotypes (traits) in individuals, and the mode of inheritance is described simply by Mendel's principle of segregation. In other words, if our initial individual has a mutation in only one paired allele on a set of homologous chromosomes, there will be a 50 percent chance of passing this chromosome (with the new mutation) to an offspring.

But what does all this activity have to do with *evolution?* To repeat an earlier definition, evolution is a change in allele frequency in a *population* from one generation to the next. The key point here is that we are now looking at entire groups of individuals, or populations, and it's populations that may change over time.

We know whether allele frequencies have changed in a population where sickle-cell hemoglobin is found by ascertaining the percentage of individuals with the sickling allele (Hb^S) versus those with the normal allele (Hb^A). If the relative proportions of these alleles alter with time, evolution has occurred. In addition to discovering that evolution has occurred, it's important to know why. Several possibilities arise. First, we know that the only way the new allele Hb^S could have arisen is by mutation, and we have shown how this process can happen in a single individual. This change, however, is not yet really an evolutionary one, for in a relatively large population, the alteration of one individual's genes will not significantly alter allele frequencies of the entire population. Somehow, this new allele must *spread* in the population.

One way this can happen is in a small population, where mutations in one or just a few individuals and their offspring may indeed alter the overall frequency quite quickly. This case would be representative of genetic drift. As discussed, drift acts in small populations, where random factors may cause significant changes in allele frequency. With a small population size, there is not likely to be a balance of factors affecting individual survival or reproduction. Consequently, some alleles may be completely removed from the population, while others may become established as the only allele present at that particular locus (and are said to be "fixed" in the population).

In the course of human evolution, drift has probably played a significant role at times, and it's important to remember that at this microevolutionary level, drift and/or gene flow can (and will) produce evolutionary change, even in the absence of natural selection. However, directional evolutionary trends could only have been sustained by *natural selection*. The way this has worked in the past and still operates today (as in sickle-cell) is through differential reproduction. That is, individuals who carry a particular allele or combination of alleles produce more offspring than other individuals with different alleles. Hence, they cause the frequency of the new allele in the population to increase slowly from generation to generation. When this process is compounded over hundreds of generations for numerous loci, the result is significant evolutionary change. The levels of organization in the evolutionary process are summarized in Table 4–4.

TABLE 4–4 Levels of Organization in the Evolutionary Process

EVOLUTIONARY FACTOR	LEVEL	EVOLUTIONARY PROCESS	TECHNIQUE OF STUDY
Mutation	DNA	Storage of genetic information; ability to replicate; influences phenotype by production of proteins	Biochemistry, electron microscope, recombinant DNA
Mutation	Chromosomes	A vehicle for packaging and transmitting genetic material (DNA)	Light or electron microscope
Recombination (sex cells only)	Cell	The basic unit of life that contains the chromosomes and divides for growth and for production of sex cells	Light or electron microscope
Natural selection	Organism	The unit, composed of cells, that reproduces and which we observe for phenotypic traits	Visual study, biochemistry
Drift, gene flow	Population	A group of interbreeding organisms; changes in allele frequencies between generations; it's the population that evolves	Statistical analysis

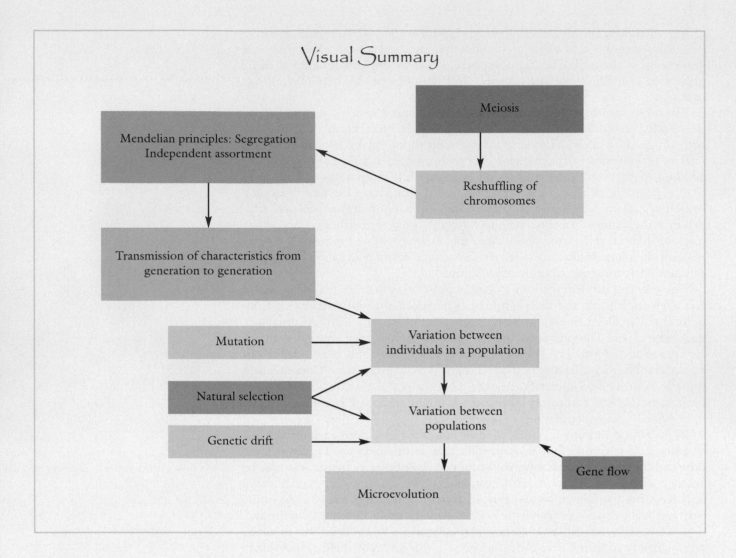

Visual Summary

Summary

We have seen how Gregor Mendel discovered the principles of segregation, independent assortment, and dominance and recessiveness by conducting experiments on garden peas. Although the field of genetics progressed dramatically during the twentieth century, the concepts first put forth by Gregor Mendel remain as the basis of our current knowledge of how traits are inherited.

Basic Mendelian principles are applied to the study of the various modes of inheritance we are familiar with today. We have presented three of these in some detail: autosomal dominant, autosomal recessive, and X-linked recessive. The most important factor in all the Mendelian modes of inheritance is the role of segregation of chromosomes, and the alleles they carry, during meiosis. Although our understanding of human inheritance has virtually exploded in the last 50 years, the very foundation of our knowledge rests on the basic rules as set forth by Gregor Mendel almost 150 years ago.

Building on fundamental nineteenth-century contributions by Charles Darwin and his contemporaries and the rediscovery in 1900 of Mendel's work, further refinements later in the twentieth century added to contemporary evolutionary thought. In particular, the combination of natural selection with Mendel's principles of inheritance and experimental evidence concerning the nature of mutation have all been synthesized into a modern understanding of evolutionary change, appropriately termed the Modern Synthesis. In this, the central contemporary theory of evolution, evolutionary change is seen as a two-stage process. The first stage is the production and redistribution of variation. The second stage is the process whereby natural selection acts on the accumulated genetic variation.

Mutation is crucial to all evolutionary change because it's the only source of completely new genetic material (which increases variation). In addition, the factors of recombination, genetic drift, and gene flow redistribute variation within individuals (recombination), within populations (genetic drift), and between populations (gene flow).

Natural selection is the central determining factor influencing the long-term direction of evolutionary change. How natural selection works can best be explained as differential reproductive success—in other words, how successful

For Further Thought

1. Give some examples of how selection, gene flow, genetic drift, and mutation have acted on populations or species in the past. Try to think of at least one human and one nonhuman example. Why do you think genetic drift might be important today to endangered species?

2. Try to construct a pedigree chart for your family regarding some Mendelian trait. Try to include your siblings (if any), your parents, and your grandparents. If you are really ambitious, also consider aunts, uncles, and cousins.

Go to the book website at **http://www.anthropology.wadsworth.com** for resources to help you explore these questions further. Click on "For Further Thought" for this chapter.

individuals are in leaving offspring to succeeding generations. To more fully illustrate the mechanics of evolutionary change through natural selection, comprehensive and well-understood examples from other organisms are most helpful. The detailed history of the evolutionary spread of the sickle-cell allele provides the best-documented example of natural selection among recent human populations. It must be remembered that evolution is an integrated process, and this chapter concluded with a discussion of how the various evolutionary factors can be integrated into a single, comprehensive view of evolutionary change.

Questions for Review

1. Why do you think the existence of different alleles at many genetic loci is important for evolution?
2. Explain dominance and recessiveness. In what ways are these concepts misunderstood by the general public? How are these concepts changing in the views of geneticists?
3. If two people with blood type A, both with the *AO* genotype, have children, what *proportion* of these children would be expected to have blood type O? Why? Can these two parents have a child with AB blood? Why or why not?
4. Can you think of some polygenic traits not mentioned in this chapter? How does the inheritance of polygenic characteristics differ from the inheritance of Mendelian traits?
5. We mentioned in this chapter that with regard to polygenic traits, inheritance at the individual loci that influence such traits still follow Mendelian principles. Explain why and give an example.
6. What role does genetic variation play in evolution? Where does variation come from? Try to discuss the source of variation as something *completely new* in a

species and also as it is introduced into one of many populations *within* a species.
7. How has natural selection acted to increase the frequency of HB^S, the allele that causes sickle-cell anemia in homozygotes, in some populations? In other words, how can selection favor a recessive allele that is harmful in homozygotes?

Suggested Further Reading

Cummings, Michael R. 2000. *Human Heredity. Principles and Issues.* 5th ed. Pacific Grove, CA: Brooks/Cole.
Little, Peter. 1999. "The Book of Genes." *Nature* 402: 467–468.
Ridley, Mark. 1993. *Evolution.* Cambridge, MA: Blackwell Scientific.
Ridley, Matt. 2000. *Genome.* New York: Perennial.
Wake, David B. 2001. "Evolution: Speciation in the Round." *Nature* 409: 299–300.

Online Anthropology Resource Center

Go to the Anthropology Resource Center at **http://www.anthropology.wadsworth.com** for a wealth of online resources, including a companion website for your text that provides study aids such as self-quizzes for each chapter and a practice final exam, as well as links to anthropology websites and information on the latest theories and discoveries in the field. Also, check out InfoTrac College Edition®, your online library that offers full-length articles from thousands of scholarly and popular publications. Just click on the InfoTrac button at the companion website and use the passcode that came with your book.

Molecular Applications in Forensic Anthropology

No doubt, you know of instances where DNA analysis is used in forensic circumstances to identify a criminal. Likewise, you've no doubt heard of cases where mistakenly imprisoned individuals have been released when DNA evidence cleared them of criminal involvement—sometimes several years following conviction.

Since the 1980s, molecular applications have greatly assisted law enforcement agencies. In fact, immediately following development of the polymerase chain reaction (PCR) technique in the mid-1980s, the first widely applied examples of precise DNA genotyping were for forensic purposes.

Forensic anthropologists, from the outset, have been central contributors in these molecular applications. It must be emphasized that forensic science is a coordinated *team effort*. Thus, forensic anthropologists work in close collaboration with law enforcement agencies, medical examiners, forensic odontologists (i.e., dental experts), entomologists, and DNA identification laboratories.

The standard methods used in these laboratories include PCR and DNA fingerprinting (see pp. 67 and 68). Both mitochondrial and nuclear DNA are used to identify individuals. PCR makes it possible to reliably identify individuals from exceedingly small samples of tissue (e.g., blood, semen, teeth, and bone). Thus, even in cases where the remains have deteriorated badly over time or were crushed or burned in a mass disaster, proper collection and precise laboratory controls can often yield useful results. For example, a person missing for several years can be identified from just a small scrap of bone if the DNA fingerprint can be matched with that of a close relative. Anthropologists provide crucial assistance in the identification process, because initial analysis of physical attributes of the skeleton (e.g., age, sex, stature) can greatly narrow the range of possibilities (so that fewer potential relatives need to be tested for a match). At present, existing data banks are insufficient to accomplish the task without such initial corroborating clues.

To successfully make a positive genetic ID, the DNA must be (1) extracted (from bone, by cutting a small section with a saw); (2) purified to remove chemicals that interfere with PCR; (3) amplified (i.e., replicated millions of times by PCR); and (4) sequenced (usually by use of "fingerprinting"—that is, characterizing for particular chromosomal regions, unique repeated arrays of small DNA segments).

One renowned case of DNA identification from skeletal remains was that of the last tsar of Russia, Nicholas II. As is well known, Nicholas and all his immediate family were executed in July 1918. The bodies were long thought to

have been completely destroyed, but the true location of the graves of the Russian royal family was discovered several years ago. Only after the fall of communism, however, were the skeletal remains finally exhumed in 1991.

A team, led by the late William Maples, was permitted to examine the remains and attempt to establish the exact identities of all the individuals (more than 1,000 bone fragments were mixed together) (Fig. 1). Anthropological analysis of the skeletons suggested that five members of the royal family were represented among the remains (Tsar Nicholas, Empress Alexandra, and their three oldest daughters). Agreeing with documents from the time of the execution, the two youngest children (Anastasia and Alexei) were missing (because they had been buried elsewhere).

In 1992 the first DNA testing was done on small bone samples taken to England. Molecular results agreed with the anthropological findings (Gill et al., 1994), except that some lingering questions remained concerning the identification of the tsar's mtDNA. To provide absolute confirmation, additional bone and tooth samples were taken and further DNA analysis was done at the Armed Forces DNA

FIGURE 1 Forensic anthropologist Bill Maples examining the cranium of Tsar Nicholas II (inset).

Identification Laboratory (AFDIL) in Washington, D.C. Moreover, because the DNA thought to come from the tsar's skeleton showed a highly unusual pattern, permission was given by the Russian Orthodox Church to exhume the body of his younger brother (who had died in 1899) and compare his DNA with that taken from the presumed tsar's skeleton. The results showed beyond any doubt that the skeleton was indeed that of the executed tsar, Nicholas II (Ivanov et al., 1996).

Scenes of mass disaster (such as fires, earthquakes, explosions, or plane crashes) are another context in which both forensic anthropology and DNA analysis play crucial roles. To respond quickly and effectively to such disasters, the federal government has organized regional disaster reaction work groups called DMORT (Disaster Mortuary Operational Response Team). A forensic anthropologist is included in all these teams, and sometimes the anthropologist is the team leader. In fact, following the tragic events of September 11, 2001, Paul Sledzik (a forensic anthropologist at the Armed Forces Institute of Pathology) was the DMORT leader at the Pennsylvania crash site of United Flight 93.

During the recovery, the team followed strict procedures in the collection and analysis of the human remains and other evidence. It must be remembered that in addition to a site of immense personal tragedy, this was also a crime scene. Accordingly, as in all such circumstances, close interaction with law enforcement agencies is essential; in this case, the FBI led the criminal investigation. (For a detailed documentation of the procedures followed at the Flight 93 crash site, see the website provided with other sources at the end of this feature.)

Forensic anthropologists also assisted in the recovery of human remains at the World Trade Center. Here, procedures differed, as millions of tons of debris had to be sifted through; and the few human remains that were present were extremely fragmentary and severely burned.

In Pennsylvania, although broken and burned, the remains of victims were much more complete. Thus, the DMORT staff could select the material most likely to provide the best DNA results. Moreover, clothing and other personal items found with the remains could provide an exact identification (which could be further corroborated through basic anthropological observations of age, sex, etc.). Where identification was unambiguous, DNA analysis was not required.

From the World Trade Center, few remnants of associated clothing or personal effects were found. Moreover, since the bone and tooth fragments were so small and were often altered by intense heat, few of the standard anthropological skeletal observations were possible. As a result, basically all the presumed bone and dental remains are being analyzed for DNA.

Major tragedies leading to large numbers of civilian deaths also occur during wars and ethnic conflicts. Forensic anthropologists are often asked to assist in these circumstances as well, since victims of atrocities sometimes are left in mass graves. When possible, these graves are intensively investigated, often revealing decomposed bodies as well as partial skeletons. Such work has sadly become more commonplace, keeping pace with the increase in brutality seen throughout the world. (Consider, for example, the tragedies of Argentina, Guatemala, Rwanda, and the Balkans; and as of this writing, a few teams are conducting recovery efforts in Iraq—and more are on the way.)

Recovery efforts are concerned first with identifying the victims. Successful personal identification allows family members to learn the fate of missing loved ones. Second, the evidence obtained can be used in legal proceedings in which perpetrators are tried for genocide or other crimes against humanity (such trials are now being conducted in Africa and at the World Court).

As with the circumstances at the 9/11 disaster sites, DNA analyses are sometimes required; but in other cases, accurate personal identification can be done more quickly and more economically using standard anthropological criteria and from associated personal items (the latter corroborated by relatives of the deceased). Such methods are especially important in very poor, war-torn regions (where large-scale DNA testing is not affordable) (Baraybar, 2004). However, international agencies have recently stepped up aid; for example, in Bosnia and Herzegovina, the International Commission on Missing Persons is overseeing large-scale DNA testing (Drukier et al., 2004; Klanowski, 2004). An analogous approach is also being implemented in the United States to identify bodies of hundreds of immigrants who died while trying to cross the Mexican-U.S. border (Baker and Baker, 2004).

In addition to the field collection and analysis contexts discussed above, forensic anthropologists are also becoming directly involved in molecular research in the laboratory. Several anthropologists working in cooperation with molecular biologists are investigating how to refine procedures to make DNA sequencing more accurate (Kontanis, 2004; Latham et al., 2004). For example, at AFDIL, anthropologist Heather Thew is a DNA analyst. Here she is directly involved in all steps of sample preparation and molecular analysis. Much of her work concerns the mtDNA testing of the remains of military personnel—some of whom have been missing since World War II; thus, the physical remains consist only of very fragmented bone pieces. Thew credits her anthropology training in human skeletal analysis and modern population biology as providing her with both a solid background and specialized skills that allow her to better perform many of the laboratory duties at AFDIL (Fig. 2.).

Molecular Applications in Forensic Anthropology (continued)

Craig King, Armed Forces DNA Identification Laboratory

FIGURE 2 DNA analyst Heather Thew prepares a bone sample at the Armed Forces DNA Identification Laboratory.

Sources

Baker, Lori E., and Erich Baker. 2004. "Reuniting Families: Using Phenotypic and Genotypic Forensic Evidence to Identify Unknown Immigrant Remains." Paper presented at Annual Meetings of the American Academy of Forensic Sciences, Dallas, February 2004.

Druikier, Piotr. 2004. "Anthropological Review of Remains from Srebrenica as Part of the Identification Process." Paper presented at Annual Meetings of the American Academy of Forensic Sciences, Dallas, February 2004.

Flight 93 Morgue Protocols. See website: www.dmort. org/FilesforDownload/Protocol_flight_93.pdf

Gill, P., P.L. Ivanov, C. Kimpton, et al. 1994. "Identification of the Remains of the Romanov Family by DNA Analysis." *Nature Genetics* 6:130–135.

Ivanov, Pavel L., Mark J. Wadhams, Rhonda K. Roby, et al. 1996. "Mitochondrial DNA Sequence Heteroplasmy in the Grand Duke of Russia Georgij Romanov Establishes the Authenticity of the Remains of Tsar Nicholas II." *Nature Genetics* 12:417–420.

Klanowski, Eva. 2004. "Exhumation—and What After? ICMP Model in Bosnia and Herzegovina." Paper presented at Annual Meetings of the American Academy of Forensic Sciences, Dallas, February 2004.

Kotanis, Elias J. 2004. "Using Real-Time PCR Quantifications of Nuclear and Mitochondrial DNA to Develop Degradation Profiles for Various Tissues." Paper presented at Annual Meetings of the American Academy of Forensic Sciences, Dallas, February 2004.

Latham, Krista E. 2004. "The Ability to Amplify Skeletal DNA After Heat Exposure Due to Maceration." Paper presented at Annual Meetings of the American Academy of Forensic Sciences, Dallas, February 2004.

Macroevolution: Processes of Vertebrate and Mammalian Evolution

5

A human chromosome
© Biophoto Associates / Photo Researchers, Inc.

Introduction

See the following sections of the CD-ROM for topics covered in this chapter: Virtual Lab 7, sections I and II.

Many people view paleontology as a pretty boring endeavor, practiced by overly serious academics. But have you ever been to a natural history museum—or perhaps to one of the larger, more elaborate toy stores? If so, you may have seen a full-size mock-up of *Tyrannosaurus,* one that might even have moved its head and arms and screamed threateningly. These displays are usually encircled by flocks of running, shouting children. The children seem anything but bored.

The study of the history of life on earth is full of mystery and adventure. The bits and pieces of fossils are the tantalizing remains of once living, breathing animals (some of which *were* large and dangerous). Searching for these fossils in remote corners of the globe is not a task for the faint of heart. Piecing together the tiny clues and ultimately reconstructing what *Tyrannosaurus* (or, for that matter, a small, 50-million-year-old primate) looked like and how it might have behaved is a task akin to detective work. Sure, it can be serious; but it can also be a lot of fun.

In this chapter, we review the evolution of vertebrates and, more specifically, of mammals. It is important to understand these more general aspects of evolutionary history to place our species in its proper biological context. *Homo sapiens* is but one of millions of species that have evolved. Moreover, humans have been around for just an instant in the vast expanse of time that life has existed. Where do humans fit into this long and complex story of life on earth?

In addition to the broad trends of evolutionary history, we also discuss some contemporary issues relating to evolutionary theory. In particular, we emphasize concepts that relate to large-scale evolutionary processes, that is, *macroevolution* (in contrast to the microevolutionary focus of Chapter 4). The fundamental perspectives reviewed here concern geological history, principles of classification, and modes of evolutionary change, and they serve as a basis for topics covered throughout much of the remainder of the text.

The Human Place in the Organic World

There are millions of species living today; if we were to include microorganisms, the total would likely exceed tens of millions. And if we then added in the vast multitudes of species that are now extinct, the total would be staggering—perhaps hundreds of millions!

How do we deal with all this diversity scientifically? Biologists, being human, approach complexity by attempting to simplify it. One way to do this is to construct a system of **classification** that organizes diversity into categories to reduce complexity and at the same time indicate evolutionary relationships.

Organisms that move about and ingest food (but do not photosynthesize, as do plants) are called animals. More precisely, the multicelled animals are placed within the group called the **Metazoa** (Fig. 5–1). Within the Metazoa there are more than 20 major groups termed *phyla* (*sing.,* phylum). One of these phyla is

classification In biology, the ordering of organisms into categories, such as orders, families, and genera, to show evolutionary relationships.

Metazoa Multicellular animals; a major division of the animal kingdom.

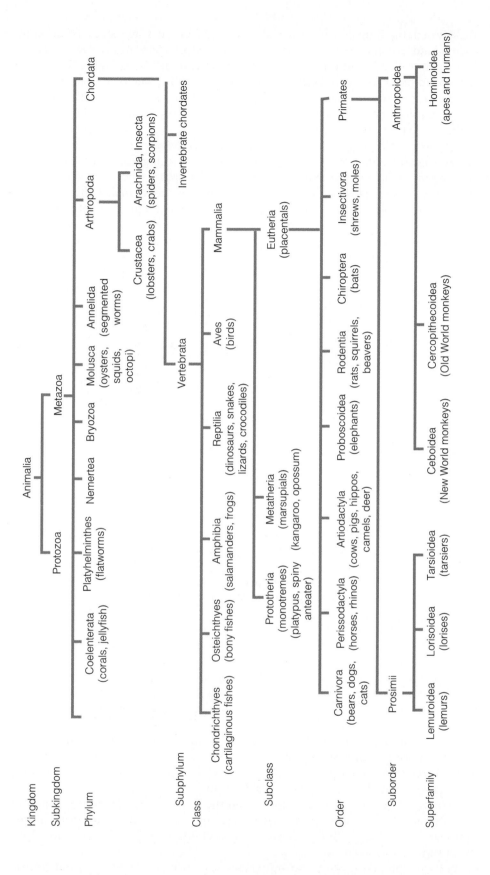

FIGURE 5–1 Classification chart, modified from Linnaeus. All animals are placed in certain categories based on structural similarities. Not all members of categories are shown. For example, there are up to 20 orders of placental mammals (8 are depicted). A more comprehensive classification of the primate order is presented in Chapter 6.

Chordata The phylum of the animal kingdom that includes vertebrates.

vertebrates Animals with segmented boney spinal columns; includes fishes, amphibians, reptiles, birds, and mammals.

the **Chordata,** animals with a nerve cord, gill slits (at some stage of development), and a supporting cord along the back. Most chordates today are **vertebrates,** so called because they have a vertebral column. Vertebrates also have a developed brain and paired sensory structures for sight, smell, and balance.

The vertebrates themselves are subdivided into six classes: bony fishes, cartilaginous fishes, amphibians, reptiles, birds, and mammals. We will discuss mammalian classification later in this chapter.

By categorizing organisms into increasingly narrow groupings, this hierarchical arrangement not only organizes diversity into categories, but also makes statements about evolutionary and genetic relationships between species and groups of species. Dividing placental mammals into orders makes the statement that, for example, all carnivores (Carnivora) are more closely related to each other than they are to any species placed in another order. Consequently, bears, dogs, and cats are more closely related to each other than they are to cattle, pigs, or deer (Artiodactyla). At each succeeding level (suborder, superfamily, family, subfamily, genus, and species), finer distinctions are made between categories until, at the species level, only those animals that can interbreed and produce viable offspring are included.

Principles of Classification

Before we go any further, we need to discuss the basis of animal classification. The field that specializes in establishing the rules of classification is called *taxonomy*. Organisms are classified first, and most traditionally, on the basis of physical similarities. Such was the basis of the first systematic classification devised by Linnaeus in the eighteenth century (see Chapter 2).

Today, basic physical similarities are still considered a good starting point. But for similarities to be useful, they *must* reflect evolutionary descent. For example, the bones of the forelimb of all terrestrial air-breathing vertebrates (tetrapods) are so similar in number and form (Fig. 5–2) that the obvious explanation for the striking resemblance is that all four kinds of air-breathing vertebrates ultimately derived their forelimb structure from a common ancestor.

The way such seemingly major evolutionary modifications in structure could occur likely begins with only relatively minor genetic changes. For example, recent research shows that forelimb development in all vertebrates is directed by just a few regulatory genes, what are called *Hox* genes (see p. 56) (Shublin et al., 1997; Riddle and Tabin, 1999). A few mutations among early vertebrates in certain *Hox* genes led to the basic limb plan seen in all subsequent vertebrates. Additional small mutations in these genes could produce the varied structures that make up the wing of a chicken, the flipper of a porpoise, or the upper limb of a human. You should recognize that *basic* genetic regulatory mechanisms are highly conserved in animals; that is, they have been maintained relatively unchanged for hundreds of millions of years. Like a musical score with a basic theme, small variations on the pattern can produce the different "tunes" that define one organism from another. This is the essential genetic foundation for most macroevolutionary change. Large anatomical modifications, therefore, don't always require major genetic rearrangements.

homologies Similarities between organisms based on descent from a common ancestor.

Structures that are shared by species on the basis of descent from a common ancestor are called **homologies**. Homologies alone are reliable indicators of evolutionary relationship. But we have to be careful not to draw hasty conclusions from superficial similarities.

For example, both birds and butterflies have wings, but they should not be grouped together on the basis of this single characteristic; butterflies (as insects) differ dramatically from birds in a number of other, even more fundamental

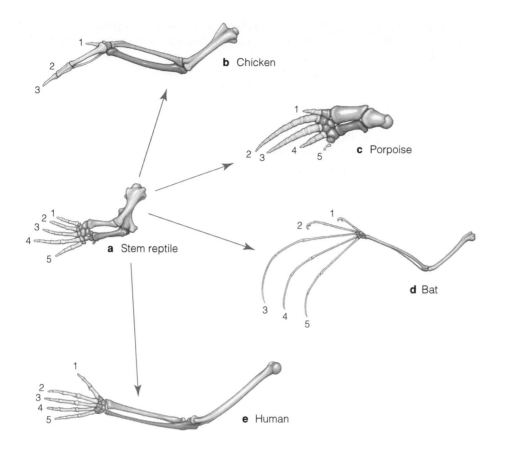

FIGURE 5–2 Homologies. The similarities in the forelimb bones of these animals can be most easily explained by descent from a common ancestor.

ways. (For example, birds have an internal skeleton, central nervous system, and four limbs; insects don't.)

What has happened in evolutionary history is that from quite distant ancestors, both butterflies and birds have developed wings *independently*. Thus, their (superficial) similarities are a product of separate evolutionary response to roughly similar functional demands; such similarities, based on independent functional adaptation and not on shared evolutionary descent, are called **analogies**. The process that leads to the development of analogies (also called analogous structures) such as wings in birds and butterflies is termed **homoplasy**. In the case of butterflies and birds, the homoplasy has occurred in evolutionary lines that share only very remote ancestry. Here, homoplasy has produced analogous structures separately from any homology. In some cases, however, homoplasy can occur in lineages that are more closely related (and which also share considerable homology as well). Examples of homoplasy in closely related lineages are evident among the primates (e.g., among New and Old World monkeys and also among the great apes; see Chapter 6).

CONSTRUCTING CLASSIFICATIONS AND INTERPRETING EVOLUTIONARY RELATIONSHIPS

There are two major approaches, or "schools," by which evolutionary biologists interpret evolutionary relationships and thus produce classifications. The first of these, called **evolutionary systematics,** is the more traditional approach, whereas the second approach, called **cladistics,** has emerged primarily in the last two decades. While aspects of both approaches are still used by most evolutionary biologists, in recent years cladistic methodologies have predominated among

analogies Similarities between organisms based strictly on common function with no assumed common evolutionary descent.

homoplasy (*homo,* meaning "same," and *plasy,* meaning "growth") The separate evolutionary development of similar characteristics in different groups of organisms.

evolutionary systematics A traditional approach to classification (and evolutionary interpretation) in which presumed ancestors and descendants are traced in time by analysis of homologous characters.

cladistics An approach to classification that attempts to make rigorous evolutionary interpretations based solely on analysis of certain types of homologous characters (those considered to be derived characters).

See Virtual Lab 7, section II, for a discussion of taxonomy and classification.

ancestral (primitive) Referring to characters inherited by a group of organisms from a remote ancestor and thus not diagnostic of groups (lineages) that diverged after the character first appeared.

clade A group of organisms sharing a common ancestor. The group includes the common ancestor and all descendants.

derived (modified) Referring to characters that are modified from the ancestral condition and thus *are* diagnostic of particular evolutionary lineages.

anthropologists. Indeed, one noted primate evolutionist recently commented that "virtually all current studies of primate phylogeny involve the methods and terminology" of cladistics (Fleagle, 1998, p. 1).

Before drawing distinctions between these two approaches, it is first helpful to note features shared by both evolutionary systematics and cladistics. First, both schools are interested in tracing evolutionary relationships and constructing classifications that reflect these relationships. Second, both schools recognize that organisms must be compared for specific features (called *characters*) and that some of these characters are more informative than others. And third (and deriving directly from the previous two points), both approaches focus exclusively on homologies.

However, there are also significant differences between these approaches in terms of how characters are chosen, which groups are compared, and how the results are interpreted and eventually incorporated into evolutionary schemes and classifications. The primary difference is that cladistics more explicitly and more rigorously defines the kinds of homologies that yield the most useful information. For example, at a very basic level, all life (except for some viruses) shares DNA as the molecule that underlies all organic processes. However, beyond inferring that all life most likely derives from a single origin (a most intriguing point), the presence of DNA tells us nothing further regarding more specific relationships among different kinds of life forms. To draw further conclusions, we need to look at particular characters that are shared by certain groups as the result of more recent ancestry.

This perspective emphasizes an important point: Some homologous characters are much more informative than others. We saw earlier that all terrestrial vertebrates share homologies in the number and basic arrangement of bones in the forelimb. Thus, while these similarities are broadly useful in showing that these large evolutionary groups (amphibians, reptiles, birds, and mammals) are all related through a distant ancestor, they do not provide information we can use to distinguish one from another (a reptile from a mammal, for example). These kinds of characters (also called traits) that are shared through such remote ancestry are said to be **primitive,** or **ancestral.** We prefer the term *ancestral* because it does not carry a negative connotation regarding the evolutionary value of the character in question. In biological anthropology, the term *primitive* or *ancestral* simply means that a character seen in two organisms is inherited in both of them from a distant ancestor.

In most circumstances, analysis of ancestral characters does not provide enough information to make accurate evolutionary interpretations regarding relationships between different groups. In fact, misinterpretation of ancestral characters can easily lead to quite inaccurate evolutionary conclusions. The traits that cladistics focuses on, and which are far more informative, are those that distinguish particular evolutionary lineages. Lineages that share a common ancestor are called a **clade,** giving the name *cladistics* to the field that seeks to identify and interpret these groups. The characters of interest are said to be **derived,** or **modified.** Thus, while the general ancestral bony pattern of the forelimb in land animals with backbones does not allow us to distinguish among them, the further modification in certain groups (as hooves, flippers, or wings, for instance) does.

A simplified example might help clarify the basic principles used in cladistic analysis. Figure 5–3a shows a hypothetical "lineage" of passenger vehicles. All of the "descendant" vehicles share a common ancestor, the prototype passenger vehicle. The first major division (I) is that differentiating passenger cars from trucks. The second split (i.e., diversification) is between luxury cars and sports cars (you could, of course, imagine many other subcategories). Modified (derived) traits that distinguish trucks from cars might include type of frame,

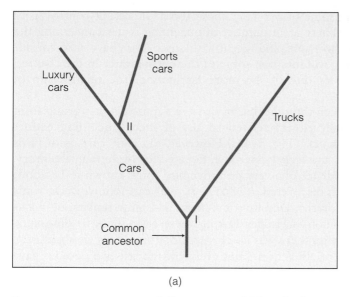

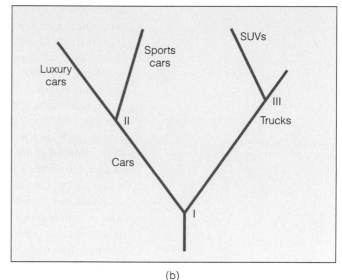

From a common ancestor of all passenger vehicles, the first major divergence is that between cars and trucks (I). A later divergence also occurs between luxury cars and sports cars (II). Derived features of each grouping ("lineage") appear only after its divergence from other groups (e.g., cargo beds are found only in trucks, cushioned suspension only in cars; likewise, only sports cars have a decorative racing stripe).

In this "tree," SUVs diverge from trucks, but like sports cars, they have a decorative racing stripe. This feature is a homoplasy and does *not* make SUVs sports cars. The message is that classifications based on just one characteristic that can appear independently in different groups can lead to an *incorrect* conclusion. *Note:* In (a), two clades are defined (I and II), while in (b), three clades (I, II, and III) are recognized.

suspension, wheel size, and, in some forms, an open cargo bed. Derived characters that might distinguish sports cars from luxury cars could include engine size and type, wheel base size, and a decorative racing stripe.

Now let us assume that you are presented with an "unknown" vehicle (i.e., one as yet unclassified). How do you decide what kind of vehicle it is? You might note such features as four wheels, a steering wheel, and a seat for the driver, but these are *ancestral* characters of all passenger vehicles (and ones found in the common ancestor). If, however, you note that the vehicle lacks a cargo bed and raised suspension (i.e., is not a truck) but has a racing stripe, you might conclude that it is a car, and more than that, a sports car (since it has a derived feature presumably of *only* that group).

All this seems fairly obvious, and you probably have noticed that this simple type of decision making characterizes much of human mental organization. Still, there are frequently complications that are not so obvious. What if you are presented with a sports utility vehicle (SUV) with a racing stripe (Fig. 5–3b)? SUVs are basically trucks, but the presence of the racing stripe could be seen as a homoplasy with sports cars. The lesson here is that we need to be careful, to look at several traits, to decide which are ancestral and which are derived, and finally to try to recognize the complexity (and confusion) introduced by homplasy.

The preceding example is useful up to a point. Because it concerns human inventions, the groupings possess characters that humans can add and delete in almost any combination. Naturally occurring organic systems are more limited in this respect. Any species can only possess characters that have been inherited from its ancestor or that have been subsequently modified (derived) from those shared with the ancestor. Thus, any modification in *any* species is constrained by that species' evolutionary legacy—that is, what the species starts out with.

Another example, one drawn from paleontological (fossil) evidence of actual organisms, can help clarify these points. Most people know something about

FIGURE 5–3 Evolutionary "trees" showing development of passenger vehicles.

dinosaur evolution, and some of you may know about the recent controversies surrounding this topic. There are a number of intriguing issues concerning the evolutionary history of dinosaurs, and recent fossil discoveries have shed considerable light on them. We will mention some of these issues later in the chapter, but here we will consider one of the more fascinating: the relationship of dinosaurs to birds.

Traditionally, it had been thought that birds were a quite distinct group from reptiles and not especially closely related to any of them (including extinct forms, such as the dinosaurs) (Fig. 5–4a). However, the early origins of birds were clouded in mystery and have been much debated for more than a century. In fact, the first fossil evidence of a very primitive bird (now known to be about 150 million years old) was discovered in 1861, just two years following Darwin's publication of *Origin of Species.* Despite some initial and quite remarkably accurate interpretations by Thomas Huxley linking these early birds to dinosaurs, most experts concluded that there was no close relationship. This view persisted through most of the twentieth century, but events of the last two decades have swung the consensus back to the hypothesis that birds *are* closely related to some dinosaurs. Two developments in particular have influenced this change of opinion: the remarkable discoveries in the 1990s from China, Madagascar, and elsewhere and the application of cladistic methods to the interpretation of these and other fossils.

Recent finds from Madagascar of chicken-size very primitive birds dated to 70–65 million years ago (m.y.a.) show an elongated second toe (similar, in fact, to that in the dinosaur *Velociraptor,* made infamous in the film *Jurassic Park*). Indeed, these primitive birds from Madagascar show many other similarities to *Velociraptor* and its close cousins, which together comprise a group of small- to medium-sized ground-living, carnivorous dinosaurs called **theropods.** Even more extraordinary finds have been unearthed recently in China, where embossed in fossilized sediments are traces of what were once *feathers!* For many researchers, these new finds have finally solved the mystery of bird origins, leading some experts to conclude that this evidence "shows that birds are not only *descended* from dinosaurs, they *are* dinosaurs (and reptiles)—just as humans are mammals, even though people are as different from other mammals as birds are from other reptiles" (Padian and Chiappe, 1998, p. 43) (Fig. 5–4b).

theropods Small- to medium-sized ground-living dinosaurs, dated to approximately 150 m.y.a. and thought to be related to birds.

FIGURE 5–4 Evolutionary relationships of birds and dinosaurs. (a) Traditional view, showing no close relationship. (b) Revised view, showing common ancestry of birds and dinosaurs.

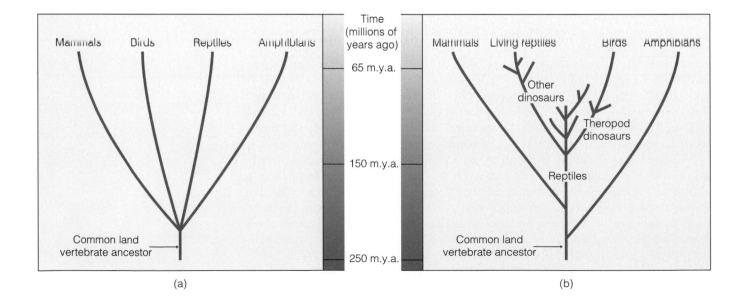

(a)   (b)

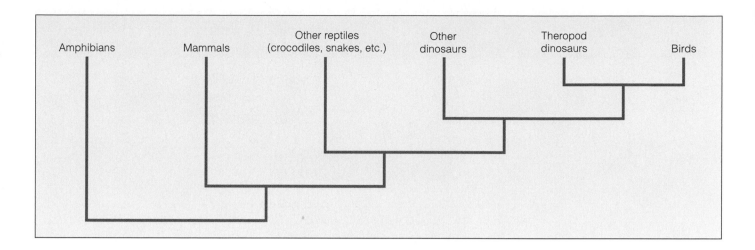

There are some doubters who remain concerned that the presence of feathers in dinosaurs (145–125 m.y.a.) might simply be a homoplasy (i.e., these creatures developed the trait independently from its appearance in birds). Certainly, the possibility of homoplasy must always be considered, as it can add considerably to the complexity of what seems like a straightforward evolutionary interpretation. Indeed, strict cladistic analysis assumes that homoplasy is not a common occurrence; if it were, perhaps no evolutionary interpretation could be very straightforward! In the case of the proposed relationship between some (theropod) dinosaurs and birds, the presence of feathers looks like an excellent example of a shared derived characteristic, which therefore *does* link the forms. Moreover, cladistic analysis emphasizes that several characteristics should be examined, since homoplasy might muddle an interpretation based on just one or two shared traits. In the bird-dinosaur case, several other characteristics further suggest their evolutionary relationship.

One last point needs to be mentioned. Traditional evolutionary systematics illustrates the hypothesized evolutionary relationships using a *phylogeny,* more properly called a **phylogenetic tree.** Strict cladistic analysis, however, shows relationships in a **cladogram** (Fig. 5–5). If you examine these charts, you will see some obvious differences. A phylogenetic tree incorporates the dimension of time, shown approximately in Figure 5–4. (Numerous other examples can be found in this and subsequent chapters.) A cladogram does not indicate time; all forms (fossil and modern) are indicated along one dimension. Phylogenetic trees usually attempt to make some hypotheses regarding ancestor-descendant relationships (e.g., theropods are ancestral to modern birds). Cladistic analysis (through cladograms) makes no attempt whatsoever to discern ancestor-descendant relationships. In fact, strict cladists are quite skeptical that the evidence really permits such specific evolutionary hypotheses to be scientifically confirmed (since there are many more extinct species than living ones).

In practice, most physical anthropologists (and other evolutionary biologists) utilize cladistic analysis to identify and assess the utility of traits and to make testable hypotheses regarding the relationships of groups of organisms. Moreover, they frequently extend this basic cladistic methodology to further hypothesize likely ancestor-descendant relationships shown relative to a time scale (i.e., in a phylogenetic tree). In this way, aspects of both traditional evolutionary systematics and cladistic analysis are combined to produce a more complete picture of evolutionary history.

FIGURE 5–5 Cladogram showing relationships of birds, dinosaurs, and other terrestrial vertebrates. Note that no time scale is utilized, and both living and fossil forms are shown along the same dimension (i.e., there is *no* indication of ancestor-descendant relationships).

phylogenetic tree A chart showing evolutionary relationships as determined by phylogenetic systematics. It contains a time component and implies ancestor-descendant relationships.

cladogram A chart showing evolutionary relationships as determined by cladistic analysis. It is based solely on interpretation of shared derived characters. No time component is indicated, and ancestor-descendant relationships are *not* implied.

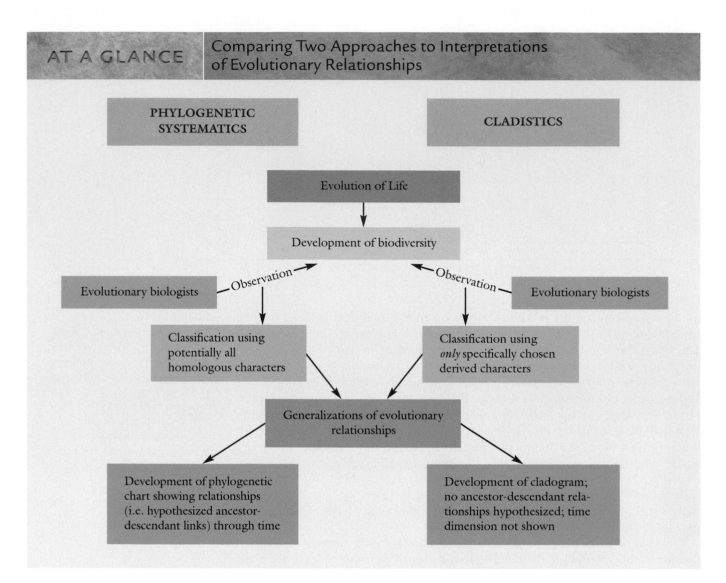

AT A GLANCE   Comparing Two Approaches to Interpretations of Evolutionary Relationships

PHYLOGENETIC SYSTEMATICS

CLADISTICS

Evolution of Life

Development of biodiversity

Evolutionary biologists —Observation→

←Observation— Evolutionary biologists

Classification using potentially all homologous characters

Classification using *only* specifically chosen derived characters

Generalizations of evolutionary relationships

Development of phylogenetic chart showing relationships (i.e. hypothesized ancestor-descendant links) through time

Development of cladogram; no ancestor-descendant relationships hypothesized; time dimension not shown

Definition of Species

Whether biologists are doing a cladistic or more traditional phylogenetic analysis, they are comparing groups of organisms—that is, different species, genera*, families, orders, and so forth. Fundamental to all these levels of classification is the most basic, the species.

It is appropriate, then, to ask, How do biologists define species? We addressed this issue briefly in Chapter 1, and there we used the most common definition, one that emphasizes interbreeding and reproductive isolation. While not the only definition of species (others will be discussed shortly), this view, called the **biological species concept** (Mayr, 1970), is the one preferred by most zoologists.

The best way to understand what species are is to consider how they come about in the first place—what Darwin called "origin of species." This most fundamental of macroevolutionary processes is called **speciation.** According to the biological species concept, the way new species are first produced involves some form of isolation. Picture a single species (baboons, for example) composed of

biological species concept A depiction of species as groups of individuals capable of fertile interbreeding, but reproductively isolated from other such groups.

speciation The process by which a new species evolves from a prior species. Speciation is the most basic process in macroevolution.

---

*Plural of *genus.*

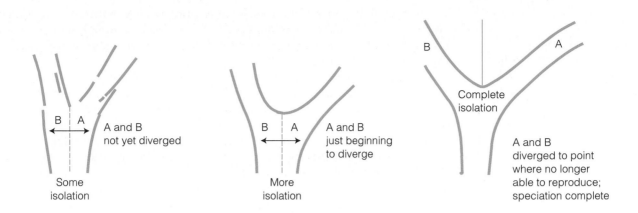

several populations distributed over a wide geographical area. Gene exchange between populations (gene flow) will be limited if a geographical barrier, such as an ocean or mountain range, effectively separates these populations. This extremely important form of isolating mechanism is called *geographical isolation.*

If one baboon population (A) is separated from another baboon population (B) by a mountain range, individual baboons of population A will not mate with individuals from B (Fig. 5–6). As time passes (perhaps hundreds or thousands of generations), genetic differences will accumulate in both populations. If population size is small, we can assume that genetic drift will also cause allele frequencies to change in both populations. Moreover, since drift is *random*, we would not expect the effects to be the same. Consequently, the two populations will begin to diverge genetically.

As long as gene exchange is limited, the populations can only become more genetically different with time. Moreover, further difference can be expected if the baboon groups are occupying slightly different habitats. These additional genetic differences would be incorporated through the process of natural selection. Certain individuals in population A would be most reproductively fit in their own environment, but would show less reproductive success in the environment occupied by population B. Thus, allele frequencies will shift further, and the results, again, will be divergent in the two groups.

With the cumulative effects of genetic drift and natural selection acting over many generations, the result will be two populations that—even if they were to come back into geographical contact—could no longer interbreed. More than just geographical isolation might now apply. There may, for instance, be behavioral differences that interfere with courtship—what we call *behavioral isolation.* Using our *biological* definition of species, we now would recognize two distinct species where initially only one existed.

Another related process that can contribute to the further differentiation of populations into incipient species concerns mate recognition. Sometimes called the **recognition species concept,** the crucial process again concerns reproduction (i.e., who is mating with whom) (Ridley, 1993).

Assume in our baboon example that some isolation has already occurred and that phenotypic (and genotypic) differences have begun to be established between two populations. In this situation, coloration patterns of faces or the size, location, coloration, or even smell of the estrous swelling might vary from group to group. If so, then a female from population A might not recognize a male from population B as an appropriate mate (and vice versa, of course). Natural selection would quickly favor such discrimination if hybrids were less reproductively successful than within-population crosses. Indeed, once such "selective breeding" became established, speciation would be accelerated considerably.

FIGURE 5–6 A speciation model. This model of speciation is called branching evolution, or cladogenesis.

recognition species concept A depiction of species in which the key aspect is the ability of individuals to identify members of their own species for purposes of mating (and to avoid mating with members of other species). In theory, this type of selective mating is a component of a species concept emphasizing mating and is therefore compatible with the biological species concept.

ecological species concept The concept that a species is a group of organisms exploiting a single niche. This view emphasizes the role of natural selection in separating species from one another.

Another definition of species focuses primarily on natural selection and emphasizes that speciation is the result of influences of varied habitats. Called the **ecological species concept,** a species is here defined as a group of organisms exploiting a single niche.

For each population, initially the habitats will vary slightly, and different phenotypes will be slightly more advantageous in each. For example, one population might be more arboreal and another more terrestrial; but there would not be an intermediate population equally successful on the ground and in the trees.

In recent years, the ecological species concept has attracted support from a number of evolutionary biologists, especially among physical anthropologists. While the biological species concept emphasizes gene flow and reproductive isolation, the ecological species concept stresses the role of natural selection. Clearly, our approach in this text has been to focus on the evolutionary contribution of natural selection; thus, the ecological species concept has much to offer here. Nevertheless, our understanding of species need not entail an either/or choice between the biological species concept and the ecological species concept. Some population isolation could indeed *begin* the process of speciation. The process might then be reinforced by natural selection through habitat differentiation as well as mate recognition.

A final approach that biologists use to define species is mostly a practical one. How can species be defined when neither reproductive isolation nor ecological separation can be clearly tested? This type of difficulty plagues the interpretation of fossil organisms but sometimes crops up in discussions of contemporary species as well. For example, Colin Groves, of the Australian National University, has advocated splitting many populations of primates into separate species (Groves, 2001). He utilizes a definition of species called the *phylogenetic species concept,* based on an identifiable parental pattern of ancestry.

For living species, characteristics that define a phylogenetic species could be phenotypic or more directly genotypic (identifying shared patterns in the karotype or in specific DNA sequences). For extinct groups, with a few notable exceptions (from which ancient DNA has been extracted), the *only* evidence available comes from phenotypic characters (see p. 120 for further discussion).

PROCESSES OF SPECIATION

Now that we have seen how species can be defined in somewhat varied ways, what are some of the more specific theories that evolutionary biologists have developed to account for *how* species originate? First, you should recognize that these hypotheses are quite abstract and thus difficult to test doing conventional field biology on contemporary species. Although rates of evolution vary widely among different groups of animals, the process is, by its very nature, a slow one. Some groups, such as fruit flies, members of genus *Drosophila*), seem to speciate especially slowly, taking a million years or more for a new species to be fully separate. The fastest rate of speciation in recent times may have occurred in freshwater fishes. Extreme isolation of cichlid fish populations has periodically occurred in African lakes, producing "explosive speciation" in just the last few thousand years (Seehausen, 2002). It must be emphasized, however, that such extreme isolation has likely never been a factor in the evolution of other vertebrates. Mammals seem to fall somewhere in between the slowly evolving fruit flies and the explosively speciating cichlids. As suggested by fossil evidence, it likely takes tens of thousands of years for speciation to occur in a free-ranging mammalian species.

allopatric Living in different areas; important in the divergence of closely related species from each other and from their shared ancestral species because it leads to reproductive isolation.

Given the constraints of field testing in such a slowly occurring phenomenon, biologists have hypothesized that speciation could occur in three different ways: by **allopatric** speciation, *parapatric* speciation, or *sympatric* speciation.

By far, the most widely accepted view of speciation emphasizes an allopatric pattern. This model requires complete reproductive isolation within a population, leading to the formation of an incipient species separated (geographically) from its ancestral population.

In parapatric speciation, only *partial* reproductive isolation is required, so that the ranges of the populations may be partially overlapping. In this situation hybrid zone would form in an area between the two partially separated populations. More complete separation could then occur through reinforcement of mate recognition and selective breeding.

Interestingly, in some areas of East Africa, there is good evidence that parapatric speciation might be currently (and slowly) taking place between populations of savanna baboons and hamadryas baboons. Long-term research by Jane Phillips-Conroy and Clifford Jolly has carefully documented hybrid individuals produced by the mating of savanna baboons with hamadryas baboons. Traditionally, these two types of baboons have been placed in separate species (savanna as *Papio cynocephalus* and hamadryas as *Papio hamadryas*). Yet, the hybrids appear quite functional and are *fertile* (Phillips-Conroy et al., 1992; Jolly, 1993). Thus, what we are likely seeing here is speciation in process—and probably following a parapatric pattern. Thus, we might regard these two types of baboons as incipient species. It is also possible that some mate recognition differentiation may be operating as well, since male-female interactions differ considerably between savanna and hamadryas baboons.

The third type of speciation proposed, sympatric speciation, is theorized to occur completely within one population with *no* necessary reproductive isolation. However, this form of speciation, while possible, is not well supported by contemporary evidence and is thus considered the least significant of the three models.

A fourth type of speciation has also been recognized and may have played a role in the evolution of certain species. In this pattern, called *instantaneous speciation,* chromosomal rearrangements occur (by chromosomal mutation), producing reproductive barriers immediately. As well documented in plants, this type of speciation can be very rapid, with varieties emerging with completely different numbers of chromosomes. Here, the process is one of multiplication of chromosome sets (due to mistakes in meiosis), producing a condition called *polyploidy.* While common in plants, such drastic reorganization of chromosome number is not a factor in speciation of animals, where polyploidy is always lethal. However, somewhat less dramatic chromosomal alterations, such as inversions and translocations (including fusions; see p. 151), could accelerate speciation in animals. Certainly, chromosomal alterations may be important in speciation, and some researchers have even suggested that such processes may be a central factor in macroevolution.

Nevertheless, demonstration in animals of the systematic influence of such large-scale mutation has been difficult. Indeed, theoretical models suggest that major mutational change could not *by itself* produce speciation in animals, but would require some further mechanism to help "fix" the genetic changes within populations. Inbreeding within small population segments has been suggested by some investigators as a possible mechanism that could reinforce rapid speciation by chromosomal mutation. Moreover, some theoretical support for this process (from data concerning relative amounts of within-species chromosomal variation) has been found in those species divided into small social groupings. And, perhaps of greatest interest, the best evidence of this type of patterning has been shown in species of horses and primates.

INTERPRETATION OF SPECIES AND OTHER GROUPS IN THE FOSSIL RECORD

Throughout much of this text, we will be using a variety of taxonomic terms for fossil primates (including fossil hominids); consequently, you will be introduced to such terms as *Proconsul, Sivapithecus, Australopithecus,* and *Homo.* Of course, *Homo* is still a living primate. But it is especially complex to make these types of designations from remains of animals that are long dead (and only partially preserved as skeletal remains). In these contexts, what do such names mean in evolutionary terms?

Our goal when applying species, genus, or other taxonomic labels to groups of organisms is to make meaningful biological statements about the variation that is present. When looking at populations of living or long-extinct animals, we certainly are going to see variation. The situation is true of *any* sexually reproducing organism because of the factors of recombination (see Chapter 3). As a result of recombination, each individual organism is a unique combination of genetic material, and the uniqueness is usually reflected to some extent in the phenotype.

In addition to such *individual variation,* we see other kinds of systematic variation in all biological populations. *Age changes* alter overall body size as well as shape in many mammals. One pertinent example for fossil hominoid studies is the change in number, size, and shape of teeth from deciduous (milk) teeth (only 20 present) to the permanent dentition (32 present). It would be an obvious error to differentiate fossil forms solely on the basis of such age-dependent criteria. If one individual were represented just by milk teeth and another (seemingly very different) individual were represented just by adult teeth, they easily could be different-aged individuals from the *same* population. Variation due to sex also plays an important role in influencing differences among individuals observed in biological populations. Differences in physical characteristics between males and females of the same species are called **sexual dimorphism,** and these can result in marked variation in body size and proportions in adults of the same species.

Recognition of Fossil Species   Keeping in mind all the types of variation present within interbreeding groups of organisms, the minimum biological category we would like to define in fossil primate samples is the *species.* As already defined (according to the biological species concept), a species is a group of interbreeding or potentially interbreeding organisms that is reproductively isolated from other such groups. In modern organisms, this concept is theoretically testable by observations of reproductive behavior. In animals long extinct, such observations are obviously impossible. Therefore, to get a handle on the interpretation of variation seen in fossil groups, we must refer to living animals.

We know without doubt that variation is present. The question is, What is its biological significance? Two immediate answers come to mind. Either the variation is accounted for by individual, age, and sex differences seen within every biological species (it is **intraspecific**) or the variation represents differences between reproductively isolated groups (it is **interspecific**). How do we decide which answer is correct? We clearly must refer to already defined groups where we can observe reproductive behavior—in other words, contemporary species.

If the amount of morphological variation observed in fossil samples is comparable to that seen today *within species of closely related forms,* then we should not "split" our sample into more than one species. We must, however, be careful in choosing modern analogues, for rates of morphological evolution vary widely among different groups of mammals. So, for example, when interpreting past primates, we do best comparing them with well-known species of modern primates.

Nevertheless, studies of such living groups have shown that delimiting exactly where species boundaries begin and end is often difficult. In dealing with extinct species, the uncertainties are even greater. In addition to the overlapping patterns of variation *over space,* variation also occurs *through time.* In other words, even more variation will be seen in **paleospecies,** since individuals may be separated by thousands or even millions of years. Applying strict Linnaean taxonomy to such a situation presents an unavoidable dilemma. Standard Linnaean classification, designed to take account of variation present at any given time, describes a static situation. However, when we deal with paleospecies, the time frame is

sexual dimorphism Differences in physical characteristics between males and females of the same species. For example, humans are slightly sexually dimorphic for body size, with males being taller, on average, than females of the same population.

intraspecific Within species; refers to variation seen within the same species.

interspecific Between species; refers to variation beyond that seen within the same species to include additional aspects seen between two different species.

paleospecies Species defined from fossil evidence, often covering a long time span.

expanded, and the situation can be dynamic (i.e., later forms might be different than earlier ones). In such a dynamic situation, taxonomic decisions (where to draw species boundaries) are ultimately going to be somewhat arbitrary.

It is precisely because the task of interpreting paleospecies is so difficult that paleoanthropologists have sought various practical solutions. Most researchers today define species using clusters of derived traits (identified cladistically). However, owing to the ambiguity of how many derived characters are required to identify a fully distinct species (as opposed to a subspecies), the frequent mixing of characters into novel combinations, and the nagging problem of homoplasy, there continues to be disagreement. A good deal of the dispute is driven by philosophical orientation. Exactly how much diversity should one *expect* among fossil hominids?

Researchers who assume that speciation occurred frequently during hominid evolution will tend to identify numerous species among samples of fossil hominid populations. (These paleoanthropologists are often called "splitters.") Alternatively, those who presume less frequent speciation will interpret more of the observed variation as *intraspecific,* leading to fewer hominid species identified, named, and eventually plugged into evolutionary schemes. (Paleoanthropologists adopting this approach are called "lumpers.") As we will see in succeeding chapters, debates of this sort pervade paleoanthropology—perhaps more so than any other branch of evolutionary biology.

Recognition of Fossil Genera   The next, more inclusive level of taxonomic classification, the **genus,** presents another problem. To have more than one genus, we obviously must have at least two species (reproductively isolated groups), and the species of one genus must differ in a basic way from the species of another genus. A genus is therefore defined as a group of species composed of members more closely related to each other than they are to species from any other genus.

Grouping species together into genera is largely a subjective procedure wherein the degree of relatedness becomes a relative judgment. One possible test for contemporary animals is to check for results of hybridization between individuals of different species—rare in nature but quite common in captivity. If two normally separate species interbreed and produce live, though not necessarily fertile, offspring, they probably are not too different genetically and should therefore be grouped together in the same genus. A well-known example of such a cross is horses with donkeys (*Equus caballus* x *Equus asinus*), which normally produces live but sterile offspring (mules).

As previously mentioned, we cannot perform breeding experiments with extinct animals, but another definition of genus becomes highly relevant. Species that are members of the same genus share the same broad adaptive zone. What this represents is a general ecological lifestyle more basic than the narrower ecological niches characteristic of individual species. This ecological definition of genus can be an immense aid in interpreting fossil primates. Teeth are the most frequently preserved parts, and they often can provide excellent general ecological inferences. Moreover, cladistic analysis (see pp. 111–115) also provides assistance in making judgments about evolutionary relationships. That is, members of the same genus should all share derived characters not seen in members of other genera.

As a final comment, we should point out that classification by genus is not always a straightforward decision. Indeed, the argument among primatologists over whether the chimpanzee and gorilla represent one genus (*Pan troglodytes, Pan gorilla*) or two different genera (*Pan troglodytes, Gorilla gorilla*) demonstrates that even with living, breathing animals, the choices are not always clear. For that matter, many current researchers (Wildman et al., 2003), pointing to the very close genetic similarities between humans and chimpanzees, would place both in the same genus (*Homo sapiens, Homo troglodytes*). When it gets this close to home, it is even more difficult to remain objective!

genus A group of closely related species.

Vertebrate Evolutionary History: A Brief Summary

geological time scale The organization of earth history into eras, periods, and epochs; commonly used by geologists and paleoanthropologists.

In addition to the staggering array of living and extinct life forms, biologists must also contend with the vast amount of time that life has been evolving on earth. Again, scientists have devised simplified schemes—but in this case to organize *time,* not organic diversity.

Geologists have formulated the **geological time scale** (Fig. 5–7), in which very large time spans are organized into eras and periods. Periods, in turn, can be broken down into epochs. For the time span encompassing vertebrate evolution, there are three eras: the Paleozoic, the Mesozoic, and the Cenozoic. The first vertebrates are present in the fossil record dating to early in the Paleozoic 500 m.y.a. and probably go back considerably further. It is the vertebrate capacity to form bone that accounts for their more complete fossil record *after* 500 m.y.a.

During the Paleozoic, several varieties of fishes (including the ancestors of modern sharks and bony fishes), amphibians, and reptiles appeared. In addition, at the end of the Paleozoic, close to 250 m.y.a., several varieties of mammal-like

FIGURE 5–7 Geological time scale.

ERA	PERIOD	(Began m.y.a.)	EPOCH	(Began m.y.a.)
CENOZOIC	Quaternary	1.8	Holocene Pleistocene	0.01 1.8
CENOZOIC	Tertiary	65	Pliocene Miocene Oligocene Eocene Paleocene	5 23 34 55 65
MESOZOIC	Cretaceous	136		
MESOZOIC	Jurassic	190		
MESOZOIC	Triassic	225		
PALEOZOIC	Permian	280		
PALEOZOIC	Carboniferous	345		
PALEOZOIC	Devonian	395		
PALEOZOIC	Silurian	430		
PALEOZOIC	Ordovician	500		
PALEOZOIC	Cambrian	570		
PRE-CAMBRIAN				

See Virtual Lab 7, section I, for a discussion of geological time.

reptiles were also diversifying. It is widely thought that some of these forms gave rise to the mammals.

The evolutionary history of vertebrates and other organisms during the Paleozoic and Mesozoic was profoundly influenced by geographical events. We know that the positions of the earth's continents have dramatically shifted during the last several hundred million years. This process, called **continental drift,** is explained by the geological theory of *plate tectonics,* which views the earth's crust as a series of gigantic moving and colliding plates. Such massive geological movements can induce volcanic activity (as, for example, all around the Pacific rim), mountain building (e.g., the Himalayas), and earthquakes. Living on the edge of the Pacific and North American plates, residents of the Pacific coast of the United States are acutely aware of some of these consequences, as illustrated by the explosive volcanic eruption of Mt. St. Helens or the frequent earthquakes in Alaska and California.

Geologists, in reconstructing the earth's physical history, have established the prior (significantly altered) positions of major continental landmasses. During the late Paleozoic, the continents came together to form a single colossal landmass called *Pangea.* In actuality, the continents had been drifting on plates, coming together and separating, long before the end of the Paleozoic (circa 225 m.y.a.), and to be more precise, the large landmass at this time should be called Pangea II. During the early Mesozoic, the southern continents (South America, Africa, Antarctica, Australia, and India) began to split off from Pangea, forming a large southern continent called *Gondwanaland* (Fig. 5–8a). Similarly, the northern continents (North America, Greenland, Europe, and Asia) were consolidated into a northern landmass called *Laurasia.* During the Mesozoic, Gondwanaland and Laurasia continued to drift apart and to break up into smaller segments. By the end of the Mesozoic (circa 65 m.y.a.), the continents were beginning to assume their current positions (Fig. 5–8b).

The evolutionary ramifications of this long-term continental drift were profound. Groups of land animals became effectively isolated from each other by large water boundaries, and the distribution of reptiles and mammals was significantly influenced by continental movements. Although not producing such dramatic continental realignments, the process continued into the Cenozoic. The more specific effects of continental drift on early primate evolution are discussed in Chapter 10.

continental drift The movement of continents on sliding plates of the earth's surface. As a result, the positions of large landmasses have shifted dramatically during the earth's history.

FIGURE 5–8 Continental drift. Changes in positions of the continental plates from late Paleozoic to the early Cenozoic. (a) The positions of the continents during the Mesozoic (c. 125 m.y.a.). Pangea is breaking up into a northern landmass (Laurasia) and a southern landmass (Gondwanaland). (b) The positions of the continents at the beginning of the Cenozoic (c. 65 m.y.a.).

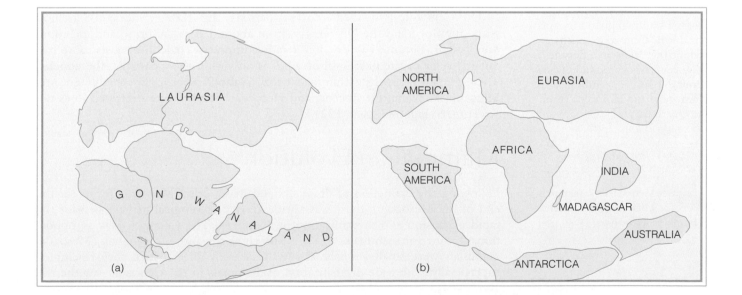

PALEOZOIC						MESOZOIC		
Cambrian	Ordovician	Silurian	Devonian	Carbon-iferous	Permian	Triassic	Jurassic	Cretaceous
Trilobites abundant; also brachiopods, jellyfish, worms, and other invertebrates	First fishes; trilobites still abundant; graptolites and corals become plentiful; possible land plants	Jawed fishes appear; first air-breathing animals; definite land plants	Age of Fish; first amphibians; first forests	First reptiles; radiation of amphibians; modern insects diversify	Reptile radiation; mammal-like reptiles	Reptiles further radiate; first dinosaurs; egg-laying mammals	Great Age of Dinosaurs; flying and swimming dinosaurs; first toothed birds	Placental and marsupial mammals appear; first modern birds

Major extinction event (between Permian and Triassic)

Major extinction event (after Cretaceous)

570 m.y.a   500 m.y.a   430 m.y.a   395 m.y.a   345 m.y.a   280 m.y.a   225 m.y.a   190 m.y.a   136 m.y.a   65 m.y.a

FIGURE 5–9 Time line of major events in early vertebrate evolution.

ecological niches The positions of species within their physical and biological environments, together making up the *ecosystem*. A species' ecological niche is defined by such components as diet, terrain, vegetation, type of predators, relationships with other species, and activity patterns, and each niche is unique to a given species.

epochs Categories of the geological time scale; subdivisions of periods. In the Cenozoic, epochs include the Paleocene, Eocene, Oligocene, Miocene, and Pliocene (from the Tertiary) and the Pleistocene and Holocene (from the Quaternary).

See Virtual Lab 7, section II, for a discussion of placental mammal relationships.

During most of the Mesozoic, reptiles were the dominant land vertebrates, and they exhibited a broad expansion into a variety of **ecological niches,** which included aerial and marine habitats. No doubt, the most famous of these highly successful Mesozoic reptiles were the dinosaurs, which themselves evolved into a wide array of sizes and lifestyles. Dinosaur paleontology, never a boring field, has advanced several startling notions in recent years: that many dinosaurs were warm-blooded; that some varieties were quite social and probably also engaged in considerable parental care; that many forms became extinct as the result of major climatic changes to the earth's atmosphere from collisions with comets or asteroids; and finally, as previously discussed, that not all dinosaurs became entirely extinct, with many descendants still living today (i.e., all modern birds). (See Figure 5–9 for a summary of major events in early vertebrate evolutionary history.)

The earliest mammals are known from fossil traces fairly early in the Mesozoic, but the first *placental* mammals cannot be positively identified until quite late in the Mesozoic, approximately 70 m.y.a. This highly successful mammalian adaptive radiation is thus almost entirely within the most recent era of geological history, the Cenozoic.

The Cenozoic is divided into two periods, the Tertiary (about 63 million years duration) and the Quaternary, from about 1.8 m.y.a. up to and including the present. Because this division is rather imprecise, paleontologists more frequently refer to the next level of subdivision within the Cenozoic, the **epochs**. There are seven epochs within the Cenozoic: the Paleocene, Eocene, Oligocene, Miocene, Pliocene, Pleistocene, and Holocene, the last often referred to as the Recent (see Fig. 5–7, page 122).

Mammalian Evolution

Following the extinction of dinosaurs and many other Mesozoic forms (at the end of the Mesozoic), there was a wide array of ecological niches open for the rapid expansion and diversification of mammals. The Cenozoic was an opportunistic time for mammals, and it is known as the Age of Mammals. Mesozoic mammals were small animals, about the size of mice, which they resembled superficially. The wide diversification of mammals in the Cenozoic saw the rise

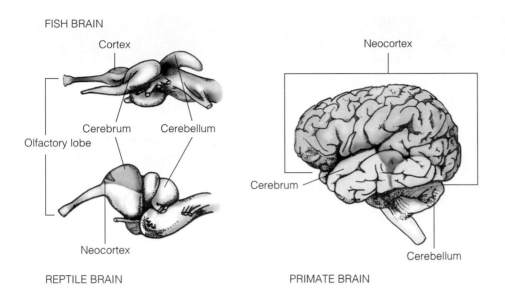

FIGURE 5–10 Lateral view of the brain. The illustration shows the increase in the cerebral cortex of the brain. The cerebral cortex integrates sensory information and selects responses.

of the major lineages of all modern mammals. Indeed, mammals, along with birds, replaced reptiles as the dominant terrestrial vertebrates.

How do we account for the rapid success of the mammals? Several characteristics relating to learning and general flexibility of behavior are of prime importance. To process more information, mammals were selected for larger brains than those typically found in reptiles. In particular, the cerebrum became generally enlarged, especially the outer covering, the neocortex, which controls higher brain functions (Fig. 5–10). In some mammals, the cerebrum expanded so much that it came to comprise the majority of brain volume; moreover, the number of surface convolutions increased, creating more surface area and thus providing space for even more nerve cells (neurons). As we will see shortly (in Chapter 6), this is a trend even further emphasized among the primates.

For such a large and complex organ as the mammalian brain to develop, a longer, more intense period of growth is required. Slower development can occur internally (*in utero*) as well as after birth. While internal fertilization and internal development are not unique to mammals, the latter is a major innovation among terrestrial vertebrates. Other forms (birds, most fishes, and reptiles) incubate their young externally by laying eggs (i.e., they are oviparous), while mammals, with very few exceptions, give birth to live young and are thus said to be **viviparous.** Even among mammals, however, there is considerable variation among the major groups in how mature the young are at birth. As you will see, it is in mammals like ourselves, the *placental* forms, where development *in utero* goes the furthest.

Another distinctive feature of mammals is seen in the dentition. While living reptiles consistently have similarly shaped teeth (called a *homodont* dentition), mammals have differently shaped teeth (Fig. 5–11). This varied pattern, termed a **heterodont** dentition, is reflected in the primitive (ancestral) mammalian array of dental elements, which includes 3 incisors, 1 canine,

REPTILIAN (alligator): homodont

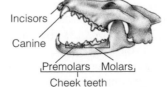

MAMMALIAN: heterodont

Incisors
Canine
Premolars Molars
Cheek teeth

viviparous Giving birth to live young.

heterodont Having different kinds of teeth; characteristic of mammals, whose teeth consist of incisors, canines, premolars, and molars.

FIGURE 5–11 Reptilian and mammalian teeth.

A CLOSER LOOK

Deep Time

The vast expanse of time during which evolution has occurred on earth staggers the imagination. Indeed, this fundamental notion of what John McPhee has termed "deep time" is not really understood or, in fact, widely believed. Of course, as we have emphasized beginning in Chapter 1 (see Issue, pp. 20–21), *belief*, as such, is not part of science. But observation, theory building, and testing are. Nevertheless, in a world populated mostly by nonscientists, the concept of deep time, crucial as it is to geology and anthropology, is resisted by many people. This situation is really not surprising; as an idea that can be truly understood (i.e., internalized and given some personal meaning), deep time is in many ways counterintuitive. As individuals, human beings measure their existence in months, years, or in the span of human lifetimes.

But what are these durations, measured against geological or galatic phenomena? In a real sense, these vast time expanses are beyond human comprehension. We can reasonably fathom the reaches of human history, stretching to about 5,000 years ago. In a leap of imagination, we can perhaps even begin to grasp the stretch of time back to the cave painters of France and Spain, approximately 17,000 to 25,000 years ago. How do we relate, then, to a temporal span 10 times this, back to 250,000 years ago, about the time of the earliest *Homo sapiens*—or to 10 times this span to 2,500,000 years ago (about the time of the appearance of our genus, *Homo*)? We surely can respond that any of these time blocks are vast—and then *more* vast. But multiply this last duration another 1,000 times (to 2,500,000,000), and we are back to a time of fairly early life forms. And we would still have to reach further into earth's past another 1.5 billion years to approach the *earliest* documented life.

The dimensions of these intervals are humbling, to say the least. The discovery in the nineteenth century of deep time (as we documented in Chapter 2) in what the late Stephen Jay Gould called "geology's greatest contribution to human thought" plunged one more dagger into humanity's long-cherished special view of itself. Astronomers had previously established how puny our world was in the physical expanse of space, and then geologists showed that even on our own small planet, we were but residues dwarfed within a river of time "without a vestige of a beginning or prospect of an end" (from James Hutton, a founder of modern geology and one of the discoverers of deep time). It is no wonder that there is resistance to the concept of deep time; it not only stupefies our reason, but implies a sense of collective meaninglessness and reinforces our individual mortality.

Geologists, astronomers, and other scholars have struggled for over a century, with modest success, to translate the tales told in rocks and hurtling stars in terms that can be understood by everyone. Various analogies have been attempted—metaphors, really—drawn from common experience. Among the most successful of these attempts is

4 premolars, and 3 molars for each quarter of the mouth. Since the upper and lower jaws are usually the same and are symmetrical for both sides, the "dental formula" is conventionally illustrated by dental quarter (see p. 145 for a more complete discussion of dental patterns as they apply to primates). Thus, with 11 teeth per quarter segment, the primitive (i.e., ancestral) mammalian dental complement includes a total of 44 teeth. Such a heterodont arrangement allows mammals to process a wide variety of foods. Incisors can be used for cutting, canines for grasping and piercing, and premolars and molars for crushing and grinding.

A final point regarding teeth relates to their disproportionate representation in the fossil record. As the hardest, most durable portion of a vertebrate skeleton, teeth have the greatest likelihood of becoming fossilized (i.e., mineralized). As a result, the vast majority of the available fossil data for most vertebrates, including primates, consists of teeth.

a "cosmic calendar" devised by eminent astronomer Carl Sagan in his book *Dragons of Eden* (1977). In this version of time's immensity, Sagan likens the passage of geological time to that of one calendar year. The year begins on January 1 with the "Big Bang," the cosmic explosion marking the beginning of the universe and the beginning of time. In this version, the Big Bang is set at 15 billion years ago,* with some of the major events in the geological past as follows:

*Recent evidence gathered by the Hubble Space Telescope has questioned the established date for the Big Bang. However, even the most recent data are somewhat contradictory, suggesting a date from as early as 16 billion years ago (indicated by the age of the oldest stars) to as recent as 8 billion years ago (indicated by the rate of expansion of the universe). Here, we will follow the conventional dating of 15 billion years; if you apply the most conservative approximation (8 billion years), the calibrations shift as follows: 1 day = 22,000,000 years; 1 hour = 913,000 years; 1 minute = 15,000 years. Using these calculations, for example, the first hominids appear on Dec. 31 at 7:37 P.M., and modern *Homo sapiens* are on the scene at 11:42 P.M.

TIME UNIT CONVERSIONS USING THE COSMIC CALENDAR

1 year = 15,000,000,000 years   1 hour = 1,740,000 years
1 month = 1,250,000,000 years   1 minute = 29,000 years
1 day = 41,000,000 years   1 second = 475 years

Event	Date	Event	*December 31 Events*
Big Bang	January 1		
Formation of the earth	September 14	Appearance of early hominoids (apes and humans)	12:30 P.M.
Origin of life on earth (approx.)	September 25	First hominids	9:30 P.M.
Significant oxygen atmosphere begins to develop	December 1	Extensive cave painting in Europe	11:59 P.M.
		Invention of agriculture	11:59:20 P.M.
Precambrian ends; Paleozoic begins; invertebrates flourish	December 17	Renaissance in Europe: Ming Dynasty in China; emergence of scientific method	11:59:59 P.M.
Paleozoic ends and Mesozoic begins	December 25		
Cretaceous period: first flowers; dinosaurs become extinct	December 28	Widespread development of science and technology; emergence of a global culture; first steps in space exploration	NOW: the first second of the New Year
Mesozoic ends; Cenozoic begins; adaptive radiation of placental mammals	December 29		

Another major adaptive complex that distinguishes contemporary mammals from reptiles is the maintenance of a constant internal body temperature. Also colloquially (and incorrectly) called warm-bloodedness, this central physiological adaptation is also seen in contemporary birds (and was also perhaps characteristic of many dinosaurs as well). In fact, many contemporary reptiles are able to approximate a constant internal body temperature through behavioral means (especially by regulating activity and exposing the body to the sun). In this sense, reptiles (along with birds and mammals) could be said to be *homeothermic.* Thus, the most important distinction in contrasting mammals (and birds) with reptiles is how the energy to maintain body temperature is produced and channeled. In reptiles, this energy is obtained directly from exposure (externally) to the sun; reptiles are thus said to be *ectothermic.* In mammals and birds, however, the energy is generated *internally* through metabolic activity (by processing food or by muscle action); mammals and birds are hence referred to as **endothermic.**

endothermic (*endo,* meaning "within" or "internal") Able to maintain internal body temperature through the production of energy by means of metabolic processes within cells; characteristic of mammals, birds, and perhaps some dinosaurs.

The Emergence of Major Mammalian Groups

There are three major subgroups of living mammals: the egg-laying mammals, or monotremes (Fig. 5–12), the pouched mammals, or marsupials (Fig. 5–13), and the placental mammals. The monotremes are extremely primitive and are considered more distinct from marsupials or placentals than these latter are from each other.

The most notable distinction differentiating the marsupials from the placentals is the type of fetal development. In marsupials, the young are born extremely immature and must complete development in an external pouch. It has been suggested (Carroll, 1988) that such a reproductive strategy is more energetically costly than retaining the young for a longer period *in utero*. In fact, the latter is exactly what placental mammals have done through a more advanced placental connection (from which the group gets its popular name). But perhaps even more basic than fetal nourishment are the means to allow the mother to *tolerate* her young internally over an extended period. Marsupial young are born so quickly after conception that there is little chance for the mother's system to recognize and have an immune rejection of the fetal "foreign" tissue. But in placental mammals, such an immune response would occur were it not for the development of a specialized tissue that isolates the fetus from the mother's immune detection, thus preventing tissue rejection. Quite possibly, this innovation is the central factor in the origin and initial rapid success of placental mammals (Carroll, 1988).

In any case, with a longer gestation period, the central nervous system could develop more completely in the fetus. Moreover, after birth, the "bond of milk" between mother and young also allows more time for complex neural structures to form. It should also be emphasized that from a *biosocial* perspective, this

FIGURE 5–12 The spiny anteater (a monotreme).

FIGURE 5–13 A wallaby with an infant in the pouch (marsupials).

dependency period not only allows for adequate physiological development, but also provides for a wider range of learning stimuli. That is, the young mammalian brain receives a vast amount of information channeled to it through observation of the mother's behavior and through play with age-mates. It is not sufficient to have evolved a brain capable of learning. Collateral evolution of mammalian social systems has ensured that young mammal brains are provided with ample learning opportunities and are thus put to good use.

Processes of Macroevolution

As noted earlier, evolution operates at both microevolutionary and macroevolutionary levels. We discussed evolution primarily from a microevolutionary perspective in Chapter 4; in this chapter, our focus is on macroevolution. Macroevolutionary mechanisms operate more on the whole species than on individuals or populations and take much longer than microevolutionary processes to have a noticeable impact.

ADAPTIVE RADIATION

The potential capacity of a group of organisms to multiply is practically unlimited; its ability to increase its numbers, however, is regulated largely by the available resources of food, shelter, and space. As the size of a population increases, its food supply, shelter, and space decrease, and the environment will ultimately prove inadequate. Depleted resources engender pressures that may induce some members of the population to seek an environment in which competition is considerably reduced and the opportunities for survival and reproductive success are increased. This evolutionary tendency to exploit unoccupied habitats may eventually produce an abundance of diverse species.

A good example of the evolutionary process known as **adaptive radiation** is seen in the divergence of the stem reptiles into the profusion of different forms of the late Paleozoic and especially those of the Mesozoic. It is a process that has taken place many times in evolutionary history when a life form has rapidly taken advantage, so to speak, of the many newly available ecological niches.

The principle of evolution illustrated by adaptive radiation is fairly simple, but important. It may be stated thus: *A species, or group of species, will diverge into as many variations as two factors allow: (1) its adaptive potential and (2) the adaptive opportunities of the available zones.*

In the case of reptiles, there was little divergence in the very early stages of evolution, when the ancestral form was little more than one among a variety of amphibian water dwellers. In reptiles, a more efficient egg than that of amphibians (i.e., one that could incubate out of water) had developed, but although it had great adaptive potential, there were few zones to invade. However, once reptiles became fully terrestrial, there was a sudden opening of available zones—ecological niches—accessible to them.

This new kind of egg provided the primary adaptive trait that freed reptiles from their attachment to water. The adaptive zones for reptiles were not limitless; nevertheless, continents were now open to them with no serious competition from any other animal. The reptiles moved into the many different ecological niches on land (and to some extent in the air and sea), and as they adapted to these areas, they diversified into a large number of species. This spectacular radiation burst forth with such evolutionary rapidity that it may well be termed an adaptive explosion.

The rapid expansion of placental mammals at the beginning of the Cenozoic and the diversification of lemurs in Madagascar are other good examples of

adaptive radiation The relatively rapid expansion and diversification of life forms into new ecological niches.

adaptive radiation. This latter (primate) example is particularly instructive. As we will see in Chapter 6, the contemporary array of 61 lemur species shows considerable diversity, both in size and in lifestyle (diet, degree of arboreality, etc.). Indeed, if we also include several other species that have become extinct in the last 1,000 years (following intensive human occupation of the island), the degree of lemur biodiversity was even greater—even including a ground-living form the size of a gorilla! The diversification of so many different kinds of lemur in Madagascar is explained by their adaptive radiation from a common ancestor, beginning up to 50 m.y.a. Without competition from other types of mammals, the lemurs fairly rapidly diversified and expanded into a number of varied niches in their isolated island home.

GENERALIZED AND SPECIALIZED CHARACTERISTICS

Another aspect of evolution closely related to adaptive radiation involves the transition from generalized characteristics to specialized characteristics. These two terms refer to the adaptive potential of a particular trait. A trait that is adapted for many functions is said to be generalized; a trait that is limited to a narrow set of functions is said to be specialized.

For example, a generalized mammalian limb has five fairly flexible digits adapted for many possible functions (grasping, weight support, digging). In this respect, human hands are still quite generalized. On the other hand (or foot), there have been many structural modifications in our feet suited for the specialized function of stable weight support in an upright posture.

The terms *generalized* and *specialized* are also sometimes used when speaking of the adaptive potential of whole organisms. For example, the aye-aye of Madagascar is a highly specialized animal structurally adapted in its dentition for an ecologically narrow rodent/woodpecker-like niche—digging holes with prominent incisors and removing insect larvae with an elongated finger.

The notion of adaptive potential is a relative judgment and can estimate only crudely the likelihood of one form evolving into one or more other forms. Adaptive radiation is a related concept, for only a generalized ancestor can provide the flexible evolutionary basis for such rapid diversification. Only a generalized species with potential for adaptation to varied ecological niches can lead to all the later diversification and specialization of forms into particular ecological niches.

An issue that we have already raised also bears on this discussion: the relationship of ancestral and derived characters. While not always the case, ancestral characters *usually* tend to be more generalized than specialized. And specialized characteristics are almost always also derived ones.

MODES OF EVOLUTIONARY CHANGE

Until recently, the general consensus among evolutionary biologists was that microevolutionary mechanisms could be translated directly into the larger-scale macroevolutionary changes, especially the most central of all macroevolutionary processes, speciation (also called *transspecific evolution*). A smooth gradation of change was assumed to run directly from microevolution into macroevolution. A representative view was expressed by a leading synthesist, Ernst Mayr: "The proponents of the synthetic theory maintain that all evolution is due to accumulation of small genetic changes, guided by natural selection, and that transspecific evolution is nothing but an extrapolation and magnification of events that take place within populations and species" (Mayr, 1970, p. 351).

In the last two decades, this view has been seriously challenged. Many theorists now believe that macroevolution cannot be explained solely in terms of accumulated microevolutionary changes. Consequently, these researchers are convinced that macroevolution is only partly understandable through microevolutionary models.

Gradualism vs. Punctuated Equilibrium   The traditional view of evolution has emphasized that change accumulates gradually in evolving lineages—the idea of phyletic gradualism. Accordingly, the complete fossil record of an evolving group (if it could be recovered) would display a series of forms with finely graded transitional differences between each ancestor and its descendant. The fact that such transitional forms are only rarely found is attributed to the incompleteness of the fossil record, or, as Darwin called it, "a history of the world, imperfectly kept, and written in changing dialect."

For more than a century, this perspective dominated evolutionary biology, but in the last 25 years, some biologists have called this notion into serious question. The evolutionary mechanisms operating on species over the long run are often not continuously gradual. In some cases, species persist for thousands of generations basically unchanged. Then, rather suddenly, at least in evolutionary terms, a "spurt" of speciation occurs. This uneven, nongradual process of long stasis and quick spurts has been termed **punctuated equilibrium** (Gould and Eldredge, 1977).

What the advocates of punctuated equilibrium are disputing are the tempo (rate) and mode (manner) of evolutionary change as commonly understood since Darwin's time. Rather than a slow, steady tempo, this alternate view postulates long periods of no change punctuated only occasionally by sudden bursts. From this observation, it was concluded that the mode of evolution, too, must be different from that suggested by classical Darwinists. Rather than gradual accumulation of small changes in a single lineage, advocates of punctuated equilibrium believe that an additional evolutionary mechanism is required to push the process along. They thus postulate *speciation* as the major influence in bringing about rapid evolutionary change.

How well does the paleontological record agree with the predictions of punctuated equilibrium? Indeed, considerable fossil data show long periods of stasis punctuated by occasional quite rapid changes (on the order of 10,000 to 50,000 years). The best supporting evidence for punctuated equilibrium has come from the fossilized remains of marine invertebrates. Intermediate forms are rare, not so much because the fossil record is poor, but because the speciation events and longevity of these transitional species were so short that we should not expect to find them very often.

And while some of the fossil evidence of other animals, including primates (Gingerich, 1985; Brown and Rose, 1987; Rose, 1991), does not fit the expectations of punctuated equilibrium, it would be a fallacy to assume that evolutionary change in these groups must therefore be of a completely gradual tempo. Such is clearly not the case. In all lineages, the pace assuredly speeds up and slows down as a result of factors that influence the size and relative isolation of populations. In addition, environmental changes that influence the pace and direction of natural selection must also be considered. Nevertheless, in general accordance with the Modern Synthesis, microevolution and macroevolution need not be "decoupled," as some evolutionary biologists have recently suggested.

punctuated equilibrium The concept that evolutionary change proceeds through long periods of stasis punctuated by rapid periods of change.

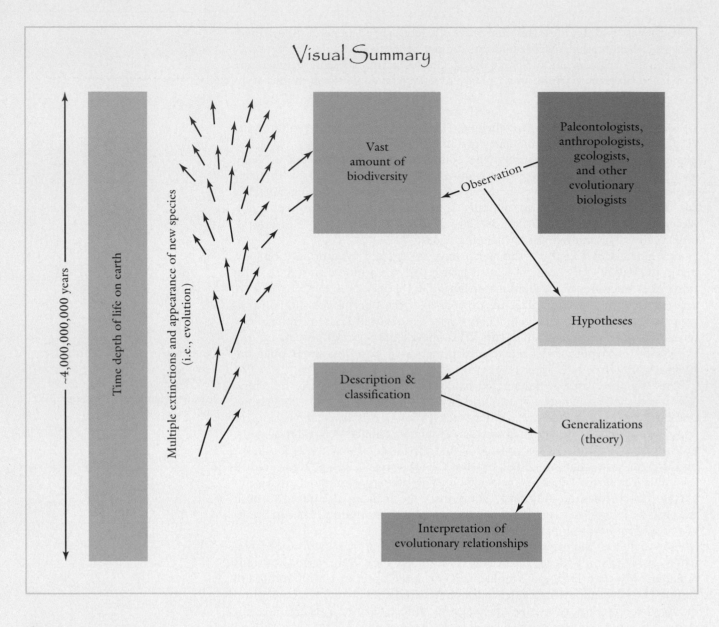

Summary

This chapter has surveyed the basics of vertebrate and mammalian evolution, emphasizing a macroevolutionary perspective. Given the huge amount of organic diversity displayed, as well as the vast time involved, two major organizing perspectives prove indispensable: schemes of formal classification to organize organic diversity and the geological time scale to organize geological time. The principles of classification were reviewed in some detail, contrasting two differing approaches: evolutionary systematics and cladistics. Because primates are vertebrates and, more specifically, mammals, these broader organic groups were briefly reviewed, emphasizing major evolutionary trends.

Theoretical perspectives relating to contemporary understanding of macroevolutionary processes (especially the concepts of species and speciation) are crucial to interpreting any long-term aspect of evolutionary history, be it vertebrate, mammalian, or primate. As genus and species designation is the common form of reference for both living and extinct organisms (and will be used frequently throughout the text), its biological significance was discussed in depth. From a more general theoretical perspective, evolutionary biologists have postulated two different modes of evolutionary change: gradualism and punctuated equilibrium. At present, the available fossil record does not conform entirely to the predictions of punctuated equilibrium, but one should not conclude that evolutionary tempo was necessarily strictly gradual (which it certainly was not).

For Further Thought

1. Given that life has been evolving on earth for upward of 4 billion years, how would you try to explain this amount of time to a nonscientist?

Go to the book website at **http://www.anthropology.wadsworth.com** for resources to help you explore these questions further. Click on "For Further Thought" for this chapter.

Questions for Review

1. What are the two goals of organic classification? What happens when meeting both goals simultaneously becomes difficult or even impossible?
2. What do we mean when we say that an animal is a vertebrate? What are the major groups of vertebrates, and where do humans fit in?
3. Remains of a fossil mammal have been found on your campus. If you adopt a cladistic approach, how would you determine (a) that it is a primate rather than some other kind of vertebrate (discuss specific characters), (b) what kind of primate it is (again, discuss specific characters), and (c) how it *might* be related to one or more living mammals (again, discuss specific characters).
4. For the same fossil find (and your interpretation) in question 3, draw an interpretive figure using cladistic analysis (i.e., draw a cladogram). Next, using more traditional phylogenetic systematics, construct a phylogeny. Lastly, explain the differences between the cladogram and the phylogeny (be sure to emphasize the fundamental ways the two schemes differ).
5. a. Humans are fairly generalized mammals. What do we mean by this—and what specific features (characters) would you select to illustrate this statement?
   b. Humans, more precisely, are *placental* mammals. How do humans, and generally all other placental mammals, differ from the other two major groups of mammals?
6. Return to the fossil find in question 3. Examine every character you mentioned in parts a–c, and evaluate whether each character you named is an ancestral character or a derived character. What types of characters are most useful in your analysis? Why? (*Note:* For the three different parts of question 3, the comparative analysis differs, and so, necessarily, does your selection of characters that convey the most information.)
7. While studying contemporary primates in their native habitat in West Africa, you observe two populations of small monkeys that differ somewhat in appearance and behavior. (They vary in the color of facial hair, and one population displays unimale groups, while the other is multimale.) How would you decide if these two monkey populations are members of one or two different species? To test your hypothesis, devise a methodology and analysis using the biological species concept. Then, discuss a somewhat different approach using another definition of species (either the ecological species concept or the recognition species concept).

Suggested Further Reading

Carroll, Robert L. 1988. *Vertebrate Paleontology and Evolution.* New York: Freeman.

Fleagle, John. 1999. *Primate Adaptation and Evolution,* 2nd ed. New York: Academic Press.

Mayr, Ernst. 2001. *What Evolution Is.* New York: Basic Books.

Padian, Kevin, and Luis M. Chiappe. 1998. "The Origin of Birds and Their Flight." *Scientific American* 278: 38–47.

Ridley, Mark. 1993. *Evolution.* Boston: Blackwell Scientific Publications.

🌏 Online Anthropology Resource Center

Go to the Anthropology Resource Center at **http://www.anthropology.wadsworth.com** for a wealth of online resources, including a companion website for your text that provides study aids such as self-quizzes for each chapter and a practice final exam, as well as links to anthropology websites and information on the latest theories and discoveries in the field. Also, check out InfoTrac College Edition®, your online library that offers full-length articles from thousands of scholarly and popular publications. Just click on the InfoTrac button at the companion website and use the passcode that came with your book.

Just When We Thought Things Couldn't Get Any Worse: Bushmeat and Ebola

Several major extinction events have occurred throughout the course of vertebrate evolution, and each of these decimated tens of thousands of species in a relatively short period of time. The best-documented of these extinction events occurred approximately 65 m.y.a., at the end of the Mesozoic. Geological evidence indicates that at this time a large asteroid collided with the earth, causing major climatic changes and widespread extinctions of many life forms, including the dinosaurs. Geologists have also found evidence of an earlier mass extinction, dating to the end of the Paleozoic (c.250 m.y.a.). That event, perhaps caused by a volcanic eruption or other geological forces, is estimated to have wiped out over 90 percent of all marine life.

Today, we're in the midst of another mass extinction crisis, one that could match the other two events of the last 250 million years. However, unlike the earlier mass extinctions, the current one is due to the environmentally destructive influence of a single expanding species. That species is, of course, *Homo sapiens.* Many primatologists and conservationists were taken off guard when, in the 1990s, they became aware of the devastating effects of a rapidly developing trade in *bushmeat* (meat derived from wild animals) in West and central Africa. (The problem has now expanded to East Africa.) Actually, as early as the 1960s and '70s, primatologists began reporting that monkeys in many West African forests were becoming scarce because of a developing commercial trade in monkey meat (Oates, 1999). But the current slaughter is unprecedented. In fact, some observers have likened the killing of primates and other species in parts of Africa to the near extermination of the American bison in the 19th century.

Wherever they occur, nonhuman primates have traditionally been an important source of food for people. In the past, subsistence hunting by indigenous peoples, armed with snares and bows and arrows, didn't usually constitute a serious threat to nonhuman primate populations, and certainly not to entire species. But now, hunters have greater access to firearms, and with shotguns and automatic rifles, they can wipe out an entire group of monkeys, gorillas, or chimpanzees in minutes.

The underlying factor that has produced the current bushmeat catastrophe is human population growth. The current human population of West and central Africa (approximately 24 million) increases at an annual rate of 2 to 4 percent. Traditionally, the people of these regions were not pastoralists, and while today some households may keep a few cattle, goats, and chickens, the primary dietary source of animal protein is still meat from wild animals.

Another key factor in the rapidly developing bushmeat trade is logging, which occurs because of the high demand for tropical hardwoods in Europe and the United States. (We encourage you to consider this the next time you are tempted to buy anything made of wood from any tropical area.)

The construction of logging roads, mainly by French, German, and Belgian lumber companies, has opened up vast tracts of forest that, until recently, were inaccessible to local hunters. Once the roads are cut, hunters hitch rides to previously inaccessible areas. (Of course, the truck drivers receive a fee, ultimately derived from the sale of bushmeat.) Logging trucks also carry meat out of the forest, which allows hunters to kill more animals because they don't have to carry the meat. Lastly, the loggers themselves consume bushmeat. In one logging camp in Gabon, 1,200 loggers consumed an estimated 80 tons of bushmeat in just one year! In another camp in Congo, over 8,000 animals were consumed. What has emerged is a profitable trade in bushmeat, a trade in which logging company employees and local government officials participate with hunters, villagers, market vendors, and smugglers who cater to growing overseas markets.

As you can see, the hunting of wild animals for food, particularly in Africa, has quickly shifted from being a subsistence activity to a commercial enterprise of international scope. The carcasses of primates and other species are common sights in local African markets (Fig. 1). Gorilla and chimpanzee meat is considered a delicacy in the restaurants of some West African cities, and the trade extends beyond Africa. Wildlife carcasses are smuggled into European countries to be illegally sold at high prices, and chimpanzee and gorilla meat is reportedly sometimes served in some Belgian and French restaurants.

With unprecedented access to the forests, hunters currently take over 1 million metric tons of meat (equivalent to over 4 million cattle) from the forests annually. Most of this meat comes from elephants, duikers (small forest antelopes), monkeys, porcupines, reptiles, and rodents. About 1 percent comes from great ape carcasses, but much more comes from monkeys. Given the very slow

FIGURE 1 Red-eared guenons (with red tails) and Preuss' guenons for sale in bushmeat market, Malabo, Equatorial Guinea.

reproductive rate of primates, and great apes in particular, this level of hunting far exceeds the replacement capacity of these species and also of many nonprimate species.

It's impossible to know how many animals are slaughtered each year. But estimates for monkeys and apes are in the thousands. In addition to those killed, hundreds of infants are orphaned and sold in the markets as pets (Fig. 2). Although a few of these traumatized orphans make it to sanctuaries, most die of injury, starvation, disease, and neglect within days or weeks of capture.

But it gets worse. About 80 percent of the world's remaining gorillas and most of the common chimpanzees are found in two west African countries, Gabon and the Republic of Congo (Walsh, et al., 2003). Between 1983 and 2000, ape populations in Gabon declined by half, mostly because of hunting. But, these populations are now faced with another threat, the viral disease ebola. This severe disease, first recognized in 1976, is believed to be maintained in wild animals, but exactly which species is unknown. Furthermore, ebola is transmitted to humans through contact (butchering, eating) with infected animals. In humans, ebola is frequently fatal and symptoms include fever, vomiting, diarrhea, and sometimes, severe bleeding.

Since 1994, there have been four outbreaks of ebola in Gabon, and ape carcasses have been found near affected human settlements in three. In one area of Gabon where large-scale hunting has not occurred, ape populations declined by an estimated 90 percent between 1991 and 2000! Quite simply, faced with the combination of ebola and commercial hunting, great ape populations in western Africa cannot be sustained.

The problems of deforestation, disease, and overhunting are overwhelming, and if solutions are to be found, they will need to focus on the needs of millions of people living in poverty and facing starvation. At the local level, it's nearly impossible to convince a poor farmer not to kill monkeys he can sell in the market for a higher price than his crops will bring. But selling primate carcasses represents only short-term gain because there can be no long-term profit.

Conservation organizations are encouraging logging companies to set aside refuges for threatened species. Logging companies are also being urged to stop employees from transporting hunters and to provide employees with sources of protein other than bushmeat. So far, one company has complied. Some governments are also considering ways to practice sustainable management of natural resources, including wildlife.

Locally, efforts are being directed at encouraging people to eat meat from domestic animals, but this transition will not be easy. Also, there are education programs that teach people about the substantial health risks (e.g., HIV/AIDS and ebola) associated with bushmeat.

Perhaps most encouraging is the establishment of the Great Ape Survival Project (GRASP) in 2000 by the United Nations Environmental Program (UNEP). GRASP is an alliance of many of the world's major great ape conservation and research organizations. Under its auspices, three internationally recognized primatologists, Jane Goodall, Russell Mittermeir, and Toshisada Nishida were named as United Nations Special Envoys for Great

FIGURE 2 These orphaned chimpanzee infants are being bottle-fed at a sanctuary near Pointe Noir, Congo. Probably, they will never be returned to the wild and they face a very uncertain future.

Just When We Thought Things Couldn't Get Any Worse: Bushmeat and Ebola (continued)

Apes. Richard Leakey, the world famous paleoanthropologist and wildlife conservationist was also named as a special advisor. These envoys and other members of the project hope to persuade heads of state throughout the world to take actions to end the slaughter and trade in bushmeat.

In 2003, GRASP appealed for $25 million to be used in attempts to prevent all the great apes (including non-African orangutans) from going extinct. The money (in reality, a paltry sum) would be used to increase enforcement of laws that regulate hunting and illegal logging; and satellite surveillance would help monitor deforestation. It goes without saying that GRASP and other organizations must succeed.

Unless deforestation, the spread of ebola, and the slaughter of nonhuman primates are curtailed *very, very, soon,* many species will certainly disappear. In fact, primatologists and conservationists fear that several primate species, certainly the great apes, could be exterminated from parts of Indonesia and West and central Africa by the year 2010. And by the year 2030, they could be extinct in the wild.

Critical Thinking Questions

1. Can you suggest ways in which the bushmeat trade might be slowed? How would you suggest that the needs of the people be addressed while encouraging them not to kill or sell nonhuman primates and other animals?
2. How have industrialized nations contributed to the development of the bushmeat trade?
3. What are some things you can do that might help stop the bushmeat trade?
4. Can you think of other examples of trade in endangered species, including primates, in other parts of the world? Can you suggest ways in which these activities can be curtailed?

Sources

"Bushmeat. A Wildlife Crisis in West and Central Africa and Around the World." Bushmeat Crisis Task Force (BCTF). Online version at www.bushmeat.org.

"Bushmeat Factsheet." The Jane Goodall Institute. Online version at www.janegoodall.org/.

Hearn, Josephine. 2001. "Unfair Game. The Bushmeat Trade Is Wiping Out Large African Mammals." *Scientific American* June: 24–26.

Strier, Karen B., 1999. *Primate Behavioral Ecology.* (2nd ed.) New York: Allyn & Bacon.

United Nations Environmental Program for Great Ape Survival Program website: www.unep.org/grasp

Walsh, Peter D., et al. 2003. "Catastrophic Ape Decline in Western Equatorial Africa." *Nature.* 422: 611–614

An Overview of the Primates

6

Orangutan (*Pongo pygmaeus*)
Ryan McVay/Getty Images

Key Questions

What are the major characteristics of primates? Why are humans considered primates?

Why is it important to study nonhuman primates?

Introduction

See the following sections of the CD-ROM for topics covered in this chapter: Virtual Lab 1, sections II, III, and IV; Virtual Lab 3; Virtual Lab 4, sections I and II; and Virtual Lab 5.

Chimpanzees are not monkeys. Neither are gorillas or orangutans. They are apes, and there are many differences between monkeys and apes. Yet, how many times have you seen a greeting card or magazine ad with a picture of a chimpanzee and a phrase that goes something like, "Don't monkey around" or "No more monkey business"? Or you may have noticed how people at zoos find captive primates especially funny, particularly when they tease and provoke them. While these issues may seem trivial, they aren't, because they illustrate how ill informed most people are about their closest relatives. This lack of knowledge is extremely unfortunate, because by better understanding these relatives, not only can we better know ourselves, but we can also attempt to preserve the many primate species that are critically endangered.

To gain an understanding of any organism, it's necessary, whenever possible, to compare its anatomy and behavior with those of other, closely related forms. This comparative approach helps explain the significance of physiological and behavioral systems as adaptive responses to various selective pressures throughout the course of evolution. This statement applies to *Homo sapiens* just as it does to any other species, and if we wish to identify the components that have shaped the evolution of our species, a good starting point is a comparison between humans and our closest living relatives, the approximately 230 species of nonhuman primates (**prosimians,** monkeys, and apes). (Groves, 2001b, suggests that there may be as many as 350 primate species.)

prosimians Members of a suborder of Primates, the *Prosimii* (pronounced "pro-sim´-ee-eye"). Traditionally, the suborder includes lemurs, lorises, and tarsiers.

This chapter describes the physical characteristics that define the order Primates, gives a brief overview of the major groups of living primates, and introduces some methods of comparing living primates through genetic data. (For a comparison of human and nonhuman skeletons, see Appendix A.) But before we go any further, we again want to call attention to a few common misunderstandings about evolutionary processes.

anthropoids Members of a suborder of Primates, the *Anthropoidea* (pronounced "ann-throw-poid´-ee-uh"). Traditionally, the suborder includes monkeys, apes, and humans.

Evolution is *not* a goal-directed process; thus, the fact that prosimians evolved before **anthropoids** does not mean that prosimians "progressed," or "advanced," to become anthropoids. Living primate species are in no way "superior" to their evolutionary predecessors or to one another. Consequently, in discussions of major groupings of contemporary nonhuman primates, there is no implied superiority or inferiority of any of these groups. Each grouping (lineage, or species) has come to possess unique qualities that make it better suited than others to a particular habitat and lifestyle. Given that all contemporary organisms are "successful" results of the evolutionary process, it's best to avoid altogether the use of such loaded terms as "superior" and "inferior." Finally, you shouldn't make the mistake of thinking that contemporary primates (including humans) necessarily represent the final stage or apex of a lineage. Actually, the only species that represent final evolutionary stages of particular lineages are the ones that become extinct.

See Virtual Lab 1, section I, for a discussion of the inclusion of the primate order within the class Mammalia.

Characteristics of Primates

All primates possess numerous characteristics they share in common with other placental mammals. Some of these traits are body hair; a relatively long gestation period followed by live birth; mammary glands (thus the term *mammal*); different types of teeth (incisors, canines, premolars, and molars); the ability to maintain a constant internal body temperature through physiological means (*homeothermy*); increased brain size; and a considerable capacity for learning and behavioral flexibility. Therefore, to differentiate primates, as a group, from other mammals, we need to describe those characteristics that, taken together, set primates apart from other mammalian groups.

Identifying single traits that define the primate order isn't a simple task, for among mammals, primates have remained quite *generalized*. That is, primates have retained many ancestral or primitive mammalian traits that some other mammalian species have lost over time. In response to particular selective pressures, many mammalian groups have become increasingly **specialized.** For example, through the course of evolution, horses and cattle have undergone a reduction of the number of digits (fingers and toes) from the ancestral pattern of five to one and two respectively. Moreover, these species have developed hard, protective coverings over their feet in the form of hooves (see Fig. 6–1). While this type of limb structure is adaptive in prey species, whose survival depends on speed and stability, it restricts the animal to only one type of locomotion. Moreover, limb function is limited entirely to support and movement, while the ability to manipulate objects is completely lost.

specialized Evolved for a particular function; usually refers to a specific trait (e.g., incisor teeth), but may also refer to the entire way of life of an organism.

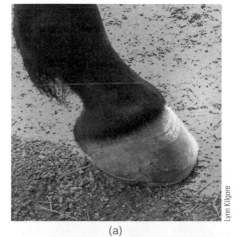
(c)

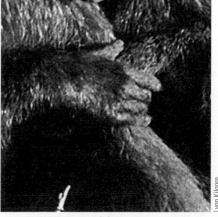
(a)

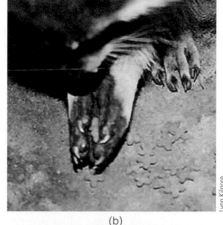
(b)

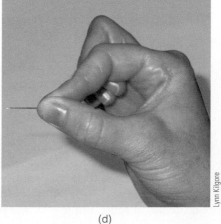
(d)

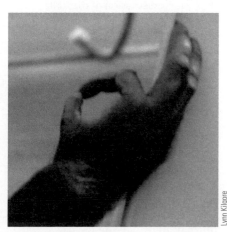
(e)

FIGURE 6–1 (a) A horse's front foot, homologous with a human hand, has undergone reduction from 5 digits to one. (b) While raccoons are capable of considerable manual dexterity and can readily pick up small objects with one hand, they have no opposable thumb. (c) Many monkeys are able to grasp objects with an opposable thumb, while others have very reduced thumbs. (d) Humans are capable of a "precision grip." (e) Chimpanzees with their reduced thumbs are capable of a precision grip but frequently use a modified form.

Primates, precisely because they are *not* so specialized, can't be simply defined by one or even two traits they share in common. As a result, anthropologists have pointed to a group of characteristics that, taken together, more or less characterize the entire order. But, you should keep in mind that these are a set of *general* tendencies and are not all equally expressed in all primates. Moreover, while some of these traits are unique to primates, many others are retained ancestral mammalian characteristics. These latter are useful in contrasting the generalized primates with the more specialized varieties of other placental mammals. Thus, the following list is intended to give an overall structural and behavioral picture of that kind of animal we call "primate," focusing on those characteristics that tend to set primates apart from other mammals. Concentrating on certain retained (ancestral) mammalian traits along with more specific, derived, ones has been the traditional approach of **primatologists**. Some contemporary primatologists (Fleagle, 1999) believe that it is useful to enumerate all these features to better illustrate primate adaptations. Thus, a common evolutionary history with adaptations to similar environmental challenges is seen to be reflected in the limbs and locomotion, teeth and diet, senses, brain, and behaviors of those animals that make up the primate order.

primatologists Scientists who study the evolution, anatomy, and behavior of nonhuman primates. Those who study behavior in noncaptive animals are usually trained as physical anthropologists.

A. *Limbs and Locomotion*
  1. *A tendency toward erect posture (especially in the upper body).* Shown to some degree in all primates, this tendency is variously associated with sitting, leaping, standing, and, occasionally, bipedal walking.
  2. *A flexible, generalized limb structure, permitting most primates to engage in a number of locomotor behaviors.* Primates have retained some bones (e.g., the clavicle, or collarbone) and certain abilities, (e.g., rotation of the forearm) that have been lost in some more specialized mammals. Various aspects of hip and shoulder **morphology** also provide primates with a wide range of limb movement and function. Thus, by maintaining a generalized locomotor anatomy, primates are not restricted to one form of movement, as are many other mammals. Primate limbs are also used for activities other than locomotion.

morphology The form (shape, size) of anatomical structures; can also refer to the entire organism.

  3. *Hands and feet with a high degree of **prehensility** (grasping ability).* All primates use the hands, and frequently the feet, to grasp and manipulate objects (Fig. 6–1). This capability is variably expressed and is enhanced by a number of characteristics, including:
    a. *Retention of five digits on hands and feet.* This trait varies somewhat throughout the order. Some species show marked reduction of the thumb or second digit.
    b. *An opposable thumb and, in most species, a divergent and partially opposable big toe.* Most primates are capable of moving the thumb so that it comes in contact (in some fashion) with the second digit or the palm of the hand.
    c. *Nails instead of claws.* This characteristic is seen in all primates except some New World monkeys. All prosimians also possess a claw on one digit.
    d. *Tactile pads enriched with sensory nerve fibers at the ends of digits.* This enhances the sense of touch.

prehensility Grasping, as by the hands and feet of primates.

See Virtual Lab 1, section III, for a discussion of the traits typically used to define the primate order. Section IV presents mammalian life history variables.

B. *Diet and Teeth*
  1. *Lack of dietary specialization.* This is typical of most primates, who tend to eat a wide assortment of food items.
  2. *A generalized dentition.* The teeth are not specialized for processing only one type of food, a pattern correlated with the lack of dietary specialization. In general, primates are **omnivorous.**
C. *The senses and the brain.* Primates (**diurnal** ones in particular) rely heavily on the visual sense and less on the sense of smell, especially compared to

omnivorous Having a diet consisting of many food types (i.e., plant materials, meat, and insects).

diurnal Active during the day.

many other mammals. This emphasis is reflected in evolutionary changes in the skull, eyes, and brain.

1. *Color vision.* This is characteristic of all diurnal primates. **Nocturnal** primates lack color vision.

2. *Depth perception.* **Stereoscopic vision,** or the ability to perceive objects in three dimensions, is made possible through a variety of mechanisms, including:

   a. *Eyes positioned toward the front of the face (not to the sides).* This configuration provides for overlapping visual fields, or **binocular vision** (Fig. 6–2).

   b. *Visual information from each eye transmitted to visual centers in both hemispheres of the brain.* In nonprimate mammals, most optic nerve fibers cross to the opposite hemisphere through a structure at the base of the brain. In primates, about 40 percent of the fibers remain on the same side (see Fig. 6–2).

   c. *Visual information organized into three-dimensional images by specialized structures in the brain itself.* The capacity for stereoscopic vision is dependent on each hemisphere of the brain receiving visual information from both eyes and from overlapping visual fields.

3. *Decreased reliance on the sense of smell (olfaction).* This trend is seen in an overall reduction in the size of olfactory structures in the brain (see p. 205). Corresponding reduction of the entire olfactory apparatus has also resulted in decreased size of the snout. In some species, such as

nocturnal Active during the night.

stereoscopic vision The condition whereby visual images are, to varying degrees, superimposed on one another. This provides for depth perception, or the perception of the external environment in three dimensions. Stereoscopic vision is partly a function of structures in the brain.

binocular vision Vision characterized by overlapping visual fields provided by forward-facing eyes. Binocular vision is essential to depth perception.

hemispheres The two halves of the cerebrum that are connected by a dense mass of fibers. (The cerebrum is the large rounded outer portion of the brain.)

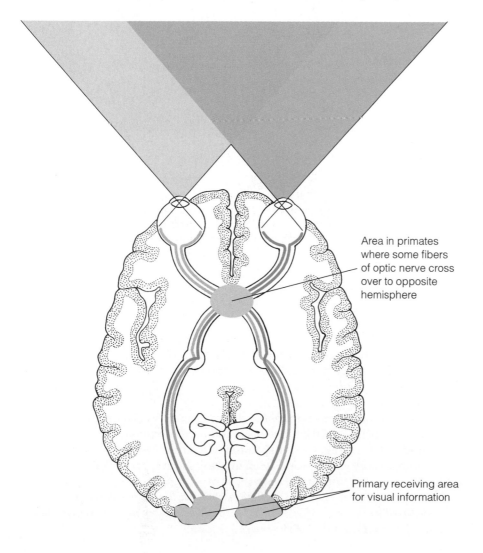

Area in primates where some fibers of optic nerve cross over to opposite hemisphere

Primary receiving area for visual information

FIGURE 6–2 Simplified diagram showing overlapping visual fields that permit binocular vision in primates and many predators with eyes positioned at the front of the face. (The green shaded area represents the area of overlap.) Stereoscopic vision (three-dimensional vision) is provided in part by binocular vision and in part by the transmission of visual stimuli from each eye to *both* hemispheres of the brain. (In nonprimate mammals, most, if not all, visual information crosses over to the hemisphere opposite the eye in which it was initially received.)

A CLOSER LOOK

Primate Cranial Anatomy

Several significant anatomical features of the primate cranium help us distinguish primates from other mammals. The mammalian trend toward increased brain development has been further emphasized in primates, as shown by a relatively enlarged braincase. In addition, the primate emphasis on vision is reflected in generally large eye sockets; and the decreased dependence on olfaction is indicated by reduction of the snout and corresponding flattening of the face (Fig. 1)

Here are some of the specific anatomical details seen in modern and most fossil primate crania:

1. The primate face is shortened, and the size of the braincase, relative to that of the face, is enlarged compared to other mammals (see Fig. 1).

2. Eye sockets are enclosed at the sides by a ring of bone called the *postorbital bar* (see Fig. 1). In most other mammals, there is no postorbital bar. In addition, in tarsiers, monkeys, apes, and humans, there is a plate of bone at the back of the eye orbit called the *postorbital plate*. The postorbital plate is not present in lemurs and lorises. The functional significance of these structures has not been thoroughly explained, but it may be related to stresses on the eye orbits imposed by chewing (Fleagle, 1999).

3. The region of the skull that contains the structures of the middle ear is completely encircled by a bony structure called the *auditory bulla*. In primates, the floor of the auditory bulla is derived from a segment of the temporal bone (Fig. 2). Of the skeletal structures, most primate paleontologists consider the postorbital bar and the derivation of the auditory bulla to be the two best diagnostic traits of the primate order.

4. The base of the skull in primates is somewhat flexed, so that the muzzle (mouth and nose) is positioned lower relative to the braincase (Fig. 3). This arrangement provides for the exertion of greater force during chewing, particularly as needed for the crushing and grinding of tough vegetable fibers, seeds, and hard-shelled fruits.

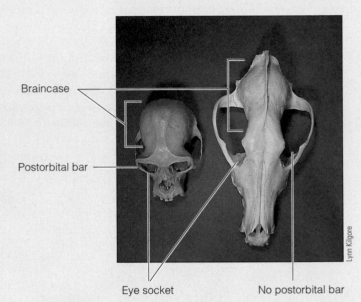

Braincase

Postorbital bar

Eye socket   No postorbital bar

Lynn Kilgore

FIGURE 1 The skull of a gibbon (left) compared to that of a red wolf (right). Note that the absolute size of the braincase in the gibbon is slightly larger than that of the wolf, even though the wolf (at about 80 to 100 pounds) is six times the size of the gibbon (about 15 pounds).

---

sensory modalities Different forms of sensation (e.g., touch, pain, pressure, heat, cold, vision, taste, hearing, and smell.

baboons, the large muzzle is not related to olfaction, but to the presence of large teeth, especially the canines. (See A Closer Look above.)

4. *Expansion and increased complexity of the brain.* This is a general trend among placental mammals, but it is especially true of primates. In primates, this expansion is most evident in the visual and association areas of the neocortex (portions of the brain where information from different **sensory modalities** is integrated). Expansion in regions involved with the hand (both sensory and motor) is seen in many species, particularly humans.

D. *Maturation, learning, and behavior*

1. *A more efficient means of fetal nourishment, longer periods of gestation, reduced numbers of offspring (with single births the norm), delayed maturation, and extension of the entire life span.*

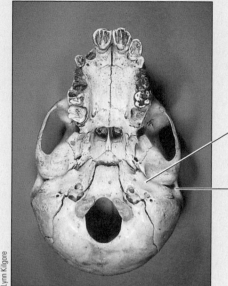

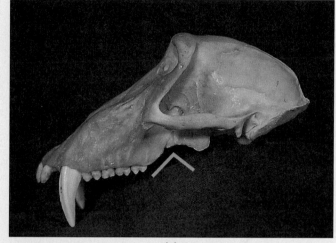

Portion of temporal bone enclosing auditory bulla

External opening to ear (external auditory meatus)

(a)

FIGURE 2 The base of an adolescent chimpanzee skull. (Note that in an adult animal, the bones of the skull would be fused together and would not appear as separate elements as shown here.)

FIGURE 3 The skull of a male baboon (a) compared to that of a red wolf (b). The angle at the base of the baboon skull is due to flexion. The corresponding area of the wolf skull is relatively flat. Note the forward-facing position of the eye orbits above the snout in the baboon. Also, be aware that in the baboon, the enlarged muzzle does *not* reflect a heavy reliance on the sense of smell. Rather, it serves to support very large canine teeth, the roots of which curve back through the bone for as much as 1½ inches.

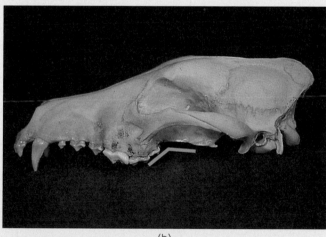

(b)

2. *A greater dependence on flexible, learned behavior.* This trend is correlated with delayed maturation and consequently longer periods of infant and child dependency on the parent. As a result of both these trends, parental investment in each offspring is increased, so that although fewer offspring are born, they receive more intense and efficient rearing.

3. *The tendency to live in social groups and the permanent association of adult males with the group.* Except for some nocturnal species, primates tend to associate with other individuals. The permanent association of adult males with the group is uncommon in mammals but widespread in primates.

4. *The tendency to diurnal activity patterns.* This is seen in most primates; only one monkey species and some prosimians are nocturnal.

Primate Adaptations

EVOLUTIONARY FACTORS

arboreal Tree-living: adapted to life in the trees.

adaptive niche The entire way of life of an organism: where it lives, what it eats, how it gets food, how it avoids predators, etc.

intelligence Mental capacity; the ability to learn, reason, or comprehend and interpret information, facts, relationships, meanings, etc.; the capacity to solve problems, whether through the application of previously acquired knowledge or through insight.

arboreal hypothesis The traditional view that primate characteristics can be explained as a consequence of primate diversification into arboreal habitats.

Traditionally, the suite of characteristics shared by primates has been explained as the result of adaptation to **arboreal** living. While other placental mammals were adapting to various ground-dwelling lifestyles and even marine environments, the primates found their **adaptive niche** in the trees. Indeed, some other mammals were also adapting to arboreal living, but while many of these species nested in trees, they continued to come to the ground to forage for food. But throughout the course of evolution, primates came increasingly to exploit foods (leaves, seeds, fruits, nuts, insects, and small mammals) found in the branches themselves. The exploitation of these varied foods enhanced the general trend toward *omnivory* in primates and, correspondingly, toward the generalized dentition characteristic of primates.

This adaptive process is also reflected in the primate reliance on vision. In a complex, three-dimensional environment with uncertain footholds, acute color vision with depth perception is, to say the least, extremely beneficial. The presence of grasping hands and feet is also an indicator of the adaptation to living in the trees. Climbing can be accomplished by either digging in with claws (as in many successful species, such as squirrels or raccoons) or grasping around branches with prehensile hands and feet. Primates adopted this latter strategy, which allowed a means of moving about, sometimes very rapidly, on small, unstable surfaces, and grasping abilities were further enhanced by the appearance of flattened nails instead of claws.

Finally, increased **intelligence** may be, in part, a primate solution to coping with the complexities of an arboreal habitat. Jerison (1973) also suggested that the crucial development of increased behavioral flexibility in primates may have been further stimulated by a shift from nocturnal (nighttime) to diurnal (daytime) activity patterns. But, perhaps, the most important factor was the adoption of social living and the many complexities involved in social interactions (see p. 204).

An alternative to this traditional **arboreal hypothesis,** called the *visual predation hypothesis* (Cartmill, 1972, 1992), points out that forward-facing eyes are characteristic not only of primates, but also of predators, such as cats and owls, that prey on small animals. Furthermore, forward-facing eyes, grasping hands and feet, and the presence of nails instead of claws may *not* have arisen as adaptive advantages in a purely arboreal environment. According to the visual predation hypothesis, primates may first have adapted to shrubby forest undergrowth and the lowest tiers of the forest canopy, where they hunted insects and other small prey primarily through stealth.

A third scenario (Sussman, 1991) proposes that the basic primate traits developed in conjunction with another major evolutionary occurrence, the rise of the *angiosperms* (flowering plants). Flowering plants provided numerous resources, including nectar, seeds, and fruits, and their appearance and diversification were accompanied by the appearance of ancestral forms of major groups of modern birds and mammals. Sussman argues that visual predation isn't common among modern primates and that forward-facing eyes, grasping extremities, and omnivory may have arisen in response to the demand for fine visual and tactile discrimination, necessary when feeding on small food items such as fruits, berries, and seeds among branches and stems.

These hypotheses are not mutually exclusive. The complex of primate characteristics might well have begun in nonarboreal settings and certainly may have been stimulated by the new econiches provided by evolving angiosperms. But at some point, the primates did take to the trees, and that is where the majority of them still live today. Whereas the basic primate structural complexes may have been adapted for visual predation and/or omnivory in shrubby undergrowth and terminal branches, they became ideally suited for the arboreal adaptations that followed. We would say, then, that the early primates were *preadapted* for arboreal living and that those early adaptations have served them long and well in the trees.

GEOGRAPHICAL DISTRIBUTION AND HABITATS

With just a couple of exceptions, primates are found in tropical or semitropical areas of the New and Old Worlds. In the New World, these areas include southern Mexico, Central America, and parts of South America. Old World primates are found in Africa, India, Southeast Asia (including numerous islands), and Japan (see Fig. 6–4 on pp. 146–147).

The majority of primates are, as we have discussed, mostly arboreal and live in forest or woodland habitats. However, some Old World monkeys (e.g., baboons) have, to varying degrees, adapted to life on the ground in areas where trees are sparsely distributed. Moreover, among the apes, gorillas, chimpanzees, and bonobos spend a considerable amount of time on the ground in forested and wooded habitats. Nevertheless, no nonhuman primate is adapted to a fully terrestrial lifestyle, and all spend some time in the trees.

DIET AND TEETH

As noted, primates are generally *omnivorous*. In fact, the tendency toward omnivory is one example of the overall lack of specialization in primates. Although the majority of primate species tend to emphasize some food items over others, most eat a combination of fruit, nuts, seeds, leaves, other plant materials, and insects. Many also obtain animal protein from birds and amphibians. Some (capuchins, baboons, bonobos, and especially chimpanzees) occasionally kill and eat small mammals, including other primates. Others, such as African colobus monkeys and the leaf-eating monkeys (langurs) of India and Southeast Asia, have become more specialized and subsist primarily on leaves. Such a wide array of choices is highly adaptive, even in fairly predictable environments.

Like the majority of other mammals, most primates have four kinds of teeth: incisors and canines for biting and cutting and premolars and molars for chewing. Biologists use a device called a *dental formula* to describe the number of each type of tooth that typifies a species. A dental formula indicates the number of each tooth type in each quadrant of the mouth (Fig. 6–3). For example, all Old World *anthropoids* have two incisors, one canine, two premolars, and three molars on each side of the **midline** in both the upper and lower jaws, or a total of 32 teeth. This is represented as a dental formula of

> 2.1.2.3. (upper)
> 2.1.2.3. (lower)

The dental formula for a generalized placental mammal is 3.1.4.3. (three incisors, one canine, four premolars, and three molars). Primates have fewer teeth than this ancestral pattern because there has been a general evolutionary trend toward reduction of the number of teeth in many mammal groups. Consequently, the number of each type of tooth varies between lineages. For example, in the majority of New World monkeys, the dental formula is 2.1.3.3. (two incisors, one canine, three premolars, and three molars). Humans, apes, and all Old World monkeys have the same

See Virtual Lab 1, section III, for interactive exercises regarding the global distribution and habitats of nonhuman primates.

See Virtual Lab 5 for an in-depth discussion of primate diets and dental adaptations.

midline An anatomical term referring to a hypothetical line that divides the body into right and left halves.

FIGURE 6–3 Dental formulae. The number of each kind of tooth is given for one-quarter of the mouth.

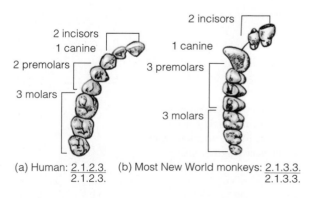

2 incisors
1 canine
2 premolars
3 molars

2 incisors
1 canine
3 premolars
3 molars

(a) Human: 2.1.2.3.
2.1.2.3.

(b) Most New World monkeys: 2.1.3.3.
2.1.3.3.

FIGURE 6–4 Geographical distribution of living nonhuman primates. Much original habitat is now very fragmented.

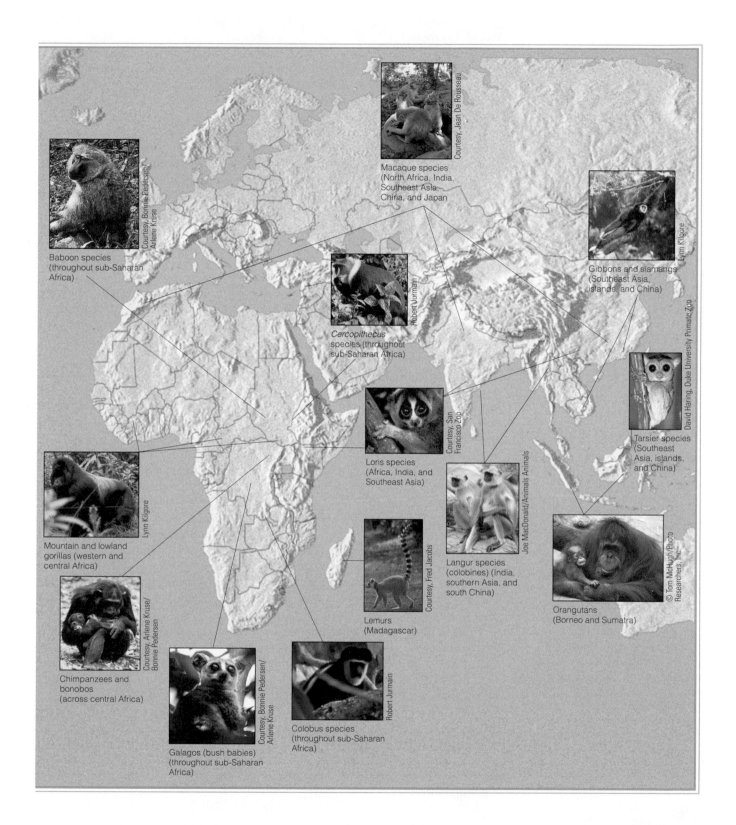

Macaque species (North Africa, India, Southeast Asia, China, and Japan

Courtesy, Jean De Rousseau

Baboon species (throughout sub-Saharan Africa)

Courtesy, Bonnie Pedersen/ Arlene Kruse

Gibbons and siamangs (Southeast Asia, islands, and China)

Lynn Kilgore

Cercopithecus species (throughout sub-Saharan Africa)

Robert Jurmain

Tarsier species (Southeast Asia, islands, and China)

David Haring, Duke University Primate Zoo

Loris species (Africa, India, and Southeast Asia)

Courtesy, San Francisco Zoo

Mountain and lowland gorillas (western and central Africa)

Lynn Kilgore

Langur species (colobines) (India, southern Asia, and south China)

Joe MacDonald/Animals Animals

Orangutans (Borneo and Sumatra)

© Tom McHugh/Photo Researchers, Inc.

Chimpanzees and bonobos (across central Africa)

Courtesy, Arlene Kruse/ Bonnie Pedersen

Lemurs (Madagascar)

Courtesy, Fred Jacobs

Galagos (bush babies) (throughout sub-Saharan Africa)

Courtesy, Bonnie Pedersen/ Arlene Kruse

Colobus species (throughout sub-Saharan Africa)

Robert Jurmain

cusps The elevated portions (bumps) on the chewing surfaces of premolar and molar teeth.

dental formula: 2.1.2.3. (Note that there is one less premolar than in New World monkeys.)

The overall lack of dietary specialization in primates is correlated with minimal specialization in the size and shape of the teeth. This is because tooth form is directly related to diet. For example, carnivores typically have premolars and molars with high pointed **cusps** adapted for tearing meat, while the premolars of herbivores, such as cattle and horses, have broad, flat surfaces suited to chewing tough grasses and other plant materials. Most primates have premolars and molars with low, rounded cusps, a molar morphology that enables them to process most types of foods. Thus, throughout their evolutionary history, the primates have developed a dentition adapted to a varied diet, and the capacity to exploit many foods has contributed to their overall success during the last 50 million years.

LOCOMOTION

quadrupedal Using all four limbs to support the body during locomotion; the basic mammalian (and primate) form of locomotion.

macaques (muh-kaks′) Group of Old World monkeys comprising several species, including rhesus monkeys.

Almost all primates are, at least to some degree, **quadrupedal,** meaning they use all four limbs to support the body during locomotion. However, most primates use more than one form of locomotion, and they owe this important ability to their generalized structure.

Although the majority of quadrupedal primates are arboreal, terrestrial quadrupedalism is fairly common and is typical of some lemurs, baboons, and **macaques.** Typically, the limbs of terrestrial quadrupeds are approximately the same length, with forelimbs being 90 percent (or more) as long as hind limbs (Fig. 6–5a). In arboreal quadrupeds, forelimbs are shorter and may be only 70 to 80 percent as long as hind limbs (Fig. 6–5b).

Quadrupeds are also characterized by a relatively long and flexible *lumbar spine* (lower back). This lumbar flexibility permits the animal to bend the body during running, positioning the hind limbs and feet well forward under the body and enhancing their ability to propel forward. (Watch for this the next time you see slow-motion footage of cheetahs or lions on television.)

Vertical clinging and leaping, another form of locomotion, is characteristic of many prosimians and tarsiers. As the term implies, vertical clingers and leapers support themselves vertically by grasping onto trunks of trees while their knees and ankles are tightly flexed (Fig. 6–5c). Forceful extension of their long hind limbs allows them to spring powerfully away in either a forward or backward direction.

brachiation A form of locomotion in which the body is suspended beneath the hands and support is alternated from one forelimb to the other; arm swinging.

Brachiation, or arm swinging, is yet another type of primate locomotion is where the body is alternatively supported under either forelimb. Because of anatomical modifications at the shoulder joint, apes and humans are capable of true brachiation. However, only the small gibbons and siamangs of Southeast Asia use this form of locomotion almost exclusively (Fig. 6–5d).

Brachiation is seen in species characterized by arms longer than legs, a short stable lumbar spine, long curved fingers, and reduced thumbs. Because these are traits seen in all the apes, it's believed that, although none of the great apes (orangutans, gorillas, bonobos, and chimpanzees) habitually brachiates today, they most likely inherited these characteristics from brachiating or perhaps climbing ancestors.

See Virtual Lab 4, section I, for video clips of primate locomotion.

Some New World monkeys (e.g. muriquis and spider monkeys) are called *semibrachiators,* as they practice a combination of leaping with some arm swinging. And in some New World species, arm swinging and other suspensory behaviors are enhanced by use of a *prehensile tail,* which in effect serves as an effective grasping fifth "hand." It should be noted that prehensile tails are strictly a New World phenomenon and are not seen in any Old World primate species.

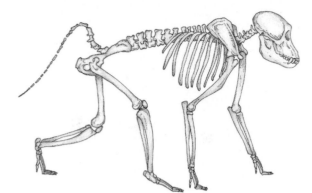

(a) Skeleton of a terrestrial quadruped (savanna baboon).

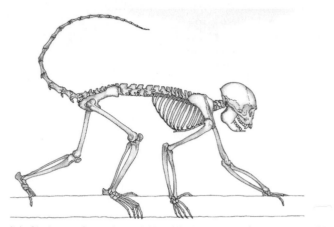

(b) Skeleton of an arboreal New World monkey (bearded saki).

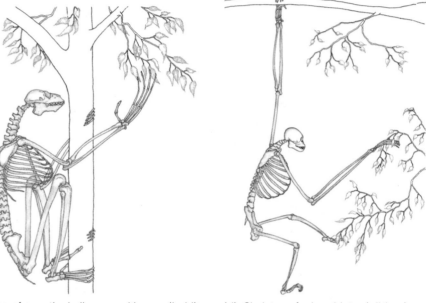

(c) Skeleton of a vertical clinger and leaper (indri).

(d) Skeleton of a brachiator (gibbon).

FIGURE 6–5 (a–d) Differences in skeletal anatomy and limb proportions reflect differences in locomotor patterns. (Redrawn by Stephen Nash from original art in John G.Fleagle, *Primate Adaptation and Evolution,* 2nd ed., 1999. Reprinted by permission of publisher and Stephen Nash.)

Primate Classification

The living primates are commonly categorized into their respective subgroups as shown in Figure 6–6. This taxonomy is based on the system originally established by Linnaeus. (Remember that the primate order, which includes a diverse array of approximately 230 species, belongs to a larger group, the class *Mammalia.*)

As you learned in Chapter 5, in any taxonomic system, animals are organized into increasingly specific categories. For example, the order *Primates* includes *all* primates. However, at the next level down—the *suborder*—the primates have conventionally been divided into two large categories, Prosimii (all the prosimians: lemurs, lorises, and, customarily, the tarsiers) and Anthropoidea (all the monkeys, apes, and humans). Therefore, the suborder distinction is more specific and more precise than the order.

At the level of the suborder, the prosimians are distinct as a group from all the other primates, and this classification makes the biological and evolutionary statement that all the prosimian species are more closely related to one another

See Virtual Lab 3 for a presentation of anatomical terms. See Virtual Lab 4, sections I and II, for a discussion of the relationship between relative limb proportions and locomotion.

FIGURE 6–6 Primate taxonomic classification. This abbreviated taxonomy illustrates how primates are grouped into increasingly specific categories. Only the more general categories are shown, except for the great apes and humans.

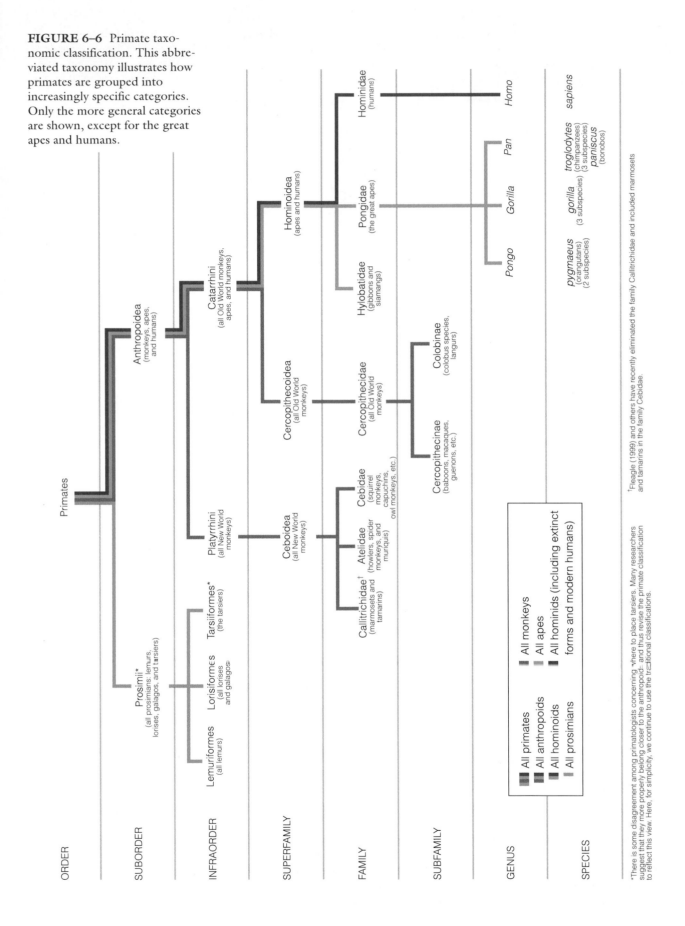

*There is some disagreement among primatologists concerning where to place tarsiers. Many researchers suggest that they more properly belong closer to the anthropoid and thus revise the primate classification to reflect this view. Here, for simplicity, we continue to use the traditional classifications.

†Fleagle (1999) and others have recently eliminated the family Callitrichidae and included marmosets and tamarins in the family Cebidae.

than they are to any of the anthropoids. Likewise, all anthropoid species are more closely related to one another than they are to the prosimians.

The taxonomy presented in Figure 6–6 is the traditional one and is based on physical similarities between species and lineages. However, since the goal of any classification system is to clarify biological and evolutionary relationships between groups of organisms, this technique can be problematic. For example, two primate species that resemble each other anatomically (e.g., some New and Old World monkeys) may in fact not be very closely related. Looking only at physical characteristics overlooks the unknown effects of separate evolutionary history. But genetic evidence avoids this problem and indeed shows Old and New World monkeys to be evolutionarily quite distinct.

Primate classification is currently in a state of transition, mainly because of genetic evidence that certain relationships, especially between humans and chimpanzees, are even closer than previously thought. Beginning in the 1970s, scientists began to apply genetic analysis to help identify biological and phylogenetic relationships between species.

One way to identify genetic relationships between species is to examine the sequence of amino acids that make up specific proteins. This approach is based on the fact that proteins evolve. In fact, we really can't overstate the importance of this concept. It is critical in the study of evolution to know that speciation occurs because *genes, proteins, and genomes evolve.* Over time, alterations in the sequence of amino acids in proteins produce slightly different forms of proteins in different species. So while proteins serve the same basic functions in different species, they may vary somewhat in their structure. The more closely related two species are, the more structurally similar their proteins will be.

Comparisons between human and African ape proteins show great similarity. For example, in the 146 amino acids that make up the hemoglobin beta chain, chimpanzees and humans differ in only one amino acid. However, comparisons between human hemoglobin and that of various Old World monkeys reveal differences in 4 to 9 amino acids, and the even more distantly related tarsiers differ by 15 amino acid substitutions.

Sibley and Alquist (1984) used another technique called *DNA hybridization* to show that humans and chimpanzees are closer genetically than either is to the gorilla. For that matter, chimpanzees and humans share more genetic similarities than do zebras and horses or goats and sheep. DNA hybridization involves matching strands of DNA from two species to determine what percentage of bases match. The higher the percentage, the closer the genetic relationship. In the Sibley and Alquist study, 98.4 percent of the human and chimpanzee DNA base sequences that were studied were identical.

Another way of making genetic comparisons between species has been to examine their karyotypes to identify similarities and differences in chromosome shape, size, number, and banding patterns. (These banding patterns are formed when segments of DNA differentially take up certain stains They are not the same patterns as those illustrated on page 68 in our discussion of DNA fingerprinting.)

Humans and chimpanzees have 46 and 48 chromosomes, respectively. The banding patterns of human chromosome 2 correspond to those of two much smaller chimpanzee chromosomes (numbers 12 and 13). This finding led to the speculation that in an ancestral hominoid, these two chromosomes fused to produce what became, in some populations, human chromosome 2 (Fig. 6–7).

Amino acid sequencing, DNA hybridization, and chromosomal comparisons have reaffirmed the basic tenets of traditional primate classification. But as useful as these techniques have been, they are *indirect* methods of comparing DNA sequences between species. However, the techniques of DNA sequencing used in the Human Genome Project make it entirely possible to make direct

See Virtual Lab 1, section II, for an interactive discussion of primate taxonomy and the issue of ape and human classification.

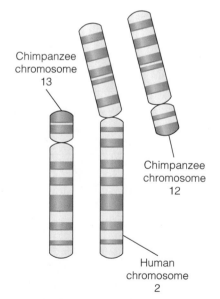

Chimpanzee chromosome 13

Chimpanzee chromosome 12

Human chromosome 2

FIGURE 6–7 Human chromosome 2 has banding patterns that correspond to those of chimpanzee chromosomes 12 and 13. These similarities suggest that human chromosome 2 resulted from the fusion of these two ape chromosomes during the course of hominid evolution.

between-species comparisons of DNA sequences! This approach is called *comparative genomics.*

The completion of a draft sequence of the chimpanzee genome in December, 2003 was a major advance in human comparative genomics. But prior to this achievement, molecular anthropologists had already compared the sequences of several chimpanzee and human genes or groups of genes.

These studies are vital because they reveal such differences in DNA as the number of nucleotide substitutions and/or deletions that have occurred since related species last shared a common ancestor. They can also demonstrate that some genes that are shared by living species are the result of fusion of two or more genes that were present in their most recent common ancestor. Geneticists calculate the rate of genetic change and use this information, combined with the degree of change, to estimate when related species diverged from a common ancestor. For example, Wildman et al. (2003) compared 97 human genes with their chimpanzee, gorilla, and orangutan counterparts and determined that humans are most closely related to chimpanzees and that they are between 98.4 and 99.4 percent identical. Using their data, they calculated that humans and chimpanzees last shared a common ancestor with gorillas around 6–7 m.y.a. and that the chimpanzee and human lineages diverged between 5 and 6 m.y.a.

These results are consistent with the findings of several other studies (Chen and Li, 2001; Clark, et al., 2003), and they have prompted many primatologists to change the way the hominoids are classified (Goodman et al., 1998; Wildman et al., 2003). Although there is no formal acceptance of suggested changes, many anthropologists support placing all great apes in the family Hominidae along with humans.

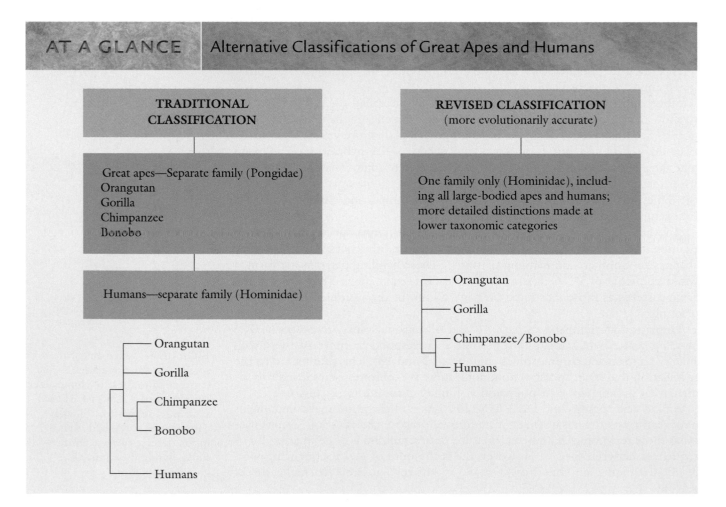

AT A GLANCE   Alternative Classifications of Great Apes and Humans

TRADITIONAL CLASSIFICATION

Great apes—Separate family (Pongidae)
Orangutan
Gorilla
Chimpanzee
Bonobo

Humans—separate family (Hominidae)

- Orangutan
- Gorilla
- Chimpanzee
- Bonobo
- Humans

REVISED CLASSIFICATION
(more evolutionarily accurate)

One family only (Hominidae), including all large-bodied apes and humans; more detailed distinctions made at lower taxonomic categories

- Orangutan
- Gorilla
- Chimpanzee/Bonobo
- Humans

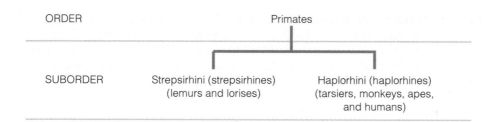

ORDER   Primates

SUBORDER   Strepsirhini (strepsirhines)   Haplorhini (haplorhines)
            (lemurs and lorises)   (tarsiers, monkeys, apes,
                                                 and humans)

FIGURE 6–8 Revised partial classification of the primates. In this system, the terms *Prosimii* and *Anthropoidea* have been replaced by *Strepsirhini* and *Haplorhini*, respectively. The tarsier is included in the same suborder with monkeys, apes, and humans to reflect a closer relationship with these species than with lemurs and lorises. (Compare with Fig. 6–6.)

Yet another area where modifications have been suggested concerns tarsiers (see p. 155). Tarsiers are highly specialized animals that display several unique physical characteristics. Because they possess a number of prosimian traits, tarsiers traditionally have been classified as prosimians (with lemurs and lorises); but they also share certain anthropoid features. Moreover, biochemically, tarsiers are more closely related to anthropoids than to prosimians (Dene et al., 1976); but with regard to chromosomes and several anatomical traits, they are distinct from both groups.

Today, most primatologists consider tarsiers to be more closely related to anthropoids than to prosimians. But instead of simply moving them into the suborder Anthropoidea, one scheme places lemurs and lorises in a different suborder, Strepsirhini (instead of Prosimii), while tarsiers are included with monkeys, apes, and humans in another suborder, Haplorhini (Szalay and Delson, 1979) (Fig. 6–8). In this classification, the conventionally named suborders Prosimii and Anthropoidea are replaced by Strepsirhini and Haplorhini, respectively. While this designation has not been universally accepted, the terminology is now common, especially in technical publications. So if you see the term *strepsirhine,* you know the author is referring specifically to lemurs and lorises.

We have presented the traditional system of primate classification in this chapter, even though we acknowledge the need for modification. Until the new designations are formally adopted, we think it appropriate to use the standard taxonomy along with discussion of some proposed changes. We also want to point out that while specific details and names have not yet been worked out, the vast majority of experts do accept the evolutionary implications of the revised groupings.

A Survey of the Living Primates

PROSIMIANS (LEMURS AND LORISES)

The most primitive of the primates are the lemurs and lorises (we do not include tarsiers here.) Remember that by "primitive" we mean that prosimians, taken as a group, are more similar anatomically to their earlier mammalian ancestors than are the other primates (monkeys, apes, and humans). Therefore, they tend to exhibit certain more ancestral characteristics, such as a more pronounced reliance on *olfaction* (sense of smell). Their greater olfactory capabilities (compared to other primates) are reflected in the presence of a moist, fleshy pad (**rhinarium**) at the end of the nose and in a relatively long snout. Moreover, prosimians actively mark territories with scent in a manner not seen in many other primates.

There are numerous other characteristics that distinguish lemurs and lorises from the anthropoids, including somewhat more laterally placed eyes, differences in reproductive physiology, and shorter gestation and maturation periods. Lemurs and lorises also possess a dental specialization known as the "dental comb." The dental comb is formed by forward-projecting lower incisors and canines, and together these modified teeth are used in both grooming and feeding (Fig. 6–9). One other characteristic that sets lemurs and lorises apart from anthropoids is the retention of a claw (called a "grooming claw") on the second toe.

rhinarium (rine-air´-ee-um) The moist, hairless pad at the end of the nose seen in most mammalian species. The rhinarium enhances an animal's ability to smell.

FIGURE 6–9 Prosimian dental comb, formed by forward-projecting incisors and canines.

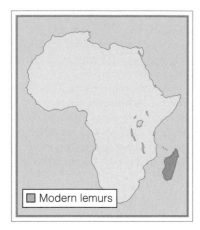

FIGURE 6-10 Geographical distribution of modern lemurs.

Lemurs   Lemurs are found only on the island of Madagascar and adjacent islands off the east coast of Africa (Fig. 6–10). As the only nonhuman primates on Madagascar, which comprises some 227,000 square miles, lemurs diversified into numerous and varied ecological niches without competition from monkeys and apes. Thus, the approximately 60 surviving species of lemurs, today restricted to Madagascar, represent an evolutionary pattern that has vanished elsewhere.

Lemurs range in size from the small mouse lemur, with a body length (head and trunk) of only 5 inches, to the indri, with a body length of 2 to 3 feet (Nowak, 1999). While the larger lemurs are diurnal and exploit a wide variety of dietary items, such as leaves, fruit, buds, bark, and shoots, the smaller forms (mouse and dwarf lemurs) are nocturnal and insectivorous.

Lemurs display considerable variation regarding numerous other aspects of behavior. While many are primarily arboreal, others, such as the ring-tailed lemur (Fig. 6–11), are more terrestrial. Some arboreal species are quadrupeds, and others (sifakas and indris) are vertical clingers and leapers (Fig. 6–12). Socially, several species (e.g., ring-tailed lemurs and sifakas) are gregarious and live in groups of 10 to 25 animals composed of males and females of all ages. Others (the indris) live in monogamous family units, and several nocturnal forms are mostly solitary.

Lorises   Lorises (Fig. 6–13), which are similar in appearance to lemurs, were able to survive in mainland areas by adopting a nocturnal activity pattern at a time when most other prosimians became extinct. In this way, they were (and are) able to avoid competition with more recently evolved primates (the diurnal monkeys).

There are at least eight loris species, all of which are found in tropical forest and woodland habitats of India, Sri Lanka, Southeast Asia, and Africa. Also included in the same general category are six to nine (Bearder, 1987; Nowak, 1999) galago species (Fig. 6–14), which are widely distributed throughout most of the forested and woodland savanna areas of sub-Saharan Africa.

Locomotion in lorises is a slow, cautious climbing form of quadrupedalism, and flexible hip joints permit suspension by hind limbs while the hands are used in feeding. All galagos, however, are highly agile and active vertical clingers and leapers. Some lorises and galagos are almost entirely insectivorous; others supplement their diet with various combinations of fruit, leaves, gums, and slugs. Lorises and galagos frequently forage for food alone (females leave infants behind in nests until they are older). However, ranges overlap, and two or more females occasionally forage together or share the same sleeping nest.

Lemurs and lorises represent the same general adaptive level. Both groups exhibit good grasping and climbing abilities and a fairly well developed visual

FIGURE 6-11 Ring-tailed lemur.

FIGURE 6-12 Sifakas in their native habitat in Madagascar.

FIGURE 6–13 Slow loris.   **FIGURE 6–14** Galago, or "bush baby."

apparatus, although vision is not completely stereoscopic, and color vision may not be as well developed as in anthropoids. Most lemurs and lorises also have prolonged life spans as compared to most other small-bodied mammals, averaging about 14 years for lorises and 19 years for lemurs.

TARSIERS

There are five recognized tarsier species (Nowak, 1999) (Fig. 6–15), all restricted to island areas in Southeast Asia (Fig. 6–16), where they inhabit a wide range of forest types, from tropical forest to backyard gardens. Tarsiers are nocturnal insectivores, leaping onto prey (which may also include small vertebrates) from lower branches and shrubs. They appear to form stable pair bonds, and the basic tarsier social unit is a mated pair and their young offspring (MacKinnon and MacKinnon, 1980).

As we have already mentioned, tarsiers present a complex blend of characteristics not seen in other primates. Moreover, they are unique in that their enormous eyes, which dominate much of the face, are immobile within their sockets. To compensate for this inability to move the eyes, tarsiers are able to rotate their heads 180° as owls do.

ANTHROPOIDS (MONKEYS, APES, AND HUMANS)

Although there is much variation among anthropoids, there are certain features that, when taken together, distinguish them as a group from prosimians (and other placental mammals). Here is a partial list of these traits:

1. Generally larger body size
2. Larger brain (in absolute terms and relative to body weight)
3. Reduced reliance on the sense of smell, indicated by absence of rhinarium and other structures
4. Increased reliance on vision, with forward-facing eyes placed at front of face
5. Greater degree of color vision
6. Back of eye socket formed by a bony plate
7. Blood supply to brain different from that of prosimians
8. Fusion of the two sides of the mandible at the midline to form one bone (in prosimians and tarsiers they are joined by fibrous tissue)
9. Less specialized dentition, as seen in absence of dental comb and some other features
10. Differences with regard to female internal reproductive anatomy
11. Longer gestation and maturation periods
12. Increased parental care
13. More mutual grooming

FIGURE 6–15 Tarsier.

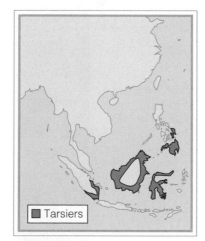

☐ Tarsiers

FIGURE 6–16 Geographical distribution of tarsiers.

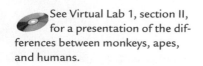

See Virtual Lab 1, section II, for a presentation of the differences between monkeys, apes, and humans.

Approximately 85 percent of all primates are monkeys (about 195 species). It is frequently impossible to give precise numbers of species because the taxonomic status of some primates remains in doubt, and primatologists are still making new discoveries. (In fact, between 1990 and 2001, 22 species and subspecies of monkeys were discovered and described.) Monkeys are divided into two groups separated by geographical area (New World and Old World), as well as by several million years of separate evolutionary history.

FIGURE 6–17 New World monkeys.

New World Monkeys The New World monkeys exhibit a wide range of size, diet, and ecological adaptation (Fig. 6–17). In size, they vary from the tiny marmosets and tamarins (about 12 ounces) to the 20-pound howler monkeys (Figs.

Squirrel monkeys

Female muriqui with infant

Prince Bernhard's titi monkey (discovered in 2002)

White-faced capuchins

Male uakari

FIGURE 6–18 A pair of golden lion tamarins.

FIGURE 6–19 Howler monkeys.

6–18 and 6–19). New World monkeys are almost exclusively arboreal, and some never come to the ground. Like Old World monkeys, all except one species (the owl monkey) are diurnal. New World monkeys can be found in a wide range of arboreal environments throughout most forested areas in southern Mexico and Central and South America (Fig. 6–20).

One of the characteristics distinguishing New World monkeys from Old World monkeys is the shape of the nose. New World forms have broad noses with outward-facing nostrils. Conversely, Old World monkeys have narrower noses with downward-facing nostrils. This difference in nose form has given rise to the terms *platyrrhine* (flat-nosed) and *catarrhine* (downward-facing nose) to refer to New and Old World anthropoids, respectively.

New World monkeys have traditionally been divided into two families: **Callitrichidae** (marmosets and tamarins) and **Cebidae** (all others). But molecular data along with recently reported fossil evidence indicate that a major regrouping of New World monkeys is in order (Fleagle, 1999).*

Of the roughly 70 New World monkey species, marmosets and tamarins are the smallest. They have claws instead of nails and usually give birth to twins instead of one infant. They are mostly insectivorous, although the marmoset diet includes gums from trees, and tamarins also eat fruit. Locomotion is quadrupedal, and their claws assist in climbing, just as in squirrels. Moreover, some tamarins use vertical clinging and leaping as a form of travel. Socially, these small monkeys live in family groups composed usually of a mated pair, or a female and two adult males, and their offspring. In fact, marmosets and tamarins are among the few primate species in which males are extensively involved in infant care.

Cebid and atelid species (see Fig. 6–6) range in size from the squirrel monkey (body length 12 inches) to the howler (body length 24 inches). Diet varies, with most relying on a combination of fruit and leaves supplemented, to varying degrees, by insects. Most are quadrupedal, but some—for example, muriquis and spider monkeys (Fig. 6–21)—are semibrachiators. Muriquis, howlers, and spider monkeys also have powerful prehensile tails that are used not only in locomotion

EQUATOR

☐ New World monkeys

FIGURE 6–20 Geographical distribution of modern New World monkeys.

Callitrichidae
(kal-eh-trick´-eh-dee)

Cebidae (see´-bid-ee)

---

*One possibility is to include spider monkeys, howler monkeys, and muriquis (woolly spider monkeys) in a third family, Atelidae (see Fig. 6–6). Another is to eliminate the family Callitrichidae altogether and include marmosets and tamarins as a subfamily within the family Cebidae.

FIGURE 6–21 Spider monkey. Note the prehensile tail.

ischial callosities Patches of tough, hard skin on the buttocks of Old World monkeys and chimpanzees.

Cercopithecidae (serk-oh-pith´-eh-sid-ee)

cercopithecines (serk-oh-pith´ -eh-seens) The subfamily of Old World monkeys that includes baboons, macaques, and guenons.

colobines (kole´-uh-beans) The subfamily of Old World monkeys that includes the African colobus monkeys and Asian langurs.

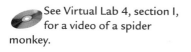
See Virtual Lab 4, section I, for a video of a spider monkey.

FIGURE 6–22 Geographical distribution of modern Old World monkeys.

but also for suspension under branches while feeding. Socially, most cebids and atelids are found in groups of both sexes and all age categories. Some (e.g., titis) form monogamous pairs and live with their subadult offspring.

Old World Monkeys   Except for humans, Old World monkeys are the most widely distributed of all living primates. They are found throughout sub-Saharan Africa and southern Asia, ranging from tropical jungle habitats to semiarid desert and even to seasonally snow-covered areas in northern Japan (Fig. 6–22).

Most Old World monkeys are quadrupedal and primarily arboreal, but some (e.g., baboons) are also adapted to life on the ground. Whether in trees or on the ground, these monkeys spend a good deal of time sleeping, feeding, and grooming while sitting with their upper bodies held erect. Usually associated with this sitting posture are areas of hardened skin on the buttocks (**ischial callosities**) that serve as sitting pads.

All Old World monkeys are placed in one taxonomic family: **Cercopithecidae.** In turn, this family is divided into two subfamilies: the **cercopithecines** and **colobines.**

The cercopithecines are the more generalized of the two groups, showing a more omnivorous dietary adaptation and cheek pouches for storing food. As a group, the cercopithecines eat almost anything, including fruit, seeds, leaves, grasses, tubers, roots, nuts, insects, birds' eggs, amphibians, small reptiles, and small mammals (the last seen in baboons).

The majority of cercopithecine species, such as the mostly arboreal guenons (Fig. 6–23) and the more terrestrial savanna (Fig. 6–24) and hamadryas baboons are found in Africa. However, the several macaque species, which include the well-known rhesus monkey, are widely distributed in southern Asia and India.

Colobine species have a narrower range of food preferences and feed mainly on mature leaves, a behavior that has led to their designation as "leaf-eating monkeys." The colobines are found mainly in Asia, but both the red colobus and the black-and-white colobus are exclusively African (Fig. 6–25). Other colobines include several Asian langur species and the proboscis monkey of Borneo.

Locomotor behavior among Old World monkeys includes arboreal quadrupedalism in guenons, macaques, and langurs; terrestrial quadrupedalism in baboons, patas, and macaques; and semibrachiation and acrobatic leaping in colobus monkeys.

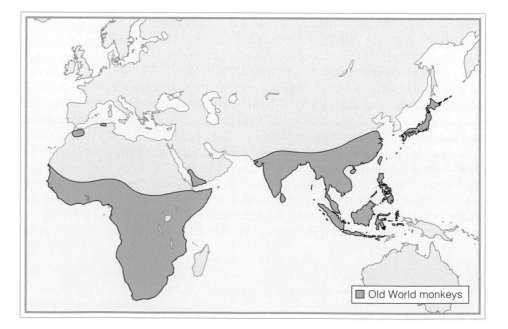
Old World monkeys

FIGURE 6–23 Adult male sykes monkey, one of several guenon species.

Robert Jurmain

(a)

(b)

Courtesy, Bonnie Pedersen/Arlene Kruse

FIGURE 6–24 Savanna baboons. (a) Male. (b) Female.

Marked differences in body size or shape between the sexes, referred to as **sexual dimorphism,** are typical of some terrestrial species and are particularly pronounced in baboons and patas (see Fig. 7–10, p. 189). In these species, male body weight (up to 80 pounds in baboons) may be twice that of females.

sexual dimorphism Differences in physical characteristics between males and females of the same species. For example, humans are slightly sexually dimorphic for body size, with males being taller, on average, than females of the same population.

Lynn Kilgore

See Virtual Lab 1, section IV, for a discussion of sexual dimorphism.

FIGURE 6–25 Black-and-white colobus monkey.

estrus (ess´-truss) Period of sexual receptivity in female mammals (except humans), correlated with ovulation. When used as an adjective, the word is spelled "estrous."

Females of several species (especially baboons and some macaques) exhibit pronounced cyclical changes of the external genitalia. These changes, including swelling and redness, are associated with **estrus,** a hormonally initiated period of sexual receptivity in female nonhuman mammals correlated with ovulation.

Several types of social organization characterize Old World monkeys, and there are uncertainties among primatologists regarding some species. In general, colobines tend to live in small groups, with only one or two adult males. Savanna baboons and most macaque species are found in large social units comprising several adults of both sexes and offspring of all ages. Monogamous pairing is not common in Old World monkeys, but is seen in a few langurs and possibly one or two guenon species.

Old and New World Monkeys: A Case of Homoplasy We have mentioned several differences between Old World monkeys and New World monkeys, but the fact remains that they are all monkeys. That is, they all are adapted to a similar (primarily arboreal) way of life. Except for the South American owl monkey, they are all diurnal, and all are social, usually fairly omnivorous, and quadrupedal, though with variations of this general locomotor pattern.

These similarities are all the more striking when we consider that Old and New World monkeys have gone their separate evolutionary paths for at least 30 million years. It was once believed that both lineages evolved independently from separate prosimian ancestors. The current consensus among researchers, however, disputes this claim (Hoffstetter, 1972; Ciochon and Chiarelli, 1980) and postulates that both Old and New World monkeys arose in Africa from a common monkey ancestor and later reached South America by "rafting" over on chunks of land that had broken away from mainland areas.

There have been various reports of large "floating islands" of vegetation and trees on the open ocean, but there are few accounts of vertebrates being transported across large bodies of water. However, over-water dispersal hypotheses gained support in a report by Censky et al. (1998) that describes the probable introduction, in 1995, of a species of iguana to an island in the Caribbean. The dispersal of this species was attributed to ocean currents and, more specifically, to two hurricanes that struck the region about one month prior to the appearance of the lizards on the island.

A number of conditions that existed 50–30 m.y.a. could have facilitated a trans-Atlantic crossing from Africa to South America. South America and Africa were somewhat closer together than they are today, and prevailing ocean currents are thought to have been favorable. In fact, it's believed that a voyage of around 600 miles could have been accomplished in less than three weeks. In addition, a series of large volcanic islands that existed in the Caribbean and South Atlantic may have served as "stepping stones" for would-be immigrants.

Whether the last common ancestor shared by New and Old World monkeys was a prosimian or a monkey-like animal, what is most remarkable is that the two forms have not diverged more than they have over the last 30 million years or so. The arboreal adaptations we see in the monkeys of both hemispheres are examples of homoplasy (see p. 111) resulting from adaptation in geographically distinct populations that have responded to similar selective pressures.

Hominoidea The formal designation for the superfamily of anthropoids that includes apes and humans.

Hylobatidae (high-lo-baht´-id-ee)

Pongidae (ponj´-id-ee)

HOMINOIDS (APES AND HUMANS)

The other large grouping of anthropoids (the hominoids) includes apes and humans. The superfamily **Hominoidea** includes the so-called "lesser" apes in the family **Hylobatidae** (gibbons and siamangs); the great apes in the family **Pongidae** (orangutans, gorillas, bonobos, and chimpanzees); and humans in the family Hominidae.

Apes and humans differ from monkeys in numerous ways:

1. Generally larger body size, except for gibbons and siamangs
2. Absence of a tail
3. Shortened trunk (lumbar area shorter and more stable)
4. Differences in position and musculature of the shoulder joint (adapted for suspensory locomotion)
5. More complex behavior
6. More complex brain and enhanced cognitive abilities
7. Increased period of infant development and dependency

Gibbons and Siamangs   The eight gibbon species and the closely related siamang are today found in the southeastern tropical areas of Asia (Fig. 6–26). These are the smallest of the apes, with a long, slender body weighing 13 pounds in the gibbon (Fig. 6–27) and 25 pounds in the larger siamang.

The most distinctive structural feature of gibbons and siamangs is related to an adaptation for brachiation. They have extremely long arms, long, permanently curved fingers, short thumbs, and powerful shoulder muscles. These highly specialized locomotor adaptations may be related to feeding behavior while hanging beneath branches. The diet of both species is largely composed of fruit. Both (especially the siamang) also eat a variety of leaves, flowers, and insects.

The basic social unit of gibbons and siamangs comprises an adult male and female with dependent offspring. Although these small apes have been described as monogamous, in reality they sometimes do mate with other individuals. As in marmosets and tamarins, male gibbons and siamangs are very much involved in rearing their young. Both males and females are highly territorial and protect their territories with elaborate whoops and siren-like "songs."

Orangutans   Orangutans (*Pongo pygmaeus*) (Fig. 6–28) are represented by two subspecies found today only in heavily forested areas on the Indonesian islands of Borneo and Sumatra (see Fig. 6–26). Due to poaching by humans and continuing habitat loss on both islands, orangutans are severely threatened by extinction in the wild.

Orangutans are slow, cautious climbers whose locomotor behavior can best be described as "four-handed," referring to the tendency to use all four limbs for grasping and support. Although they are almost completely arboreal, orangutans sometimes travel quadrupedally on the ground. Orangutans are also very large

FIGURE 6–26 Geographical distribution of modern Asian apes.

FIGURE 6–27 White-handed gibbon.

Lynn Kilgore

FIGURE 6–28 Female orangutan.

Robert Jurmain, photo by Jill Matsumoto/Jim Anderson

frugivorous (fru-give´-or-us) Having a diet composed primarily of fruit.

animals with pronounced sexual dimorphism (males may weigh 200 pounds or more and females less than 100 pounds).

In the wild, orangutans lead largely solitary lives, although adult females are usually accompanied by one or two dependent offspring. They are primarily **frugivorous,** but bark, leaves, insects, and meat (on rare occasions) may also be eaten.

Gorillas The largest of all living primates, gorillas (*Gorilla gorilla*) are today confined to forested areas of western and eastern equatorial Africa (Fig. 6–29). There are three generally recognized subspecies, although molecular data suggest that one of these, the western lowland gorilla (Fig. 6–30), is perhaps sufficiently genetically distinct to warrant designation as a separate species (Ruvolo et al., 1994; Garner and Ryder, 1996). The western lowland gorilla is found in several countries of western central Africa and is the most numerous of the three subspecies. Doran and McNeilage (1998) reported an estimated population size of perhaps 110,000. However, a recently published report (Walsh et al., 2003) suggests that numbers may be far lower. The eastern lowland gorilla is found

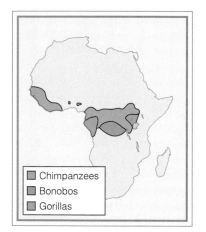

☐ Chimpanzees
☐ Bonobos
☐ Gorillas

FIGURE 6–29 Geographical distribution of modern African apes.

Lynn Kilgore

Lynn Kilgore

FIGURE 6–30 Western lowland gorillas. (a) Male. (b) Female.

(a)   (b)

(a)

(b)

near the eastern border of the Democratic Republic of the Congo (DRC—formerly Zaire) and numbers about 12,000. Mountain gorillas (Fig. 6–31), the most extensively studied of the three subspecies, are found in the mountainous areas of central Africa in Rwanda, the DRC, and Uganda. Mountain gorillas have probably never been very numerous, and today they are among the more endangered primates, numbering only about 600.

Gorillas exhibit marked sexual dimorphism, with males weighing up to 400 pounds and females around 150 to 200 pounds. Because of their weight, adult gorillas, especially males, are primarily terrestrial and adopt a semiquadrupedal (knuckle-walking) posture on the ground.

Mountain gorillas live in groups consisting of one (or sometimes two) large *silverback* males, a variable number of adult females, and their subadult offspring. The term *silverback* refers to the saddle of white hair across the back of full adult (at least 12 or 13 years of age) male gorillas. Additionally, the silverback male may tolerate the presence of one or more young adult *blackback* males, probably his sons. Typically, but not always, both females and males leave their **natal group** as young adults. Females join other groups, and males, who appear to be less likely to emigrate, may live alone for a while, or they may join up with other males before eventually forming their own group.

Systematic studies of free-ranging western lowland gorillas were not initiated until the mid-1980s; thus, our knowledge of their social structure and behavior is still in its infancy. In general, it appears that their social structure is similar to that of mountain gorillas, but groups are smaller and somewhat less cohesive.

All gorillas are almost exclusively vegetarian. Mountain gorillas concentrate primarily on leaves, pith, and stalks. These foods are also important for western lowland gorillas, but western lowland gorillas also eat considerably more fruit, depending on seasonal availability. Recent studies also report that western lowland gorillas, unlike mountain gorillas (which avoid water), frequently wade through swamps while foraging on aquatic plants.

Perhaps because of their large body size and enormous strength, gorillas have long been considered ferocious. But in reality, they are usually shy and gentle. This is not to imply that gorillas are never aggressive. Among males, competition for females can be extremely violent. Moreover, when threatened, males will attack, and they will certainly defend their group from any perceived danger, whether it be another male gorilla or a human hunter. Still, the reputation of gorillas as murderous beasts is the result of uninformed myth making and little else.

FIGURE 6–31 Mountain gorillas. (a) Male. (b) Female.

natal group The group in which animals are born and raised. (*Natal* pertains to birth.)

Chimpanzees Chimpanzees are probably the best known of all nonhuman primates (Fig. 6–32). Often misunderstood because of zoo exhibits, circus acts, television shows, and movies, the true nature of chimpanzees didn't become known until years of fieldwork with wild groups provided a reliable picture. Today, chimpanzees are found in equatorial Africa, stretching in a broad belt from the Atlantic Ocean in the west to Lake Tanganyika in the east. Their range, however, is patchy within this large geographical area, and with further habitat destruction, it is becoming even more so.

In many ways, chimpanzees are anatomically similar to gorillas, with corresponding limb proportions and upper-body shape. This similarity is due to commonalities in locomotion when on the ground (quadrupedal knuckle walking). However, the ecological adaptations of chimpanzees and gorillas differ, with chimpanzees spending more time in the trees. Moreover, whereas gorillas are typically placid and quiet, chimpanzees are highly excitable, active, and noisy.

Chimpanzees are smaller than orangutans and gorillas, and although they are sexually dimorphic, sex differences are not as pronounced as in these other species. While male chimpanzees may weigh over 100 pounds, females can weigh at least 80.

In addition to quadrupedal knuckle walking, chimpanzees (particularly youngsters) may brachiate while in the trees. When on the ground, they frequently walk bipedally for short distances when carrying food or other objects.

Chimpanzees eat an amazing variety of foods, including fruit, leaves, insects, nuts, birds' eggs, berries, caterpillars, and small mammals. Moreover, both males and females occasionally take part in group hunting efforts to kill small mammals such as red colobus, young baboons, bushpigs, and antelope. When hunts are successful, the prey is shared by the group members.

Chimpanzees live in large, fluid communities of as many as 50 individuals or more. At the core of a chimpanzee community is a group of bonded males. Although relationships between them are not always peaceful or stable, these males nevertheless act as a group to defend their territory and are highly intolerant of unfamiliar chimpanzees, especially nongroup males.

Even though chimpanzees are said to live in communities, there are few times, if any, when all members are together. Rather, chimpanzees tend to come and go, so that the individuals they encounter vary from day to day. Moreover, adult females usually forage either alone or in the company of their offspring. The latter foraging group could comprise several chimpanzees, as females with infants sometimes accompany their own mothers and their younger siblings. A female may also leave her group, either permanently to join another community

FIGURE 6–32 Chimpanzees. (a) Male. (b) Female.

(a)

(b)

FIGURE 6–33 Female bonobos with young.

Courtesy, Ellen Ingmanson

or temporarily while she's in estrus. This behavioral pattern may reduce the risk of mating with close male relatives, because males apparently never leave the group in which they were born.

Chimpanzee social behavior is complex, and individuals form lifelong attachments with friends and relatives. Indeed, the bond between mothers and infants can remain strong until one or the other dies. This may be a considerable period, because many wild chimpanzees live into their mid-30s and a few into their 40s.

Bonobos   Bonobos (*Pan paniscus*) are found only in an area south of the Zaire River in the DRC (see Fig. 6–29). Not officially recognized by European scientists until the 1920s, they remain among the least studied of the great apes. Although ongoing field studies have produced much information (Susman, 1984; Kano, 1992), research has been hampered by civil war. There are no accurate counts of bonobos, but their numbers are believed to be between 10,000 and 20,000 (IUCN, 1996), and these are highly threatened by human hunting, warfare, and habitat loss.

Because bonobos bear a strong resemblance to chimpanzees but are somewhat smaller, they have been called "pygmy chimpanzees." However, differences in body size are not striking, although bonobos have a more linear body build, longer legs relative to arms, a relatively smaller head, a dark face from birth, and tufts of hair at the side of the face (Fig. 6–33).

Bonobos are more arboreal than chimpanzees, and are less excitable and aggressive. While aggression is not unknown, it appears that physical violence both within and between groups is uncommon. Like chimpanzees, bonobos live in geographically based, fluid communities, and they eat many of the same foods, including occasional meat derived from small mammals (Badrian and Malinky, 1984). But bonobo communities are not centered around a group of closely bonded males. Instead, male-female bonding is more important than in chimpanzees (and most other nonhuman primates), and females are not peripheral to the group (Badrian and Badrian, 1984). This may be related to bonobo sexuality, which differs from that of other nonhuman primates in that copulation is frequent and occurs throughout a female's estrous cycle.

HUMANS

Humans are the only living representatives of the habitually bipedal hominids (genus *Homo*, species *sapiens*). Our primate heritage is evident in our overall anatomy and genetic makeup and in many aspects of human behavior. With the exception of reduced canine size, human teeth are typical primate teeth; indeed, in overall morphology, they very much resemble ape teeth. The human dependence on vision and decreased reliance on olfaction, as well as flexible limbs and grasping hands, are rooted in our primate, arboreal past. Humans can even brachiate, and playgrounds often accommodate this ability in children.

Humans in general are omnivorous, although all societies observe certain culturally based dietary restrictions. Nevertheless, as a species with a rather generalized digestive system, we are physiologically adapted to digest an extremely wide assortment of foods. Perhaps to our detriment, given how humans tend to go to extremes, we also share with our relatives a fondness for sweets that originates from the importance of high-energy fruits in the diets of many nonhuman primates.

But quite obviously, humans are unique among primates and indeed among all animals. For example, no member of any other species has the ability to write or think about issues such as how they differ from other life forms. This ability is rooted in the fact that human evolution, during the last 800,000 years or so, has been characterized by dramatic increases in brain size and other neurological changes.

Humans are also completely dependent on culture. Without cultural innovation, it would have been impossible for us to have ever left the tropics. As it is, humans inhabit every corner of the planet with the exception of Antarctica, and we have even established outposts there. And lest we forget, a fortunate few have even walked on the moon. None of the technologies (indeed, none of the other aspects of culture) that humans have developed over the last several thousand years would have been possible without the highly developed cognitive abilities we alone possess. Nevertheless, the neurological basis for intelligence is rooted in our evolutionary past, and it's something we share with other primates. Indeed, research has demonstrated that several nonhuman primate species—most notably chimpanzees, bonobos, and gorillas—display a level of problem solving and insight that most people would have considered impossible 25 years ago (see Chapter 8).

Humans are uniquely predisposed to use spoken language, and for the last 5,000 years or so, we have used written language as well. This ability exists because human evolution has modified certain neurological and anatomical structures in ways not observed in any other animal (see p. 210). But while nonhuman primates aren't anatomically capable of producing speech, research has demonstrated that to varying degrees the great apes are able to communicate through the use of symbols. And basically, that's a foundation for language that humans and the great apes (to a limited degree) have in common.

Aside from cognitive abilities, the one other trait that sets humans apart from other primates is our unique (among mammals) form of *habitual* bipedal locomotion. This particular trait appeared early in the evolution of our lineage, and over time, we have become more efficient at it because of related changes in the musculoskeletal anatomy of the pelvis, leg, and foot (see Chapter 9). But for whatever reasons, early hominids increasingly adopted bipedalism because they were already preadapted for it. That is, as primates, and especially as ape-like primates, they were already behaviorally predisposed to, and anatomically capable of, at least short-term bipedal walking before they adopted it wholeheartedly.

Thus, while it is certainly true that human beings are unique intellectually, and in some ways anatomically, we are still primates. In fact, fundamentally, humans are somewhat exaggerated African apes.

Endangered Primates

In September 2000, scientists announced that a subspecies of red colobus, named Miss Waldron's red colobus, had officially been declared extinct. This announcement came after a six-year search for the 20-pound monkey that had not been seen for 20 years (Oates, et al., 2000). Thus, this species, indigenous to the West African countries of Ghana and the Ivory Coast, has the distinction of being the first nonhuman primate to be declared extinct in the twenty-first century. But it will certainly not be the last. In fact, as of this writing, over half of all nonhuman primate species are now in jeopardy, and some face almost immediate extinction in the wild (Table 6–1).

Population estimates of free-ranging primates are difficult to obtain, but some species (hapalemur, diadem sifaka, aye-aye, lion tamarin, muriqui, red colobus subspecies, lion-tailed macaque, and mountain gorilla) now number

See Virtual Lab 1, section III, for a stark contrast between the restricted geographical ranges of nonhuman primates and humans.

TABLE 6–1 African Primates in Danger of Extinction

SPECIES/ SUBSPECIES COMMON NAME	LOCATION	ESTIMATED SIZE OF REMAINING POPULATION
Barbary macaque	North Africa	23,000
Tana River mangabey	Tana River, Kenya	800–1,100
Sanje mangabey	Uzungwa Mts., Tanzania	1,800–3,000
Drill	Cameroon, Bioko	?
Preuss' guenon	Cameroon, Bioko	?
White-throated guenon	Southwest Nigeria	?
Pennant's red colobus	Bioko	?
Preuss' red colobus	Cameroon	8,000
Bouvier's red colobus	Congo Republic	?
Tana River red colobus	Tana River, Kenya	200–300
Uhehe red colobus	Uzungwa Mts., Tanzania	10,000
Zanzibar red colobus	Zanzibar	1,500
Mountain gorilla	Virunga Volcanoes (Rwanda, Uganda, and Democratic Republic of the Congo) and Impenetrable Forest (Uganda)	550–650

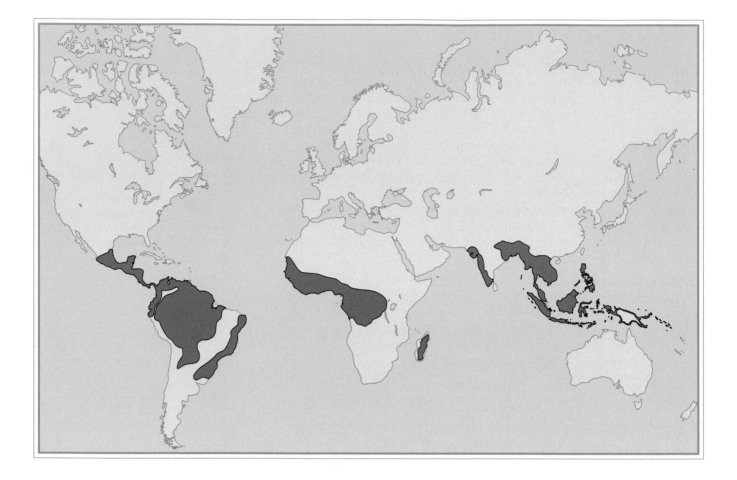

FIGURE 6–34 Tropical rain forests of the world (distribution before recent massive destruction).

only in the hundreds. Others are believed to be represented in the wild by a few thousand (agile mangabey, mentawi langur, red colobus subspecies, moloch gibbon, Kloss' gibbon, orangutan, lowland gorilla, chimpanzee, and bonobo).

There are three basic reasons for the worldwide depletion of nonhuman primates: habitat destruction, hunting for food, and live capture for export or local trade. Underlying these three causes is one major factor: unprecedented human population growth, which is occurring at a faster rate in developing countries than in the developed world. The developing nations of Africa, Asia, and Central and South America are home to over 90 percent of all nonhuman primate species, and these countries, aided in no small part by the industrialized countries of Europe and the United States, are cutting their forests at a rate of about 30 million acres per year (Fig. 6–34). Unbelievably, in the year 2002, deforestation of the Amazon increased by 40 percent over that of 2001. This increase, in large part, was due to land clearing for the cultivation of soybeans. In Brazil, the Atlantic rain forest originally covered some 385,000 square miles. Today, an estimated 7 percent is all that remains of what was once home to countless New World monkeys and thousands of other species.

Much of the motivation behind the devastation of the rain forests is, of course, economic: the short-term gains from clearing forests to create immediately available (but poor) farmland or ranchland; the use of trees for lumber and paper products; and large-scale mining operations (with their necessary roads, digging, etc., all of which cause habitat destruction). Regionally, the loss of rain forest ranks as a national disaster for some countries. For example, the West African nation Sierra Leone had an estimated 15,000 square miles of rain forest early in the twentieth century. Today, less than 530 square miles remain, and most of this destruction has occurred since World War II. People in many developing countries are also short of fuel and frequently use whatever firewood is obtainable. And, of course, the demand for tropical hardwoods (e.g., mahogany, teak, and rosewood) in the United States, Europe, and Japan continues unabated, creating an enormously profitable market for rain forest products.

Primates have also been captured live for zoos, biomedical research, and the exotic pet trade. Live capture has declined since the implementation of the Convention on Trade in Endangered Species of Wild Flora and Fauna (CITES) in 1973. Currently, 87 countries have signed this treaty, agreeing not to allow trade in species listed by CITES as being endangered. However, even some CITES members are still occasionally involved in the illegal primate trade (Japan and Belgium, among others).

In many areas, habitat loss has been, and continues to be, the single greatest cause of declining numbers of nonhuman primates. But everywhere primates occur, human hunting for food now poses an even greater threat. This tragic turn of events occurred rather quickly, but during the 1990s, primatologists became increasingly aware of the immense scope of the slaughter, which now accounts for the loss of thousands of nonhuman primates and other species annually (see Issue, pp. 134–136).

Although the slaughter may be most extreme in Africa, it is by no means limited to that continent. In South America, for example, hunting nonhuman primates for food is common (Fig. 6–35). And one report documents that in less than two years, one family of Brazilian rubber tappers killed almost 500 members of various large-bodied species, including spider monkeys, woolly monkeys, and howler monkeys (Peres, 1990). Moreover, live capture and (illegal) trade in endangered primate species continues unabated in China and Southeast Asia, where nonhuman primates are not only eaten but also funneled into the exotic pet trade. But perhaps most important is the fact that primate body parts also figure prominently in traditional medicines, and with increasing human population size, the enormous demand for these products (and products from other, nonprimate species, such as tigers) has placed many species in extreme jeopardy.

Fortunately, steps are being taken to ensure the survival of some species. Many developing countries, such as Costa Rica and the Malagasy Republic (Madagascar), are designating national parks and other reserves for the protection of natural resources, including primates. There are also several private international efforts aimed at curbing the bushmeat trade. It is only through such practices and through educational programs that many primate species have a chance of escaping extinction, at least in the immediate future.

If you are in your 20s or 30s, you will live to hear of the extinction of some of our marvelously unique and clever cousins. Many more will undoubtedly slip away unnoticed. Tragically, this will occur, in most cases, before we have even had the opportunity to get to know them.

Each species on earth is the current result of a unique set of evolutionary events that, over millions of years, has produced a finely adapted component of a diverse ecosystem. When it becomes extinct, that adaptation and that part of biodiversity is lost forever. What a tragedy it will be if, through our own mismanagement and greed, we awaken to a world without chimpanzees, mountain gorillas, or the tiny, exquisite lion tamarin. When this day comes, we truly will have lost a part of ourselves, and we will certainly be the poorer for it.

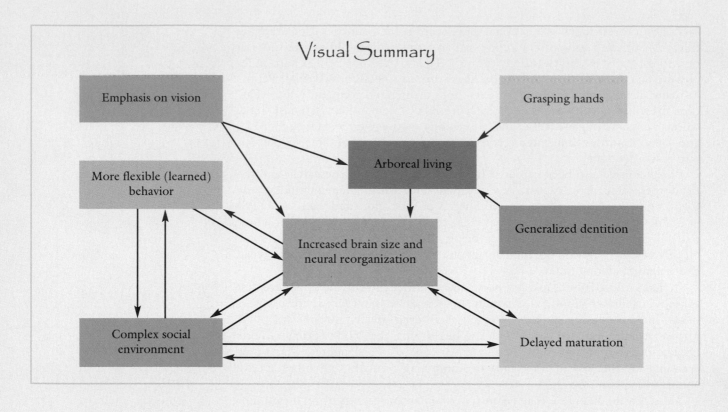

Summary

In this chapter, we have introduced you to the primates, the mammalian order that includes prosimians, monkeys, apes, and humans. We discussed how primates, including humans, have retained a number of ancestral characteristics that have permitted them, as a group, to be generalized in terms of diet and locomotor patterns. You also were presented with a general outine of traits that differentiate primates from other mammals.

We also discussed primate classification and how primatologists are redefining relationships between some lineages. In particular, we mentioned the removal of tarsiers from the suborder Prosimii, placing them with the anthropoids in a grouping called the haplorhines. The lemurs and lorises would be kept together under the suborder distinction of strepsirhine. Also, chimpanzees, gorillas, and orangutans would be placed with humans in the family Hominidae. These changes reflect increasing knowledge of the genetic relationships between primate lineages and, particularly in the case of tarsiers, reconsideration of various anatomical characteristics.

You also became acquainted with the major groups of nonhuman primates, especially with regard to their basic social structure, diet, and locomotor patterns. Most primates are diurnal and live in social groups. The only nocturnal primates are lorises, some lemurs, tarsiers, and owl monkeys. Nocturnal species tend to forage for food alone or with offspring and one or two other animals. Diurnal primates live in a variety of social groupings, including monogamous pairs, and groups consisting of one male with several females and offspring or those composed of several males and females and offspring.

Finally, we talked about the precarious existence of most nonhuman primates today as they face hunting, capture, and habitat loss. These threats are all imposed by only one primate species, one that arrived fairly late on the evolutionary stage. In the next two chapters, where we discuss various aspects of human and nonhuman primate behavior, you will become better acquainted with the fairly recently evolved primate species, of which you are a member.

Questions for Review

1. How has genetic research clarified biological relationships between species? How can we determine what genetic similarities and differences exist between species? Why is it important to examine how genes and proteins change over time?
2. How does a classification scheme reflect biological and evolutionary changes in a lineage? Can you give an example of suggested changes to how primates are classified? What is the basis of these suggestions?
3. What are some basic differences between lemurs and lorises and anthropoids? What do we mean when we

For Further Thought

1. How do you think continued advances in genetic research will influence how we look at our species' relationships with nonhuman primates in 10 years?

2. What factors are threatening the existence of nonhuman primates in the wild? What can you do to help in the efforts to save nonhuman primates from extinction?

Go to the book website at **http://www.anthropology.wadsworth.com** for resources to help you explore these questions further. Click on "For Further Thought" for this chapter.

say that lemurs and lorises are more primitive than anthropoids?

4. What are the characteristics, taken as a group, that distinguish primates from other mammals? In which type of environment did these traits evolve?

5. When we say that primates are generalized when compared to many other mammals, what do we mean? Provide at least two examples.

Suggested Further Reading

Fleagle, John. 1999. *Primate Adaptation and Evolution*. New York: Academic Press.

Mittermeier, Russell A., Ian Tattersall, William R. Konstant, David M. Meyers, and Roderick B. Mast. 1994. *Lemurs of Madagascar*. Washington, DC: Conservation International.

Nowak, Ronald M. 1999. *Walker's Primates of the World*. Baltimore: The Johns Hopkins University Press.

Rowe, Noel. 1996. *The Pictorial Guide to the Living Primates*. Charlestown, RI: Pogonias Press.

Online Anthropology Resource Center

Go to the Anthropology Resource Center at **http://www.anthropology.wadsworth.com** for a wealth of online resources, including a companion website for your text that provides study aids such as self-quizzes for each chapter and a practice final exam, as well as links to anthropology websites and information on the latest theories and discoveries in the field. Also, check out InfoTrac College Edition®, your online library that offers full-length articles from thousands of scholarly and popular publications. Just click on the InfoTrac button at the companion website and use the passcode that came with your book.

7 Primate Behavior

Orangutan (*Pongo pygmaeus*)
Ryan McVay/Getty Images

Introduction

People are so intrigued by nonhuman animal **behavior** that nature shows are one of the more popular forms of television entertainment, and you may watch some of these programs yourself. These shows perform a good service because they may be the only source of information about nonhuman animal behavior for a majority of people. Unfortunately, much of this information is doled out in short segments that are little more than sound bites crammed between commercials. That fact, coupled with the necessarily superficial presentation of scientific data results in misleading narration that reinforces many misconceptions people have about other species.

In truth, behavior, especially in mammals and birds, is extremely complex because in all species, it has been shaped over evolutionary time by countless interactions between genetic and environmental processes. But not everyone has accepted this premise. Social scientists, in particular, have objected to the notion of genetic influences on human behavior because of concerns that it implies that behaviors are fixed entities that can't be modified by experience (i.e., learning).

Furthermore, among the general public, there is the prevailing notion of a fundamental division between humans and all other animals. In some cultures, this view is fostered by religion, but even when religion isn't a factor, most people see themselves as uniquely set apart from all other species. This is unfortunate, because people judge other species from a human perspective, which of course isn't a valid thing to do. For example, many people think cats are cruel because they play with mice before they kill them. Horses are skittish if they leap aside when a breeze rattles the leaves of a shrub. But this kind of thinking is based on uninformed opinion, and the truth is that most people have no real understanding of why other species do what they do.

Sometimes cats do play with mice before killing them because that's how, as kittens, they learn to hunt small prey, and hunting small prey is how they survive in an undomesticated environment. Cruelty doesn't enter into it because the cat has no concept of cruelty and no idea of what it's like to be the mouse. Likewise, the horse that tosses you onto a cactus doesn't do it deliberately. She does it because her behavior has been shaped by thousands of generations of horse ancestors who jumped first and asked questions later. Horses evolved as prey animals, and their evolutionary history is littered with unfortunate individuals that didn't respond quickly to a sound in a shrub. In many cases, they learned, too late, that the sound wasn't caused by a breeze at all. This is a mistake prey animals don't usually survive, and those that don't leap first leave few descendants.

Actually, this chapter isn't about cats and horses. It's about what we currently know and hypothesize about the individual and social behaviors of nonhuman primates. But we begin with the familiar examples of cats and horses because we want to point out that many basic behaviors have been shaped by the evolutionary history of particular species. Likewise, the same factors that have influenced many types of behavior in nonprimate animals also apply to primates. Consequently, if we wish to discover the underlying principles of behavioral evolution, we first need to identify the interactions between a number of environmental and physiological variables.

behavior Anything organisms do that involves action in response to internal or external stimuli. The response of an individual, group, or species to its environment. Such responses may or may not be deliberate and they aren't necessarily the results of conscious decision making, as in one-celled organisms, insects, and many other species.

See the following sections of the CD-ROM for topics covered in this chapter: Virtual Lab 1; Virtual Lab 2, section I; Virtual Lab 5, section I; Virtual Lab 6, sections I, II, and IV; and Virtual Labs 9–12.

Primate Field Studies

free-ranging Pertaining to non-captive animals living in their natural habitat. Ideally, the behavior of wild study groups would be free of human influence.

See Virtual Lab 6, sections I and II, for discussion of primate behavior and field methods used by primatologists.

The primary goal of primate field studies is to collect information on **free-ranging** animals, whose behavior is unaffected by human activities. Unfortunately, most, if not all, primate populations have now been exposed to human activities that influence their behavior (Janson, 2000). Moreover, wild primates aren't easy to study until they've been habituated to the presence of humans, whom they generally fear, and the habituation process can take a very long time. And once accomplished, habituation itself can change primate behavior! Until the last two decades, the most systematic information on free-ranging primates came from species that spend a lot of time on the ground (baboons, macaques, some lemurs, chimpanzees, and gorillas) (Fig. 7-1a). This is because arboreal primates are difficult to identify and observe as they flit through the forest canopy (Fig. 7-1b). Now, however, primatologists have accumulated a great deal of data on many arboreal species, including black and white colobus, red colobus, some guenons, capuchins, howlers, spider monkeys, muriquis, marmosets and tamarins. Others have focused on nocturnal prosimians and tarsiers. Thanks to these efforts, many of the gaps in our knowledge of nonhuman primates are being filled. However, with each new discovery come new questions, so the process will continue as long as there are wild primates to study.

The earliest studies of nonhuman primates in their natural habitats began with an American psychologist named Roberts Yerkes who, in the late 1920s and 1930s, sent students into the field to study gorillas, chimpanzees, and howler monkeys. Japanese scientists began their pioneering work with Japanese macaques in 1948 (Sugiyama, 1965). In 1960, Jane Goodall started her now-famous field study of chimpanzees at Gombe National Park, Tanzania, and this project was closely followed by Diane Fossey's work with mountain gorillas in Rwanda, and Birute Galdikas' research on orangutans in Borneo. All three projects, initiated by paleoanthropologist Louis Leakey, are still ongoing, but today they aren't all directly supervised by these women.

(a)

FIGURE 7–1 (a) Rhesus macaques spend much of their time on the ground and are much easier to observe than black and white colobus. (b) Imagine trying to recognize the colobus monkeys as individuals. What tools and techniques would you use to identify them?

(b)

Courtesy, Jean De Rousseau

Courtesy, John Oates

In the early l960s almost nothing was known of nonhuman primate behavior, so initial studies were, of necessity, largely descriptive in nature. Still, some early studies of savanna baboons (DeVore and Washburn, 1963), hamadryas baboons (Kummer, 1968), and geladas (Crook and Gartlan, 1966) related aspects of **social structure** and individual behavior to **ecological** factors. Most early work emphasized male behaviors, partly because of the role of males in group defense. But, by the late 1970s and early 1980s primatologists were focusing more attention on females, not solely as mothers, but also because they have an enormous influence on group dynamics.

Since then, primatologists have studied and continue to study well over 100 nonhuman primate species. Because most primates live in social groups, extensive research is devoted to primate social behavior, the costs and benefits of living in bisexual groupings, and the advantages and disadvantages of specific behaviors to individuals and groups. Behavioral research is done within an evolutionary framework, so primatologists test hypotheses relating to how behaviors have evolved. Moreover, the application of genetic techniques to primate behavioral research is beginning to provide answers to many questions, especially those that relate to paternity and to reproductive success.

The Evolution of Behavior

Scientists who study behavior in free-ranging primates do so from an ecological and evolutionary perspective, meaning that they focus on the relationship between individual and social behaviors, the natural environment, and various physiological traits of the species in question. This approach is called **behavioral ecology,** and it's based on the underlying assumption that all of the biological components of ecological systems (animals, plants, and even microorganisms) evolved together. Therefore, behaviors are adaptations to environmental circumstances that existed in the past as well as in the present.

Briefly, the cornerstone of this perspective is that *behaviors have evolved through the operation of natural selection.* That is, if behaviors are influenced by genes, then they are subject to natural selection in the same way physical characteristics are. (Remember that within a specific environmental context, natural selection favors traits that provide a reproductive advantage to the individuals who possess them.) Therefore, behavior constitutes a phenotype, and those individuals whose behavioral phenotypes increase reproductive fitness will pass on their genes at a faster rate than others. But this certainly doesn't mean that primatologists think that genes code for specific behaviors, such as a gene for aggression, another for cooperation, and so on. Studying complex behaviors from an evolutionary viewpoint does not imply a one gene–one behavior relationship, nor does it suggest that those behaviors that are influenced by genes can't be modified through learning.

Much of the behavior of insects and other invertebrates is largely under genetic control. In other words, most behavioral patterns in those species aren't learned. However, in many vertebrates, especially birds and mammals, the proportion of behavior that is due to learning, is substantially increased, while the proportion under genetic control is reduced. This is especially true of primates. And, in humans, who are so much a product of culture, most behavior is learned. But at the same time, we also know that in higher organisms, some behaviors are at least partly influenced by certain gene products such as hormones. You may be aware that numerous studies have shown that increased levels of testosterone increase aggression in many species. You may also have heard that some conditions such as depression, schizophrenia, and bipolar disorder are caused by abnormal levels of certain neurotransmitters. Neurotransmitters are chemicals produced by brain cells. These neurotransmitters are then sent from one cell to another to cause a

social structure The composition, size, and sex ratio of a group of animals. Social structures are the results of natural selection in specific habitats, and they influence individual interactions and social relationships. In many species, social structure varies, depending on different environmental factors. Therefore, in most primate species, social structure should be viewed as flexible, not fixed.

ecological Pertaining to the relationships between organisms and all aspects of their environment (temperature, predators, nonpredators, vegetation, availability of food and water, types of food, disease organisms, parasites, etc.).

behavioral ecology The study of the evolution of behavior, emphasizing the role of ecological factors as agents of natural selection. Behaviors and behavioral patterns have been selected for because they increase the reproductive fitness of individuals (i.e., they are adaptive) in specific environmental contexts.

See Virtual Lab 5, section I, for a discussion of ecological factors.

response, (i.e., they transmit information from cell to cell). These responses range from muscle activity to release of hormones elsewhere in the body.

Brain cells manufacture neurotransmitters because of the action of functional genes within them, and in this way, genes can influence aspects of behavior. In some cases many genetic loci are involved and at each locus there may be one or more alleles, each of which can influence the amount of a given neurotransmitter a cell will produce. In turn, abnormal levels of neurotransmitters are the basis of drug therapies for many conditions. For example, depression can be caused by inadequate levels of the chemical serotonin and may respond to a class of drugs that includes Prozac or Zoloft. These drugs act by increasing the availability of serotonin to receiving cells.

Behavioral genetics, or the study of how genes influence behavior, is a relatively new field and we currently don't know the degree to which genes influence behavior in humans or, indeed, other species. But we do know that behavior must be viewed as the product of *complex interactions between genetic and environmental factors.* Between species, there is considerable variation in the limits and potentials for learning and for behavioral **plasticity** or flexibility. In some species, the potentials are extremely broad; in others, they aren't. Ultimately, those limits and potentials are set by genetic factors that have been selected for throughout the evolutionary history of every species. That history, in turn, has been shaped by the ecological setting, not only of living species, *but also that of their ancestors.*

plasticity The capacity to change. In a behavioral context, the ability of animals to modify behaviors in response to differing circumstances.

One of the major goals of primatology is to determine how behaviors influence reproductive fitness and how ecological factors have influenced their development. While the actual mechanics of behavioral evolution aren't yet fully understood, new technologies and methodologies are beginning to answer numerous questions. For example, genetic analysis has recently been used to establish paternity in a few primate groups, and this has helped support hypotheses about some behaviors (see p. 224). But, in general, an evolutionary approach to the study of behavior doesn't provide definitive answers to many research questions. Rather, it provides a valuable framework within which primatologists analyze data to generate and test hypotheses concerning behavioral patterns.

Because primates are among the most social of animals, social behavior is one of the major topics in primate research. This is a broad subject and it includes *all* aspects of behavior that occur in social groupings, even some you may not think of as social behaviors like feeding or mating. In order to understand the function of one behavioral element, it's necessary to determine how it is influenced by numerous interrelated factors. As an example, we will discuss some of the more important variables that influence social structure (see A Closer Look). But we must remember that we're discussing complex interactions and that social structure also influences individual behavior so that, in many cases, the distinctions between social and individual behaviors are blurred.

FIGURE 7–2 Dwarf mouse lemur

Russ Mittermeir

SOME FACTORS THAT INFLUENCE SOCIAL STRUCTURE

Body size   Among the living primates, body size is extremely diverse, ranging from the dwarf mouse lemur (Fig. 7–2) (about 66 grams or 2.4 ounces) to the gorilla (117 kilograms or about 260 pounds). As a general rule, larger animals require fewer calories per unit of weight than smaller animals. This is because larger animals have a smaller ratio of surface area to mass than do smaller animals. Since body heat is lost at the surface, they are able to retain heat more efficiently, and therefore they require less energy overall. It may seem strange, but two five kilogram (11 pound) monkeys require more food than one 10 kg (22 pound) monkey (Fleagle, 1999).

Types of Nonhuman Primate Social Groups*

1. One male-multifemale. A single adult male, several adult females, and their offspring. This is the most common primate mating structure, in which only one male actively breeds. Usually formed by a male joining a kin group of females. Females usually form the permanent nucleus of the group. Examples: guenons, gorillas, some pottos, some spider monkeys, patas, some langurs, and some colobus. In many species, several one-male groups may form large congregations.

2. *Multimale-multifemale.* Several adult males, several adult females, and their young. Many of the males reproduce. The presence of several males in the group may lead to tension and to the formation of a dominance hierarchy. Examples: some lemurs, macaques, mangabeys, savanna baboons, vervets, squirrel monkeys, some spider monkeys, and chimpanzees. In some species (e.g., vervets, baboons and macaques, females are members of matrilines, or groups composed of a female, her female offspring and their offspring. These kin groups are arranged in a hierarchy, thus each matriline is dominant to some other matrilines and, at the same time, subordinate to others.

3. *Monogamous pair.* A mated pair and its young. The term "monogamous" is somewhat misleading because extra-pair matings aren't uncommon. Usually arboreal, minimal sexual dimorphism, frequently territorial. Adults don't normally tolerate other adults of the same sex. Not found among the great apes, and least common of the breeding structures among nonhuman primates. Examples: siamangs, gibbons, indris, titis, sakis, owl monkeys, and pottos. Males may directly participate in infant care.

4. *Polyandry.* One female and two males. Seen only in some New World monkeys (marmosets and tamarins). Males participate in care of infants.

5. *Solitary.* Individual forages for food alone. Seen in some nocturnal prosimians (aye-ayes, lorises, and galagos). In some species, adult females may forage in pairs or may be accompanied by offspring. Also seen in orangutans.

---

*There are also other groupings, such as foraging groups, hunting groups, all female or male groups, and so on. Like humans, nonhuman primates do not always maintain one kind of group; single-male, multifemale groups may sometimes form multimale-multifemale groups and vice versa. Hamadryas baboons, for example, are described as living in one-male groups but they form herds of 100 or more at night as they move to the safety of sleeping cliffs.

Basal metabolic rate (BMR)   The BMR concerns **metabolism** and it is the rate at which energy is used by the body at a resting state to maintain all bodily functions. It's closely correlated with body size so, in general, smaller animals have a higher BMR than larger ones. Consequently, smaller primates like galagos, tarsiers, marmosets, and tamarins require an energy rich diet high in protein (insects), fats (nuts and seeds), and carbohydrates (fruits and seeds). Some larger primates, which tend to have a lower BMR and reduced energy requirements relative to body size, can benefit from less energy-rich foods.

Diet   The nutritional requirements of animals are related to the previous two factors and all three have evolved together. When primatologists study the relationships between diet and behavior, they consider the benefits in terms of energy (calories) derived from various food items against the costs (energy expended) of obtaining and digesting them.

   As we discussed in Chapter 6, most primates eat a wide variety of food items, but each species concentrates on some more than others. And almost all consume some animal protein even if it's just in the form of insects and other invertebrates. While small-bodied primates focus on high-energy foods, larger

metabolism The chemical processes within cells that breakdown nutrients and release energy for the body to use. (When nutrients are broken down into their component parts, such as amino acids, energy is released and made available for the cell to use.)

Lynn Kilgore

FIGURE 7–3 This male mountain gorilla has only to reach out to find something to eat.

bodied species don't necessarily need to. For instance, mountain gorillas exploit leaves, pith from bamboo stems, and other types of vegetation. Lowland gorillas do likewise, but they exploit a wider range of materials that includes a number of water plants. These foods have less caloric value than fruits, nuts, and seeds, but they still serve these animals well because gorillas tend to spend much of the day eating. Moreover, gorillas don't need to expend much energy searching for food since they are literally surrounded by it (Fig. 7–3).

Some monkeys, especially colobines (colobus and langur species), are primarily leaf eaters. Compared to many other monkeys, they are fairly large-bodied and they've also evolved elongated intestines and pouched stomachs that enable them, with the assistance of intestinal bacteria, to digest the tough fibers and cellulose in leaves. Moreover, in at least two langur species, there is a duplicated gene that produces an enzyme which assists in the digestive process. Importantly, this gene duplication is not found in other primates that have been studied and therefore the duplication event probably occurred after colobines and cercopithecines (see p. 152) last shared a common ancestor (Zhang, et al., 2002). Since having a second copy of the gene was advantageous to colobine ancestors who were probably already exploiting leaves, natural selection favored it to the point it was established in the lineage.

Distribution of resources   Different kinds of foods are distributed in various ways. Food items such as leaves can be abundant and dense and will therefore support large groups of animals. (Think also of immense herds of grazing animals that can be supported on large expanses of grassland.) Other foods, such as insects, may be widely scattered. Thus, the animals that rely on them usually feed alone or perhaps in the company of one or two others.

Fruit and nuts in dispersed trees, or berries on shrubs, are foods that occur in clumps. These can most efficiently be exploited by smaller groups of animals, so large groups frequently break up into smaller subunits while feeding. Such subunits may consist of one-male groups (hamadryas baboons) or matrilines (macaques). Species that subsist on abundantly distributed resources may also live in one-male groups, and because food is plentiful, these one-male units are able to join with others, to form large, stable communities (howlers and some colobines). To the casual observer, these communities can appear to be multimale-multifemale groups.

Some species that rely on foods distributed in small clumps tend to be protective of resources, especially if their feeding area is small enough to be defended. Some of these species live in small groups, composed of monogamous pairs (siamangs) or a female with one or two males (marmosets and tamarins). Naturally, dependent offspring are also included. Lastly, many kinds of food are only seasonally available. These include fruits, nuts, seeds, berries, etc. Primates that rely on seasonally available foods must exploit a number of different types and must move about to obtain food throughout the year. This is another factor that tends to favor smaller feeding groups.

The distribution and seasonality of water are also important variables. Water supplies may be stable year-round as in continuously flowing rivers and streams, or where there is abundant rainfall. But in areas that have a dry season, water may only exist in widely dispersed ponds that primates must share with other animals, including predators.

Predation   Primates are vulnerable to many types of predators, including snakes, birds of prey, leopards, wild dogs, lions, and even other primates. Their responses to predation depend on the type of predator, body size and social structure. Typically, where predation pressure is high and body size is small, large communities are advantageous. These may be multimale-multifemale groups or congregations of one-male groups (see p. 182).

Relationships with other, non-predatory species   Many primate species associate with other primate and nonprimate species for various reasons including predator avoidance (see p. 183). When they do share habitats with other species they exploit somewhat different resources (see p. 181).

Dispersal   Another factor that greatly influences social structure and also relationships within groups is dispersal. As is true of most mammals (and indeed, most vertebrates), members of one sex leave the group in which they were born (their *natal group*) about the time they reach puberty. There is considerable variability within and between species regarding which sex leaves, but male dispersal is the most common pattern in primates (e.g., ring-tailed lemurs, vervets, and macaques, to name a few). Female dispersal is seen in some colobus species, hamadryas baboons, chimpanzees, and mountain gorillas.

Dispersal may have more than one outcome. Typically, when females leave, they join another group. Males may do likewise, but in some species they may remain solitary for a time, or they may temporarily join an all-male "bachelor" group until they are able to establish a group of their own. But one common theme that emerges is that those individuals who disperse usually find mates outside their natal group. This commonality has led primatologists to conclude that the most valid explanations for dispersal are probably related to two major factors: reduced competition for mates (particularly between males) and, perhaps even more important, decreased likelihood of close inbreeding.

Members of the **philopatric** sex enjoy certain advantages. Individuals (of either sex) who remain in their natal group are able to establish long-term bonds with relatives and other animals, with whom they cooperate to protect resources or enhance their position within the social structure. This is well illustrated by chimpanzee males who permanently reside in their natal groups (see further discussion in Chapter 8). Also, because female macaques are philopatric, they form stable matrilineal subgroups. Larger matrilines can have greater access to foods, and these females support each other in conflict situations.

Because some individuals remain together over a long period of time, members of a primate group get to know each other well. They learn—as they must—how to respond to a variety of actions that may be threatening, friendly, or neutral. In such social groups, individuals must be able to evaluate situations before they act. Evolutionarily speaking, this would have placed selective pressure on social intelligence, which in turn would have selected for brains capable of assessing social situations and storing relevant information. One of the results of such selection would be the evolution of proportionately larger and more complex brains, especially among the higher primates (i.e., anthropoids).

Life histories   **Life history traits** contribute to primate social structure. Life history traits are characteristics or developmental stages that typify members of a given species and that influence potential reproductive rates. Examples of life history traits are length of gestation; length of time between pregnancies (interbirth interval); period of infant dependency and age at weaning; age of sexual maturity; and life expectancy. But the importance of life history traits to social

philopatric Remaining in one's natal group or home range as an adult. In most species, members of one sex disperse from their natal group as young adults, and members of the philopatric sex remain. In the majority of nonhuman primate species, the philopatric sex is female.

Virtual Lab 1, section IV, presents a discussion of several life history variables.

life history traits Also called *life history strategies;* characteristics and developmental stages that influence rates of reproduction.

organization can't be analyzed in the absence of long-term data on primate groups, since primates have such long life spans. Fortunately, in addition to the Gombe chimpanzees, there are groups of many species that have now been studied more or less continuously for more than 30 years.

Life history traits have important and complex consequences for many aspects of social life and social structure. They can also be critical to species survival. Shorter life histories are advantageous to species that live in marginal or unpredictable habitats (Strier, 2003). Since these species mature early and have short interbirth intervals, reproduction can occur at a relatively fast rate. Conversely, species with extended life histories are well suited to stable environmental conditions. The extended life histories of the great apes in particular, characterized by later sexual maturation and long interbirth intervals (three to five years), means that most females will raise only three or four offspring to maturity. Today, this slow rate of reproduction increases the threat to great ape populations now being hunted at a devastating rate that far outpaces their replacement capacities (see Issue, p. 167).

strategies Behaviors or behavioral complexes that have been favored by natural selection to increase individual reproductive fitness.

Strategies   **Strategies** are behavioral phenotypes that increase individual reproductive fitness, and they, too, influence the structure and dynamics of primate social groups. We are accustomed to using the word strategies to mean deliberate schemes or plans purposefully designed to achieve goals. But in the context of nonhuman behavioral ecology, strategies are seen as products of natural selection, and no conscious planning or motivation is implied (Strier, 2003). Several kinds of strategies are discussed in behavioral studies, including *life history strategies, feeding strategies, social strategies, reproductive strategies,* and *predator avoidance strategies.*

Distribution and types of sleeping sites   Gorillas are the only nonhuman primates that sleep on the ground. Primate sleeping sites can be in trees or on cliff faces, and their spacing can be related to social structure and to predator avoidance.

Activity patterns   Most primates are diurnal, but several small-bodied prosimians and one New World monkey (the owl monkey) are nocturnal. Nocturnal species tend to forage for food alone or in groups of 2 or 3 and many use concealment to avoid predators.

Human activities   We stated earlier that virtually all nonhuman primate populations are now impacted by human hunting and forest clearing (see pp. 134 and 168). These activities severely disrupt and isolate groups, reduce numbers, reduce resource availability, and eventually can cause extinction.

Sympatric Species

FIVE MONKEY SPECIES IN THE KIBALE FOREST, UGANDA

sympatric Living in the same area; pertaining to two or more species whose habitats partly or largely overlap.

Another issue that is basic to the behavioral ecology of primates is the differential exploitation of resources by **sympatric** species. This strategy provides a way to maximize access to food while at the same time reducing competition between different species.

An early study of sympatric relationships was undertaken in the Kibale Forest (Fig. 7–4) of western Uganda (Struhsaker and Leyland, 1979). The five species studied are all varieties of Old World monkeys and include the black-and-white colobus (*Colobus guereza*), red colobus (*Colobus badius*), mangabey (*Cercocebus albigena*), blue monkey (*Cercopithecus mitis*), and redtail monkey (*Cercopithecus ascanius*). In addition to these five, the Kibale Forest is home to two other monkey species as well as pottos, two galago species, and chimpanzees (for a discussion of the latter, see Ghiglieri, 1984). Altogether there are 11 different nonhuman primate species at Kibale.

Although the five species studied are sympatric, they differ with regard to anatomy, behavior, and dietary preference. Body weights vary considerably (3 to 4 kg for redtails and up to 7 to 10 kg for the mangabey and colobus species). Diet also differs, with the two colobus species primarily eating leaves (i.e., they are folivorous) and the other three species showing more concentration on fruits supplemented by insects.

Courtesy, John Oates

FIGURE 7–4 Kibale Forest habitat, Uganda.

Several aspects of social organization also vary among the five species. For example, red colobus and mangabeys live in multimale-multifemale groups, while only one fully adult male is typically present in the other species. Furthermore, all five species occasionally have solitary males moving independently of the bisexual groups, but bachelor groups do not typically form. Even among the mostly multimale-multifemale species, there is a marked difference. In mangabeys, females constitute the permanent core of the group, with males transferring out. In red colobus, it's the females who transfer (with the males remaining the long-term residents) (Struhsaker and Leyland, 1987). Indeed, there is so much variability that there was little correlation between social organization and feeding ecology.

More detailed analysis of feeding patterns showed still other differences. For instance, while both colobus species eat mostly leaves, they nevertheless exploit different resources. Black-and-white colobus eat mature leaf blades, some high in protein. Red colobus, on the other hand, eat a wider variety of leaves, but usually not mature ones, as well as fruits and shoots. Perhaps correlated with these dietary differences are the observations that black-and-white colobus spend less time feeding but more time resting; in contrast, red colobus range farther and live in higher density.

Ecological patterns and social ramifications are unquestionably complicated. In the same forest at Kibale, the closely related colobus species show marked differences in social organization. Black-and-white colobus are found in one-male groups, while red colobus form multimale-multifemale associations (see A Closer Look on p. 177). Yet in another area (the Tana River Forest of Kenya), red colobus live in one-male groups, like black-and-white colobus at Kibale. The distinct impression one gets from all this is that many primate species are exceedingly flexible regarding group composition, a fact that makes generalizing extremely tentative.

Still, the highly controlled nature of the Kibale study makes some comparisons and provisional generalizations possible:

1. The omnivores (mangabeys, redtail and blue monkeys) move about more than the folivores (the two colobus species).
2. Among the omnivores there is an inverse relationship between body size and group size (i.e., the smaller the body size, the larger the group tends to be). Also among the omnivores, there is a direct relationship between body size and **home range.**

home range The total area exploited by an animal or social group; usually given for one year—or for the entire lifetime—of an animal.

3. Omnivores are more spatially dispersed than folivores.
4. Female sexual swelling (see p. 189) is obvious only in those species (red colobus and mangabeys) that live in multimale-multifemale groups.
5. Feeding, spacing, group residency, dispersal, and reproductive strategies may be very different for males and females of the same species. These considerations have become a central focus of ecological and evolutionary research.

Why Be Social?

See Virtual Lab 6, section IV, for an in-depth presentation, including video of savanna baboon behavior.

As you can see, the topic of primate behavior is very complicated. Primatologists have to consider an animal's relative brain size, BMR, and reproductive physiology in addition to such ecological factors as the distribution of food resources and the nutritional value of foods and how they are selected and processed. (See Fleagle, 1999, and Strier, 2003, for detailed discussions of these factors.) Moreover, the variability in ecological adaptations seen in closely related species, or even within the same species, must be understood. And it's important to know how primates interact with other species, including other primates.

But there is an even more basic question. Group living exposes primates to competition with other group members for resources, so why don't they live alone? After all, competition can lead to injury or even death, and it's costly in terms of energy expenditure. If they lived alone, females would be free to forage without competition, and occasional encounters with males would still ensure reproductive success. Indeed, females of some diurnal species do forage alone, or usually with offspring (e.g., orangutans, chimpanzees). These females, being relatively large-bodied, have little to fear from predators, and by feeding alone or with only one or two youngsters, they maximize their access to food, free from competition with others. In the case of the orangutan, this may be particularly important, as the female is effectively removing herself from competition with males who may be twice her size.

One widely accepted answer to the question of why primates live in groups is that the costs of competition are compensated for by the benefits of predator defense provided by associating with others. Groups composed of several adult males and females (multimale-multifemale groups) have traditionally been viewed as advantageous in areas where predation pressure is high, particularly in mixed woodlands and on open savannas, where there are a number of large predators. Leopards are the most significant predator of terrestrial primates, but they also take a substantial number of arboreal monkeys (Fig. 7–5). Where members of prey species occur in larger groups, the chances of early predator detection (and thus, avoidance) are increased simply because there are more pairs of eyes looking about. This also has the advantage of giving individuals more time to feed, because the amount of time each one spends in surveillance is reduced (Janson, 1990; Isbell and Young, 1993).

Savanna baboons have long been cited as an example of this principle. Savanna baboons are found in semiarid grassland and broken woodland habitats throughout sub-Saharan Africa. During the day, they forage in large multimale-multifemale groups, and if they detect nonhuman predators, they flee to the safety of trees. However, if they are at some distance from safety or if the predator is nearby, adult males may join forces to chase the intruder away. The effective-

FIGURE 7–5 When a baboon strays too far from its troop, as this one has done, it's more likely to fall prey to predators. Leopards are the most serious nonhuman threat to terrestrial primates.

Time Life Pictures/Getty Images

ness of male baboons in this regard should not be underestimated, because they've been known to kill domestic dogs and even to attack leopards and lions.

Examples of increased group size as a defense against predators have been reported in vervets (Isbell, 1993) and capuchins (de Ruiter, 1986). In these species, vigilance was seen to increase as group size increased. Hamadryas baboons forage in small groups consisting of one male and a few females and offspring. But when predators are seen, such one-male units join with others to mobilize against the intruder.

The benefits of larger groups are also apparent in reports of polyspecific (more than one species) associations that function to reduce predation. In the Tai National Park, Ivory Coast, red colobus monkeys, a favorite prey of chimpanzees (see Chapter 8), frequently associate with Diana monkeys (a guenon species) as a predator avoidance strategy (Bshary and Noe, 1997; Noe and Bshary, 1997). Normally, these two species don't form close associations, but when chimpanzee predation increases, new groupings develop and preexisting ones remain intact for longer than normal periods of time. McGraw and Bshary (2002) report that a third species, the sooty mangabey, sometimes provides additional support. The more terrestrial mangabeys live in multimale groups of up to 100 individuals, and they detect predators earlier than the other two species. Mangabeys are in proximity to red colobus and Diana monkeys only about 5 to 10 percent of the time, but when they are present, the other two species modify their foraging strategies. The normally arboreal red colobus monkeys even come to the ground (McGraw and Bshary, 2002). Consequently, through the strategy of interspecific associations, potential prey animals are able to spend more time feeding and increase their opportunities for foraging.

As effective as increased numbers can be in preventing predation, there are other explanations for primate sociality. One is that larger social groups can outcompete smaller groups of **conspecifics** when foraging in the same area

conspecifics members of the same species.

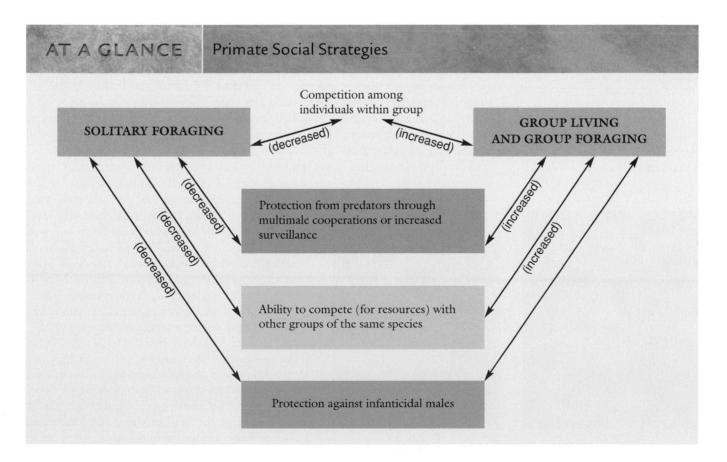

AT A GLANCE   Primate Social Strategies

SOLITARY FORAGING

GROUP LIVING AND GROUP FORAGING

Competition among individuals within group

(decreased)   (increased)

Protection from predators through multimale cooperations or increased surveillance

(decreased)   (increased)

Ability to compete (for resources) with other groups of the same species

(decreased)   (increased)

(decreased)

Protection against infanticidal males

See Virtual Lab 6, section II, for a discussion of ethograms or catalogs of behavior.

(Wrangham, 1980). Wrangham (1980) also suggests that large multimale-multifemale groups evolved because males were attracted to related females living in association with one another. And lastly, females may tolerate familiar males, since they can provide protection against infanticidal males.

As you learned in the previous chapter, not all primates are found in large groups. Solitary foraging is typical of many species and is probably related to diet and distribution of resources. In the case of insectivorous lorises, solitary feeding reduces competition, which results in less distance traveled (and thus less energy expended) in the search for prey. Moreover, because insects usually don't occur in dense patches, they are more efficiently exploited by widely dispersed animals rather than by groups. Solitary foraging may also be related to predator avoidance in species that rely chiefly on concealment, rather than escape for protection.

There is probably no single answer to the question of why primates live in groups. More than likely, predator avoidance is a major factor but not the only one. Group living evolved as an adaptive response to a number of ecological variables, and it has served primates well for a very long time.

Primate Social Behavior

Because primates solve their major adaptive problems in a social context, we might expect them to participate in a number of activities to reinforce the integrity of the group. The better known of these activities are described in the sections that follow. And remember, all these behaviors have evolved as adaptive responses more than 50 million years of primate evolution.

DOMINANCE

dominance hierarchies Systems of social organization wherein individuals within a group are ranked relative to one another. Higher-ranking individuals have greater access to preferred food items, and mating partners than lower-ranking individuals. Dominance hierarchies are sometimes referred to as "pecking orders."

A number of primate societies are organized into **dominance hierarchies.** Dominance hierarchies impose a certain degree of order within groups by establishing parameters of individual behavior. Although aggression is frequently a means of increasing one's status, dominance usually serves to reduce the amount of actual physical violence. Not only are lower-ranking animals unlikely to attack or even threaten a higher-ranking one, but dominant animals are also frequently able to exert control simply by making a threatening gesture.

Individual rank or status may be measured by access to resources, including food items and mating partners. Dominant individuals are given priority by others, and they usually don't give way in confrontations.

Many primatologists think that the primary benefit of dominance is the increased reproductive success of high ranking animals. This may be true for some species, but there is good evidence that lower-ranking males of some species also successfully mate. For example, subordinate baboon males frequently establish friendships with females and, simply because of this close association they are able to mate surreptitiously with their female friend when she comes into estrus.

Low ranking male orangutans also mate frequently. These young males don't develop certain secondary sex characteristics such as wide cheek pads, and heavier musculature as long as they live in proximity to a dominant male (Fig. 7–6). One theory is that this arrested development serves to protect them from the dominant male who doesn't view them as a threat. But, they are a threat in terms of reproductive success because their strat-

FIGURE 7–6 Fully mature, breeding male orangutan with well-developed cheek pads (a) compared to a suppressed adult male without cheek pads (b).

(a)   (b)

egy is to force females to mate with them. In fact, the degree of force these males use has caused primatologists to use the term "rape" to describe it.

Increased reproductive success is also postulated for high-ranking females, who have greater access to food than subordinate females. High-ranking females are provided with more energy for offspring production and care (Fedigan, 1983), and presumably their reproductive success is greater. Altmann et al. (1988) reported that while dominant female yellow baboons in one study group didn't have higher birthrates than lower-ranking females, they did reach sexual maturity earlier (presumably because of their enhanced nutritional status), thus increasing their potential number of offspring throughout the course of their lives.

In one other example, during a drought in Kenya, dominant female vervets in two groups prevented a third group from gaining access to their water hole. The deprived third group resorted to licking dew from tree trunks, but the lower-ranking members of this group were denied access to even this resource by higher-ranking members. Consequently, over half of this group died, and all of those were either adolescents or low-ranking adults (Cheney et al., 1988):

Pusey, et al. (1997) demonstrated that the offspring of high-ranking female chimpanzees at Gombe had significantly higher rates of infant survival. Moreover, their daughters matured faster, which meant they had shorter inter-birth intervals and consequently produced more offspring.

An individual's rank is not permanent and changes throughout life. It is influenced by many factors, including sex, age, level of aggression, amount of time spent in the group, intelligence, perhaps motivation, and sometimes the mother's social position (particularly true of macaques).

In species organized into groups containing a number of females associated with one or several adult males, the males are generally dominant to females. Within such groups, males and females have separate hierarchies, although very high ranking females can dominate the lowest-ranking males (particularly young males). There are exceptions to this pattern of male dominance. Among many lemur species, females are the dominant sex. Moreover, in species that form monogamous pairs (e.g., indris, gibbons), males and females are codominant.

All primates *learn* their position in the hierarchy. From birth, an infant is carried by its mother, and it observes how she responds to every member of the group. Just as importantly, it sees how others react to her. Dominance and subordination are indicated by gestures and behaviors, some of which are universal throughout the primate order (including humans), and this gestural repertoire is part of every youngster's learning experience.

Young primates also acquire social rank through play with age peers. As they spend more time with play groups, their social interactions widen. Competition and rough-and-tumble play allow them to learn the strengths and weaknesses of peers, and they carry this knowledge with them throughout their lives. Thus, through early contact with the mother and subsequent exposure to peers, young primates learn to negotiate their way through the complex web of social interactions that make up their daily lives.

COMMUNICATION

Communication is universal among animals and includes scents and unintentional, **autonomic** responses and behaviors that convey meaning. Such attributes as body posture convey information about an animal's emotional state. For example, a crouched position indicates a certain degree of insecurity or fear, while a purposeful striding gait implies confidence. Moreover, autonomic responses to threatening or novel stimuli, such as raised body hair (most species) or enhanced body odor (gorillas), indicate excitement.

Many intentional behaviors also serve as communication. In primates, these include a wide variety of gestures, facial expressions, and vocalizations, some of

Virtual Lab 6, section IV, includes several video exercises about baboon behavior.

communication Any act that conveys information, in the form of a message, to another individual. Frequently, the result of communication is a change in the behavior of the recipient. Communication may not be deliberate but may instead be the result of involuntary processes or a secondary consequence of an intentional action.

autonomic Pertaining to physiological responses not under voluntary control. An example in chimpanzees would be the erection of body hair during excitement. An example in humans is blushing. Both convey information regarding emotional states, but neither is a deliberate behavior, and communication is not intended.

FIGURE 7–7 An adolescent male savanna baboon threatens the photographer with a characteristic "yawn" that shows the canine teeth. Note also that the eyes are closed briefly to expose light, cream-colored eyelids. This has been termed the "eyelid flash."

displays Sequences of repetitious behaviors that serve to communicate emotional states. Nonhuman primate displays are most frequently associated with reproductive or agonistic behavior.

FIGURE 7–8 One young male savanna baboon mounts another as an expression of dominance.

which we humans share. Among many primates, a mild threat is indicated by an intense stare, and indeed, we humans find prolonged eye contact with strangers very uncomfortable. (For this reason, people should avoid eye contact with captive primates.) Other threat gestures are a quick yawn to expose canine teeth (baboons, macaques) (Fig. 7–7); bobbing back and forth in a crouched position (patas monkeys); and branch shaking (many monkey species). High-ranking baboons *mount* the hindquarters of subordinates to express dominance (Fig. 7–8). Mounting may also serve to defuse potentially tense situations by indicating something like, "It's okay, I accept your apology, I know you didn't intend to offend me."

There is also a variety of behaviors that indicate submission, reassurance, or amicable intentions. Submission is indicated by a crouched position (most primates) or presenting the hindquarters (baboons). Reassurance takes the form of touching, patting, hugging, and holding hands. Grooming also serves in a number of situations to indicate submission or reassurance.

A wide variety of facial expressions indicating emotional state is seen in chimpanzees and, especially, in bonobos (Fig. 7–9). These include the well-known play face (also seen in several other primate and nonprimate species), associated with play behavior, and the fear grin (seen in *all* primates) to indicate fear and submission.

Primates also use a wide array of vocalizations for communication. Some, such as the bark of a baboon that has just spotted a leopard, are unintentional startled reactions. Others, such as the chimpanzee food grunt, are heard only in specific contexts. Nevertheless, both serve the same function: They inform others, although not necessarily deliberately, of the possible presence of predators or food.

Primates (and other animals) also communicate through **displays,** which are more complicated, frequently elaborate combinations of behaviors. For example, the exaggerated courtship dances of many male birds, often enhanced by colorful plumage, are displays. Common gorilla displays are chest slapping and the tearing of vegetation to indicate threat. Likewise, an angry chimpanzee, with hair bristling, may charge an opponent while screaming, waving its arms, and tearing vegetation.

By describing a few communicative behaviors shared by many primates (including humans), we don't mean that these gestures are dictated solely by genetic factors. Indeed, if primates aren't reared within a relatively normal social context, such behaviors may not be performed appropriately, because the contextual manifestations of communicatory actions are *learned*. But the underlying *predisposition* to learn and use them and the motor patterns involved in their execution are genetically influenced, and these factors do have adaptive significance. Therefore, theories about how such expressive devices evolved focus on motor patterns and the original context in which they occurred.

Over time, certain behaviors and motor patterns that originated in specific contexts have assumed increasing importance as communicatory signals.

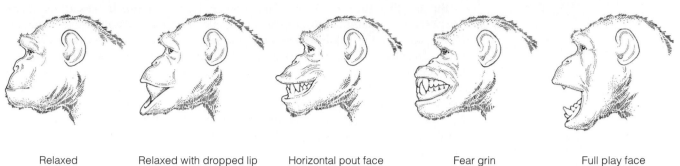

Relaxed   Relaxed with dropped lip   Horizontal pout face (distress)   Fear grin (fear/excitement)   Full play face

For example, crouching (seen also in many nonprimate species, such as dogs) initially helped avoid physical attack. But this behavior also conveyed that the individual was fearful, submissive, and nonaggressive. Thus, crouching became valuable not only for its primary function, but for its role in communication as well, and natural selection increasingly favored it for this secondary role. In such a manner, over time, the expressions of specific behaviors may thus become elaborated or exaggerated because of their value in enhancing communication. Moreover, many complex displays incorporate various combinations of **ritualized behaviors.**

Mounting, as seen in baboons, is a good example of a ritualized behavior. Higher-ranking individuals mount the hindquarters of more subordinate animals, not to mate, but to express dominance. (It should be noted that when mounting serves a communicatory function, mounters and mountees may be members of the same sex.) In most anthropoid species characterized by one-male or multimale groups, males (the mounters in the mating context) are socially dominant to females. Thus, in the context of communication, the mounter assumes the male reproductive role. Likewise, presentation of the hindquarters to solicit mounting indicates submission or subordination by the mountee. As communication, these behavior patterns are entirely removed from their original reproductive context, and they function instead to reinforce and clarify the respective social roles of individuals in specific interactions.

All nonhuman animals employ various vocalizations, body postures, and, to some degree, facial expressions that transmit information. However, the array of communicative devices is much richer among nonhuman primates, even though they don't use language the way humans do. Communication is important, for it truly is what makes social living possible. Through submissive gestures, aggression is reduced and physical violence is less likely. Likewise, friendly intentions and relationships are reinforced through physical contact and grooming. Indeed, we humans can see ourselves in other primate species most clearly in the familiar uses of nonverbal communication.

AGGRESSIVE AND AFFILIATIVE INTERACTIONS

Within primate societies, there is an interplay between **affiliative** behaviors, which promote group cohesion, and aggressive behaviors, which can lead to group disruption. Conflict within a group frequently develops out of competition for resources, including mating partners and food items. Instead of actual attacks or fighting, most intragroup aggression occurs in the form of various signals and displays, frequently within the context of a dominance hierarchy. The majority of such situations are resolved through various submissive and appeasement behaviors.

FIGURE 7–9 Chimpanzee facial expressions.

ritualized behaviors Behaviors removed from their original context and sometimes exaggerated to convey information.

affiliative Pertaining to amicable associations between individuals. Affiliative behaviors, such as grooming, reinforce social bonds and promote group cohesion.

But conflict isn't always resolved peacefully, and it can have serious consequences. For example, high-ranking female macaques frequently intimidate, harass, and even attack lower-ranking females, in order to restrict their access to food. Dominant females consistently chase subordinates away from food and have even been observed to take food from their mouths. Eventually, these behaviors can result in weight loss and poorer nutrition in low-ranking females. Even more important, subordinant females exhibit lower reproductive success because they are less able to successfully rear offspring to maturity, in part because of their inability to obtain food (Silk et al., 2003).

Competition between males for mates frequently results in injury and occasionally in death. In species that have a distinct breeding season (e.g., squirrel monkeys), conflict between males is most common during that time. Male squirrel monkeys form coalitions to compete with other males, and when outright fighting occurs, injuries can be severe. In species not restricted to a mating season, competition between males can be an ongoing process. As you have seen, one-male social groups are common in primates, and a male who gains control of a group of females must constantly protect his own interests against the interests of other males attempting to overthrow him. While a majority of conflicts don't result in death, it does occur. In one well-known example, Dian Fossey once found the skull of an adult male mountain gorilla in which was embedded a canine tooth of another male gorilla!

Even though conflict can be destructive, a certain amount of aggression is useful in maintaining order within groups and protecting either individual or group resources. Fortunately, to reinforce bonds between individuals, promote group cohesion, minimize actual violence, and defuse potentially dangerous situations, there is an array of affiliative, or friendly, behaviors that serve to reinforce bonds between individuals and enhance group stability.

Common affiliative behaviors include reconciliation, consolation, and simple amicable interactions between friends and relatives. Most such behaviors involve various forms of physical contact, such as touching, hand holding, hugging, and, among chimpanzees, kissing. In fact, physical contact is one of the most important factors in primate development and is crucial in promoting peaceful relationships in many primate social groups.

Grooming is one of the most important affiliative behaviors in many primate species. Although grooming occurs in other animal species, social grooming is mostly a primate activity, and it plays an important role in day-to-day life (Fig. 7–10). Because grooming involves using the fingers to pick through the fur of another individual (or one's own) to remove insects, dirt, and other materials, it serves hygienic functions. But it's also an immensely pleasurable activity that members of some species (especially chimpanzees) engage in for long periods of time.

Grooming occurs in a variety of contexts. Mothers groom infants. Males groom sexually receptive females. Subordinate animals groom dominant ones, sometimes to gain favor. Friends groom friends. In general, grooming is comforting. It restores peaceful relationships between animals who have quarreled and provides reassurance during tense situations. In short, grooming reinforces social bonds and consequently helps to maintain and strengthen the structure of the group.

Conflict resolution through reconciliation is another important aspect of primate social behavior. Following a conflict, chimpanzee opponents frequently move, within minutes, to reconcile (de Waal, 1982). Reconciliation takes many forms, including hugging, kissing, and grooming. Even uninvolved individuals may take part, either grooming one or both participants or forming their own grooming parties. In addition, bonobos are unique in their use of sex to promote group cohesion, restore peace after conflicts, and relieve tension within the group (de Waal, 1987, 1989).

See Virtual Lab 6, section IV, for video clips depicting affiliative behaviors.

grooming Picking through fur to remove dirt, parasites, and other materials that may be present. Social grooming is common among primates and reinforces social relationships.

(a)

(b)

(c)

(d)

Social relationships are crucial to nonhuman primates, and the bonds between individuals can last a lifetime. These relationships serve a variety of functions. Individuals of many species form alliances in which one supports another against a third. Alliances, or coalitions, as they are also called, can be used to enhance the status of members. For example, at Gombe, the male chimpanzee Figan achieved alpha status because of support from his brother (Goodall, 1986, p. 424). In fact, chimpanzees so heavily rely on coalitions and are so skillful politically that an entire book, appropriately titled *Chimpanzee Politics* (de Waal, 1982), is devoted to the topic.

FIGURE 7–10 Grooming primates. (a) Patas monkeys; female grooming male. (b) Longtail macaques. (c) Savanna baboons. (d) Chimpanzees.

Reproduction and Reproductive Strategies

In most primate species, sexual behavior is tied to the female's reproductive cycle, with females being sexually receptive to males only when they're in estrus. Estrus is characterized by behavioral changes that indicate a female is receptive. In Old World monkeys and apes that live in multimale groups, estrus is also accompanied by swelling and changes in color of the skin around the genital area. These

See Virtual Lab 2, section I, for a discussion of reproductive strategies and reproductive success.

FIGURE 7–11 Estrous swelling of genital tissues in a female chimpanzee.

reproductive strategies The complex of behavioral patterns that contributes to individual reproductive success. The behaviors need not be deliberate, and they often vary considerably between males and females.

K-selected Pertaining to an adaptive strategy whereby individuals produce relatively few offspring, in whom they invest increased parental care. Although only a few infants are born, chances of survival are increased for each individual because of parental investments in time and energy. Examples of nonprimate K-selected species are birds and canids (e.g., wolves, coyotes, and dogs).

r-selected Pertaining to an adaptive strategy that emphasizes relatively large numbers of offspring and reduced parental care (compared to K-selected species). *K-selection* and *r-selection* are relative terms; e.g., mice are r-selected compared to primates but K-selected compared to many fish species.

changes serve as visual cues of a female's readiness to mate (Fig 7–11).

Permanent bonding between males and females isn't common among nonhuman primates. However, male and female savanna baboons sometimes form mating *consortships*. These temporary relationships last while the female is in estrus, and the two spend most of their time together, mating frequently. Moreover, as we mentioned earlier, lower-ranking baboon males often form "friendships" (Smuts, 1985) with females and occasionally may mate with them, although they may be driven away by high-ranking males when the female is most receptive.

Mating consortships are sometimes seen in chimpanzees and are particularly common among bonobos. In fact, a male and female bonobo may spend several weeks primarily in each other's company. During this time, they mate often, even when the female is not in estrus. These relationships of longer duration are not typical of chimpanzee (*Pan troglodytes*) males and females.

Such a male-female bond may result in increased reproductive success for both sexes. For the male, there is the increased likelihood that he will be the father of any infant the female conceives. At the same time, the female potentially gains protection from predators or others of her group and perhaps assistance in caring for offspring she may already have.

FEMALE AND MALE REPRODUCTIVE STRATEGIES

Reproductive strategies, and especially how they differ between the sexes, have been a primary focus of primate research. The goal of such strategies is to produce and successfully rear to adulthood as many offspring as possible.

Primates are among the most **K-selected** of mammal species. By this we mean that individuals produce only a few young, in whom they invest a tremendous amount of parental care. Contrast this pattern with **r-selected** species, where individuals produce large numbers of offspring but invest little or no energy in parental care. Good examples of r-selected species include insects, most fishes, and, among mammals, mice and rabbits.

When we consider the degree of care required by young, dependent primates offspring, it is clear that enormous investment by at least one parent is necessary, and, in a majority of species, the mother carries most of the burden both before and after birth. Primates are totally helpless at birth. They develop slowly and are thus exposed to expanded learning opportunities within a *social* environment. This trend has been elaborated most dramatically in great apes and humans, and especially in the latter. Thus, what we see in ourselves and our close primate kin (and presumably in our more recent ancestors as well) is a strategy wherein a few "high-quality," slowly maturing offspring are produced through extraordinary investment by at least one parent, usually the mother.

Finding food and mates, avoiding predators, and caring for and protecting dependent young are difficult challenges for nonhuman primates. Moreover, in most species, males and females employ different strategies to meet these challenges.

Female primates spend almost all their adult lives either pregnant, lactating, and/or caring for offspring, and the resulting metabolic demands are enormous.

A pregnant or lactating female, although perhaps only half the size of her male counterpart, may require about the same number of calories per day. Even if these demands are met, her physical resources may be drained. For example, analysis of chimpanzee skeletons from Gombe National Park, in Tanzania, showed significant loss of bone and bone mineral in older females (Sumner et al., 1989).

Given these physiological costs, and the fact that her reproductive potential is limited by lengthy intervals between births, a female's best strategy is to maximize the amount of resources available to her and her offspring. Indeed, as we just discussed, females of many primate species (gibbons, marmosets, and macaques, to name a few) are viciously competitive with other females and aggressively protect resources and territories. In other species, as we have seen, females distance themselves from others to avoid competition. Males, however, face a separate set of challenges. Having little investment in the rearing of offspring and the continuous production of sperm, it is to the male's advantage to secure as any mates and produce as many offspring as possible.

SEXUAL SELECTION

One outcome of different mating strategies is **sexual selection,** a phenomenon first described by Charles Darwin. Sexual selection is a type of natural selection that operates on only one sex, usually males, whereby the selective agent is male competition for mates and, in some species, mate choice in females. The long-term effect of sexual selection is to increase the frequency of those traits that lead to greater success in acquiring mates.

In the animal kingdom, there are numerous male attributes that result from sexual selection. In some bird species, for example, males are much more brightly colored than females. For various reasons, female birds find those males with more vividly colored plumage more attractive as mates; thus, selection has increased the frequency of alleles that influence brighter coloration in males. However, not all bird species exhibit color dimorphism. Moreover, in some species, such as phalaropes, females compete for males, and the males sit on developing eggs. In these species, sexual selection acts on females, who are more brightly colored than males. This example illustrates the fact that given the necessity for predator avoidance, it is beneficial for those responsible for hatching the eggs to be as inconspicuous as possible.

Sexual selection in primates is most important in species in which mating is polygynous and male competition for females is prominent. In these species, sexual selection produces dimorphism with regard to a number of traits, most noticeably body size. As you have seen, the males of many primate species are considerably larger than females and males also have larger canine teeth. Males of multimale-multifemale societies also have relatively larger testes than males of other types of groups, presumably because of the potential need to produce greater numbers of sperm, which may ultimately compete with the sperm of other males when females mate with more than one partner.

Conversely, in species that live in pairs (e.g., gibbons) or where male competition is reduced, sexual dimorphism in canine and body size is either reduced or nonexistent, and relative testis size is smaller. For these reasons, the presence or absence of sexually dimorphic traits in a species can be a reasonably good indicator of mating structure.

INFANTICIDE AS A REPRODUCTIVE STRATEGY?

Paradoxically, one way males may increase their chances of reproducing is by killing infants fathered by other males. This explanation was first offered in an early study of Hanuman langurs in India (Hrdy, 1977). Hanuman langurs (Fig. 7–12) typically live in groups composed of one adult male, several females, and

sexual selection A type of natural selection that operates on only one sex within a species. It is the result of competition for mates, and it can lead to sexual dimorphism with regard to one or more traits.

FIGURE 7–12 Hanuman langurs.

their offspring. Other males without mates form "bachelor" groups which frequently forage within sight of the one-male associations. These peripheral males occasionally attack and defeat a reproductive male and drive him from his group. Sometimes, following such takeovers, some or all of the group's infants (fathered by the previous male) are killed by the new male.

Such behavior would appear to be counterproductive, especially for a species as a whole. However, individual animals act to maximize their *own* reproductive success, no matter what the effect may be on the population or ultimately the species. And that's what the male langur may be doing, albeit unknowingly. While a female is producing milk and nursing an infant, she doesn't come into estrus, and therefore she isn't sexually available. But, when an infant dies, its mother stops lactating and, within two or three months, she resumes cycling and becomes sexually receptive. Consequently, by killing nursing infants, a new male avoids waiting two to three years for them to be weaned before he can mate with their mothers. This could be advantageous to him since chances are good that his tenure in the group won't even last two or three years. Moreover, he doesn't expend energy and put himself at risk defending infants who don't carry his genes,

Hanuman langurs aren't the only primates that engage in infanticide. Infanticide has been observed (or surmised) in many species, such as redtail monkeys, red colobus, blue monkeys, savanna baboons, howlers, orangutans, gorillas, chimpanzees (Struhsaker and Leyland, 1987) and humans. In the majority of reported nonhuman primate examples, infanticide coincides with the transfer of a new male into a group or, as in chimpanzees, an encounter with an unfamiliar female and infant. (It should also be noted that infanticide occurs in numerous nonprimate species, including rodents, cats, and horses.

Numerous objections to this explanation of infanticide have been raised. Alternative explanations have included competition for resources (Rudran, 1973), aberrant behaviors related to human-induced overcrowding (Curtin and Dohlinow, 1978), and inadvertent killing during aggressive episodes, where it wasn't clear that the infant was actually the target animal (Bartlett et al., 1993). Sussman and colleagues (1995), as well as others, have questioned the actual prevalence of infanticide, arguing that although it does occur, it's not particularly common. These authors have also suggested that if indeed male reproductive fitness is increased through the killing of infants, such increases are negligible. Yet others (Struhsaker and Leyland, 1987; Hrdy, 1995), maintain that the incidence and patterning of infanticide by males are not only significant, but consistent with the assumptions established by theories of behavioral evolution.

Henzi and Barrett (2003) report that when chacma baboon males migrate into a new group they ". . . deliberately single out females with young infants and hunt them down" (Fig. 7–13), (Henzi and Barrett, 2003). These authors also state that resident males (presumed fathers) move closer to older, but still vulnerable, subadults, so that most attacks don't result in the death of an infant.

FIGURE 7–13 An immigrant male chacma baboon chases a terrified female and her infant (clinging to her back). Resident males interceded to stop the chase.

© Peter Henzi

The importance of these findings is the conclusion that, at least in chacma baboons, the attempts at infanticide are consistently made by newly arrived males, and that the attacks are highly aggressive and purposeful. These observations indicate that the incoming males are very motivated and are engaging in a goal-directed behavior, although they most certainly don't understand the possible reproductive advantages they may later gain.

However, reports such as this don't prove that infanticide increases a male's reproductive fitness. In order to do this, primatologists must demonstrate two crucial facts:

1. Infanticidal males *don't* kill their own offspring.
2. Once a male has killed an infant, he subsequently fathers another infant with the victim's mother.

Borries et al. (1999) collected DNA samples from the feces of infanticidal males and their victims in several groups of free-ranging Hanuman langurs specifically to determine if these males killed their own offspring. Their results showed that in all 16 cases where infant and male DNA was available, the males were not related to the infants they either attacked or killed. Secondly, DNA analysis also showed that in four out of five cases where victim's mothers subsequently gave birth, their new infants were fathered by the infanticidal males. Although still more evidence is needed, this DNA evidence, strongly suggests that infanticide may indeed give males an increased chance of fathering offspring.

Mothers, Fathers, and Infants

The basic social unit among all primates is the female and her infants (Fig. 7–14). Except in those species in which monogamy or, **polyandry** occurs, males don't directly participate in the rearing of offspring. Observations both in the field and in captivity suggest that the mother-offspring core provides the social group with its stability.

The mother-infant bond begins at birth. Although the exact nature of the bonding process is not fully known, there appear to be predisposing innate factors that strongly attract the female to her infant, so long as she herself has had sufficiently normal experience with her own mother. This doesn't mean that primate mothers possess innate knowledge of how to care for an infant. Monkeys and apes raised in captivity without contact with their own mothers not only don't know how to care for a newborn infant, but they may also be afraid of it and attack and even kill it. Thus, learning is critically important in the establishment of a mother's attraction to her infant.

The crucial role of bonding between primate mothers and infants was clearly demonstrated by the University of Wisconsin psychologist Harry Harlow (1959), who raised infant monkeys with surrogate mothers fashioned from wire or a combination of wire and cloth. Other monkeys were raised with no mother at all. In one experiment, infants retained an attachment to their cloth-covered surrogate mother (Fig.7–15). But those raised with no mother were incapable of forming lasting affectional ties. These deprived monkeys sat passively in their cages and stared vacantly into space. None of the motherless males ever successfully copulated, and those females who were (somewhat artificially) impregnated either paid little attention to offspring or reacted aggressively toward them (Harlow and Harlow, 1961). The point is that monkeys reared in isolation were denied opportunities to *learn* the rules of social and maternal behavior. Moreover, and just as essential, they were denied the all-important physical contact so necessary for normal primate psychological and emotional development.

The importance of a normal relationship with the mother is demonstrated by field studies as well. From birth, infant primates are able to cling to their

polyandry A mating system wherein a female continuously associates with more than one male (usually two or three) with whom she mates. Among nonhuman primates, this pattern is seen only in marmosets and tamarins. It also occurs in a few human societies.

See Virtual Lab 6 for examples of the interactions between males, females, and infants.

(a)

(b)

(c)

(d)

(e)

FIGURE 7-14 Primate mothers with young. (a) Mongoose lemur. (b) Chimpanzee. (c) Patas monkey. (d) Orangutan. (e) Sykes monkey.

See Virtual Lab 6, section II, for a video clip showing interactions between a female baboon and her infant.

mother's fur, and they are in more or less constant physical contact with her for several months. During this critical period, the infant develops a closeness with its mother that doesn't always end with weaning. This closeness is often maintained throughout life (especially among some Old World monkeys). And it's reflected in grooming behavior that continues between mother and offspring even after the young reach adulthood and have infants of their own.

In later studies, Suomi and colleagues emphasized that social isolation initiated early in life could have devastating effects on subsequent development and behavior for many primate species. The primate deprivation syndrome that results from early isolation is characterized by displays of abnormal self-directed behavior, such as hugging oneself or rocking back and forth, and by gross deficits in all aspects of social behavior (Suomi et al., 1983, p. 190).

Although infants are mainly cared for by their mothers, in some species, presumed fathers also participate. Male siamangs are actively involved in the care of offspring, and among marmosets and tamarins, males provide most of the direct infant care. In fact, marmoset and tamarin offspring (frequently twins), are usually carried on the male's back and are transferred to their mother only for nursing.

Even in species where adult males aren't directly involved in infant care, they may take more than a casual interest in them, and this has been frequently noted in hamadryas and savanna baboons. But to establish that baboons exhibit paternal care, it's necessary to establish paternity. Buchan et al. (2003) have done just that by analyzing DNA to firmly establish paternity. They then showed that during disputes, the fathers intervened on behalf of their offspring significantly more often than for unrelated juveniles. Because disputes can lead to severe injury, Buchan and colleagues considered the male intervention an example of true paternal care. (Although this study also demonstrates that nonhuman primates can recognize relatives, the exact mechanisms of kin recognition have not been fully identified (see p. 224 for further discussion).

What may be an extension of the mother-infant relationship has been called **alloparenting** (Fig. 7–16). This type of behavior occurs in many animal species but is most richly expressed in primates, and some researchers believe that it's found among all social primates. Usually, alloparents crowd around an infant and attempt to groom, hold, or touch it. Some species, langurs, for example, are well known for their "aunts," and as many as eight females may hold an infant during its first day of life. Occasionally, rough treatment by inexperienced or aggressive animals can result in injury or death to the infant. For this reason, mothers may attempt to shield infants from overly attentive individuals.

Several functions are suggested for alloparenting. If the mother dies, the infant stands a chance of being adopted by an alloparent or other individual of the group. Moreover, the practice may bind together the adults of the group. Also, it may simply be convenient for the mother to leave her infant occasionally with another female. Finally, the practice of alloparenting may help train young females in the skills of motherhood.

Because the survival of offspring is the key to individual reproductive success, parenting strategies have evolved throughout the animal kingdom. In many r-selected species such as fishes, parenting may involve nothing more than laying large numbers of eggs. But in birds and mammals, as you have seen, there is increased care of dependent young. Alloparenting is important in some mammalian species besides primates (e.g., elephants) but even so, it's most highly developed in several primate species. Likewise, males provide group defense in many mammal species, but actual paternal care is most common in primates. And with further use of genetic technologies, the role of males and other related individuals in infant care will undoubtedly become more clear.

FIGURE 7–15 Infant macaque clinging to cloth mother.

alloparenting A common behavior in many primate species whereby individuals other than the parent(s) hold, carry, and in general interact with infants.

FIGURE 7–16 Male savanna baboon carrying an infant. This is an example of alloparenting—or perhaps parental care.

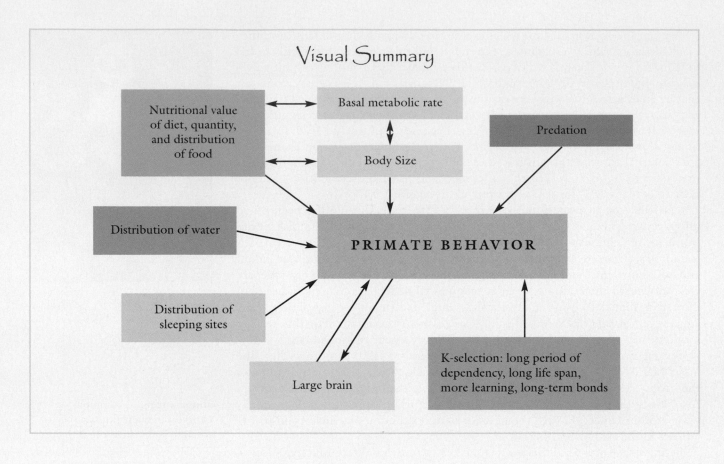

Visual Summary

Nutritional value of diet, quantity, and distribution of food

Basal metabolic rate

Predation

Body Size

Distribution of water

PRIMATE BEHAVIOR

Distribution of sleeping sites

Large brain

K-selection: long period of dependency, long life span, more learning, long-term bonds

Summary

In this chapter, we have presented the major theoretical models for the evolution of behavior in primates and we have discussed some of the evidence, including some reports that use genetic data to support these models. The subject of the evolution of behavior is extremely complex because it requires research into the interactions of dozens, if not hundreds, of ecological and physiological variables.

The fundamental principle of behavioral evolution is that aspects of behavior (including social behavior) are influenced by genetic factors. And because some behavioral elements are therefore inherited, natural selection can act on them in the same way it acts on physical and anatomical characteristics. We pointed out that in more primitive organisms, such as insects and most other invertebrates, the proportion of behavior that is directly influenced by genes is much greater than in mammals and birds.

Behavioral ecology is the discipline that examines behavior from the perspective of complex ecological relationships and the role of natural selection as it favors behaviors that increase reproductive fitness. This approach generates many models of behavioral evolution that can be applied to all species, including humans. Members of each species inherit a genome that is species-specific, and some part of that genome influences behaviors. But in more complex animals, the genome allows for greater degrees of behavioral flexibil-

ity and learning. And, in humans, who rely on cultural adaptations for survival, most behavior is learned.

Life history traits or strategies (developmental stages that characterize a species) are important to the reproductive success of individuals. These include length of gestation, number of offspring per birth, interbirth interval, age of sexual maturity, and longevity. Although these characters are strongly influenced by the genome of any species, they are also influenced by environmental and social factors such as nutrition and social status. In turn, nutritional requirements are affected by body size, diet, and basal metabolic rate (BMR).

We also described the various types of primate social groups: one male-multifemale groups; multimale-multifemale groups; so-called monogamous pairs; polyandry; and more or less solitary individuals. And we presented various explanations for why primates live in social groups (e.g., predator avoidance and competition for resources with other groups). There was also discussion of the various strategies primates have adopted to facilitate social living, including affiliative and aggressive interactions. And lastly, we talked about the relationships between mothers and infants and how there is increasing evidence that male primates provide more parental care than was previously thought.

For Further Thought

1. Apply some of the topics presented in this chapter to some nonprimate species with which you are familiar. Can you develop some hypotheses to explain the behavior of some domestic species? You might want to speculate on how behavior in domestic animals may differ from that of their wild ancestors. (Chapter 2 might help you here.)

2. In anticipation of the next chapter, can you speculate on how the behavioral ecology of nonhuman primates may be helpful in explaining human behavior?

Go to the book website at **http://www.anthropology.wadsworth.com** for resources to help you explore these questions further. Click on "For Further Thought" for this chapter.

Questions for Review

1. How does basal metabolic rate relate to diet and body size?
2. What are the disadvantages and advantages of living in social groups? Can you make similar statements about some nonprimate species, both predators and prey animals?
3. What are the major characteristics that influence social structure?
4. How can infanticide contribute to an individual's reproductive success? Is it more advantageous to males or females? Can you relate infanticide to any of the life history traits we discussed. and if so, which ones?
5. What are some of the ways nonhuman primates regulate behavior in social groups in order to mitigate conflict?
6. What is philopatry, and how can it be beneficial to the philopatric sex of a species? What species do not exhibit philopatry?

Suggested Further Reading

Cartmill, Matt. 1990. "Human Uniqueness and Theoretical Content in Paleoanthropology." *International Journal of Primatology* 11(3): 173–192.

Cheney, Dorothy L., and Robert M. Seyfarth. 1990. *How Monkeys See the World*. Chicago: University of Chicago Press.

Goodall, Jane. 1986. *The Chimpanzees of Gombe*. Cambridge, MA: The Belknap Press of Harvard University Press.

Maggioncalda, Anne Nacey, and Robert M. Sapolsky. 2002. "Disturbing Behaviors of the Orangutan." *Scientific American* 286: 60–65.

Napier, J. R., and P. H. Napier. 1985. *The Natural History of the Primates*. Cambridge, MA: The MIT Press.

Packer, C., and A. E. Pusey. 1997. "Divided We Fall: Cooperation Among Lions." *Scientific American* 276(5); 52–59.

Rowe, Noel. 1996. *The Pictorial Guide to the Living Primates*. Charlestown, R.I.: Pogonias Press.

Smuts, Barbara B., Dorothy L. Cheney, Robert M. Seyfarth, Richard W. Wrangham, and Thomas T. Struhsaker (eds.). 1987. *Primate Societies*. Chicago: University of Chicago Press.

Strier, Karen B. 2000. *Primate Behavioral Ecology*. Boston: Allyn Bacon.

Online Anthropology Resource Center

Go to the Anthropology Resource Center at **http://www.anthropology.wadsworth.com** for a wealth of online resources, including a companion website for your text that provides study aids such as self-quizzes for each chapter and a practice final exam, as well as links to anthropology websites and information on the latest theories and discoveries in the field. Also, check out InfoTrac College Edition®, your online library that offers full-length articles from thousands of scholarly and popular publications. Just click on the InfoTrac button at the companion website and use the passcode that came with your book.

Primates in Biomedical Research: Ethics and Concerns

The use of nonhuman animals for experimentation is an established practice, long recognized for its benefits to human beings as well as to nonhuman animals. Currently, an estimated 17 to 22 million animals are used annually in the United States for the testing of new vaccines and other methods of treating or preventing disease, as well as for the development of innovative surgical procedures. Nonhuman animals are also used in psychological experimentation and in the testing of consumer products.

Because of biological and behavioral similarities shared with humans, nonhuman primates are among the species most desired for biomedical research. In the United States, about 50,000 nonhuman primates are used annually in laboratory research, with approximately 3,000 being involved in more than one study. This figure is more than five times the number used in all the European Union member countries combined, and in the year 2000, United States labs used over 57,000 nonhuman primates.

The most commonly used primates are baboons, vervets, various macaque species, squirrel monkeys, marmosets, and tamarins. Because they are more costly than other species (such as mice, rats, rabbits, cats, and dogs), primates are usually reserved for medical and behavioral studies and not for the testing of consumer goods such as cosmetics or household cleaners. (It should be noted that many cosmetic companies say they no longer perform tests on animals.)

Although work with primates has certainly benefited humankind, these benefits are expensive, not only monetarily but in terms of suffering and animal lives lost. The development of the polio vaccine in the 1950s serves as one example of the costs involved. Prior to the 1950s, polio had killed and crippled millions of people worldwide. Now the disease is almost unheard of, at least in developed nations. But included in the price tag for the polio vaccine were the lives of 1.5 *million* rhesus macaques, mostly imported from India.

Unquestionably, the elimination of polio and other diseases is a boon to humanity, and such achievements are part of the obligation of medical research to promote the health and well-being of people. But at the same time, serious questions have been raised about medical advances made at the expense of millions of nonhuman animals, many of whom are primates. Indeed, one well-known primatologist, speaking at a conference some years ago, questioned whether we can morally justify depleting populations of threatened species solely for the benefit of a single, highly overpopulated one. This question will seem outrageous to many readers, especially in view of the fact that the majority of people would argue that *whatever* is necessary to promote human health and longevity is justified.

Leaving the broader ethical issues aside for a moment, one area of controversy regarding laboratory primates is housing. Traditionally, lab animals were kept in small metal cages, usually one or two per cage. Cages were usually bare, except for food and water, and they were frequently stacked one on top of another, so that their inhabitants find themselves in the unnatural situation of having animals above and below them, as well as on each side.

The primary reason for small cage size is simple. Small cages are less expensive than large ones and they require less space (space is also costly). Moreover, sterile, unenriched cages (i.e., lacking objects for manipulation or play) are easier and therefore cheaper to clean. But for such curious, intelligent animals as primates, these easy-to-maintain facilities result in a deprivation that leads to depression, neurosis, and psychosis.

Chimpanzees, reserved primarily for AIDS and hepatitis B research, probably suffer more than any other species from inadequate facilities. In 1990, Jane Goodall published a description of conditions she encountered in one lab she visited in Maryland. In this facility, she saw two- and three-year-old chimpanzees housed, two together, in cages measuring 22 inches square and 24 inches high.

Obviously, movement for these youngsters was virtually impossible, and they had been kept this way for over three months! At this same lab, adult chimps, infected with HIV or hepatitis, were confined alone for several years in small isolation chambers, where they rocked back and forth, seeing little and hearing nothing of their surroundings.

Fortunately, conditions are improving. There has been increased public awareness of existing conditions; and there is, among some members of the biomedical community, a growing sensitivity toward the special requirements of primates.

In 1991, amendments to the Animal Welfare Act (first enacted in 1966) required all labs to provide minimum standards for the humane care of all "warm-blooded" animals. (For some reason, birds and rodents aren't included in this category.) These minimum standards provide specific requirements for cage size based on weight of the animal. For example, primates weighing less than 2.2 pounds must have 1.6 square feet of floor space per animal, and the cage must be at least 20 inches high. Those weighing more than 77 pounds are allotted at least 25 square feet of floor space per animal and at least 84 inches (7 feet) of vertical space.

Clearly, the enclosures described above aren't large enough for most normal locomotor activities, and this contributes to psychological stress. One method of reducing such stress is to provide cages with objects and climbing structures (even part of a dead branch is a considerable improvement and costs nothing).

Several facilities now implement such procedures. Also, many laboratory staff members are now trained to provide enrichment for the animals in their care. Moreover, the Maryland lab that Dr. Goodall visited no longer maintains chimpanzees in isolation chambers. Now they are housed with other animals in areas measuring 80 cubic feet and they're provided with various forms of enrichment.

Aside from the treatment of captive primates, there continues to be concern over the depletion of wild populations in order to provide research animals. Actually, the number of wild-caught animals used in research today is small compared to the numbers lost to habitat destruction and hunting for food. However, in the past, particularly in the 1950s and 1960s, the numbers of primates captured for research were staggering. In 1968, for example, 113,714 were received in the United States alone!

On average, the United States annually imports some 20,000 (some from breeding colonies in the country of origin). Although it would be best if no free-ranging primates were involved, at least these figures represent a substantial improvement since the 1960s. And there is mounting concern over primates provided by breeding colonies in countries where they occur naturally. For example, Chinese breeding centers obtain their breeding animals from free-ranging populations.

In response to concerns for diminishing wild populations and regulations to protect them, a number of breeding colonies have been established in the United States and other countries to help meet demands for laboratory animals. Additionally, in 1986, the National Institutes of Health established the National Chimpanzee Breeding Program to provide chimpanzees primarily for AIDS and hepatitis B research.

Furthermore, in 1989, the United States Fish and Wildlife Service upgraded the status of wild chimpanzees from "threatened" to "endangered." Although the endangered status was not applied to animals born in captivity, the upgrade was intended to provide additional protection for free-ranging populations. Unfortunately, even with all the policies now in place, there is no absolute guarantee that some wild-born chimpanzees will not find their way into research labs.

The animal rights movement has been described by many in the scientific community as "antiscience" or "anti-intellectual." Certainly, there are extremists in the animal rights movement and these labels are appropriate for them. But there are many members of the biomedical and scientific communities, including the authors of this text, to whom these labels don't apply. It's neither antiscience nor anti-intellectual to recognize that humans who derive benefits from the use of nonhuman species have an obligation to reduce suffering and provide adequate facilities for highly intelligent, complex animals. This obligation in no way necessitates laboratory break-ins. But improvement does mean that individual members of the biomedical community must become yet more aware of the requirements of captive primates. Moreover, those involved in primate testing, as well as the granting agencies that fund them, should be kept well informed as to the status of wild primate populations. Lastly, and perhaps most importantly, existing laws that regulate the capture, treatment, and trade of wild-caught animals *must* be more strictly enforced.

Undoubtedly, humankind has much to gain by using nonhuman primates for experimentation. But we also have a moral obligation to ensure their survival in the wild, as well as to provide them with humane treatment and enriched captive environments. (One sign of progress is the 200 acre "retirement center" for former lab chimpanzees. This center is scheduled to open sometime in 2004 in Louisiana.) And most of all, we owe them respect as complex, intelligent, and sensitive animals that are not so different from ourselves. If we grant them this, the rest should follow.

Critical Thinking Questions

1. What do you see as the benefits derived from using nonhuman primates in biomedical research? Have you personally benefited from this type of research? If so, how?
2. Do you personally have concerns regarding the use of nonhuman primates in biomedical research? Explain your views.
3. Delineate the issues surrounding habitat enrichment for laboratory primates. Do you think enrichment is an important concern? Why or why not? If so, how would you address this issue, bearing in mind that there are constraints on funding?

Sources

Cyranoski, D. 2003. "China Launches Primate Centre to Broaden Medical Use of Monkeys." *Nature,* 424:239–240.

Goodall, Jane. 1990. *Through a Window*. Boston: Houghton-Mifflin.

Goodman, S. and E. Check, 2002. "The Great Primate Debate." *Nature,* 417:684–687.

Holden, Constance. 1988. "Academy Explores Use of Laboratory Animals." *Science* 242 (October): 185.

United States Department of Agriculture. Subchapter A— Animal Welfare. Washington, DC: U.S. Government Printing Office, Publication Number 311–364/60638, 1992.

Note: We would like to express special appreciation to Dr. Shirley MacGreal, President, International Primate Protection League, and to Dr. Thomas L. Wolfle, Director, Institute of Laboratory Animal Resources, for providing information for this issue.

8 Primate Models for Human Evolution

Orangutan (*Pongo pygmaeus*)
Ryan McVay/Getty Images

Key Questions

Which patterns of nonhuman primate behavior are the most important for understanding human evolution?

How are humans unique among primates? In what ways are we not unique?

Introduction

In Chapter 1, we said that chimpanzees, in particular, are often used as models for early hominid behavior. But once the human and chimpanzee lineages diverged from a common ancestor, they traveled down different evolutionary paths and continued to evolve in response to different environmental pressures. Consequently, no living species, not even chimpanzees, can perfectly serve as a representative of early hominid adaptations.

Anyone who is even slightly curious about the beginnings of humankind would like to know more about our early ancestors. Artists' renditions of early hominids, based on fossil remains, may give a fairly accurate depiction of what they looked like, but what did they *really* look like? What were their lives like? Did they have the same diseases people have today? What kinds of social groups did they form? What did they eat? How long did they live? How did they die?

We will never have definitive answers to all these questions. But we can continue to enhance our understanding of the complex interactions that influence many behaviors in living nonhuman primates. And through continued discovery and analysis of fossil material, we can put our exploration of behavioral evolution on an even firmer scientific footing.

In the last chapter, we considered many of the factors that have guided the evolutionary history of nonhuman primate behaviors. In the last two decades, primatologists have agreed that certain human behavioral predispositions reflect patterns also seen in other primates (Cartmill, 1990; King, 1994; de Waal, 1996). However, just because both chimpanzees and humans exhibit a particular behavior, we still can't say for certain that it's a definite and direct result of shared ancestry. What's important in these inquiries is to closely examine the patterns of behavior that have evolved as adaptive responses in nonhuman primates, while keeping in mind the enormous degree of flexibility in primate behavior. Then researchers can look for similar patterns in modern humans and attempt to draw conclusions about the ecological and genetic factors that may have produced similarities (and differences) between ourselves and our closest relatives. This approach places the study of human behavior firmly within an evolutionary context.

We've discussed how primates show a propensity for forming long-term social bonds that frequently include complex alliances and friendships. This predisposition for complex social life provided a foundation for the evolution of the earliest hominids. One of the hallmarks of later hominid evolution is increased relative brain size, but the foundations of neurological complexity were laid long before hominids began making stone tools. These foundations are still evident today in behavioral patterns shared by humans and nonhuman primates.

Certainly, human behavior is predominantly learned. But the *ability* to learn and behave in complex ways is ultimately rooted in biological factors, and natural selection has favored increased learning capacities and behavioral modification in the human lineage. This biological perspective doesn't assume that all

See the following sections of the CD-ROM for topics covered in this chapter: Virtual Lab 1, section I, and Virtual Labs 9–12.

human abilities and behaviors are genetically determined or unalterable. Rather, it helps explain *how* certain patterns may have come about and what their adaptive significance might be. Within this framework, the plasticity of human behavior is clearly recognized and emphasized.

Human Origins and Behavior

The evolution of many human traits is discussed in Virtual Labs 9–12.

What does it mean to be human? Clearly, it's behavioral attributes that most dramatically set humans apart from other species. Long ago, culture became our strategy for coping with life's challenges. If suddenly stripped of all cultural attributes, modern humans would not be able to survive in much of the world. And no other primate even comes close to the human ability to modify the environment.

Although we humans share more than 98 percent of our DNA sequences and many anatomical and behavioral characteristics with chimpanzees, we are undeniably quite different from them, physically as well as behaviorally. Humans have different limb proportions, flatter faces, smaller teeth, and, most importantly, relatively and absolutely bigger brains than any other primate. Anatomical differences, such as limb proportions, are the results of changes in the behavior of regulatory genes that guide the direction of embryonic development. These homeotic genes (see p. 56) are highly conserved throughout the animal kingdom, and they govern the same developmental processes in all animals. But the length of time they operate to establish patterns and proportions of anatomical structures is determined by still other genes, and these genes do vary between species. Indeed, alterations in the activities of these developmental genes through the course of evolution may be the single most important factor in speciation. For example, chimpanzees have longer faces and larger teeth than humans, since the genes that control the development of these structures cause them to develop at different rates (Fig. 8–1).

In spite of these differences, humans and apes are sufficiently similar anatomically that we can identify many shared derived traits they both inherited from their last common ancestor. Human and ape shoulders are anatomically quite similar but different from those of monkeys. Likewise, apes and humans have fewer lumbar vertebrae than monkeys, which results in a shorter, more stable lower back. But, in humans, as in many species, some systems evolved at different times and rates than others. As a consequence, human hands are less derived than ape hands because our thumbs are not as reduced and our fingers not as elongated. In fact, humans have the hands of a generalized cercopithecine monkey.

So what does all this mean in terms of behavior? It means that to some extent, we shouldn't limit our behavioral comparisons to chimpanzees, but we should include many species in our behavioral analogies. The selective pressures that acted on ancestral monkeys have played a role in our evolution, too, and that is something we should not forget.

In the 1970s, the prevailing theory was that early hominids diverged from the apes as they moved out of a forested environment and adapted to a savanna environment. Such a move meant that they were subjected to increased predation pressure and that the adoption of bipedality arose partly out of the need to stand upright

FIGURE 8–1 Developmental changes in the skull of (a) chimpanzees and (b) humans illustrate morphological differences between two closely related species. These differences are due to differences in the timing of development due to regulatory genes.

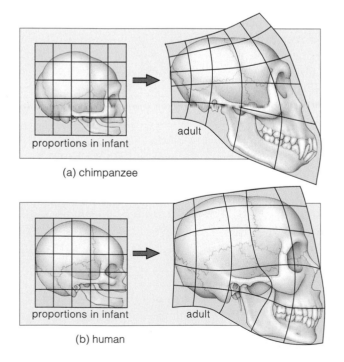
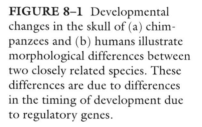

while looking for predators (see Chapter 9). The first hominids were already predisposed to adopting a bipedal stance because standing upright is something many earlier primates were anatomically capable of doing. The same principle applies to behavior. Although we now believe that early hominid ancestors probably exploited a more mixed woodland habitat rather than a savanna environment, they still had to have possessed anatomical and behavioral capacities that allowed them to go there in the first place. But as a separate lineage, their own evolutionary story probably began with a behavioral shift to exploiting an econiche different from other hominoids, and this new adaptation required spending more time on the ground and exploiting different types of food resources. These factors in turn selected for further behavioral and anatomical adaptations, while other hominoids were responding to different environmental pressures.

Because modern terrestrial primates, such as baboons, live on the savanna, they were used initially as a model for early hominid behavior and adaptation (Washburn and deVore, 1961). For example, because savanna baboons live in large multimale-multifemale groups partly as an adaptive response to predation, it was hypothesized that early hominids also had a similar social structure (and they probably did). But because we're closely related to chimpanzees, they, too, were used as an analogue for the development of many human behaviors, including tool use and competition for social rank. Thus, several species have been chosen for comparison on the basis of both behavioral ecology and biological relatedness (Dunbar, 2001).

Today, while primatologists still use nonhuman primate behavior to examine the evolution of human behavior, they now use statistical tests as well to examine the relationships between two or more variables. For example, it is important to establish if there is a correlation between body size and BMR (see p. 177). Then, having demonstrated a positive correlation, we might add another variable, such as diet. Subsequently, we could add other factors, such as increased brain size and social structure. In other words, we look for correlations between life history traits and sociality. Once positive (or negative) correlations are ascertained, we can postulate certain principles to apply to the study of human behavioral evolution.

Brain and Body Size

The one characteristic that clearly differentiates humans from other animal species is *relative brain size,* by which we mean the proportion of some measure of body size, such as weight, that is accounted for by the brain. Brain size and body size are closely correlated. Clearly, an animal the size of a chimpanzee (about 45 kg, or 100 pounds) has a larger brain than a squirrel monkey, which weighs almost 1 kg, or about 2 pounds. But in cross-species comparisons, as body weight increases, brain size does not necessarily increase at the same rate.

The predictable relationship between body and brain size has been called the index of **encephalization** (Jerison, 1973). The degree of encephalization can be a very powerful analytical tool, since it provides a gauge of the expected brain size for any given body size. Most primates fall close to the predicted curve, but there is one notable exception: *Homo sapiens.* Modern humans have a brain size well beyond that expected for a primate of similar body weight. It's this degree of encephalization that must be explained as a unique and central component of recent human evolution. Using these same analytical perspectives as applied to the fossil materials in the next several chapters, you will see that early members of the genus *Homo* as well as more primitive hominids (*Australopithecus*) weren't nearly as encephalized as modern *H. sapiens.*

encephalization The proportional size of the brain relative to some other measure, usually some estimate of overall body size, such as weight. More precisely, the term refers to increases in brain size beyond that which would be expected given the body size of a particular species.

allometry Also called "scaling," the differential proportion among various anatomical structures. For example, the size of the brain in proportion to overall body size changes during the development of an individual. Moreover, scaling effects must also be considered when comparing species.

cortex Layer. In the brain, the cortex is the layer that covers the cerebral hemispheres which, in turn, cover more primitive or older structures related to bodily functions and the sense of smell. It is composed of nerve cells called neurons, which communicate with each other and also send and receive messages to and from all parts of the body.

neocortex The more recently evolved portions of the cortex of the brain that are involved with higher mental functions and composed of areas that integrate incoming information from different sensory organs.

Carefully controlled comparisons are essential in making cross-species generalizations regarding animals of differing sizes (a point to keep in mind when we discuss early hominids, most of which varied notably from *Homo sapiens* in body size). Such controls relate to considerations of what is called *scaling,* or (more technically) **allometry.** These allometric comparisons have become increasingly important in understanding contemporary primate life history variables and adaptations. Moreover, similar approaches, as directly borrowed from these primate models, are now also routinely applied to interpretation of the primate/hominid fossil record.

Beyond simple brain size comparisons between different species, it's more appropriate to emphasize the relative size of certain structures in the brain. Primitive brains, such as those of reptiles, are mostly composed of structures related to basic physiological functions, and there is a small **cortex** that receives sensory information (especially olfaction). As discussed in Chapter 5, in primitive mammals, the most recently evolved layer of the cortex, called the **neocortex,** is enlarged to deal with more complex sensory information. And in primates, the expansion of the neocortex has accounted for much of the increase in brain size (Fig. 8–2). The primate neocortex comprises many complex association areas, and it's the part of the brain that, in humans, is associated with cognitive functions related to reasoning, complex problem solving, forethought, and language. In humans, the neocortex accounts for about 80 percent of total brain volume (Dunbar, 1998).

Timing of brain growth is also important. In nonhuman primates, the most rapid period of brain growth occurs shortly before birth; but in humans, it occurs after birth. Restraints on prenatal brain growth in humans are necessary if the infant is to pass through the birth canal. As it is, owing to the size of the head in human neonates, childbirth is more difficult in humans than in any other primate (see p. 453). Thus, human infants show considerable brain expansion for at least the first five years after birth. Because brain tissue is the most costly of all body tissues in terms of energy consumed, the metabolic costs of such rapid and sustained neurological growth are enormous, requiring more than 50 percent of an infant's metabolic output (Aiello, 1992).

In evolutionary terms, the metabolic costs of a large brain must be compensated for by benefits. That is, large brains would not have evolved if they didn't offer some advantage (Dunbar, 1998). Various hypotheses have been proposed for the evolution of large brains in primates, and these have mostly focused on solutions to problems related to food getting and the kinds of foods a species eats. For example, some monkeys (with a smaller relative brain size) primarily eat leaves, which, although plentiful, are not an energy rich food. Primates also need a complex brain to be familiar with their home range; to be aware of when seasonal foods are available; and to solve the problem of extracting foods from shells, hard peels, and even underground roots. But one could argue that these are problems for all foraging species, squirrels and raccoons for example, and yet these animals have *not* evolved such relatively large brains.

Another explanation, the *social brain hypothesis* proposes that primate brains increased in relative size and complexity because primates live in social groups. The demands of social living are many, and primates must be able to negotiate a complex web of interactions, including competition, alliance formation, and forming and maintaining friendships, avoiding certain individuals, etc.

But at the same time, group size is limited by brain size to the extent that a group can't be made up of more animals than individuals can recognize and interact with. Hence, brain and group size probably coevolved (Dunbar, 1998, 2001).

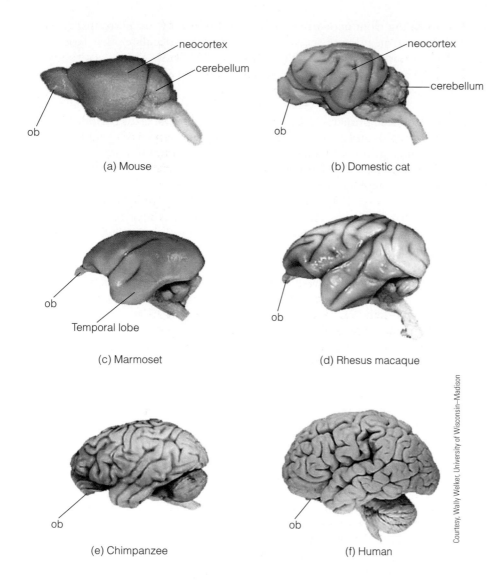

neocortex

cerebellum

ob

(a) Mouse

neocortex

cerebellum

ob

(b) Domestic cat

ob

Temporal lobe

(c) Marmoset

ob

(d) Rhesus macaque

ob

(e) Chimpanzee

ob

(f) Human

Courtesy, Wally Welker, University of Wisconsin–Madison

FIGURE 8–2 Comparisons of mammalian brains as seen in these left lateral views (front is to left). Expansion of the neocortex, the outer layers of the cerebral hemispheres, has been the most significant trend during the evolution of the mammalian brain. This is especially evident in the size of the neocortex relative to that of the olfactory bulb (ob) at the front of the brain. The olfactory bulb is the termination point of sensory fibers that send olfactory information from the nose to the brain. A relatively large olfactory bulb indicates a greater dependence on the sense of smell. Compare the size of this organ, relative to the neocortex, in these brains. In the mouse and cat it is particularly large, but it becomes smaller in primates, and in humans, it's barely visible. In fact, in chimpanzees and humans the neocortex is all that is visible from the top and sides except for the cerebellum. Another thing to note is the increasingly convoluted surface of the neocortex. This is due to cortical folding which allows more neurons to be packed into a limited space. Increasing the number of neurons provides more interconnections between areas of the brain and allows more information to be processed. Although the marmoset exhibits less cortical folding than the cat, the temporal lobe (part of the neocortex) is better defined and brain size compared to body size is greater. As you can see, *cortical folding* is most pronounced in humans. (Illustrations are shown approximately the same size and not to scale.) (Photos provided by the University of Wisconsin-Madison Comparative Mammalian Brain Collection: http://brainmuseum.org. Preparation of these images and specimens was funded by the National Science Foundation and the National Institutes of Health.)

Extrapolating from neocortical volume to the size of social groups, as seen in several nonhuman primate species, Dunbar (1998) speculates that large group size in some early members of the genus *Homo* is likely. This is not to say that early humans always lived in large groups, but that considerable aggregations were formed by periodic associations of smaller groups. This hypothesis is supported by observations of recent hunter-gatherer groups (e.g., aboriginal Australians) whose primary social unit was a clan. Several clans periodically came together for rituals and other occasions, forming gatherings of roughly 150 people. This overall group size seems to reflect the maximum number of individuals people can recognize and be acquainted with, and it also correlates well with nonhuman primate data.

Bergman, et al. (2003) showed that savanna baboons in a study group in Botswana recognized that the female social hierarchy is divided into matrilines, and that the matrilines are ranked relative to one another. In addition, they also recognized dominance relationships within each matriline. In other words, they understand the arrangement of hierarchies within hierarchies. Hence, interactions between individuals are influenced by the social position of individuals within matrilines and of matrilines within the entire group. Emphasizing the implications of such behavioral complexity for the evolution of increased intelligence in humans, these authors state, "The selective pressures imposed by complex societies may therefore have favored cognitive skills that constitute an evolutionary precursor to some components of human cognition (Bergman et al., 2003:1234).

University of Southern California primatologist Craig Stanford (1999; 2001) proposes that meat eating was also important to the development of increased cognitive abilities in the human lineage. Hunting, especially of big game, was a topic of considerable interest in early hominid studies in the 1960s (Washburn and Lancaster, 1968) but those theories were eventually discounted for various reasons, one of which is that the earliest hominids weren't capable of hunting large prey.

Most nonhuman primates that do kill and eat small mammals don't actually hunt them. Chimpanzees, however, do hunt and their favorite prey is red colobus monkeys (see p. 183) (Fig. 8–3). Stanford and others (Aiello and Wells, 2002) argue that if early hominids relied on a diet that increasingly contained a high proportion of meat, rich in protein and fats, such a diet would meet the nutritional demands of a lineage in which relatively large brains were becoming important. But, as Stanford also points out, relatively large brain size has not developed in social carnivores such as wolves and lions. Moreover, the percentage of meat in chimpanzee diets is small and may be similar to what early hominids obtained.

Hence, if meat was important in the evolution of large brains in hominids, some factor other than nutrition would have had to be important. Among chimpanzees, once a kill has been made, the meat is often shared with relatives, allies, and females. Negotiating the complexities and strategies involved in the politics of sharing meat, might be viewed as one aspect of the social brain hypothesis where neurological complexity evolved as a response to complicated behavioral challenges.

In addition to what we know about the differences in meat consumption by chimpanzees (not much) and humans (a lot), there is recent evidence that strongly suggests meat became an important dietary component in human ancestors sometime after chimpanzees and humans went their separate ways. In a preliminary analysis of the chimpanzee genome rough draft, Clark et al.,

FIGURE 8–3 Male chimpanzees eating a red colobus monkey they have killed.

David Bygott, Anthro Photo

(2003) discovered that several of the genes that produce enzymes involved in amino acid metabolism have changed over time in both species. (Animal protein is a major source of amino acids.) This finding adds support to theories that increased meat consumption may have been important for increased brain size in early humans (Penny, 2004). At the very least it indicates that, as the two lineages diverged, both responded to different selective pressures and selection favored enzyme mutations that enabled some hominids to digest meat more efficiently.

Language

One of the most significant events in human evolution was the development of language. In the previous chapter, we described several behaviors and autonomic responses that convey information among primates. But although we emphasized the importance of communication to nonhuman primate social life, we also said that nonhuman primates don't use language in the way that humans do.

FIGURE 8–4 Group of free-ranging vervets.

The view traditionally held by most linguists and behavioral psychologists has been that nonhuman communication consists of mostly involuntary vocalizations and actions that convey information solely about the emotional state of the animal (anger, fear, etc.). Nonhuman animals have not been considered capable of communicating about external events, objects, or other animals, either in close proximity or removed in space or time. For example, when a startled baboon barks, other group members know only that it is startled. They don't know what prompted the bark, and this they can only ascertain by looking around. In general, then, it has been assumed that nonhuman animals, including primates, use a *closed system* of communication, where the use of vocalizations and other modalities doesn't include references to specific external phenomena.

But for several years, these views have been challenged (Steklis, 1985; King, 1994). For example, vervet monkeys (Fig. 8–4) use specific vocalizations to refer to particular categories of predators, such as snakes, birds of prey, and leopards (Struhsaker, 1967; Seyfarth, Cheney, and Marler, 1980a, 1980b). When researchers made tape recordings of various vervet alarm calls and played them back within hearing distance of free-ranging vervets, they saw different responses to various calls. In response to leopard-alarm calls, the monkeys climbed trees; eagle-alarm calls caused them to look up and they responded to snake-alarm calls by looking around at nearby grass.

These results demonstrate that vervets use distinct vocalizations to refer to specific components of the external environment. These calls are not involuntary, and they do not refer solely to the emotional state (alarm) of the individual, although this information is also conveyed. While these findings dispel certain long-held misconceptions about nonhuman communication (at least for some species), they also indicate certain limitations. Vervet communication is restricted to the present; as far as we know, no vervet can communicate about a predator it saw yesterday or one it might see in the future.

Other studies have demonstrated that numerous nonhuman primates, including cottontop tamarins (Cleveland and Snowdon, 1982), Goeldi's monkeys (Masataka, 1983), red colobus (Struhsaker, 1975), and gibbons (Tenaza and Tilson, 1977), produce distinct calls that have specific references. There is also growing evidence that many birds and some nonprimate mammals use specific predator alarm calls (Seyfarth, 1987).

In contrast, humans use *language,* a set of written and/or spoken symbols that refer to concepts, other people, objects, and so on. This set of symbols is said to be *arbitrary* in that the symbol itself has no inherent relationship with whatever it stands for. For example, the English word for *flower* when written or spoken neither looks, sounds, smells, nor feels like the thing it represents. Moreover, humans can recombine their linguistic symbols in an infinite number of ways to create new meanings, and we can use language to refer to events, places, objects, and people far removed in both space and time. For these reasons, language is described as an *open system* of communication, based on the human ability to think symbolically.

Language, as distinct from other forms of communication, has always been considered a uniquely human achievement, setting humans apart from the rest of the animal kingdom. But work with captive apes has raised some doubts about some aspects of this notion. Although many people were skeptical about the capacity of nonhuman primates to use language, reports from psychologists, especially those who work with chimpanzees, leave little doubt that apes can learn to interpret visual signs and use them in communication. No mammal other than humans has the ability to speak. However, the fact that apes can't speak has less to do with lack of intelligence than to differences in the anatomy of the vocal tract and *language-related structures in the brain.*

Because of unsuccessful attempts by others to teach young chimpanzees to speak, psychologists Beatrice and Allen Gardner designed a study to test language capabilities in chimpanzees by teaching an infant female named Washoe to use ASL (American Sign Language for the deaf). The project began in 1966, and in three years, Washoe acquired at least 132 signs. "She asked for goods and services, and she also asked questions about the world of objects and events around her" (Gardner et al., 1989, p. 6).

Years later, an infant chimpanzee named Loulis was placed in Washoe's care. Psychologist Roger Fouts and colleagues wanted to know if Loulis would acquire signing skills from Washoe and other chimpanzees in the study group. Within just eight days, Loulis began to imitate the signs of others. Moreover, Washoe also deliberately *taught* Loulis some signs. For example, instructing him to sit, "Washoe placed a small plastic chair in front of Loulis, and then signed CHAIR/SIT to him several times in succession, watching him closely throughout" (Fouts et al., 1989, p. 290).

There have been other chimpanzee language experiments. A chimpanzee called Sara was taught by David Premack to recognize plastic chips as symbols for various objects. Importantly, the chips did not resemble the objects they represented. For example, the chip that represented an apple was neither round nor red. Sara's ability to associate chips with concepts and objects to which they bore no similarity implies some degree of symbolic thought.

At the Yerkes Regional Primate Research Center in Atlanta, Georgia, another chimp, Lana, worked with a specially designed computer keyboard with chips attached to keys. After six months, Lana recognized symbols for 30 words and was able to ask for food and answer questions through the machine (Rumbaugh, 1977). Also at Yerkes, two male chimpanzees, Sherman and Austin, learned to communicate using a series of lexigrams, or geometric symbols, imprinted on a computer keyboard (Savage-Rumbaugh, 1986).

Dr. Francine Patterson, who taught ASL to Koko, a female lowland gorilla, reports that Koko uses more than 500 signs. Furthermore, Michael, an adult male gorilla who was also involved in the study until his death in 2000, had a considerable sign vocabulary, and the two gorillas communicated with each other via signs.

In the late 1970s, a two-year-old male orangutan named Chantek (also at Yerkes) began to use signs after one month of training. Eventually, he acquired approximately 140 signs, which were sometimes used to refer to objects and people not present. Chantek also invented signs and recombined them in novel ways, and he appeared to understand that his signs were *representations* of items, actions, and people (Miles, 1990).

Questions have been raised about this type of experimental work. Do the apes really understand the signs they learn, or are they merely imitating their trainers? Do they learn that a symbol is a name for an object or simply that executing a symbol will produce that object? Other unanswered questions concern the apes' use of grammar, especially when they combine more than just a few "words" to communicate.

Partly in an effort to address some of these questions and criticisms, psychologist Sue Savage-Rumbaugh taught the two chimpanzees Sherman and Austin to use symbols to categorize *classes* of objects, such as "food" or "tool." This was done in recognition of the fact that in previous studies, apes had been taught symbols for *specific* items. Savage-Rumbaugh recognized that using a symbol as a label is not the same thing as understanding the *representational value* of the symbol. But if the chimpanzees could classify things into groups, it would indicate that they can use symbols referentially.

Sherman and Austin were taught to recognize familiar food items, for which they routinely used symbols, as belonging to a broader category referred to by yet another symbol, "food." They were then introduced to unfamiliar food items, for which they had no symbols, to see if they would place them in the food category. The fact that they both had perfect or nearly perfect scores further substantiated that they could categorize unfamiliar objects. More importantly, it was clear that they were capable of assigning to unknown objects symbols that denoted membership in a broad grouping. This ability was a strong indication that the chimpanzees understood that the symbols were being used referentially.

However, subsequent work with Lana, who had different language experiences, didn't prove as successful. Although Lana was able to sort actual objects into categories, she was unable to assign generic symbols to novel items (Savage-Rumbaugh and Lewin, 1994). Thus, it became apparent that the manner in which chimpanzees are introduced to language influences their ability to understand the representational value of symbols.

Throughout the relatively brief history of ape language studies, one often repeated criticism was that young chimpanzees must be *taught* to use symbols. This pattern was contrasted with the ability of human children to learn language through exposure, without being deliberately taught. Therefore, it was significant when Savage-Rumbaugh and her colleagues reported that Kanzi, an infant male bonobo, was *spontaneously* acquiring and using symbols at the age of 2½ years (Savage-Rumbaugh et al., 1986) (Fig. 8–5). In the same way, his younger half-

FIGURE 8–5 The bonobo Kanzi, as a youngster, using lexigrams to communicate with human observers.

sister began to use symbols spontaneously when she was only 11 months old. Both animals had been exposed to the use of lexigrams when they accompanied their mother to training sessions, but neither had received instruction and in fact they weren't even involved in these sessions.

While Kanzi and his sister showed a remarkable degree of cognitive complexity, it nevertheless remains evident that apes don't acquire and use language in the same way humans do. Moreover, it appears that not all signing apes understand the referential relationship between symbol and object, person, or action. Nonetheless, there is now abundant evidence that humans are not the only species capable of some degree of symbolic thought and complex communication.

THE EVOLUTION OF LANGUAGE

From an evolutionary perspective, the ape language experiments may suggest clues to the origins of human language. It's quite likely that the last common ancestor we share with the living great apes had communication capabilities similar to those we see in these species. If so, we need to identify the factors that enhanced the adaptive significance of these characteristics in our own lineage. And, at the same time, it's equally important to explore why these pressures didn't operate to the same degree in our closest relatives.

While increased brain size played a crucial role in human evolution, it was changes in preexisting neurological structures that permitted the development of language. Current evidence suggests that *new* structures and novel connections have not generally been the basis for most of the neurological differences we see among species. Rather, reorganization, elaboration, and/or reduction of existing structures, as well as shifts in the proportions of existing connections, have been far more important (Deacon, 1992). And, it's important to understand that the neurological changes that enhanced language development in humans would not have happened if early hominids had not already possessed the behavioral and neurological foundations that made them possible. For reasons we don't yet fully understand, communication became increasingly important during the course of human evolution, and natural selection favored anatomical and neurological changes that enhanced our ancestors' ability to use spoken language.

Some researchers argue that language capabilities appeared late in human evolution (i.e., with the wide dispersal of modern *Homo sapiens* some 100,000 to 30,000 years ago). Others favor a much earlier origin, possibly with the appearance of the genus *Homo* some 2 m.y.a. Whichever scenario is correct, language came about as complex and efficient forms of communication gained selective value in our lineage.

As you have already learned, the metabolic costs of producing and maintaining brain tissues are high, and those costs must be offset by benefits. So we have to assume that there was intense selective pressure that favored the ability of early humans to communicate at increasingly precise levels.

In most people, language function is located in the left hemisphere, meaning it is **lateralized.** (The left hemisphere is the dominant hemisphere in most people and, since it controls motion on the right side of the body, most people are right-handed.) In particular, two regions, *Broca's area* in the left frontal lobe, and *Wernicke's area* in the left temporal lobe, are directly involved in the production and perception, respectively, of spoken language (Fig. 8-6).

Broca's area is located in the **motor cortex** immediately adjacent to a region that controls movement of muscles in the face, lips, larynx, and tongue. During speech, information is sent to Broca's area where it is organized *specifically for communication.* Then it's transmitted to the adjacent motor areas, which in turn activate the muscles involved in speech. We know that Broca's area operates this way because when it is damaged speech production is impaired, but there is no muscle paralysis. Paralysis occurs only when there is damage to the nearby motor areas themselves.

Wernicke's area is an *association area* that lies near structures involved in the reception of sound. A lesion in Wernicke's area doesn't impair hearing, but it severely affects language comprehension. This, in turn, interferes with speech production, because auditory information specifically related to language is sent from Wernicke's area to Broca's area by way of a bundle of nerve fibers that connects the two regions.

But the perception and production of speech involves much more than these two areas, and the use of written language requires still other neurological structures. Eventually, information relating to all the senses (visual, olfactory, tactile,

lateralized Pertaining to lateralization, the functional specialization of the hemispheres of the brain for specific activities.

motor cortex That portion of the cortex involved in sending outgoing signals involved in muscle use. The motor cortex is located at the back of the frontal lobe.

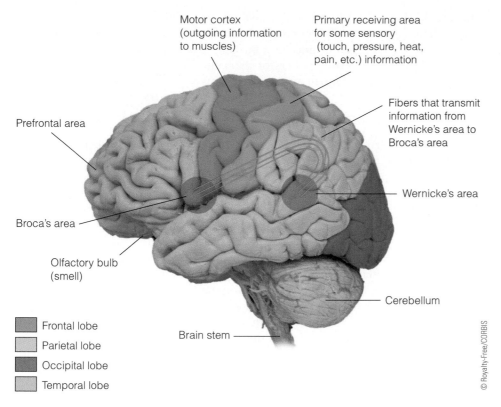

Motor cortex
(outgoing information
to muscles)

Primary receiving area
for some sensory
(touch, pressure, heat,
pain, etc.) information

Fibers that transmit
information from
Wernicke's area to
Broca's area

Prefrontal area

Wernicke's area

Broca's area

Olfactory bulb
(smell)

Cerebellum

Frontal lobe
Parietal lobe
Occipital lobe
Temporal lobe

Brain stem

© Royalty-Free/CORBIS

FIGURE 8–6 Left lateral view of the human brain, showing major regions and areas involved in language. Information that is to be used in speech is sent from Wernicke's area, via a bundle of nerve fibers, to Broca's area.

and auditory) is combined and relayed to Broca's area, where it is translated for speech production. This remarkable human ability depends on the interconnections between receiving areas for all sensory stimuli. While the brains of other species have such areas, they don't have the ability to transform sensory information for the purpose of using language. Or, maybe they do, at least to some degree.

Cantalupo and Hopkins (2001) report that magnetic resonance imaging of chimpanzee, bonobo, and gorilla brains demonstrates that, as in humans, a region analogous to part of Broca's area is larger on the left side than on the right. In humans, this particular area is involved in some of the motor aspects of speech production, and the report suggests that it also may have been important to the development of gestural language. These authors further note that in captive great ape studies, gestures are preferentially made by the right hand (controlled by the left hemisphere) most especially when gestures are combined with vocalizations. Therefore, this study suggests, that perhaps the anatomical basis for the development of left-hemisphere dominance in speech production in humans was present, at least to an incipient degree, in the last common ancestor of humans and the African great apes

Specialization of auditory centers of the left hemisphere for language may have preceded the evolutionary divergence of humans and apes and may even have had its beginnings in the earliest mammals. A team of neuroscientists has shown that this type of lateralization is present in rhesus macaques (Poremba et al., 2004). These researchers demonstrated that, like humans and other species, rhesus macaques receive and process auditory information in the temporal lobes of both hemispheres. But, these monkeys show greater metabolic activity in the left hemisphere *specifically when they hear vocalizations of other rhesus macaques.* This indicates that in macaques the left temporal lobe is specialized for processing the vocalizations of conspecifics in particular.

But this specialization may even have an evolutionary history that extends back before the emergence of primates. Poremba et al. point to other studies that imply that mice and birds also analyze *conspecific* vocalizations in the left hemisphere (Ehret, 1987; George et al., 2002). These studies don't state that this trait is as developed in mice and birds as it is in macaques. And since they only concern the calls of members of the same species, they don't explain the origins of language in human ancestors. However, these discoveries do indicate that, in human evolution, the development of *language specific centers* in the left hemisphere occurred as an elaboration of a trend that has a very long evolutionary history.

The recent identification of a gene that is involved in speech may provide another piece to the puzzle of the evolution of language in humans. The gene, called FOXP2, produces a protein that regulates the expression of other genes. These genes, in turn, influence the embryological development of circuits in the brain that relate to language in humans. People who inherit a particular FOXP2 mutation are afflicted with developmental disorders in the brain that cause severe speech and language impairment (Lai et al., 2001).

The FOXP2 gene is not unique to humans. In fact, it's extremely conserved and, since it's present in mice, it undoubtedly occurs in all mammals. But, while FOXP2 is important to neurological development in nonhuman mammals, it has nothing to do with language in these species. When researchers compared the human form of the *FOXP2* protein to that of chimpanzees and gorillas, they found that the human protein differed from the two ape versions by two amino acid substitutions. This means that since humans last shared a common ancestor with chimpanzees and gorillas, the gene has undergone two point mutations during the course of human evolution. But in chimpanzees and gorillas it hasn't changed.

The FOXP2 gene is the first gene demonstrated to influence language development. The fact that it varies between humans and closely related species indicates that natural selection has acted on it in our lineage, and that perhaps the FOXP2 protein may have played a role in the development of language capacities in humans. But even if it didn't play such a role, the discovery of the relationship between language and FOXP2 illustrates how a gene that is present in many species can mutate in one lineage and begin to perform a slightly different function. If that function confers some advantage, natural selection should favor it and eventually it can come to have enormous evolutionary significance.

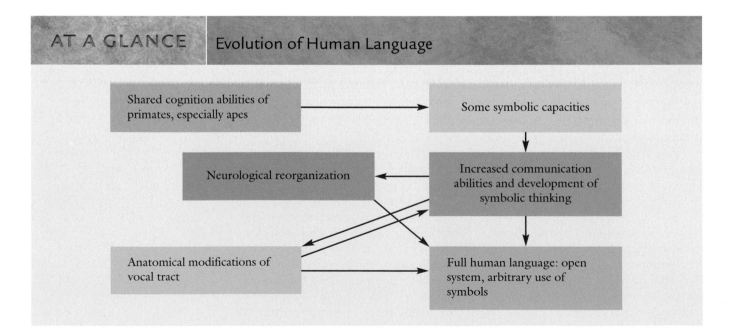

AT A GLANCE   Evolution of Human Language

Shared cognition abilities of primates, especially apes → Some symbolic capacities

Neurological reorganization

Increased communication abilities and development of symbolic thinking

Anatomical modifications of vocal tract

Full human language: open system, arbitrary use of symbols

Primate Cultural Behavior

One important trait that makes primates, and especially chimpanzees and bonobos, attractive as models for behavior in early hominids may be called *cultural behavior*. Although many cultural anthropologists and others prefer to use the term *culture* to refer specifically to human activities, most biological anthropologists consider it appropriate to use the term in discussions of nonhuman primates as well (McGrew, 1992, 1998; de Waal, 1999; Whiten et. al., 1999). In fact, the term *cultural primatology* is now being used more frequently.

Undeniably, most aspects of culture are uniquely human, and one must be cautious when interpreting nonhuman animal behavior. But again, since humans are products of the same evolutionary forces that have produced other species, they can be expected to exhibit some of the same *behavioral patterns,* particularly of other primates. However, because of increased brain size and learning capacities, humans express many characteristics to a greater degree. We would argue that the *aptitude for culture* as a means of adapting to the natural environment is one such characteristic.

Among other things, cultural behavior is *learned;* it is passed from generation to generation not biologically, but through learning. Whereas humans deliberately teach their young, free-ranging nonhuman primates (with the exception of a few reports) don't appear to do so. But at the same time, like young nonhuman primates, human children also acquire a tremendous amount of knowledge through observation rather than instruction (Fig. 8–7a). Nonhuman primate infants, through observing their mothers and others, learn about food items, appropriate behaviors, and how to use and modify objects to achieve certain ends (Fig. 8–7b). In turn, their own offspring will observe their activities. What emerges is a *cultural tradition* that may eventually come to typify an entire group or even a species.

The earliest reported example of cultural behavior concerned a study group of Japanese macaques on Koshima Island. In 1952, Japanese researchers began provisioning the 22-member troop with sweet potatoes. The following year, a young female named Imo began washing her potatoes in a freshwater stream prior to eating them. Within three years, several monkeys had adopted the

FIGURE 8–7 (a) This little girl is learning the basic skills of computer use by watching her older sister. (b) A chimpanzee learns the art of termiting (see p. 214) through intense observation.

(a)

(b)

practice, but they had switched from using the stream to taking their potatoes to the ocean nearby. Maybe they liked the salt seasoning!

The researchers proposed that dietary habits and food preferences are learned and that potato washing was an example of nonhuman culture. Because the practice arose as an innovative solution to a problem (removing dirt) and gradually spread through the troop until it became a tradition, it was seen as containing elements of human culture.

A study of orangutans in six areas (4 Bornean and 2 Sumatran) listed 19 behaviors that showed sufficient regional variation to be classed as "very likely cultural variants" (van Schaik et al., 2003). Four activities in the "very likely" category involved the use of nests. In five localities, nests were built exclusively for play activities and not for resting or sleeping. There was also variation in the construction of nests above resting nests (as in bunk beds) to provide shelter from bright sun or rain. While tool use didn't seem to be as elaborate as in chimpanzees, in one Bornean locality, orangutans used sticks to scratch themselves and leaves as "napkins." And in one Sumatran area, they pushed sticks into tree holes to obtain insects. Other behaviors that varied included the use of branches to swat insects, and pressing leaves or hands to the mouth to amplify sounds.

Chimpanzees exhibit more elaborate examples of *tool use*. This point is very important, because traditionally, tool use (along with language) was said to set humans apart from other animals.

Chimpanzees insert twigs and grass blades into termite mounds in a practice called "termite fishing." When termites seize the twig, the chimpanzee withdraws it and eats the attached insects. Chimpanzees modify some of their stems and twigs by stripping the leaves—in effect, manufacturing a tool from the natural material. To some extent, chimpanzees even alter objects to a "regular and set pattern" and have been observed preparing objects for later use at an out-of-sight location (Goodall, 1986, p. 535). For example, a chimpanzee will very carefully select a piece of vine, bark, twig, or palm frond and modify it by removing leaves or other extraneous material, then break off portions until it is the proper length. Chimpanzees have also been seen making these tools even before the termite mound is in sight.

All this preparation has several implications. First, the chimpanzees are engaged in an activity that prepares them for a future (not immediate) task at a somewhat distant location, and this action implies planning and forethought. Second, attention to the shape and size of the raw material indicates that chimpanzees have a preconceived idea of what the finished product needs to be in order to be useful. To produce a tool, even a simple tool, based on a concept is an extremely complex behavior. Scientists previously believed that such behavior was the exclusive domain of humans, but now we question this assumption.

Chimpanzees also crumple and chew handfuls of leaves, which they dip into tree hollows where water accumulates. Then they suck the water that would otherwise be inaccessible from their newly made "leaf sponges." Leaves are also used to wipe substances from fur; twigs are sometimes used as toothpicks; stones may be used as weapons; and various objects, such as branches and stones, may be dragged or rolled to enhance displays. Lastly, sticks or leaves are used to help process mammalian prey, but with one exception these practices appear to be incidental. The one exception is in the Tai Forest (Ivory Coast), where chimpanzees use sticks to extract marrow from long bones (Boesch and Boesch, 1989).

Chimpanzees in numerous West African study groups use hammerstones with platform stones to crack nuts and hard-shelled fruits (Boesch et al, 1994) (Fig. 8–8). However, it's important to note that neither the hammerstone nor the platform stone is deliberately manufactured.* Wild capuchin monkeys use leaves

See Virtual Lab 11, section I, for a discussion of chimpanzee tool use.

---

*Observers of nonhuman primates rarely distinguish natural objects used as tools from modified objects deliberately manufactured for specific purposes. The term *tool* is usually employed in both cases.

to extract water from cavities in trees (Phillips, 1998) and also smash objects against stones (Izawa and Mizuno, 1977), and their use of stones in captivity (both as hammers and anvils) has been reported (Visalberghi, 1990). (Stones serve as anvils when fruit or other objects are bashed against the rock surface.) Chimpanzees are the only nonhuman animal to use stones both as hammers and anvils to obtain food. And they are the only nonhuman primate that consistently and habitually makes and uses tools (McGrew, 1992).

It's important that chimpanzees exhibit regional variation regarding both the types and methods of tool use. Stone hammers and platforms are used only in West African groups. And at central and eastern African sites, chimpanzees "fish" for termites with stems and sticks, but they don't at some West African locations (McGrew, 1992).

Chimpanzees also show regional dietary preferences (Nishida et al., 1983; McGrew, 1992, 1998). For example, oil palms are exploited for their fruit and nuts at many locations, including Gombe, but even though they are present in the Mahale Mountains, they aren't eaten by the chimpanzees there. Such regional patterns in tool use and food preferences that are not related to environmental variation are reminiscent of the cultural variations characteristic of humans.

McGrew (1992) presents eight criteria for cultural behaviors in nonhuman species (Table 8–1). Of these, the first six were established by the pioneering cultural anthropologist Alfred Kroeber (1928); the last two were added by McGrew and Tutin (1978). McGrew (1992) demonstrates that Japanese macaques meet the first six criteria. However, all the macaque examples have developed within the context of human interference (which is not to say they all resulted directly from human intervention). To avoid this difficulty, the last two criteria were added.

Chimpanzees unambiguously meet the first six criteria, although not all groups meet the last two because most study groups have been at least minimally provisioned. However, all criteria are met by at least some chimpanzees in some instances (McGrew, 1992). While it is obvious that chimpanzees don't possess human culture, we can't overlook the implications that tool use and local traditions of learned behavior have for early hominid evolution.

Courtesy, Tetsuro Matsuzawa

FIGURE 8–8 Chimpanzees in Bossou, Guinea, West Africa, use a pair of stones as hammer and anvil to crack oil-palm nuts.

TABLE 8–1 Criteria for Cultural Acts in Others Species

Innovation	New pattern is invented or modified.
Dissemination	Pattern is acquired (through imitation) by another from an innovator.
Standardization	Form of pattern is consistent and stylized.
Durability	Pattern is performed without presence of demonstrator.
Diffusion	Pattern spreads from one group to another.
Tradition	Pattern persists from innovator's generation to the next.
Nonsubsistence	Pattern transcends subsistence.
Naturalness	Pattern is shown in absence of direct human influence.

Source: Adapted from Kroeber, 1928, and McGrew and Tutin, 1978. In McGrew, 1992.

Using sticks, twigs, and stones enhances the ability of chimpanzees to exploit resources. Learning these behaviors occurs during infancy and childhood, partly as a result of prolonged contact with the mother. It's also important that exposure to others in social groupings provides additional learning opportunities. These statements also apply to early hominids. While sticks and unmodified stones don't remain to tell tales, our early ancestors surely used these same objects as tools in much the same manner as chimpanzees still do today.

While chimpanzees in the wild have not been observed modifying the stones they use, the male bonobo Kanzi (see p. 209) learned to strike two stones together to produce sharp-edged flakes. In a study conducted by Sue Savage-Rumbaugh and archaeologist Nicholas Toth, Kanzi was allowed to watch as Toth produced stone flakes, which were then used to open a transparent plastic food container (Savage-Rumbaugh and Lewin, 1994). Although bonobos apparently don't commonly use objects as tools in the wild, Kanzi readily appreciated the usefulness of the flakes in obtaining food. Moreover, he was able to master the basic technique of producing flakes without having been taught the various components of the process, although initially his progress was slow. Eventually, Kanzi realized that if he threw the stone onto a hard floor, it would shatter and he would have an abundance of cutting tools. Although his solution wasn't necessarily the one that Savage-Rumbaugh and Toth expected, it perhaps more importantly provided an excellent example of bonobo insight and problem-solving ability. Moreover, Kanzi did eventually learn to produce flakes by striking two stones together, and these flakes were then used to obtain food. Not only is this behavior an example of tool manufacture and tool use, albeit in a captive situation; it's also a very sophisticated goal-directed activity.

Human culture has become the environment in which modern *Homo sapiens* lives. Quite clearly, the use of sticks in termite fishing and hammerstones to crack nuts is hardly comparable to modern human technology. However, modern human technology had its beginnings in these very types of behaviors. But, this doesn't mean that nonhuman primates are "on their way" to becoming human. Remember, evolution is not goal directed, and if it were, there is nothing to dictate that modern humans necessarily constitute an evolutionary goal. Such a conclusion is a purely **anthropocentric** view, and it has no validity in discussions of evolutionary processes.

Moreover, nonhuman primates have probably practiced certain cultural behaviors for millions of years. As we have stated, the common ancestor that humans share with chimpanzees undoubtedly used sticks and stones to exploit resources perhaps even as weapons. The fact that we have only recently discovered and described these behaviors doesn't mean that our close relatives recently developed them. Thus, we must continue to study these capabilities in nonhuman primates in their social and ecological context so that we may eventually understand more clearly how cultural traditions emerged in our own lineage.

Aggressive Interactions Between Groups

Interactions between groups of conspecifics can be just as revealing as those that take place within groups. For many primate species, especially those whose ranges are small, contact with one or more other groups of the same species is a daily occurrence, and as you read in Chapter 7, the nature of these encounters can vary from species to species.

Between groups, aggression is used to protect resources through defense of **territories.** Primate groups are associated with a *home range* where they remain permanently. (Although individuals may leave their home range and join another community, the group itself remains in a particular area.) Within the home range is a portion called the **core area.** This area contains the highest concentration of

anthropocentric Viewing nonhuman organisms in terms of human experience and capabilities; emphasizing the importance of humans over everything else.

territories Portions of an individual's or group's home range actively defended against intrusion, particularly by conspecifics.

core area The portion of a home range containing the highest concentration and most reliable supplies of food and water. The core area is frequently the area that will be defended.

predictable resources, and it's where the group most frequently may be found. Although portions of the home range may overlap with that of one or more other groups, core areas of adjacent groups don't overlap. The core area can also be said to be a group's territory, and it's the portion of the home range defended against intrusion. However, in some species, other areas of the home range may also be defended. Whatever area is defended is termed the *territory*.

Not all primates are territorial. In general, territoriality is associated with species whose ranges are sufficiently small to permit patrolling and protection (e.g., gibbons and vervets). And, you already know that in many species, group encounters are frequently nonaggressive.

But male chimpanzees are highly intolerant of unfamiliar chimpanzees, especially other males, and will fiercely defend their territories and resources. Therefore, chimpanzee intergroup interactions are almost always characterized by aggressive displays, chasing, and frequently, actual fighting.

Members of chimpanzee communities commonly travel to areas where their range borders or overlaps those of other communities. These peripheral areas are not entirely safe, and before entering them, chimpanzees usually hoot and display to determine if other animals are present. They then remain silent, listening for a response. If members of another community should appear, some form of aggression will occur until one group retreats.

Male chimpanzees (sometimes accompanied by one or two females) also patrol their borders. During patrols, party members travel silently in compact groupings. They stop frequently to sniff, look around, or climb tall trees, where they may sit for an hour or more surveying the region. During such times, individuals are tense, and a sudden sound, such as a snapping twig, causes them to touch or embrace in reassurance (Goodall, 1986). It's quite apparent from their tension and very uncharacteristic silence that the chimpanzees are very aware that they have ventured into a potentially dangerous situation.

If a border patrol happens to come upon one or two strangers, the patrollers most surely will attack. However, if they encounter a group larger than their own, they themselves may be attacked, or at least chased as they retreat.

Recent discussion among primatologists has focused on aggression between groups of conspecifics and whether the primary motivation is solely territoriality (i.e., protection of resources in a given area) or whether other factors are also involved (Cheney, 1987; Manson and Wrangham, 1991; Nishida, 1991). Much of this discussion has centered on intergroup aggression and lethal raiding in chimpanzees and has emphasized implications for the evolution of human aggressive behavior as well (Fig. 8–9).

FIGURE 8–9 Members of a chimpanzee "border patrol" at Gombe survey their territory from a tree.

Beginning in 1974, Jane Goodall and her colleagues witnessed at least five unprovoked and extremely brutal attacks by groups of chimpanzees (usually, but not always, males) upon lone individuals. To explain these attacks, it's necessary to point out that by 1973, the original Gombe community had divided into two distinct groups, one located in the north and the other in the south of what had once been the original group's home range. In effect, the southern splinter group had denied the others access to part of their former home range.

By 1977, all seven males and one female of the splinter group were either known or suspected to have been killed. All observed incidents involved several animals, usually adult males, who brutally attacked lone individuals. Although it isn't possible to know exactly what motivated the attackers, it was clear that they intended to incapacitate their victims (Goodall, 1986). In fact, Goodall (1986) has suggested that the attacks strongly imply that although chimpanzees don't possess language and do not wage war as we know it (i.e., armed conflict between nations), they do exhibit behaviors that, if present in early hominids, could have been precursors to war.

A situation similar to the one at Gombe was also reported for a group of chimpanzees in the Mahale Mountains south of Gombe. Over a 17-year period, all the males of a small community disappeared. Although no attacks were actually observed, there was circumstantial evidence that most of these males met the same fate as the Gombe attack victims (Nishida et al., 1985, 1990).

Lethal, unprovoked aggression between groups of conspecifics is *known* to occur in only two mammalian species: humans and chimpanzees. Prior to its discovery in chimpanzees, such lethal aggression was thought to be an exclusively human endeavor, motivated by territoriality. In the past few years, a number of researchers have posed various questions within the theoretical framework that specific aggressive patterns may be explained by similar factors operating in both species. According to Manson and Wrangham (1991, p. 370), "These similarities between chimpanzees and humans suggest a common evolutionary background. Thus, they indicate that lethal male raiding could have had precultural origins and might be elicited by the same set of conditions among humans as among chimpanzees."

In chimpanzees and most traditional human cultures, males are *philopatric* and form lifelong bonds within their social group. Indeed, the core of a chimpanzee community is a group of closely bonded males who, because of their long-term association, act cooperatively in various endeavors, including hunting and attack. In most other primate species, females are the philopatric sex, and in some species (notably macaques and baboons), females may cooperate in aggressive encounters against females from other groups. (Usually these conflicts develop as contests for resources, and they don't result in fatalities.) Generally, then, conflicts between groups of conspecifics involve members of the philopatric sex. In fact, Manson and Wrangham (1991) suggest that in chimpanzees, lethal aggression is a male activity because males are the philopatric sex.

Efforts to identify the social and ecological factors that predispose human and chimpanzee males to engage in lethal attacks have led to hypotheses that attempt to explain the function and adaptive value of these activities. In this context, the benefits and costs of extreme aggression must be identified. The principal benefit to aggressors is acquisition of mating partners, food, and water. Costs include risk of injury or death and loss of energy expended in performing aggressive acts.

Although the precise motivation of chimpanzee intergroup aggression may never be fully explained, it appears that resource acquisition and protection are involved (Nishida et al., 1985, 1990; Goodall, 1986; Manson and Wrangham, 1991; Nishida, 1991). Through careful examination of shared aspects of human and chimpanzee social life, we can develop hypotheses regarding how intergroup conflict may have arisen in our own lineage.

Cultural anthropologist Napoleon Chagnon (1979, 1988) has argued that among the Yanomamo Indians of Brazil, competition for mates between males is the motivation behind warfare between groups. Among the Yanomamo, over 30 percent of male deaths are attributed to violence, and Chagnon believes that the majority of hostilities either *within* or *between* villages (with raids leading to deaths, then revenge raids leading to more fatalities) are caused initially by competition for females. These phenomena are explained as functions of some of the same evolutionary principles that operate in chimpanzees, in full recognition of the obvious differences between the two species regarding weaponry, language, and mating systems (Manson and Wrangham, 1991). Chagnon (1988, p. 986) states that "men who demonstrate their willingness to act violently and exact revenge for the deaths of kin may have higher marital and reproductive success."

Early hominids and chimpanzees may well have inherited from a common ancestor the predispositions that have resulted in shared patterns of strife between populations. It isn't possible to draw direct comparisons between chimpanzee conflict and modern human warfare owing to later human elaborations of culture, use of symbols (e.g., national flags), and language. But it is important and intriguing to speculate on the fundamental issues that may have led to the development of similar patterns in both species.

Affiliation, Altruism, and Cooperation

In Chapter 7, we briefly discussed affiliative behaviors and the role they play in maintaining group cohesion by reinforcing bonds between individuals. There are also behaviors that indicate just how important such bonds are, and some of them can perhaps be said to be examples of caregiving, or compassion.

The use of the term *compassion* is a bit risky, because in humans, compassion is motivated by empathy for another. Whether nonhuman primates can empathize with the suffering or misfortune of another is not known, but laboratory research has indicated that some do. Certainly there are numerous examples, mostly from chimpanzee studies, of caregiving actions that resemble compassionate behavior in humans. Examples include protection of others during attacks, helping younger siblings, and staying near ill or dying relatives or friends.

In a poignant example from Gombe, the young adult female Little Bee brought food to her mother on at least two occasions while the latter lay dying of wounds inflicted by attacking males (Goodall, 1986). When chimpanzees have been observed sitting near a dying relative, they were seen occasionally to shoo flies away or groom the other, as if attempting to assist in some way.

FIGURE 8–10 Adolescent savanna baboons holding hands.

ALTRUISM

Altruism, behavior that benefits another while involving some risk or sacrifice to the performer, is common in many primate species, and altruistic acts sometimes contain elements of compassion and cooperation. The most fundamental of altruistic behaviors, the protection of dependent offspring, is ubiquitous among mammals and birds, and in the majority of species, altruistic acts are confined to this context. However, among primates, recipients of altruistic acts may include individuals who are not offspring and who may not even be closely related to the performer. Chimpanzees routinely come to the aid of relatives and friends; female langurs join forces to protect infants from infanticidal males; and male baboons protect infants and cooperate to chase predators. In fact, the primate literature abounds with examples of altruistic acts, whereby individuals place themselves at some risk to protect others from attacks by conspecifics or predators.

altruism Behavior that benefits another individual but at some potential risk or cost to oneself.

Virtual Lab 1, section 1, provides a comparison of Darwinian and inclusive fitness.

Adoption of orphans is a form of altruism that has been reported for macaques and baboons, and it's common in chimpanzees. When chimpanzee youngsters are orphaned, they are routinely adopted, usually by older siblings who are solicitous and highly protective. Adoption is crucial to the survival of orphans, who would certainly not survive on their own. In fact, it is extremely rare for a chimpanzee orphan less than three years of age to survive even if it is adopted.

One striking and poignant report concerns the attempted rescue of a young adult male baboon who, at some distance from his group, was being chased by a hyena. Suddenly, observers saw an adult female racing toward the hyena in what turned out to be a vain attempt to rescue the male (Stelzner and Strier, 1981; Strier, 2003). The female was not the victim's mother, and a female baboon is no match for a hyena. So we ask, "Why would she place herself in serious danger to help an animal to whom, as far as we know, she was not closely related?"

Evolutionary explanations of altruism are based on the premise that risky or self-sacrificing behaviors are more likely to be performed for the benefit of a relative, who shares genes with the performer. According to this hypothesis, known as *kin selection,* an individual's reproductive success may be enhanced by saving the life of a relative, with whom genes are shared. Even if the performer's life is lost as a result of the act, the relative may survive to reproduce and pass on genes that both individuals share.

There is also the idea of *reciprocal altruism,* when the recipient of an altruistic act (i.e., the one who benefits) may later return the favor (the debt to be paid in the future). The formation of coalitions or alliances between two or more individuals is an often-cited example of reciprocal altruism and is common in baboons and chimpanzees. As we mentioned in Chapter 7, members of alliances support and defend one another in conflicts with others and/or to increase their status within the group hierarchy. In chimpanzees, members of coalitions are sometimes related, but this isn't always the case. But, while reciprocal altruism may exist, we still haven't explained it, and so it remains as a hypothesis still to be tested.

Group selection is another hypothesis that has had some support among primatologists over the years. According to this model, an individual may act altruistically to benefit other group members because ultimately it's to the performer's benefit that the group be maintained. (In humans, one could see group selection in action when people sacrifice their lives for their country or some cause.) If the altruist dies, genes he or she shares with other group members may still be passed on (as in kin selection).

But the problem with the group selection theory is that, according to natural selection theory, individual reproductive success is enhanced by acting selfishly, and it's the individual that is the object of natural selection. Consequently, supporters of the group selection explanations argue that natural selection acts, not only at the level of the individual, but also at that of the species. This issue has not been resolved, nor is it likely to be any time soon. But we do know that for a number of reasons discussed in Chapter 7, primates, including humans, have a better chance of surviving and reproducing if they live in groups. And we also know that, even though it frequently isn't obvious, people succeed better when they use their highly developed communication skills to solve problems through cooperation instead of aggression.

The Primate Continuum

It is an unfortunate fact that humans generally view themselves as separate from the rest of the animal kingdom. This perspective is, in no small measure, due to a prevailing lack of knowledge of the behavior and abilities of other species. Moreover, these notions are continuously reinforced through exposure to advertising, movies, and television.

FIGURE 8–11 This unfortunate advertising display is a good example of how humans misunderstand and thus misrepresent our closest relatives.

For decades, behavioral psychology taught that animal behavior represents nothing more than a series of conditioned responses to specific stimuli. (This perspective is very convenient for those who wish to exploit nonhuman animals, for whatever purposes, and remain free of guilt.) Fortunately, this attitude has begun to change in recent years to reflect a growing awareness that humans, although in many ways unquestionably unique, are nevertheless part of a **biological continuum.** Indeed, we are also a part of a behavioral continuum.

Where do humans fit, then, in this biological continuum? Are we at the top? The answer depends on the criteria used. Certainly, we are the most intelligent species if we define intelligence in terms of problem-solving abilities and abstract thought. However, if we look more closely, we recognize that the differences between ourselves and our primate relatives, especially chimpanzees and bonobos, are primarily quantitative and not qualitative.

Although the human brain is absolutely and relatively larger, neurological processes are functionally the same. The necessity of close bonding with at least one parent and the need for physical contact are essentially the same. Developmental stages and dependence on learning are strikingly similar. Indeed, even in the capacity for cruelty and aggression combined with compassion, tenderness, and altruism exhibited by chimpanzees, we see a close parallel to the dichotomy between "evil" and "good" so long recognized in ourselves. The main difference between how chimpanzees and humans express these qualities (and therefore the dichotomy) is one of degree. Humans are much more adept at cruelty and compassion, and we can reflect on our behavior in ways that chimpanzees can't. Like the cat that plays with a mouse, chimpanzees don't seem to understand the suffering they inflict on others, but humans do. Likewise, while an adult chimpanzee may sit next to and protect a dying relative or friend, it doesn't seem to feel intense grief and a sense of loss to the extent a human normally does.

To arrive at any understanding of what it is to be human, it is vastly important to recognize that many of our behaviors are but elaborate extensions of those of our hominid ancestors and close primate relatives. The fact that so many of us prefer to bask in the warmth of the "sun belt" with literally millions of others reflects our heritage as social animals adapted to life in the tropics. And the "sweet tooth" seen in so many humans is a direct result of our earlier primate ancestors' predilection for high-energy sugar contained in desirably sweet, ripe fruit. Thus, it's important to recognize our primate heritage as we explore how humans came to be and how we continue to adapt.

biological continuum Refers to the fact that organisms are related through common ancestry and that behaviors and traits seen in one species are also seen in others to varying degrees. (When expressions of a phenomenon continuously grade into one another so that there are no discrete categories, they are said to exist on a continuum. Color is such a phenomenon.)

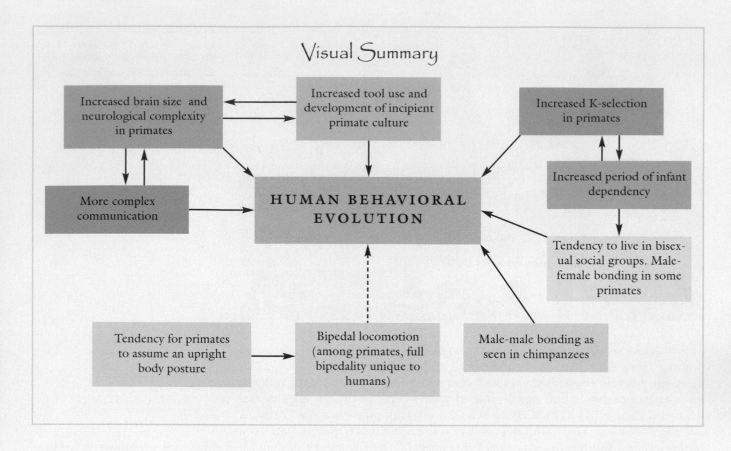

Visual Summary

Increased brain size and neurological complexity in primates

Increased tool use and development of incipient primate culture

Increased K-selection in primates

More complex communication

HUMAN BEHAVIORAL EVOLUTION

Increased period of infant dependency

Tendency to live in bisexual social groups. Male-female bonding in some primates

Tendency for primates to assume an upright body posture

Bipedal locomotion (among primates, full bipedality unique to humans)

Male-male bonding as seen in chimpanzees

Summary

In this chapter, we have discussed how biological anthropologists (including primatologists) apply what they have learned about nonhuman primate evolution, life history traits, and behavior to the study of early hominid behavior and adaptations. Although we humans share a common ancestry with all nonhuman primates and over 98 percent of our DNA sequences with chimpanzees, we are unique with regard to complex behavior and language use. This uniqueness is related to expansion of the neocortex of the brain since the divergence of the hominid lineage from that of the African great apes.

Because of the importance of neocortical expansion in human evolution, we emphasized some of the evolutionary changes that have occurred in the brain, particularly as they relate to language. Because the brain is such a metabolically expensive organ to maintain, selective pressures favoring increased behavioral complexity would have been enormous, and an important source of this pressure may have been living in social groups.

We also described some of the evidence for cultural behavior in nonhuman primates, particularly with regard to tool use in various populations. For example, while West African chimpanzees use stones to crack palm nuts, East African populations don't. Variation in cultural behavior

and the transmission of these behaviors from one individual to another through observation and learning are hallmarks of human culture. But while nonhuman primates exhibit certain aspects of culture, so do several nonprimate species, although none of these species have adopted culture as an adaptive strategy the way humans have.

Questions for Review

1. How do primatologists extrapolate general principles that have guided human evolution from examples of nonhuman primate behavior?

2. Why is it important not to focus only on great ape behavior when studying aspects of early hominid behavior?

3. What are the factors that have contributed to the development of language in humans? Using what you learned in Chapter 7, how would you compare human and nonhuman primate forms of communication?

4. Why is the evolution of the brain important to the development of language?

5. How does philopatry influence many aspects of human behavior? Give two nonhuman primate examples.

For Further Thought

1. Do you think that knowing about nonhuman primate cultural behavior can help explain the evolution of culture in human ancestors? Why or why not?

2. What are some examples of cultural behavior in nonprimate species that weren't mentioned in this chapter? Have you personally witnessed such behaviors?

Go to the book website at **http://www.anthropology.wadsworth.com** for resources to help you explore these questions further. Click on "For Further Thought" for this chapter.

Suggested Further Reading

Evolutionary Anthropology, 2003, Vol. 12, Issue 2. Entire issue devoted to cultural behavior in nonhuman primates.

Cartmill, Matt. 1990. "Human Uniqueness and Theoretical Content in Paleoanthropology: *International Journal of Primatology* 11(3): 173–192.

Cheney, Dorothy L., and Robert M. Seyfarth. 1990. *How Monkeys See the World.* Chicago: University of Chicago Press.

de Waal, Frans B. M. (ed.) 2001. *Tree of Origin. What Primate Behavior Can Tell Us about Human Social Evolution.* Cambridge, MA: Harvard University Press.

Fouts, Roger (with Stephen Tukel Mills). 1997. *Next of Kin. What Chimpanzees Have Taught Me About Who We Are.* New York: Morrow.

Goodall, Jane. 1986. *The Chimpanzees of Gombe.* Cambridge, MA. The Belknap Press of Harvard University Press.

King, Barbara J. 1994. *The Information Continuum: Social Information Transfer in Monkeys, Apes, and Hominids.* Santa Fe: SAR Press.

McGrew, W. C. 1992. *Chimpanzee Material Culture.* Cambridge, England: Cambridge University Press.

Savage-Rumbaugh, S., and Roger Lewin. 1994. *Kanzi: The Ape at the Brink of the Human Mind.* New York: Wiley.

Stanford, Craig. 2001. *Significant Others. The Ape-Human Continuum and the Quest for Human Nature.* New York: Basic Books.

Wrangham, R. W. and D. Peterson. 1996. *Demonic Males: Apes and the Evolution of Human Aggression.* Boston: Houghton Mifflin.

Online Anthropology Resource Center

Go to the Anthropology Resource Center at **http://www.anthropology.wadsworth.com** for a wealth of online resources, including a companion website for your text that provides study aids such as self-quizzes for each chapter and a practice final exam, as well as links to anthropology websites and information on the latest theories and discoveries in the field. Also, check out InfoTrac College Edition®, your online library that offers full-length articles from thousands of scholarly and popular publications. Just click on the InfoTrac button at the companion website and use the passcode that came with your book.

Molecular Applications in Primatology

Primatologists have recently used molecular biological techniques to compare the DNA sequences of a wide range of contemporary primates. From these data, new insights have been gained concerning sensory perception, physiology, social relationships, and evolutionary relationships.

One crucial source of information concerns the precise identification of kin relationships within primate societies. Recognizing maternity is almost always obvious (to primatologists studying primate social groups and probably to all members of these groups as well). Tracing paternity, however, has always been problematic. And without knowing who fathered individuals within the group, testing behavioral ecological hypotheses (e.g., those relating to kin selection, infanticide, and the selective advantage of dominance, etc.) has been severely hampered.

Recently, great strides have been made to overcome these difficulties. Biologist Phillip Morin and anthropologist Jim Moore (of the University of California, San Diego) did the first molecularly based study on the Gombe chimpanzees (Morin et al., 1994). An important aspect of this research was that DNA samples could be obtained *without* interfering with the animals themselves (Fig. 1). Previously, it was necessary to capture the animals (usually by darting with a sedative), retrieve a blood sample, and then release them. Clearly, such procedures are dangerous for the animals, and they can seriously disrupt the social group.

However, the development of PCR techniques (see p. 67) has made it possible to use much smaller samples; in this study, for example, Moore retrieved shed hairs from abandoned chimpanzee nests (if the follicle is present, enough DNA can usually be retrieved). Back in the laboratory, following PCR, individual identification and recognition of close kin was accomplished by DNA fingerprinting (see p. 68).

Expanding on this initial research, primatologists have used molecular analysis to identify kin relationships and mating patterns in the West African Tai Forest chimpanzees (Gagneux et al., 1999). Surprisingly, the results showed that about half of the offspring appeared to have been sired by nongroup males (i.e., the mothers must have been mating frequently with males from outside the group). More recently, a more complete follow-up study was done by researchers from the Max Planck Institute for Evolutionary Anthropology (MPIEA). Founded in Leipzig, Germany, in 1997, this institution has quickly become the leading center for a variety of groundbreaking applications within anthropology. Consisting of molecular biologists, primatologists, and molecular anthropologists, MPIEA has contributed significantly to many aspects of molecular research discussed in this text (see website provided at the end of this feature).

The follow-up study, led by primatologist Linda Vigilant, found that most of the chimpanzee offspring within the Tai Forest community were, in fact, fathered by resident males (Vigilant et al., 2001). Moreover, it appeared that the females might be bonded more closely and over longer time spans than previously recognized. Such a conclusion could force revision of the traditional view that the most central cohesive influence on chimpanzee group structure derives from male-male bonds.

FIGURE 1 Physical anthropologist Jim Moore collecting hair samples from a chimpanzee sleeping nest at Gombe.

Lastly, and supporting the more recent results from West Africa, a further study of the Gombe chimpanzees, using DNA from both shed hair and fecal samples, found that *all* offspring were fathered by resident males (Constable et al., 2001). Moreover, detailed examination of social relationships within the Gombe community showed that a variety of male strategies could lead to reproductive success (including dominance, but also possessiveness, opportunistic mating, and consortships). The degree of inbreeding can also be assessed. At Gombe, 13 of 14 offspring were not closely inbred; but in one case, a male had successfully mated with his mother.

Similar molecular research on paternity and its social correlates has recently been conducted on savanna baboons (Buchan et al., 2003). Among groups of baboons in Kenya, males displayed paternal care by supporting their juvenile offspring in disputes with other baboons more than they supported unrelated juveniles. Given that baboon society is polygynous and estrous females usually mate with more than one male, how could fathers distinguish their offspring from unrelated individuals? Clues to how nonhuman primates might recognize kin could come from new, molecularly based research.

Led by Leslie Knapp, the Primate Immunogenetics and Molecular Ecology Research Group at Cambridge University is investigating aspects of human and nonhuman primate genetic mechanisms—and how these, in turn, might influence immunity, disease, and potentially social behavior as well (The focus of their investigations is a genetic system called the major histocompatibility complex, or more simply, the MHC). Currently, these studies are examining MHC variation in chimpanzees, gorillas, mandrills, several New World monkeys, lemurs, and humans. Techniques of analysis include PCR and nucleotide sequencing (Fig. 2.). Results are used to test hypotheses regarding the effects of natural selection on particular allele combinations, the antiquity of these genes in different primate groups, and possible influences on how individuals signal each other information regarding their genotype (which, in turn, could facilitate kin recognition, mate choice, and inbreeding avoidance) (Knapp, personal communication; also see website listing below for the Primate Immunogenetics and Molecular Ecology Research Group).

Members of the Cambridge research team work both in the laboratory and in the field (where they assist in collecting appropriate samples and collaborate in long-term behavioral studies). Such intensive investigations are necessary in this work—and also for all the investigations discussed above. Clearly, it is not very helpful to know, for example, that two chimpanzees are brothers if we don't have detailed long-term data on how they *behave* (relative to each other as compared to other members of the group).

Exactly how nonhuman primates detect information concerning kin is not yet fully understood. However, olfac-

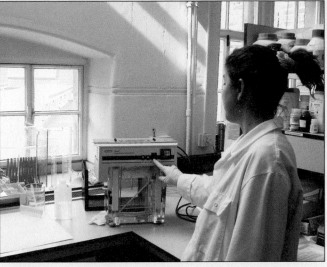

FIGURE 2 Variation in DNA sequences can be studied using a variety of molecular genetic techniques. A graduate student at the University of Cambridge uses gradient gel electrophoresis (DGGE) to study variability in the chromosomal region involved in immune response (the area of DNA which helps provide protection against infection).

tory (smell) cues may be crucial in many circumstances, and this hypothesis is currently being tested by many researchers who are discovering some fascinating genetic patterns that influence olfactory perception in contemporary primates—including humans.

Several genes and their protein products that directly control olfactory reception in mammals have recently been recognized. One of these directly influences a particular form of scent perception. This gene is present and fully active in most mammals and in some primates (prosimians and New World monkeys), but is completely dysfunctional in all Old World anthropoids (i.e., in Old World monkeys, apes, and humans). These observations were discovered separately by two pairs of investigators, one at the University of Southern California (Liman and Innan, 2003) and the other at the University of Michigan (Zhang and Webb, 2003). Moreover, both research teams have reached the same conclusions regarding *when* in evolution such olfactory capabilities were lost and *why* it occurred. The evolutionary timing of the genetic mutations that made this type of olfaction no longer possible is placed just before the divergence of Old World monkeys and hominoids (about 25–20 m.y.a.). Furthermore, the reason hypothesized for such altered selection in primate evolution is the parallel development of full color vision (which has also recently been investigated in different primates using molecular techniques). The researchers suggest that the advantages provided by full color vision relaxed the selection pressure that favored pheromone detection—eventually leading to deactivation of genes controlling it.

225

Molecular Applications in Primatology

(continued)

If the ability shown by many primates to recognize kin is partly influenced by olfactory detection, it is not tied primarily to pheromone perception (at least not among Old World anthropoids). Perhaps, in many Old World monkeys and apes, other olfactory mechanisms are at work. Indeed, hundreds of other genes have been shown to directly influence olfactory reception (in fact, these constitute the largest gene family currently known within mammalian genomes). However, there is one major exception—*Homo sapiens*.

In pioneering research, Yoav Gilad (also at MPIEA) has shown that humans have far fewer functional olfactory receptor genes than any other primate (including our closest African ape cousins) (Gilad et al., 2003a, 2003b). When in hominid evolution this extreme reduction in olfactory ability occurred is not known. However, at least for modern *H. sapiens*, a reduced sense of smell could be added to the list of characteristics distinguishing us from other primates.

Sources

Buchan, Jason C., Susan Alberts, Joan B. Silk, and Jeanne Altman. 2003. "True Paternal Care in Multi-Male Primate Society. *Nature* 425:179–181.

Constable, Julie L., Mary V. Ashley, Jane Goodall, and Anne E. Pusey. 2001. "Noninvasive Paternity Assignment in Gombe Chimpanzees." *Molecular Ecology* 10:1279–1300.

Gagneux, Pascal, Christophe Boesch, and David Woodruff. 1999. "Female Reproductive Strategies, Paternity, and Community Structure in Wild West African Chimpanzees." *Animal Behaviour* 57:19–32.

Gilad, Yoav, Orna Man, Svante Paabo, and Doran Lancet. 2003a. "Human Specific Loss of Receptor Genes." *Proceedings of the National Academy of Sciences* 100:3324–3327.

Gilad, Yoav, Carlos D. Bustamante, Doran Lancet, and Svante Paabo. 2003b. "Natural Selection on the Olfactory Receptor Gene Family in Humans and Chimpanzees." *American Journal of Human Genetics*, 73:489–501.

Grob, B., L. A. Knapp, R. D. Martin, and G. Anzenberger. 1998. "The Major Histocompatibility Complex and Mate Choice: Inbreeding Avoidance and Selection of Good Genes." *Exp. Clin. Immunogenet.* 15(3):119–129.

Liman, Emily R., and Hideki Innan. 2003. "Relaxed Selective Pressure on an Essential Component of Pheromone Transduction in Primate Evolution." *Proceedings of the National Academy of Sciences* 100:3328–3332.

Max Planck Institute for Evolutionary Anthropology website: www.eva.mpg.de

Morin, P. A., J. Wallis, J. Moore, and D. S. Woodruff. 1994. "Paternity Exclusion in a Community of Wild Chimpanzees Using Hypervariable Simple Sequence Repeats." *Molecular Evolution* 3:469–477.

Primate Immunogenetics and Molecular Ecology Research Group website: www-prime.bioanth.cam.ac.uk.

Vigilant, Linda, Michael Hofreiter, Heike Siedel, and Christophe Boesch. 2001. "Paternity and Relatedness in Wild Chimpanzee Communities." *Proceedings of the National Academy of Sciences* 98:12890–12895.

Zhang, Jianzhi, and David Webb. 2003. "Evolutionary Deterioration of the Vomeronasal Pheromone Transduction Pathway in Catarrrhine Primates." *Proceedings of the National Academy of Sciences* 100:8337–8341.

Paleoanthropology:
Reconstructing Early Hominid Behavior and Ecology

9

Taung child's cranium held by South African paleo-anthropologist Phillip Tobias

Robert Jurmain

What are the central aspects of paleoanthropology?

Why, from a biocultural perspective, do we want to learn about *both* the behavior and the anatomy of ancient hominids?

Introduction

See the following sections of the CD-ROM for topics covered in this chapter: Virtual Lab 7, sections I and II; Virtual Lab 8, section 1; and Virtual Lab 2.

A portion of a pig's tusk, a small sample of volcanic sediment, a battered cobble, a primate's molar tooth: What do these seemingly unremarkable remains have in common, and more to the point, why are they of interest to paleoanthropologists? First of all, if they are all discovered at certain sites in Africa, they *may* be quite ancient—indeed, perhaps millions of years old. Further, some of these materials actually inform scientists directly of quite precise dating of the finds—in this case, 2.2 million years old. Lastly, and most exciting, some of these finds may have been modified, used, and discarded by bipedal creatures who looked and behaved in some ways like ourselves (but were, in other respects, very different). And what of that molar tooth? Is it a fossilized remnant of an ancient hominid? These are the kinds of questions asked by paleoanthropologists, and to answer them, these researchers travel to remote locales on the African continent.

How do we identify possible hominids from other types of animals, especially when all we have are fragmentary fossil remains from just a small portion of a skeleton? How do humans and our most distant ancestors compare with other animals? In the last four chapters, we have seen how humans are classified as primates, both structurally and behaviorally, and how our evolutionary history coincides with that of other mammals and, specifically, other primates. However, we are a unique kind of primate, and our ancestors have been adapted to a particular lifestyle for several million years. Some primitive hominoid probably began this process close to 7 m.y.a., but with better-preserved fossil discoveries, there is now more definitive evidence of hominids shortly after 5 m.y.a.

The hominid nature of these remains is revealed by more than the structure of teeth and bones; we know that these animals are hominids also because of the way they behaved—emphasizing once again the *biocultural* nature of human evolution. In this chapter, we will discuss the methods scientists use to explore the secrets of early hominid behavior and ecology, and we will demonstrate these methods through the example of the best-known early hominid site in the world: Olduvai Gorge, in East Africa.

Definition of Hominid

Dating to the end of the Miocene, the earliest evidence of hominids that has been found mainly include dental and cranial pieces. But dental features alone don't describe the special features of hominids and certainly aren't the most distinctive of the later stages of human evolution. Modern humans, as well as our most immediate hominid ancestors, are distinguished from the great apes by more obvious features than tooth and jaw dimensions. For example, various scientists have pointed to such distinctive hominid characteristics as bipedal loco-

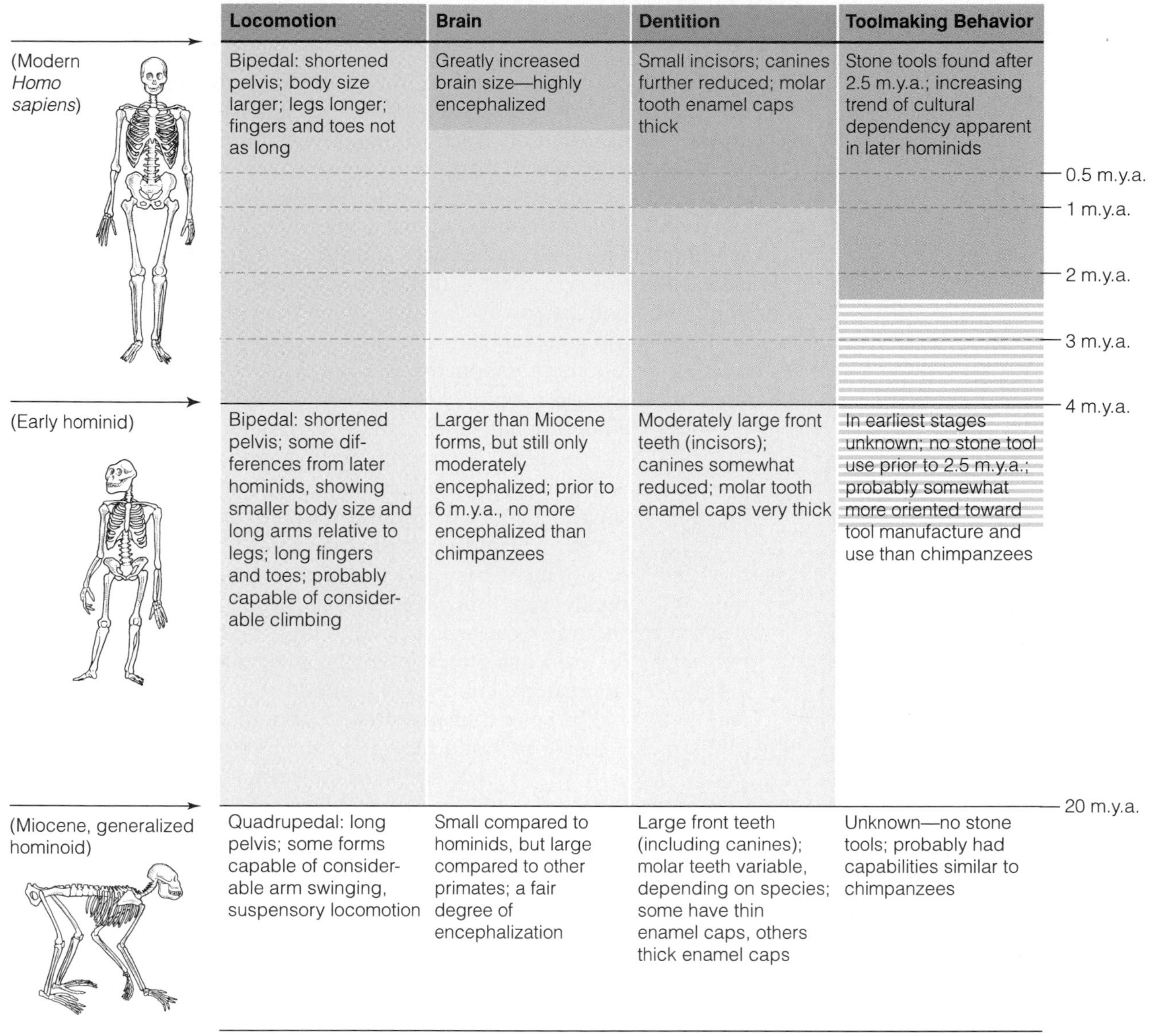

	Locomotion	Brain	Dentition	Toolmaking Behavior
(Modern *Homo sapiens*)	Bipedal: shortened pelvis; body size larger; legs longer; fingers and toes not as long	Greatly increased brain size—highly encephalized	Small incisors; canines further reduced; molar tooth enamel caps thick	Stone tools found after 2.5 m.y.a.; increasing trend of cultural dependency apparent in later hominids
(Early hominid)	Bipedal: shortened pelvis; some differences from later hominids, showing smaller body size and long arms relative to legs; long fingers and toes; probably capable of considerable climbing	Larger than Miocene forms, but still only moderately encephalized; prior to 6 m.y.a., no more encephalized than chimpanzees	Moderately large front teeth (incisors); canines somewhat reduced; molar tooth enamel caps very thick	In earliest stages unknown; no stone tool use prior to 2.5 m.y.a.; probably somewhat more oriented toward tool manufacture and use than chimpanzees
(Miocene, generalized hominoid)	Quadrupedal: long pelvis; some forms capable of considerable arm swinging, suspensory locomotion	Small compared to hominids, but large compared to other primates; a fair degree of encephalization	Large front teeth (including canines); molar teeth variable, depending on species; some have thin enamel caps, others thick enamel caps	Unknown—no stone tools; probably had capabilities similar to chimpanzees

Timeline markers: 0.5 m.y.a. — 1 m.y.a. — 2 m.y.a. — 3 m.y.a. — 4 m.y.a. — 20 m.y.a.

FIGURE 9–1 Mosaic evolution of hominid characteristics: a postulated time line.

motion, large brain size, and toolmaking behavior as being significant (at some stage) in defining what makes a hominid a hominid.

All these characteristics didn't develop simultaneously. Quite the opposite, in fact, has been apparent in hominid evolution over the last 7 million years. This pattern, in which different physiological systems (and behavioral correlates) evolve at different rates, is called **mosaic evolution.** As we first pointed out in Chapter 1 and will discuss in more detail in Chapter 10, the most defining characteristic for all of hominid evolution is *bipedal locomotion.* Certainly for the earliest stages of the hominid lineage, skeletal evidence of bipedal locomotion is the only truly reliable indicator of hominid status. However, in later stages of hominid evolution, other features, especially those relating to neurology and behavior, do become highly significant (Fig. 9–1).

These behavioral aspects of hominid emergence—particularly toolmaking—is what we wish to emphasize in this chapter. The important structural attributes of the hominid brain, teeth, and especially locomotor apparatus will be discussed in the next chapter, where we investigate early hominid anatomical adaptations in greater detail.

mosaic evolution A pattern of evolution in which the rate of evolution in one functional system varies from that in other systems. For example, in hominid evolution, the dental system, locomotor system, and neurological system (especially the brain) all evolved at markedly different rates.

BIOCULTURAL EVOLUTION: THE HUMAN CAPACITY FOR CULTURE

See Virtual Lab 2 for a discussion of the archaeological record.

When compared with other animals, the most distinctive behavioral feature of humans is our extraordinary elaboration of and dependence on culture. Certainly, other primates, and many other animals for that matter, modify their environments. As we saw in Chapter 7, chimpanzees especially are known for such behaviors as using termite sticks and sponges and even transporting rocks to crush nuts. Given such observations, it becomes difficult to draw sharp lines between hominid toolmaking behavior and that exhibited by other animals.

Another point to remember is that human culture, at least as it is defined in contemporary contexts, involves much more than toolmaking capacity. For humans, culture integrates an entire adaptive strategy involving cognitive, political, social, and economic components. The *material culture,* that is the tools and other items humans use, is only a small portion of this cultural complex.

Nevertheless, when examining the archaeological record of earlier hominids, what is available for study is almost exclusively certain remains of material culture, especially residues of stone tool manufacture. Consequently, it is extremely difficult to learn anything about the earliest stages of hominid cultural development prior to the regular manufacture of stone tools. As you will see, this most crucial cultural development has been traced to approximately 2.5 m.y.a. Yet, hominids undoubtedly were using other kinds of tools (such as sticks) and displaying an array of other cultural behaviors long before this time. However, without any "hard" evidence preserved in the archaeological record, the development of these nonmaterial cultural components remains elusive.

The fundamental basis for human cultural elaboration relates directly to cognitive abilities. Again, we are not dealing with an absolute distinction, but a relative one. As you have learned, some other primates possess some of the symboling capabilities exhibited by humans. Nevertheless, modern humans display these abilities in a complexity several orders of magnitude beyond that of any other animal. Moreover, only humans are so completely dependent on symbolic communication and its cultural by-products that contemporary *Homo sapiens* could not survive without them.

When did the unique combination of cognitive, social, and material cultural adaptations become prominent in human evolution? To answer this question, we must be careful to recognize the nature of culture in a broad sense and not expect it always to contain the same elements across species (for instance, as compared with nonhuman primates) or through time (when trying to reconstruct ancient hominid behavior). Richard Potts (1993) has critiqued this overly simplistic perspective and suggests a more dynamic approach, one that incorporates many subcomponents (including aspects of behavior, cognition, and social interaction).

We know that the earliest hominids almost certainly did *not* regularly manufacture stone tools (at least, none that has been found!). The earliest members of the hominid lineage, probably dating back to approximately 7–5 m.y.a., could be referred to as **protohominids.** These protohominids may have carried objects such as naturally sharp stones or stone flakes, parts of carcasses, and pieces of wood. At minimum, we would expect them to have displayed these behaviors at least to the same degree as living chimpanzees.

Moreover, as you will see in the next chapter, by 6 m.y.a., and perhaps as early as 7 m.y.a., hominids had developed one crucial advantage: They were bipedal and therefore could more easily carry all kinds of objects from place to place. Ultimately, the efficient exploitation of resources widely distributed in time and space would most likely have led to using "central" spots where key components, especially stone objects, were cached (Potts, 1991) (see A Closer Look on pp. 242–243).

protohominids The earliest members of the hominid lineage, as yet only poorly represented in the fossil record; thus, their structure and behavior are reconstructed mostly hypothetically.

A CLOSER LOOK

What Is a Hominid?

At first glance, this is a simple question, and so far our discussion has provided a straightforward answer: A hominid is a bipedal primate—more specifically, a bipedal hominoid. But who are our closest relatives? This, too, at least superficially, is pretty easy: The great apes are our closest relatives.

But which apes? Now things get a bit stickier. Traditionally, classifications contrasted humans (and our immediate predecessors) in the hominid family (technically called the Hominidae) with the pongid family of great apes (including chimpanzees, bonobos, gorillas, and orangutans, all technically called the Pongidae). We discussed this classification in Chapter 6 (see p. 152) but also noted that there were some serious problems with it. In particular, the *African great apes* are considerably more closely related to humans than is the orangutan. More specifically yet, accumulating genetic evidence has shown that chimpanzees and bonobos are slightly more closely related to humans than gorillas are.

This order of relationships, most particularly the extremely close genetic/evolutionary relationship of the human line to other African large-bodied hominoids, is exceedingly important to recognize. Indeed, no other observation in this text more clearly illuminates the human place in a biological continuum. It would not be an overstatement, in fact, to describe hominids as "bipedal African apes." We could show the oder of relationships in a chart, using simple terminology:

[A]
Hominoids = Us* and all apes

[B]
Small-bodied hominoids
(the gibbon and siamang)

[C]
Large-bodied hominoids
(*Us* and great apes)

[D]
Orangutan

[E]
Gorillas

[F]
Us and chimpanzees/
bonobos

[G]
Chimpanzees/bonobos

[H]
Us

Scientists, of course, use standardized terminology, and this is especially rigorous for names used in formal classifications. The rules followed in naming make good sense. But unfortunately, nobody considered the burden on introductory students when these names were first suggested. Here is how the preceding classification appears using the technicial

names now preferred by a growing number of paleoanthropologists (for example, Wood and Richmond, 2000):[†]

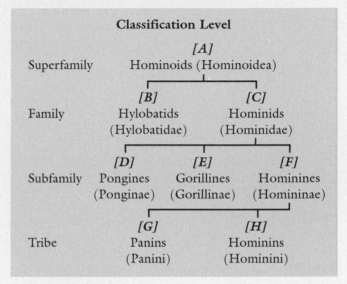

Classification Level		
	[A]	
Superfamily	Hominoids (Hominoidea)	
	[B]	**[C]**
Family	Hylobatids (Hylobatidae)	Hominids (Hominidae)
	[D]	**[E]**	**[F]**
Subfamily	Pongines (Ponginae)	Gorillines (Gorillinae)	Hominines (Homininae)
	[G]	**[H]**
Tribe	Panins (Panini)	Hominins (Hominini)

In this scheme, a hominid includes us (and our immediate predecessors) but *also* all the great apes (and their immediate predecessors, back to a common ancestor). What we call "hominid" in this book ("us") is now (following this system) technically referred to as hominin.

Two final points can be made. First, classification *must* accurately reflect evolutionary relationships. Thus, the traditionally recognized family of great apes (Pongidae) should be scrapped. That will, in turn, require a major reshuffling of the entire hominoid superfamily. However, evolutionary biologists have not yet agreed on the best way to do this.[‡] Consequently, in this book we continue to refer to "us" as hominids. If you see the term *hominin* in other publications, recognize that it is being used synonymously with our use of the term *hominid*.

---

* Us = bipedal hominoids, including *H. sapiens* and all our predecessors, back to the split with our closest relatives, the chimpanzee/bonobo lineage.

†Even this seemingly highly detailed classification fails to make an important distinction (between the Asian and the African large-bodied hominoids, a distinction emphasized in the next chapter; see p. 261). The classification shown is not inaccurate; it is simply incomplete and probably will necessitate further refining.

‡The recent annual meetings of the American Association of Physical Anthropologists (2003) gives evidence as to how little consensus there is regarding terminology. Eight different sessions dealt with fossil evidence of our immediate precursors—and were all entitled "Hominid Evolution." Included in these sessions were more than 100 presentations. A total of 26 of these used either "hominid" or "hominin" in their titles, and these were equally split (13 preferring each term). Many other presentations avoided the problem in their titles by referring to "human fossils" or to "human evolution."

What is certain is that over a period of several million years, during the early stages of hominid emergence, numerous components interacted, but not all developed simultaneously. As cognitive abilities developed, more efficient means of communication and learning resulted. Largely as a result of such neural reorganization, more elaborate tools and social relationships also emerged. These, in turn, selected for greater intelligence, which in turn selected for further neural elaboration. Quite clearly, then, these mutual dynamics are at the very heart of what we call hominid *biocultural* evolution.

The Strategy of Paleoanthropology

To understand human evolution adequately, we obviously need a broad base of information. The task of recovering and interpreting all the clues left by early hominids is the work of paleoanthropologists. Paleoanthropology is defined as the study of ancient humans. As such, it is a diverse *multidisciplinary* pursuit seeking to reconstruct every possible bit of information concerning the dating, structure, behavior, and ecology of our hominid ancestors. In the last few decades, the study of early humans has marshaled the specialized skills of many different kinds of scientists. Included in this growing and exciting adventure are geologists, archaeologists, physical anthropologists, and **paleoecologists** (Table 9–1).

Geologists, usually working with anthropologists, do the initial surveys to locate potential early hominid sites. Many sophisticated techniques can aid in this search, including aerial and satellite photography. Paleontologists are usually involved in this early survey work, for they can help find geological beds containing fossilized remains. Where conditions are favorable for the preservation of bone from such species as pigs and elephants, conditions may also be favorable for the preservation of hominid material. In addition, paleontologists can (through comparison with known faunal sequences) give fairly quick estimates of the approximate age of fossil sites without having to wait for the more expensive and time-consuming analyses. In this way, fossil beds of appropriate geological ages (i.e., where hominid finds are most likely) can be identified.

Once potential early hominid localities have been found, much more extensive surveying begins. At this point, at least for some sites postdating 2.5 m.y.a., archaeologists take over in the search for hominid "traces." We do not necessarily have to find remains of early hominids themselves to know that they consistently occupied a particular area. Preserved material clues, or **artifacts,** also inform us directly and unambiguously about early hominid activities. Modifying rocks according to a consistent plan or simply carrying them around from one place to another (over fairly long distances) is characteristic of no other animal but a hominid. Therefore, when we see such behavioral evidence at a site, we know absolutely that hominids were present.

paleoecologists (*paleo,* meaning "old," and *ecology,* meaning "environmental setting") Scientists who study ancient environments.

artifacts Material traces of hominid behavior. Very old ones are usually made of stone or, occasionally, bone.

TABLE 9–1 Subdisciplines of Paleoanthropology

PHYSICAL SCIENCES	BIOLOGICAL SCIENCES	SOCIAL SCIENCES
Geology	Physical anthropology	Archaeology
Stratigraphy	Paleoecology	Ethnoarchaeology
Petrology	Paleontology (fossil	Cultural anthropology
(rocks, minerals)	animals)	Ethnography
Pedology (soils)	Palynology (fossil pollen)	Psychology
Geomorphology	Primatology	
Geophysics		
Chemistry		
Taphonomy		

Because organic materials such as sticks and bones do not usually preserve in the archaeological record, we have no solid evidence of the earliest stages of hominid cultural modifications. On the other hand, our ancestors at some point came to depend more and more on stone because stone provided not only an easily accessible and transportable material (to use as convenient projectiles to throw or to hold down objects, such as skins and windbreaks), but also the most durable and sharpest cutting edges available at that time. Luckily for us, stone is almost indestructible, and some early hominid sites are strewn with thousands of stone artifacts. The earliest artifact sites now documented are from the Gona and Bouri areas in northeastern Ethiopia, dating to 2.5 m.y.a. (Semaw et al., 1997; de Heinzelin et al., 1999).

If an area is clearly demonstrated to be a hominid site, much more concentrated research will then begin. We should point out that a more mundane but very significant aspect of paleoanthropology not shown in Table 9–1 is the financial one. Just the initial survey work in usually remote areas costs many thousands of dollars, and mounting a concentrated research project costs several hundred thousand dollars. Therefore, for such work to go on, massive financial support is required from government agencies and private donations. A significant amount of a paleoanthropologist's efforts and time is necessarily devoted to writing grant proposals or speaking on the lecture circuit to raise the required funds for this work.

Once the financial hurdle has been cleared, a coordinated research project can begin. Usually headed by an archaeologist or physical anthropologist, the field crew will continue to survey and map the target area in great detail. In addition, field crew members will begin to search carefully for bones and artifacts eroding out of the soil, take pollen and soil samples for ecological analysis, and carefully recover rock samples for use in various dating techniques. If, in this early stage of exploration, members of the field crew find a fossil hominid, they will feel very lucky indeed. The international press usually considers human fossils the most exciting kind of discovery, a situation that produces wide publicity, often ensuring future financial support. More likely, the crew will accumulate information on geological setting, ecological data (particularly faunal remains), and, with some luck, hominid artifacts.

After long and arduous research in the field, even more time-consuming and detailed analysis is required back in the laboratory. Archaeologists must clean, sort, label, and identify all artifacts, and paleontologists must do the same for all faunal remains. Knowing the kinds of animals represented, whether forest browsers, woodland species, or open-country forms, will greatly help in reconstructing the local *paleoecological* settings in which early hominids lived. In addition, analysis of pollen remains by a palynologist will further aid in a detailed environmental reconstruction. All these paleoecological analyses can assist in reconstructing the diet of early humans. Also, the **taphonomy** of the site must be worked out to understand its depositional history—that is, whether the site is part of a *primary* or *secondary* **context.**

In the concluding stages of interpretation, the paleoanthropologist will draw together the following essentials:

1. *Dating*
   geological
   paleontological
   geophysical
2. *Paleoecology*
   paleontology
   palynology
   geomorphology
   taphonomy
3. *Archaeological traces of behavior*
4. *Anatomical evidence from hominid remains*

taphonomy (*taphos,* meaning "dead") The study of how bones and other materials came to be buried in the earth and preserved as fossils. A taphonomist studies the processes of sedimentation, the action of streams, preservation properties of bone, and carnivore disturbance factors.

context The environmental setting where artifacts are found. A *primary* context is a setting in which archaeological material was originally deposited. A *secondary* context is one to which it has been moved (e.g., by the action of a stream).

From all this information, scientists will try to "flesh out" the kind of animal that may have been our direct ancestor, or at least a very close relative. In this final analysis, still further comparative scientific information may be needed. Primatologists may assist here by showing the detailed relationships between the anatomical structure and behavior of humans and that of contemporary nonhuman primates (see Chapters 6 through 8). Cultural anthropologists may contribute ethnographic information concerning the varied nature of human behavior, particularly ecological adaptations of those contemporary hunter-gatherer groups exploiting roughly similar environmental settings as those reconstructed for a hominid site.

The end result of years of research by dozens of scientists will (we hope) produce a more complete and accurate understanding of human evolution—how we came to be the way we are. Both biological and cultural aspects of our ancestors pertain to this investigation, each process developing in relation to the other.

Paleoanthropology in Action— Olduvai Gorge

Several paleoanthropological projects of the scope just discussed have recently been pursued in diverse places in the Old World (Fig. 9–2). The most important of these include David Pilbeam's work in the Miocene beds of the Potwar Plateau of western Pakistan (c. 13–7 m.y.a.); Don Johanson's projects at Hadar and other areas of Ethiopia (c. 3.7–1.6 m.y.a.), sponsored by the Institute of Human Origins; a recently intensified effort just south of Hadar in Ethiopia in an area called the Middle Awash (c. 6–4 m.y.a.), led by Berkeley paleoanthropologist Tim White; a now completed research project along the Omo River of southern Ethiopia (c. 4–1.5 m.y.a.), directed by F. Clark Howell; Richard and Meave Leakey's fantastically successful research near Lake Turkana in northern Kenya (c. 4.2–1.5 m.y.a.); Mary Leakey's famous investigations at Olduvai Gorge in northern Tanzania (c. 1.85 m.y.a. to present); and finally the recent exploration by Phillip Tobias and Ron Clarke of hominid localities in southern Africa (the most important being Sterkfontein and Swartkrans, discussed in Chapter 10).

Of all these localities, the one that has yielded the finest quality and greatest abundance of paleoanthropological information concerning the behavior of early hominids has been Olduvai Gorge. First "discovered" in the early twentieth century by a German butterfly collector, Olduvai was soon scientifically surveyed and its wealth of paleontological evidence recognized. In 1931, Louis Leakey made his first trip to Olduvai Gorge and almost immediately realized its significance for studying early humans. From 1935, when she first worked there, until she retired in 1984, Mary Leakey directed the archaeological excavations at Olduvai.

Located in the Serengeti Plain of northern Tanzania, Olduvai is a steep-sided valley resembling a miniature version of the Grand Canyon. A deep ravine cut into an almost mile-high grassland plateau of East Africa, Olduvai extends more than 25 miles in total length. Climatically, the semiarid pattern of present-day Olduvai is believed to be similar to what it has been for the last 2 million years. The surrounding countryside is a grassland savanna broken occasionally by scrub bushes and acacia trees.

Geographically, Olduvai is located on the eastern branch of the Great Rift Valley of Africa. The geological

FIGURE 9–2 Major paleoanthropological projects.

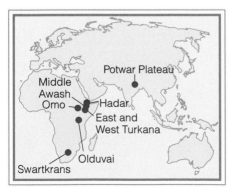

processes associated with the formation of the Rift Valley make Olduvai (and other East African sites) extremely important to paleoanthropological investigation. Three results of geological rifting are most significant:

See Virtual Lab 7, section I, for a discussion of geological processes.

1. Faulting, or earth movement, exposes geological beds near the surface that are normally hidden by hundreds of feet of accumulated overburden.
2. Active volcanic processes cause rapid sedimentation, which often yields excellent preservation of bone and artifacts that normally would be scattered by carnivore activity and erosion forces.
3. Volcanic activity provides a wealth of radiometrically datable material.

As a result, Olduvai is the site of superb preservation of ancient hominids, portions of their environment, and their behavioral patterns in datable contexts, all of which are readily accessible.

The greatest contribution Olduvai has made to paleoanthropological research is the establishment of an extremely well-documented and correlated *sequence* of geological, paleontological, archaeological, and hominid remains over the last 2 million years. At the very foundation of all paleoanthropological research is a well-established geological context. At Olduvai, the geological and paleogeographical situation is known in minute detail. Olduvai is today a geologist's delight, containing sediments in some places 350 feet thick, accumulated from lava flows (basalts), tuffs (windblown or waterborne fine deposits from nearby volcanoes), sandstones, claystones, and limestone conglomerates, all neatly stratified (Fig. 9–3). A hominid site can therefore be accurately dated relative to other sites in the Olduvai Gorge by cross-correlating known marker beds. At the most general geological level, the stratigraphic sequence at Olduvai is broken down into four major beds (Beds I–IV).

Paleontological evidence of fossilized animal bones also has come from Olduvai in great abundance. More than 150 species of extinct animals have been recognized, including fish, turtles, crocodiles, pigs, giraffes, horses, and many birds, rodents, and antelopes. Careful analysis of such remains has yielded voluminous information concerning the ecological conditions of early human habitats. In addition, the precise analysis of bones directly associated with artifacts can sometimes tell us about the diets and bone-processing techniques of early hominids. (There are some reservations, however; see pp. 242–243.)

The archaeological sequence is also well documented for the last 2 million years. Beginning at the earliest hominid site (c. 1.85 m.y.a.), there is already a

FIGURE 9–3 View of the main gorge at Olduvai. Note the clear sequence of geological beds. The discontinuity to the right is a major fault line.

Robert Jurmain

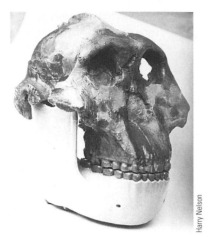

Harry Nelson

FIGURE 9–4 *Zinjanthropus* skull, discovered by Mary Leakey at Olduvai Gorge in 1959. The skull and reconstructed jaw depicted here are casts at the National Museums of Kenya, Nairobi. As we will see in Chapter 10, this fossil is now included as part of the genus *Australopithecus*.

chronometric dating (*chrono,* meaning "time," and *metric,* meaning "measure") A dating technique that gives an estimate in actual numbers of years.

stratigraphy Study of the sequential layering of deposits.

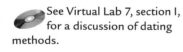 See Virtual Lab 7, section I, for a discussion of dating methods.

well-developed stone tool kit, including primarily numerous small flake tools (Leakey, 1971). Such a tool industry is called *Oldowan* (after Olduvai), and it continues into later beds with some small modifications.

Finally, partial remains of several fossilized hominids have been found at Olduvai, ranging in time from the earliest occupation levels to fairly recent *Homo sapiens*. Of the more than 40 individuals represented, many are quite fragmentary, but a few are excellently preserved. While the center of hominid discoveries has now shifted to other areas of East Africa, it was the initial discovery by Mary Leakey of the *Zinjanthropus* skull at Olduvai in July 1959 that focused the world's attention on this remarkably rich area (Fig. 9–4).

Dating Methods

One of the essentials of paleoanthropology is placing sites and fossils into a time frame. In other words, we want to know how old they are. How, then, do we date sites—or, more precisely, the geological strata in which sites are found? The question is both reasonable and important, so let us examine the dating techniques used by paleontologists, archaeologists, and other scientists involved in paleoanthropological research.

Scientists use two kinds of dating for this purpose: relative dating and **chronometric dating** (also known as *absolute dating*). Relative dating methods tell us that something is older or younger than something else, but not by how much. If, for example, a cranium is found at a depth of 50 feet and another cranium at 70 feet at the same site, we usually assume that the specimen discovered at 70 feet is older. We may not know the date (in years) of either one, but we would know that one is older (or younger) than the other. Although this may not satisfy our curiosity about the actual number of years involved, it would give some idea of the evolutionary changes in cranial morphology (structure), especially if a number of crania at different levels are found and compared.

This method of relative dating is based on **stratigraphy** and was one of the first techniques to be used by scientists working with the vast period of geological time. Stratigraphy, in turn, is based on the law of superposition, which states that a lower stratum (layer) is older than a higher stratum. Given the fact that much of the earth's crust has been laid down by layer after layer of sedimentary rock, much like the layers of a cake, stratigraphy has been a valuable aid in reconstructing the history of the earth and the life upon it.

Stratigraphic dating does, however, have a number of problems. Earth disturbances, such as volcanic activity, river activity, and mountain building, may shift strata and the objects within them, and the chronology of the material may be difficult or even impossible to reconstruct. Furthermore, the time period of a particular stratum—that is, the length of time it took to accumulate—is not possible to determine with much accuracy.

Another method of relative dating is *fluorine analysis,* which applies only to bones (Oakley, 1963). Bones in the earth are exposed to the seepage of groundwater that usually contains fluorine. The longer a bone lies in the earth, the more fluorine it will incorporate during the fossilization process. Therefore, bones deposited at the same time in the same location should contain the same amount of fluorine. The use of this technique by Professor Oakley of the British Museum in the early 1950s exposed the Piltdown (England) hoax by demonstrating that a human skull was considerably older than the jaw (ostensibly also human) found with it (Weiner, 1955). A discrepancy in fluorine content led Oakley and others to a closer examination of the bones, and they found that the jaw was not that of a hominid at all but of a young adult orangutan! (See Issue, p. 254.)

Unfortunately, fluorine is useful only with bones found at the same location. Because the amount of fluorine in groundwater is based on local conditions, it varies from place to place. Also, some groundwater may not contain any fluorine. For these reasons, comparing bones from different localities by fluorine analysis is impossible.

In both stratigraphy and fluorine analysis, the actual age of the rock stratum and the objects in it is impossible to calculate. To determine the age in years, scientists have developed a variety of chronometric techniques based on the phenomenon of radioactive decay. Actually, the theory is pretty simple: Certain radioactive isotopes of elements are unstable, disintegrate, and form an isotopic variation of another element. Since the rate of disintegration follows a definite mathematical pattern, the radioactive material forms an accurate geological time clock. By measuring the amount of disintegration in a particular sample, scientists can calculate the number of years it took for that amount of decay to accumulate. Chronometric techniques have been used for dating the immense age of the earth as well as artifacts less than 1,000 years old. Several techniques have been employed for a number of years and are now quite well known.

The most important chronometric technique used to date early hominids involves potassium-40 (^{40}K), which has a **half-life** of 1.25 billion years and produces argon-40 (^{40}Ar). Known as the K/Ar or potassium-argon method, this procedure has been extensively used by paleoanthropologists in dating materials in the 1- to 5-million-year range, especially in East Africa. In addition, a variant of this technique, the $^{40}Ar/^{39}Ar$ method, has recently been used to date a number of hominid localities. The $^{40}Ar/^{39}Ar$ method allows analysis of smaller samples (even single crystals), reduces experimental error, and is more precise than standard K/Ar dating. Consequently, it can be used to date a wide chronological range—indeed, the entire hominid record, even up to modern times. Recent applications have provided excellent dates for several early hominid sites in East Africa (discussed in Chapter 10) as well as somewhat later sites in Java (discussed in Chapter 11). In fact, the technique was recently used to date the famous Mt. Vesuvius eruption of A.D. 79 (which destroyed the city of Pompeii). Remarkably, the midrange date obtained by the $^{40}Ar/^{39}Ar$ technique was A.D. 73, just six years from the known date (Deino et al., 1998)! Organic material, such as bone, cannot be measured by these techniques, but the rock matrix in which the bone is found can be. K/Ar was used to provide a minimum date for the deposit containing the *Zinjanthropus* cranium by dating a volcanic layer above the fossil.

Rocks that provide the best samples for K/Ar and $^{40}Ar/^{39}Ar$ are those heated to an extremely high temperature, such as that generated by volcanic activity. When the rock is in a molten state, argon, a gas, is driven off. As the rock cools and solidifies, potassium-40 continues to break down to argon, but now the gas is physically trapped in the cooled rock. To obtain the date of the rock, it is reheated and the escaping gas measured.

A well-known radiometric method popular with archaeologists makes use of carbon-14 (^{14}C), with a half-life of 5,730 years. Carbon-14 has been used to date material from less than 1,000 years to as old as 75,000 years, although accuracy is reduced for materials more than 40,000 years old. Since this technique applies to the latter stages of hominid evolution, its applications relate to material discussed in Chapters 12 and 13. In addition, other dating techniques (thermoluminescence and electron spin resonance) that are used for calibrating these latter time periods will be discussed in Chapter 13.

You should realize that none of these methods is entirely precise, and each has problems that must be carefully considered during laboratory measurement and the collection of material to be analyzed. Because the methods are not perfectly

half-life The time period in which a radioactive isotope is converted chemically (into a daughter product). For example, after 1.25 billion years half the ^{40}K remains; after 2.5 billion years one-fourth remains.

A CLOSER LOOK

Chronometric Dating Estimates

Chronometric dates are usually determined after several geological samples are tested. The dates that result from such testing are combined and expressed statistically. For example, say that five different samples are used to give the K/Ar date 1.75 ± 0.2 m.y. for a particular geological bed. The individual results from all five samples are totaled together to give an average date (here, 1.75 m.y.), and the standard deviation is calculated (here, 0.20 m.y.; that is, 200,000 years). The dating estimate is then reported as the mean plus or minus (±) one standard deviation. For those of you who have taken statistics, you realize that (assuming a normal distribution) 67 percent of a distribution of dates is included within 1 standard deviation (±) of the mean. Thus, the chronometric results, as shown in the reported range, is simply a probability statement that 67 percent of the dates from all the samples tested fell within the range of dates from 1.55 to 1.95 m.y.a. You should carefully read chronometric dates and study the reported ranges. The smaller the range, probably the more samples that were analyzed. Smaller ranges mean more precise estimates; better laboratory controls will also increase precision.

accurate, approximate dates are given as probability statements with a plus or minus factor. For example, a date given as 1.75 ± 0.2 million years should be read as having a 67 percent chance that the actual date lies somewhere between 1.55 and 1.95 million years (see A Closer Look).

There are, then, two ways in which the question of age may be answered. We can say that a particular fossil is *x* number of years old, a date determined usually either by K/Ar or ^{14}C chronometric dating techniques. Or we can say that fossil X lived before or after fossil Y, a relative dating technique.

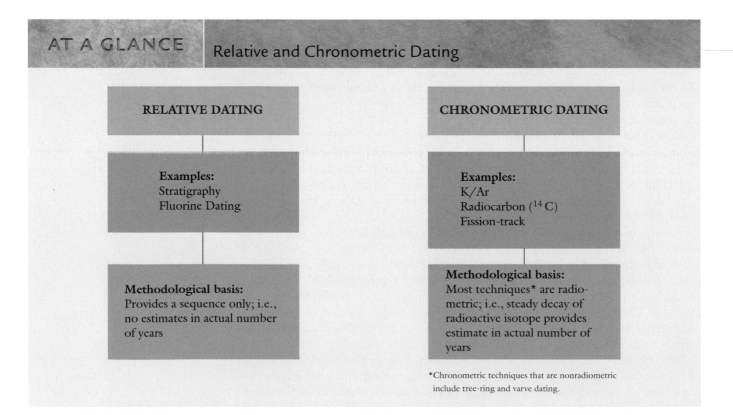

AT A GLANCE   Relative and Chronometric Dating

RELATIVE DATING	CHRONOMETRIC DATING
Examples: Stratigraphy Fluorine Dating	**Examples:** K/Ar Radiocarbon (^{14}C) Fission-track
Methodological basis: Provides a sequence only; i.e., no estimates in actual number of years	**Methodological basis:** Most techniques* are radiometric; i.e., steady decay of radioactive isotope provides estimate in actual number of years

*Chronometric techniques that are nonradiometric include tree-ring and varve dating.

APPLICATIONS OF DATING METHODS: EXAMPLES FROM OLDUVAI

Olduvai has been a rich proving ground for numerous dating techniques, and as a result, it has some of the best-documented chronology for any hominid site in the Lower or Middle Pleistocene.

As noted, the potassium-argon (K/Ar) method is an extremely valuable tool for dating early hominid sites and has been widely used in areas containing suitable volcanic deposits (mainly in East Africa). At Olduvai, K/Ar has given several reliable dates of the underlying basalt and several tuffs in Bed I, including the one associated with the "Zinj" find (now dated at 1.79 ± 0.03 m.y.a.).

Due to several potential sources of error, K/Ar dating must be cross-checked using other independent methods. Once again, the sediments at Olduvai provide some of the best examples of the use of many of these other dating techniques.

Fission-track dating is one of the most important techniques for cross-checking K/Ar determinations. The key to fission-track dating is that uranium-238 (^{238}U) decays regularly by spontaneous fission. By counting the proportion of uranium atoms that have fissioned (shown as microscopic tracks caused by explosive fission of ^{238}U nuclei), researchers can estimate the age of a mineral or natural glass sample. One of the earliest applications of this technique was on volcanic pumice from Olduvai, giving a date of 2.30 (±0.28 m.y.a.)—in good accord with K/Ar dates. Fission-track dating has also been used to date baked earth and pottery from contexts as recently as 5,000 years ago from a site in Iran (Wagner, 1996).

Another important means of cross-checking dates is called **paleomagnetism.** This technique is based on the constantly shifting nature of the earth's magnetic pole. Of course, the earth's magnetic pole is now oriented in a northerly direction, but this hasn't always been so. In fact, the orientation and intensity of the geomagnetic field have undergone numerous documented changes in the last few million years. From our present point of view, we call a northern orientation "normal" and a southern one "reversed." Major epochs (also called "*chrons*") of recent geomagnetic time are:

0.7 m.y.a.–present	Normal
2.6–0.7 m.y.a.	Reversed
3.4–2.6 m.y.a.	Normal
?–3.4 m.y.a.	Reversed

Paleomagnetic dating is accomplished by carefully taking samples of sediments that contain magnetically charged particles. Since these particles maintain the magnetic orientation they had when they were consolidated into rock (millions of years ago), we have a kind of "fossil compass." Then the paleomagnetic *sequence* is compared against the K/Ar dates to check if they agree. Some complications may arise, for during an epoch, a relatively long period of time can occur when the geomagnetic orientation is the opposite of what is expected. For example, during the reversed epoch from 2.6 to 0.7 m.y.a. (the Matuyama epoch), there was an *event* lasting about 210,000 years when orientations were normal. (Because this phenomenon was first conclusively demonstrated at Olduvai, it is appropriately called the *Olduvai event.*) However, once these oscillations in the geomagnetic pole are worked out, the sequence of paleomagnetic orientations can provide a valuable cross-check for K/Ar and fission-track age determinations.

A final dating technique used at Olduvai and other African sites is based on the regular evolutionary changes in well-known groups of mammals. This technique, called *faunal correlation* or **biostratigraphy,** provides yet another means of cross-checking the other methods. Animals that have been widely used in biostratigraphic analysis in East and South Africa are fossil pigs, elephants, antelopes, rodents, and

paleomagnetism Dating method based on shifts in the positions of the magnetic poles.

biostratigraphy Dating method based on evolutionary changes within an evolving lineage.

carnivores. From areas where dates are known (by K/Ar, for instance), approximate ages can be extrapolated to other lesser-known areas by noting which genera and species are present.

All these methods—potassium-argon, fission-track, paleomagnetism, and biostratigraphy—have been used in dating sites at Olduvai. So many different dating techniques are necessary because no single one is perfectly reliable by itself. Sampling error, contamination, and experimental error can all introduce ambiguities into our so-called "absolute" dates. However, the sources of error are different for each technique; therefore, cross-checking among several independent methods is the most reliable way of authenticating the chronology for early hominid sites.

Excavations at Olduvai

Because the vertical cut of the Olduvai Gorge provides a cross section of 2 million years of earth history, sites can be excavated by digging "straight in" rather than first having to remove tons of overlying dirt (Fig. 9–5). In fact, sites are usually discovered by merely walking the exposures and observing what bones, stones, and so forth, are eroding out.

Several dozen hominid sites (at a minimum, they are bone and tool scatters) have been surveyed at Olduvai, and Mary Leakey extensively excavated close to 20 of these. An incredible amount of paleoanthropological information has come from these excavated areas, data that can be generally grouped into three broad categories of site types, depending on implied function:

1. *"Butchering" localities,* areas containing one or only a few individuals of a single species of large mammal associated with a scatter of archaeological traces. Two "butchering" sites, one containing an elephant and another containing a *Deinotherium* (a large extinct relative of the elephant), have been found at levels approximately 1.7 m.y.a. Both sites contain parts of only a single animal, and it is impossible to ascertain whether the hominids actually killed these animals or exploited them after they were already dead. A third butchering locality dated at approximately 1.2 m.y.a. shows more consistent and efficient exploitation of large mammals by this time.

FIGURE 9–5 Excavations in progress at Olduvai. This site, more than 1 million years old, was located when a hominid ulna (arm bone) was found eroding out of the side of the gorge.

Robert Jurmain

FIGURE 9–6 A dense scatter of stone and some fossilized animal bone from a site at Olduvai, dated at approximately 1.6 m.y.a. Some of these remains are the result of hominid activities.

2. *Quarry localities,* areas where early hominids extracted stone to make tools. At such sites, thousands of small stone fragments of only one type of rock are found, usually associated with no or very little bone refuse. At Olduvai, a 1.6- to 1.7-million-year-old area was apparently a chert (a rock resembling flint) factory site, where hominids came repeatedly to obtain this material.

3. *Multipurpose localities* (also called "campsites"), general-purpose areas where hominids possibly ate, slept, and put the finishing touches on their tools. The accumulation of living debris, including broken bones of many animals of several different species and many broken stones (some complete tools, some waste flakes), is a basic human pattern. As Glynn Isaac noted:

> The fact that discarded artifacts tend to be concentrated in restricted areas is itself highly suggestive. It seems likely that such patches of material reflect the organization of movement around a camp or home base, with recurrent dispersal and reuniting of the group at the chosen locality. Among living primates this pattern in its full expression is distinctive of man. The coincidence of bone and food refuse with the artifacts strongly implies that meat was carried back—presumably for sharing. (Isaac, 1976, pp. 27–28)

(See A Closer Look on pp. 242–243 for a different interpretation.)

Several multipurpose areas have been excavated at Olduvai, including one that is over 1.8 million years old. This site has a circle of large stones forming what at one time was thought to be a base for a windbreak; however, this interpretation is now considered unlikely. Whatever its function, without the meticulous excavation and recording of modern archaeological techniques, the presence of such an archaeological feature would never have been recognized. This point requires further emphasis. Many people assume that archaeologists derive their information simply from analysis of objects (stone tools, gold statues, or whatever). However, it is the *context* and **association** of objects (i.e., precisely where the objects are found and what is found associated with them) that give archaeologists the information they require to understand the behavioral patterns of ancient human populations. Once pot hunters or looters pilfer a site, proper archaeological interpretation is never again possible.

The types of activities carried out at these multipurpose sites remain open to speculation (Fig. 9–6). Archaeologists had thought, as the quote by Glynn Isaac

See Virtual Lab 2, section III, for a discussion of the factors that influence the development of archaeological localities.

association Relationships between components of an archaeological site. All the things artifacts are found with.

A CLOSER LOOK

Who Was Doing What at Olduvai and Other Plio-Pleistocene Sites?

The long-held interpretation of the bone refuse and stone tools discovered at Olduvai has been that most, if not all, of these materials are the result of hominid activities. More recently, however, a comprehensive reanalysis of the bone remains from Olduvai localities has challenged this view (Binford 1981, 1983). Archaeologist Lewis Binford criticizes those drawn too quickly to the conclusion that these bone scatters are the remnants of hominid behavior patterns while simultaneously ignoring the possibility of other explanations.

From information concerning the kinds of animals present, which body parts were found, and the differences in preservation among these skeletal elements, Binford has concluded that much of what is preserved could be explained by carnivore activity. This conclusion has been reinforced by certain details observed by Binford himself in Alaska—details on animal kills, scavenging, the transportation of elements, and preservation that are the result of wolf and dog behaviors. Binford describes his approach thus:

> I took as "known," then, the structure of bone assemblages produced in various settings by animal predators and scavengers; and as "unknown" the bone deposits excavated by the Leakeys at Olduvai Gorge. Using mathematical and statistical techniques I considered to what degree the finds from Olduvai Gorge could be accounted for in terms of the results of predator behavior and how much was "left over." (Binford, 1983, pp. 56–57)

Binford is not arguing that all of the remains found at Olduvai resulted from nonhominid activity. In fact, he recognizes that "residual material" was consistently found on surfaces with high tool concentration "which could not be explained by what we know about African animals" (Binford, 1983).

Support for the idea that at least some of the bone refuse was utilized by early hominids has come from a totally different perspective. Researchers have analyzed (both macroscopically and microscopically) the cut marks left on fossilized bones. By experimenting with modern materials, they have further been able to delineate clearly the differences between marks left by stone tools and those left by animal teeth (or other factors) (Bunn, 1981; Potts and Shipman, 1981). Analysis of bones from several early localities at Olduvai have shown unambiguously that these specimens were utilized by hominids, who left telltale cut marks from stone tool usage. The sites thus far investigated reveal a somewhat haphazard cutting and chopping, apparently unrelated to deliberate disarticulation. It has thus been concluded (Shipman, 1983) that hominids scavenged carcasses (probably of carnivore kills) and did *not* hunt large animals themselves.

Following and expanding on the experimental approaches pioneered by Binford, Bunn, and others, more detailed analysis of the Olduvai material has recently been done by Robert Blumenschine of Rutgers University. Like his predecessors, Blumenschine has also concluded that the cut

indicates (and as also argued by Mary Leakey), that the sites functioned as "campsites." Lewis Binford has forcefully critiqued this view and has alternatively suggested that much of the refuse accumulated is the result of nonhominid (i.e., predator) activities. Another possibility, suggested by Richards Potts (1984), postulates that these areas served as collecting points (caches) for some tools. This last interpretation has received considerable support from other archaeologists in recent years.

A final interpretation, incorporating aspects of the hypotheses proposed by Binford and Potts, has been suggested by Robert Blumenschine. He argued that early hominids were gatherers and scavengers, and the bone and stone scatters reflect these activities (Blumenschine, 1986; Blumenschine and Cavallo, 1992; see A Closer Look).

marks on animal bones are the result of hominid processing (Blumenschine, 1995). Moreover, Blumenschine and colleagues surmise that most meat acquisition (virtually all from large animals) was the result of scavenging (from remains of carnivore kills or from animals who died from natural causes). In fact, these researchers suggest that scavenging was a critically important adaptive strategy for early hominids and considerably influenced their habitat usage, diet, and stone tool utilization (Blumenschine and Cavallo, 1992; Blumenschine and Peters, 1998). Of notable scientific merit, Blumenschine and colleagues have developed a model detailing how scavenging and other early hominid adaptive strategies integrate into patterns of land use (i.e., differential utilization of various niches in and around Olduvai). From this model they formulated specific hypotheses concerning the predicted distribution of artifacts and animal remains in different areas at Olduvai. Ongoing excavations at Olduvai are now aimed specifically at *testing* these hypotheses.

If early hominids (close to 2 m.y.a.) were not hunting consistently, what did they obtain from scavenging the kills of other animals? One obvious answer is, whatever meat was left behind. However, the position of the cut marks suggests that early hominids were often hacking at non-meat-bearing portions of the skeletons. Perhaps they were after bone marrow and brain, substances not fully exploited by other predators and scavengers (Binford, 1981; Blumenschine and Cavallo, 1992).

Exciting new discoveries from the Bouri Peninsula of the Middle Awash of Ethiopia provide the best evidence yet for meat and marrow exploitation by early hominids. Dated to 2.5 m.y.a. (i.e., as old as the oldest known artifacts), antelope and horse fossils from Bouri show telltale incisions and breaks indicating that bones were smashed to extract marrow and also cut, ostensibly to retrieve meat (de Heinzelin et al., 1999). The researchers who analyzed these materials have suggested that the greater dietary reliance on animal products may have been important in stimulating brain enlargement in the lineage leading to genus *Homo*.

Another new research twist relating to the reconstruction of early hominid diets has come from biochemical analysis of hominid teeth from South Africa (dating to about the same time range as hominids from Olduvai—or perhaps slightly earlier). In an innovative application of stable carbon isotope analysis (see p. 247), Matt Sponheimer of University of Colorado, Boulder, and Julia Lee-Thorp of the University of Cape Town found that these early hominid teeth revealed telltale chemical signatures relating to diet (Sponheimer and Lee-Thorp, 1999). In particular, the proportions of stable carbon isotopes indicated that these early hominids either ate grass products (such as seeds) or ate meat/marrow from animals that in turn had eaten grass products (i.e., the hominids might well have derived a significant portion of their diet from meat or other animal products). This evidence comes from an exciting new perspective, for it provides a more *direct* indicator of early hominid diets. While it is not clear how much meat these early hominids consumed, these new data do suggest they were consistently exploiting more open regions of their environment.

Experimental Archaeology

Simply classifying artifacts into categories and types is not enough. We can learn considerably more about our ancestors by understanding how they made and used their tools. It is, after all, the artifactual traces of prehistoric tools of stone (and, to a lesser degree, bone) that provide much of our information concerning early human behavior. Tons of stone debris litter archaeological sites worldwide. A casual walk along the bottom of Olduvai Gorge could well be interrupted every few seconds by tripping over prehistoric tools!

Thus, archaeologists are presented with a wealth of information revealing at least one part of human material culture. What do these artifacts tell us about our ancestors? How were these tools made and how were they used? To answer these questions, contemporary archaeologists have tried to reconstruct prehistoric techniques of stone toolmaking, butchering, and so forth. In this way, experimental archaeologists are, in a sense, trying to re-create the past.

STONE TOOL (LITHIC) TECHNOLOGY

Since stone is by far the most common residue of prehistoric cultural behavior, archaeologists have long been keenly interested in this material.

When struck properly, certain types of stone will fracture in a controlled way. The smaller piece that comes off is called a **flake,** while the larger remaining chunk is called a **core** (Fig. 9–7). Both core and flake have sharp edges useful for cutting, sawing, or scraping. The earliest hominid cultural inventions probably used nondurable materials that did not survive archaeologically (such as a digging stick or an ostrich eggshell used as a watertight container). Still, a basic human invention was the recognition that stone can be fractured to produce sharp edges.

For many years it has been assumed that in the earliest known stone tool industry (i.e., the Oldowan), both core and flake tools were deliberately manufactured as final, desired products. Such core implements as "choppers" were thought to be central artifactual components of these early **lithic** assemblages (indeed, the Oldowan has often been depicted as a "chopping tool industry"). However, detailed reevaluation of these artifacts has thrown these traditional assumptions into doubt. From careful analysis of the attributes of Oldowan artifacts from Olduvai, Potts (1991, 1993) concluded that the so-called core tools were really not tools after all. He suggests rather that what early hominids were deliberately producing were flake tools, and the various stone nodules (choppers) were simply "incidental stopping points in the process of removing flakes from cores" (Potts, 1993, p. 60). Potts summarizes his reevaluation: "The flaked stones of the Oldowan thus cannot be demonstrated to constitute discrete target designs, but can be shown to represent simple by-products of the repetitive act of producing sharp flakes" (Potts, 1993, pp. 60–61).

Breaking rocks by bashing them together is one thing. Producing consistent results, even apparently simple flakes, is quite another. You might want to give it a try, just to appreciate how difficult making a stone tool can be. It takes years of practice before modern stone **knappers** learn the intricacies of the type of rock to choose, the kind of hammer to employ, the angle and velocity with which to strike, and so on. Such experience allows us to appreciate how skilled in stoneworking our ancestors truly were.

Flakes can be removed from cores in a variety of ways. The object in making a tool, however, is to produce a usable cutting surface. By reproducing results similar to those of earlier stoneworkers, experimental archaeologists can infer which kinds of techniques *might* have been employed.

For example, the nodules (now thought to be blanks) found in sites in Bed I at Olduvai (c. 1.85–1.2 m.y.a.) are flaked on one side only (i.e., *unifacially*). It is possible, although by no means easy, to produce such implements by hitting one stone—the hammerstone—against another—the core—in a method called **direct percussion** (Fig. 9–8).

In Bed IV sites (c. 400,000 y.a.*), however, the majority of tools are flaked on both sides (i.e., *bifacially*) and have long sinuous edges. Such a result cannot be reproduced by direct percussion with just a hammerstone. The edges must have been straightened ("retouched") with a "soft" hammer, such as bone or antler.

To reproduce implements similar to those found in later stages of human cultural development, even more sophisticated techniques are required. Tools such

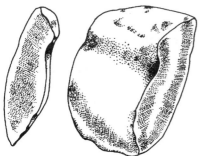

Flake   Core

FIGURE 9–7 Flake and core.

flake Thin-edged fragment removed from a core.

core Stone reduced by flake removal; a core may or may not be used as a tool itself.

lithic (*lith,* meaning "stone") Referring to stone tools.

knappers People (frequently archaeologists) who make stone tools.

direct percussion Striking a core or flake with a hammerstone.

microliths (*micro,* meaning "small," and *lith,* meaning "stone") Small stone tools usually produced from narrow blades punched from a core; found especially in Africa during the latter part of the Pleistocene.

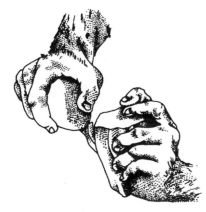

FIGURE 9–8 Direct percussion.

*y.a. stands for "years ago."

as the delicate **microliths** found in the uppermost beds at Olduvai (c. 17,000 y.a.), the superb Solutrean blades from Europe (c. 20,000 y.a.), and the expertly crafted Folsom projectile points from the New World (c. 10,000 y.a.) all require a mastery of stone matched by few knappers today.

Reproducing implements such as those mentioned above requires removal of extremely thin flakes, possible only through **pressure flaking**—for example, using a pointed piece of bone, antler, or hard wood and pressing firmly against the stone (Fig. 9–9).

Once the tools were manufactured, the ways our ancestors used them can be inferred through further experimentation. For example, archaeologists from the Smithsonian Institution successfully butchered an entire elephant (which had died in a zoo) using stone tools they had made for that purpose (Park, 1978). Others have cut down trees using stone axes they had made.

Ancient tools themselves may carry telltale signs of how they were used. Lawrence Keeley performed a series of experiments in which he manufactured flint tools and then used them in diverse ways—whittling wood, cutting bone, cutting meat, and scraping skins. Viewing those implements under a microscope at fairly high magnification revealed patterns of polishes, striations, and other kinds of **microwear** (Fig. 9–10). What is most intriguing is that these patterns varied, depending on how the implement was used and which material was worked. For example, Keeley was able to distinguish among implements used on bone, antler, meat, plant materials, and hides. In the latter case, he was even able to determine if the hides were fresh or dried! In addition, orientations of microwear markings are also indicative of the way in which the tool was used (e.g., for cutting or scraping). Evidence of microwear polish has been examined on even the extremely early hominid stone tools from Koobi Fora (East Lake Turkana), in Kenya (Keeley and Toth, 1981).

Recent advances in tool use studies include the application of scanning electron microscopy (SEM). Working at 10,000× magnification, researchers have found that the working edges of stone implements sometimes retain plant fibers and amino acids, as well as nonorganic residues, including **phytoliths.** Because phytoliths produced by different plant species are morphologically distinctive, there is good potential for identifying the botanical materials that came in contact with the tool during use (Rovner, 1983). Such work is most exciting, since for the first time, we may be able to make definite statements concerning the uses of ancient tools.

ANALYSIS OF BONE

Experimental archaeologists are also interested in the ways bone is altered by human and natural forces. Other scientists are vitally concerned with this process as well; in fact, it has engendered an entire new branch of paleoecology—taphonomy. Taphonomists have carried out comprehensive research on how natural factors influence bone deposition and preservation. In South Africa, C. K. Brain collected data on contemporary African butchering practices, carnivore (dog) disturbances, and so forth, and correlated these factors with the kinds and numbers of elements usually found in bone accumulations (Brain, 1981). In this way, he was able to account for the accumulation of most (if not all) of the bones in South African cave sites. Likewise, in East African game parks, observations have been made on decaying animals to measure the effects of weathering, predator chewing, and trampling (Behrensmeyer et al., 1979; Perkins, 2003).

Further insight into the many ways bone is altered by natural factors has come from experimental work in the laboratory (Boaz and Behrensmeyer, 1976). In an experiment conducted at the University of California, Berkeley, human bones were put into a running-water trough. Researchers observed how far different

FIGURE 9–9 Pressure flaking.

pressure flaking A method of removing flakes from a core by pressing a pointed implement (e.g., bone or antler) against the stone.

microwear Polishes, striations, and other diagnostic microscopic changes on the edges of stone tools.

phytoliths (*phyto*, meaning "hidden," and *lith*, meaning "stone") Microscopic silica structures formed in the cells of many plants, particularly grasses.

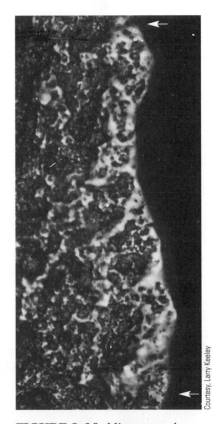

Courtesy, Larry Keeley

FIGURE 9–10 Microwear: the polish left on an experimental flint implement by scraping wood for 10 minutes. Bright, smooth areas are the microwear polish; dark, grainy areas are the unworn flint surface. Arrows indicate implement edge. (Magnification 200×)

pieces were transported and how much damage was done. Application of such information is extremely useful in interpreting early hominid sites. For example, the distribution of hominid fossils at Olduvai suggests that less active water transport was prevalent there than in the Omo River Valley.

Detailed examination of bones may also provide evidence of butchering and bone breakage by hominids, including cut marks and percussion marks left by stone tools. Great care must be taken to distinguish scars left on bone by carnivore or rodent gnawing, weathering processes, hoof marks, or even normal growth. High magnification of a cut made by a stone tool may reveal a minutely striated and roughened groove scored into the bone's surface. Many such finds have been recognized at early hominid sites, including Olduvai Gorge (Bunn et al., 1980; Bunn, 1981; Potts and Shipman, 1981) (see pp. 242–243).

Reconstruction of Early Hominid Environments and Behavior

Now that we have reviewed the various methods used by paleoanthropologists to *collect* their varied data, we can look at the intriguing ways this information is *interpreted*. We must caution that much of this interpretation is quite speculative and not as amenable to scientific verification as are more concrete sources of data (e.g., that relating to dating, geology, or hominid anatomy). (In Chapter 1, we discussed how hypotheses are developed and tested by scientists, noting the requirement that *scientific* explanations be falsifiable.)

However, paleoanthropologists are keenly interested in not just *how* early hominids evolved, but also *why* the process occurred the way that it did. Accordingly, the data available are frequently used as a basis for broad, speculative **scenarios** that try to explain both early hominid adaptations to a changing environment and the new behaviors that these hominids adopted. Such scenarios are fascinating, and paleoanthropologists enjoy constructing them (and certainly many in the general public enjoy reading them). Without doubt, for scientists and laypersons alike, our curiosity inevitably leads to intriguing and sweeping generalizations. Nevertheless, in the following discussion, we will focus on what is *known* from the paleoanthropological record itself and to separate that from the more speculative conclusions. You, too, should evaluate these explanations with a critical eye and attempt to discern the empirical basis for each type of reconstruction. It is important to go beyond accepting views merely because they are appealing (often because they are simple) or just because they seem *plausible*. We always need to ask ourselves what kinds of evidence support a particular contention, how generally the explanation fits the evidence (i.e., how consistent it is with different types of data from varied sources), and what types of *new* evidence might either help verify or potentially falsify the interpretation.

scenarios General, speculative reconstructions derived from various scientific data. In paleoanthropology, scenarios are usually presented as imaginative reconstructions of early hominid behavior. Such interpretations are broader than typical scientific hypotheses and theories and are not as rigorously amenable to verification.

ENVIRONMENTAL EXPLANATIONS FOR HOMINID ORIGINS

As we will discuss in the next chapter, the earliest hominids evolved late in the Miocene or very early in the Pliocene (7–5 m.y.a.). What were the environmental conditions at this time? Can these general ecological patterns help explain the origins of the first hominids (as they diversified from other kinds of hominoids)?

Before continuing, we should provide one further caution. A common misconception that many students have is that a single large environmental change is related clearly to a major adaptive change in a type of organism (in other words, environmental change X produced adaptation Y in a particular life form).

This oversimplification is a form of **environmental determinism,** and it grossly underestimates the true complexity of the evolutionary process. It is clear that the environment does influence evolutionary change, as seen in the process of natural selection. But organisms are highly complex systems, composed of thousands of genes, and any adaptive shift to changing environmental circumstances is likely to be a compromise, balancing several selective factors simultaneously (such as temperature requirements, amount and distribution of food and water, predators, and safe sleeping sites). Our discussion of the socioecological dynamics of nonhuman primate adaptations in Chapter 7 made this same point.

There is some evidence that at about the same time the earliest hominids were diverging, there *may* have been some major ecological changes occurring in Africa. Could these ecological and evolutionary changes be related to each other? As we will see, there is much debate regarding such a sweeping generalization. For most of the Miocene, Africa was generally tropical, with heavy rainfall persisting for most of the year; consequently, most of the continent was heavily forested. However, beginning later in the Miocene and intensifying up to the end of the epoch (about 5 m.y.a.), the climate became cooler, drier, and more seasonal.

We should mention as well that there were other regions of the world where paleoecological evidence reveals a distinct cooling trend at the end of the Miocene. However, our focus is on Africa, particularly eastern and central Africa, for it is from these regions that we have the earliest evidence of hominid diversification. As already noted, one method used by paleoanthropologists to reconstruct environments is to analyze animal (faunal) remains and fossilized pollen. In addition, an innovative technique also studies the chemical pathways utilized by different plants. In particular, **stable carbon isotopes** are produced by plants in differing proportions, depending partly on temperature and aridity (plants adapted to warmer, wetter climates, such as most trees, shrubs, and tubers, versus plants requiring hotter, drier conditions, as typified by many types of grasses). Animals eat the plants, and the differing concentrations of the stable isotopes of carbon are incorporated into their bones and teeth, thus providing a "signature" of the general type of environment in which they lived.

It is from a combination of these analytical techniques that paleoecologists have gained a reasonably good handle on worldwide and continentwide environmental patterns of the past. For example, one model postulates that as climates grew cooler in East Africa 12–5 m.y.a., forests became less continuous. As a result, forest "fringe" habitats and transitional zones between forests and grasslands became more widespread. It is hypothesized that in such transitional environments, some of the late Miocene hominoids may have exploited more intensively the drier grassland portions of the fringe (these would be the earliest hominids); conversely, other hominoids concentrated more on the wetter portions of the fringe (these presumably were the ancestors of African great apes). In the incipient protohominids, further adaptive strategies would have followed, including bipedalism, increased tool use, dietary specialization (perhaps on hard items such as seeds and nuts), and changes in social organization.

Such assertions concerning interactions of habitat, locomotion, dietary changes, and social organization are not really testable (since we do not know which changes came first). Still, some of the more restricted contentions of this "climatic forcing" theory are amenable to testing; in fact, some of the more basic predictions of the model have not been verified. Most notably, further analyses using stable carbon isotopes from several East African localities suggest that during the late Miocene, environments across the area were consistently quite densely forested (i.e., grasslands never predominated, except perhaps at a local level).

environmental determinism An interpretation that links simple environmental changes directly to a major evolutionary shift in an organism. Such explanations tend to be extreme oversimplifications of the evolutionary process.

stable carbon isotopes Isotopes of carbon that are produced in plants in differing proportions, depending on environmental conditions. Through analyzing the proportions of the isotopes contained in fossil remains of animals (who ate the plants), it is possible to reconstruct aspects of ancient environments (particularly temperature and aridity).

You should be aware that there can be wide fluctuations at the local level pertaining to such factors as temperature, rainfall, vegetation, and the animals exploiting the vegetation. For example, local uplift can produce a rain shadow, dramatically altering rainfall and temperature in a region. River and related lake drainages also have major impacts in some areas, and these topographical features are often influenced by highly localized geological factors. To generalize about climates in Africa, good data from several regions are required.

It would thus appear, given current evidence and available analytical techniques, that our knowledge of the factors influencing the appearance of the *earliest* hominids is very limited. Considering the constraints, most hypotheses relating to potential factors are best kept restricted in scope and directly related to actual data. In this way, their utility can be more easily evaluated and they can be modified and built upon.

Other environmentally oriented hypotheses have also been proposed for somewhat later stages of hominid evolution in Africa. Analysis of faunal remains from South African sites led Elizabeth Vrba of Yale University to suggest an *evolutionary pulse theory*. In this view, at various times during the Pliocene and early Pleistocene, the environment all across Africa became notably more arid. Vrba hypothesized that these major climatic shifts may have played a central role in stimulating hominid evolutionary development at key stages.

However, more complete data derived from thousands of fossils in East Africa (Behrensmeyer et al., 1997) have failed to show that these environmental transitions were as widespread as initially proposed. Further detailed analysis by Richard Potts of the Smithsonian Institution has, in fact, shown that ecosystems (the communities of plants and animals changed rapidly and often predictably throughout Africa (Bower, 2003; Potts, 2003). Rather than large-scale environmental changes "forcing" hominids into new adaptive strategies, perhaps our ancestors flourished and evolved because they were flexible opportunists.

WHY DID HOMINIDS BECOME BIPEDAL?

As we have noted several times, the adaptation of hominids to bipedal locomotion was *the* most fundamental adaptive shift among the early members of our family. But what were the factors that initiated this crucial change? Ecological theories, similar to some of those just discussed, have long been thought to be central to the development of bipedalism. Clearly, however, environmental influences would have to occur *before* documented evidence of well-adapted bipedal behavior. In other words, the major shift would have been at the end of the Miocene. Although the evidence indicates that no *sudden* wide ecological change took place at this time, locally forests probably did become patchier as rainfall became more seasonal. Given the changing environmental conditions, did hominids come to the ground to seize the opportunities offered in these more open habitats? Did bipedalism then quickly ensue, stimulated by this new way of life? At a very general level, the answer to these questions is yes. Obviously, hominids did at some point become bipedal, and this adaptation took place on the ground. Likewise, hominids are more adapted to mixed and open-country habitats than are our closest ape cousins. Successful terrestrial bipedalism probably made possible the further adaptation to more arid, open-country terrain. Still, this rendition simply tells us *where* hominids found their niche, not *why*.

As always, one must be cautious when speculating about causation in evolution. It is all too easy to draw superficial conclusions. For example, it is often surmised that the mere fact that ground niches were available (and perhaps lacked direct competitors) inevitably led the earliest hominids to terrestrial bipedalism. But consider this: There are plenty of mammalian species, including some nonhuman primates, that also live mostly on the ground in open country—and they are not bipedal. Clearly, beyond such simplistic environmental determinism, some more complex explanation for hominid bipedalism is required. There must have been something *more* than just an environmental opportunity to explain this adaptation to such a unique lifestyle.

Another issue sometimes overlooked in the discussion of early hominid bipedal adaptation is that these creatures did not suddenly become *completely* terrestrial. We know, for example, that all terrestrial species of nonhuman primates (e.g., savanna baboons, hamadryas baboons, patas monkeys; see Chapter 7) regularly seek out "safe sleeping sites" off the ground. These safe havens help protect against predation and are usually found in trees or on cliff faces. Likewise, early hominids almost certainly sought safety at night *in the trees,* even after they became well adapted to terrestrial bipedalism during daytime foraging. Moreover, the continued opportunities for feeding in the trees would most likely have remained significant to early hominids, well after they were also utilizing ground-based resources.

A variety of hypotheses to explain why hominids initially became bipedal have been suggested and are summarized in Table 9–2. The primary influences claimed to have stimulated the shift to bipedalism include the ability to carry objects (and offspring); hunting on the ground; gathering of seeds and nuts; feeding from bushes; improved thermoregulation (i.e., keeping cooler on the open savanna); better view of open country (to spot predators); long-distance walking; and provisioning by males of females with dependent offspring.

These are all creative scenarios, but once again are not very conducive to rigorous testing and verification. Nevertheless, two of the more ambitious scenarios proposed by Clifford Jolly (1970) and Owen Lovejoy (1981) deserve further mention. Both of these views sought to link several aspects of early hominid ecology, feeding, and social behavior, and both utilized models derived from studies of contemporary nonhuman primates.

Jolly's seed-eating hypothesis used the feeding behavior and ecology of gelada baboons as an analogy for very early hominids. In this view, early hominids are hypothesized to have adapted to open country and bipedalism as a consequence of their *primary* adaptation to eating seeds and nuts (found on the ground). The key assumption is that early hominids were eating seeds acquired in similar ecological conditions to those of contemporary gelada baboons.

Lovejoy, meanwhile, has combined *presumed* aspects of early hominid ecology, feeding, pair bonding, infant care, and food sharing to devise his creative scenario. This view hinges on the following assumptions: (1) that the earliest hominids had offspring at least as K-selected (see p. 190) as other large-bodied hominoids; (2) that hominid males ranged widely and provisioned females and their young, who remained more tied to a "home base"; and (3) that males were paired *monogamously* with females.

As we have noted, while not strictly testable, such scenarios do make certain predictions (which can be verified). Accordingly, aspects of each scenario can be evaluated in light of more specific data (obtained from the paleoanthropological record). As pertaining to the seed-eating hypothesis, predictions relating to size of the back teeth in most early hominids are met; however, the proportions of the front teeth in many forms are not what would be expected in a committed seed eater. Moreover, the analogy with gelada baboons is not as informative as once thought, since these animals actually do not eat that many seeds. Finally, many of the characteristics suggested by Jolly to be restricted to hominids (and geladas) are also found in several late Miocene hominoids (who were not hominids). Thus, regarding the seed-eating hypothesis, the proposed dental and dietary adaptations do not appear to be linked specifically to hominid origins or bipedalism.

TABLE 9–2 Possible Factors Influencing the Initial Evolution of Bipedal Locomotion in Hominids

FACTOR	SPECULATED INFLUENCE	COMMENTS
Carrying (objects, tools, weapons, infants)	Upright posture freed the arms to carry various objects (including offspring)	Charles Darwin emphasized this view, particularly relating to tools and weapons; however, evidence of stone tools is found much later in record than first evidence of bipedalism
Hunting	As correlated with above theory, carrying weapons made hunting more efficient; in addition, long-distance walking may have been more energetically efficient (see below)	Systematic hunting is now thought not to have been practiced until after the origin of bipedal hominids (see Issue, Chapter 11)
Seed and nut gathering	Feeding on seeds and nuts occurred while standing upright	Model initially drawn from analogy with gelada baboons (see text)
Feeding from bushes	Upright posture provided access to seeds, berries, etc., in lower branches; analogous to adaptation seen in some specialized antelope	Climbing adaptation already existed as prior ancestral trait in earliest hominids (i.e., bush and tree feeding already was established prior to bipedal adaptation)
Thermoregulation (cooling)	Vertical posture exposes less of the body to direct sun; increased distance from ground facilitates cooling by increased exposure to breezes	Works best for animals active midday on savanna; moreover, adaptation to bipedalism may have initially occurred in woodlands, not on savanna
Visual surveillance	Standing up provided better view of surrounding countryside (view of potential predators as well as other group members)	Behavior seen occasionally in terrestrial primates (e.g., baboons); probably a contributing factor, but unlikely as "prime mover"
Long-distance walking	Covering long distances was more efficient for a biped than for a quadruped (during hunting or foraging); mechanical reconstructions show that bipedal walking is less energetically costly than quadrupedalism (this is not the case for bipedal *running*)	Same difficulties as with hunting explanation; long-distance foraging on ground also appears unlikely adaptation in *earliest* hominids
Male provisioning	Males carried back resources to dependent females and young	Monogamous bond suggested; however, most skeletal data appear to falsify this part of the hypothesis (see text)

Further detailed analyses of data have also questioned crucial elements of Lovejoy's male-provisioning scenario. The evidence that appears to most contradict this view is that *all* early hominids were quite sexually dimorphic. According to Lovejoy's model (and analogies with contemporary monogamous nonhuman primates such as gibbons), there should not be such dramatic differences in body size between males and females. A recent study (Reno et al., 2003) has questioned this view, suggesting, at least for one species, that sexual dimorphism was only very moderate. This conclusion appears at odds with most of the evidence regarding early hominids. Furthermore, the notions of food sharing (presumably including considerable meat), home bases, and long-distance provisioning are questioned by more controlled interpretations of the archaeological record (see A Closer Look on p. 242).

Another imaginative view is also relevant to this discussion of early hominid evolution, since it relates the adaptation to bipedalism (which was first) to increased brain expansion (which came later). This interpretation, proposed by Dean Falk, of the State University of New York at Albany, suggests that an upright posture put severe constraints on brain size (since blood circulation and drainage would have been altered and thus cooling would have been more limited than in quadrupeds). Falk thus hypothesizes that new brain-cooling mechanisms must have coevolved with bipedalism, articulated in what she calls the "radiator theory" (Falk, 1990). Falk further surmises that the requirements for better brain cooling would have been particularly marked as hominids adapted to open-country ground living on the hot African savanna. Another interesting pattern observed by Falk concerns two different cooling adaptations found in different early hominid species. She thus suggests that the type of "radiator" adapted in the genus *Homo* was particularly significant in reducing constraints on brain size—which presumably limited some other early hominids. The radiator theory works well, since it not only helps explain the relationship of bipedalism to later brain expansion, but also explains why only some hominids became dramatically encephalized.

The radiator theory, too, has been criticized by some paleoanthropologists. Most notably, the presumed species distinction concerning varying cooling mechanisms is not so obvious as suggested by the hypothesis. Both types of venous drainage systems can be found in contemporary *Homo sapiens* as well as within various early hominid species (i.e., the variation is intraspecific, not just interspecific). Indeed, in some early hominid specimens, both systems can be found in the *same* individual (expressed on each side of the skull). Moreover, as Falk herself has noted, the radiator itself did not lead to larger brains; it simply helped reduce constraints on increased encephalization among hominids. It thus requires some *further* mechanism (prime mover) to explain why, in some hominid species, brain size increased in the manner it did.

As with any such ambitious effort, it is all too easy to find holes. Falk aptly reminds us that "the search for such 'prime movers' is highly speculative and these theories do not lend themselves to hypothesis testing" (Falk, 1990, p. 334). Nevertheless, the attempt to interrelate various lines of evidence, the use of contemporary primate models, and predictions concerning further evidence obtained from paleoanthropological contexts all conform to sound scientific methodology. All the views discussed here have contributed to this venture— one not just aimed at understanding our early ancestors, but one also seeking to refine its methodologies and scientific foundation.

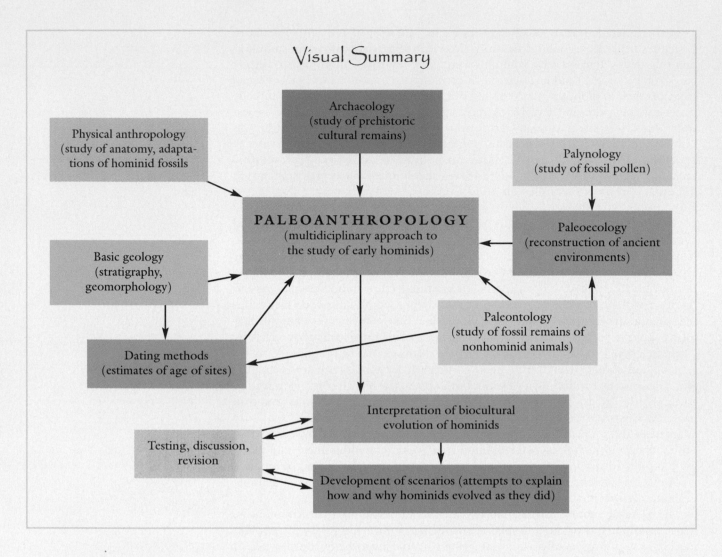

Visual Summary

Summary

The biocultural nature of human evolution requires that any meaningful study of human origins examine both biological and cultural information. The multidisciplinary approach of paleoanthropology is designed to bring together varied scientific specializations to reconstruct the anatomy, behavior, and environments of early hominids. Such a task is centered around the skills of the geologist, paleontologist, paleoecologist, archaeologist, and physical anthropologist.

Much of what we know about the origins of human culture between 2 and 1 m.y.a. comes from archaeological excavations by Mary Leakey at Olduvai Gorge, in East Africa. Olduvai's well-documented stratigraphic sequence, its superior preservation of remains, and the varied dating techniques possible there have made it an information bonanza for paleoanthropologists. Excavated sites have yielded a wealth of bones of fossil animals, as well as artifact traces of hominid behavior. Ecological reconstructions of habitat and dietary preferences are thereby possible and

inform us in great detail concerning crucial evolutionary processes affecting early hominid populations.

Archaeologists are better able to interpret the "bones and stones" of earlier populations through experimentation. In recent years, much new light has been shed on the techniques of making stone tools as well as the factors affecting preservation of bone.

Broader interpretations, leading to several speculative scenarios, have also been attempted to help us understand the environmental influences and behavioral adaptations exhibited by early hominids. Most notably, attempts have been made to link the earliest origins of hominids as well as somewhat later diversifications to general ecological changes in Africa. Finally, many researchers have speculated concerning the factors influencing that most fundamental of all early hominid adaptations, the development of bipedal locomotion. In the next chapter, we will survey the fossil hominid evidence in South and East Africa that informs us directly about human origins during the Plio-Pleistocene.

For Further Thought

1. Why does the discovery of fossil hominids often get front-page media coverage?

Go to the book website at **http://www.anthropology.wadsworth.com** for resources to help you explore these questions further. Click on "For Further Thought" for this chapter.

Questions for Review

1. You are leading a paleoanthropological expedition aimed at discovering an early hominid site dating to the Pliocene. In what part of the world will you pick your site, and why? Once you have identified a particular region, how will you identify which area(s) to survey on foot?

2. Refer to the expedition proposed in question 1. Once you have settled on a particular area to investigate intensively, what types of experts will you include on your team for the initial survey? Let's assume that your team is very lucky (as well as skilled), and you discover a hominid fossil in the first year of exploration. How will you alter your research strategy for you second season, and which further experts will you include in the field (as well as in laboratory phases of the work)?

3. Why is it important to have accurate dates for paleoanthropological localities? Why is it necessary to use more than one kind of dating technique?

4. What do we mean when we say that early hominids displayed *cultural behavior*? What types of behavior do you think this would have included? (Imagine that you have transported yourself back by time machine, and you are sitting in a tree watching a group of hominids at Olduvai Gorge 1.5 m.y.a.)

5. Now put yourself in the same place leading an archaeological excavation. What would be left for you to detect of the cultural behavior you observed in question 4? What happened to the remainder of this behavioral repertoire?

6. What do we mean when we say that human evolution is biocultural? How do paleoanthropologists investigate early hominids using such a biocultural perspective?

7. Devise a scenario to explain why bipedal locomotion first evolved in hominids. First do it as though you were presenting your scenario to classmates. Then redo the scenario in a form to present to a group of professional paleoanthropologists. How will you go about making your scenario more "scientific"?

Suggested Further Reading

Delson, Eric, Ian Tattersall, and John A. Van Couvering. 1999. *Encyclopedia of Human Evolution and Prehistory.* 2nd ed. New York: Garland.

Klein, Richard G. 1999. *The Human Career: Human Biological and Cultural Origins.* 2nd ed. Chicago: University of Chicago Press.

Leakey, Mary. 1984. *Disclosing the Past. An Autobiography.* Garden City, NJ: Doubleday.

Panger, Melissa A., Alison S. Brooks, Brian G. Richmond, and Bernard Wood. 2002. "Older than the Oldowan? Rethinking the Emergence of Hominin Tool Use." *Evolutionary Anthropology* 11:235–242.

Schick, Kathy, and Nicholas Toth. 1993. *Making Stone Tools Speak: Human Evolution and the Dawn of Technology.* New York: Simon and Schuster.

Scientific American. 2003. "New Look at Human Evolution." *Scientific American,* Special Edition 13(2).

Tattersall, Ian, and Jeffrey H. Schwartz. 2001. *Extinct Humans.* Boulder, CO: Westview Press.

Online Anthropology Resource Center

Go to the Anthropology Resource Center at **http://www.anthropology.wadsworth.com** for a wealth of online resources, including a companion website for your text that provides study aids such as self-quizzes for each chapter and a practice final exam, as well as links to anthropology websites and information on the latest theories and discoveries in the field. Also, check out InfoTrac College Edition®, your online library that offers full-length articles from thousands of scholarly and popular publications. Just click on the InfoTrac button at the companion website and use the passcode that came with your book.

The Piltdown Caper: Who Dunnit?

When first announced to the world in 1912, *Eoanthropus dawsoni* (Dawson's Dawn Man) created an anthropological sensation. Found during 1911 in Sussex in the south of England by Charles Dawson, a lawyer and amateur geologist, this "fossil" was to bewilder two generations of anthropologists. "Piltdown man," as he popularly came to be called, was composed of a fragmented skull and parts of a lower jaw. The enigma of the fossil from the very beginning was the combination of a large *sapiens*-like partial skull with an apelike lower jaw.

Most tantalizing of all, Piltdown was apparently extremely ancient, associated with long extinct fauna, such as mastodon, hippo, and rhino, all suggesting a date of early Pleistocene. A puzzling feature was the presence of these early fossils mixed in with clearly late Pleistocene fauna. The prevailing consensus, however, was that Piltdown was indeed ancient, "the earliest known representative of man in western Europe."

Despite its seeming incongruities, Piltdown was eagerly accepted by British scientists, including A. Keith, G. Elliot Smith, and A. Smith Woodward (all later knighted). What made the fossil such a delectable treat was that it confirmed just what had been expected, a combination of *modern* ape and *modern* human characteristics—a true "missing link." We, of course, know that no ancestral fossil form is a 50-50 compromise between modern ones, but represents its own unique adaptation. Besides inciting enthusiasm for a missing link, the fossil also represented a "true man" as opposed to the obviously primitive beasts (Java "man," Neandertals) found elsewhere. Such a fervently biased desire to find an "ancient modern" in the human lineage has obscured evolutionary studies for decades and still causes confusion in some circles.

While generally accepted in England, experts in France, Germany, and the United States felt uneasy about Piltdown. Many critics, however, were silenced when a second fragmentary find was announced in 1917 (actually found in 1915) in an area 2 miles away from the original site. The matter stood in limbo for years, with some scientists as enthusiastic supporters of the Piltdown man and others remaining doubters. The uneasiness continued to fester as more hominid material accumulated in Java, China, and (particularly in regard to australopithecines) South Africa. None of these hominids showed the peculiar combination of a human cranium with an apelike jaw seen in Piltdown, but actually indicated the reverse pattern.

The final proof of the true nature of the Dawn Man came in the early 1950s, when British scientists began an intensive reexamination of the Piltdown material. In particular, fluorine analysis performed by Kenneth Oakley showed both the skull and jaw to be relatively recent. Later, more extensive tests showed the jaw to be younger than the skull and *very* recent in date. Now a much more critical eye was turned to all the material. The teeth, looking initially as though they had been worn down flat in the typical hominid fashion, were apparently ape teeth filed down deliberately to give that impression. The mixed bag of fauna had apparently been acquired from all manner of places (a fossil elephant came from Tunisia in North Africa), and the fossils had been chemically stained so that they were all the same color. Finally, some "tools" found at Piltdown had also met the hand of a forger, for the bone implements showed modifications that apparently could have been made only by a metal knife.

The "fossil" itself had probably been purchased from local dealers. The skull probably came from a moderately ancient grave (a few thousand years old), and the jaw was a specially broken, filed, and stained mandible of a fairly recently deceased adolescent orangutan! The evidence was indisputable: a deliberate hoax. But who did it?

Just about everyone connected with the "crime" has at one time or another been implicated, beginning with Piltdown's discoverer, Charles Dawson. Yet Dawson was an amateur and thus may have lacked the expertise to carry out the admittedly crafty job of anatomical modification.

In addition, at various times, suspicions have been cast toward neuroanatomist Sir Grafton Elliot Smith, geologist W. J. Sollas, anatomist Sir Arthur Keith, and French philosopher and archaeologist Father Pierre Teilhard de Chardin. Even the legendary mystery writer and physician, Sir Arthur Conan Doyle (creator of Sherlock Holmes), was at one time suspected (Winslow and Meyer, 1983).

An unsolved mystery is always an irresistible temptation; so the Piltdown "affair" has remained a challenge to several generations of amateur sleuths (especially those otherwise employed as academics). But it seemed that there was little hope of solving the mystery, as the forgery had been perpetrated 90 years ago (and its demonstration as a hoax announced 50 years ago). Without some new clues, the case seemed unsolvable and the trail stone cold.

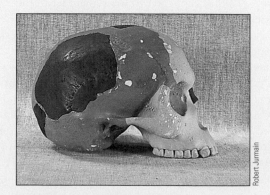

FIGURE 1 The Piltdown skull.

Enter, however, Professor Brian Gardinier of King's College, London, and a startling piece of new evidence. First, the evidence: While cleaning the attic at London's Natural History Museum, workers came across a trunk with the initials of Martin Hinton, a curator of zoology at the museum at the time of the fraud. Contained within the trunk were several pieces of artificially carved and chemically stained fossil bones. The trunk was found in the mid-1970s, but its contents required meticulous analysis and corroboration. Here is where Professor Gardinier comes in. His own investigations had led him to circumstantial evidence implicating Hinton. The contents of the trunk, however, proved to be the final conclusive evidence—as the fossils had been deliberately modified employing exactly the same combination of chemicals as that used on the Piltdown material (it seems that the pieces in the trunk were used in "trial runs" by the forger—Hinton—to practice his technique). Hinton's motives are now difficult to establish, but there is some reason to believe he had a grudge against Smith Woodward, who had been his supervisor at the museum. If, indeed, the goal was to embarrass Smith Woodward, Hinton did succeed spectacularly—since Smith Woodward spent most of his professional career (he died in 1944) in a spirited defense of the significance and validity of the Piltdown find.

After years of study, Professor Gardinier was prepared to announce his findings—which he did in 1996 to much fanfare and media attention. Has the mystery finally been solved? Since the riddle has survived for nine decades, it is difficult now for some to abandon the hunt. There are still a great number of sleuths out there yearning to keep the mystery alive!

Critical Thinking Questions

1. Why do you think hoaxes are occasionally perpetrated in science?
2. Why are such hoaxes inevitably discovered, even if it is years later?
3. More importantly, *how* are such further discoveries made?
4. If you had suspicions regarding the authenticity of a scientific study, how would you check it?

Sources

Gee, Henry. 1996. "Box of Bones 'Clinches' Identity of Piltdown Palaeontology Hoaxer." *Nature* 381: 261–262.

Spencer, Frank. 1990. *Piltdown: A Scientific Forgery.* New York: Oxford University Press.

Weiner, J. W. 1955. *The Piltdown Forgery.* London: Oxford University Press.

Winslow, John Hathaway, and Alfred Meyer. 1983. "The Perpetrator at Piltdown." *Science* '83 (September): 33–43.

10 Hominid Origins in Africa

Taung child's cranium held by South African paleo-anthropologist Phillip Tobias

Robert Jurmain

Key Questions

Who are the oldest members of the human family, and how do these early hominids compare with modern humans? With modern apes? How do they fit within a biological continuum?

Introduction

Our species today dominates our planet, as we use our brains and cultural inventions to invade every corner of the earth. Yet, 5 million years ago, our ancestors were little more than bipedal apes, confined to a few regions in Africa. What were these creatures like? When and how did they begin their evolutionary journey?

In Chapter 9, we discussed the techniques paleoanthropologists use to locate and excavate sites as well as the multidisciplinary approaches used to interpret discoveries. In this chapter, we turn first to the physical evidence of earlier primates and then to the hominid fossils themselves. The earliest fossils identifiable as hominids are all from Africa. During the early Pliocene (by 4 m.y.a.), the fossil discoveries become fairly abundant and are considered by paleoanthropologists as unambiguously members of the hominid family. Indeed, the fossil evidence becomes more complete over the next several million years, encompassing the Pliocene and the first half of the Pleistocene epochs. Together, this time period is usually referred to as the **Plio-Pleistocene**.

Hominids, of course, evolved from earlier primates (dating from the Eocene to late Miocene), and we will briefly review this prehominid fossil record to provide a better context to understand the subsequent evolution of the human family. From new discoveries, the earliest hominids are now thought to date as far back as the end of the Miocene (7–5 m.y.a.). This fossil material is extremely exciting, extending, as it does, the evidence of the human family back 2 million years into prehistory. Moreover, these discoveries have all been made very recently—just in the last five years. As a result, detailed evaluations are still in process, and conclusions must remain tentative.

One thing is certain, however. The earliest members of the human family were confined to Africa. Only much later do their descendants disperse from the African continent to other areas of the Old World (this "out of Africa" saga will be the topic of the next chapter).

See the following sections of the CD-ROM for topics covered in this chapter: Virtual Lab 7, sections I and II; Virtual Lab 8, section I; Virtual Labs 9 and 10; Virtual Lab 12, section I.

Plio-Pleistocene Pertaining to the Pliocene and first half of the Pleistocene, a time range of 5–1 m.y.a. For this time period, numerous fossil hominids have been found in Africa.

Early Primate Evolution

Long before bipedal hominids first evolved in Africa, more primitive primates had diverged from even more distant mammalian ancestors. The roots of the primate order go back to the beginnings of the placental mammal radiation circa 65 m.y.a. Thus, the earliest primates were diverging from quite early primitive placental mammals. We have seen (in Chapter 6) that strictly defining living primates using clear-cut derived features is not an easy task. The further back we go in the fossil record, the more primitive and, in many cases, the more generalized the fossil primates become. Such a situation makes classifying them all the more difficult.

In fact, we only have scarce traces of the earliest primates. Some anthropologists have suggested that recently discovered bits and pieces from North Africa *may* be those of a very small primitive primate. But until more evidence is found, we will just have to wait and see.

See Virtual lab 7, section III, for a detailed discussion of early primate evolution.

Fortunately, a vast number of fossil primates from the Eocene (55–34 m.y.a.) have been discovered and now total more than 200 recognized species (see Fig. 5–7, p. 122, for a geological chart). Unlike the available Paleocene forms, those from the Eocene display distinctive primate features. Indeed, primatologist Elwyn Simons (1972, p. 124) called them "the first primates of modern aspect." These animals have been found primarily in sites in North America and Europe (which were then still connected). It is important to recall that the landmasses that connect continents, as well as the water boundaries that separate them, have obvious impact on the geographical distribution of such terrestrially bound animals as primates (see p. 123).

Some interesting late Eocene forms have also been found in Asia, which was joined to Europe by the end of the Eocene epoch. Looking at the whole array of Eocene primates, it is certain that they were (1) primates, (2) widely distributed, and (3) mostly extinct by the end of the Eocene. What is less certain is how any of them might be related to the living primates. Some of these forms are probably ancestors of the *prosimians*—the lemurs and lorises.* Others are probably related to the tarsier. New evidence of Eocene *anthropoid* origins has also recently been discovered in several sites from North Africa, the Persian Gulf, and China. These newly discovered fossils demonstrate that anthropoid origins were well established by 35 m.y.a.

Some new discoveries of very small primates from China are particularly interesting. Dating from the early Eocene (55–45 m.y.a.), some of these Chinese fossils are among the earliest definite primates yet known. They show three particularly interesting and somewhat surprising features. First, because of certain characteristics such as forward rotation of the eyes, they are thought to be on the evolutionary lineage leading to tarsiers and anthropoids (i.e., haplorhines; see p. 150) and thus already distinct from the lemur-loris lineage (i.e., strepsirhines). Second, a newly discovered cranium shows small eye sockets, suggesting early primates may have been diurnal (Ni et al., 2004). (Note: it had previously been assumed the earliest primates were nocturnal.) And, last, these ancient Chinese haplorhine primates were all apparently extremely small, weighing less than one ounce (Gebo et al., 2000).

The Oligocene (34–23 m.y.a.) has yielded numerous additional fossil remains of several different species of early anthropoids. Most of these forms are *Old World anthropoids,* all discovered at a single locality in Egypt, the Fayum (Fig. 10–1). In addition, from North and South America, there are a few known bits that relate only to the ancestry of New World monkeys. By the early Oligocene, continental drift had separated the New World (i.e., the Americas) from the Old World (Africa and Eurasia). Some of the earliest Fayum forms, nevertheless, *may* potentially be close to the ancestry of both Old and New World anthropoids. It has been suggested that late in the Eocene or very early in the Oligocene, the first anthropoids (primitive "monkeys") arose in Africa and later reached South America by "rafting" over the water separation on drifting chunks of vegetation. What we call "monkey," then, may have a common Old World origin, but the ancestry of New and Old World varieties remains separate after about 35 m.y.a. The closest evolutionary affinities humans have after this time are with other Old World anthropoids, that is, with Old World monkeys and apes.

The possible roots of anthropoid evolution are illustrated by different forms from the Fayum; one is the genus *Apidium*. Well known at the Fayum, *Apidium*

FIGURE 10–1 Location of the Fayum, an Oligocene primate site in Egypt.

---

*In strict classification terms, especially from a cladistic point of view, lemurs and lorises should be referred to as strepsirhines.

TABLE 10–1 Inferred General Paleobiological Aspects of Oligocene Primates

	WEIGHT RANGE	SUBSTRATUM	LOCOMOTION	DIET
Apidium	750–1,600 g (2–3 lb)	Arboreal	Quadruped	Fruit, seeds
Aegyptopithecus	6,700 g (15 lb)	Arboreal	Quadruped	Fruit, some leaves?

Source: After Fleagle, 1999.

is represented by several dozen jaws or partial dentitions and more than 100 specimens from the limb and trunk skeleton. Because of its primitive dental arrangement, some paleontologists have suggested that *Apidium* may lie near or even before the evolutionary divergence of Old and New World anthropoids. As so much fossil material of teeth and limb bones of *Apidium* has been found, some informed speculation regarding diet and locomotor behavior is possible. It is thought that this small, squirrel-sized primate ate mostly fruits and some seeds and was most likely an arboreal quadruped, adept at leaping and springing (Table 10–1).

The other genus of importance from the Fayum is *Aegyptopithecus*. This genus, also well known, is represented by several well-preserved crania and abundant jaws and teeth. The largest of the Fayum anthropoids, *Aegyptopithecus* is roughly the size of a modern howler monkey (13 to 20 pounds) (Fleagle, 1983) and is thought to have been a short-limbed, slow-moving arboreal quadruped (see Table 10–1). *Aegyptopithecus* is important because, better than any other known form, it bridges the gap between the Eocene fossils and the succeeding Miocene hominoids.

Nevertheless, *Aegyptopithecus* is a very primitive Old World anthropoid, with a small brain and long snout and not showing any derived features of either Old World monkeys or hominoids. Thus, it may be close to the ancestry of *both* major groups of living Old World anthropoids. Found in geological beds dating to 35–33 m.y.a., *Aegyptopithecus* further suggests that the crucial evolutionary divergence of hominoids from other Old World anthropoids occurred *after* this time (Fig. 10–2).

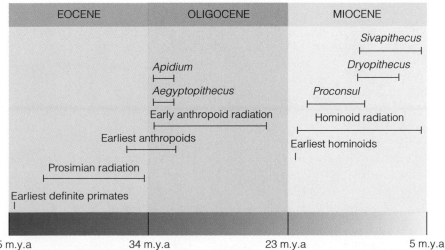

FIGURE 10–2 Major events in early primate evolution.

See Virtual Lab 7 glossary, for a phylogeny and pronunciation guide of primate fossils.

Miocene Fossil Hominoids

During the approximately 18 million years of the Miocene (23–5 m.y.a.), a great deal of evolutionary activity took place. In Africa, Asia, and Europe, a diverse and highly successful group of hominoids emerged (Fig. 10–3). Indeed, there were many more forms of hominoids from the Miocene than are found today (now represented by the highly restricted groups of apes and one species of humans). In fact, the Miocene could be called "the golden age of hominoids." Many thousands of fossils have been found from dozens of sites scattered in East Africa, southwest Africa, southwest Asia, into western and southern Europe, and extending into southern Asia and China.

During the Miocene, significant transformations relating to climate and repositioning of landmasses took place. By 23 m.y.a., *major* continental locations approximated those of today (except that North and South America were separate). Nevertheless, the movements of South America and Australia further away from Antarctica significantly altered ocean currents. Likewise, the continued movement of the South Asian plate into Asia produced the Himalayan Plateau. Both of these paleogeographical modifications had significant impact on the climate, and the early Miocene was considerably warmer than the preceding Oligocene. Moreover, by 16 m.y.a., the Arabian Plate (which had been separate) "docked" with northeastern Africa. As a result, migrations of animals from Africa directly into southwest Asia (and in the other direction as well) became possible. Among the earliest transcontinental migrants (soon after 16 m.y.a.) were African hominoids who colonized Asia and later Europe.

A problem arises in any attempt to simplify the complex evolutionary situation regarding Miocene hominoids. For example, for many years paleontologists tended to think of these fossil forms as either "apelike" or "humanlike" and used modern examples as models. But as we have just noted, very few hominoids remain. Therefore, we should not hastily generalize from the living forms to the much more diverse fossil forms; otherwise, we obscure the evolutionary uniqueness of these animals. In addition, we should not expect all fossil forms to be directly or even particularly closely related to living species. Indeed, we should expect the opposite; that is, most lines vanish without descendants.

Over the last three decades, the Miocene hominoid assemblage has been interpreted and reinterpreted. As more fossils are found, the evolutionary picture grows more complicated. The vast array of fossil forms has not yet been

See Virtual lab 7, section III, for a discussion of Miocene hominoid fossils.

FIGURE 10–3 Miocene hominoid distribution, from fossils thus far discovered.

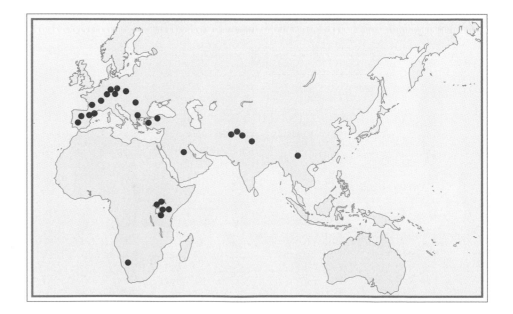

completely studied, so conclusions remain tenuous. Given this uncertainty, it is probably best, for the present, to group Miocene hominoids geographically:

1. *African forms (23–14 m.y.a.)*   Known especially from western Kenya, these include quite generalized, and in many ways primitive, hominoids. The best-known genus is *Proconsul* (Fig. 10–4). In addition to the well-known East African early Miocene hominoids, a more recent discovery (in 1992) from Namibia has further extended by over 1,800 miles the known range of African Miocene hominoids (Conroy et al., 1992).

2. *European forms (16–11 m.y.a.)*   Known from widely scattered localities in France, Spain, Italy, Greece, Austria, Germany, and Hungary, most of these forms are quite derived. However, this is a varied and not well understood group. The best known of the forms are placed in the genus *Dryopithecus;* the Hungarian and Greek fossils are usually assigned to other genera. The Greek fossils are called *Ouranopithecus,* and remains date to sites 9 to 10 million years of age. Evolutionary relationships are uncertain, but several researchers have suggested a link with the African ape/hominid group. New discoveries in 1999 and 2003 from sites in Germany and Turkey of yet another hominoid genus (called *Griphopithecus*) have helped bolster this hypothesis (Begun, 2003).

3. *Asian forms (16–7 m.y.a.)*   The largest and most varied group from the Miocene fossil hominoid assemblage, geographically dispersed from Turkey through India/Pakistan and east to the highly prolific site Lufeng, in southern China, most of these forms are *highly* derived. The best-known genus is *Sivapithecus* (known from Turkey and Pakistan). The Lufeng material (now totaling more than 1,000 specimens) is usually placed in a separate genus from *Sivapithecus* (and is referred to as *Lufengpithecus*).

Four general points are certain concerning Miocene hominoid fossils: They are widespread geographically; they are numerous; they span a considerable portion of the Miocene, with *known* remains dated between 23 and 6 m.y.a.; and at present, they are poorly understood. However, we can reasonably draw the following conclusions:

1. These are hominoids—more closely related to the ape-human lineage than to Old World monkeys.
2. They are mostly **large-bodied hominoids,** that is, more akin to the lineages of orangutans, gorillas, chimpanzees, and humans than to smaller-bodied apes (i.e., gibbons).
3. Most of the Miocene forms thus far discovered are so derived that they are probably not ancestral to *any* living form.
4. One lineage that appears well established relates to *Sivapithecus* from Turkey and Pakistan. This form shows some highly derived facial features similar to the modern orangutan, suggesting a fairly close evolutionary link (Fig. 10–5).

Robert Jurmain

FIGURE 10–4 *Proconsul africanus* skull (from early Miocene deposits on Rusinga Island, Kenya).

large-bodied hominoids Those hominoids including the great apes (orangutans, chimpanzees, gorillas) and hominids, as well as all ancestral forms back to the time of divergence from small-bodied hominoids (i.e., the gibbon lineage).

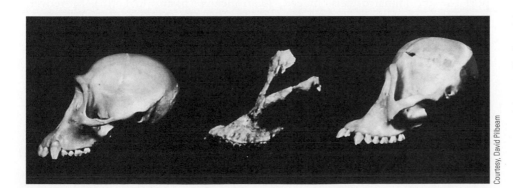

Courtesy, David Pilbeam

FIGURE 10–5 Comparison of *Sivapithecus* cranium (center) with that of modern chimpanzee (left) and orangutan (right). The *Sivapithecus* fossil is specimen GSP 15000, from the Potwar Plateau, Pakistan, c. 8 m.y.a.

hominids Colloquial term for members of the family Hominidae, which includes all bipedal hominoids back to the divergence from African great apes.

morphological Pertaining to the form and structure of organisms.

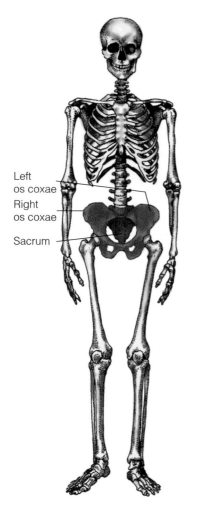

See Virtual Lab 9, section I, for a discussion of the evolution of bipedalism.

Left os coxae

Right os coxae

Sacrum

FIGURE 10–6 The human pelvis: various elements shown on a modern skeleton.

5. Evidence of *definite* **hominids** from the Miocene has not yet been absolutely confirmed. However, exciting new (and not fully studied) finds from Kenya, Ethiopia, and Chad (the latter dating as far back as 7 m.y.a.) strongly suggest that hominids diverged sometime in the latter Miocene (see pp. 267–269 for further discussion). The most fundamental feature of the early hominids is the adaptation to bipedal locomotion.

The Bipedal Adaptation

In our overview in Chapter 9 of behavioral reconstructions of early hominids, we highlighted several hypotheses that attempt to explain *why* bipedal locomotion first evolved in the hominids. Here we turn to the specific anatomical (i.e., **morphological**) evidence that shows us when, where, and how hominid bipedal locomotion evolved.

In our discussion of primate anatomical trends in Chapter 6, we noted that there is a general tendency in all primates for erect body posture and some bipedalism. However, of all living primates, efficient bipedalism as the primary form of locomotion is seen *only* in hominids. Functionally, the human mode of locomotion is most clearly shown in our striding gait, where weight is alternately placed on a single fully extended hind limb. This specialized form of locomotion has developed to a point where energy levels are used to near peak efficiency. Such is not the case in nonhuman primates, who move bipedally with hips and knees bent and maintain balance in a clumsy and inefficient manner.

Our mode of locomotion is indeed extraordinary, involving as it does an activity in which "the body, step by step, teeters on the edge of catastrophe" (Napier, 1967, p. 56). The problem is to maintain balance on the "stance" leg while the "swing" leg is off the ground. In fact, during normal walking, both feet are simultaneously on the ground only about 25 percent of the time, and as speed of locomotion increases, this figure becomes even smaller.

To maintain a stable center of balance in this complex form of locomotion, many drastic structural/anatomical alterations in the basic primate quadrupedal pattern are required. The most dramatic changes are seen in the pelvis. The pelvis is composed of three elements: two *ossa coxae* (*sing.,* os coxae) joined at the back to the sacrum (Fig. 10–6). In a quadruped, the ossa coxae are elongated bones positioned along each side of the lower portion of the spine and oriented more or less parallel to it. In hominids, the pelvis is comparatively much shorter and broader and extends around to the side (Fig. 10–7). This configuration helps to stabilize the line of weight transmission, in a bipedal posture, from the lower back to the hip joint (Fig. 10–8).

A number of consequences resulted from the remodeling of the pelvis during early hominid evolution. Broadening the two sides and extending them around to the side and front of the body produced a basin-shaped structure that helps support the abdominal organs (indeed, *pelvis* means "basin" in Latin). Moreover, these alterations repositioned the attachments of several key muscles that act on the hip and leg, changing their mechanical function. Probably the most important of these altered relationships is that involving the *gluteus maximus,* the largest muscle in the body, which in humans forms the bulk of the buttocks. In quadrupeds, the gluteus maximus is positioned to the side of the hip and functions to pull the thigh to the side, away from the body. But in humans, this muscle acts, along with the hamstrings, to extend the thigh, pulling it to the rear during walking and running (Fig 10–9). Indeed, the gluteus maximus is a powerful extensor of the thigh and provides additional force, particularly during running and climbing.

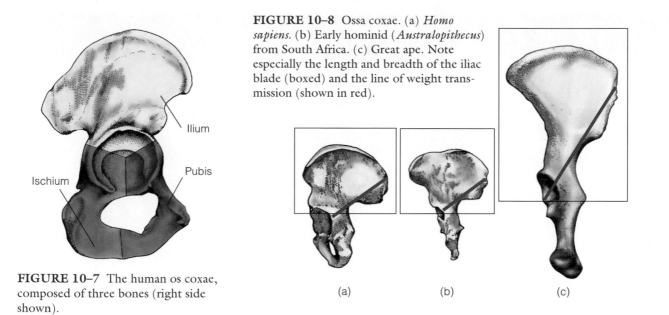

FIGURE 10–8 Ossa coxae. (a) *Homo sapiens.* (b) Early hominid (*Australopithecus*) from South Africa. (c) Great ape. Note especially the length and breadth of the iliac blade (boxed) and the line of weight transmission (shown in red).

(a)   (b)   (c)

FIGURE 10–7 The human os coxae, composed of three bones (right side shown).

Ilium
Ischium
Pubis

Modifications also occurred in other parts of the skeleton as a result of the shift to bipedalism. The most significant of these are summarized in A Closer Look on page 264 and include (1) repositioning of the **foramen magnum,** the opening at the base of the skull through which the spinal cord emerges; (2) the addition of spinal curves that facilitate the transmission of the weight of the upper body to the hips in an upright posture; (3) shortening and broadening of the pelvis and the stabilization of weight transmission (discussed earlier); (4) lengthening of the hind limb, thus increasing stride length; (5) angling of the femur (thighbone) inward to bring the knees and feet closer together under the body; and (6) several structural changes in the foot, including the development of a longitudinal arch and realignment of the big toe in parallel with the other toes (i.e., it was no longer divergent).

foramen magnum The opening at the base of the skull through which the spinal cord passes as it enters the body to descend through the vertebral column. In quadrupeds, it is located more to the rear of the skull, while in bipeds, it is located farther beneath the skull.

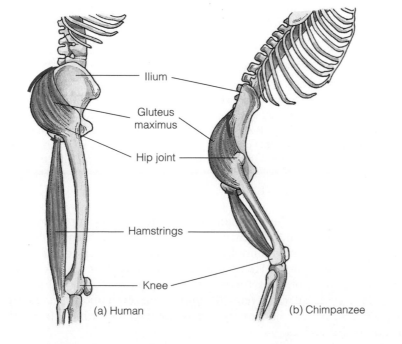

(a) Human   (b) Chimpanzee

Ilium
Gluteus maximus
Hip joint
Hamstrings
Knee

FIGURE 10–9 Comparisons of important muscles that act to extend the hip. Note that the attachment surface (origin, shown in red) of the gluteus maximus in humans (a) is farther in back of the hip joint than in a chimpanzee standing bipedally (b). Conversely, in chimpanzees, the hamstrings are farther in back of the knee.

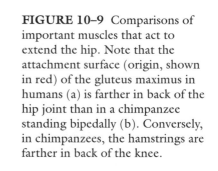

A CLOSER LOOK

Major Features of Bipedal Locomotion

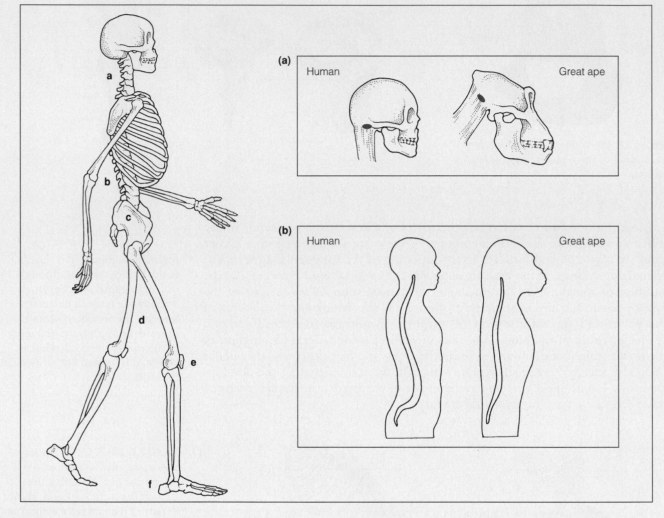

During hominid evolution, several major structural features throughout the body have been reorganized (from that seen in other primates) to facilitate efficient bipedal locomotion. These are illustrated here, beginning with the head and progressing to the foot: (a) The foramen magnum (shown in red) is repositioned farther underneath the skull, so that the head is more or less balanced on the spine (and thus requires less robust neck muscles to hold the head upright). (b) The spine has two distinctive curves—a backward (thoracic) one and a forward (lumbar) one—that keep the trunk (and weight) centered above the pelvis. (c) The pelvis is shaped more in the form of a basin to support internal organs;

As you can appreciate, the evolution of hominid bipedalism required complex anatomical reorganization. For natural selection to produce anatomical change of the magnitude seen in hominids, the benefits of bipedal locomotion must have been significant indeed. We mentioned in Chapter 9 several possible adaptive advantages that bipedal locomotion *may* have conferred upon early hominids. However, these all remain hypotheses (even more accurately, they could be called scenarios), and we lack adequate data with which to test the various proposed alternatives.

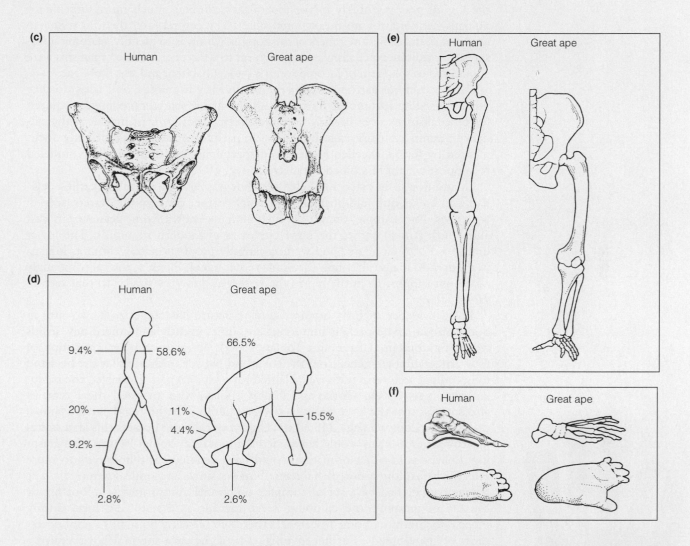

moreover, the ossa coxae (specifically, iliac blades) are shorter and broader, thus stabilizing weight transmission. (d) Lower limbs are elongated, as shown by the proportional lengths of various body segments (e.g., in humans the thigh comprises 20 percent of body height, while in gorillas it comprises only 11 percent). (e) The femur is angled inward, keeping the legs more directly under the body; modified knee anatomy also permits full extension of this joint. (f) The big toe is enlarged and brought in line with the other toes; in addition, a distinctive longitudinal arch forms, helping absorb shock and adding propulsive spring.

Still, given the anatomical alterations that efficient bipedalism necessitated, there must have been some major behavioral stimuli influencing its development. In the interpretation of evolutionary history, biologists are fond of saying that form follows function. In other words, during evolution, organisms do not undergo significant reorganization in structure *unless* these changes (over many generations) assist individuals in some functional capacity (and, in so doing, increase their reproductive success). Such changes did not necessarily occur all at once, but probably evolved over a fairly long period of time. Nevertheless, once behavioral influences initiated certain structural modifications, the process gained momentum and proceeded irreversibly.

We say that hominid bipedalism is *habitual* and *obligate*. By habitual, we mean that hominids, unlike any other primate, move bipedally as their standard and most efficient mode of locomotion. By obligate, we mean that hominids are committed to bipedalism and cannot locomote efficiently in any other manner. For example, the loss of grasping ability in the foot makes climbing much more difficult for humans (although by no means impossible). The central task, then, in trying to understand the earliest members of the hominid family is to identify anatomical features that indicate bipedalism and to interpret to what degree these organisms were committed to this form of locomotion (i.e., was it habitual and was it obligate?).

What structural patterns are observable in early hominids, and what do they imply regarding locomotor function? All the major structural changes required for bipedalism are seen in early hominids from Africa (at least insofar as the evidence permits conclusions to be made). In particular, the pelvis, as clearly documented by several excellently preserved specimens, was dramatically remodeled to support weight in a bipedal stance (see Fig. 10–8b).

In addition, other structural changes shown after 4 m.y.a. in the earliest relatively complete hominid postcranial remains further confirm the pattern seen in the pelvis. For example, the vertebral column (as known from specimens in East and South Africa) shows the same curves as in modern hominids. The lower limbs were also elongated and were apparently proportionately about as long as in modern humans (although the arms were longer). Further, the carrying angle of weight support from the hip to the knee was also very similar to that seen in *Homo sapiens*.

Fossil evidence of early hominid foot structure has come from two sites in South Africa, and especially important are some recently announced new fossils from Sterkfontein (Clarke and Tobias, 1995). These specimens, consisting of four articulating elements from the ankle and big toe, indicate that the heel and longitudinal arch were both well adapted for a bipedal gait. However, the paleoanthropologists (Ron Clarke and Phillip Tobias) who analyzed these remains also suggest that the large toe was *divergent*, unlike the hominid pattern shown in A Closer Look on page 265. If the large toe really did possess this anatomical position, it most likely would have aided the foot in grasping. In turn, this grasping ability (as in other primates) would have enabled early hominids to more effectively exploit arboreal habitats. Finally, since anatomical remodeling is always constrained by a set of complex functional compromises, a foot highly capable of grasping and climbing is *less* capable as a stable platform during bipedal locomotion. Some researchers therefore see early hominids as not necessarily obligate bipeds. Further investigation of the cave site in 1998 revealed a remarkable find, the remains of a nearly complete skeleton belonging to the same individual from which the foot came (see p. 283).

Further evidence for evolutionary changes in the foot skeleton comes from Olduvai Gorge in Tanzania, where a nearly complete hominid foot is preserved (Fig. 10–10), and from Hadar in Ethiopia, where numerous foot elements have been recovered. As in the remains from South Africa, the East African fossils suggest a well-adapted bipedal gait. The arches are developed, but some differences in the ankle also imply that considerable flexibility was possible (again, suggested for continued adaptation to climbing). As we will see, some researchers have recently concluded that many early forms of hominids probably spent considerable time in the trees. Moreover, they may not have been quite as efficient bipeds as has previously been suggested. Nevertheless, to this point, *all* the early hominids that have been identified from Africa are thought by most researchers to have been both habitual and obligate bipeds (notwithstanding the new evidence from South Africa and the earliest traces from central and East Africa, all of which will require further study).

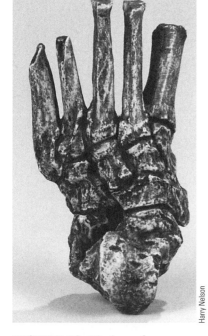

Harry Nelson

FIGURE 10–10 A nearly complete hominid foot (OH 8) from Olduvai Gorge, Tanzania.

Early Hominids from Africa (Pre-*Australopithecus* Finds)

Over the last 80 years, a tremendous number of hominid fossils have been discovered in Africa. The first finds came from South Africa, but by the 1970s, East Africa (particularly along the Rift Valley in Ethiopia, Kenya, and Tanzania) had taken preeminence. This shift in the focus and significance of discovery came about as a result of many factors. The geological circumstances found in East Africa produce a clearer stratigraphic picture and better association of hominids with archaeological artifacts, and equally important, these materials are much more easily datable (using chronometric methods). Moreover, fossils are generally easier to find in East Africa, although it's never easy anywhere to find hominid fossils! Erosion from wind, rain, and gravity expose fossils on the ground surface, where they can simply be picked up—assuming, of course, one knows exactly *where* to look. In South Africa, by contrast, the fossils are embedded in rock matrix, making precise archaeological recovery extraordinarily difficult. Nevertheless, excavations have continued at several South African sites. From this ongoing work, some new and highly productive locales have been explored, and as of this writing, perhaps the most intact early hominid skeleton ever discovered is being excavated at Sterkfontein Cave, just outside Johannesburg.

The saga of new and more intriguing African hominid discoveries is not yet completed—indeed, not even slowed. Just in 2002, perhaps the most remarkable discovery in the last 75 years was announced. What made this discovery (from Chad) so surprising was (1) its location (in central Africa, *not* in either South or East Africa), (2) its age (estimated at close to 7 m.y.a., making it by far the earliest hominid found anywhere), and (3) its physical appearance (quite unexpected and unlike anything discovered previously; more on this presently).

Thus, if we accept the latest discoveries and provisional dating as accurate, hominid origins go back in Africa approximately 7 million years. Hominids, as far as current evidence indicates, stayed in Africa for the next 5 million years, first emigrating to other Old World locales 2 m.y.a. Thus, it appears that for the first 70 percent of hominid history, our family was restricted to Africa.

EARLIEST TRACES

The distinction of being designated "the earliest hominid" is one that draws worldwide media coverage, but it is a notoriously fickle title. When this textbook was first published in 1979, the earliest hominid was dated at between 3 and 4 m.y.a. By the seventh edition (1997), based on some Ethiopian fossils, this had been pushed back to 4.4 m.y.a. By 2000 (based on Kenyan material), the date was further extended to close to 6 m.y.a. And in 2002, the startling find from Chad suggested that the current bearer of the "earliest" title is 7 million years old.

This brief history is not intended to force unsuspecting students to memorize exactly what was found when. Our point is to illustrate how rapidly discoveries have taken place; in just the last decade, the reported span of hominid existence has increased by 60 percent.

Central Africa   The most stunning of these new finds is also the oldest. The fossil, a nearly complete cranium, was discovered in 2001 at a site called Toros-Menalla in northern Chad (Brunet et al., 2002). Provisional dating using faunal correlation (biostratigraphy; see p. 239) suggests a date nearly 7 m.y.a. (Vignaud et al., 2002). Surprisingly, the very early suggested age of this fossil places it at almost 1 million years earlier than *any* of the other proposed early hominids (and close to 3 million years earlier than the oldest well-established hominid discoveries).

See Virtual lab 8, section I, for a discussion of the fossil evidence for some of the very early hominids.

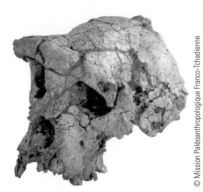

© Mission Paléoanthropologique Franco-Tchadienne

FIGURE 10–11 A nearly complete cranium of *Sahelanthropus* from Chad, dating to 7 m.y.a.

postcranial (*post,* meaning "after") In a quadruped, referring to that portion of the body behind the head; in a biped, referring to all parts of the body *beneath* the head (i.e., the neck down).

The morphology of the fossil is unusual, with a combination of characteristics unlike that found in other early hominids. The braincase is small, estimated at no larger than a modern chimpanzee's (preliminary estimate in the range of 320 to 380 cm^3), and it is massively built, with huge browridges in front, a crest on top, and large muscle attachments in the rear (Fig. 10–11). Yet, combined with these apelike features is a smallish vertical face containing front teeth very unlike an ape's. In fact, the lower face, being more tucked in under the brain vault (and not protruding, as in most other early hominids), is more of a *derived* feature more commonly expressed in much later hominids (especially members of genus *Homo*). Moreover, unlike the dentition seen in apes (and some early hominids), the upper canine is reduced and is worn down from the tip (rather than shearing along its side against the first lower premolar).

In recognition of this unique combination of characteristics, the lead researcher, Michael Brunet (of the University of Poitiers, in France), has placed the Toros-Menalla remains into a new genus and species of hominid, *Sahelanthropus tchadensis* (Sahel being the region of the southern Sahara in North Africa).

These new finds from Chad have forced an immediate and significant reassessment of early hominid evolution. Two cautionary comments, however, are in order. First, the dating is only approximate, based, as it is, on biostratigraphic correlation with sites in Kenya (1,500 miles to the east). The faunal sequences, nevertheless, seem to be clearly bracketed by two very well-dated sequences in Kenya. Second, and perhaps more serious, is the hominid status of the Chad fossil. Given the facial structure and dentition, it is difficult to see how *Sahelanthropus* could be anything but a hominid. However, some researchers (Wolpoff et al., 2002) have raised questions regarding the evolutionary interpretation of *Sahelanthropus*, suggesting that this fossil may represent an ape rather than a hominid. As we have previously said, the best-defining anatomical characteristics of hominids relate to bipedal locomotion. Unfortunately, no **postcranial** elements have been recovered from Chad—at least not yet. Consequently, we do not yet know the locomotor behavior of *Sahelanthropus*, and this raises even more fundamental questions: What if further finds show this form not to be bipedal? Should we still consider it a hominid? What, then, are the defining characteristics of our family?

East Africa   Two areas in East Africa, one in central Kenya and the other from the Middle Awash area of northeastern Ethiopia, have also quite recently yielded very early hominid remains. The oldest of these finds come from sites in the Tugen Hills of central Kenya, near Lake Baringo (Pickford and Senut, 2001; Senut et al., 2001). Good radiometric determinations place the age of the remains at close to 6 m.y.a.

The fossil remains are a mixed assortment, with a couple of pieces of lower jaw and several isolated teeth. Most intriguing, however, are a few limb bone pieces, including two excellently preserved femora. From these latter fossils especially, French paleontologist Brigitte Senut (of the Museum of Natural History in Paris) and her colleagues are convinced that these 6-million-year-old primates walked *bipedally* and are thus hominids. However, there are also some unusual aspects of the teeth, mostly suggesting a primitive, apelike morphology. This curious combination of features has led the French scientists to assign the remains to a completely new genus and species (*Orrorin tugenensis*).

Since the Tugen Hills fossils were first discovered in 2000, the popular press has dubbed this form "Millennium Man." The initial reports, published early in 2001, were rather sketchy and did not initially receive much support from other scholars. To establish satisfactorily whether "Millennium Man" is indeed the earliest hominid yet found will require further study. Nevertheless, the well-preserved lower limb bones should help considerably in determining clearly whether (or not) these animals moved about bipedally.

Coming from a few hundred miles north of the Tugen Hills, in the Middle Awash region of Ethiopia, another group of quite early fossils was also first described in 2001. Yohannes Haile-Selassie, an anthropology graduate student at the University of California, Berkeley, discovered the first remains in 1997, with further discoveries extending to 2001 and 2002 (Haile-Selassie, 2001; Haile-Selassie et al., 2004). Well-controlled radiometric dating determinations place the fossils in the late Miocene (at 5.8–5.2 m.y.a.), just a little later than the Tugen Hills finds. These latter fossil remains are quite fragmentary, including mostly teeth, a jaw fragment, and just a few pieces of the limb skeleton, the latter including one toe bone, a phalanx from the middle of the foot (see Appendix A, Fig. A–8). From suggestive clues seen in this toe bone, Haile-Selassie concludes that this primate was a well-adapted *biped* (once again, the best supporting evidence of hominid status).

There are other, more complete remains from the Middle Awash area discovered at the Aramis site (discussed shortly), originating a little later in time. These remains have been assigned to the genus *Ardipithecus,* and Haile-Selassie and colleagues (Haile-Selassie et al., 2004) have determined that the earlier fossils from this same region should be placed in this same genus (but a different species) from the later fossils. Moreover, these same researchers caution that the late Miocene hominids discussed here (from Chad, Kenya, and Ethiopia) are all quite similar and could thus belong to the same genus. Clearly, these exciting, but still enigmatic, hominids will require much more study before their relationships with each other as well as their potential relationship with later hominids can be worked out.

Aramis (air´-ah-miss)

Other Early Discoveries   In addition to the reasonably complete remains from the Tugen Hills and the Middle Awash, there are several scattered finds of what many researchers think may be other very early hominids. In the time range 5–4 m.y.a., there are three additional localities (two from central Kenya and one from Ethiopia). However, none of this further material is particularly informative (or diagnostic), since only a single (fragmentary) specimen has been recovered from each locality.

ARDIPITHECUS FROM ARAMIS (ETHIOPIA)

The Middle Awash sites are in one of the most exciting areas for future research in East Africa, the Afar Triangle of northeastern Ethiopia, where the Red Sea, Rift Valley, and Gulf of Aden all intersect. From this region have come many of the most important recent discoveries bearing on human origins. Several areas have yielded fossil remains in recent decades, and many potentially very rich sites are currently being explored. One of these sites quite recently discovered, located in the Middle Awash (along the banks of the Awash River), is called **Aramis.** Initial radiometric dating of the sediments places the hominid remains at 4.4 m.y.a., making this the earliest substantial *collection* of hominids yet discovered.

Fossil remains from Aramis were excavated between 1992 and 1995 and include up to 50 different individuals (Wolpoff, 1999). This crucial and quite large fossil assortment includes several dental specimens as well as an upper arm bone (humerus) and some fragmentary cranial remains. Most exciting of all, in 1995, 40 percent of a skeleton was discovered; however, the bones are all encased in limestone matrix, thus requiring a long and tedious process to remove the fossils intact from the cementlike material surrounding them. In fact, as of this writing, the Aramis remains (including the skeleton) have not yet been fully scientifically described. Nevertheless, details from initial reports are highly suggestive that these remains are, in fact, very early hominids.

First of all, in an Aramis partial cranium, the *foramen magnum* is positioned farther forward in the base of the skull than is the case in quadrupeds (Fig. 10–12). Second, features of the humerus also differ from those seen in quadrupeds, indicating that the Aramis humerus did not function in locomotion

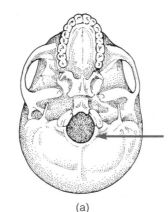

(a)

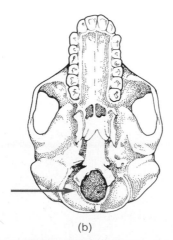

(b)

FIGURE 10–12 Position of the foramen magnum in (a) a human and (b) a chimpanzee. Note the more forward position in the human cranium.

to support weight (i.e., the upper limbs were free). From these two features, the provisional interpretation by Tim White, of the University of California, Berkeley, and his colleagues was that the Aramis individuals were *bipedal*. Moreover, initial interpretation of the partial skeleton (while not yet fully cleaned and reported) also suggests obligate bipedalism (Wolpoff, 1999).

Nevertheless, these were clearly quite primitive hominids, displaying an array of characteristics quite distinct from other members of our family. These primitive characteristics include flattening of the cranial base and relatively thin enamel caps on the molar teeth. From measurements of the humerus head, Wolpoff (1999) estimates a body weight of 42 kg (93 pounds); if this humerus comes from a male individual, this weight estimate is very similar to that hypothesized for other Plio-Pleistocene hominids (see Table 10–2, p. 286).

Thus, current conclusions (which will be either unambiguously confirmed or falsified as the skeleton is fully cleaned and studied) interpret the Aramis remains as among the earliest hominids yet known. These primitive hominids from Aramis were apparently bipedal, although not necessarily in the same way that later hominids were.

As a result of their analyses, Tim White and colleagues have concluded (White et al., 1995) that the fossil hominids from Aramis are so primitive and so different from other early hominids that they should be assigned to a new genus (and, necessarily, a new species as well): *Ardipithecus ramidus*. Most especially, the thin enamel caps on the molars are in dramatic contrast to all other confirmed early hominids, who show quite thick enamel caps. These other early hominid forms (all somewhat later than *Ardipithecus*) are placed in the genus **Australopithecus**. Moreover, White and his associates have further suggested that as the earliest and most primitive hominid yet discovered, *Ardipithecus* may possibly be the root species for all later hominids.

This view does not take into account the recently discovered fossils from Toros-Menalla and the Tugen Hills, which are each provisionally assigned to other early hominid genera (*Sahelanthropus* and *Orrorin*, respectively). However, this interpretation does encompass the earlier remains from the Middle Awash—which, for the moment, are also included within *Ardipithecus*.

Another intriguing aspect of all these late Miocene/early Pliocene locales (i.e., Tugen Hills, early Middle Awash sites, and Aramis) relates to the ancient environments associated with the suggested earliest of hominids. Rather than the more open grassland savanna habitats so characteristic of most later hominid sites, the environments at these early locales are more heavily forested. The oldest of the hominid localities, Toros-Menalla, shows (from initial analysis) a mosaic of environments (Vignaud et al., 2002). The hominids almost certainly died near a lakeshore, but apparently forest and grassland habitats were also nearby. The general ecological association of the very early hominids with forested habitats is not surprising. After all, hominids almost certainly diverged from a line of forest-living hominoids—and likely did so not long before these late Miocene hominids came on the scene.

Australopithecus An early hominid genus, known from the Plio-Pleistocene of Africa, characterized by bipedal locomotion, a relatively small brain, and large back teeth.

AT A GLANCE	In Summary: Key Very Early Fossil Hominid Discoveries (pre-*Australopithecus*; (prior to 4 m.y.a.)		
	Site	Dates (m.y.a.)	Hominids
East Africa	Middle Awash (Ethiopia; five localities)	5.8–5.2	*Ardipithecus*
	Aramis (Ethiopia)	4.4	*Ardipithecus ramidus*
	Tugen Hills	~6.0	*Orrorin tugenensis*
Central Africa	Toros-Menalla	~7.0	*Sahelanthropus tchadenis*

Australopithecus from East Africa

Several sites in Ethiopia, Kenya, and Tanzania have yielded remains of somewhat later hominids than the *Ardipithecus* remains from Aramis. Dating from 4.2 m.y.a. to approximately 1.4 m.y.a., most of these later East African fossils are included in the genus *Australopithecus*.* Note, however, that in the later half of this time span, some other specimens are placed by many paleoanthropologists in the genus *Homo*.

The earliest members of *Australopithecus* found to date come from two sites near Lake Turkana in northern Kenya (Allia Bay and Kanapoi). Like the other sites we have been reviewing, these localities have only recently been fully explored, with the majority of discoveries coming during 1994 and 1995 (Leakey et al., 1995). Not as many specimens have been found at these two sites as at Aramis, but from what has been discovered, Meave Leakey and her colleagues have detected some interesting patterns. First, as with the Aramis specimens, limb bones indicate that these individuals were bipedal. Moreover, the molar teeth have thick enamel, like other members of *Australopithecus*.

However, there are also some primitive characteristics in these still quite early hominid specimens (dated 4.2–3.9 m.y.a.). For example, Leakey and colleagues point to such primitive features as a large canine, a **sectorial** lower first premolar (Fig. 10–13), and a small opening for the ear canal. Since these particular *Australopithecus* individuals have initially been interpreted as more primitive than all the later members of the genus, Meave Leakey and associates have provisionally assigned them to a separate species (*Australopithecus anamensis*). Further study and (with some luck) additional more complete remains will help decide whether such a distinction is warranted.

Slightly later and much more complete remains of *Australopithecus* have come from the sites of Hadar (in Ethiopia) and Laetoli (in Tanzania). Much of this material has been known for some time (since the mid-1970s), and the fossils have been very well studied; indeed, in certain instances, they are quite famous. For example, the Lucy skeleton was discovered at Hadar in 1974, and the Laetoli footprints were first found in 1978.

Literally thousands of footprints have been found at Laetoli, representing more than 20 different kinds of animals (Pliocene elephants, horses, pigs, giraffes, antelope, hyenas, and an abundance of hares). Several hominid footprints have also been found, including a trail more than 75 feet long, made by at least two—and perhaps three—individuals (Leakey and Hay, 1979) (Fig 10–14). Such discoveries of well-preserved hominid footprints are extremely important in furthering our understanding of human evolution. For the first time, we can make *definite* statements regarding the locomotor pattern and stature of early hominids. Analyses of these Pliocene footprints suggests a stature of about 4 feet 9 inches for the larger individual and 4 feet 1 inch for the smaller individual.

Studies of these impression patterns clearly show that the mode of locomotion of these hominids was bipedal (Day and Wickens, 1980). As we have discussed, the development of bipedal

---

*Moreover, some paleoanthropologists place portions of the *Australopithecus* sample into another genus designated *Paranthropus* (see p. 294).

sectorial Adapted for cutting or shearing; among primates, refers to the compressed (side-to-side) first lower premolar, which functions as a shearing surface with the upper canine.

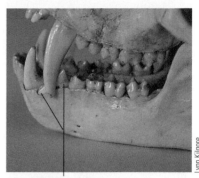

Sectorial lower first premolar

FIGURE 10–13 Left lateral view of the teeth of a male patas monkey. Note how the large upper canine shears against the elongated surface of the *sectorial* lower first premolar.

FIGURE 10–14 Hominid footprint from Laetoli, Tanzania. Note the deep impression of the heel and the large toe (arrow) in line (adducted) with the other toes.

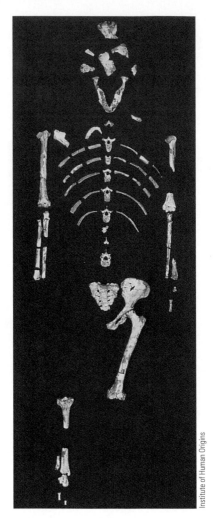

Institute of Human Origins

FIGURE 10–15 "Lucy," a partial hominid skeleton, discovered at Hadar in 1974. This individual is assigned to *Australopithecus afarensis*.

australopithecine
(os-tra-loh-pith´-e-seen) The colloquial name for members of the genus *Australopithecus*. The term was first used as a subfamily designation, but it is now most commonly used informally.

See Virtual lab 8, section I, for a discussion of *Australopithecus afarensis*.

locomotion is the most important defining characteristic of early hominid evolution. Some researchers, however, have concluded that these early hominids were not bipedal in quite the same way that modern humans are. From detailed comparisons with modern humans, estimates of stride length, cadence, and speed of walking have been ascertained, indicating that the Laetoli hominids moved in a slow-moving ("strolling") fashion with a rather short stride (Chateris et al., 1981).

Two extraordinary discoveries at Hadar are most noteworthy. First, there is the Lucy skeleton (Fig. 10–15), found by Don Johanson eroding out of a hillside. This fossil is scientifically designated as Afar Locality (AL) 288-1, but is usually just called Lucy (after the Beatles' song "Lucy in the Sky with Diamonds"). Representing almost 40 percent of a skeleton, this is one of the three most complete individuals from anywhere in the world for the entire period before about 100,000 years ago.*

The second find, a phenomenal discovery, came to light in 1975 at another Hadar locality. Don Johanson and his amazed crew found dozens of hominid bones scattered along a hillside. These bones represented at least 13 individuals, including 4 infants. Possibly members of one social unit, it has been argued that the members of this group died at about the same time, thus representing a "catastrophic" assemblage (White and Johanson, 1989). However, the precise deposition of the site has not been completely explained, so this assertion must be viewed as quite tentative. (In geological time, an "instant" could represent many decades or centuries.) Considerable cultural material has been found in the Hadar area, mostly washed into stream channels, but some stone tools have been reported in context at a site dated at 2.5 m.y.a., potentially making the findings among the oldest cultural evidence yet discovered.

Because the Laetoli area was covered periodically by ashfalls from nearby volcanic eruptions, accurate dating is possible and has provided dates of 3.7–3.5 m.y.a. Dating from the Hadar region has not proved as straightforward; however, more complete dating calibration, using a variety of techniques (see Chapter 9), has determined a range of 3.9–3.0 m.y.a. for the hominid discoveries from this area.

AUSTRALOPITHECUS AFARENSIS FROM LAETOLI AND HADAR

Several hundred specimens, representing a minimum of 60 individuals (and perhaps as many as 100), have been removed from Laetoli and Hadar. At present, these materials represent the largest *well-studied* collection of early hominids. Moreover, it has been suggested that fragmentary specimens from other locales in East Africa are remains of the same species as that found at Laetoli and Hadar. Most anthropologists refer to this species as *Australopithecus afarensis*.

Without question, *A. afarensis* is more primitive than any of the other **australopithecine** fossils from South or East Africa (discussed subsequently), although the recently described materials from Kanapoi and Allia Bay (*Australopithecus anamensis*) are even more primitive yet. By "primitive," we mean that *A. afarensis* is less evolved in any particular direction than are later occurring hominid species. That is, *A. afarensis* shares more primitive features with other early homin*oids* and with living great apes than do later hominids, who display more derived characteristics.

For example, the teeth of *A. afarensis* are quite primitive. The canines are often large, pointed teeth. Moreover, the lower first premolar is semisectorial (i.e., it provides a shearing surface for the upper canine), and the tooth rows are parallel, even converging somewhat toward the back of the mouth (Fig. 10–16).

*The others are a specimen from Sterkfontein in South Africa (see p. 283) and a *H. erectus* skeleton from west of Lake Turkana, Kenya (see p. 316). Also note that the crushed and embedded skeleton from Aramis may be nearly as complete as Lucy.

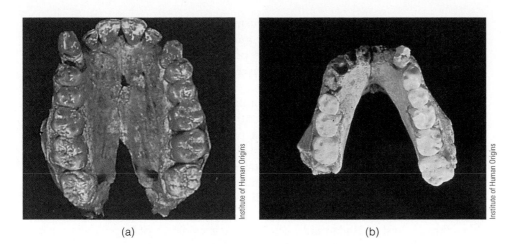

FIGURE 10–16 Jaws of *Australopithecus afarensis.* (a) Maxilla, AL 200-1a, from Hadar, Ethiopia. (Note the parallel tooth rows and large canines.) (b) Mandible, LH 4, from Laetoli, Tanzania. This fossil is the type specimen for the species *Australopithecus afarensis.*

(a)   (b)

Institute of Human Origins

The cranial portions that are preserved, including a more recently discovered specimen, also display several primitive hominoid characteristics, including a compound crest in the back as well as several primitive features of the cranial base. Cranial capacity estimates for *A. afarensis* show a mixed pattern when compared to later hominids. A provisional estimate for the one partially complete cranium—apparently a large individual—gives a figure of 500 cm³, but another, even more fragmentary cranium is apparently quite a bit smaller and has been estimated at about 375 cm³ (Holloway, 1983). Thus, for some individuals (males?), *A. afarensis* is well within the range of other australopithecine species (see A Closer Look),

See Virtual Lab 10, section IV, for a discussion of the evolution of hominid brain size.

A CLOSER LOOK

Cranial Capacity

Cranial capacity, usually reported in cubic centimeters, is a measure of brain size, or volume. The brain itself, of course, does not fossilize. However, the space once occupied by brain tissue (the inside of the cranial vault) does sometimes preserve, at least in those cases where fairly complete crania are recovered.

For purposes of comparison, it is easy to obtain cranial capacity estimates for contemporary species (including humans) from analyses of skeletonized specimens in museum collections. From studies of this nature, estimated cranial capacities for modern hominoids have been determined as follows (Tobias, 1971, 1983):

	Range (cm³)	Average (cm³)
Human	1150–1750*	1325
Chimpanzee	285–500	395
Gorilla	340–752	506
Orangutan	276–540	411
Bonobo	—	350

These data for living hominoids can then be compared with those obtained from early hominids:

	Average (cm³)
Sahelanthropus	~350
Orrorin	Not presently known
Ardipithecus	Not presently known
Australopithecus anamensis	Not presently known
Australopithecus afarensis	438
Later australopithecines	410–530
Early members of genus *Homo*	631

As the tabulations indicate, cranial capacity estimates for australopithecines fall within the range of most modern great apes, and gorillas actually average slightly more than *A. afarensis*. It must be remembered, however, that gorillas are very large animals, whereas australopithecines probably weighed on the order of 100 pounds (see Table 10–2, p. 286). Since brain size is partially correlated with body size, comparing such different-sized animals cannot be justified. Compared to living chimpanzees (most of which are slightly larger than early hominids) and bonobos (which are somewhat smaller), australopithecines had *proportionately* about 10 percent bigger brains, and we would therefore say that these early hominids were more *encephalized*.

---

*The range of cranial capacity for modern humans is very large—in fact, even greater than that shown (which approximates cranial capacity for the *majority* of contemporary *H. sapiens*).

but others (females?) may have a significantly smaller cranial capacity. However, a detailed depiction of cranial size for *A. afarensis* is not possible at this time; this part of the skeleton is unfortunately too poorly represented. One thing is clear: *A. afarensis* had a small brain, probably averaging for the whole species not much over 420 cm³.

On the other hand, a large assortment of postcranial pieces has been found at Hadar. Initial impressions suggest that relative to lower limbs, the upper limbs are longer than in modern humans (also a primitive hominoid condition). (This statement does not mean that the arms of *A. afarensis* were longer than the legs.) In addition, the wrist, hand, and foot bones show several differences from modern humans (Susman et al., 1985). Stature can now be confidently estimated: *A. afarensis* was a short hominid. From her partial skeleton, Lucy is figured to be only 3½ to 4 feet tall. However, Lucy—as demonstrated by her pelvis—was probably a female, and at Hadar and Laetoli, there is evidence of larger individuals as well. The most economical hypothesis explaining this variation is that *A. afarensis* was quite sexually dimorphic: The larger individuals are male and the smaller ones, such as Lucy, are female. Estimates of male stature can be approximated from the larger footprints at Laetoli, inferring a height of not quite 5 feet. If we accept this interpretation, *A. afarensis* was a very sexually dimorphic form indeed. In fact, for overall body size, this species may have been as dimorphic as *any* living primate (i.e., as much as gorillas, orangutans, or baboons). A recent reanalysis of the *A. afarensis* fossils (Reno et al., 2003) has come to a dramatically different conclusion. Phillip Reno and colleagues at Kent State University used a larger sample and a different statistical approach from that utilized by other researchers. This new study concluded that *A. afarensis* was not very sexually dimorphic at all—finding, in fact, about the same degree of male-female body size difference as seen in modern *H. sapiens*. It must be noted, however, that this revised interpretation is inconsistent not just with prior consensus views of *A. afarensis*, but with those of virtually all early hominids (see Table 10–2, p. 286).

See Virtual Lab 9, section V, for a discussion of the locomotion of *A. afarensis*.

AT A GLANCE	Abbreviations Used for Fossil Hominid Specimens

For those hominid sites where a number of specimens have been recovered, standard abbreviations are used to designate the site as well as the specimen number (and occasionally museum accession information as well). In this chapter, the following abbreviations are used.

Abbreviation	Explanation	Example
AL	Afar locality	AL-288-1
LH	Laetoli hominid	LH4
OH	Olduvai hominid	OH5
KNM-ER (or simply ER)	Kenya National Museums, East Rudolf*	ER 1470
KNM-WT (or simply WT)	Kenya National Museums, West Turkana	WT 17000
Sts	Sterkfontein, main site	Sts 5
Stw	Sterkfontein, west extension	Stw 53
SK	Swartkrans	SK 48

*East Rudolf is the former name for Lake Turkana; the abbreviation was first used before the lake's name was changed. All these fossils (as well as others from sites throughout Kenya) are housed in Nairobi at the National Museums of Kenya.

In a majority of dental and cranial features, *A. afarensis* is clearly more primitive than later hominids. In fact, from the neck up, *A. afarensis* is so primitive that without any evidence from the limbs, one would be hard-pressed to call it a hominid at all (although the back teeth are large and heavily enameled, unlike those of the great apes, and the position of the foramen magnum indicates an upright posture).

What, then, makes *A. afarensis* a hominid? The answer is revealed by its manner of locomotion. From the abundant limb bones recovered from Hadar and those beautiful footprints from Laetoli, we know unequivocally that *A. afarensis* walked bipedally when on the ground. Whether Lucy and her contemporaries still spent considerable time in the trees and just how efficiently they walked, have become topics of some controversy. Most researchers, however, agree that *A. afarensis* was an efficient habitual biped while on the ground. These hominids were also clearly obligate bipeds, which would have hampered their climbing abilities but would not necessarily have precluded arboreal behavior altogether. As one physical anthropologist has surmised: "One could imagine these diminutive early hominids making maximum use of *both* terrestrial and arboreal resources in spite of their commitment to exclusive bipedalism when on the ground. The contention of a mixed arboreal and terrestrial behavioral repertoire would make adaptive sense of the Hadar australopithecine forelimb, hand, and foot morphology without contradicting the evidence of the pelvis" (Wolpoff, 1983b, p. 451).

ANOTHER EAST AFRICAN HOMINID

The pace of hominid discoveries in East Africa has dramatically intensified in recent years, and many of these new discoveries have revealed a different combination of anatomical features from those recognized in remains discovered previously. Among the most distinctive and intriguing of these new finds is a cranium unearthed in 1999 on the west side of Lake Turkana in northern Kenya (Leakey et al., 2001).

Dated to 3.5 m.y.a., this fossil hominid is thus contemporaneous with *Australopithecus afarensis*. Yet, it shows a quite distinctive combination of facial and dental features (most especially, a flat lower face and fairly small molar teeth). In these respects, this newly discovered Kenyan hominid is different from *A. afarensis*, and, in fact, from *all* known australopithecines. Because the skull has been severely distorted, cranial capacity is difficult to establish clearly. However, the best estimates suggest that the cranial capacity is similar to that of *Australopithecus* (i.e., in the range of 400 to 500 cm^3.).

Because of its unusual anatomical features, Meave Leakey and her colleagues have proposed an entirely new hominid genus (*Kenyanthropus*) for this exceptional cranium. Whether this designation will be substantiated by further, more detailed analysis remains to be seen. At minimum, this and all the other discoveries from recent years are forcing a major reassessment of the early stages of hominid evolution (see Appendix B).

LATER EAST AFRICAN AUSTRALOPITHECINE FINDS

An assortment of fossil hominids, including many specimens of later members of the genus *Australopithecus*, has been recovered from geological contexts with dates after 3 m.y.a. at several localities in East Africa. Up to 10 different such sites are now known (in the time range of 3–1 m.y.a.), but here we will concentrate on the three most significant ones: East Lake Turkana, West Lake Turkana (both in northern Kenya), and Olduvai Gorge (in northern Tanzania).

A significant new hominid discovery from another site in East Africa was announced in 1999 (Asfaw et al., 1999). Behane Asfaw, Tim White, and

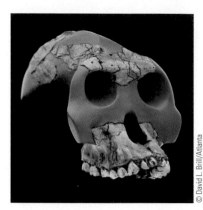

FIGURE 10-17 Reconstructed cranium of *Australopithecus garhi* from Bouri, Ethiopia; estimated date, 2.5 m.y.a.

colleagues have discovered several fossils, dated to 2.5 m.y.a., of what they suggest may be yet another species of *Australopithecus,* termed *A. garhi, garhi* meaning "surprise" in the Afar language (Fig. 10–17). These important new finds come from the Bouri site also in the Middle Awash region of Ethiopia, just south of Aramis. The hominid fossils, including an incomplete cranium and much of the limb skeleton (from another individual), are in several ways quite different from any other Plio-Pleistocene hominid. For example, the cranium combines a projecting face, fairly large front teeth, and very large back teeth. The limb proportions are also unusual, with long forelimbs (as in *A. afarensis*) but also with quite long hind limbs (as in *Homo*). Finally, the hominids at Bouri were found close to animal bones displaying clear signs of butchering (see p. 243).

Located very near the considerably older Allia Bay site on the east shore of Lake Turkana is Koobi Fora (Fig. 10–18). This latter locality, with sediments dating to 1.8–1.3 m.y.a., has provided specimens representing at least 100 individuals, and this fine sample includes several complete crania, many jaws, and an assortment of postcranial bones. Next to Olduvai, Koobi Fora has yielded the most information concerning the behavior of early hominids. More than 20 archaeological sites have been discovered, and excavation or testing has been done at 10 localities.

Across the lake, on the west side of Lake Turkana, are other deposits that recently have yielded new and very exciting discoveries—including the earlier *Kenyanthropus* finds (discussed previously). In addition, Olduvai Gorge (discussed in detail in Chapter 9) has also yielded a considerable collection of early hominid fossils.

AUSTRALOPITHECINES FROM OLDUVAI AND LAKE TURKANA

Most fossil hominids from Olduvai, West Lake Turkana, and especially Koobi Fora are later in time than the *A. afarensis* remains from Laetoli and Hadar (by at least 500,000 years). It is thus not surprising that they are more derived, in some cases dramatically so. Also, these later hominids are considerably more diverse. Most researchers accept the interpretation that all the hominids from Laetoli and Hadar are members of a single taxon, *A. afarensis.* However, it is clear that the remains from the Turkana area and Olduvai collectively represent

FIGURE 10-18 Excavations in progress at Koobi Fora, in East Lake Turkana, northern Kenya.

multiple taxa—two different genera and perhaps up to five or six different species. Current discussion on how best to sort this complex material is among the most vehement in paleoanthropology. Here we summarize the broad patterns of physical morphology. At the end of this chapter, we will take up the various schemes that attempt to interpret the fossil remains in a broader evolutionary context.

Following 2.5 m.y.a., later (and more derived) representatives of *Australopithecus* are found in East Africa. This is a most distinctive group that has popularly been known for some time as "robust" australopithecines. By "robust" it had generally been meant that these forms—when compared to other australopithecines—were larger in body size. However, more recent and better controlled studies (Jungers, 1988; McHenry, 1988, 1992) have shown that all the species of *Australopithecus* overlapped considerably in body size. As you will see shortly, "robust" australopithecines have also been found in South Africa.

As a result of these new weight estimates, many researchers have either dropped the use of the term *robust* (along with its opposite, *gracile*) or presented it in quotation marks to emphasize its conditional application. We believe that the term *robust* can be used in this latter sense, as it still emphasizes important differences in the scaling of craniodental traits. In other words, even if they are not larger overall, robust forms are clearly robust in the skull and dentition.

Dating to approximately 2.5 m.y.a., the earliest representative of this robust group comes from northern Kenya on the west side of Lake Turkana. A complete cranium (WT 17000—"the black skull") was unearthed there in 1985 and has proved to be a most important discovery (Fig. 10–19). This skull, with a cranial capacity of only 410 cm³, is among the smallest for any hominid known, and it has other primitive traits reminiscent of *A. afarensis.* For example, there is a compound crest in the back of the skull, the upper face projects considerably, the upper dental row converges in back, and the cranial base is extensively pneumatized—that is, it possesses air pockets (Kimbel et al., 1988).

What makes the black skull so fascinating, however, is that mixed with this array of distinctively primitive traits are a host of derived ones linking it to other members of the robust group (including a broad face, a very large palate, and a large area for the back teeth). This mosaic of features seems to place skull WT 17000 between earlier *A. afarensis* on the one hand and the later robust species on the other. Because of its unique position in hominid evolution, WT 17000 (and the population it represents) has been placed in a new species, *Australopithecus aethiopicus.*

Around 2 m.y.a., different varieties of even more derived members of the robust lineage were on the scene in East Africa. As well documented by finds at Olduvai and Koobi Fora, robust australopithecines have relatively small cranial capacities (ranging from 510 to 530 cm³) and very large, broad faces with massive back teeth and lower jaws. The larger (probably male) individuals also show a raised ridge, called a **sagittal crest,** along the midline of the cranium. The first find of a recognized Plio-Pleistocene hominid in East Africa, in fact, was of a nearly complete robust australopithecine cranium, discovered in 1959 by Mary Leakey at Olduvai Gorge (see p. 236). As a result of Louis Leakey's original naming of the fossil (as *Zinjanthropus*), this find is still popularly referred to as "Zinj." However, it and other members of the same species in East Africa are now usually classified as *Australopithecus boisei.*

FIGURE 10–19 The "black skull," WT 17000, discovered at West Lake Turkana in 1985. This specimen is provisionally assigned to *Australopithecus aethiopicus.* It is called the "black skull" owing to the dark color from the fossilization (mineralization) process.

sagittal crest Raised ridge along the midline of the cranium where the temporal muscle (which closes the jaw) is attached.

AT A GLANCE	In Summary: Key East African *Australopithecus* and Early *Homo* Discoveries		
Site	**Dates (m.y.a.)**	**Hominids**	
Olduvai (N. Tanzania)	1.85–1.0	Australopithecines, early *Homo*	
Turkana (N. Kenya; eastern side of Lake Turkana) (West side of Lake Turkana)	1.9–1.3 (3.5–1.6)	Many australopithecines; several early *Homo* *Australopithecus* (*A. aethiopicus*); also *Kenyanthropus** 2 nearly complete crania; 3 jaw fragments, isolated teeth; 1 nearly complete skeleton (*H. erectus*)	
Bouri (N.E. Ethiopia)	2.5	Australopithecines (*A. garhi*)	
Hadar (N.E. Ethiopia)	3,9–3.0	Many early australopithecines (*A. afarensis*);	
Laetoli (N. Tanzania)	3.7–3.5	Early australopithecines (*A. afarensis*); also, well-preserved footprints	

*The genus *Kenyanthropus* has not been accepted as a separate taxon by all researchers.

Early *Homo*

See Virtual Lab 10 for a discussion of the evolution of the genus *Homo*.

In addition to the robust australopithecine remains in East Africa, there is another contemporaneous Plio-Pleistocene hominid that is quite distinctive. In fact, as best documented by fossil discoveries from Olduvai and Koobi Fora, these materials have been placed by most paleoanthropologists in the genus *Homo*—and thus are seen as different from all species assigned to *Australopithecus*.*

The earliest appearance of genus *Homo* in East Africa may be as ancient as that of the robust australopithecines. (As we have discussed, the black skull from West Turkana has been dated to approximately 2.5 m.y.a.) Reinterpretations of a temporal fragment from the Lake Baringo region of central Kenya have suggested that early *Homo* may also be close to this same antiquity (estimated age of 2.4 m.y.a.) (Hill et al., 1992). More diagnostic remains of a lower jaw of early *Homo* have also recently been reported from Hadar, in Ethiopia, and are dated to 2.3 m.y.a. (Kimbel et al., 1996). Given that the robust australopithecine lineage was probably diverging at this time, it is not surprising to find the earliest representatives of the genus *Homo* also beginning to diversify.

The presence of a Plio-Pleistocene hominid with a significantly larger brain than seen in *Australopithecus* was first suggested by Louis Leakey in the early 1960s on the basis of fragmentary remains found at Olduvai Gorge. Leakey and his colleagues gave a new species designation to these fossil remains, naming them **Homo habilis**.

Homo habilis (hab´-ih-liss) A species of early *Homo*, well known from East Africa but perhaps also found in other regions.

The *Homo habilis* material at Olduvai ranges in time from 1.85 m.y.a. for the earliest to about 1.6 m.y.a. for the latest. Due to the fragmentary nature of the fossil remains, interpretations have been difficult and much disputed. The most immediately obvious feature distinguishing the *H. habilis* material from the australopithecines is cranial size. For all the measurable *H. habilis* skulls, the estimated average cranial capacity is 631 cm^3, compared to 520 cm^3 for all measurable robust australopithecines and 442 cm^3 for the less robust species (McHenry, 1988) (see A Closer Look on p. 273). *Homo habilis*, therefore, shows an increase in cranial size of about 20 percent over the larger of the aus-

---

*As we will discuss shortly, the status of "early *Homo*" has recently been reevaluated by several researchers.

tralopithecines and an even greater increase over some of the smaller-brained forms (from South Africa, discussed shortly). In their initial description of *H. habilis*, Leakey and his associates also pointed to differences from australopithecines in cranial shape and in tooth proportions (larger front teeth relative to back teeth and narrower premolars).

The naming of this fossil material as *Homo habilis* ("handy man") was meaningful from two perspectives. First of all, Leakey inferred that members of this group were the early Olduvai toolmakers. If true, how do we account for a robust australopithecine like "Zinj" lying in the middle of the largest excavated area known at Olduvai? What was he doing there? Leakey suggested that he was the remains of a *habilis* meal! Excepting those instances where cut marks are left behind (see pp. 242–243), we must point out again that there is no clear way archaeologically to establish the validity of such a claim. However, the debate over this assertion serves to demonstrate that cultural factors as well as physical morphology must be considered in the interpretation of hominids as biocultural organisms. Secondly, and most significantly, by calling this group *Homo,* Leakey was arguing for at least *two separate branches* of hominid evolution in the Plio-Pleistocene. Clearly, only one could be on the main branch eventually leading to *Homo sapiens.* By labeling this new group *Homo* rather than *Australopithecus,* Leakey was guessing that he had found our ancestors.

Because the initial evidence was so fragmentary, most paleoanthropologists were reluctant to accept *H. habilis* as a valid taxon distinct from *all* australopithecines. Later discoveries, especially from Lake Turkana, of better-preserved fossil material have shed further light on early *Homo* in the Plio-Pleistocene. The most important of this additional material is a nearly complete cranium (ER 1470) discovered at Koobi Fora (Fig. 10–20). With a cranial capacity of 775 cm^3, this individual is well outside the known range for australopithecines and actually overlaps the lower boundary for *Homo erectus.* In addition, the shape of the skull vault is in many respects unlike that of australopithecines. However, the face is still quite robust (Walker, 1976), and the fragments of tooth crowns that are preserved indicate that the back teeth in this individual were quite large. Dating of the Koobi Fora early *Homo* material places it contemporaneous with the Olduvai remains—that is, about 1.8–1.6 m.y.a.

On the basis of evidence from Olduvai and particularly from Koobi Fora, we can reasonably postulate that one or more species of early *Homo* were present in East Africa probably by 2.4 m.y.a., developing in parallel with at least one line of australopithecines (Fig. 10–21). These two hominid lines lived contemporaneously for a minimum of 1 million years, after which the australopithecine lineage apparently disappeared forever.

Recently, this widely supported interpretation of early *Homo* has been significantly challenged. Most notably, Bernard Wood (of George Washington University) and colleague Mark Collard (of University College, London) have argued that all the early *Homo* specimens are very different from other (later) members of *Homo.* Pointing to primitive features of the face and limb proportions, these researchers have reassigned everything previously assigned as early *Homo* back into *Australopithecus.*

This radical reinterpretation of the status of early *Homo* is highly controversial. Many paleoanthropologists flatly disagree (Walker, 2002; Cela-Conde and Ayala, 2003), while others remain cautious (e.g., Foley, 2002). Such differences in interpretation of variation in the fossil record are not unusual (quite the opposite, in fact!). The problems are first of all due to the considerable variation present in what has been called early *Homo.* The specimens collectively lumped into early *Homo* are indeed a very mixed bag, and some of the fossils might well belong to an australopithecine. This difficulty is heightened when attempting to relate one part of the body to another. A key aspect of Wood and Collard's reinterpretation is based on the apparent primitive limb proportions (i.e., proportionately long

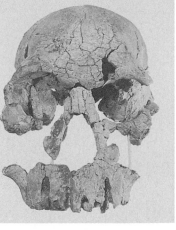

(a)

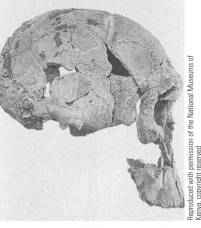

(b)

FIGURE 10–20 A nearly complete early *Homo* cranium from East Lake Turkana (ER 1470), one of the most important single fossil hominid discoveries from East Africa. (a) frontal view (b) lateral view.

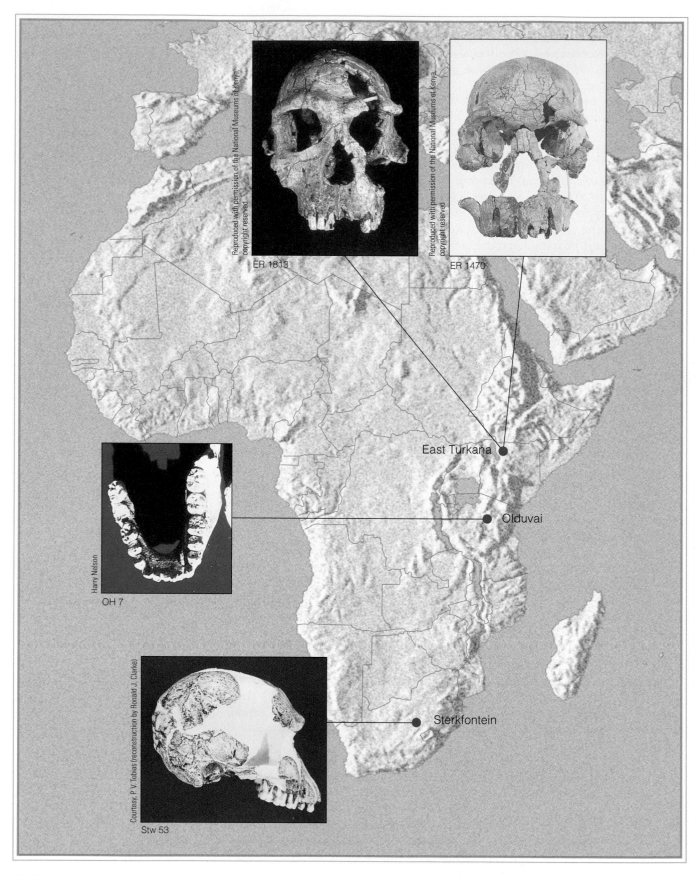

ER 1813

ER 1470

East Turkana

Olduvai

OH 7

Stw 53

Sterkfontein

FIGURE 10–21 Early *Homo* fossil finds.

arms). However, it is not at all certain which fossil limb bones go with which cranial remains. Thus, it is possible to assign a cranium like ER 1470 to early *Homo,* while unassociated limb bones *might* come from the same species—or, just as easily, they may have belonged to a contemporaneous *Australopithecus boisei* individual (explaining why the limb proportions would look like an australopithecine).

The degree of encephalization shown by the early *Homo* cranial remains argues that at least some of these specimens do not belong in *Australopithecus* (indeed, Wood and Collard concede that their placement of these fossils into *Australopithecus* is tentative and probably will need to be revised further). For the moment, then, it seems prudent to continue to include those specimens with good cranial preservation from Olduvai, Koobi Fora, and elsewhere as early *Homo.* Nevertheless, we should always recognize that, as in any such decision, a classification is merely a hypothesis—and one easily prone to eventual falsification.

South African Sites

EARLIEST DISCOVERIES

The first quarter of the twentieth century saw the discipline of paleoanthropology in its scientific infancy. Informed opinions considered the likely origins of the human family to be in Asia, where fossil forms of a primitive kind of *Homo* had been found in Indonesia in the 1890s. Europe was also considered a center of hominid evolution, for spectacular discoveries there of premodern humans (including the famous Neandertals) and millions of stone tools had come to light, particularly in the early 1900s.

Few scholars would have given much credence to Darwin's prediction:

> In each region of the world the living mammals are closely related to the extinct species of the same region. It is, therefore, probable that Africa was formally inhabited by extinct apes closely allied to the gorilla and chimpanzee, and as these two species are now man's nearest allies, it is somewhat more probable that our early progenitors lived on the African continent than elsewhere. (Darwin, *The Descent of Man,* 1871)

Moreover, it would be many more decades before the East African discoveries would come to light. It was in such an atmosphere of preconceived biases that the discoveries of a young Australian-born anatomist were to jolt the foundations of the scientific community in the 1920s. Raymond Dart (Fig. 10–22) arrived in South Africa in 1923 at the age of 30 to take up a teaching position in Johannesburg. Fresh from his evolution-oriented training in England, Dart had developed a keen interest in human evolution. Consequently, he was well prepared when startling new evidence began to appear at his very doorstep.

The first clue came in 1924, when Dart received a shipment of fossils from the commercial limeworks quarry at Taung (200 miles southwest of Johannesburg). He immediately recognized something that was quite unusual, a natural **endocast** of a higher primate. The endocast fit into another limestone block containing the fossilized front portion of the skull, face, and lower jaw (Fig. 10–23). However, these were difficult to see clearly, for the bone was hardened into a cemented limestone matrix. Dart patiently chiseled away for weeks, later describing the task:

> No diamond cutter ever worked more lovingly or with such care on a precious jewel—nor, I am sure, with such inadequate tools. But on the seventy-third day, December 23, the rock parted. I could view the face from the front, although the right side was still imbedded. . . . What emerged was a baby's face, an infant with a full set of milk teeth and its

FIGURE 10–22 Raymond Dart, shown working in his laboratory.

endocast A solid impression of the inside of the skull, often preserving details relating to the size and surface features of the brain.

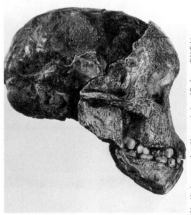

FIGURE 10–23 The Taung child, discovered in 1924. The endocast is in back, with the fossilized bone mandible and face in front.

permanent molars just in the process of erupting. I doubt if there was any parent prouder of his offspring than I was of my Taung baby on that Christmas. (Dart, 1959, p. 10)

See Virtual Lab 8, section I, for a discussion of South African early hominids.

As indicated by the formation and eruption of the teeth, the Taung child was probably about three to four years old. Interestingly, the rate of development of this and many other Plio-Pleistocene hominids was more like that of apes than of modern *Homo* (Bromage and Dean, 1985). Dart's initial impression that this form was a hominoid was confirmed when he could observe the face and teeth more clearly. However, as it turned out, it took considerably more effort before the teeth could be seen completely, since Dart worked for four years to separate the upper and lower jaws.

But Dart was convinced long before he had an unimpeded view of the dentition that this discovery was a remarkable one, an early hominoid from South Africa. The question was, What kind of hominoid? Dart realized that it was extremely improbable that this specimen could have been a forest ape, for South Africa has had a relatively dry climate for millions of years. Even though the climate at Taung may not have been as dry as Dart initially speculated (Butzer, 1974), it was still a very unlikely spot to find an ape!

If not an ape, then what was it? Features of the skull and teeth of this small child held clues that Dart seized on almost immediately. The entrance of the spinal cord into the brain (the *foramen magnum* at the base of the skull; see Fig. 10–12) was farther forward in the Taung skull than in modern great apes, though not as much as in modern humans. From this fact Dart concluded that the head was balanced *above* the spine, indicating erect posture. In addition, the slant of the forehead was not as receding as in apes, the milk canines were exceedingly small, and the newly erupted permanent molars were very large, broad teeth. In all these respects, the Taung fossil was more akin to hominids than to apes. There was, however, a disturbing feature that was to confuse many scientists for several years: The brain was quite small. More recent studies have estimated the Taung child's brain size at approximately 405 cm³ (which translates to a full adult estimate of 440 cm³), not very large (for a hominid) when compared to modern great apes (see A Closer Look on p. 273).

The estimated cranial capacity of the Taung fossil falls within the range of modern great apes, and gorillas actually average about 10 percent greater. It must, however, be remembered that gorillas are very large animals, whereas the Taung specimen derives from a population in which adults may have averaged less than 80 pounds. Since brain size is partially correlated with body size, comparing such differently sized animals is unjustified. A more meaningful comparison would be with the bonobo (*Pan paniscus*), whose body weight is comparable. Bonobos have adult cranial capacities averaging 356 cm³ for males and 329 cm³ for females, and thus the Taung child, versus a *comparably sized* ape, displays a 25 percent increase in cranial capacity.

Despite the relatively small size of the brain, Dart saw that it was no ape. Realizing the immense importance of his findings, Dart promptly reported them in the British scientific weekly *Nature* on February 7, 1925—a bold venture, since Dart, only 32, was presumptuously proposing a whole new view of human evolution. The small-brained Taung child was christened by Dart ***Australopithecus africanus*** (southern ape of Africa), which he saw as a kind of halfway "missing link" between modern apes and humans. This concept of a single "missing link" was a fallacious one, but Dart correctly emphasized the hominid-like features of the fossil.

Not all scientists were ready for such a theory from such an "unlikely" place. Hence, Dart's report was received with indifference, disbelief, and even caustic scorn. Dart realized that more complete remains were needed. The skeptical world would not accept the evidence of one partial immature individual, no matter how suggestive the clues. Most scientists in the 1920s regarded this little

Australopithecus africanus
(os-tral-oh-pith´-e-kus af-ri-kan´-us)

Taung child as an interesting aberrant form of ape. Clearly, more fossil evidence was needed, particularly adult crania (since these would show more diagnostic features). Not an experienced fossil hunter himself, Dart sought further assistance in the search for more australopithecines.

FURTHER DISCOVERIES OF SOUTH AFRICAN HOMINIDS

Soon after publication of his controversial theories, Dart found a strong ally in Robert Broom (Fig. 10–24). A Scottish physician and part-time paleontologist, Broom's credentials as a fossil hunter had been established earlier with his highly successful paleontological work on early mammal-like reptiles in South Africa.

Although interested, Broom was unable to participate actively in the search for additional australopithecines until 1936. From two of Dart's students, Broom learned of another commercial limeworks site, called **Sterkfontein,** not far from Johannesburg. Here, as at Taung, the quarrying involved blasting out large sections with dynamite, leaving piles of debris that often contained fossilized remains. Accordingly, Broom asked the quarry manager to keep his eyes open for fossils, and when Broom returned to the site in August 1936, the manager asked, "Is this what you are looking for?" Indeed it was, for Broom held in his hand the endocast of an adult australopithecine—exactly what he had set out to find! Looking further over the scattered debris, Broom was able to find most of the rest of the skull of the same individual.

Such remarkable success, just a few months after beginning his search, was not the end of Broom's luck, for his magical touch was to continue unabated for several more years. In the 1930s and 1940s, Broom discovered two further hominid sites, including **Swartkrans,** the most prolific of all South African Plio-Pleistocene locales (it has since yielded hundreds of fossils). In the 1940s, Raymond Dart discovered another hominid site, bringing the total to five.

Numerous extremely important discoveries came from these additional sites, discoveries that would eventually swing the tide of intellectual thought to the views that Dart expressed back in 1925. Particularly important was a nearly complete cranium and pelvis, both found at Sterkfontein in 1947. As the number of discoveries accumulated, it became increasingly difficult to simply write the australopithecines off as aberrant apes.

By 1949, at least 30 hominid individuals were represented from five South African sites, and leading scientists were coming to accept the australopithecines as hominids. With this acceptance also came the necessary recognition that hominid brains had their greatest expansion *after* earlier changes in teeth and locomotor systems. In other words, once again we see that the rate of evolution in one functional system of the body varies from that of other systems, thus displaying the *mosaic* nature of human evolution.

Since the 1950s, exploration of the South African hominid sites has continued, and numerous important discoveries were made in the 1970s and 1980s. The most spectacular new find was made in 1998 at Sterkfontein, where the remains of a virtually complete australopithecine skeleton were found by Ron Clarke and his associates from the University of Witwatersrand. Most of the remains are still embedded in the surrounding limestone matrix and may require years for removal, cleaning, and reconstruction (Fig. 10–25).

As we will discuss in more detail shortly, dating of all the South African Plio-Pleistocene sites has proved most difficult; estimates for the Sterkfontein australopithecine skeleton are between 3.6 and 2.5 m.y.a. Even before the remains have been fully excavated, this is still recognized as an unusual and highly significant find. Because such complete individuals are so rare in the hominid fossil record, this discovery has tremendous potential to shed more light on the precise nature of early hominid locomotion. For example, will the rest of the skeleton confirm what foot bones of the same individual have implied regarding arboreal climbing in this bipedal

FIGURE 10–24 Robert Broom.

Sterkfontein (sterk´-fon-tane)

Swartkrans (swart´-kranz)

FIGURE 10–25 Australopithecine skeleton embedded in limestone matrix at Sterkfontein. Much of the skeleton still is not visible. Clearly seen are the cranium (with articulated mandible) and part of an upper limb.

hominid (see p. 264)? Moreover, relative proportion of brain size compared to body size, better estimates of overall body size, relative proportions of the limbs, and much more can be more accurately assessed from such a completely preserved skeleton.*

REVIEW OF HOMINIDS FROM SOUTH AFRICA

The Plio-Pleistocene hominid discoveries from South Africa are most significant. First, they were the initial hominid discoveries in Africa and helped point the way to later finds in East and central Africa. Second, morphology of the South African hominids shows broad similarities to the forms in East Africa, but with several distinctive features, which argues for separation at least at the species level. Finally, there is a large assemblage of hominid fossils from South Africa, and exciting discoveries are still being made (see Fig. 10–25).

Further discoveries are also coming from entirely new sites. In the 1990s, the site known as Drimolen was found in South Africa, very near to Sterkfontein and Swartkrans (Keyser, 2000). While only provisionally published thus far, we do know that up to 80 specimens have been recovered—including the most complete *Australopithecus* cranium found anywhere in Africa.

A truly remarkable collection of early hominids, the remains from South Africa coming from nine different caves, exceed 1,000 (counting all teeth as separate items), and the number of individuals is now more than 200. From an evolutionary point of view, the most meaningful remains are those of the pelvis, which now include portions of nine ossa coxae (see p. 262). Remains of the pelvis are so important because, better than any other area of the body, this structure displays the unique requirements of a bipedal animal (as in modern humans *and* in our hominid forebears).

"Robust" Australopithecines   In addition to the discoveries of *A. aethiopicus* and *A. boisei* in East Africa, there are also numerous finds of robust australopithecines in South Africa. Like their East African cousins, the South African robust forms also have small cranial capacities. (The only measurable specimen equals 530 cm^3; the Drimolen cranium is smaller and might come from a female, but no cranial measurements have as yet been published.) They also possess large broad faces and very large premolars and molars (although not as massive as in East Africa). Owing to the differences in dental proportions, as well as important differences in facial architecture (Rak, 1983), most researchers now agree that there is a species-level difference between the later East African robust variety (*A. boisei*) and the South African group (*A. robustus*).

Despite these differences, all members of the robust lineage appear to be specialized for a diet made up of hard food items, such as seeds and nuts. For many years, paleoanthropologists (e.g., Robinson, 1972) had speculated that robust australopithecines concentrated their diet on heavier vegetable foods than those seen in the diet of other early hominids. More recent research that included examining microscopic polishes and scratches on the teeth (Kay and Grine, 1988) has confirmed this view.

"Gracile" Australopithecines   Another variety of australopithecine (also small-brained, but not as large-toothed as the robust varieties) is known from Africa. However, while the robust lineage is represented in both East and South Africa, this other (gracile) australopithecine form is known only from the southern part of the continent. First named *A. africanus* by Dart for the single individual at Taung, this australopithecine is also found at other sites, especially Sterkfontein (Figs. 10–26 and 10–27).

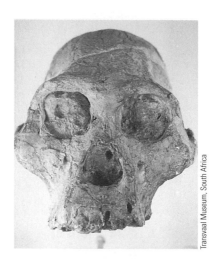

FIGURE 10–26 A gracile australopithecine cranium from Sterkfontein (Sts 5). Discovered in 1947, this specimen is the best-preserved gracile skull yet found in South Africa.

Transvaal Museum, South Africa

---

*It is a lack of *association* of cranial with postcranial remains that causes such difficulties in the interpretation of early *Homo* (see p. 241).

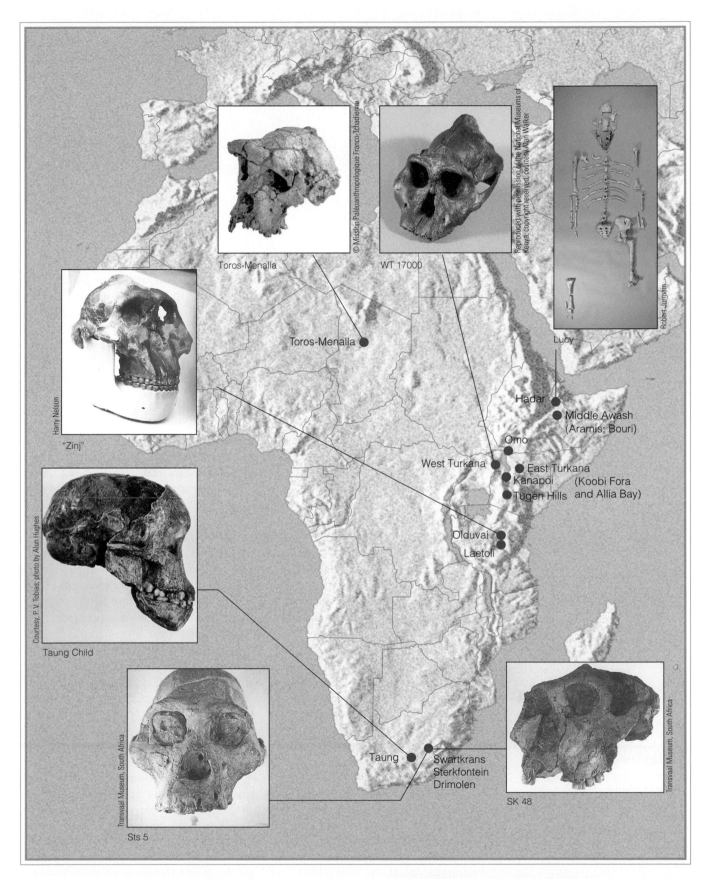

Toros-Menalla

WT 17000

Lucy

"Zinj"

Taung Child

Sts 5

SK 48

Toros-Menalla

Hadar

Middle Awash
(Aramis; Bouri)

Omo

West Turkana

East Turkana

Kanapoi

(Koobi Fora

Tugen Hills   and Allia Bay)

Olduvai

Laetoli

Taung

Swartkrans
Sterkfontein
Drimolen

FIGURE 10–27 Early hominid fossil finds and localities
(pre-*Australopithecus* and *Australopithecus* discoveries).

TABLE 10–2 Estimated Body Weights and Stature in Plio-Pleistocene Hominids

| | BODY WEIGHT | | STATURE | |
	MALE	FEMALE	MALE	FEMALE
A. afarensis	45 kg (99 lb)	29 kg (64 lb)	151 cm (59 in.)	105 cm (41 in.)
A. africanus	41 kg (90 lb)	30 kg (65 lb)	138 cm (54 in.)	115 cm (45 in.)
A. robustus	40 kg (88 lb)	32 kg (70 lb)	132 cm (52 in.)	110 cm (43 in.)
A. boisei	49 kg (108 lb)	34 kg (75 lb)	137 cm (54 in.)	124 cm (49 in.)
H. habilis	52 kg (114 lb)	32 kg (70 lb)	157 cm (62 in.)	125 cm (49 in.)

Source: After McHenry, 1992. *Note:* Reno et al. (2003) conclude that sexual dimorphism in *A afarensis* was considerably less than shown here.

See Virtual Lab 10, section III, for a discussion of the methods used to establish body mass in early hominids.

(a) Hominid (robust australopithecine)

Temporal muscle fibers oriented toward back teeth

(b) Pongid (male gorilla)

Temporal muscle fibers oriented toward front teeth

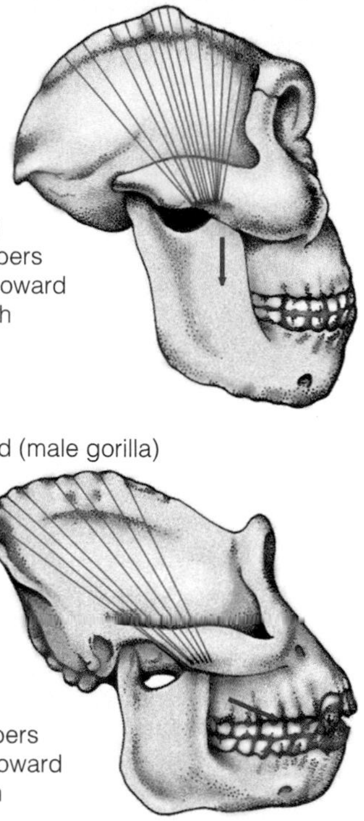

FIGURE 10–28 Sagittal crests and temporal muscle orientations. Hominid compared to pongid. (Line of greatest muscle force is shown in red.)

Traditionally, it had been thought that there was a significant variation in body size between the gracile and robust forms. But as mentioned earlier and shown in Table 10–2, there is not much difference in body size among the australopithecines. In fact, most of the differences between the robust and gracile forms are found in the face and dentition.

The facial structure of the gracile australopithecines is more lightly built and somewhat dish-shaped compared to the more vertical configuration seen in robust specimens. As we noted earlier, in robust individuals, a raised ridge along the midline of the skull is occasionally observed. Indeed, at Sterkfontein, among the larger individuals (males?), a hint of such a sagittal crest is also seen. This structure provides additional attachment area for the large temporal muscle, which is the primary muscle operating the massive jaw below. Such a structure is also seen in some modern apes, especially male gorillas and orangutans; however, in most australopithecines, the temporal muscle acts most efficiently on the back of the mouth and is therefore not functionally equivalent to the pattern seen in great apes, where the emphasis is more on the front teeth (Fig 10–28).

The most distinctive difference observed between gracile and robust australopithecines is in the dentition. Compared to modern humans, they both have relatively large teeth, which are, however, definitely hominid in pattern. In fact, more emphasis is on the typical back-tooth grinding complex among these early forms than is seen in modern humans; therefore, if anything, australopithecines are "hyperhominid" in their dentition. (In other words, they are dentally more *derived* than are modern humans.) Robust forms emphasize this trend to an extreme degree, showing deep jaws and much-enlarged back teeth, particularly the molars, leaving little room in the front of the mouth for the anterior teeth (incisors and canines). Conversely, the gracile australopithecines have proportionately larger front teeth compared to the size of their back teeth. The contrast is seen most clearly in the relative size of the canine compared to the first premolar: In robust individuals, the first premolar is clearly a much larger tooth than the small canine (about twice as large), whereas in gracile specimens, it only averages about 20 percent larger than the fairly good-sized canine (Howells, 1973).

These differences in the relative proportions of the teeth and jaws best define a gracile, as compared to a robust, australopithecine. In fact, most of the differences in skull shape we have discussed can be directly attributed to contrasting jaw function in the two forms. Both the sagittal crest and broad vertical face of the robust form are related to the muscles and biomechanical requirements of the heavy back-tooth chewing adaptation seen in this animal (see Fig. 10–29).

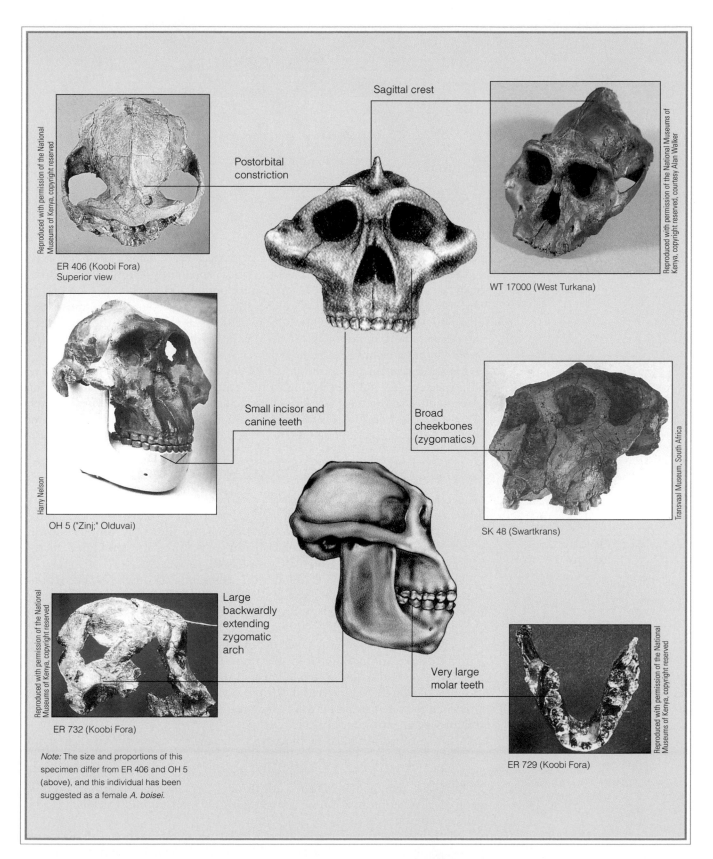

ER 406 (Koobi Fora)
Superior view

Sagittal crest

Postorbital
constriction

WT 17000 (West Turkana)

OH 5 ("Zinj;" Olduvai)

Small incisor and
canine teeth

Broad
cheekbones
(zygomatics)

SK 48 (Swartkrans)

ER 732 (Koobi Fora)

Note: The size and proportions of this
specimen differ from ER 406 and OH 5
(above), and this individual has been
suggested as a female *A. boisei.*

Large
backwardly
extending
zygomatic
arch

Very large
molar teeth

ER 729 (Koobi Fora)

FIGURE 10–29 Morphology and variation of robust
australopithecines. (Note both the typical features and
the range of variation as shown in different specimens.)

AT A GLANCE	In Summary: Key South African Pliocene and Early Pleistocene Hominid Discoveries	
Site	**Site**	**Hominids**
Swartkrans	1.8–1.0	*Australopithecus robustus* (also called *Paranthropus*); early *Homo?*
Drimolen	2.0–1.5	*Australopithecus* (*Paranthropus robustus*)
Taung	3.0–2.0??	*Australopithecus africanus*
Sterkfontein	3.3–2.6	*Australopithecus africanus;* early *Homo?*

Early *Homo* in South Africa   As in East Africa, early members of the genus *Homo* have also been found in South Africa, apparently living contemporaneously with australopithecines. At both Sterkfontein and Swartkrans, and perhaps Drimolen as well, fragmentary remains have been recognized as most likely belonging to *Homo*. In fact, Ron Clarke (1985) has shown that the key fossil of early *Homo* from Sterkfontein (Stw 53) is nearly identical to the OH 24 *Homo habilis* cranium from Olduvai.

However, a problem with both OH 24 and Stw 53 is that while many (but not all) experts agree that they belong to the genus *Homo,* there is considerable disagreement as to whether they should be included in the species *habilis.* The relationships of the Plio-Pleistocene fossil hominids to one another and the difficulties of such genus and species interpretation will be discussed in the following sections.

GEOLOGY AND DATING PROBLEMS IN SOUTH AFRICA

While the geological and archaeological context in East Africa is often straightforward, the South African early hominid sites are much more complex geologically. Except for the newly discovered sites, all the sites were found following commercial quarrying activity, which greatly disrupted the geological picture and, in the case of Taung, completely destroyed the site.

The hominid remains are found with thousands of other fossilized bones embedded in limestone cliffs, caves, fissures, and sinkholes. The limestone was formed by millions of generations of shells of marine organisms during the Precambrian—more than 2 billion years ago—when South Africa was submerged under a shallow sea. Once deposited, the limestones were cut through by percolating groundwater from below and rainwater from above, forming a maze of caves and fissures often connected to the surface by narrow shafts (Fig. 10–30). Through these vertical shafts and horizontal cave openings, bones either fell or were carried in, where they conglomerated with sand, pebbles, and soil into a cementlike matrix called *breccia.*

As the cave fissures filled in, they were constantly subjected to further erosion forces from above and below, so that caves would be partially filled, then closed to the surface for a considerable time, then reopened again to commence accumulation thousands of years later. All this activity yields an incredibly complex geological situation that can be worked out only after the most detailed kind of paleoecological analysis.

Since bones accumulated in these caves and fissures largely by accidental processes, it seems likely that none of the South African australopithecine sites are *primary* hominid localities. In other words, unlike the East African sites, these are not areas where hominids organized activities, scavenged food, and so on.

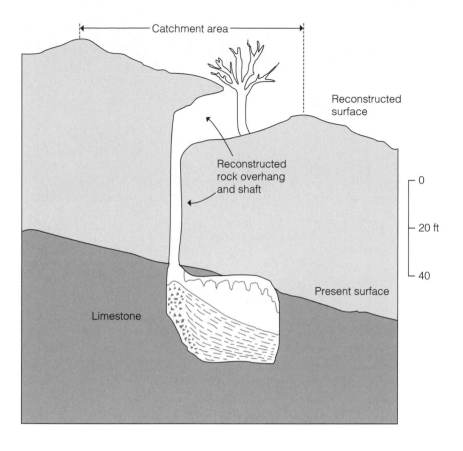

FIGURE 10–30 Swartkrans, geological section. The upper (reconstructed) part has been removed by erosion since the accumulation of the fossil-bearing deposit. (After Brain, 1970.)

Just how did all the fossilized bone accumulate, and, most particularly, what were the ancient hominids doing there? In the case of Swartkrans and Sterkfontein, the bones probably accumulated through the combined activities of carnivorous leopards, saber-toothed cats, and hyenas. Moreover, the unexpectedly high proportion of primate (baboon and hominid) remains suggests that these localities were the location (or very near the location) of primate sleeping sites, thus providing ready primate prey for various predators (Brain, 1981).

Raymond Dart argued enthusiastically for an alternative explanation, suggesting that the hominids regularly used bone, tooth, and horn remains as tools, which he called the **osteodontokeratic** culture complex. However, analogies with the food habits of modern African foragers indicate that the bone accumulation may be accounted for simply by hominid and carnivore eating practices.

osteodontokeratic (*osteo,* meaning "bone," *donto,* meaning "tooth," and *keratic,* meaning "horn")

Owing to the complex geological picture as well as a lack of appropriate material (such as volcanic deposits) for chronometric techniques, dating the South African early hominid sites has posed tremendous problems. Without chronometric dating, the best that can be done is to correlate the faunal sequences in South Africa with areas in East Africa where dates are better known (this approach is called biostratigraphy; see p. 239). Faunal sequencing of this sort on pigs, bovids such as antelope, and Old World monkeys has provided the following tenuous chronology:

Location	Age
Swartkrans	1 m.y.
Taung	2 m.y.
Sterkfontein	3 m.y.

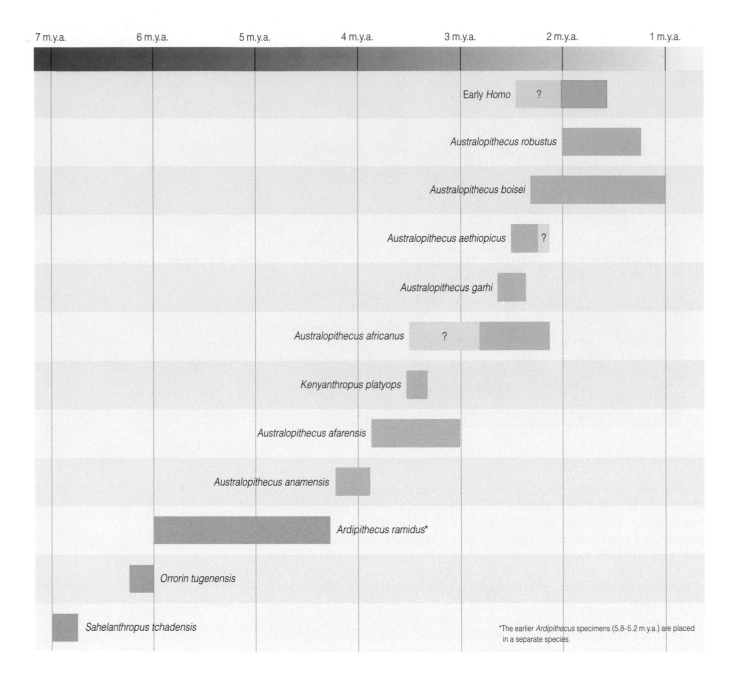

FIGURE 10–31 Time line of Plio-Pleistocene hominids. Note that most dates are approximations. Question marks indicate those estimates that are most tentative.

Attempts at paleomagnetic dating (see p. 239) suggest an age of 3.3–2.8 m.y.a. for the oldest South African hominid (Brock et al., 1977), thus pushing the estimates to the extreme limits of those provided by biostratigraphy. In fact, some researchers believe that the paleomagnetic results are ambiguous and continue to "put their money" on the biostratigraphic data, especially those dates determined by analysis of pig and monkey fossils. From such consideration, they place the oldest South African early hominid sites at perhaps as much as half a million years later (i.e., around 2.5 m.y.a.) (White et al., 1981). This is crucial, since it places *all* the South African hominids after *Australopithecus afarensis* in East Africa (Fig. 10–31). Recent excavations at Sterkfontein have suggested that the earliest hominids *may* come from levels as early as 3.5 m.y.a. (Clarke and Tobias, 1995). However, this date, which would be as early as *A. afarensis* in East Africa, has not yet been corroborated.

Interpretations: What Does It All Mean?

By this time, it may seem that anthropologists are obsessed with finding small scraps buried in the ground and then assigning them confusing numbers and taxonomic labels impossible to remember. We must realize that the collection of all the basic fossil data is the foundation of human evolutionary research. Without fossils, our speculations would be completely hollow. Several large, ongoing paleoanthropological projects are now collecting additional data in an attempt to answer some of the more perplexing questions about our evolutionary history.

The numbering of specimens, which may at times seem somewhat confusing, is an attempt to keep the designations neutral and to make reference to each individual fossil as clear as possible. The formal naming of finds as *Australopithecus, Homo habilis,* or *Homo erectus* should come much later, since it involves a lengthy series of complex interpretations. Assigning generic and specific names to fossil finds is more than just a convenience; when we attach a particular label, such as *A. africanus,* to a particular fossil, we should be fully aware of the biological implications of such an interpretation.

From the time that fossil sites are first located to the eventual interpretation of hominid evolutionary events, several steps are necessary. Ideally, they should follow a logical order, for if interpretations are made too hastily, they confuse important issues for many years. Here is a reasonable sequence:

1. Selecting and surveying sites
2. Excavating sites and recovering fossil hominids
3. Designating individual finds with specimen numbers for clear reference
4. Cleaning, preparing, studying, and describing fossils
5. Comparing with other fossil material—in chronological framework if possible
6. Comparing fossil variation with known ranges of variation in closely related groups of living primates and analyzing ancestral and derived characteristics
7. Assigning taxonomic names to fossil material

The task of interpretation is still not complete, for what we really want to know in the long run is what happened to the populations represented by the fossil remains. Indeed, in looking at the fossil hominid record, we are looking for our ancestors. In the process of eventually determining those populations that are our most likely antecedents, we may conclude that some hominids are on evolutionary side branches. If this conclusion is accurate, those hominids necessarily must have become extinct. It is both interesting and relevant to us as hominids to try to find out what influenced some earlier members of our family to continue evolving while others died out.

CONTINUING UNCERTAINTIES—TAXONOMIC ISSUES

As previously discussed, paleoanthropologists are concerned with making biological interpretations of variation found in the hominid fossil record. Most especially, researchers endeavor to assign extinct forms to particular genera and species. We saw that for the diverse array of Miocene hominoids, the evolutionary picture is exceptionally complex. As new finds accumulate, there is continued uncertainty even as to family assignment, to say nothing of genus and species!

For the very end of the Miocene and for the Plio-Pleistocene, the situation is considerably clearer. First, there is a larger fossil sample from a more restricted geographical area (South, central, and East Africa) and from a more concentrated time period (spanning about 6 million years, from 7 to 1 m.y.a.). Second, more complete specimens exist (e.g., Lucy), and we thus have good evidence for most parts of the body. Accordingly, there is considerable consensus on several basic aspects of evolutionary development during the Plio-Pleistocene. For materials prior to 4 m.y.a., not all scholars are as yet convinced of clear hominid status. However, for fossils dating later than 4 m.y.a., researchers agree unanimously that these forms are hominids (members of the family Hominidae or an equivalent taxon; see p. 231). And as support for this point, all these forms are seen as habitual, well-adapted bipeds, committed at least in part to a terrestrial niche. Moreover, researchers generally agree as to genus-level assignments for most of the forms, although *Sahelanthropus, Orrorin, Kenyanthropus,* and *Ardipithecus* have all been so recently named as to not yet be fully evaluated and accepted (there is also some disagreement regarding how to group the robust australopithecines as well as the status of early *Homo*).

As for species-level designations, little consensus can be found. Indeed, as new fossils have been discovered, the picture seems to muddy further. Once again, we are faced with a complex evolutionary process. In attempts to deal with it, we impose varying degrees of simplicity. In so doing, we hope that the evolutionary processes will become clearer—not just for introductory students, but for professional paleoanthropologists and textbook authors as well! Nevertheless, evolution is not a simple process, and disputes and disagreements are bound to arise, especially in making such fine-tuned interpretations as species-level designations.

It may prove impossible to work out clear patterns of relationships among the early hominids. Despite our best attempts, the number and complexity of hominid groups (more technically called *taxa*), which seem to increase monthly, may frustrate all attempts at simplification.

One particularly difficult obstacle is the varied combination of anatomical characteristics, seen especially in the earliest suggested members of the hominid family. For example, *Sahelanthropus* has a very primitive-looking braincase (especially in the back) combined with a fairly advanced hominid-looking face and canine teeth. Similarly, *Orrorin* combines what some claim are very chimpanzee-looking teeth with a highly efficient bipedal gait. Lastly, *Ardipithecus* combines some aspects of primitive-looking teeth with other components of a suggested bipedal gait. Moreover, from preliminary conclusions by some researchers familiar with the *Ardipithecus* finds, the manner of locomotion is thought to have been very different from any other hominid (suggesting it might have been a very derived hominid and thus an unlikely ancestor of later forms).

Fueled by all these admittedly confusing combinations of characteristics is the suspicion by some researchers (e.g., Bernard Wood, 2002) that roughly similar characteristics (like some form of bipedality or reduction of the canine teeth) could have evolved more than once—that is, separately in different lineages of hominids (or possibly even in other hominoids closely related to hominids). This evolutionary process results from what we have called *homoplasy* (see p. 111). If, indeed, this inherently messy evolutionary factor was widespread among our late Miocene and Pliocene relatives, it may prove almost impossible to discern which forms are related to others and which ones are more closely related to us. Worse yet, it may prove extremely tricky even to be able to identify some of these forms as hominids at all.

PUTTING IT ALL TOGETHER

Despite all the difficulties, paleoanthropologists still want to understand the broad patterns of early hominid evolution. The interpretation of our paleontological past in terms of which fossils are related to other fossils and how they might be related to modern humans is usually shown diagrammatically in the form of a *phylogeny*. Such a diagram is a family tree of fossil evolution. (Note that strict practitioners of cladistics prefer to use cladograms; see pp. 111–115.) This kind of interpretation is the eventual goal of evolutionary studies, but it is the final goal, only after adequate data are available to understand what is going on.

Another, more basic way to handle these data is to divide the fossil material into subsets. This avoids (for the moment) what are still problematic phylogenetic relationships. Accordingly, for the Plio-Pleistocene hominid material from Africa, we can divide the data into three broad groupings:

Set I. Pre-*Australopithecus*/basal hominids (7.0–4.4 m.y.a.)   The earliest (and most primitive) collection of remains that have been classified as hominids are those from Toros-Menalla, the Tugen Hills, and the Middle Awash, the latter area also including the site of Aramis. These fossils have, for the moment, been assigned to three separate (and newly proposed) genera—*Sahelanthropus, Orrorin,* and *Ardipithecus*—and are hence each provisionally interpreted as being generically distinct from all the other early hominid forms (listed in sets II and III). Analysis thus far indicates that at least for the later Aramis fossils, these forms were likely bipedal, but with a primitive dentition. Brain size of *A. ramidus* is not yet known, but was almost certainly quite small.

Set II. *Australopithecus*
Subset A. Early primitive forms (4.2–3.0 m.y.a.)   This grouping comprises one well-known species, *A. afarensis,* especially well documented at Laetoli and Hadar. Slightly earlier, closely related forms (perhaps representing a distinct second species) come from two other sites and are provisionally called "*Australopithecus anamensis.*" Best known from analysis of the *A. afarensis* material, the hominids in this set are characterized by a small brain, large teeth (front and back), and a bipedal gait (probably still allowing for considerable climbing).

Subset B. Later, more derived *Australopithecus* (2.5–1.4 m.y.a.; possibly as early as 3.5 m.y.a.)   This group is composed of numerous species. (Most experts recognize at least three; some subdivide this material into five or more species.) Remains have come from several sites in both South and East Africa. All of these forms have very large back teeth and do not show appreciable brain enlargement (i.e., encephalization) compared to *A. afarensis.* A growing majority of researchers view the robust australopithecines as more specialized and showing a greater dependence on a diet of coarse vegetable foods. As such, these early hominids reflect a different adaptation than other australopithecines and are thus best placed in a separate genus (*Paranthropus*).

Set III. Early *Homo* (2.4–1.8 m.y.a.)   The best-known specimens are from East Africa (East Turkana and Olduvai), but early remains of *Homo* have also been found in South Africa (Swartkrans and possibly Sterkfontein and Drimolen). This group is composed of possibly just one, but probably more than one, species. Early *Homo* is characterized (compared to

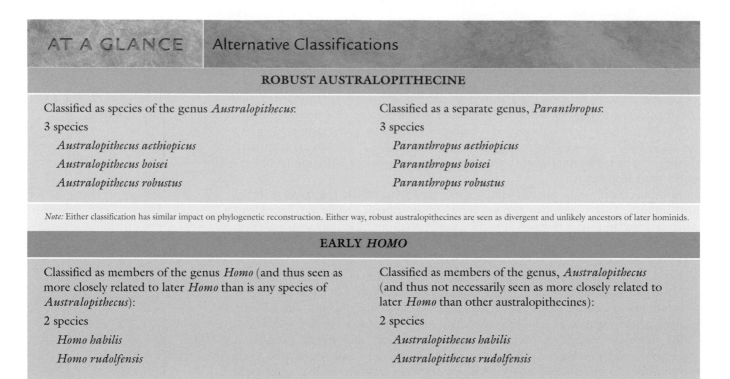

AT A GLANCE | Alternative Classifications

ROBUST AUSTRALOPITHECINE

Classified as species of the genus *Australopithecus*:	Classified as a separate genus, *Paranthropus*:
3 species	3 species
Australopithecus aethiopicus	*Paranthropus aethiopicus*
Australopithecus boisei	*Paranthropus boisei*
Australopithecus robustus	*Paranthropus robustus*

Note: Either classification has similar impact on phylogenetic reconstruction. Either way, robust australopithecines are seen as divergent and unlikely ancestors of later hominids.

EARLY *HOMO*

Classified as members of the genus *Homo* (and thus seen as more closely related to later *Homo* than is any species of *Australopithecus*):	Classified as members of the genus, *Australopithecus* (and thus not necessarily seen as more closely related to later *Homo* than other australopithecines):
2 species	2 species
Homo habilis	*Australopithecus habilis*
Homo rudolfensis	*Australopithecus rudolfensis*

Note: These differing classifications have potentially dramatic impact on phylogenetic reconstruction.

Australopithecus) by greater encephalization, altered cranial shape, and smaller (especially molars) and narrower (especially premolars) teeth. As discussed on p. 279, there is considerable variation seen among different specimens, so much so that some paleoanthropologists have removed this group from *Homo* altogether and temporarily reassigned it to *Australopithecus*.

Although hominid fossil evidence has accumulated in great abundance, the fact that so much of the material has been discovered so recently makes any firm judgments concerning the route of human evolution premature. However, paleoanthropologists are certainly not deterred from making their "best guesses," and diverse hypotheses have abounded in recent years. The vast majority of the hundreds of recently discovered fossils from Africa is still in the descriptive and early analytical stages. At this time, the construction of phylogenies of human evolution is analogous to building a house with only a partial blueprint. We are not even sure how many rooms there are! Until the existing fossil evidence has been adequately studied, to say nothing about possible new finds, speculative hypotheses must be viewed with a critical eye.

Adaptive Patterns of Early African Hominids

As you are by now aware, there are several different African hominid genera and certainly lots of species. This, in itself, is interesting. Speciation was occurring quite frequently among the various lineages of early hominids, more frequently, in fact, than among later hominids. What explains this pattern?

Evidence has been accumulating at a furious pace in the last decade, but is still far from complete. It is clear that we will never have anything approaching a complete record of early hominid evolution—and thus, significant gaps will remain. After all, we are able to discover hominids only in those special environmental contexts where fossilization was likely. All the other potential habitats they might have exploited are now invisible to us.

Nevertheless, patterns are emerging from the fascinating data we do have. First, it appears that early hominid species (pre-*Australopithecus;* australopithecines, including *Paranthropus;* and early *Homo*) all had restricted ranges. It is therefore likely that each hominid species exploited a relatively small area and could easily have become separated from other populations of its own species. Consequently, genetic drift (and, to some extent, natural selection as well) could have led to rapid genetic divergence and eventual speciation.

Second, most of these species appear to be at least partially tied to arboreal habitats, although there is disagreement on this point regarding early *Homo* (see Wood and Collard, 1999b; Foley 2002). Moreover, robust australopithecines (*Paranthropus*) were probably somewhat less arboreal than *Ardipithecus* or *Australopithecus*. These highly megadont hominids apparently concentrated on a diet of coarse fibrous plant foods, such as roots. Exploiting such resources may have routinely taken these hominids farther away from the trees than their dentally more gracile—and perhaps more omnivorous—cousins.

Third, with the exception of some early *Homo* individuals, there is very little in the way of an evolutionary trend of increased body size or of markedly greater encephalization. Beginning with *Sahelanthropus,* brain size was no more than that in chimpanzees—although when controlling for body size, this earliest of all known hominids may have had a proportionately larger brain than any living ape. Close to 6 million years later (i.e., the time of the last surviving australopithecine species), relative brain size increased by no more than 10 to 15 percent. Perhaps, tied to this relative stasis in brain capacity, there is no absolute association of any of these hominids with patterned stone tool manufacture (see Chapter 9).

Although conclusions are becoming increasingly controversial, for the moment, early *Homo* appears to be a partial exception, showing both increased encephalization and numerous occurrences of likely association with stone tools (though at many of the sites, australopithecine fossils were *also* found).

Lastly, all of these early African hominids show an accelerated developmental pattern (similar to that seen in African apes), one quite different from the *delayed* developmental pattern characteristic of *Homo sapiens* (and our immediate precursors). Moreover, this apelike development is also seen in some early *Homo* individuals (Wood and Collard, 1999a). Rates of development can be accurately reconstructed through examination of dental growth markers (Bromage and Dean, 1985), and these data perhaps provide a crucial window into understanding this early stage of hominid evolution.

These African hominid predecessors were rather small, able bipeds, but still closely tied to arboreal/climbing niches. They had fairly small brains and, compared to later *Homo,* matured rapidly. It would take a major evolutionary jump to push one of their descendants in a more human direction. For the next chapter in this more human saga, read on.

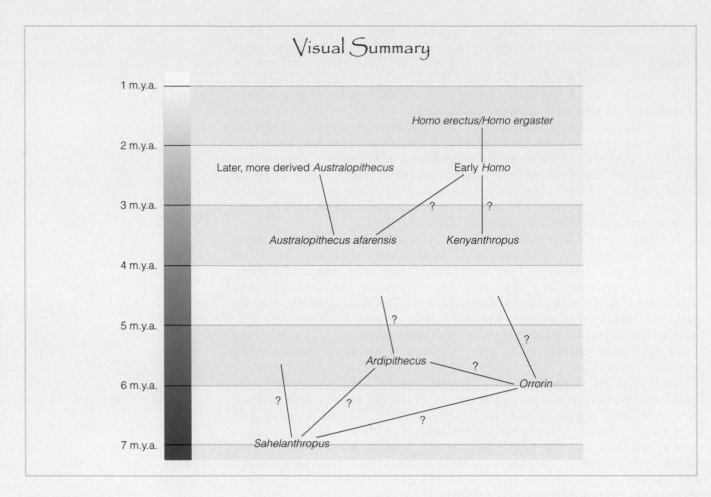

Visual Summary

Summary

The earliest evidence of the evolutionary radiation of the primates dates to the Eocene, approximately 50 m.y.a. These early primates are quite prosimian-like, but during the Oligocene, there was a broad adaptive radiation of early anthropoids. Throughout the Miocene, a wide array of hominoids evolved in the Old World. Most of these are large-bodied forms—that is, they are closely related to great apes and hominids. Although most of these hominoids went extinct by the late Miocene, it is likely that some of the fossils discovered are fairly closely related to ancestors of the great apes and early hominids.

In the Visual Summary, we present a simplified scheme showing tentative relationships among the early African fos-

TABLE 10–3 Chronological Summary of Most Significant Hominid Fossils Discussed in this Chapter

EPOCH	SITE	DATES (M.Y.A.)	TAXONOMIC DESIGNATION	COMMENTS
Plio-Pleistocene	East Turkana (Koobi Fora) and Olduvai	1.8–1.0	Derived *Australopithecus* and early *Homo*	Highly derived *Australopithecus* and first relatively complete fossils of early *Homo*
	Taung and Sterkfontein	3.3–2.0?	*Australopithecus africanus*	Best-known early hominid from South Africa; many well-preserved fossils
	Hadar and Laetoli	3.7–3.0	*Australopithecus afarensis*	Earliest well-documented group of early hominids; potentially ancestral to later *Australopithecus* and early *Homo*
	Aramis	4.4	*Ardipithecus ramidus*	Earliest large sample of hominid fossils; not yet well described; likely shows very unusual mosaic of characteristics (some highly derived)
Miocene	Toros-Menalla	~7.0	*Sahelanthropus*	Earliest proposed hominid fossils; unusual mosaic of characteristics

For Further Thought

1. Where do you think the next major early hominid discovery will occur? What do you think it will look like?

Go to the book website at **http://www.anthropology.wadsworth.com** for resources to help you explore these questions further. Click on "For Further Thought" for this chapter.

---

sil hominids discussed in this chapter. Question marks indicate those relationships that are most tentative, particularly obvious for all the earliest material (the pre-*Australopithecus* fossils, dated prior to 4 m.y.a.). Indeed, at present, with all this material so recently discovered and seemingly displaying highly complex patterns of hominid evolution, it is unwise to make anything but the most general of hypotheses.

The picture after 4 m.y.a. is somewhat clearer. It appears, for the moment, that *Australopithecus afarensis* still can be viewed as a good potential common ancestor of most (if not all) later hominids. The relationships among the later, more derived australopithecines are not as clear, nor is it certain which of the earlier Pliocene fossils is most closely related to *Homo*. As a further study aid, Table 10–3 presents the early hominid materials we consider the most significant. For those keen to pursue a more detailed evaluation of the early hominids, see Appendix B.

Science is a journey of discovery, seeking to find as many documented facts as possible. Science is also a search for clarity. The last few years of paleoanthropological research have immensely enriched our record of facts. The search for clarity continues. No doubt, more discoveries are in the offing. We certainly live in interesting times.

Questions for Review

1. (a) Why is postcranial evidence (particularly the lower limb) so crucial in showing the australopithecines (or other early forms) as definite hominids? (b) What particular aspects of the australopithecine pelvis and lower limb are hominid-like?
2. In what ways are the remains of *Sahelanthropus* and *Ardipithecus* primitive? How do we know that these forms are hominids? How sure are we?
3. Assume that you are in the laboratory analyzing the "Lucy" *A. afarensis* skeleton. You also have complete skeletons from a chimpanzee and a modern human. (a) Which parts of the Lucy skeleton are more similar to the chimpanzee? Which are more similar to the human? (b) Which parts of the Lucy skeleton are *most informative*?
4. Why are some Plio-Pleistocene hominids from East Africa called "early *Homo*"? What does this imply for the evolutionary relationships of the australopithecines? What alternative interpretations have been proposed, and why?

5. Discuss the first thing you would do if you found an early hominid fossil and were responsible for its formal description and publication. What would you include in your publication?
6. Discuss two current disputes regarding taxonomic issues concerning early hominids. Try to give support for alternative positions.
7. Why would one use the taxonomic term *Paranthropus* instead of *Australopithecus*?
8. What is a phylogeny? Construct one for early hominids (7.0–1 m.y.a.). Make sure you can describe what conclusions your scheme makes. Also, try to defend it.
9. What are the most recently discovered of the earliest hominid materials, and how are they, for the moment, incorporated into a phylogenetic scheme? How secure do you think this interpretation is?

Suggested Further Reading

Begun, David R. 2003. "Planet of the Apes." *Scientific American* 289: 74–83.

Conroy, Glenn C. 1997. *Reconstructing Human Origins. A Modern Synthesis.* New York: Norton.

Tattersall, Ian, and Jeffrey H. Schwartz. 2000. *Extinct Humans.* Boulder, CO: Westview Press.

Wolpoff, Milford H. 1999, *Paleoanthropology.* 2nd ed. Boston: McGraw-Hill.

Wong, Kate. 2003. "An Ancestor to Call Our Own." *Scientific American*, Special Edition 13 (2): 4–13.

Online Anthropology Resource Center

Go to the Anthropology Resource Center at **http://www.anthropology.wadsworth.com** for a wealth of online resources, including a companion website for your text that provides study aids such as self-quizzes for each chapter and a practice final exam, as well as links to anthropology websites and information on the latest theories and discoveries in the field. Also, check out InfoTrac College Edition®, your online library that offers full-length articles from thousands of scholarly and popular publications. Just click on the InfoTrac button at the companion website and use the passcode that came with your book.

11

The Earliest Dispersal of the Genus *Homo:*

Homo erectus and Contemporaries

Taung child's cranium held by South African paleo-anthropologist Phillip Tobias

Robert Jurmain

Introduction

Sometime, close to 2 million years ago, something decisive occurred in human evolution. As the title of this chapter suggests, for the first time, hominids expanded widely out of Africa into other areas of the Old World.

See the following section of the CD-ROM for topics covered in this chapter: Virtual Lab 10.

All the early hominids are found *only* in Africa—being restricted to this continent for perhaps 5 million years. Moreover, the later, more widely dispersed hominids are quite different both anatomically and behaviorally from their African ancestors. They were much larger, were more committed to a completely terrestrial habitat, used more elaborate stone tools, and perhaps included more meat as a regular part of their diets.

There continues to be some variation among the different geographical groups of these highly successful hominids, and debates regarding the best way to classify them continue. Discoveries continue as well. In particular, new finds from Europe are forcing a major reevaluation of exactly *who* were the first hominids to emigrate from Africa (Fig. 11–1).

Nevertheless, after 2 m.y.a., there is less diversity seen in these hominids than was apparent in their pre-*Australopithecus* and *Australopithecus* predecessors. Consequently, there is universal agreement that these hominids outside of Africa are all members of genus *Homo*. Thus, taxonomic debates focus solely on how many species are represented. The species known the longest and for which there is the most evidence is called *Homo erectus*. Furthermore, this is the one group that almost all paleoanthropologists distinguish. Thus, in this chapter we will concentrate our discussion on *Homo erectus*. We will, however, also discuss alternative interpretations that "split" the fossil sample into more species.

A New Kind of Hominid

The discoveries of fossils now referred to as *H. erectus* go back to the nineteenth century. Later in this chapter, we will discuss in some detail the historical background of these earliest discoveries in Java and the somewhat later discoveries in China. From this work, as well as presumably related finds in Europe and North Africa, a variety of taxonomic names were suggested. The most significant of these earlier terms were *Pithecanthropus* (for the Javanese remains) and *Sinanthropus* (for the fossils from northern China).

It is important to realize that such taxonomic *splitting* (which this terminology reflects) was quite common in the early years of paleoanthropology. Only after World War II and with the incorporation of the Modern Synthesis into paleontology (see p. 92) did more systematic biological thinking come to the fore. Most of the fossils previously given these varied names are today placed within the species *Homo erectus*. At minimum, all the fossils have been lumped into one genus (*Homo*).

In the last few decades, discoveries from East Africa of well-established chronometrically dated finds have established the clear presence of *Homo erectus* by 1.8 m.y.a. Some researchers (most notably, Andrews, 1984; Wood, 1991) see several anatomical differences between these African representatives of an

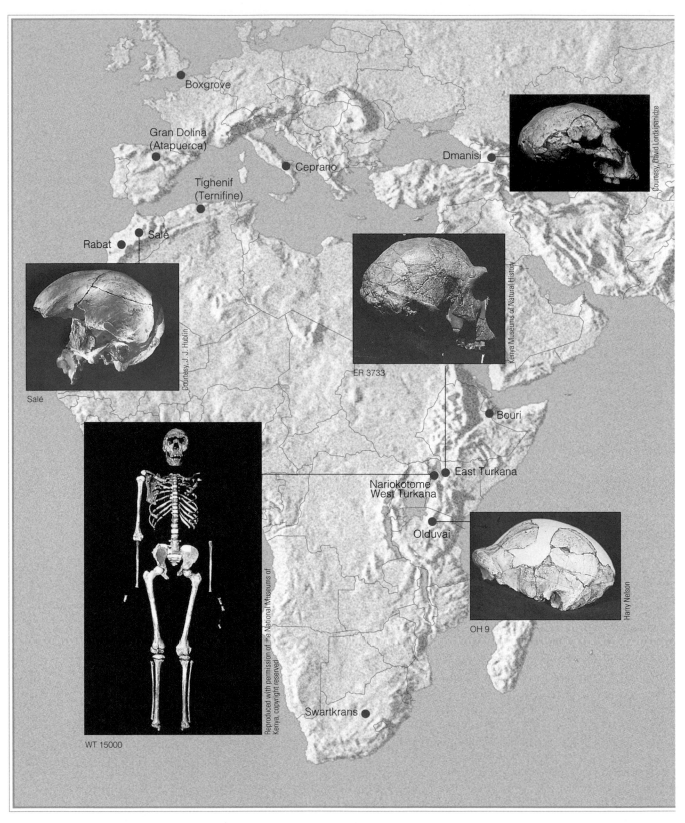

FIGURE 11–1 Major *Homo erectus* sites and localities of other contemporaneous hominids.

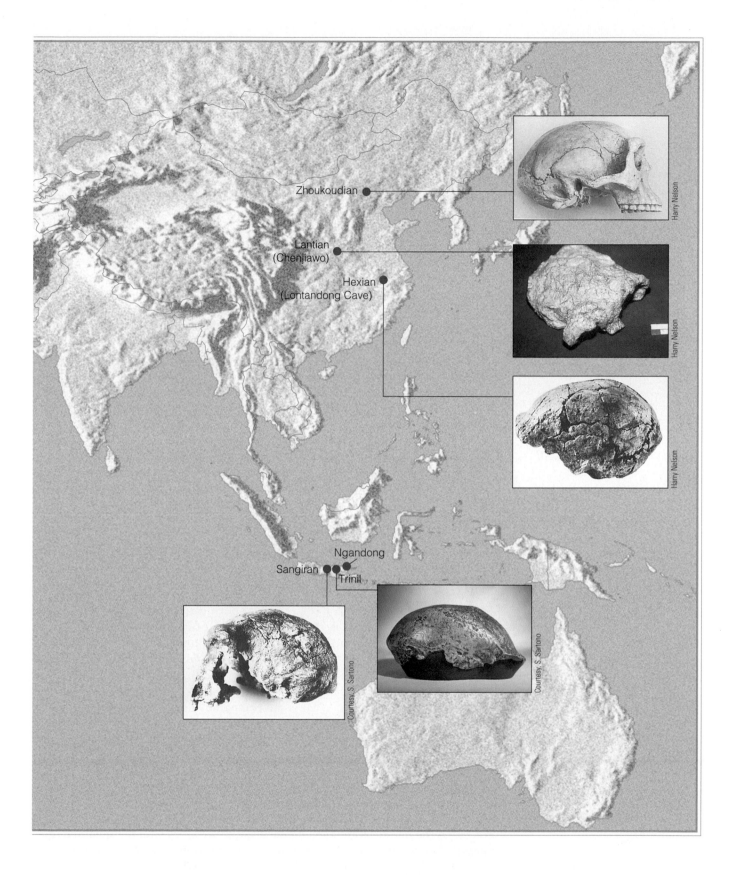

Zhoukoudian

Lantian
(Chenjiawo)

Hexian
(Lontandong Cave)

Ngandong

Sangiran

Trinil

Harry Nelson

Harry Nelson

Harry Nelson

Courtesy, S. Sartono

Courtesy, S. Sartono

See Virtual Lab 10 for an interactive map showing the distribution of *Homo erectus.*

grade A grouping of organisms sharing a similar adaptive pattern. It is not necessarily based on closeness of evolutionary relationship, but does contrast organisms in a useful way (e.g., *H. erectus* with *H. sapiens*).

erectus-like hominid and their Asian cousins (hominids that almost everybody* refers to as *Homo erectus*). Drs. Bernard Wood and Peter Andrews (as well as many other paleoanthropologists) thus place the African fossils into a separate species, one they call *Homo ergaster.*

While there are some anatomical differences between the African specimens and those from Asia, they are all clearly *closely* related (either members of one species or of two closely related species). We will refer to the full complement of these fossils as either *Homo erectus* (in the broad sense) or as *Homo erectus/ergaster.* When referring to just the Asian fossils (and at least one find from Europe), we will call these hominids *Homo erectus* (in the strict sense).

All analyses have shown that *H. erectus/ergaster* represents a different **grade** of evolution than their more ancient African predecessors. A grade is an evolutionary grouping of organisms showing a similar adaptive pattern. Increase in body size and robustness, changes in limb proportions, and greater encephalization all indicate that these hominids were more like modern humans in their adaptive pattern than were their African ancestors.[†] We should point out that a grade only implies general adaptive aspects of a group of animals; it implies nothing directly about shared ancestry (organisms that share common ancestry are said to be in the same *clade;* see p. 112). For example, orangutans and African great apes could be said to be in the same grade, but they are not in the same clade (see p. 152).

The hominids discussed in this chapter are not only members of a new and distinct grade of human evolution; they are also closely related to each other. Whether they all belong to the same clade is debatable. Nevertheless, a major adaptive shift has taken place—one setting hominid evolution in a distinctly more human direction.

We mentioned that there is considerable variation in different regional populations of hominids broadly defined as *Homo erectus.* New discoveries are showing even more dramatic variation, suggesting that some of these hominids may not fit closely at all with this general adaptive pattern (more on this presently). For the moment, however, let us review what *most* of these hominids look like.

The Morphology of *Homo erectus*

BRAIN SIZE

Homo erectus differs in several respects from both early *Homo* and *Homo sapiens.* The most obvious feature is cranial size (which, of course, is closely related to brain size). Early *Homo* had cranial capacities ranging from as small as 500 cm^3 to as large as 800 cm^3. *H. erectus,* on the other hand, shows considerable brain enlargement, with a cranial capacity of 750[††] to 1,250 cm^3 (and a mean of approximately 900 cm^3). However, in making such comparisons, we must bear in mind two key questions: What is the comparative sample, and what were the overall body sizes of the species being compared?

In relation to the first question, you should recall that many scholars are now convinced that there was more than one species of early *Homo* in East Africa around 2 m.y.a. If so, only one of these could have been ancestral to *H. erectus.* (Indeed, it is possible that neither species gave rise to *H. erectus* and that perhaps we have yet to find direct evidence of the ancestral species.) Taking a more optimistic view that at least one of these fossil groups is a likely ancestor of later hominids, the question still remains—which one? If we choose the smaller-bodied sample of early *Homo* as our presumed ancestral group, then *H. erectus* shows as

---

*At least one researcher (Wolpoff, 1999) refers to all the hominids discussed in this chapter as *Homo sapiens.*

† We did note in Chapter 10 that early *Homo* is a partial exception, being transitional in some respects.

††Considerably smaller cranial capacities have been found in recently discovered fossils from Europe.

much as a 40 percent increase in cranial capacity. However, if the comparative sample is the larger-bodied group of early *Homo* (as exemplified by skull 1470, from East Turkana), then *H. erectus* shows a 25 percent increase in cranial capacity.

As we previously discussed, brain size is closely tied to overall body size. We have made a point of the increase in *H. erectus* brain size; however, it must be realized that *H. erectus* was also considerably larger overall than earlier members of the genus *Homo*. In fact, when *H. erectus* is compared with the larger-bodied early *Homo* sample, *relative* brain size is about the same (Walker, 1991). Furthermore, when considering the relative brain size of *H. erectus* in comparison with *H. sapiens*, it is seen that *H. erectus* was considerably less encephalized than later members of the genus *Homo*.

BODY SIZE

As we have mentioned, *H. erectus* was larger than earlier hominids, as was conclusively shown by the discovery of a nearly complete skeleton in 1984 from **Nariokotome** (on the west side of Lake Turkana in Kenya). From this specimen (and from less complete individuals at other sites), some *Homo erectus* adults are estimated to have weighed well over 100 pounds, with an average adult stature of about 5 feet 6 inches (McHenry, 1992; Ruff and Walker, 1993; Walker and Leakey, 1993). Another point to keep in mind is that *Homo erectus* was quite sexually dimorphic—at least as indicated by the East African specimens. Thus, for male adults, weight and stature in some individuals may have been considerably greater than the average figures just mentioned. In fact, it is estimated that if the Nariokotome boy had survived, he would have attained an adult stature of over 6 feet (Walker, 1993).

Nariokotome
(nar´-ee-oh-koh´-tow-may)

Associated with the large stature (and explaining the significant increase in body weight) is also a dramatic increase in robusticity. In fact, this characteristic of very heavy body build was to dominate hominid evolution not just during *H. erectus* times, but through the long transitional era of premodern forms as well. Only with the appearance of anatomically modern *H. sapiens* do we see a more gracile skeletal structure, which is still characteristic of most modern populations.

CRANIAL SHAPE

The cranium of *Homo erectus* displays a highly distinctive shape, partly as a result of increased brain size, but probably more correlated with significant body size (robusticity). The ramifications of this heavily built cranium are reflected in thick cranial bone (most notably in Asian specimens) and large browridges (supraorbital tori) in the front of the skull and a projecting **nuchal torus** at the rear (Fig. 11–2).

nuchal torus (nuke´-ul, pertaining to the neck) A ridge or elevated line of bone in the back of the cranium to which the muscles of the back of the neck are attached. These muscles hold the head upright.

The vault is long and low, receding back from the large browridges with little forehead development. Moreover, the cranium is wider at the base compared with earlier *or* later species of genus *Homo*. The maximum breadth is below the ear opening, giving a pentagonal contour to the cranium (when viewed from behind). In contrast, both early *Homo* crania and *H. sapiens* crania have more vertical sides, and the maximum width is *above* the ear openings.

DENTITION

The dentition of *Homo erectus* is much like that of *Homo sapiens*, but the earlier species exhibits somewhat larger teeth. However, compared with early *Homo*, *H. erectus* does show some dental reduction.

Another interesting feature of the dentition of some *H. erectus* specimens is seen in the incisor teeth. On the back (lingual) surfaces, the teeth are scooped

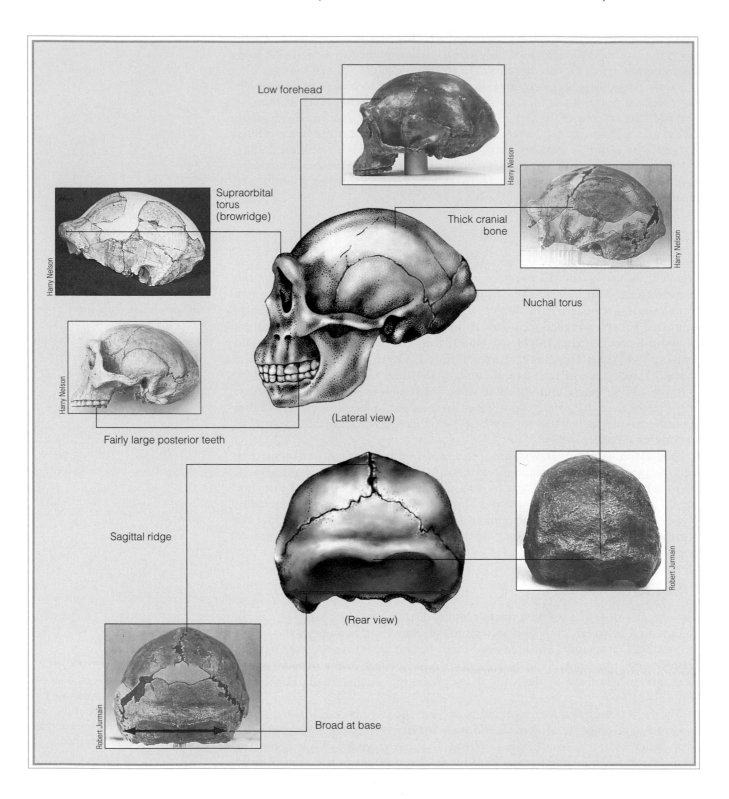

Low forehead

Supraorbital torus (browridge)

Thick cranial bone

Nuchal torus

Harry Nelson

Fairly large posterior teeth

(Lateral view)

Sagittal ridge

(Rear view)

Robert Jurmain

Broad at base

FIGURE 11–2 Morphology and variation in *Homo erectus.*

out in appearance, forming a surface reminiscent of a shovel. Accordingly, such teeth are referred to as "shovel-shaped" incisors, and they are also found in several modern human populations (Fig. 11–3). It has been suggested that teeth shaped in this manner are an adaptation in hunter-gatherers for processing foods, a contention not yet proved (or really even framed in a testable manner). One thing does seem likely: Shovel-shaped incisors are probably an ancestral feature of the species *H. erectus,* as the phenomenon has been found not just in many Chinese specimens, but also in an early individual from Kenya.

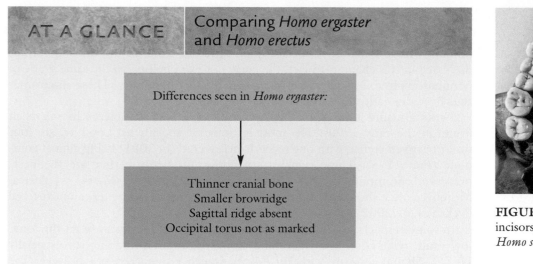

AT A GLANCE   Comparing *Homo ergaster* and *Homo erectus*

Differences seen in *Homo ergaster:*

↓

Thinner cranial bone
Smaller browridge
Sagittal ridge absent
Occipital torus not as marked

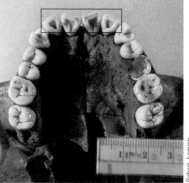

FIGURE 11–3 Shovel-shaped incisors, shown here in a modern *Homo sapiens* individual.

Who Were the Earliest African Emigrants?

The fossils from East Africa imply that a new grade of human evolution was first attained in Africa not long after 2 m.y.a. Thus, the hominids who migrated to Asia and Europe are generally assumed to be their immediate descendants. This conclusion makes good sense on at least three levels: geography, anatomy, and behavior. Geographically, Africa is the region of *all* the earlier hominids, so *H. erectus/ergaster* very likely would have first appeared here (and East Africa especially would have been a likely locality). Moreover, these are now bigger, brainier hominids capable of traveling longer distances. Finally, they likely also possessed a more advanced tool kit, allowing these hominids to exploit a wider range of resources.

Consider the following reasonable hypothesis: *Homo erectus/ergaster* first evolved in East Africa close to 2 m.y.a. and with its new physical/behavioral capacities soon emigrated to other areas of the Old World.

This hypothesis helps pull together several aspects of hominid evolution, and much of the fossil evidence after 2 m.y.a. supports it. Nevertheless, there are some difficulties, and recently discovered evidence seriously challenges this tidy view.

First, while 1.8 m.y.a. is a well-established date for the appearance of *H. erectus/ergaster* in East Africa, these hominids also appear at just about the same time in Indonesia and soon thereafter in eastern Europe (see Fig. 11–1). Radiometric dates on sediments on the island of Java have recently placed *H. erectus* (strictly defined) at sites 1.8 and 1.6 million years old. It is possible for our hypothesis to explain these hominids in Asia this early *if* we assume that *H. erectus* evolves in East Africa by 1.8 m.y.a. (or slightly earlier) and, in just a few thousand years, expands very rapidly to other regions.

Moreover, at almost as early a date, hominids are also present in the Caucasus region of easternmost Europe. Newly discovered fossils from the Dmanisi site in the Republic of Georgia (see Figs. 11–1 and 11–4) have been radiometrically dated to 1.75 m.y.a. Could this occurrence at yet another distant locality from the presumptive East African homeland still be accommodated within our hypothesis? Perhaps, but we are beginning to stretch the limits of how quickly these hominids could have migrated.

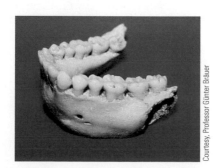

FIGURE 11–4 Dmanisi mandible.

THE DMANISI HOMINIDS

Even more problematic for our hypothesis is the physical appearance of the hominids from Dmanisi. They are quite different from all the other hominids discussed in this chapter. In fact, they may not even belong to the same grade of hominid evolution as all these other (*H. erectus*) hominids. These discoveries thus have dramatic implications.

These Dmanisi finds are all quite recent, the first few pieces having been found in the early 1990s. The most informative specimens, however, are four well-preserved crania, with one recently discovered (in 2001) being almost complete (Fig. 11–5). These remains are important because they are the best-preserved hominids of this antiquity found anywhere *outside* of Africa. Moreover, they show a mixed pattern of characteristics, some quite unexpected (Vekua et al., 2002).

In some respects, the Dmanisi crania are similar to *H. erectus* (e.g., the long, low vault, wide base, and thickening along the sagittal midline; see especially Fig. 11–5b and compare with Fig. 11–2). In other characteristics, however, the Dmanisi individuals are different from other hominid finds outside of Africa. In particular, the most complete specimen (specimen 2700; see Fig. 11–5c) has a less robust and thinner browridge, a projecting lower face, and a large upper canine. Thus, at least from the front, this skull is more reminiscent of the smaller early *Homo* specimens from East Africa than of *Homo erectus*. Moreover, cranial capacity in this individual is very small (estimated at only 600 cm³, well within the range of early *Homo*). In fact, all three Dmanisi crania show small cranial capacities (the other two estimated at 650 cm³ and 780 cm³).

A number of stone tools have also been recovered at Dmanisi. The tools are similar to early African implements and are quite different from the ostensibly more advanced technology of the Acheulian (the latter broadly associated with *H. erectus* in much of the Old World).

From these recent, startling revelations from Dmanisi, several questions can be raised:

1. Was *Homo erectus* the first hominid to leave Africa—or was it an earlier form of *Homo*?
2. Did hominids require a large brain and sophisticated stone tool culture to disperse out of Africa?
3. Was the large, robust body build of *H. erectus* a necessary adaptation for the initial occupation of Eurasia?

Of course, the Dmanisi discoveries are very new, so any conclusions we draw must be seen as highly tentative. Nevertheless, the recent evidence raises important and exciting possibilities. It now seems likely that the first transcontinental hominid migrants were a form of early *Homo* (similar to the smaller East African species, *Homo habilis;* see p. 278). At best, and as exemplified at Dmanisi, the

FIGURE 11–5 Dmanisi crania discovered in 1999 and 2001 and dated to 1.8–1.7 m.y.a. (a) Specimen 2282. (b) Specimen 2280. (c) Specimen 2700.

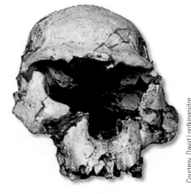

(a)

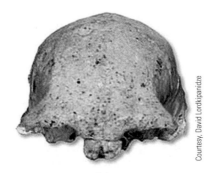

(b)

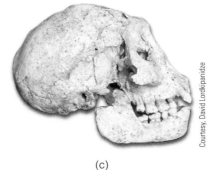

(c)

Courtesy, David Lordkipanidze

first hominids to leave Africa were a very early form of *H. erectus,* much more primitive than any of the other specimens from Africa, Asia, or Europe discussed in this chapter.

Certainly the smaller individuals from Dmanisi did not have a large brain (by *H. erectus* standards), nor did they have an advanced stone tool culture (possessing instead tools very similar to the earliest ones from East and South Africa).

Thus far, only a few isolated postcranial remains have been found at Dmanisi, so we do not know as yet the body structure of the earliest hominids to leave Africa. It is possible, however, that the overall body proportions (as with the face of the smallest Dmanisi cranium) resemble *Homo habilis* more than they do *H. erectus.* Thus, these first pioneers to leave Africa may have been, in the words of Phillip Rightmire (of the State University of New York, Binghamton, and a coauthor of the first article announcing the 2001 Dmanisi discovery), "little people." That is, they may have been very different from the big-bodied, long-legged, full-blown *H. erectus* body plan. Given these startling and still provisional observations, it appears that these Dmanisi hominids do not meet any of the criteria used to define the more human evolutionary grade of all the other *Homo erectus/ergaster* individuals. At minimum, we have to admit that our hypothesis is not looking nearly so tidy as we might have hoped!

Accordingly, major reappraisals regarding the status of early *Homo* as well as what constitutes membership in the genus *Homo* itself will be required. Moreover, the core of our hypothesis, explaining those factors that "propelled" hominids out of Africa, may well be largely falsified. All this evidence is so new, however, that it is premature even to predict what further revisions may be required.

Historical Overview of *Homo erectus* Discoveries

Homo erectus (broadly defined) is found widely distributed across three continents. It is, however, difficult to organize these materials in a clear chronological order (as we did for African hominids in Chapter 10). First, we have the problem of complexity. As already noted, the earliest members of the group all appear on the scene nearly simultaneously, around 1.8 m.y.a., in Africa, Asia, and Europe. And second, for most of the later representatives, radiometric dating is not possible. Thus, our knowledge of the chronological placement of many specimens is highly tenuous.

The best way to proceed is to discuss these fossil hominids from a historical perspective—that is, in the order in which they were discovered. We believe that this approach is useful, as the discoveries cover a broad range of time—indeed, almost the entire history of paleoanthropology. Given this relatively long history of scientific discovery, the later finds were assessed in the light of earlier ones (and thus can still be best understood within a historical context).

JAVA

Dutch anatomist Eugene Dubois (1858–1940) (Fig. 11–6) was the first scientist to deliberately design a research plan that would take him from his anatomy lab to where fossil bones might be buried. Up until this time, embryology and comparative anatomy were considered the proper methods of studying humans and their ancestry, and the research was done in the laboratory. Dubois changed all this.

The publication of Darwin's *On the Origin of Species* in 1859 had ushered in a period of intellectual excitement. This stimulating intellectual climate surrounded the youthful Dubois, who left Holland for Sumatra in 1887 to search for, as he phrased it, "the missing link."

FIGURE 11–6 Eugene Dubois, discoverer of the first *H. erectus* fossil to be found.

In October 1891, along the Solo River, near the town of Trinil, the field crew unearthed a skullcap that was to become internationally famous. The following year, a human femur was recovered about 15 yards upstream in what Dubois claimed was the same level as the skullcap. Dubois assumed that the skullcap (with a cranial capacity of slightly over 900 cm³) and the femur belonged to the same individual.

After studying these discoveries for a few years, Dubois startled the world in 1894 with a paper provocatively titled "*Pithecanthropus erectus,* A Manlike Species of Transitional Anthropoid from Java." Dubois' views were harshly criticized; yet, after other scholars examined the original fossils, his views were taken more seriously. Eventually, there was general acceptance that Dubois was correct in identifying the skull as representing a previously undescribed species; that his estimates of cranial capacity were reasonably accurate; that *Pithecanthropus erectus,* or *H. erectus* as we call it today, is a close relative and perhaps an ancestor of *H. sapiens;* and that bipedalism preceded enlargement of the brain.

By 1930, the controversy had faded, especially in light of important new discoveries near Peking (Beijing), China, in the late 1920s (discussed shortly). Similarities between the Beijing skulls and Dubois' *Pithecanthropus* were obvious, and scientists pointed out that the Java form was not an "apeman," as Dubois contended, but rather was closely related to modern *Homo sapiens.*

One might expect that Dubois would welcome the finds from China and the support they provided for the human status of *Pithecanthropus,* but Dubois would have none of it. He refused to recognize any connection between Beijing and Java and described the Beijing fossils as "a degenerate Neanderthaler" (von Koenigswald, 1956, p. 55). He also refused to accept the classification of "*Pithecanthropus*" in the same species with later finds from Java.

HOMO ERECTUS FROM JAVA

Six sites in eastern Java have yielded all the *H. erectus* fossil remains found to date on that island. The dating of these fossils has been hampered by the complex nature of Javanese geology. It has been generally accepted that most of the fossils belong in the Middle **Pleistocene** and are less than 800,000 years old. However, as we noted earlier, new dating estimates have suggested one find (from Modjokerto) to be close to 1.8 million years old and another fossil from the main site of Sangiran to be approximately 1.6 million years old.

At Sangiran, where the remains of at least five individuals have been excavated, the cranial capacities of the fossils range from 813 cm³ to 1,059 cm³. Another site called Ngandong has also been fruitful, yielding the remains of 12 crania (Fig. 11–7). The dating here is also confusing, but the Upper Pleistocene has been suggested, which may explain the larger cranial measurements of the Ngandong individuals as well as features that are more modern than those found on other Javanese crania. Recently published dates for the Ngandong site are very recent, remarkably so, in fact. Using two specialized dating techniques (discussed in Chapter 13; see p. 376), Carl Swisher of Rutgers University and his colleagues from the Berkeley Geochronology Laboratory have determined from animal bones found at the site (and presumably associated with the hominids) a date ranging from about 50,000 years ago to as recently as 25,000 years ago (Swisher et al., 1996). These dates are controversial, but further confirmation is now establishing a *very* late survival of *Homo erectus* in Java, long after these hominids had disappeared elsewhere. They would thus be contemporary with *Homo sapiens*—which, by this time, had expanded widely in the Old World.

We cannot say much about the *H. erectus* way of life in Java. Very few artifacts have been found, and those have come mainly from river terraces, not from primary sites: "On Java there is still not a single site where artifacts can be associated with *H. erectus*" (Bartstra, 1982, p. 319).

Pleistocene The epoch of the Cenozoic from 1.8 m.y.a. until 10,000 y.a. Frequently referred to as the Ice Age, this epoch is associated with continental glaciations in northern latitudes.

Courtesy, S. Sartono

FIGURE 11–7 Rear view of a Ngandong skull. Note that the cranial walls slope downward and outward (or upward and inward), with the widest breadth low on the cranium, giving it a pentagonal form.

PEKING (BEIJING)

The story of Peking *H. erectus* is another saga filled with excitement, hard work, luck, and misfortune. Europeans had known for a long time that "dragon bones," used by the Chinese as medicine and aphrodisiacs, were actually ancient mammal bones. Scientists eventually located one of the sources of these dragon bones near Beijing at the remarkable site of **Zhoukoudian.** Serious excavations were begun in the 1920s under the direction of a young Chinese geologist, Pei Wenshong. In 1929, a fossil skull was discovered, and Pei brought the specimen to anatomist Davidson Black (Fig. 11–8). Because the fossil was embedded in hard limestone, it took Black four months of hard, steady work to free it from its tough matrix. The result was worth the labor. The skull, that of a juvenile, was thick, low, and relatively small, but in Black's mind there was no doubt that it belonged to an early hominid. The response to this discovery, quite unlike that which greeted Dubois almost 40 years earlier, was immediate and enthusiastically favorable.

Franz Weidenreich (Fig. 11–9), a distinguished anatomist well known for his work on European fossil hominids, succeeded Black. After Japan invaded China in 1933, Weidenreich decided to move the fossils from Beijing to prevent them from falling into the hands of the Japanese. Weidenreich left China in 1941, taking excellent prepared casts, photographs, and drawings of the fossil material with him. After he left, the bones were packed, and arrangements were made for the U.S. Marine Corps in Beijing to take them to the United States. The bones never reached the United States, and they have never been found. To this day, no one knows what happened to them, and their location remains a mystery.

ZHOUKOUDIAN *HOMO ERECTUS*

The fossil remains of *H. erectus* discovered by the earlier work in the 1920s and 1930s as well as some more recent excavations at Zhoukoudian (Fig. 11–10) constitutes by far the largest collection of *H. erectus* material found anywhere. Included in this excellent sample are 14 skullcaps (Fig. 11–11), other cranial pieces, and more than 100 isolated teeth, but only a scattering of postcranial elements (Jia and Huang, 1990). Various interpretations to account for this unusual pattern of preservation have been offered, ranging from ritualistic treatment or cannibalism by the hominids themselves to the more mundane suggestion that the *H. erectus* remains are simply the leftovers of the meals of giant hyenas (discussed shortly).

FIGURE 11–8 Davidson Black, responsible for the first study of the Zhoukoudian fossils.

FIGURE 11–9 Franz Weidenreich.

Zhoukoudian
(Zhoh´-koh-dee´-en)

FIGURE 11–10 Zhoukoudian Cave. The grid on the wall was drawn for purposes of excavation. The entrance to the cave can be seen near the grid.

FIGURE 11–11 *H. erectus* (cast of specimen from Zhoukoudian). From this view, the supraorbital torus, low vault of the skull, and nuchal torus can clearly be seen.

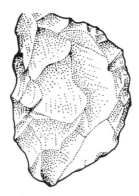

See Virtual Lab 10, section I, for a 3-D animation of a Zhoukoudian cranium.

FIGURE 11–12 Chinese tools from Middle Pleistocene sites. (Adapted from Wu and Olsen, 1985.)

Nevertheless, the hominid remains belong to upward of 40 male and female adults and children and constitute a considerable amount of evidence. With the meticulous work by Weidenreich, the Zhoukoudian fossils have led to a good overall picture of the eastern *H. erectus* of China. Peking *H. erectus,* like that from Java, possesses typical *H. erectus* features, including the supraorbital torus in front and the nuchal torus behind; also, the skull is thick and is keeled by a sagittal ridge, the face protrudes, the incisors are shoveled, and, like the Javanese forms, the skull shows the greatest breadth near the bottom.

Cultural Remains More than 100,000 artifacts have been recovered from this vast site that was occupied intermittently for almost 250,000 years. According to the Chinese (Wu and Lin, 1983, p.86), Zhoukoudian "is one of the sites with the longest history of habitation by man or his ancestors." The occupation of the site has been divided into three cultural stages:

> *Earliest Stage* (460,000–420,000 y.a.)* The tools are large, close to a pound in weight, and made of soft stone, such as sandstone.
> *Middle Stage* (370,000–350,000 y.a.) Tools become smaller and lighter (under a pound), and these smaller tools comprise approximately two-thirds of the sample.
> *Final Stage* (300,000–230,000 y.a.) Tools are still small, and the tool materials are of better quality. The coarse quartz of the earlier periods is replaced by a finer quartz, sandstone tools have almost disappeared, and flint tools increase in frequency by as much as 30 percent.

As you can see, the early tools are crude and shapeless but become more refined over time. Common tools at the site are choppers and chopping tools, but retouched flakes were fashioned into scrapers, points, burins, and awls (Fig. 11–12).

The way of life at Zhoukoudian has traditionally been described as that of hunter-gatherers who killed deer and horses as well as other animals and gathered fruits, berries, and ostrich eggs. Fragments of charred ostrich eggshells, the abundant deposits of hackberry seeds unearthed in the cave, and the flourishing plant growth surrounding the cave all suggest that meat was supplemented by the gathering of herbs, wild fruits, tubers, and eggs. Layers of what has long been thought to be ash in the cave, over 18 feet deep at one point, suggest to some researchers the use of fire by *H. erectus;* however, whether Beijing hominids could actually make fire is unknown. Wu and Lin (1983, p. 94) state that "Peking Man was a cave dweller, a fire user, a deer hunter, a seed gatherer and a maker of specialized tools," but several questions about Zhoukoudian *H. erectus* remain unanswered.

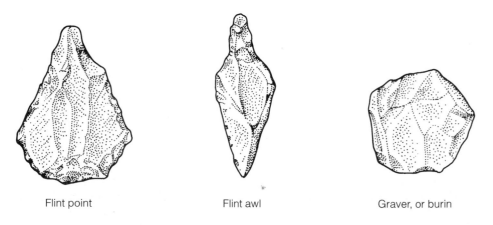

Quartzite chopper   Flint point   Flint awl   Graver, or burin

*These dates should be considered tentative until more precise chronometric determinations are available.

Did *H. erectus* at Zhoukoudian use language? If by language we mean articulate speech, it is unlikely. Nevertheless, some scholars believe that speech originated early in hominid evolution; others argue that speech did not originate until up to 200,000 years later in the Upper Paleolithic, with the origin of anatomically modern humans (see Chapter 13). We agree with Dean Falk when she writes, "Unfortunately, what it is going to take to *settle* the debate about when language originated in hominids is a time machine. Until one becomes available, we can only speculate about this fascinating and important question" (1989, p. 141).

Did these hominids wear clothes? Almost surely clothing of some type, probably in the form of animal skins, was worn. Winters in Beijing are harsh today and appear to have been bitter during the Middle Pleistocene as well. Moreover, awls were found at Zhoukoudian, and one of the probable bone tools may be a needle.

What was the life span of *H. erectus* at Zhoukoudian? Apparently, not very long, and infant and childhood mortality was probably very high. Studies of the fossil remains reveal that almost 40 percent of the bones belong to individuals under the age of 14, and only 2.6 percent are estimated to be in the 50- to 60-year age-group (Jia, 1975).

Several researchers have challenged this picture of Zhoukoudian life. Lewis Binford and colleagues (Binford and Ho, 1985; Binford and Stone, 1986a, 1986b) reject the description of Beijing *H. erectus* as hunters and argue that the evidence clearly points to them as scavengers.

Using techniques of taphonomy (discussed in Chapter 9), Noel Boaz and colleagues have even questioned whether the *H. erectus* remains at Zhoukoudian represent evidence of hominid habitation of the cave. By carefully comparing the types of bones as well as the damage to the bones found at Zhoukoudian with that seen in contemporary carnivore dens, Boaz and Ciochon (2001) have suggested that much of the materials in the cave likely accumulated through the activities of a giant extinct hyena. Indeed, they hypothesize that most of the *H. erectus* remains, too, are the food refuse of hyenic meals!

Boaz and his associates do recognize that the tools in the cave and possibly cut marks on some of the animal bones do provide evidence of hominid activities at Zhoukoudian. They also recognize that more detailed analysis is required to test their hypotheses and to "determine the nature and scope" of the *H. erectus* presence at Zhoukoudian.

Probably the most intriguing archaeological aspect of the presumed hominid behavior at Zhoukoudian has been the long-held assumption that *H. erectus* deliberately utilized fire inside the cave. The technological control of fire was one of the major cultural breakthroughs of all prehistory. By providing warmth, a means of cooking, an aid to further modify tools, and so forth, controlled fire would have been a giant technological innovation. While some potential early African sites have been suggested as giving evidence of hominid control of fire, it has long been concluded that the first *definite* evidence of hominid fire use comes from Zhoukoudian.

Now, new evidence has radically altered this assumption. Much more detailed excavations at Zhoukoudian were carried out in 1996 and 1997 by biologist Steve Weiner and colleagues. These researchers also carefully analyzed the soil samples they collected for distinctive chemical signatures (which would show whether fire had occurred in the cave) (Weiner et al., 1998). Weiner and his colleagues found that only rarely was any burnt bone found associated with tools, and in most cases the burning appeared to have taken place *after* fossilization (i.e., the bones were not cooked). Moreover, the "ash" layers mentioned earlier are not ash at all, but rather naturally accumulated organic sediment. This last conclusion was derived from chemical testing showing no sign whatsoever of wood burning inside the cave. Finally, the "hearths" that have figured so prominently in archaeological reconstructions of the fire control at this site are apparently not hearths at all. They simply are round depressions formed in the past by water collecting when the cave was more open to the elements.

Indeed, another provisional interpretation of the cave's geology suggests that the cave did not open in the manner of habitation sites, but had access only through a vertical shaft, leading archaeologist Alison Brooks to remark, "It wouldn't have been a shelter, it would have been a trap" (quoted in Wuethrich, 1998).

These serious doubts regarding control of fire, coupled with the suggestive evidence of bone accumulation by carnivores, have led anthropologists Noel Boaz and Russell Ciochon to conclude, "Zhoukoudian cave was neither hearth nor home" (Boaz and Ciochon, 2001) (see A Closer Look).

OTHER CHINESE SITES

More work has been done at Zhoukoudian than at any other Chinese site. Nevertheless, there are other hominid sites worth noting. Three of the more important sites, besides Zhoukoudian, include two sites in Lantian County (often simply referred to as Lantian) and another site in Hexian County (usually referred to as the Hexian find).

A CLOSER LOOK

The Control of Fire

An important distinction exists between the *making* of fire and the *use* of fire captured from natural sources. Some very ancient methods that could have been used deliberately to make fire might have included striking hard rocks together or rubbing wood together to create sparks through friction. Without such technological innovations, earlier hominids would have been limited to obtaining and transporting fire from natural sources, such as lightning strikes and geothermal localities.

The archaeological evidence, however, may never be sufficiently complete to allow this distinction to be made with much precision. Nevertheless, *at minimum,* the consistent use of fire would have been a major technological breakthrough and could have had potentially marked influence on hominid biological evolution as well. For example, as a result of cooking, food items would have been more tender; thus, chewing stresses would have been reduced, perhaps leading to selection for reduced size of the dentition.

It is possible that australopithecines took advantage of and used naturally occurring fire, but the evidence relating to the use of fire is not always easy to interpret. At open-air sites, for example, remains suggesting an association between hominids and burning may be found. However, ashes may already have been blown away, and stones and bones blackened by fire could be the result of a natural brush fire, as could charcoal and baked earth. Furthermore, remains found on the surface of a site might be the result of a natural fire that occurred long after the hominids had left.

There are several possible advantages that controlled use of fire may have provided to earlier hominids, including:

1. Warmth
2. Cooking meat and/or plant foods, thus breaking down fibers and, in the case of many plants, neutralizing toxins
3. Fire-hardening wood, such as the end of a spear
4. Facilitating the predictable flaking of certain stone materials, thus aiding in the production of stone tools
5. Chasing competing predators (such as bears) from caves and keeping dangerous animals at bay
6. Providing illumination in caves and, more fundamentally, extending usable light into the night

This last implication of human control of fire may have had a profound effect on human sleep cycles and with it alterations in activity patterns, neurological functioning, and hormonal balance. In fact, recent experiments have suggested that humans still today can readily (and comfortably) adjust to "natural" light/dark cycles with periods of inactivity of up to 14 hours (thus simulating winter conditions *prior* to the systematic control of fire).

Since controlling fire is so important to humans, it would be useful to know who tamed the wild flames and when, where, and how they did it. With that knowledge we

At Chenjiawo, in Lantian, an almost complete mandible containing several teeth was found in 1963. It is quite similar to those from Zhoukoudian but has been provisionally dated at about 650,000 y.a. If the dating is correct, this specimen is older than the Beijing material. The following year, a partial cranium was discovered at Gongwangling, not far from Chenjiawo. Provisionally dated to as much as 1.15 m.y.a. (Etler and Tianyuan, 1994), the Gongwangling specimen may be the oldest Chinese *Homo erectus* fossil yet known.

Perhaps the most significant find was the 1980 Hexian discovery, where remains of several individuals were recovered. One of the specimens is a well-preserved cranium (with a cranial capacity of about 1,025 cm^3) lacking much of its base. Dated roughly at 250,000 y.a., it is not surprising that this Hexian cranium displays several advanced features. The cranial constriction, for example, is not as pronounced as in earlier forms, and certain temporal and occipital characteristics are "best compared with the later forms of *H. erectus* at Zhoukoudian" (Wu and Dong, 1985, p. 87).

In 1993, Li Tianyuan and Dennis Etler reported that two relatively complete skulls were discovered in 1989 at a hominid site in Yunxian County. The date given for the site is 350,000 y.a., which, if correct, would make these the most complete crania of this great antiquity in China (Fig. 11–13).

could learn much more about the culture of our ancient ancestors and their evolution. Archaeologists are not certain who the first fire makers were. Two of the earliest presumed examples of fire use come from Africa, and both have been suggested as indicating deliberate hominid pyrotechnics *prior* to 1 m.y.a. At Chesowanja in southern Kenya, patches of burned clay dated at 1.4 m.y.a. were found in association with stone tools. John Gowlett and his colleague, Jack Harris, have suggested that the burned clay is the residue of ancient campfires. And recent excavations from upper levels at Swartkrans in South Africa by C. K. Brain and Andrew Sillen have recovered many pieces of burnt bone, again in association with stone tools dated at 1.3–1 m.y.a. (For a further discussion of Swartkrans, see pp. 283–284.) Both of these possible occurrences of hominid control of fire in Africa are thought to be associated with *Homo erectus*. However, neither of the early African contexts has yet to fully convince other experts.

True caves* may be a more probable source for finding human-made fire, because caves, except at the entrance, are damp, very dark, and impossible for habitation without light. Also, by the time humans began to occupy caves, they may have invented a method of making fire. It is possible, of course, to carry a natural fire into a cave, which is another snag in determining whether the fire was deliberately made or natural.

Probably the most famous cave site is Zhoukoudian (discussed in this chapter), where both Chinese and Western archaeologists have been working for more than 70 years. Evidence of supposed fire is abundant, but this evidence (such as charred animal bones, layers of ash, charcoal, and burned stone artifacts) has led to differing interpretations and recent reassessments by archaeologists (see discussion in text).

There appears to be evidence of fire at other open sites in China and several caves in Europe, provisionally dated to about 300,000 years ago. They have yielded evidence of fire possibly made by later hominids. But again, not all archaeologists are persuaded that humans were responsible.

Other prehistorians are sure that Neandertals (discussed in Chapter 12), who built hearths, were the first to make fire toward the end of the Middle Pleistocene (c. 125,000 y.a.). A deliberately built hearth is probably the best evidence for human-controlled fire. Ancient hearths are usually built with stone cobbles arranged in a circular or oval shape to contain the fire. The presence of numerous hearths at a site (like finding a box of matches near a fire) tends to serve as proof that the fires were probably started by humans. It is the absence of identifiable hearths that is so troublesome at the older sites and which immediately signals a doubt that the fire was made (or even systematically used) by hominids. It will take the development of carefully constructed interpretive techniques to overcome the difficulties of solving the case of the first significant controllers of fire.

---

*Swartkrans was not a cave during the time of hominid archaeological accumulation, but has been shown to have been a natural fissure into which animals and other objects fell.

FIGURE 11–13 (a) EV 9002 (Yunxian, China). The skull is in better shape than its companion, and its lateral view clearly displays features characteristic of *H. erectus:* flattened vault, receding forehead (frontal bone), angulated occiput, and supraorbital torus. (b) EV 9001 (Yunxian). Unfortunately, the skull was crushed, but it preserves some lateral facial structures absent in EV 9002.

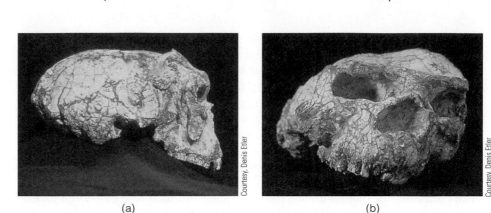

(a)   (b)

The Yunxian crania are both large and robust, considerably exceeding in size those from Zhoukoudian. In general, the Yunxian individuals fit within *Homo erectus,* but in the facial region especially they also show some differences. Unfortunately, both skulls are still covered with a hard calcareous matrix, and critics argue that until the skulls are cleaned and the crushed parts properly put together, it is too early to make accurate assessments. In any case, these Yunxian crania will ultimately provide considerable data to help clarify hominid evolution in China and perhaps elsewhere in the Old World as well

The Asian crania from both Java and China share many similar features, which may be explained by *H. erectus* migration from Java to China perhaps around 1 million years ago. African *H. erectus* forms are generally older than most Asian forms and are not as similar to them as Asian forms (i.e., from Java and China) are to each other.

EAST AFRICA

Olduvai Back in 1960, Louis Leakey unearthed a fossil skull at Olduvai (OH 9) that he identified as *H. erectus.* Skull OH 9 from Upper Bed II is dated at 1.4 m.y.a. and preserves a massive cranium but is faceless except for a bit of nose below the supraorbital torus. Estimated at 1,067 cm³, the cranial capacity of OH 9 is the largest of all the African *Homo erectus* specimens (defined in the broad sense; these specimens are also referred to as *H. ergaster*). The browridge is huge, the largest known for any hominid in both thickness and projection, but the vault walls are thin. This latter characteristic of fairly thin cranial vault bones is seen in most East African *H. erectus* specimens, and in this respect they differ from Asian *H. erectus,* in which cranial vaults are thick (this and other differences have led some researchers to place East African specimens in a separate species).

East Turkana Some 400 miles north of Olduvai Gorge, on the northern boundary of Kenya, is Lake Turkana. Explored by Richard Leakey and colleagues since 1969, the eastern shore of the lake has been a virtual gold mine for australopithecine, early *Homo,* and *H. erectus* fossil remains.

The most significant *H. erectus/ergaster* discovery from East Turkana is a nearly complete skull (Fig. 11–14) dated at 1.8 m.y.a. (i.e., as early as the earliest *H. erectus* from Java). The cranial capacity is estimated at 848 cm³, at the lower end of the range for *H. erectus,* but this is not surprising considering its early date. The cranium generally resembles Asian *H. erectus* in many features (but with some important differences, discussed shortly).

Not many tools have been found at *H. erectus* sites in East Turkana. Oldowan types of flakes, cobbles, and core tools have been found, and the introduction of **Acheulian** tools about 1.4 m.y.a. replaced the Oldowan tradition.

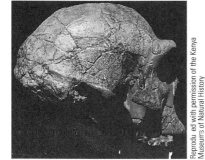

FIGURE 11–14 ER 3733, the most complete East Turkana *H. erectus* cranium.

Acheulian (ash´-oo-lay-en) Pertaining to a stone tool industry of the Lower and Middle Pleistocene characterized by a large proportion of bifacial tools (flaked on both sides). Acheulian tool kits are very common in Africa, Southwest Asia, and western Europe, but are less common elsewhere. (Also spelled "Acheulean.")

West Turkana* In August 1984, Kamoya Kimeu, a member of Richard Leakey's team, added to his reputation as an outstanding fossil hunter when he discovered a small piece of skull near the base camp on the west side of Lake Turkana. Leakey and his colleague, Alan Walker of Pennsylvania State University, excavated the site known as Nariokotome in 1984 and again in 1985.

The dig was a resounding success. The workers unearthed the most complete *H. erectus* skeleton yet found (Fig. 11–15). Known properly as WT 15000, the all but complete skeleton includes facial bones and most of the postcranial bones, a rare finding indeed for *H. erectus* (broadly defined), since these elements are scarce at other *H. erectus* sites.

Another remarkable feature of the find is its age. Its dating is based on the chronometric dates of the geological formation in which the site is located and is set at about 1.6 million years. The skeleton is that of a boy about 12 years of age and 5 feet 3 inches tall. Had he grown to maturity, his height, it is estimated, would have been more than 6 feet, taller than *H. erectus* was heretofore thought to have been. The postcranial bones appear to be quite similar, though not identical, to those of modern humans. The cranial capacity of WT 15000 is estimated at 880 cm^3; brain growth was nearly complete, and it is estimated that the boy's adult cranial capacity would have been approximately 909 cm^3 (Begun and Walker, 1993) (see A Closer Look on p. 316).

Bouri Two sites from Ethiopia have yielded *H. erectus* fossils, the most significant coming from the Bouri locale in the Middle Awash region (the same area from which numerous remains of earlier hominids have come; see Chapter 8 and Appendix B). The recent discovery of a mostly complete cranium from Bouri is important because this individual (dated at approximately 1 m.y.a.) is more like Asian *H. erectus* than are most of the earlier East African remains we have discussed (Asfaw et al., 2002). Consequently, the suggestion by several researchers that East African fossils are a different species from (Asian) *Homo erectus* is not supported by the morphology of the Bouri cranium (or, for that matter, by OH 9).

SUMMARY OF EAST AFRICAN *H. ERECTUS/ERGASTER*

The *Homo erectus* remains from East Africa show several differences from the fossil samples from Java and China. Some African specimens (particularly exemplified by ER 3733, presumably a female, and WT 15000, presumably a male) are not as strongly buttressed in the cranium (by supraorbital or nuchal tori) and do not have such thick cranial bones as seen in Asian representatives of *H. erectus*. As noted, these differences, as well as others observed in the postcranial skeleton, have so impressed some researchers that they in fact argue for a *separate* species status for the African *H. erectus* remains (as distinct from the Asian samples).[†] Bernard Wood, the leading proponent of this view, has suggested that the name *Homo ergaster* be used for the African remains; *H. erectus* would then be reserved solely for the Asian material (Wood, 1991). In addition, the very early dates now postulated for the dispersal of *H. erectus* into Asia (Java) would argue for a more than 1-million-year separate history for Asian and African populations.

Nevertheless, this species division has not been fully accepted, and the current consensus (and the one we prefer) is to continue to refer to all these hominids as *Homo erectus* (Kramer, 1993; Conroy, 1997; Rightmire, 1998; Asfaw et al., 2002). As with some earlier hominids, we accordingly will have to accommodate

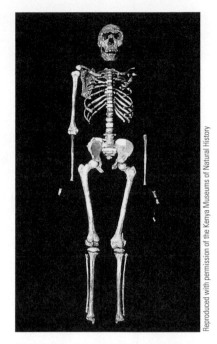

FIGURE 11–15 WT 15000 from Nariokotome, Kenya: the most complete *H. erectus* specimen yet found.

Reproduced with permission of the Kenya Museums of Natural History

See Virtual Lab 10, section I, for a 3-D animation of East African *Homo erectus* specimens.

---

*See p. 274 for an explanation of abbreviations used for fossil hominid specimens from Africa.

[†]Note, however, that other East African specimens from Olduvai, and especially from Bouri, are more like Asian fossils.

A CLOSER LOOK

The Nariokotome Skeleton– A Boy for All Seasons

The discovery of the spectacularly well-preserved skeleton from Nariokotome on the west side of Lake Turkana has allowed considerable new insight into key anatomical features of *Homo erectus*. Since its recovery in 1984 and 1985, detailed studies have been undertaken, and the published results (Walker, 1993; Walker and Leakey, 1993) have allowed some initial conclusions to be drawn. Moreover, the extraordinary quality of the remains has also allowed anthropologists to speculate on some major behavioral traits of *H. erectus** in Africa (and, more generally, of the entire species).

The remains comprise an almost complete skeleton, lacking only most of the small bones of the hands and feet and the unfused ends of long bones. This degree of preservation is remarkable, and this individual is the most complete skeleton of *any* fossil hominid yet found from before about 100,000 y.a. (after which deliberate burial facilitated much improved preservation). This superior preservation may well have been aided by rapid sedimentation in what is thought to have been an ancient shallow swamp. Once the individual died, his skeleton would have been quickly covered up, but some disturbance and breakage nevertheless occurred—from chewing by catfish, but most especially from trampling by large animals wading in the swamp 1.6 m.y.a.

As we have discussed, the individual was not fully grown when he died. His age (11 to 13 years; Walker, 1993) is determined by the stage of dental eruption (his permanent canines are not yet erupted) and by union of the ends of long bones. Moreover, as we have noted, this young *Homo erectus* male was quite tall (5 feet 3 inches), and using modern growth curve approximations, his adult stature would have been over 6 feet had he lived to full maturity.

More than simply tall, the body proportions of this boy's skeleton are intriguing. Reconstructions suggest that he had a linear build with long appendages, conforming to predictions of *Allen's rule* for inhabitants of hot climates (see Chapter 15). Further extrapolating from this observation, Alan Walker also suggests that *H. erectus* must have had a high sweating capacity to dissipate heat (in the modern human fashion). (See pp. 431–432 for a discussion of heat adaptation in humans.)

The boy's limb proportions suggest a quite warm mean annual temperature (90°F/30°C) in East Africa 1.6 m.y.a. Paleoecological reconstructions confirm this estimate of tropical conditions (much like the climate today in northern Kenya).

Another fascinating anatomical clue is seen in the beautifully preserved vertebrae. The opening through which the spinal cord passes (the neural canal; see Appendix A) is quite small in the thoracic elements. The possible behavioral corollaries of this reduced canal (as compared to modern *H. sapiens*) are also intriguing. Ann MacLarnan (1993) has proposed that the reduced canal argues for reduced size of the spinal cord, which in turn may suggest less control of the muscles between the ribs (the intercostals). One major function of these muscles is the precise control of breathing during human speech. From these data and inferences, Alan Walker has concluded that the Nariokotome youth (and *H. erectus* in general) was not fully capable of human articulate speech. (As an argument regarding language potential, this conclusion will no doubt spark considerable debate.)

A final interesting feature can be seen in the pelvis of this adolescent skeleton. It is very narrow and is thus correlated with a narrow bony birth canal. Walker (1993) again draws a behavioral inference from this anatomical feature. He estimates that a newborn with a cranial capacity no greater than a mere 200 cm^3 could have passed through this pelvis. As we showed elsewhere, the adult cranial capacity estimate for this individual was slightly greater than 900 cm^3—thus arguing for significant postnatal growth of the brain (exceeding 75 percent of its eventual size), again mirroring the modern human pattern. Walker speculates that this slow neural expansion (compared to other primates) leads to delayed development of motor skills and thus a prolonged period of infant/child dependency (what Walker terms "secondary altriciality"). This conclusion, however is not supported by more recently analyzed dental data, which show an accelerated (australopithecine-like) rate of maturation (Dean et al., 2001).

---

* H. erectus, broadly defined, and inclusive of *H. ergaster*.

a considerable degree of intraspecific variation within this species. Wood has concluded, regarding variation within such a broadly defined *H. erectus* species, "It is a species which manifestly embraces an unusually wide degree of variation in both the cranium and postcranial skeleton" (Wood, 1992a, p. 329).

SOUTH AFRICA

A mandible was found among fossil remains collected at Swartkrans in South Africa in the 1940s and 1950s. This specimen, SK 15, was originally assigned to "*Telanthropus capensis,*" but is now placed within the genus *Homo*. There is, however, disagreement about its species designation. Rightmire (1990) suggests that it may be linked with *Homo erectus,* but others are not certain. If it is *H. erectus,* it would demonstrate that *H. erectus* inhabited South Africa as well as the other regions documented by other more complete fossil finds.

NORTH AFRICA

North African remains, consisting almost entirely of mandibles (or mandible fragments) and a partial parietal bone, have been found at Ternifine (now Tighenif), Algeria, and in Morocco, at Sidi Abderrahman and Thomas Quarries. The three Ternifine mandibles and the parietal fragment are quite robust and have been dated to about 700,000 y.a. The Moroccan material is not as robust as Ternifine and may be a bit younger, at 500,000 years. In addition, an interesting cranium was found in a quarry north of Salé, in Morocco. The walls of the skull vault are thick, and several other features resemble those of *H. erectus*. Some features alternatively suggest that the Salé fossil should be placed in a later species of *Homo,* but an estimated cranial capacity of about 900 cm^3 throws doubt on that interpretation.

EUROPE

As a result of the recent discoveries from Dmanisi in the Republic of Georgia (see p. 306), the time frame for the earliest hominid occupation of Europe is being pushed back dramatically. For several decades, it had been assumed that hominids did not reach Europe until late in the Middle Pleistocene (presumably after 400,000 y.a.) and were already identifiable as a form very similar to *Homo sapiens.* It was thus concluded that *H. erectus* (and contemporaries) never expanded there. As the new discoveries are evaluated, these assumptions are being questioned, and radical revisions concerning hominid evolution in Europe are becoming necessary.

While Dmanisi is by far the earliest-dated hominid find in Europe, another recent find is extending the antiquity of hominids in the western portion of Europe. Fossil remains from Spain discovered in 1994 are the oldest hominids yet found in western Europe (see Fig. 11–1 for locations of these hominid sites). From the Gran Dolina site in the highly productive Atapuerca region of northern Spain, where numerous, somewhat more recent hominid fossils have also been discovered (discussed in Chapter 12), several fragments of at least six individuals have been found (Arsuaga et al., 1999). The dating, based on paleomagnetic determinations (see p. 239), as well as two other dating techniques, places the Gran Dolina hominids at approximately 850,000–780,000 y.a. (Parés and Pérez-González, 1995; Falguéres et al., 1999). If this dating is further corroborated, these early Spanish finds would be *at least* 250,000 years older than any other hominid yet discovered in western Europe. Because all the 80 pieces thus far identified are fragmentary, the taxonomic assignment of these fossils still remains somewhat problematic. Initial analysis, however, suggests that these fossils are *not H. erectus;* especially distinctive are remains of the face—which look much more modern than does *H. erectus*. Spanish paleoanthropologists who have studied the Gran Dolina fossils have decided to place these hominids into another (separate) species, one they call "*Homo antecessor*" (Bermúdez de Castro et al., 1997; Arsuaga et al., 1999). However, it remains to be seen whether this newly proposed species will prove to be distinct from other species of *Homo* (see p. 322 for further discussion). Another potentially early western European hominid find comes from the 500,000-year-old Boxgrove site in southern England, where a hominid tibia (shinbone) was unearthed in 1994 (the dating here, too, will require further confirmation).

Finally, the southern European discovery of a well-preserved cranium from the Ceprano site in central Italy may be the best evidence yet of *H. erectus* (strictly defined) in Europe (Ascenzi et al., 1996). Provisional dating of a partial cranium from this important site suggests a date between 800,000 and 900,000 y.a. Phillip Rightmire (1998) has concluded that cranial morphology places this specimen quite close to *H. erectus*. Italian researchers have proposed other views. Initially, they agreed with Rightmire's interpretation (Ascenzi et al., 1996), but more recently have suggested that the Ceprano cranium might belong to yet another (and separate) species (Manzi et al., 2001). This degree of "splitting" is quite extreme and is not likely to be considered favorably by most paleoanthropologists.

After about 400,000 y.a., the European fossil hominid record becomes increasingly abundant. Nevertheless, interpretations relating to the proper taxonomic assessment of many of these remains have been debated, in some cases for decades. In recent years, several of these somewhat later "premodern" specimens have been placed either as early representatives of *Homo sapiens* or as a separate species, one immediately preceding *H. sapiens*. These enigmatic premodern humans are discussed in Chapter 12. A time line for the *H. erectus* discoveries discussed in this chapter as well as other finds of more uncertain status is shown in Figure 11–16.

Technological and Population Trends in *Homo erectus*

TECHNOLOGICAL TRENDS

Many researchers have noted the remarkable stasis of the physical and cultural characteristics of *Homo erectus* populations, which seemed to change so little in the more than 1.5 million years of their existence. There is, however, dispute on this point. Some scholars (Rightmire, 1981) see almost no detectable changes in cranial dimensions over more than 1 million years of *H. erectus* evolution.* Other paleoanthropologists (e.g., Wolpoff, 1984), who use different methodologies to date and subdivide their samples, draw a different conclusion, seeing some significant long-term morphological trends. Accepting a moderate position, we can postulate that there were some changes: The brain of later *H. erectus* was somewhat larger, the nose more protrusive, and the body not as robust as in earlier forms. Moreover, there were modifications in stone tool technology.

Expansion of the brain presumably enabled *H. erectus* to develop a more sophisticated tool kit than seen among earlier hominids. The important change in this kit was a core worked on both sides, called a *biface* (known widely as a hand axe or cleaver; Fig 11–17). The biface had a flatter core than the roundish earlier Oldowan pebble tool. And, probably even more important, this *core* tool was obviously a target design, that is, the main goal of the toolmaker. This greater focus and increased control enabled the stoneknapper to produce sharper, straighter edges, resulting in a more efficient implement. This

---

*This conclusion does not take into account the Dmanisi remains, but refers to "full-blown" *H. erectus* specimens.

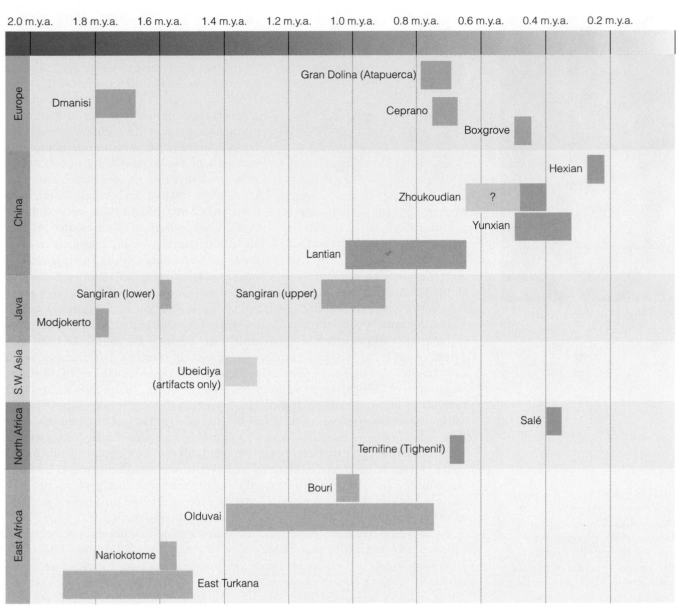

Note: Most dates are only imprecise estimates. However, the dates from East African sites are chronometrically determined and are thus much more secure. In addition, the early dates from Java are also radiometric and are gaining wide acceptance.

FIGURE 11–16 Time line for *Homo erectus* discoveries and other contemporary hominids. Note that most dates are approximations.

Acheulian stone tool became standardized as the basic *H. erectus* all-purpose tool (with only minor modification) for more than a million years. It served to cut, scrape, pound, dig, and more—a most useful tool that has been found in Africa, parts of Asia, and later in western Europe. It should also be noted that Acheulian tool kits also included several types of small tools (Fig. 11–18).

For many years, it was thought that a cultural "divide" separated the Old World—with Acheulian technology found *only* in Africa, southwest Asia, and western Europe, but not elsewhere (i.e., absent in eastern Europe and most of Asia). However, recently reported excavations from more than 20 sites in southern China have forced reevaluation of this hypothesis (Yamei et al., 2000). As noted, the most distinctive tools of the Acheulian are bifaces, and they are the very tools thought lacking throughout most of the Pleistocene in eastern Europe and most of Asia. The new archaeological assemblages from southern China are securely dated at about 800,000 y.a. and contain numerous bifaces, very similar to contemporaneous Acheulian bifaces from Africa

FIGURE 11–17 Acheulian biface ("hand axe"), a basic tool of the Acheulian tradition.

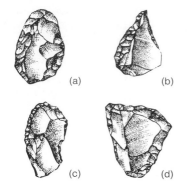

FIGURE 11–18 Small tools of the Acheulian industry. (a) Side scraper. (b) Point. (c) End scraper. (d) Burin.

FIGURE 11–19 (a) A Middle Pleistocene butchering site at Olorgesailie, Kenya, excavated by Louis and Mary Leakey, who had the catwalk built for observers. (b) A close-up of the Acheulian tools, mainly hand axes, found at the site.

(see Figs. 11–17 and 11–19b). It now appears likely that cultural traditions relating to stone tool technology were largely equivalent over the *full* geographical range of *H. erectus* and contemporaries.

While geographical distinctions are not so obvious, temporal changes in tool technology are evident. In early days, toolmakers employed a stone hammer (simply an ovoid-shaped stone about the size of an egg or a bit larger) to remove flakes from the core, thus leaving deep scars. Later, they used other materials, such as wood and bone. They learned to use these new materials as soft hammers, which gave them more control over flaking, thus leaving shallow scars, sharper edges, and a more symmetrical form. Toward the end of the Acheulian industry, toolmakers blocked out a core with stone hammers and then switched to wood or bone for defining the edges. This technique produced more elegant-appearing and pear-shaped implements.

Evidence of butchering is widespread at *H. erectus* sites, and in the past, such evidence has been cited in arguments for consistent hunting. For example, at the Olorgesailie site in Kenya (Fig. 11–19), dated at approximately 800,000 y.a., thousands of Acheulian hand axes have been recovered in association with remains of large animals, including giant baboons (now extinct). However, the assumption of consistent hunting has been challenged, especially by archaeologists who argue that the evidence does not prove the hunting hypothesis. Instead, they suggest that *H. erectus* was primarily a scavenger, a hypothesis that also has not yet been proved conclusively. We thus discuss *H. erectus* as a potential hunter *and* scavenger. It is crucial to remember, too, that *gathering* of wild plant foods was also practiced by *H. erectus* groups. Indeed, probably a majority of the calories they consumed came from such gathering activities.

Moreover, as we have seen, the mere *presence* of animal bones at archaeological sites does not prove that hominids were killing animals or even necessarily exploiting meat. Indeed, as was the case in the earlier South African sites (discussed in Chapter 10), the hominid remains themselves may have been the meal refuse of large carnivores! Thus, in making interpretations of early hominid sites,

(a)

(b)

we must consider a variety of alternatives. As Stanford University archaeologist Richard Klein has concluded regarding Middle Pleistocene sites, the interpretations are far from clear: "In sum, the available data do not allow us to isolate the relative roles of humans, carnivores, and factors such as starvation, accidents, and stream action in creating bone assemblages. . . . Certainly, as presently understood, the sites do not tell us how successful or effective *Homo erectus* was at obtaining meat"(1989, p. 221).

POPULATION TRENDS

H. erectus is the first hominid for which we have definite evidence of *wide* geographical dispersion (i.e., across more than one continent). Descendants of early *Homo* ancestors in Africa, the earliest migrants into Eurasia were similar in many ways to their early *Homo* forebears (although they may be seen as a primitive form of *H. erectus*). Once established in Eurasia, and once attaining the full physical and cultural capacities of *H. erectus,* populations dispersed far and wide in the Old World—far beyond the relatively narrow ranges of earlier hominids.

The life of hunter-scavengers (and still, no doubt, *primarily* gatherers) was nomadic, and the woodland and savanna that covered the southern tier of Asia would have been an excellent environment for *H. erectus,* as it was similar to the econiche of their African ancestors. As the population grew, small groups budded off and moved on to find their own resource areas. This process, repeated again and again, led *H. erectus* east, crossing to Java, arriving there, it seems, as early as the most ancient known sites in East Africa itself. At about the same time, another migratory route took hominids to eastern Europe. This migration, however, might have involved a more primitive form of *Homo* and did not meet with the wide success ultimately attained by *Homo erectus.*

Interpretations of *Homo erectus:* Continuing Uncertainties

There are several aspects of the geographical, physical, and behavioral patterns shown by *H. erectus* (broadly defined) that seem clear. However, new discoveries and more in-depth analyses are making some of our simpler conclusions appear tenuous. The fascinating fossil hominids discovered at Dmanisi are perhaps the most challenging piece of this puzzle.

The approach followed in this chapter and stated in our earlier hypothesis (see p. 305) suggests that *Homo erectus* was able to emigrate from Africa owing to more advanced anatomy and culture (as compared to earlier African predecessors). Yet, the Dmanisi cranial remains show that these very early Europeans still had small brains, and in one case, the cranium looks more like early *Homo* than like *Homo erectus.* Moreover, these hominids have only a very basic stone tool kit available to them, one apparently no more advanced than very early African ones.

It thus appears that part of our hypothesis is not fully accurate. At least some of the earliest emigrants from Africa did not yet show the "full-blown" *Homo erectus* physical and behavioral pattern. How different the Dmanisi hominids are from the full *H. erectus* pattern remains to be determined (discovery of more complete postcranial remains will be most illuminating).

Furthermore, the three crania from Dmanisi thus far published are extremely variable (one of them, in fact, does look more like *Homo erectus*). It would be tempting to conclude that there is more than one type of hominid represented here—but they are all found in the same geological context. The archaeologists who excavated the site are convinced that all the fossils are closely associated with each other. The simplest hypothesis is that they all are members of the *same* species. This degree of apparent intraspecific variation sends a strong message to paleoanthropologists—especially those inclined to split fossil samples into multiple species. No respectable biological scientist (including physical anthropologists) would be comfortable assigning members of the same population to different species!

This growing awareness of the broad limits of intraspecific variation among these hominids brings us to our second consideration: Is *Homo ergaster* (in Africa) a separate species from *Homo erectus* (as strictly defined in Asia)? While this interpretation has been increasingly popular in the last decade, it now seems to be losing steam. The finds from Dmanisi raise fundamental issues of interpretation. Among these three crania from one locality (see Fig. 11–5), there is more variation than between the African and Asian forms (which many researchers have interpreted as different species). Moreover, the new discovery from Bouri (Ethiopia) of a more *erectus*-looking cranium also further weakens the separate-species interpretation of *Homo ergaster.*

The separate-species status of the early European fossils from Spain (Gran Dolina) is also not yet unambiguously established. There is not much good fossil evidence yet from this site, but an early date, prior to 750,000 y.a., is well confirmed. Recall also that no other western European hominid fossils are known until at least 250,000 years later, and an ostensibly roughly contemporaneous find from Italy looks like *Homo erectus.* The more modern-looking face of the Gran Dolina hominid might be explained by a fairly early expansion (from Africa into Spain) of more modern-looking humans. Further complicating this interpretation, the best evidence comes from a young individual, estimated to have died at around 12 years of age. Thus, the "modern" facial morphology may be simply a reflection of the immature developmental stage of this adolescent. In any case, whether these hominids gained much of a foothold elsewhere in Europe remains to be seen. However, later in the Pleistocene, their possible descendants are well established both in Africa and in Europe. These later premodern humans are the topic of the next chapter.

In conclusion, we return again to our hypothesis regarding the initial dispersal of genus *Homo.* It seems that there was more than one such dispersal soon after 2 m.y.a. One, as represented by the Dmanisi fossils, involved a less derived *Homo* than the full-blown *H. erectus* pattern. These hominids, nevertheless, quite remarkably migrated as far as eastern Europe; but current evidence does not show that this more primitive *Homo* expanded much beyond this initial foothold.

Perhaps it was a second migration, deriving from early African *H. erectus,* that did disperse extremely widely. We have evidence of such an expansion from sites in East Africa, North Africa, southeastern Asia, eastern Asia, and Europe.

When we look back at the evolution of *H. erectus,* we realize how significant this early human's achievements were. It was *H. erectus* who increased in body size with more efficient bipedalism; who embraced culture wholeheartedly as a strategy of adaptation; whose brain was reshaped and increased in size to within *H. sapiens* range; who became a more efficient scavenger and likely hunter with greater dependence on meat; and who apparently established more permanent bases. In short, it was *H. erectus,* committed to a cultural way of life, who transformed hominid evolution to human evolution. As Richard Foley states, "The appearance and expansion of *H. erectus* represented a major change in adaptive strategy that influenced the subsequent process and pattern of human evolution" (1991, p. 425).

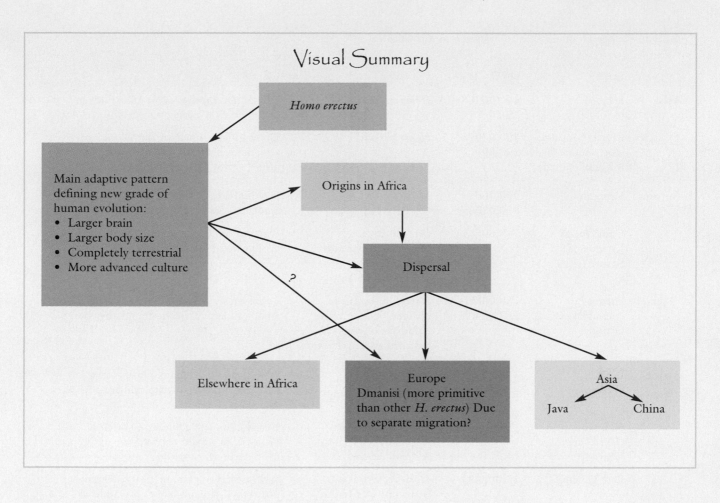

Visual Summary

Homo erectus

Main adaptive pattern defining new grade of human evolution:
- Larger brain
- Larger body size
- Completely terrestrial
- More advanced culture

Origins in Africa

Dispersal

?

Elsewhere in Africa

Europe
Dmanisi (more primitive than other *H. erectus*) Due to separate migration?

Asia
Java   China

Summary

Homo erectus remains are found in geological contexts dating from about 1.8 million to about 200,000 years ago (and perhaps much later), a period of more than 1.5 million years. While the nature and timing of migrations is uncertain, it is likely that *H. erectus* first appeared in East Africa and later migrated widely to other areas. This highly successful hominid defines a new and more advanced grade of human evolution, but some expansion out of Africa by a more primitive species of *Homo* now seems likely.

Historically, the first finds were made by Dubois in Java, and later discoveries came from China and Africa. Differences from early *Homo* are notable in *H. erectus'* larger brain, taller stature, robust build, and changes in facial structure and cranial buttressing.

The long period of *H. erectus'* existence was marked by a remarkably uniform technology over space and time. Nevertheless, compared to earlier hominids, *H. erectus* and

contemporaries introduced more sophisticated tools and probably ate novel and/or differently processed foods, using these new tools and at later sites perhaps fire as well. They were also able to move into different environments and successfully adapt to new conditions.

It is generally assumed that certain *H. erectus* populations evolved into later premodern humans, some of which, in turn, evolved into *Homo sapiens*. Evidence supporting such a series of transitions is seen in the Ngandong fossils (and others discussed in Chapter 12), which display both *H. erectus* and *H. sapiens* features. There remain questions about *H. erectus* behavior (e.g., did they hunt? did they control fire?) and about evolution to later hominids (was it gradual or rapid, and which *H. erectus* populations contributed genes?). The search for answers continues. As a further aid, the most significant hominid fossils discussed in this chapter are summarized in Table 11–1 on page 324.

TABLE 11–1 Key Hominid Fossils Discussed in this Chapter

	SITE	DATES (Y.A.)	TAXONOMIC DESIGNATION	COMMENTS
Asia	Java (6 locales)	1,8000,000–25,000	*Homo erectus*	First *H. erectus* discovery; most finds in disturbed river terrace contexts
	China (6 locales; most significant is Zhoukoudian)	400,000+–200,000?	*Homo erectus*	Up to 40 individuals at Zhoukoudian; also, many artifacts; Zhoukoudian, however, probably not primary living site
Europe	Ceprano	900,000–800,000	*Homo erectus*	One individual; well-preserved cranium; Similar to Asian *H. erectus*
	Gran Dolina (Atapuerca, Spain)	780,000?	Quite likely not *H. erectus*; referred to by discoverers as "*Homo antecessor,*"	Remains quite incomplete; oldest W. European fossil hominid discovery
	Dmanisi (Republic of Georgia)	1,800,000–1,700,000	*Homo erectus/Homo ergaster* (very primitive example—or could be classified as early *Homo*)	3 well-preserved crania plus partial mandible; among oldest *H. erectus* found anywhere
Africa	Bouri (Ethiopia)	1,000,000	*Homo erectus*	Well-preserved cranium plus postcranial bones; morphology quite similar to Asian *H. erectus*
	Nariokotome (West Turkana, Kenya)	1,600,000	*Homo erectus*, also frequently referred to as *Homo ergaster*	Nearly complete adolescent skeleton, probably of a male; shows some differences from Asian *H. erectus*
	East Turkana (Kenya)	1,800,000	*Homo erectus*, also frequently referred to as *Homo ergaster*	Well-preserved cranium plus several other postcranial remains likely coming from same group; cranium likely of female; shows several differences from Asian *H. erectus*

Questions for Review

1. How does *Homo erectus* compare with earlier hominids from Africa (geographically, physically, and behaviorally)?
2. What is meant by a "grade" of human evolution? Explain why *Homo erectus* is thought to belong to a different grade than earlier hominids.
3. Why is the nearly complete skeleton from Nariokotome so important? What kinds of evidence does it provide?
4. Assume that you are in the laboratory and have the Nariokotome skeleton as well as a skeleton of a modern human. First, given a choice, what age and sex would you choose for the human skeleton, and why? Second, what similarities and differences do the two skeletons show?
5. What fundamental questions of interpretation do the fossil hominids from Dmanisi raise? Does this evidence completely overturn the hypothesis concerning *H. erectus* dispersal from Africa? Explain why or why not.
6. What was the intellectual climate in Europe in the latter half of the nineteenth century, especially concerning human evolution? Given this climate, why do you think there was so much opposition to Dubois' interpretation of the hominid fossil he found in Java?
7. How has the interpretation of fire use by *Homo erectus* at Zhoukoudian been revised in recent years? What kinds of new evidence from this site have been used in this reevaluation, and what does that tell you about modern archaeological techniques and approaches? What kinds of archaeological evidence would convince you that *H. erectus* used fire?
8. You are interpreting the hominid fossils from three sites in East Africa (Nariokotome, Olduvai, and Bouri)—all considered possible members of *H. erectus*. What sorts of evidence would lead you to conclude that there was more than one species? What would convince you that there was just one species? Why do you think some paleoanthropologists (splitters) would tend to see more than one species, while others (lumpers) would generally not? What kind of approach would you have, and why?

For Further Thought

1. Why do physical anthropologists (and other evolutionary biologists) propose different classifications of species and genera?

2. In what ways do these different classifications affect interpretations?

Go to the book website at **http://www.anthropology.wadsworth.com** for resources to help you explore these questions further. Click on "For Further Thought" for this chapter.

Suggested Further Reading

Gore, Rick. 2002. "The First Pioneer? A New Find Shakes the Human Family Tree." *National Geographic* 202 (August), Front Supplement (not paginated).

Klein, Richard. 1999. *The Human Career* 2nd ed. Chicago: University of Chicago Press.

Leonard, William R. 2002. "Food for Thought." *Scientific American* 287(December):106–115.

Lewin, Roger. 1998. *Principles of Human Evolution: A Core Textbook*. New York: Blackwell Science.

Rightmire, G. P. 1990. *The Evolution of* Homo erectus. New York: Cambridge University Press.

Shapiro, Harry L. 1980. *Peking Man*. New York: Simon & Schuster.

Wong, Kate. 2003. "Stranger in a New Land." *Scientific American* November, 2003, vol. 299, pp. 74–83.

Online Anthropology Resource Center

Go to the Anthropology Resource Center at **http://www.anthropology.wadsworth.com** for a wealth of online resources, including a companion website for your text that provides study aids such as self-quizzes for each chapter and a practice final exam, as well as links to anthropology websites and information on the latest theories and discoveries in the field. Also, check out InfoTrac College Edition®, your online library that offers full-length articles from thousands of scholarly and popular publications. Just click on the InfoTrac button at the companion website and use the passcode that came with your book.

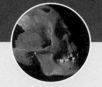

Man, the Hunter; Woman, the Gatherer?

Anthropologists have long been concerned with the behavioral evolution of our species. Accompanying changes in anatomy (limb structure, dentition, brain size and shape) were changes in mating patterns, social structure, cultural innovations, and, eventually, language. In fact, changes in these behavioral complexes are what mostly *explain* the concomitant adaptations in human biological structure.

We are, then, vitally interested in the behavioral adaptations of our early hominid ancestors. In seeking to reconstruct the behavioral patterns of these early hominids, anthropologists use inferences drawn from modern primates, social carnivores, and hunting-gathering peoples. In addition, they derive information directly from the paleoanthropological record (see Chapter 9).

Despite numerous attempts at such behavioral reconstructions, the conclusions must remain largely speculative. In point of fact, behavior does not fossilize. Accordingly, researchers must rely considerably on their imaginations in creating scenarios of early hominid behavioral evolution (see p. 246). In such an atmosphere, biases often emerge; these biased renditions, in turn, stimulate heated debates and alternative scenarios—often as narrow as those being attacked.

Among the most controversial topics in anthropology, and one that has displayed some of the most glaring biases, is the debate concerning origins of hominid gender role differences. Did early hominid males have characteristically different behavioral adaptations from their female counterparts? Did one sex dominate the frontier of early hominid cultural innovation? And if one sex did lead the way, which one?

A now well-known rendition of early hominid behavioral development was popularized in the 1960s and 1970s. According to this "man, the hunter" theory, the hunting of large animals by males was the central stimulus of hominid behavioral evolution. Such widely read works as *The Naked Ape* (1967), by Desmond Morris, and *The Hunting Hypothesis* (1976) and other books by Robert Ardrey maintain that early apish-looking forms *became* hominids as a result of a hunting way of life. As Ardrey states, "Man is man, and not a chimpanzee, because for millions upon millions of evolving years we killed for a living" (1976, p. 10).

In this reconstruction, the hunting of large, dangerous mammals by cooperating groups of males fostered the development of intelligence, language, tools, and bipedalism. In this scenario, increased intelligence accompanied by the development of weapons is also blamed for the roots of human aggressiveness, murder, and warfare.

This "man, the hunter" scenario further suggests that while the males are leading the vanguard in hominid evolution, females remain mostly sedentary, tied to the home base by the burden of dependent young. Females may have contributed some wild plant foods to the group's subsistence, but this is not seen as a particularly challenging (and certainly not a very noble) endeavor. In this situation of marked division of labor, sexual relationships quickly changed. Males, constantly away from the home base (and thus away from the females, too), could not keep a watchful eye over their mates. In order to better ensure fidelity, monogamy came into being. In this way, a male would be assured that the young in which he invested were his own. This important factor of male-female bonding as a product of differential foraging patterns has more recently been restated by Owen Lovejoy (1981) (see p. 249).

From the female's point of view, it would be beneficial to maintain a close bond with a provisioning male. Consequently, she would want to appear "attractive," and thus, through time, the female breasts and buttocks would become more conspicuous. Besides rearing their young and being attractive sex objects, females were useful to males in another way. Groups of male hunters living in the same area might occasionally come into potentially dangerous competition for the same resources. As a means of solidifying political ties between groups, the males would thus routinely exchange females (by giving or "selling" their daughters to neighboring bands).

Thus, in a single stroke, this complex of features accounts for human intelligence, sexual practices, and political organization.

As might be expected, such a male-centered scenario did not go unchallenged. Ignoring females or relegating them to a definitely inferior role in human behavioral evolution drew sharp criticism from several quarters. As Sally Slocum notes:

> So, while the males were out hunting, developing all their skills, learning to cooperate, inventing language, inventing art, creating tools and weapons, the poor dependent females were sitting back at the home base having one child after another and waiting for the males to bring home the bacon. While this reconstruction is certainly ingenious, it gives one the decided impression that only half the species—the male half—did any evolving. In addition to containing a number of logical gaps, the argument becomes somewhat doubtful in the light of modern knowledge of genetics and primate behavior. (Slocum, 1975, p. 42)

In fact, such a rigid rendering of our ancestors' behavior does not stand up to critical examination. Hunting is never defined rigorously. Does it include only large, terrestrial mammals? What of smaller mammals, sea mammals, fish, and birds? In numerous documented human societies, females actively participate in exploiting these latter resources.

Moreover, nonhuman primates do not conform to predictions derived from the "man, the hunter" model. For example, among chimpanzees, females do most of the tool-making, not the males. Finally in most nonhuman primates (most mammals, for that matter), it is the females—not the males—who choose with whom to mate.

Granting that the hunting hypothesis does not work, what alternatives have been proposed? As a reaction to male-centered views, Elaine Morgan (1972) advanced the "aquatic hypothesis." In this rendition, females are seen as the pioneers of hominid evolution. But rather than having the dramatic changes of human emergence occur on the savanna, Morgan has them take place on the seashore. As females lead the way to bipedal locomotion, cultural innovation, and intellectual development, the poor males are seen as splashing pitifully behind.

Unfortunately, this scenario has less to back it up than the hunting hypothesis. Not a shred (even a watery one) of evidence has ever been discovered in the contexts predicted by the aquatic theory. Little is accomplished by such unsubstantiated overzealous speculation. Chauvinism—whether male or female—does not elucidate our origins and only obscures the evolutionary processes that operated on the *whole* species.

Another interesting aspect of these different behavioral "theories" has been pointed out by cultural anthropologist Misia Landau. She notes that these theories are like mythical stories with a hero emerging (from the forest) and ultimately conquering the challenges of existence (by boldly going bipedally onto the savanna). It could also be noted that in most of these myths, traditionally the hero is a male who acts to defend, provide for, and inseminate the females (who otherwise are not given much consideration).

What can we conclude from all these arguments? While the pattern is not as rigid as the hunting hypothesis advocates would have us believe, in the vast majority of human societies, hunting of large, terrestrial mammals is almost always a male activity. In fact, a comprehensive cross-cultural survey shows that of 179 societies, males do the hunting exclusively in 166, both sexes participate in 13, and in *no* group is hunting done exclusively by females (Murdock, 1965).

In addition, there is some incipient division of labor in foraging patterns among chimpanzees. Females tend to concentrate more on termiting, while hunting is done mostly by males.

From his detailed studies of hunting in chimpanzees, Craig Stanford (1999) has emphasized the crucial role of meat sharing—both in chimpanzees and in early hominids.

Stanford suggests that meat is important, not so much for its nutritional value, but for its social currency. Such socially oriented sharing can foster variable gender roles, wherein males manipulate females (especially to gain reproductive advantage) and females manipulate males (to gain a desired resource or in choosing a mate).

Early hominids, expanding upon such a subsistence base, eventually adapted a greater sexual division of labor than is found in any other primate. Two points, however, must be kept in mind. First, both the gathering of wild plant foods and the hunting of animals would have been indispensable components of the diet. Consequently, *both* males and females always played a significant role. Second, the strategies must always have been somewhat flexible. With a shifting, usually unpredictable resource base, nothing else would have worked. As a result, males probably always did a considerable amount of gathering, and in most foraging societies they still do. Moreover, females—while not usually engaged in the stalking and killing of large prey—nonetheless contribute significantly to meat acquisition. Once large animals have been killed, there still remain the arduous tasks of butchering and transport back to the home base. In many societies, women and men participate equally in these activities.

A balanced view of human behavioral evolution must avoid simplistic and overly rigid scenarios. As stated by Adrienne Zihlman, a researcher concerned with reconstructing early hominid behavior:

Both sexes must have been able to care for young, protect themselves from predators, make and use tools, and freely move about the environment in order to exploit available resources widely distributed through space and time. It is this range of behaviors—the overall behavioral flexibility of both sexes—that may have been the primary ingredient of early hominids' success in the savanna environment. (Zihlman, 1981, p. 97)

Following the notion developed by Landau that much of the literature on the evolution of human behavior resembles storytelling, anthropologist Linda Fedigan concluded her own comprehensive review of the topic (1986):

People will not stop wanting to hear origin stories and scientists will not cease to write scholarly tales. But we can become aware of the symbolic content of our stories, for much as our theories are not independent of our beliefs, so our behavior is not independent of our theories of human society. In these origin tales, we try to coax the material evidence into telling us about the past, but the narrative we weave about the past also tells us about the present.

Man, the Hunter; Woman, the Gatherer?
(continued)

Critical Thinking Questions

1. What do we mean when we say, "Behavior does not fossilize"?
2. Exactly, what is it that *does* fossilize?
3. What is meant by male (or female) chauvinism? Do you detect elements of chauvinism in any of the views discussed here?
4. Select a feature of early hominid adaptation (e.g., bipedal locomotion or sexual dimorphism, where males are considerably larger than females) and construct your own behavioral explanation of how it might have evolved. (Do so in two different ways. First, restrict yourself to only firm evidence. Then be as speculative as possible, giving full vent to your imagination. Lastly, compare your two reconstructions and evaluate the *scientific* merit of each.)

Sources

Ardrey, Robert. 1976. *The Hunting Hypothesis*. New York: Atheneum.

Dahlberg, Frances (ed.). 1981. *Woman the Gatherer*. New Haven: Yale University Press.

Fedigan, Linda. 1986. "The Changing Role of Woman in Models of Human Evolution." *Annual Review of Anthropology* 15: 25–66.

Landau, Misia. 1986. "Human Evolution as Narrative." *American Scientist* 72: 262–268.

Lovejoy, C. Owen. 1981. "The Origin of Man." *Science* 211: 341–350.

Morgan, Elaine. 1972. *The Descent of Woman*. New York: Stein and Day.

Morris, Desmond. 1967. *The Naked Ape*. New York: McGraw-Hill.

Murdock, G. P. 1965. *Culture and Society*. Pittsburgh: University of Pittsburgh Press.

Slocum, Sally. 1975. "Woman the Gatherer: Male Bias in Anthropology," *Toward an Anthropology of Women*, R. R. Reiter, ed. New York: Monthly Review Press, pp. 36–50.

Stanford, Craig. 1999. The Hunting Apes. Princeton, NJ: Princeton University Press.

Zihlman, Adrienne L. 1981. "Women as Shapers of the Human Adaptation," *Woman the Gatherer*, op. cit., pp. 75–120.

Premodern Humans

Taung child's cranium held by South African paleo-anthropologist Phillip Tobias

Robert Jurmain

Key Questions

Who were the immediate precursors to modern *Homo sapiens*, and how do they compare with modern humans?

Introduction

See the following sections of the CD-ROM for topics covered in this chapter: Virtual Lab 10, section I, and Virtual Lab 11.

What does it mean to be "human"? The use of this term is highly varied, encompassing religious, philosophical, and biological considerations. Here we concentrate on the biological aspects of the human organism. Living peoples are members of one species, all showing a common anatomical pattern and similar behavioral potentials. We call hominids like us "fully modern humans," and the origin of forms essentially identical to living people will be discussed in the next chapter.

When in the past can we say our predecessors were obviously human? Certainly, the further back we go in time, hominids look less like contemporary *Homo sapiens*. This pattern is, of course, exactly what we would expect in an evolutionary sequence. Moreover, the hominid fossil record, which has become increasingly rich in recent years, now provides a detailed picture of this sequence.

We saw in the previous chapter that *Homo erectus* took crucial steps in the human direction, in so doing defining a new grade of human evolution. In this chapter, we review those hominids who continued this journey. Both physically and behaviorally they are much like modern humans. Yet, these hominids still show several significant differences. Thus, while most paleoanthropologists are comfortable calling these hominids "human," this recognition is qualified—to set them apart from fully modern people. Hence, we will refer to these fascinating immediate predecessors as "premodern humans."

When, Where, and What

THE PLEISTOCENE

Middle Pleistocene The portion of the Pleistocene epoch beginning 780,000 y.a. and ending 125,000 y.a.

Upper Pleistocene The portion of the Pleistocene epoch beginning 125,000 y.a. and ending approximately 10,000 y.a.

glaciations Climatic intervals when continental ice sheets cover much of the northern continents. Glaciations are associated with colder temperatures in northern latitudes and more arid conditions in southern latitudes (most notably in Africa).

Most of the hominids discussed in this chapter lived during the **Middle Pleistocene**, a period beginning 780,000 y.a. and ending 125,000 y.a. Some of the later premodern humans, especially the Neandertals, lived well into the **Upper Pleistocene** (125,000–10,000 y.a.).

The Pleistocene has been called the Ice Age because, as in numerous previous geological eras, periodic advances and retreats of massive continental glaciations marked this epoch. During the glacial interludes, the temperature was very cold and ice accumulated, since more snow fell each year than melted. We should mention that there were numerous advances and retreats of ice; in fact, during the Pleistocene, at least 15 major and 50 minor glacial advances are documented in Europe (Tattersall et al., 1988).

Moreover, it must be remembered that these **glaciations**, which enveloped huge swaths of Europe, Asia, and North America (as well as Antarctica), were mostly confined to northern latitudes. As a result, hominids living in these areas were severely impacted as the climate, flora, and animal life shifted during these Pleistocene oscillations. For the hominids living during this time (all restricted still to the Old World), the most dramatic of these effects were in Europe and northern Asia, but less so in southern Asia and in Africa.

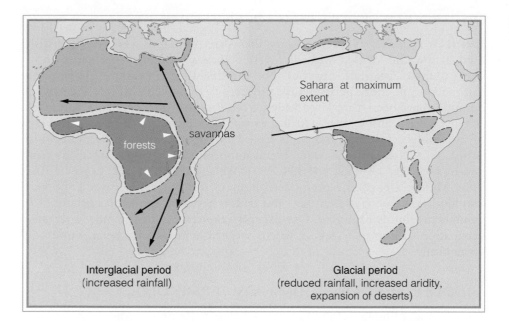

FIGURE 12–1 Changing Pleistocene environments in Africa.

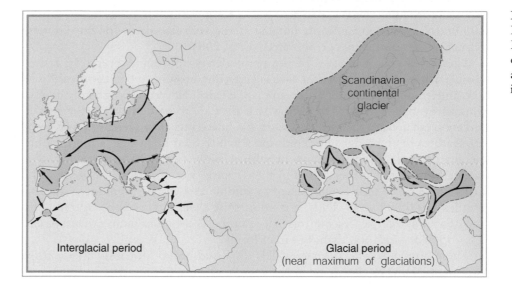
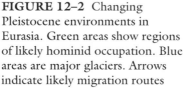

FIGURE 12–2 Changing Pleistocene environments in Eurasia. Green areas show regions of likely hominid occupation. Blue areas are major glaciers. Arrows indicate likely migration routes

In the more southerly latitudes, climates also fluctuated, but in Africa, most notably, the main effects related to changing rainfall patterns. During glacial periods, the climate in Africa became more arid, while during **interglacials**, rainfall increased. The changing availability of food resources certainly affected hominids in Africa, but perhaps even more importantly, migration routes also swung back and forth. Most crucially, in North Africa during glacial periods, the Sahara expanded, effectively blocking migration in and out of sub-Saharan Africa (Lahr and Foley, 1998) (Fig. 12–1).

In Eurasia, as well, glacial advances greatly affected migration routes. As the ice sheets expanded, sea levels dropped, more northern areas became uninhabitable, and some key passages between areas became blocked. For example, during glacial peaks, much of western Europe would have been cut off from the rest of Eurasia (Fig. 12–2).

During the warmer (and, in the south, wetter) interglacials, the ice sheets shrank, sea levels rose, and certain migration routes reopened (e.g., from central into western Europe). Clearly, to understand Middle Pleistocene hominids, it is crucial to view them within their shifting Pleistocene world.

interglacials Climatic intervals when continental ice sheets are retreating, eventually becoming much reduced in size. Interglacials in northern latitudes are associated with warmer temperatures, while in southern latitudes the climate becomes wetter.

DISPERSAL OF MIDDLE PLEISTOCENE HOMINIDS

Like their *Homo erectus* predecessors, these later hominids were widely distributed in the Old World—with discoveries likewise coming from three continents (Africa, Asia, and Europe). For the first time, in fact, it appears that Europe became more permanently and densely occupied (Middle Pleistocene hominids have been discovered widely from England, France, Spain, Germany, Italy, Hungary, and Greece). Africa, as well, likely continued as a central area of hominid occupation, and finds have come from North, East, and South Africa. Finally, Asia has yielded several important finds (most especially from China) (see Fig. 12–4 on pp. 334–335). We should point out, however, that these Middle Pleistocene premodern humans did not vastly extend the geographical range of *Homo erectus*—but largely replaced the earlier hominids in habitats previously exploited. One exception appears to be the more successful occupation of Europe, a region where earlier hominids have been found only sporadically.

MIDDLE PLEISTOCENE HOMINIDS: TERMINOLOGY

The premodern humans found in the Old World during the Middle Pleistocene (i.e., after 780,000 y.a.) generally succeed *H. erectus*. However, in some areas, especially in Asia, there apparently was a long period of coexistence, lasting 300,000 years or longer (most notably as the very late dates for the Javanese Ngandong *H. erectus* are corroborated; see p. 308).

The earlier representatives of the premoderns still retain several *H. erectus* characteristics. For example, the face is large, the brows project, the forehead is low, and in some cases the cranial vault is still thick. Nevertheless, there are other features of these hominids that show that they are more derived (in the human direction) than were their predecessors. Compared to *Homo erectus*, more modern features in premodern hominids include increased brain size, a more globular cranial vault (i.e., maximum breadth is higher up on the sides), a more vertical nose, and less angulation in the occipital area. We should note that the maximum span of time encompassed by Middle Pleistocene premodern humans is at least 500,000 years. Thus, it is no surprise that certain temporal trends are apparent. The later representatives, for example, show more brain expansion and less occipital angulation than do earlier forms.

These hominids are a diverse, widely dispersed group, distributed over three continents. How to classify them has been in dispute for decades, and disagreements still exist. However, a growing consensus concerning the classification of most of the fossils has recently emerged. Beginning perhaps as early as 850,000 y.a. and extending up to about 200,000 y.a., the fossils from Africa and Europe are placed within *Homo heidelbergensis* (named after a fossil found in Germany in 1907). Contemporaneous fossil finds from China, however, may belong to another species (discussed later).

Until recently, many researchers regarded these fossils as early but more primitive members of *Homo sapiens*. In recognition of this somewhat transitional status, these hominids were termed "archaic *Homo sapiens*." Most paleoanthropologists, however, find this terminology unsatisfactory. For example, Phillip Rightmire concludes that "simply lumping diverse ancient groups with living populations obscures their differences" (1998, p. 226).

In our own discussion, we will recognize *H. heidelbergensis* in this transitional period. Keep in mind, however, that this is a *very* closely related species to *Homo sapiens*—and one that is probably ancestral to modern humans (and to Neandertals as well). Whether these Middle Pleistocene hominid samples actually represent a fully separate species in the *biological* sense (i.e., following the biological species concept; see p. 116) is debatable. Still, researchers find it useful to give them a separate name to make this important stage of human evolution more easily identifiable. We will return to this issue later in the chapter when we discuss the theoretical implications in more detail.

Premodern Humans of the Middle Pleistocene

AFRICA

In Africa, premodern fossils have been found at several sites (Figs. 12–3 and 12–4). One of the best known is Broken Hill (Kabwe). At this site in Zambia, a complete cranium, together with other cranial and postcranial elements belonging to several individuals, was discovered.

In this and other African premodern specimens, a mixture of older and more recent traits can be seen. The skull's massive supraorbital torus (one of the largest of any hominid), low vault, and prominent occipital torus recall those of *H. erectus*. On the other hand, the occipital region is less angulated, the cranial vault bones are thinner, and the cranial base is essentially modern. Dating estimates of Broken Hill and most of the other premodern fossils from Africa have ranged throughout the Middle and Upper Pleistocene, but recent estimates have given dates for most of the localities in the range of 600,000–125,000 y.a.

A total of eight other crania from South and East Africa also show a combination of retained ancestral with more derived (modern) characteristics, and they are all mentioned in the literature as being similar to Broken Hill. The most important of these African finds come from the sites of Florisbad and Elandsfontein in South Africa, Laetoli in Tanzania, and Bodo in Ethiopia (see Fig. 12–4).

Bodo is the most significant of these other African fossils, as it is a nearly complete cranium and is dated to quite early in the Middle Pleistocene (estimated at 600,000 y.a.). The Bodo cranium is also interesting because it shows a distinctive pattern of cut marks, similar to those mentioned in Chapter 9 as evidence of butchering. Moreover, the Bodo individual was apparently defleshed by other hominids, but for what purpose is not clear. Perhaps it was cannibalism, perhaps some other purpose. In any case, this is the earliest evidence of deliberate bone processing of hominids by hominids (White, 1986).

The general similarities in all these African premodern fossils indicate a close relationship between them, almost certainly representing a single species (most commonly referred to as *H. heidelbergensis*). Moreover, these African premodern humans are quite similar to those found in Europe.

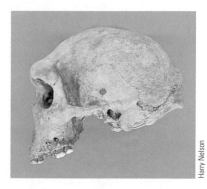

FIGURE 12–3 Broken Hill (Kabwe). Note the very heavy supraorbital torus.

AT A GLANCE	Key Middle Pleistocene Premodern Human (*H. heidelbergensis*) Fossils from Africa	
Site	**Dates (y.a.)**	**Human Remains** *Homo heidelbergensis*
Bodo (Ethiopia)	Middle Pleistocene (600,000)	Incomplete skull, part of braincase
Broken Hill (Kabwe) (Zambia)	Late Middle Pleistocene; (130,000 or older)	Nearly complete cranium, cranial fragments of second individual, miscellaneous postcranial bones

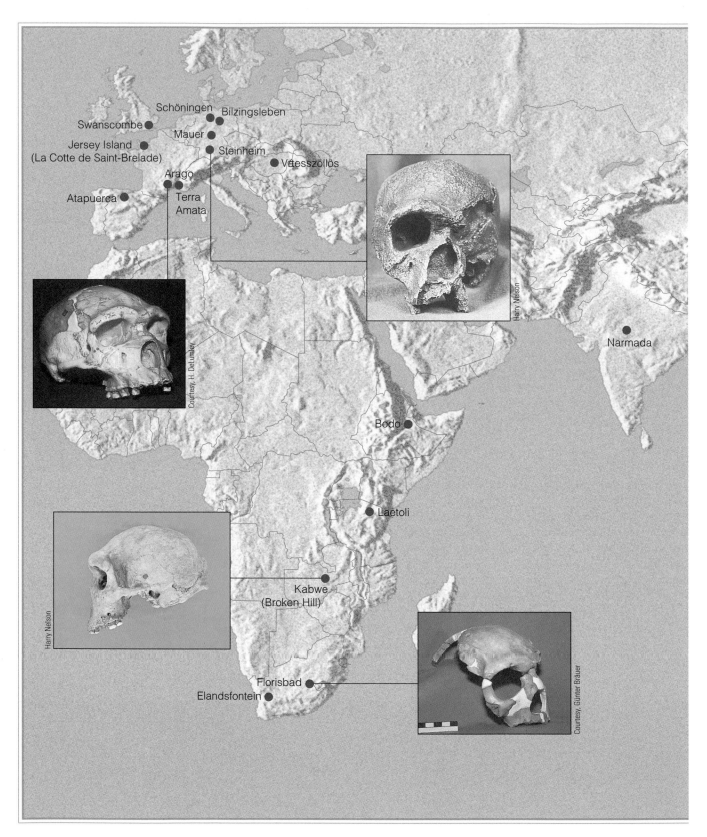

FIGURE 12–4 Fossil discoveries and archaeological localities of Middle Pleistocene premodern hominids.

Courtesy, Xinzhi Wu

EUROPE

More fossil hominids of Middle Pleistocene age have been found in Europe than in any other region. Perhaps this is because more archaeologists have been searching longer in Europe than elsewhere. In any case, during the Middle Pleistocene, Europe was more broadly and consistently occupied than it was earlier in human evolution.

The time range of European premoderns is also extremely broad, extending the full length of the Middle Pleistocene and beyond. At the earlier end, the Gran Dolina finds from northern Spain (discussed in Chapter 11; see p. 317) are definitely not *Homo erectus*. As proposed by Spanish researchers, they may be members of yet another species of hominids. Conversely, they may represent the same *grade* of hominid discussed in this chapter—that is, a population of premodern humans. As noted in the previous chapter, the Gran Dolina hominids might be representative of the same species (*H. heidelbergensis*) as their later European successors (a view also proposed by Rightmire, 1998). If such an interpretation should be further confirmed, Gran Dolina would represent the earliest well-dated occurrence of *H. heidelbergensis* (dating back as early as 850,000 y.a.).*

Later, more completely studied *H. heidelbergensis* finds are dispersed quite widely in Europe. Examples of these finds come from Steinheim and Ehringsdorf (Germany), Swanscombe (England), Arago (France), and Atapuerca (Spain). Like their African counterparts, these European premoderns show retention of *H. erectus* traits mixed with more derived ones (e.g., increased cranial capacity, more rounded occiput, parietal expansion, and reduced tooth size) (Fig. 12–5).

The hominids from Atapuerca are especially interesting. These finds come from another cave in the same area as the Gran Dolina discoveries. Dated to approximately 350,000 y.a., a total of at least 28 individuals have been recov-

(a)

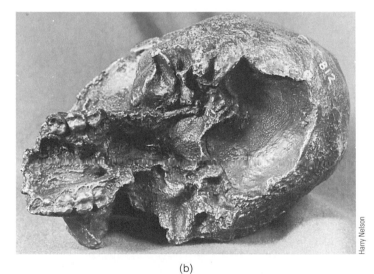

(b)

FIGURE 12–5 Cast of an archaic *Homo heidelbergensis* skull from Germany (Steinheim). (a) Frontal view showing damaged skull. (b) Basal view showing how the foramen magnum was enlarged, apparently for removal of the brain, perhaps for dietary or ritualistic purposes.

---

*Boxgrove from England, also discussed in Chapter 11, likewise would be considered *H. heidelbergensis*, but this fossil consists of only one leg bone (tibia) and is thus not very diagnostic.

AT A GLANCE	Key Middle Pleistocene Premodern Human (*H. heidelbergensis*) Fossils from Europe	
Site	**Dates (y.a.)**	**Human Remains**
Arago (Tautavel) (France)	400,000–300,000; date uncertain	Face; parietal perhaps from same person; many cranial fragments; up to 23 individuals represented
Atapuerca (Sima de los Huesos, northern Spain)	320,000–190,000, probably 300,000	Minimum of 28 individuals, including some nearly complete crania
Steinheim (Germany)	300,000–250,000; date uncertain	Nearly complete skull, lacking mandible
Swanscombe (England)	300,000–250,000; date uncertain	Occipital and parietals

ered from a site called Sima de los Huesos (literally meaning, "pile of bones"). In fact, with more than 4,000 fossils recovered, Sima de los Huesos contains more than 80% of all the Middle Pleistocene hominid remains from the whole world (Bermudez de Castro et al., 2004)! Excavations continue at this remarkable site, where bones have somehow accumulated within a deep chamber inside a cave. There are also large numbers of carnivore remains (bear, fox), but these fossils are generally in separate locations from where the hominids were found. From initial descriptions, the hominid morphology has been interpreted as showing several indications of an early Neandertal-like pattern (arching browridges, projecting midface, and other features) (Rightmire, 1998).

ASIA

China Like their contemporaries in Europe and Africa, Chinese premodern specimens also display both earlier and later characteristics. Chinese paleoanthropologists suggest that more ancestral traits, such as a sagittal ridge (see p. 304) and flattened nasal bones, are shared with *H. erectus*, especially those specimens from Zhoukoudian. They also point out that some of these features can be found in modern *H. sapiens* in China today, indicating substantial genetic continuity. That is, some Chinese researchers have argued that anatomically modern Chinese did not evolve from *H. sapiens* in either Europe or Africa, evolving instead specifically in China from a separate *H. erectus* lineage. Whether such regional evolution occurred or whether anatomically modern migrants from Africa displaced local populations is the subject of a major ongoing debate in paleoanthropology. This important controversy will be the central focus of the next chapter.

Dali, the most complete skull of the late Middle or early Upper Pleistocene fossils in China, displays *H. erectus* and *H. sapiens* traits; it also has a relatively small cranial capacity (1,120 cm³). Several other Chinese specimens also reflect both earlier and later traits and are similar to Dali. In addition, the more recently discovered (1984) partial skeleton from Jinniushan, in northeast China, has been given a provisional date of 200,000 y.a. (Tiemel et al., 1994). The cranial capacity is fairly large (approximately 1,260 cm³), and the walls of the braincase are thin—both modern features and quite unexpected in an individual this ancient (if the dating estimate does indeed hold up). How to classify these Chinese Middle Pleistocene hominids has been a subject of debate and controversy. Recently, however, a leading paleoanthropologist has concluded they are regional variants of *Homo heidelbergensis* (Rightmire, 2004).

AT A GLANCE	Key Middle Pleistocene Premodern Human (*H. heidelbergensis*) Fossils from Asia		
Site	**Dates (y.a.)**		**Human Remains**
Dali (China)	Late Middle Pleistocene (230,000–180,000)		Nearly complete skull
Jinniushan (China)	Late Middle Pleistocene (200,000)		Partial skeleton, including a cranium

India In 1982, a partial skull was discovered in the Narmada Valley, in central India. Associated with this fossil were various hand axes, cleavers, flakes, and choppers. This Narmada specimen has been dated as Middle Pleistocene with a probable cranial capacity within the range of 1,155 to 1,421 cm³. K. A. R. Kennedy (1991), who made a more recent study of the fossil, suggests that Narmada should be viewed as an early example of *H. sapiens*.

A Review of Middle Pleistocene Evolution

The premodern human fossils from Africa and Europe are more similar to each other than they are to the hominids from Asia. The mix of some ancestral characteristics (retained from *Homo erectus* ancestors) with more derived features gives these African and European fossils a distinctive look; they are usually referred to as *H. heidelbergensis*.

The situation in Asia is less tidy. To some researchers, the remains, especially those from Jinniushan, appear more modern than contemporaries from either Europe or Africa. This observation is why Chinese paleoanthropologists and American colleagues hypothesize that these hominids are early members of *H. sapiens*. Other researchers (e.g., Rightmire, 1998, 2004) suggest that these Asian premodern humans may fit as a regional branch of *H. heidelbergensis*. They may even be members of an entirely separate species.

The Pleistocene world forced many small populations into geographic isolation from other hominids. Most of these regional populations no doubt went extinct. Some, however, did evolve, and their descendants are likely traceable in the later Pleistocene fossil record. In Africa, *H. heidelbergensis* is hypothesized to have evolved into modern *H. sapiens*. In Europe, *H. heidelbergensis* evolved into Neandertals. Meanwhile, the Chinese premodern populations may all have met with extinction. At present, however, there is no consensus regarding the status or the likely fate of these enigmatic Asian Middle Pleistocene hominids (Fig. 12–6).

Middle Pleistocene Culture

The Acheulian technology of *H. erectus* carried over into the Middle Pleistocene with relatively little change until near the end of the period, when it became slightly more sophisticated. Bone, a very useful tool material, apparently went practically unused during this time. Stone flake tools similar to those of the earlier era persisted, perhaps in greater variety. Some of the later premodern humans in Africa and Europe invented a method—the Levallois technique (Fig. 12–7)—for controlling flake size and shape. Requiring several coordinated

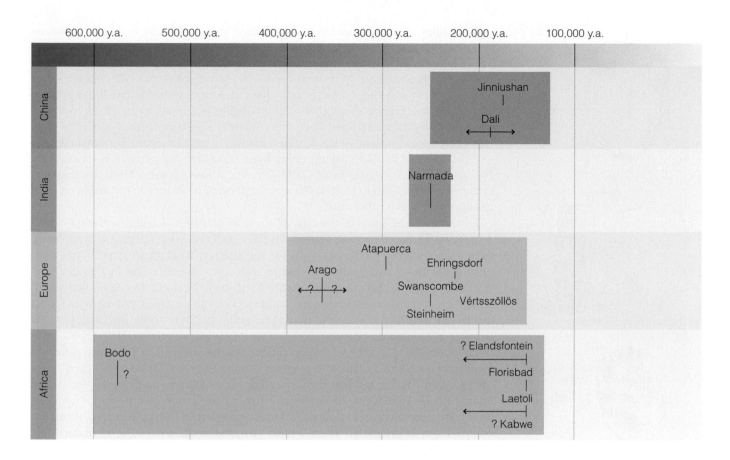

FIGURE 12–6 Time line of Middle Pleistocene hominids. Note that most dates are approximations. Question marks indicate those estimates that are most tentative.

steps, this was no mean feat and suggests to many scholars increased cognitive abilities in later premodern populations.

Interpretation of the distribution of artifacts during the later Middle Pleistocene has generated considerable discussion among archaeologists. We have noted (in Chapter 11) that there is a general geographical distribution characteristic of the Lower Pleistocene, with bifaces (mostly hand axes) found quite often at sites in Africa, but only rarely at sites in most of Asia and not at all among the rich assemblage at Zhoukoudian. Moreover, where hand axes proliferate, the stone tool industry is referred to as Acheulian, while at localities without hand axes, various other terms are used (e.g., "chopper/chopping tool"—a misnomer, since most of the tools are actually flakes).

Acheulian assemblages have been found at many African sites as well as numerous European ones (e.g., Swanscombe in England and Arago in France). Nevertheless, the broad geographical distribution of what we call Acheulian should not blind us to the considerable intraregional diversity in stone tool industries. For example, while a variety of European sites do show a typical Acheulian complex, rich in bifacial hand axes and cleavers, other contemporaneous ones—for example, Bilzingsleben in Germany and Vértesszöllös in Hungary—do not. At these latter two sites, a variety of small retouched flake tools and flaked pebbles of various sizes were found, but no hand axes.

It thus appears that different stone tool industries coexisted in some areas for long periods. Various explanations (Villa, 1983) have been offered to account for this apparent diversity: (1) The tool industries were produced by different peoples (i.e., different cultures, perhaps hominids that also differed biologically); (2) the tool industries represent different types of activities carried out at separate locales; (3) the presence (or absence) of specific tool types—bifaces—represents the availability (or unavailability) of appropriate local stone resources.

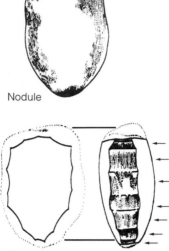

Nodule

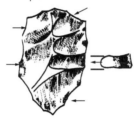

The nodule is chipped on the perimeter.

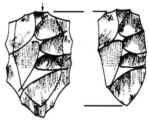

Flakes are radially removed from top surface.

A final blow at one end removes a large flake.

FIGURE 12-7 The Levallois technique.

Premodern human populations continued to live both in caves and in open-air sites, but may have increased their use of caves. Did these hominids control fire? Klein (1989, p. 255) suggests that these hominids did. He writes that there was a "concentration of burnt bones in depressions 50–60 cm across at Vértesszöllös" and that "fossil hearths have also been identified at Bilzingsleben and in several French caves that were probably occupied by early *H. sapiens.*" Chinese archaeologists insist that many Middle Pleistocene sites in China contain evidence of human-controlled fire. However, not everyone is convinced.

That Middle Pleistocene hominids built temporary structures is revealed by concentrations of bones, stones, and artifacts at several sites. Here, they manufactured artifacts and exploited the area for food. The stones may have been used to support the sides of a shelter.

In the Lazaret Cave in the city of Nice, in southern France, a shelter about 36 feet by 11 feet was built against the cave wall, and skins probably were hung over a framework of poles as walls for the shelter. Rocks and large bones supported the base, and inside the shelter were two hearths. The hearth charcoal suggests that the hominid occupants used slow-burning oak and boxwood, which produced easy-to-rekindle embers. Very little stone waste was found inside the shelter, suggesting that they manufactured tools outside, perhaps because there was more light.

Archaeological evidence clearly alludes to the utilization of many different food sources, such as fruits, vegetables, seeds, nuts, and bird eggs, each in its own season. Marine life was also exploited. From Lazaret and Orgnac (southern France) comes evidence of freshwater fishing for trout, perch, and carp. The most detailed reconstruction of Middle Pleistocene life in Europe, however, comes from evidence at Terra Amata, on the southern coast of France (de Lumley and de Lumley, 1973; Villa, 1983). From this site has come fascinating evidence relating to short-term, seasonal visits by hominid groups, who built flimsy shelters, gathered plants, exploited marine resources, and possibly hunted medium-sized and large mammals.

The hunting capabilities of premodern humans, as for earlier hominids, remain open to dispute. What seems clear is that the evidence does not yet unambiguously establish widely practiced advanced abilities. In earlier professional discussions (as well as in earlier editions of our texts), archaeological evidence from Terra Amata (in France) and Torralba and Ambrona (in Spain) was used to argue for advanced hunting skills displayed by premodern humans in Europe. However, reconstruction of these sites by Richard Klein and others has now cast doubt on those prior conclusions. Once again, we see that application of scientific rigor (which is simply good critical thinking) makes us question assumptions. And in so doing, we frequently must conclude that other less dramatic (and less romantic) explanations fit the evidence as well as or better than those based on initial imaginative scenarios.

A possible exception to the current, much more conservative view of the hunting skills of Middle Pleistocene hominids comes from an archaeological site excavated on the Channel Island of Jersey off the west coast of France (see Fig. 12–4). In a cave site called La Cotte de Saint-Brelade, many skeletal remains of large mammals (mammoth and woolly rhinoceros) were found in association with stone flakes. Unlike the remains from the sites mentioned earlier, the animals sampled at La Cotte de Saint-Brelade represent primarily subadults and adults in prime age (*not* what one would expect in naturally occurring accumulations). Moreover, the preserved elements also exhibit the kind of damage that further suggests hominid activities. Directly killing such large animals may not have been within the capabilities of the hominids (*H. heidelbergensis?*) who occupied this site. Thus, K. Scott, who led the excavations, has suggested that these early hominids may have driven their prey off a nearby cliff, bringing certain prized parts back to the cave for further butchering (Scott, 1980).

Another recent and exceptional find is also challenging assumptions regarding hunting capabilities of premodern humans in Europe. From the site of Schöningen in Germany, three remarkably well-preserved wooden spears were discovered in 1995 (Thieme, 1997). As we have noted before, fragile organic remains (such as wood) can rarely be preserved more than a few hundred years; yet these beautifully crafted implements are provisionally dated to 400,000–380,000 y.a.! Beyond this surprisingly ancient date, the spears are intriguing on a variety of other counts. Firstly, they are all large (about 6 feet long), very finely made, selected from hard spruce wood, and expertly balanced. Each spear would have required considerable planning, time, and skill to manufacture. Further, the weapons were most likely used as throwing spears, presumably to hunt large animals. Of interest in this context, bones of numerous horses were also recovered at Schöningen. Archaeologist Hartmut Thieme has thus concluded that "the spears strongly suggest that systematic hunting, involving foresight, planning and the use of appropriate technology, was part of the behavioural repertoire of pre-modern hominids" (1997, p. 807). Therefore, as with the remains from La Cotte de Saint-Brelade, these extraordinary spears from Schöningen make a strong case for advanced hunting skills practiced by at least some Middle Pleistocene populations.

As documented by the fossil hominid remains as well as artifactual evidence from archaeological sites, the long period of transitional hominids in Europe was to continue well into the Upper Pleistocene (after 125,000 y.a.). However, here the evolution of premodern humans was to take a unique turn with the appearance and expansion of the Neandertals.

Neandertals: Premodern Humans of the Upper Pleistocene

Since their discovery more than a century ago, the Neandertals have haunted the best-laid theories of paleoanthropologists. They fit into the general scheme of human evolution, and yet they are misfits. Classified either as *H. sapiens* or a sister species, they are like us and yet different. It is not an easy task to put them in their place. In classifying Neandertals as *H. sapiens*, they are included as a subspecies, *Homo sapiens neanderthalensis,** although not all paleoanthropologists agree with this interpretation (the subspecies for anatomically modern *H. sapiens* is designated as *Homo sapiens sapiens*).

While Neandertal fossil remains have been found at dates approaching 130,000 y.a., in the following discussion of Neandertals, we refer to those populations that lived especially during the last major glaciation, which began about 75,000 y.a. and ended about 10,000 y.a. (Fig. 12–8). We should also note that the evolutionary roots of Neandertals apparently reach quite far back in western Europe, as evidenced by the 300,000 y.a. remains from Sima de los Huesos, Atapuerca, in northern Spain. The majority of fossils have been found in Europe, where they have been most studied, and our description of Neandertals is based primarily on those specimens from western Europe, who are usually called *classic* Neandertals. Not all Neandertals—including others from eastern Europe and western Asia and those from the interglacial that preceded the last glacial—entirely conform to our description of the classic morphology. They tend to be less robust, perhaps because the climate in which they lived was not as cold as western Europe during the last glaciation.

See Virtual Lab 10, section I, for a discussion of Neandertals.

Thal, meaning "valley," is the old spelling and, because rules of taxonomic priority apply to spelling as well as to the names themselves, it is kept in the formal species designation (the "h" was always silent and not pronounced.) The modern spelling is *tal* and is now used this way in Germany; we shall adhere to contemporary usage in the text with the spelling Neandertal.

FIGURE 12–8 Correlation of Pleistocene subdivisions with archaeological industries and hominids. Note that the geological divisions are separate and different from the archaeological stages (e.g., Upper Pleistocene is *not* synonymous with Upper Paleolithic).

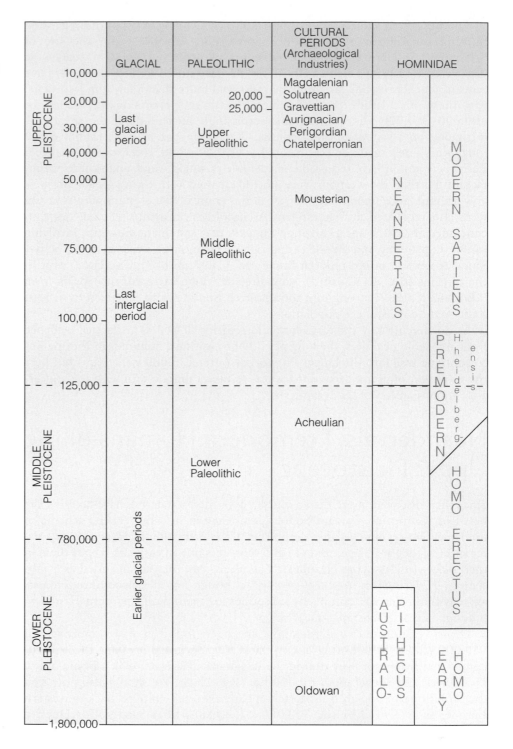

One striking feature of Neandertals is brain size, which in these hominids actually was larger than that of *H. sapiens* today. The average for contemporary *H. sapiens* is between 1,300 and 1,400 cm³, while for Neandertals it was 1,520 cm³. The larger size may be associated with the metabolic efficiency of a larger brain in cold weather. The Inuit (Eskimo) brain also averages larger than that of other modern human populations (about the size of the Neandertal brain). It should also be pointed out that the larger brain size in both premodern and contemporary human populations adapted to *cold* climates is partially correlated with larger body size, which has also evolved among these groups (see Chapter 15).

The classic Neandertal cranium is large, long, low, and bulging at the sides. Viewed from the side, the posterior portion of the occipital bone is somewhat bun-shaped, but the marked occipital angle typical of many *H. erectus* crania is absent. The forehead rises more vertically than that of *H. erectus*, and the browridges arch over the orbits instead of forming a straight bar (Fig. 12–9).

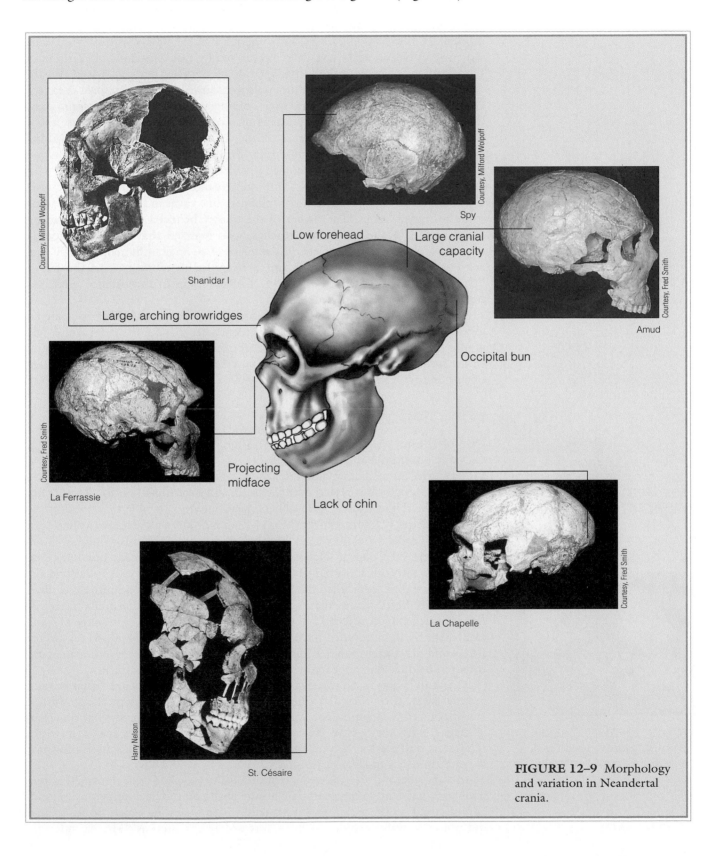

FIGURE 12–9 Morphology and variation in Neandertal crania.

Compared with anatomically modern humans, the Neandertal face stands out. It projects almost as if it were pulled forward. This feature can be seen when the distance of the nose and teeth from the eye orbits is compared with that of modern *H. sapiens*. Postcranially, Neandertals were very robust, barrel-chested, and powerfully muscled. This robust skeletal structure, in fact, dominates hominid evolution from *H. erectus* through all premodern forms. Nevertheless, the Neandertals appear particularly robust, with shorter limbs than seen in most modern *H. sapiens* populations. Both the facial anatomy and robust postcranial structure of Neandertals have been interpreted by Erik Trinkaus (of Washington University in St. Louis) to reflect adaptation to rigorous living in a cold climate.

For about 100,000 years, Neandertals lived in Europe and western Asia (see. Fig. 12–12 on pp. 346–347), and their coming and going has raised more questions and controversies than perhaps any other hominid group. As noted, Neandertal forebears date back to the later premoderns of the Middle Pleistocene. But these were transitional forms, and it is not until the Upper Pleistocene that Neandertals become fully recognizable.

Neandertal takes its name from the Neander Valley, near Düsseldorf, Germany. In 1856, workmen quarrying limestone caves in the valley came across some fossilized bones. The owner of the quarry believed them to be bear and gave them to a natural science teacher, who realized that they were not the remains of a cave bear, but rather the remains of an ancient human. Exactly what the bones represented became a *cause célèbre* for many years, and the fate of "Neandertal Man," as the bones were named, hung in the balance until later finds provided more evidence.

What swung the balance in favor of accepting the Neander Valley specimen as a genuine hominid fossil were other nineteenth-century finds similar to it. What is more important, the additional fossil remains brought home the realization that a form of human different from nineteenth-century Europeans had in fact once existed.

FRANCE AND SPAIN

One of the most important Neandertal discoveries was made in 1908 at La Chapelle-aux-Saints in southwestern France. A nearly complete skeleton was found buried in a shallow grave in a **flexed** position, with several fragments of nonhuman long bones placed over the head, and over them, a bison leg. Around the body were flint tools and broken animal bones.

The skeleton was turned over for study to a well-known French paleontologist, Marcellin Boule, who published his analysis in three copious volumes. Boule depicted the La Chapelle Neandertal as a brutish, bent-kneed, not fully erect biped. As a result of this exaggerated interpretation, some scholars, and certainly the general public, concluded that all Neandertals were highly primitive creatures.

Why did Boule draw these conclusions from the La Chapelle skeleton? Apparently, he misconstrued Neandertal posture owing to the presence of spinal osteoarthritis in this older male. In addition, and probably more important, Boule and his contemporaries found it difficult to accept fully as a human ancestor an individual who appeared to depart from the modern pattern.

The skull of this male, who was possibly at least 40 years of age when he died, is very large, with a cranial capacity of 1,620 cm³. As is typical for western European "classic" forms, the vault is low and long, the supraorbital ridges are immense, with the typical Neandertal arched shape, the forehead is low and retreating, and the face is long and projecting. The back of the skull is protuberant and bun-shaped (Figs. 12–9 and 12–10).

La Chapelle, however, is not a typical Neandertal, but is an unusually robust male that "evidently represents an extreme in the Neandertal range of variation" (Brace et al., 1979, p. 117). Unfortunately, this skeleton, which Boule claimed did not even walk completely erect, was widely accepted as "Mr. Neandertal."

flexed The position of the body in a bent orientation, with arms and legs drawn up to the chest.

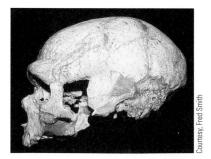

FIGURE 12–10 La Chapelle-aux-Saints. Note the occipital bun, projecting face, and low vault.

But not all Neandertal materials express the suite of "classic Neandertal" traits to the degree seen in La Chapelle.

Another Neandertal site excavated recently in southern France has revealed further fascinating details relating to Neandertal behavior. From the 100,000- to 120,000-year-old Moula-Guercy Cave site, Alban Defleur, Tim White, and colleagues have analyzed 78 broken hominid fragments representing probably six individuals (Defleur et al., 1999). The intriguing aspect of these remains concerns *how* they were broken. Detailed analysis of cut marks, pits, scars, and other features clearly suggests that the Neandertal individuals were *processed*—that is, they "were defleshed and disarticulated. After this, the marrow cavity was exposed by a hammer-on-anvil technique" (Defleur et al., 1999, p. 131). Moreover, the non-human bones at this site, especially the deer remains, were processed in an identical fashion. In other words, the Moula-Guercy Neandertals provide the best-documented evidence thus far of Neandertal *cannibalism*.

Some of the most recent of the western European Neandertals come from St. Césaire in southwestern France and are dated at about 35,000 y.a. (Fig. 12–11). The bones were recovered from a bed including discarded chipped blades, hand axes, and other stone tools of an **Upper Paleolithic** tool industry associated with Neandertals. Another site, Zafarraya Cave in southern Spain, may provide yet a more recent time range for Neandertal occupation in Europe. During the 1980s and 1990s, a few pieces of hominid individuals were found at Zafarraya that have been interpreted as Neandertal in morphology. What is most interesting, however, is the *date* suggested for the site. French archaeologist Jean-Jacques Hublin, who has excavated the site, asserts that the date is close to 29,000 y.a.—a full 6,000 years later than St. Césaire.

Another site, also recently redated, is apparently about the same age as Zafarraya but is located in central Europe. Recent recalibration by radiocarbon dating has indicated that the later Neandertal levels at Vindija, in Croatia (discussed shortly), are about 28,000 to 29,000 years old (Smith et al., 1999). If one of these dates is further confirmed, then either Zafarraya or Vindija would gain the distinction of having the most recent Neandertals thus far discovered.

Yet a more recent site in Portugal has recently been interpreted as showing hybridization between Neandertals and modern *Homo sapiens*. (We will discuss this intriguing suggestion in more detail in Chapter 13.)

The St. Césaire, Zafarraya, and Vindija sites are fascinating for several reasons. Anatomically modern humans were living in central and western Europe by about 35,000 y.a. or a bit earlier. Therefore, it is possible that Neandertals and modern *H. sapiens* were living in close proximity for several thousand years (Fig. 12–13). How did these two groups interact? Evidence from a number of French sites indicates that Neandertals borrowed technological methods and tools (such as blades) from the anatomically modern populations and thereby modified their own tools, creating a new industry, the **Chatelperronian**. However, such an example of cultural diffusion does not specify *how* the diffusion took place. Did the Neandertals become assimilated into modern populations? Did the two groups interbreed? It would also be interesting to know more precisely how long the coexistence of Neandertals and modern *H. sapiens* lasted. No one knows the answers to these questions, but it has been suggested that an average annual difference of 2 percent mortality between the two populations (i.e., modern *H. sapiens* individuals lived longer than Neandertals) would have resulted in the extinction of the Neandertals in approximately 1,000 years (Zubrow, 1989).

It should be noted that not all paleoanthropologists agree with the notion of the coexistence of Neandertals and Upper Paleolithic modern humans. For example, David Frayer of the University of Kansas states, "There is still *no human fossil evidence* which supports the coexistence of Neanderthal and Upper Paleolithic forms in Europe" (emphasis added) (1992, p. 9). That is, despite the indications of cultural diffusion noted here, no European site has yet produced directly associated remains of *both* types of humans.

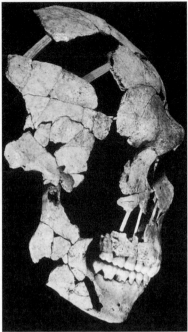

Harry Nelson

FIGURE 12–11 St. Césaire, among the "last" Neandertals.

Upper Paleolithic A cultural period usually associated with modern humans (but also found with some Neandertals) and distinguished by technological innovation in various stone tool industries. Best known from western Europe, similar industries are also known from central and eastern Europe and Africa.

Chatelperronian Pertaining to an Upper Paleolithic industry found in France and Spain, containing blade tools and associated with Neandertals.

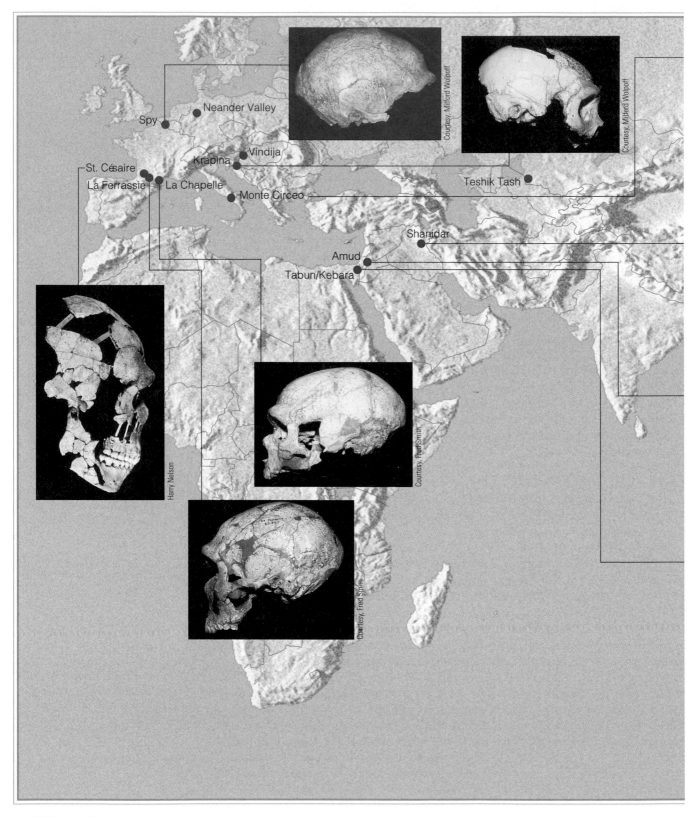

FIGURE 12–12 Fossil discoveries of Neandertals.

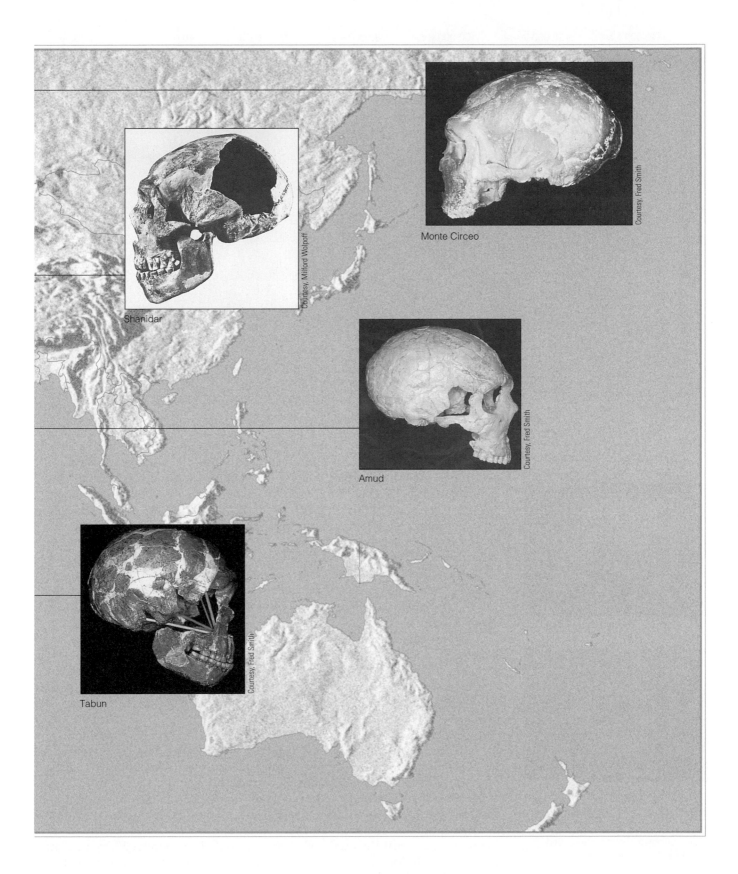

Shanidar

Courtesy, Milford Wolpoff

Monte Circeo

Courtesy, Fred Smith

Amud

Courtesy, Fred Smith

Tabun

Courtesy, Fred Smith

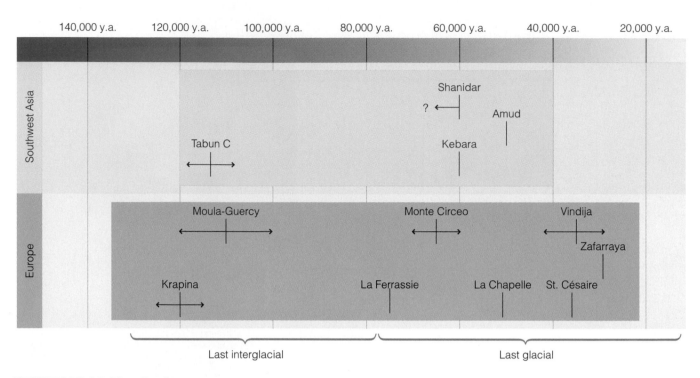

FIGURE 12–13 Time line for Neandertal fossil discoveries.

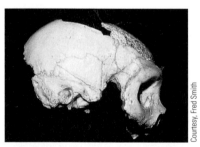

(a)

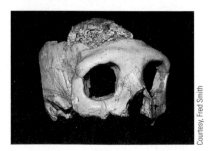

(b)

FIGURE 12–14 Krapina C. (a) Lateral view showing characteristic Neandertal traits. (b) Three-quarters view.

CENTRAL EUROPE

There are quite a few other European classic Neandertals, including significant finds in central Europe (see Fig. 12–12). At Krapina, Croatia, an abundance of bones (1,000 fragments representing up to 70 individuals) and 1,000 stone tools or flakes have been recovered (Trinkaus and Shipman, 1992). Krapina is an old site, perhaps the earliest showing the full "classic" Neandertal morphology, dating back to the beginning of the Upper Pleistocene (estimated at 130,000–110,000 y.a.). Moreover, despite the relatively early date, the characteristic Neandertal features of the Krapina specimens (although less robust) are similar to the western European finds (Fig. 12–14). Krapina is also important as an intentional burial site, one of the oldest on record.

Another interesting site in central Europe is Vindija, about 30 miles from Krapina. The site is an excellent source of faunal, cultural, and hominid materials stratified in *sequence* throughout much of the Upper Pleistocene. Neandertal fossils consisting of some 35 specimens are dated between about 42,000 and 28,000 y.a. (the latter date would be among the most recent of all Neandertal discoveries). Even though some of their features approach the morphology of early modern south-central European *H. sapiens*, the overall pattern is definitely Neandertal. However, these modified Neandertal features, such as smaller browridges and slight chin development, have led some researchers to suggest a possible evolutionary trend toward modern *H. sapiens*.

Fred Smith, for example, of Loyola University, takes the view that variation in Vindija cranial features points to a trend continuing on to the later anatomically modern specimens found in the upper levels of the cave. Does Vindija support the proposition that the origin of *H. sapiens* could have occurred here in central Europe? Smith does not insist on this interpretation and suggests that anatomically modern *H. sapiens* could have come from elsewhere. But he does believe that there is at least some morphological and genetic continuity between the samples found in the lower and upper levels of the cave.

FIGURE 12–15 Excavation of the Tabun Cave, Mt. Carmel, Israel.

WESTERN ASIA

Israel In addition to European Neandertals, there are numerous important discoveries from southwest Asia. Several specimens from Israel display some modern features and are less robust than the classic Neandertals of Europe, but again the overall pattern is Neandertal. The best known of these discoveries is from Tabun (Mugharet-et-Tabun, "Cave of the Oven") at Mt. Carmel, a short drive south from Haifa (Fig. 12–15). Tabun, excavated in the early 1930s, yielded a female skeleton, recently dated by thermoluminescence (TL) at about 120,000–110,000 y.a. If this dating proves accurate, it places the Tabun find as generally contemporary with early modern *H. sapiens* found in nearby caves. (TL dating is discussed on p. 376.)

A more recent Neandertal burial, a male discovered in 1983, comes from Kebara, a neighboring cave of Tabun at Mt. Carmel. Although the skeleton is incomplete—the cranium and much of the lower limbs are missing—the pelvis, dated to 60,000 y.a., is the most complete Neandertal pelvis so far recovered. Also recovered at Kebara is a hyoid bone, the first from a Neandertal, and this find is especially important from the point of view of reconstructing language capabilities.*

Iraq A most remarkable site is Shanidar, in the Zagros Mountains of northeastern Iraq, where partial skeletons of nine individuals—males and females, seven adults and two infants—were found, four of them deliberately buried. One of the more interesting individuals is Shanidar 1, a male who lived to be approximately 30 to 45 years old, a considerable age for a prehistoric human (Fig. 12–16). His stature is estimated at 5 feet 7 inches, while his cranial capacity is 1,600 cm^3. This individual shows several fascinating features:

> There had been a crushing blow to the left side of the head, fracturing the eye socket, displacing the left eye, and probably causing blindness on that side. He also sustained a massive blow to the right side of the body that so badly damaged the right arm that it became withered and useless; the

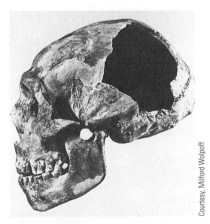

FIGURE 12–16 Shanidar 1. Does he represent Neandertal compassion for the disabled?

---

*The Kebara hyoid is identical to that of modern humans, suggesting that Neandertals did not differ from *H. sapiens sapiens* in this key element.

bones of the shoulder blade, collar bone, and upper arm are much smaller and thinner than those on the left. The right lower arm and hand are missing, probably not because of poor preservation . . . but because they either atrophied and dropped off or because they were amputated. (Trinkaus and Shipman, 1992, p. 340)

In addition to these injuries, there was damage to the lower right leg (including a healed fracture of a foot bone). The right knee and left leg show signs of pathological involvement, and these changes to the limbs and foot may have left this man with a limping gait.

How such a person could perform normal obligations and customs is difficult to imagine. However, both Ralph Solecki, who supervised the work at Shanidar Cave, and Erik Trinkaus, who has carefully studied the Shanidar remains, believe that to survive, he must have been helped by others: "A one-armed, partially blind, crippled man could have made no pretense of hunting or gathering his own food. That he survived for years after his trauma was a testament to Neandertal compassion and humanity" (Trinkaus and Shipman, 1992, p. 341).*

CENTRAL ASIA

Uzbekistan About 1,600 miles east of Shanidar in Uzbekistan, in a cave at Teshik-Tash, is the easternmost Neandertal discovery. New analyses suggest the Teshik-Tash skeleton may actually be that of a modern human, and, thus, not a Neandertal (Glantz et al., 2004). The skeleton is that of a nine-year-old boy who appears to have been deliberately buried. It was reported that five pairs of wild goat horns surrounded him, suggesting a burial ritual or perhaps a religious cult, but owing to inadequate published documentation of the excavation, this interpretation has been seriously questioned. The Teshik-Tash individual, like some specimens from Croatia and southwest Asia, also shows a mixture of Neandertal traits (heavy browridges and occipital bun) and modern traits (high vault and definite signs of a chin).

As noted, the Teshik-Tash site represents the easternmost location presently established for Neandertals. Thus, based on the assumed evidence that Teshik-Tash is a Neandertal, geographical distribution of the Neandertals extended from France eastward possibly to central Asia, a distance of about 4,000 miles.

AT A GLANCE	Key Neandertal Fossil Discoveries	
Site	**Dates (y.a.)**	**Human Remains**
Vindija (Croatia)	42,000–28,000	35 specimens; almost entirely cranial fragments
La Chapelle (France)	50,000	Nearly complete adult male skeleton
Shanidar (Iraq)	70,000–60,000	9 individuals (partial skeletons)
Tabun (Israel)	110,000 date uncertain	2 (perhaps 3) individuals, including almost complete skeleton of adult female
Krapina (Croatia)	125,000–120,000	Up to 40 individuals, but very fragmentary

*K.A. Dettwyler (1991) asserts that Shanidar I could have survived without assistance and that there is no solid evidence that compassion explains this individual's survival.

Culture of Neandertals

Neandertals, who lived in the cultural period known as the Middle Paleolithic, are almost always associated with the **Mousterian** industry (although the Mousterian industry is not always associated with Neandertals). In the early part of the last glacial period, Mousterian culture extended across Europe and North Africa into the former Soviet Union, Israel, Iran, and as far east as Uzbekistan and perhaps even China. Moreover, in sub-Saharan Africa, the contemporaneous Middle Stone Age industry is broadly similar to the Mousterian.

TECHNOLOGY

Neandertals improved on previous prepared-core techniques (i.e., the Levallois) by inventing a new variation. They trimmed a flint nodule around the edges to form a disk-shaped core. Each time they struck the edge, they produced a flake, continuing this way until the core became too small and was discarded. Thus, the Neandertals were able to obtain more flakes per core than their predecessors. They then trimmed (retouched) the flakes into various forms, such as scrapers, points, and knives (Fig. 12–17).

Neandertal craftspeople elaborated and diversified traditional methods, and there is some indication of development in the specialization of tools used in skin and meat preparation, hunting, woodworking, and hafting. There is, however, still nearly a complete absence of bone tools, in strong contrast to the succeeding cultural period, the Upper Paleolithic. Nevertheless, Neandertals advanced their technology, which tended to be similar in basic tool types over considerable geographical distances, well beyond that of earlier hominids. It is quite possible that their modifications in technology helped provide a basis for the remarkable changes of the Upper Paleolithic (discussed in the next chapter).

SETTLEMENTS

People of the Mousterian culture lived in a variety of open sites, caves, and rock shelters. Living in the open on the cold tundra suggests the building of structures, and there is some evidence of such structures (although the last glaciation must have destroyed many open sites). At the site of Moldova, in the Ukraine (now an independent state and neighbor of Russia), archaeologists found traces of an oval ring of mammoth bones enclosing an area of about 26 by 16 feet and which may have been used to weigh down the skin walls of a temporary hut or tent. Inside the ring are traces of a number of hearths, hundreds of tools, thousands of waste flakes, and many bone fragments, quite possibly derived from animals brought back for consumption.

Evidence of life in caves is abundant. Windbreaks of poles and skin were probably erected at the cave mouth for protection against severe weather. Fire was in general use by this time and was no doubt used for cooking, warmth, light, and keeping predators at bay.

How large were Neandertal settlements, and were they permanent or temporary? These questions are not yet answered, but Binford (1981) suggests that the settlements were used intermittently for short-term occupation.

SUBSISTENCE

Neandertals were successful hunters, as the abundant remains of animal bones at their sites demonstrate. But while it is clear that Neandertals could hunt large mammals, they may not have been as efficient at this task as were Upper Paleolithic hunters. Inferring from his detailed work in the Middle East,

Mousterian Pertaining to the stone tool industry associated with Neandertals and some modern *H. sapiens* groups; also called Middle Paleolithic. This industry is characterized by a larger proportion of flake tools than is found in Acheulian tool kits.

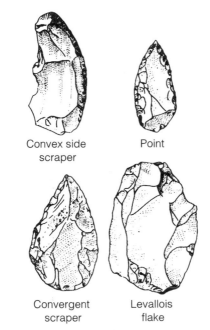

Convex side scraper   Point

Convergent scraper   Levallois flake

FIGURE 12–17 Mousterian tools. (After Bordes.)

See Virtual Lab 11 for a discussion of dietary reconstruction.

Harvard anthropologist Ofer Bar-Yosef (1994) has concluded that only after the beginning of the Upper Paleolithic was the spear-thrower, or atlatl (see p. 382), invented. Moreover, shortly thereafter, the bow and arrow may have greatly facilitated efficiency (and safety) in hunting large mammals. Lacking such long-distance weaponry, and thus mostly limited to close-proximity spears, Neandertals may have been more prone to serious injury—a hypothesis recently given some intriguing support by paleoanthropologists Thomas Berger and Erik Trinkaus. Berger and Trinkaus (1995) analyzed the pattern of trauma (particularly fractures) in Neandertals and compared it with that seen in contemporary human samples. Interestingly, the pattern in Neandertals—especially the relatively high proportion of head and neck injuries—matched most closely to that seen in contemporary rodeo performers. Berger and Trinkaus thus conclude, "The similarity to the rodeo distribution suggests frequent close encounters with large ungulates unkindly disposed to the humans involved" (Berger and Trinkaus, 1995, p. 841).

Meat was, of course, not the only component of Neandertal diet. Evidence (from Shanidar, for example) indicates that Neandertals gathered as well, consuming berries, nuts, and other plants.

It is assumed that in the bitter cold of the last glacial period, Neandertals wore clothing, and they probably had developed methods of curing skins. But since there is no evidence of sewing equipment, the clothing was probably of simple design, perhaps something like a poncho.

We know much more of European Middle Paleolithic culture than of any prior period, as it has been studied longer and by more scholars. In recent years, however, Africa has been a target not only of physical anthropologists (as we have seen copiously documented in earlier chapters), but also of archaeologists, who have added considerably to our knowledge of African Pleistocene hominid history. In many instances, the technology and assumed cultural adaptations in Africa were similar to those in Europe and southwest Asia. We will see in the next chapter that the African technological achievements also kept pace with (or even preceded) those in western Europe.

SYMBOLIC BEHAVIOR

There are a variety of hypotheses concerning the speech capacities of Neandertals. Many of these views are highly contradictory; although some scholars argue that Neandertals were incapable of human speech, the prevailing consensus has been that Neandertals *were* capable of articulate speech, perhaps even fully competent in the range of sounds produced by modern humans. However, there is new genetic evidence that may require reassessment of just when fully human language first emerged (Enard et al., 2002). In humans today, mutations in a particular gene (locus) are known to produce serious language impairments. From an evolutionary perspective, what is perhaps most significant concerns the greater variability seen in the alleles at this locus in modern humans as compared to other primates. An intriguing hypothesis explaining this increased variation postulates intensified selection acting on human populations, perhaps quite recently—and thus potentially after the evolutionary divergence of the Neandertals.

But even if we were to conclude that Neandertals *could* speak, that does not necessarily mean that they had the same language capabilities of modern *Homo sapiens*. A major contemporary focus among paleoanthropologists is the apparently sudden expansion of modern *H. sapiens* (discussed in Chapter 13) and various explanations for the success of this group. Moreover, as we attempt to explain how and why *H. sapiens sapiens* expanded its geographical range, we are left with the further problem of explaining what happened to the Neandertals.

In making these types of interpretations, a growing number of paleoanthropologists suggest that *behavioral* differences are the key. Further corroboration of a recent evolutionary shift resulting from mutation of a crucial gene influencing language will bolster this view.

Upper Paleolithic *H. sapiens* is hypothesized to have possessed some significant behavioral advantages that Neandertals (and other premodern humans) lacked. Was it some kind of new and expanded ability to symbolize, communicate, organize social activities, elaborate technology, obtain a wider range of food resources, or care for the sick or injured, or was it some other factor? Were there, compared with *H. sapiens sapiens*, neurological differences that limited the Neandertals and thus contributed to their demise?

The direct anatomical evidence derived from Neandertal fossils is not especially helpful in specifically answering these questions. Ralph Holloway (1985) has maintained that Neandertal brains (at least as far as the fossil evidence suggests) do not differ significantly from that of modern *H. sapiens*. Moreover, Neandertal vocal tracts and other morphological features, compared with our own, do not appear seriously to have limited them.

Most of the reservations about advanced cognitive abilities in Neandertals have come from archaeological data. Interpretation of Neandertal sites, when compared with succeeding Upper Paleolithic sites (especially as documented in western Europe), have led to several intriguing contrasts, as shown in Table 12–1.

TABLE 12–1 Cultural Contrasts* Between Neandertals and Upper Paleolithic Modern Humans

NEANDERTALS	UPPER PALEOLITHIC MODERN HUMANS
Tool Technology Numerous flake tools; few, however, apparently for highly specialized functions; use of bone, antler, or ivory very rare; relatively few tools with more than one or two parts	Many more varieties of stone tools; many apparently for specialized functions; frequent use of bone, antler, and ivory; many more tools comprised of two or more component parts
Hunting Efficiency and Weapons No long-distance hunting weapons; close-proximity weapons used (thus, more likelihood of injury)	Use of spear-thrower and bow and arrow; wider range of social contacts, perhaps permitting larger, more organized hunting parties (including game drives)
Stone Material Transport Stone materials transported only short distances—just "a few kilometers" (Klein, 1989)	Stone tool raw materials transported over much longer distances, implying wider social networks and perhaps trade
Art Artwork uncommon; usually small; probably mostly of a personal nature; some items perhaps misinterpreted as "art"; others may be intrusive from overlying Upper Paleolithic contexts; cave art absent	Artwork much more common, including transportable objects as well as elaborate cave art; well executed, using a variety of materials and techniques; stylistic sophistication
Burial Deliberate burial at several sites; graves unelaborated; graves frequently lack artifacts	Burials much more complex, frequently including both tools and remains of animals

*The contrasts are more apparent in some areas (particularly western Europe) than others (eastern Europe, Near East). Elsewhere (Africa, eastern Asia), where there were no Neandertals, the cultural situation is quite different. Moreover, even in western Europe, the cultural transformations were not necessarily abrupt, but may have developed more gradually from Mousterian to Upper Paleolithic times. For example, Straus (1995) argues that many of the Upper Paleolithic features were not consistently manifested until after 20,000 y.a.

On the basis of this type of behavioral and anatomical evidence, Neandertals in recent years have increasingly been viewed as an evolutionary dead end. Whether their disappearance and ultimate replacement by anatomically modern Upper Paleolithic peoples (with their presumably "superior" culture) was solely the result of cultural differences or was also influenced by biological variation cannot at present be determined.

BURIALS

It has been known for some time that Neandertals deliberately buried their dead. Indeed, the spectacular discoveries at La Chapelle, Shanidar, and elsewhere were the direct results of ancient burial, thus facilitating much more complete preservation. Such deliberate burial treatment extends back at least 90,000 years at Tabun. Moreover, some form of consistent "disposal" of the dead (but not necessarily below-ground burial) is evidenced at Atapuerca, Spain, where at least 28 individuals comprising more than 700 fossilized elements were found in a cave at the end of a deep vertical shaft. From the nature of the site and the accumulation of hominid remains, Spanish researchers are convinced that the site demonstrates some form of human activity involving deliberate disposal of the dead (Arsuaga et al., 1997).

The provisional 300,000-year-old age for Atapuerca suggests that Neandertals (more precisely, their immediate precursors) were, by the Middle Pleistocene, handling their dead in special ways, a behavior thought previously to have emerged only much later (in the Upper Pleistocene). And, as far as current data indicate, this practice is seen in western European contexts well before it appears in Africa or in eastern Asia. For example, in the premodern sites at Kabwe and Florisbad (discussed earlier), deliberate disposal of the dead is not documented. Nor is it seen in African early modern sites (e.g., Klasies River Mouth, dated at 120,000–100,000 y.a.; see p. 372).

Nevertheless, in later contexts (after 35,000 y.a.) in Europe, where anatomically modern *H. sapiens* (*H. sapiens sapiens*) remains are found in clear burial contexts, their treatment is considerably more complex than is seen in Neandertal burials. In these later (Upper Paleolithic) sites, grave goods, including bone and stone tools as well as animal bones, are found more consistently and in greater concentrations. Because many Neandertal sites were excavated in the nineteenth or early twentieth century, before the development of more rigorous archaeological methods, there are questions regarding numerous purported burials. Nevertheless, the evidence seems quite clear that deliberate burial was practiced at La Chapelle, La Ferrassie (eight graves), Tabun, Amud, Kebara, Shanidar, and Teshik Tash (as well as at several other localities, especially in France). Moreover, in many instances, the *position* of the body was deliberately modified and placed in the grave in a flexed posture (see p. 344). Such a flexed position has been found in 16 of the 20 best-documented Neandertal burial contexts (Klein, 1989).

Finally, the placement of supposed grave goods in burials, including stone tools, animal bones (such as cave bear), and even arrangements of flowers, together with stone slabs on top of the burials, have all been postulated as further evidence of Neandertal symbolic behavior. However, in many instances, again due to poor excavation documentation, these assertions are questionable. Placement of stone tools, for example, is occasionally seen, but apparently was not done consistently. In those 33 Neandertal burials for which adequate data exist, only 14 show definite association of stone tools and/or animal bones with the deceased (Klein, 1989). It is not until the next cultural period, the Upper Paleolithic, that we see a major behavioral shift, as demonstrated in more elaborate burials and development of art.

Genetic Evidence

As a result of the revolutionary advances in molecular biology (discussed in Chapter 3), fascinating new avenues of research have become possible in the study of earlier hominids. The extraction, amplification, and sequencing of ancient DNA from contexts spanning the last 10,000 years or so are now becoming fairly commonplace (e.g., the analysis of DNA from the 5,000-year-old "Iceman" found in the Italian Alps; see p. 363).

Finding usable DNA in yet more ancient remains is much more difficult because the material has become more mineralized, obliterating organic components, including (usually) the DNA. Nevertheless, in the past few years, very exciting results have been announced relating to DNA found in four different Neandertal fossils. The first of these comes from the original Neander Valley specimen, and analysis was completed in 1997 (Krings et al., 1997). New excavations at the Neander Valley site have recovered at least two further individuals, one of which had its DNA analyzed (Schmitz et al., 2002). The other two come from Mezmaiskaya Cave in Russia (Ovchinnikov et al., 2000) and from Vindija in Croatia (Krings et al., 2000). In all cases, the individuals are by far the oldest hominid remains from which DNA has been recovered. The Neander Valley fossils are dated at 40,000 years old, the Vindija remains are 42,000 y.a., and the Mezmaiskaya material is dated at 29,000 y.a. (*Note:* This places the latter among the most recent of all Neandertal discoveries.)

The technique used in the study of Neandertal fossils involved the extraction of mitochondrial DNA (mtDNA), amplification by PCR (see p. 67), and nucleotide sequencing of portions of the molecule. Results from the four specimens show that they are genetically more different from contemporary *Homo sapiens* populations than these latter populations are from each other (about three times as much). Extrapolating from these comparative data, Krings and colleagues (1997) have hypothesized that the Neandertal lineage separated from that of modern *H. sapiens* ancestors between 690,000 and 550,000 y.a.

This intriguing hypothesis, however, has not been fully confirmed and is most certainly not accepted by all paleoanthropologists. It is still not clear how rapidly mtDNA evolves, nor is it obvious how genetically different we should *expect* ancient hominids to be compared to us. (In other words, at present, we cannot rule out evolutionary relationships on the basis of available genetic evidence.) Nevertheless, such data probably offer the best hope of ultimately untangling the place of Neandertals in human evolution—and perhaps even of understanding something of their fate.

Trends in Human Evolution: Understanding Premodern Humans

The Middle Pleistocene hominids are a quite diverse group, broadly dispersed through time and space. There is thus considerable diversity among them, and a clear evolutionary picture is not readily attainable. Given that regional populations were small and frequently isolated, many of these likely went extinct without issue. To see an "ancestor" in every one of the fossil finds is a mistake.

Nevertheless, as a group, these Middle Pleistocene premoderns do reveal some general trends. In many respects, for example, they appear *transitional* between the hominid grades that preceded them (*H. erectus*) and that which followed them (*H. sapiens*). It is not a stretch to say that all these Middle Pleistocene premoderns derived from *H. erectus* forebears and that some of them, in turn, are quite likely ancestral to the earliest fully modern humans.

A CLOSER LOOK

Are They Human?

At the beginning of this chapter, we posed the question, What does it mean to be "human"? Applying this term to our extinct hominid predecessors is somewhat tricky. Various prior hominid species share with contemporary *Homo sapiens* a mosaic of physical features. For example, they are all bipedal, most (but not all) have fairly small canine teeth, some are completely terrestrial, and some are moderately encephalized (while others are much more so). Thus, the *physical* characteristics that define humanity appear at different times during hominid evolution.

Even more tenuous are the *behavioral* characteristics frequently identified as signifying human status. The most significant of these proposed behavioral traits include major dependence on culture, innovation, cooperation in acquiring food, full language, and elaboration of symbolic representations in art and body adornment. Once again, the characteristics become apparent at different stages of hominid evolution. But distinguishing when and how these behavioral characteristics became established in our ancestors is even more problematic than analysis of anatomical traits. While the archaeological record provides considerable information regarding stone tool technology, it is mostly silent on other aspects of material culture. The social organization and language capabilities of earlier hominids are as yet almost completely invisible.

From the evidence that is available, we can conclude that *H. erectus* took significant steps in the human direction—well beyond that of earlier hominids. *H. erectus* vastly expanded hominid geographical ranges, achieved the full body size and limb proportions of later hominids, had increased encephalization, and became considerably more culturally dependent.

H. heidelbergensis (in the Middle Pleistocene) and, to an even greater degree, Neandertals (in the Upper Pleistocene), maintained several of these characteristics (such as body size and proportions), while also showing further evolution in the human direction. Most particularly, relative brain size increased further, expanding on average about 22 percent beyond that of *H. erectus* (Fig. 1); note, however, that the largest "jump" in proportional brain size occurs very late in hominid evolution—only with the appearance of fully modern humans.

In addition to brain enlargement, cranial shape also was remodeled in *H. heidelbergensis* and Neandertals, producing a more globular shape of the vault (and suggesting further neurological reorganization). Stone tool technology also became more sophisticated during the Middle Pleistocene, with the manufacture of tools requiring a more complicated series of steps. Moreover, for the first time, fire was definitely controlled (and in wide use); caves were routinely occupied; hominid ranges were successfully expanded throughout much of Europe as well as into northern Asia (i.e., colder habitats were more fully exploited); structures were built; and more systematic hunting took place.

Some premoderns also were like modern humans in another significant way. Analysis of teeth from a Neandertal shows that these hominids had the same *delayed maturation* found in modern *H. sapiens* (Dean et al., 2001). We do not yet have similar data for earlier *H. heidelbergensis* individuals, but it is possible that they, too, showed this distinctively human pattern of development.

Paleoanthropologists are certainly concerned with such broad generalities as these, but they also want to focus on meaningful anatomical, environmental, and behavioral details as well as underlying processes. Thus, regional variability displayed by particular fossil samples is seen as significant—but just *how* significant is debated. Moreover, increasingly sophisticated theoretical approaches are being used to better understand the processes that shaped the evolution of later *Homo*, both at macroevolutionary and microevolutionary levels.

Scientists, like all humans, name phenomena, a point we addressed in discussing classification in Chapter 8. Paleoanthropologists are certainly no exception. Yet, working from a common evolutionary foundation, paleoanthropologists still come to highly different conclusions regarding the most appropriate way to interpret the Middle/Upper Pleistocene hominids. Consequently, a variety of species names have been proposed in recent years.

Did these Middle/Upper Pleistocene hominids have the full language capabilities and other symbolic/social skills of living peoples? It is impossible to answer this question completely, given the types of fossil and archaeological evidence available. Yet, it does seem probable that neither *H. heidelbergensis* nor the Neandertals possessed this entire array of *fully* human attributes. That is why we call them premodern humans.

So, back to our initial question: Were these hominids human? We could answer conditionally: They *were* human—at least, mostly so.

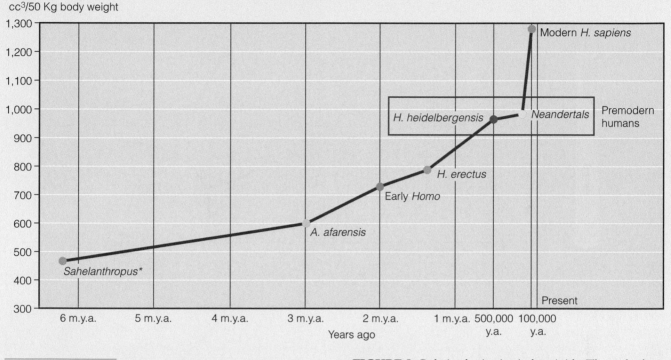

FIGURE 1 Relative brain size in hominids. The scale shows brain size as cc³ per 50 kg of body weight. Premodern humans have a more than 20% increase in relative brain size compared to *H. erectus,* but modern humans show another 30% expansion beyond that in premodern humans.

*There are no direct current data for body size in *Sahelanthropus.* Body size is estimated from tooth size in comparison with *A. afarensis.* Data abstracted from McHenry, 1992; Wood and Collard, 1999; Brunet, 2002; and Carroll, 2003.

At the extreme lumping end of the spectrum, only one species is recognized for all these premodern fossils. They are called *Homo sapiens* and are thus further lumped with modern humans (although partly distinguished by such terminology as "archaic *H. sapiens*") (see Fig. 12–18a).

At the other end of the spectrum, paleontological splitters have identified at least three species, all distinct from *H. sapiens.* Two of these were discussed earlier (*H. heidelbergensis* and *H. neanderthalensis*). A third species has recently been proposed by Robert Foley and Marta Mariazón Lahr and is called *H. helmei* (Foley and Lahr, 1997; Lahr and Foley, 1998). This last group of hominids is suggested as a possible African ancestor of *both* modern humans and Neandertals, but one that appears fairly late in the Middle Pleistocene (300,000–250,000 y.a.) and thus coming largely after *H. heidelbergensis.* This more complex evolutionary interpretation is shown in Figure 12–18b.

See the Glossary for Virtual Lab 10 for alternative phylogenies of the genus *Homo.*

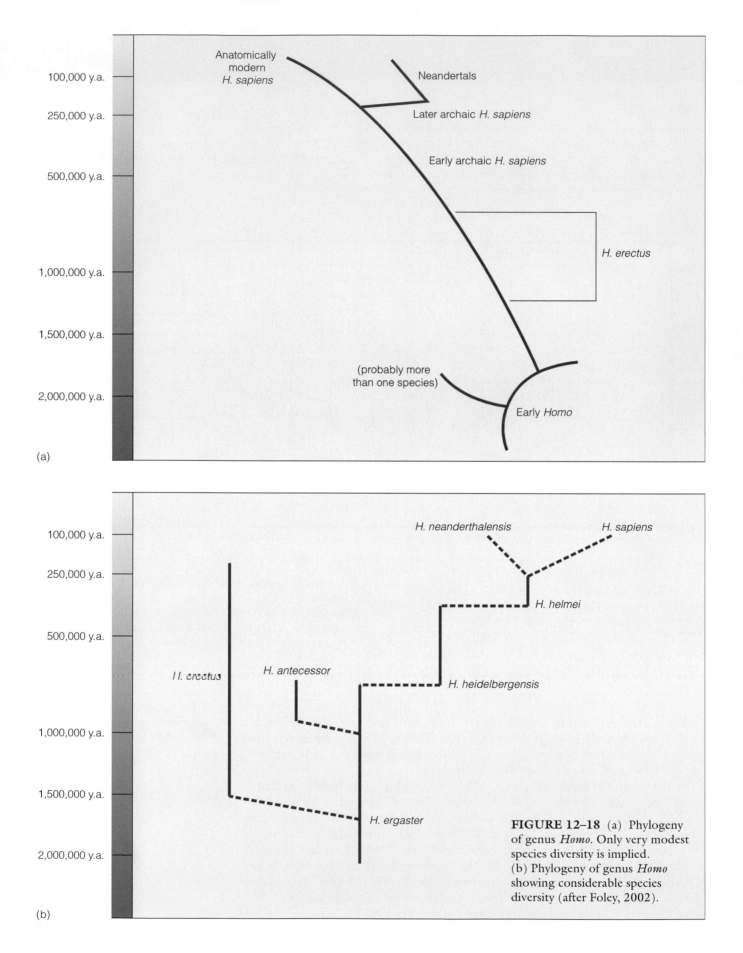

FIGURE 12–18 (a) Phylogeny of genus *Homo*. Only very modest species diversity is implied. (b) Phylogeny of genus *Homo* showing considerable species diversity (after Foley, 2002).

We addressed similar differences of interpretation in Chapters 10 and 11, and such disparity can be frustrating to students new to paleoanthropology. The proliferation of new names is confusing, and it might seem that experts in the field are endlessly arguing about what to call the fossils.

Fortunately, it is not quite that bad. There is actually more agreement than is initially apparent. No one doubts that all these hominids are quite closely related to each other as well as to modern humans. Moreover, all agree that only some of the fossil samples represent populations that left descendants. There is disagreement on which of these hominids are most likely to be most closely related to later hominids. The grouping of the hominids into evolutionary clusters (clades) and the consequent variable naming of them is a reflection of differing interpretations—and, more fundamentally, of somewhat differing philosophies.

We should not, however, place too much emphasis on the naming/classification debates. Most paleoanthropologists recognize that a large portion of these disagreements result from simple, practical considerations. Even the most enthusiastic of splitters acknowledge that the fossil "species" are not true species as defined by the biological species concept (see p. 116). For example, the scheme shown in Figure 12–18b reflects the views of Robert Foley, who readily admits: "It is unlikely they are all biological species. . . . These are probably a mixture of real biological species and evolving lineages of subspecies. In other words, they could potentially have interbred, but owing to allopatry [i.e., geographical separation] were unlikely to have had the opportunity" (Foley, 2002, p. 33).

Nevertheless, Foley, along with an increasing number of other professionals, distinguishes these different fossil samples with species names to highlight their distinct position in hominid evolution. That is, these hominid groups are seen as phylogenetic species (see p. 118) rather than as fully biological species. Giving the significantly distinct hominid samples a separate (species) name makes them more easily identifiable to other researchers and makes various cladistic hypotheses more explicit (and, equally important, more directly testable). Eminent paleoanthropologist F. Clark Howell (of the University of California, Berkeley) also recognizes these advantages, but is less emphatic about species designations. Howell recommends the term *paleo-deme* to refer to either a species or subspecies classification (Howell, 1999).

The hominids that best illustrate these issues are the Neandertals. Fortunately, they are also the best known, represented by dozens of well-preserved individuals. Consequently, many of the differing hypotheses can be systematically tested and evaluated.

Are Neandertals very closely related to modern *H. sapiens*? Certainly. Are they physically and behaviorally distinct from both ancient and recent fully modern humans? Yes. Are Neandertals, therefore, a fully separate biological species from modern humans—and therefore theoretically incapable of fertilely interbreeding with modern people? Probably not. Finally, then, should Neandertals be considered a separate species from, or a subspecies of, *H. sapiens*? For most purposes, it does not matter, since the distinction at some point is arbitrary. Speciation is, after all, a *dynamic* process. Fossil groups like the Neandertals display a point in this process.

We can view these fascinating premodern humans as a quite distinctive side branch of later hominid evolution. Like the distinction of hamadryas and savanna baboons (see p. 119), we could say that Neandertals were an "incipient species." Given enough time and enough isolation, they likely would have separated completely from their modern human contemporaries.

However, as fossil, archaeological, and genetic data are making increasingly clear, Neandertals never got this far. Their fate, in a sense, was decided for them as more successful competitors expanded into Neandertal habitats. These highly successful hominids were fully modern humans, and their story is the focus of the next chapter.

Visual Summary

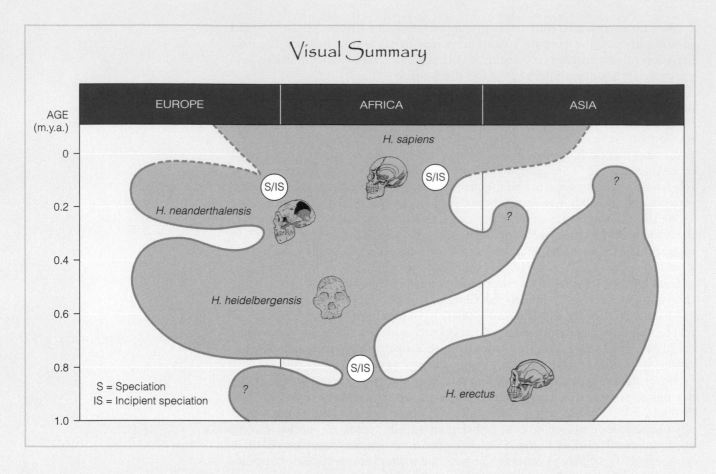

| EUROPE | AFRICA | ASIA |

H. sapiens

H. neanderthalensis S/IS S/IS ?

H. heidelbergensis ?

S/IS ?

S = Speciation
IS = Incipient speciation

H. erectus

AGE (m.y.a.): 0, 0.2, 0.4, 0.6, 0.8, 1.0

Summary

The Middle Pleistocene (780,000–125,000 y.a.) was a period of transition in human evolution. Fossil hominids from this period show similarities both with their predecessors (*H. erectus*) and with their successors (*H. sapiens*). Moreover, these transitional hominids have been found widely dispersed in the Old World, Africa, Asia, and Europe (in the latter case, representing the first truly successful occupation of that continent). Because these transitional hominids are more derived (and advanced in the human direction) than *H. erectus*, we can refer to them as premodern humans. This terminology also recognizes that these hominids display several significant anatomical and behavioral differences from modern humans.

There is some dispute concerning the best way to formally classify the majority of Middle Pleistocene hominids, but most paleoanthopologists now prefer to refer to them as *H. heidelbergensis*. Similarities between the African and European Middle Pleistocene hominid samples suggest that they all can be reasonably seen as part of this same species. The contemporaneous Asian fossils, however, do not fit as neatly into this model, and conclusions regarding these premodern humans remain more tenuous.

Some of the later *H. heidelbergensis* populations in Europe likely evolved into Neandertals. Abundant Neandertal fossil and archaeological evidence has been collected from the Upper Pleistocene time span of Neandertal existence (c. 130,000–29,000 y.a.). But, unlike their Middle Pleistocene (*H. heidelbergensis*) predecessors, Neandertals are more geographically restricted, found only in Europe and southwest Asia. Moreover, various lines of evidence—anatomical, archaeological, and genetic—suggest that Neandertals were isolated and distinct from other hominids.

These observations have led to a growing consensus among paleoanthropologists that Neandertals were largely a side branch of later hominid evolution. Nevertheless, there remain significant differences in theoretical approaches regarding how best to deal with the Neandertals; that is, should they be considered a separate species or as a subspecies of *H. sapiens*? We suggest that the best way to view the Neandertals is within a dynamic process of speciation. Accordingly, Neandertals can be interpreted as an "incipient species," one in the process of splitting from early *H. sapiens* populations.

As a further study aid, the most significant premodern human fossils discussed in this chapter are presented in Table 12–2.

For Further Thought

1. Given that Neandertals lived at the same time as populations of modern humans, what sorts of interactions might they have had?

Go to the book website at **http://www.anthropology.wadsworth.com** for resources to help you explore these questions further. Click on "For Further Thought" for this chapter.

TABLE 12–2 Most Significant Premodern Human Fossil Discoveries Discussed in this Chapter

SITE	DATES (Y.A.)	TAXONOMIC DESIGNATION	COMMENTS
La Chapelle	50,000	Neandertal (*Homo neanderthalensis, Homo sapiens neanderthalensis*)	Historically most important site in France in description of Neandertal morphology
Tabun	110,000	Neandertal (*Homo neanderthalensis, Homo sapiens neanderthalensis*)	Important early Neandertal site; shows clear presence of Neandertals in Near East
Atapuerca (Sima de los Huesos)	320,000–190,000	*Homo heidelbergensis*	Large sample; earliest evidence in Europe of Neandertal morphology; evidence of disposal of the dead
Steinheim	300,000–250,000?	*Homo heidelbergensis*	Transitional-looking fossil
Jinniushan	200,000?	*Homo heidelbergensis* Early *Homo sapiens*, as termed by the Chinese	Possibly oldest example of *H. sapiens* in China, but status uncertain
Kabwe (Broken Hill)	130,000+?	*Homo heidelbergensis*	Transitional-looking fossil; similar to Bodo
Bodo	600,000	*Homo heidelbergensis*	Earliest evidence of *H. heidelbergensis* in Africa and perhaps anywhere

Questions for Review

1. Why are the fossil hominids from the Middle Pleistocene called "transitional"? What hominids come before as well as after these hominids—and how do they compare?

2. Why are the Middle Pleistocene hominids called premodern humans? In what ways are they human?

3. How did climate in the Old World during the Middle Pleistocene differ from that of today? What effects did climate have on hominid evolution in Eurasia and Africa?

4. What is the general popular conception of Neandertals? Do you agree with this view? (Cite both anatomical and archaeological evidence to support your conclusion.)

5. Compare the skeleton of a Neandertal with that of a modern human. In which ways are they most similar? In which ways are they most different?

6. What evidence suggests that Neandertals deliberately buried their dead? What interpretations does such treatment of the dead suggest to you?

7. How are species defined, both for living animals and for extinct ones? Use the Neandertals to illustrate the problems encountered in distinguishing species among extinct hominids. Contrast specifically the interpretation of Neandertals as a distinct species with the interpretation of Neandertals as a subspecies of *H. sapiens*.

Suggested Further Reading

Arsuaga, Jean Louis de. 2002. *The Neanderthal's Necklace: In Search of the First Thinkers*. New York: Four Walls Eight Windows.

Mellars, Paul. 1995. *The Neanderthal Legacy. An Archaeological Perspective from Western Europe*. Princeton, NJ: Princeton University Press.

Shreeve, James. 1995. *The Neandertal Enigma*. New York: Morrow.

Tattersall, Ian. 1999. *The Last Neanderthal. The Rise, Success, and Mysterious Extinction of Our Closest Human Relatives*. Boulder, CO: Westview Press.

Trinkaus, Erik, and Pat Shipman. 1993. *The Neandertals: Changing the Image of Mankind*. New York: Knopf.

Online Anthropology Resource Center

Go to the Anthropology Resource Center at **http:// www.anthropology.wadsworth.com** for a wealth of online resources, including a companion website for your text that provides study aids such as self-quizzes for each chapter and a practice final exam, as well as links to anthropology websites and information on the latest theories and discoveries in the field. Also, check out InfoTrac College Edition, your online library that offers full-length articles from thousands of scholarly and popular publications. Just click on the InfoTrac button at the companion website and use the passcode that came with your book.

Ancient DNA

An exciting and potentially highly informative new direction of research has focused on extracting and analyzing DNA samples from ancient remains. Some of these finds can be extremely ancient, most notably insect tissue embedded in amber (i.e., fossilized tree resin). Some of the insect DNA derived from these sources is upward of 120 million years old, and these discoveries, first reported back in 1992, were the inspiration for Michael Crichton's *Jurassic Park*.

Amber provides a very unusual and favorable environment for long-term preservation of small organisms, a situation, unfortunately, not applicable to larger organisms such as vertebrates. Nevertheless, following the introduction of PCR technology (see p. 67), it became possible to look for *very* small amounts of DNA that just might still linger in ancient human remains.

In 1986, researchers reported results of sequenced brain DNA obtained from mummified remains found in a Florida bog dated at 7,000–8,000 y.a. (Doran et al., 1986). The famous "Iceman" mummy discovered in the Alps in 1991 also yielded widely publicized DNA information as to his population origins (shown to be not far from where he died) (Fig. 1). More recently, a group of Italian biologists, led by Franco Rollo of the Molecular Anthropology/Ancient DNA Laboratory of the University of Camerino, has analyzed the Iceman's intestinal contents using molecular techniques. Their results show that the Iceman's last meal was composed of red deer and possibly cereal grains, and that his preceding meal contained ibex, cereals, and other plant food (Rollo et al., 2002). This next-to-last meal was apparently consumed at a lower altitude than the 10,500-foot locale where he died. This observation is supported by other DNA studies of pollen found in his lungs, showing that he had recently passed through a midaltitude carboniferous forest.

In both the Florida and alpine mummies, no nuclear DNA was identified, so researchers used the more plentiful mitochondrial DNA. Their successes gave hope that more ancient remains containing preserved human DNA could be analyzed.

And indeed, in 1997, Matthias Krings and associates from the University of Munich and the Max Planck Institute of Evolutionary Anthropology (see p. 224) made a startling breakthrough. They successfully extracted, amplified, and sequenced DNA from a Neandertal skeleton. As discussed in this chapter (p. 355), three other Neandertals (ranging in date from 42,000 to 29,000 y.a.) have subsequently yielded enough mtDNA for analysis.

As we have noted, the place of Neandertals in human evolution has been and continues to be a topic of fascination and contention. It is for this reason that the Neandertal DNA evidence is so important. Moreover, comparison of Neandertal DNA patterns with those of early modern humans would be extremely illuminating. Certainly, there are numerous early *H. sapiens* skeletons from Europe and elsewhere (many of which are discussed in the next chapter) likely still to contain some DNA. As we will discuss in Chapter 13, a team of scientists from several Italian universities just recently reported DNA results from a 24,000-year-old modern human skeleton from the Paglicci Cave in southern Italy (Caramelli et al., 2003).

These new Italian finds seem to support the view that Neandertals were genetically quite distinct from modern humans and thus unlikely ancestors of any living people. Questions, however, remain concerning possible contamination of the samples. With PCR, even the tiniest amounts of extraneous DNA (even a single molecule) can be replicated millions of times; thus, there is always a chance of contamination from handling by excavators or lab investigators. Indeed, one researcher has estimated that there is more DNA in the few skin cells shed by researchers in the lab than is contained in most fossils! Even with the best attempts at contamination control, inadvertent contamination can never be ruled out.

As a result, *any* ancient human shown to be a very close genetic match to living people falls under immediate suspicion. The Italian early modern DNA was essentially identical to that of living people—thus increasing such scrutiny even further. In fact, the eminent molecular biologist Svante Pääbo (who is a director at the Max Planck Institute for Evolutionary Anthropology) has concluded that, "Cro-Magnon [early modern] DNA is so similar to modern human DNA that there is no way to say whether what has been seen is real" (Pääbo, quoted in Abbott, 2003, p. 468).

Similar difficulties have surrounded the analysis of a potentially older early modern human from the Lake

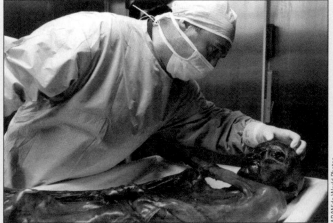

FIGURE 1 Iceman.

Ancient DNA (continued)

Mungo site in Australia (see Chapter 13, p. 379, for further discussion). In addition to possible recent contamination, there are potential problems caused by mutant mtDNA insertions into nuclear DNA (forming "pseudogenes"). Any molecular analysis using mtDNA may actually be getting readings from these altered/inserted genes rather than "real" mtDNA. This is a particular concern when results come from a single representative of an ancient group. The Neandertal DNA results largely avoid this problem, since highly consistent patterns have been found in four different individuals; but for the Italian and Australian finds, serious doubts linger.

Analysis of nuclear DNA from ancient specimens would help alleviate some of these difficulties, although none, as yet, has been obtained from any hominid older than a few thousand years. Nevertheless, positive results may be forthcoming. Nuclear DNA has been successfully extracted from a cave bear discovered at the Vindija Neandertal site in Croatia (dated to 33,000 y.a.). Moreover, the Mezmaiskaya Neandertal retained so much mtDNA that further testing might just come up with usable amounts of nuclear DNA as well.

Sources

Abbott, Alison. 2003. "Anthropologists Cast Doubt on Human DNA Evidence." *Nature* (News) 423:468.

Caramelli, David, Carles Lalueza-Fox, Cristano Vernesi, et al. 2003. "Evidence for a Genetic Discontinuity between Neandertals and 24,000-Year-Old Anatomically Modern Europeans." *Proceedings of the National Academy of Sciences* 100:6593–6597.

Doran, G. H., D. N. Dickel, W. E. Ballinger, Jr., et al. 1986. "Anatomical, Cellular, and Molecular Analysis of 8,000-Yr-Old Human Brain Tissue from the Windover Archaeological Site." *Nature* 323:803–806.

Krings, M., A. Stone, R. W. Schmitz, et al. 1997. "Neandertal DNA Sequences and the Origin of Modern Humans." *Cell* 90:19–30.

O'Rourke, Dennis H., M. Geoffrey Hayes, and Shawn W. Carlyle. 2000. "Ancient DNA Studies in Physical Anthropology." *Annual Reviews of Anthropology* 29:217–242.

Rollo, Franco, Massimo Ubaldi, Lucca Ermini, and Isolina Marota. 2002. "Otzi's Last Meals: DNA Analysis of the Intestinal Content of the Neolithic Glacier Mummy from the Alps." *Proceedings of the National Academy of Sciences* 99:12594–12599.

Schmitz, Ralf W., David Serre, Georges Bonani, et al. 2002. "The Neandertal Type Site Revisited: Interdisciplinary Investigations of Skeletal Remains from the Neander Valley, Germany." *Proceedings of the National Academy of Sciences* 99:13342–13347.

Origin and Dispersal of Modern Humans

13

Taung child's cranium held by South African paleo-anthropologist Phillip Tobias

Robert Jurmain

Introduction

See the following sections of the CD-ROM for topics covered in this chapter: Virtual Lab 11, section IV and Virtual Lab 12, sections I and II.

Sometime, probably close to 150,000 y.a., the first modern *Homo sapiens* evolved in Africa. Within 100,000 years or so, descendants of these early modern humans dispersed across most of the Old World, even expanding as far as Australia (and somewhat later to the Americas).

Who were they, and why were these early modern people so successful? Further, what was the fate of the other hominids, such as the Neandertals, who were already long established in areas outside Africa? Did they evolve as well, leaving descendants among some living human populations? Or were they completely swept aside and replaced by African emigrants?

In this chapter, we discuss the origin and dispersal of modern *H. sapiens*. All contemporary populations, encompassing the more than 6 billion living humans, are placed in the subspecies *Homo sapiens sapiens*. Most paleoanthropologists agree that several fossil forms, dating back as far as 100,000 y.a., should also be included in the same subspecies.

In addition, some recently discovered fossils from Africa also are clearly *H. sapiens,* but show some (minor) differences from living people and could thus be described as "near-modern." Nevertheless, we can think of these early African humans as well as their somewhat later kin as "us."

These first modern humans, who evolved by 150,000 y.a., are probably descendants of some of the premodern humans discussed in Chapter 12. Most especially, African populations of *H. heidelbergensis* are the most likely ancestors of the earliest modern *H. sapiens*. This transition of modern humans from more ancient premodern forms and their subsequent wide dispersal throughout most of the Old World were relatively rapid evolutionary events, and they raise several fundamental questions:

1. *When* (approximately) did modern humans first appear?
2. *Where* did the transition take place? Did it occur in just one region or in several?
3. *What* was the pace of evolutionary change? How quickly did the transition occur?
4. *How* did the dispersal of modern humans to other areas of the Old World (outside that of origin) take place?

These questions concerning the origins and early dispersal of modern *Homo sapiens* continue to fuel much controversy among paleoanthropologists. And it is no wonder, for members of early *Homo sapiens* are our *direct* kin and are thus closely related to all contemporary humans. They were much like us skeletally, genetically, and (most likely) behaviorally as well. In fact, it is the various hypotheses relating to the behavioral capacities of our most immediate predecessors that have most fired the imagination of scientists and laypeople alike. In every major respect, these are the first hominids that we can confidently refer to as "fully human."

In this chapter, we will also discuss archaeological evidence from the Upper Paleolithic (see p. 345). This evidence will allow us to better understand technological and social developments during the period when modern humans arose and quickly came to dominate the planet.

The evolutionary story of *Homo sapiens sapiens* is really a biological auto-biography of us all. It is a story that still has many unanswered questions; but several theories have been proposed that seek to organize the diverse information that is presently available.

Approaches to Understanding Modern Human Origins

There are two major theories that attempt to organize and explain modern human origins: the complete replacement model and the regional continuity model. These two views are quite distinct and in some ways diametrically opposed to each other. Moreover, the popular press has further contributed to a wide and incorrect perception of irreconcilable argument on these points by "opposing" scientists. Indeed, there is a third theory, which we call the partial replacement model, that is a compromise hypothesis incorporating some aspects of the two major theories. Because so much of our contemporary view of modern human origins is driven by the debates linked to these differing theories, let us begin by briefly reviewing each. We will then turn to the fossil evidence itself to see what it can contribute to resolving the questions we have posed.

THE COMPLETE REPLACEMENT MODEL (RECENT AFRICAN EVOLUTION)

The complete replacement model, developed by British paleoanthropologists Christopher Stringer and Peter Andrews (1988), is based on the origin of modern humans in Africa and later replacement of populations in Europe and Asia (Fig. 13–1). In brief, this theory proposes that anatomically modern populations arose in Africa within the last 200,000 years, then migrated from Africa, completely *replacing* populations in Europe and Asia. This model does not take into account any transition from premodern forms to modern *H. sapiens* anywhere in the world except Africa. A critical deduction of the Stringer and Andrews theory postulates the appearance of anatomically modern humans as a biological speciation event. Thus, in this view there could be no admixture of migrating African modern *H. sapiens* with local populations because the African modern humans were a *biologically* different species. In a taxonomic context, all of the premodern populations outside Africa would, in this view, be classified as belonging to different species of *Homo* (e.g., the Neandertals would be classified as *H. neanderthalensis;* see p. 359 for further discussion). While this speciation explanation fits nicely with, and in fact helps explain, *complete* replacement, Stringer has more recently stated that he is not dogmatic regarding this issue. Thus, he suggests that there may have been potential for interbreeding, but he argues that very little apparently took place.

Interpretations of the latter phases of human evolution have recently been greatly extended by newly available genetic techniques. Advances in molecular biology, which have so revolutionized the biological sciences (including physical anthropology), have been recently applied to the question of modern human origins. Using numerous contemporary human populations as a data source, a wide variety of DNA sequences have been precisely determined and compared. The theoretical basis of this approach assumes at least some of the genetic patterning seen today can act as a "window" on the past. In particular, the genetic patterns observed today between geographically widely dispersed humans are hypothesized partly to reflect migrations that occurred back in the late

See Virtual Lab 12, section II, for a discussion of the Complete Replacement Model.

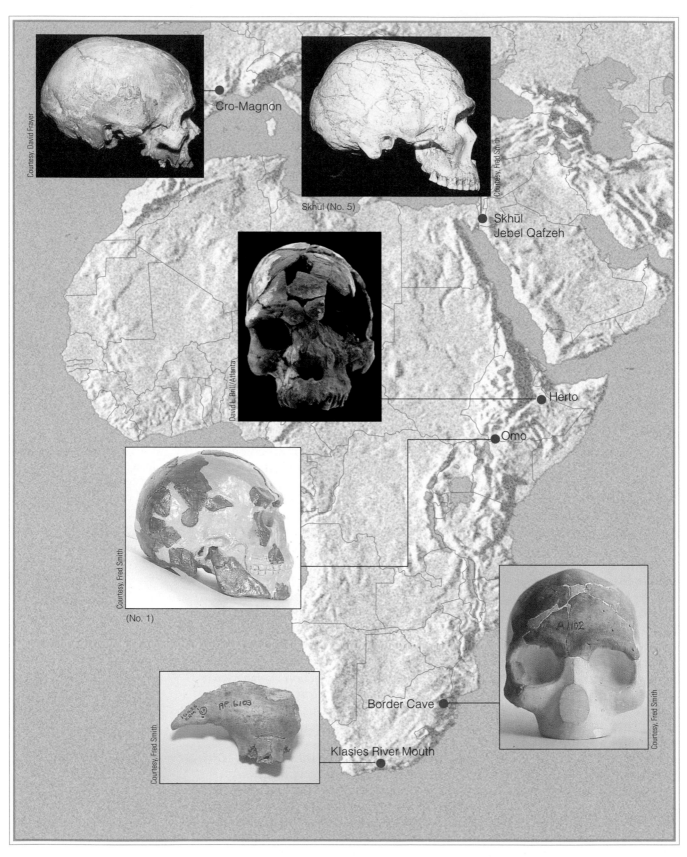

FIGURE 13–1 Anatomically modern humans in Europe, the Near East, and Africa.

Pleistocene. This hypothesis can be further tested as various types of contemporary population genetic patterning are better documented.

In pursuit of such fuller documentation, geneticists have investigated both coded and noncoded regions of DNA. Moreover, both nuclear and mitochondrial DNA have been intensively studied (see pp. 46 and 47). Y chromosome and mitochondrial patterns are considered particularly informative, since neither is significantly recombined during sexual reproduction (mitochondria recombine not at all, and the Y chromosome does so at only a few loci). As a result, inheritance of mitochondria follow a strictly maternal pattern (inherited through females), while the Y chromosome follows a paternal pattern (inherited only father to son).

As these new data have accumulated, consistent relationships have emerged, especially in showing indigenous African populations with far greater diversity than populations from elsewhere in the world. The consistency of the results is highly significant, because it strongly supports an African origin for modern humans and some mode of replacement elsewhere (see A Closer Look for further discussion).

Certainly, most molecular data come from contemporary organisms, since DNA does not *usually* preserve in long-dead individuals. Nevertheless, exceptions do occur, and these cases provide another genetic window—one that can directly illuminate the past. As discussed in the previous chapter (see p. 355), Neandertal DNA has been recovered from four Neandertal fossils.

In addition, two ancient anatomically modern skeletons from Italy (dated 24,000–23,000 y.a.) have recently had their mtDNA sequenced (Caramelli et al., 2003). The results show mtDNA sequence patterns very similar to living humans—and thus significantly different from the mtDNA patterns found in the four Neandertals thus far analyzed.

If these results are further confirmed, they provide powerful *direct* evidence of a genetic discontinuity between Neandertals (one dating as late as 29,000 y.a.) and these early fully modern humans. In other words, these data suggest that no (or very little) interbreeding took place between Neandertals and anatomically modern humans.

A potentially serious difficulty has been raised regarding these latest DNA results from the Italian early modern skeletons. The mtDNA sequences are so similar to that of modern humans that they could, in fact, be the result of contamination (i.e., the amplified and sequenced DNA could be that of some person who handled the fossil in recent years).

Despite extensive experimental precautions undertaken by the molecular biologists who did this research (which follow standard practices used by other laboratories), there is, at present, no way to rule out such contamination. Nevertheless, the results do fit with an emerging overall consensus regarding likely Neandertal distinctiveness as compared to modern humans.

PARTIAL REPLACEMENT MODELS

Various alternative perspectives also suggest an African origin of modern humans followed by population expansion out of Africa into other areas of the Old World. But unlike the complete replacement hypothesis, these partial replacement models postulate that some interbreeding occurred between emigrating Africans and resident premodern populations elsewhere. Thus, partial replacement assumes that *no* speciation event occurred, and all these hominids should be considered members of *H. sapiens.* Günter Bräuer of the University of Hamburg suggests that very little interbreeding occurred—a view supported recently by John Relethford (see A Closer Look). Fred Smith of Loyola University also favors an African origin of modern humans, but his "assimilation" model hypothesizes that in some regions more interbreeding took place (Smith, 2002).

Mitochondrial Eve, Complete Replacement, and What New Genetic Data Have to Tell Us

Gathering samples of mtDNA from placentas of women whose ancestors lived in Africa, Asia, Europe, Australia, and New Guinea, biologists Allan Wilson, Rebecca Cann, and Mark Stoneking, while they were at the University of California, Berkeley, postulated a distinctive genetic pattern for each area. They then compared the diversity of the various patterns (Cann et al., 1987).

They found the greatest variation among Africans and therefore postulated Africa to have been the home of the oldest human populations (the assumption is that the longer the time, the greater the accumulation of genetic variation). They also found that the African variants contained only African mtDNA, whereas those from other areas all included at least one African component. Therefore, the biologists concluded, there must have been a migration initially from Africa, ultimately to all other inhabited areas of the world. By counting the number of genetic mutations and applying the *rate* of mutation, Rebecca Cann and her associates calculated a date for the origin of anatomically modern humans: between 285,000 and 143,000 y.a.—in other words, an average estimate of about 200,000 y.a. Indeed, a further contention of the mtDNA researchers is that the pattern of variation argues that all modern humans shared in common a single African female lineage that lived sometime during this time range. Thus was born the popularized concept of "mitochondrial Eve."

Not all scientists, by any means, agree with this scenario. The estimated rate of mutations may be incorrect, in which case the proposed date of migration out of Africa would also be in error. Moreover, differing population size in Africa, compared to elsewhere, would complicate interpretations (Relethford and Harpending, 1994). Also, secondary migration, outside Africa, could disrupt the direct inheritance of the African maternal line. Even more troubling are the inherent biases in the statistical technique used to identify the primary population relationships ("trees"). More recent reanalyses of the data suggest that the situation is not nearly as clear-cut as originally believed.

Scrutiny of the mitochondrial DNA–based model of modern human origins came when the approach was attempted by other laboratories using similar techniques and statistical treatments. In February 1992, three different papers were published by different teams of researchers, all of which severely challenged the main tenets of the hypotheses as proposed by Wilson, Cann, and Stoneking. The most serious error was a failure to recognize how many *equally valid* results could be deduced statistically from the *same set* of original data. In science, as we have remarked before, beyond the data themselves, the methodological treatments (especially statistical models) greatly influence both the nature and *confidence limits* of the results.

The central conclusion that Africa alone was the *sole* source of modern humans could still be correct. Yet, now it had to be admitted that dozens (indeed, thousands) of other equally probable renditions could be derived from the supposedly unambiguous mitochondrial data. Thus, barely a few months after the original researchers had proposed their most systematic statement of their hypotheses, the entire perspective (especially its statistical implications) was shaken to its very foundations—and, in many people's eyes, falsified altogether.

An interesting twist regarding this entire reassessment is that the team from Pennsylvania State University that challenged the initial results was joined in its critique by Mark Stoneking, one of the original formulators of the now-questioned hypothesis. A viable scientific perspective, so well illustrated here, is that new approaches (or refined applications) often necessitate reevaluation of prior hypotheses. It takes both objectivity and courage to admit miscalculations. By so doing, an even more permanent and positive legacy helps contain the inherent personal biases that sometimes have so divided the study of human origins.

On the basis of these studies, many proclaimed that mitochondrial Eve was dead—and perhaps the complete replacement hypothesis with her. As could be expected, the proponents of the African origin view are not yet ready to bury Eve or significantly alter their confidence in the complete replacement hypothesis.

These scientific developments offer a historical perspective about ongoing debates as well as an outstanding example of the scientific process. In the last 10 years, tremendous advances have been made, many stimulated by the Human Genome Project. With new molecular techniques available (and at much reduced costs) and the publication of the first largely complete map of the human genome in 2000, expanded opportunities have opened up to investigate the detailed genetic patterning in our species. (*Note:* More precise maps of the human genome are being published; e.g., see Hillier et al., 2003).

Many researchers have seized on these opportunities to investigate modern human origins. Specific research directed at addressing this issue has now yielded comprehensive data on mitochondrial DNA (e.g., Ingman et al., 2000); the Y chromosome (e.g., Underhill et al., 2001; Jobling and Tyler-Smith, 2003); the X chromosome (e.g., Harris and Hey, 1999); and highly variable noncoding regions of autosomal nuclear DNA (e.g., Marth et al., 2003; Zhivotvsky et al., 2003). In addition, the more traditional data source revealing variation in functional loci has also continued to be used (Templeton, 2002).

The results of this research (and many other studies as well) point in a consistent direction—one largely verifying the initial findings of the Berkeley investigators back in 1987. It is generally agreed that Africa is the region from which hominid population expansion originated—perhaps in several episodes during the Pleistocene. Alan Templeton of Washington University has characterized this process of repeated African emigrations as "out of Africa, again and again."

However, there isn't full agreement on whether these genetic data indicate a complete replacement of other Old World populations or one with some interbreeding (i.e., some form of partial replacement). The majority of investigators are impressed with the consistency of data showing a strong genetic "signature" in living humans of a mostly African ancestry. Indeed, many of these researchers (e.g., Harpending et al, 1998; Marth et al., 2003) are convinced that the African emigrants completely replaced the hominids in other regions. Furthermore, there is general agreement on the timing of the latter out-of-Africa migrations(s) after 200,000 y.a. (*Note:* Many think that there was more than one.) Estimates place a likely first wave between 200,000 and 100,000 y.a. and a less clearly defined later African population expansion between perhaps 50,000 and 40,000 y.a.

A recent comprehensive review of the genetic data (Templeton, 2002) has questioned these conclusions, in terms of both the completeness of replacement and the timing of the proposed African migrations. In Templeton's view, African migrants interbred extensively with resident populations. Moreover, this researcher hypothesizes that at least one of the migrations proposed occurred at a much earlier time. From varied lines of data, Templeton concludes that one migration occurred well back in the Middle Pleistocene (c.840,000–420,000 y.a.) and thus would likely be correlated with *H. heidelbergensis*. The second migration he sees as taking place much later, between 150,000 and 80,000 y.a. (and thus is largely consistent with the earlier migration proposed above).

Because these genetic data are highly complex, it is not possible to reach unambiguous conclusions at present. Nevertheless, the soundest approach is to use a wide array of data sources (e.g., as shown by Harpending et al., 1998, Relethford, 2001; Templeton, 2002). For the moment, the best conclusion points to a major population impact coming out of Africa, leading to a largely complete replacement elsewhere (indeed, the possibility of complete replacement cannot be falsified). This conclusion agrees well with the model initially proposed by Günter Bräuer (see p. 369) as well as the model more recently proposed by John Relethford (of the State University of New York College at Oneonta) in what he calls "mostly out of Africa" (Relethford, 2001).

THE REGIONAL CONTINUITY MODEL (MULTIREGIONAL EVOLUTION)

The regional continuity model is most closely associated with paleoanthropologist Milford Wolpoff of the University of Michigan and his associates (Wolpoff et al., 1994; 2001). These researchers suggest that local populations (not all, of course) in Europe, Asia, and Africa continued their indigenous evolutionary development from premodern Middle Pleistocene forms to anatomically modern humans. A question immediately arises: How is it possible for different local populations around the globe to evolve with such similar morphology? In other words, how could anatomically modern humans arise separately in different continents and end up physically (and genetically) so similar? The multiregional model explains this phenomenon by (1) denying that the earliest modern

See Virtual Lab 12, section II, for an animation of the Regional Continuity Model.

372   **CHAPTER THIRTEEN**   Origin and Dispersal of Modern Humans

H. sapiens populations originated *exclusively* in Africa and challenging the notion of complete replacement and (2) asserting that some gene flow (migration) between premodern populations was extremely likely, in which case modern humans cannot be considered a species separate from premodern hominids.

Through gene flow and natural selection, according to the multiregional hypothesis, local populations would *not* have evolved totally independently from one another, and such mixing would have "prevented speciation between the regional lineages and thus maintained human beings as a *single,* although obviously *polytypic* (see p. 398), species throughout the Pleistocene" (Smith et al., 1989).

Advocates of the multiregional model are not dogmatic regarding the degree of regional continuity. They recognize that a likely strong influence of African migrants existed throughout the world (and is still detectable today). Agreeing with Smith's assimilation model, this modified multiregionalism hypothesizes only perhaps minimal gene continuity in several regions (e.g., western Europe), with most modern genes coming as a result of large African migration(s) and/or more incremental gene flow (Relethford, 2001; Wolpoff et al., 2001).

The Earliest Discoveries of Modern Humans

Current evidence strongly indicates that the earliest modern *H. sapiens* fossils come from Africa, but not everyone agrees on the dates or precisely which specimens are the modern forms and which are the premodern forms. With this cautionary note, we continue our discussion, but there undoubtedly will be corrections as more evidence is gathered.

AFRICA

In Africa, several early fossil finds have been interpreted as fully anatomically modern forms (see Fig. 13–1). These specimens come from the Klasies River Mouth on the south coast (which could be the earliest find), Border Cave slightly to the north, and Omo Kibish 1 in southern Ethiopia. With the use of relatively new techniques, all three sites have been dated to about 120,000–80,000 y.a. The original geological context at Border Cave is uncertain, and the fossils may be younger than at the other two sites (see Table 13–1 and Fig. 13–6). For several years some paleoanthropologists have considered these fossils the earliest known anatomically modern humans. Problems with dating, context, and differing interpretations of the evidence have led other paleoanthropologists to question whether the *earliest* modern forms (Fig. 13–2) really did evolve in Africa. Other modern *H. sapiens* individuals, possibly older than these African fossils, have been found in the Near East.

Herto   The announcement in June 2003 of well-preserved *and* well-dated *H. sapiens* fossils from Ethiopia has now gone a long way to filling long-standing gaps in the later Pleistocene African fossil record and, as a result, helping to resolve key issues regarding modern human origins. Tim White (of the University of California, Berkeley) and colleagues have been working for over a decade in the Middle Awash area of Ethiopia, discovering there a remarkable array of early fossil hominids (*Ardipithecus* and *Australopithecus garhi*) as well as somewhat later forms (*H. erectus*). From this same area in the Middle Awash (in the Herto member of the Bouri formation), highly significant new discoveries came to light in 1997. For simplicity sake, these new hominids are referred to as the Herto remains.

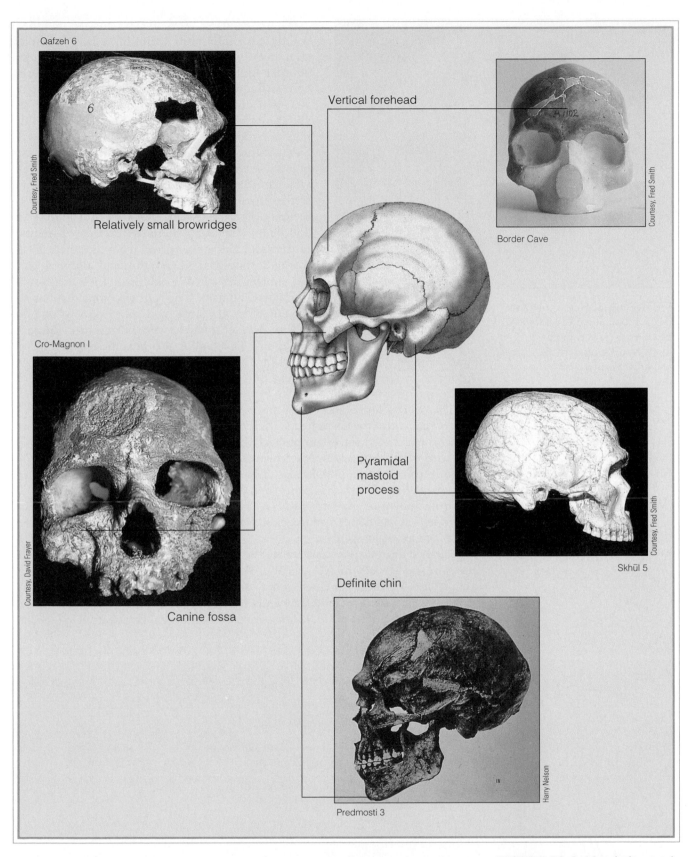

Qafzeh 6

Courtesy, Fred Smith

Relatively small browridges

Vertical forehead

Border Cave

Courtesy, Fred Smith

Cro-Magnon I

Courtesy, David Frayer

Canine fossa

Pyramidal mastoid process

Skhūl 5

Courtesy, Fred Smith

Definite chin

Predmosti 3

Harry Nelson

FIGURE 13–2 Morphology and variation in early specimens of modern *Homo sapiens.*

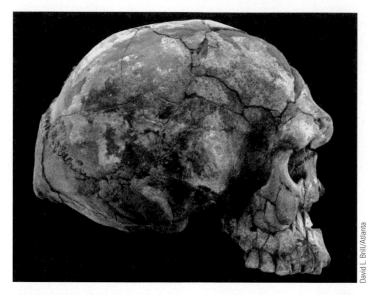

David L. Brill/Atlanta

FIGURE 13–3 Herto cranium from Ethiopia, dated 160,000–154,000 y.a. This is the best-preserved early modern *H. sapiens* cranium yet found.

These exciting new Herto fossils include a mostly complete adult cranium, a fairly complete (but heavily reconstructed) child's cranium, and another adult incomplete cranium (plus a few other cranial fragments). Following lengthy reconstruction and detailed comparative studies, White and colleagues were prepared to announce their findings in 2003.

What they found is quite remarkable and caused quite a sensation among paleoanthropologists (and was reported in the popular press as well). First, well-controlled radiometric dating ($^{40}Ar/^{39}Ar$) securely places the remains between 160,000 and 154,000 y.a., making these the best-dated hominid fossils from this time period from anywhere in the world. Second, the preservation and morphology of the remains leave little doubt as to their relationship to modern humans. The mostly complete adult cranium (Fig. 13–3) is quite dramatic; it is very large, with an extremely long cranial vault. The cranial capacity is 1,450 cm³, well within the range of contemporary *H. sapiens* populations. The skull is also in some respects heavily built, with a large arching browridge in front and a large projecting occipital protuberance in back. Nevertheless, the face is nonprojecting, in stark contrast to Eurasian Neandertals.

The overall impression is that this individual—as well as the child, aged six to seven years, and the incomplete adult cranium—is clearly *Homo sapiens*. White and his team performed comprehensive statistical studies, comparing these fossils with other early *H. sapiens* remains as well as with a large series (over 3,000 crania) from modern populations. The conclusion: While not identical to modern people, the Herto fossils are "near-modern." To distinguish these individuals from fully modern humans (*H. sapiens sapiens*), the researchers have placed them in a newly defined subspecies: *Homo sapiens idaltu* (*idaltu*, from the Afar language, means "elder").

Further analysis has shown that the morphological patterning of the crania does not specifically match that of *any* contemporary group of modern humans. What can we then conclude? First, an African origin of modern humans is strongly supported by these new finds. The Herto fossils are of the right age and come from the right place. Moreover, they look much like what we might have

AT A GLANCE	Key Early Modern *Homo sapiens* Discoveries from Africa and the Near East	
Site	**Dates (y.a.)**	**Human Remains**
Qafzeh (Israel)	110,000	Minimum of 20 individuals (*H. sapiens sapiens*)
Skhūl (Israel)	115,000	Minimum of 10 individuals (*H. sapiens sapiens*)
Klasies River Mouth (South Africa)	120,000?	Several individuals; highly fragmentary (*H. sapiens sapiens*)
Herto (Ethiopia)	160,000–154,000	Dental and cranial remains of 4 individuals (*H. sapiens idaltu*)

predicted. These new Herto finds are the most conclusive fossil evidence yet supporting an African origin of modern humans. They are thus compatible with an array of genetic data indicating some form of replacement model for human origins (see A Closer Look on p. 370).

THE NEAR EAST

In Israel, early modern *H. sapiens* fossils (the remains of at least 10 individuals) were found in the Skhūl Cave at Mt. Carmel (Figs. 13–4 and 13–5a), very near the Neandertal site of Tabun. Also from Israel, the Qafzeh Cave has yielded the remains of at least 20 individuals (Fig. 13–5b). Although their overall configuration is definitely modern, some specimens

show certain premodern (i.e., Neandertal) features. Skhūl has been dated to about 115,000 y.a., and Qafzeh has been placed around 100,000 y.a. (Bar-Yosef, 1993, 1994) (Fig. 13–6).

Such early dates for modern specimens pose some problems for those advocating local replacement (the multiregional model). How early do premodern *H. sapiens* populations (Neandertals) appear in the Near East? A recent chronometric calibration for the Tabun Cave suggests a date as early as 120,000 y.a. Neandertals thus may *slightly* precede modern forms in the Near East, but there would appear to be considerable overlap in the timing of occupation by these different humans. And recall, the modern site at Mt. Carmel (Skhūl) is very near the Neandertal site (Tabun). Clearly, the dynamics of *Homo sapiens* evolution in the Near East are highly complex (Shea, 1998), and no simple model may explain later hominid evolution adequately.

FIGURE 13–4 Mt. Carmel, studded with caves, was home to *H. sapiens sapiens* at Skhūl (and to Neandertals at Tabun and Kebara).

FIGURE 13–5 (a) Skhūl 5. (b) Qafzeh 6. These specimens from Israel are thought to be representatives of early modern *Homo sapiens*. The vault height, forehead, and lack of prognathism are modern traits.

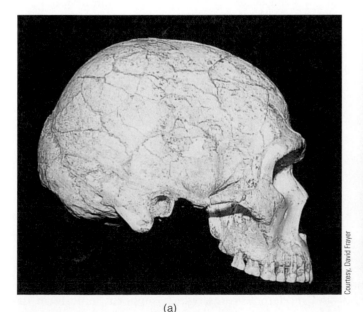

(a)

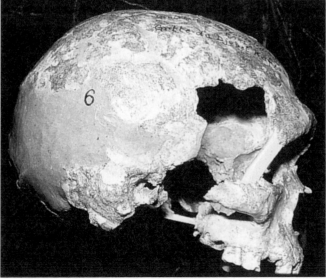

(b)

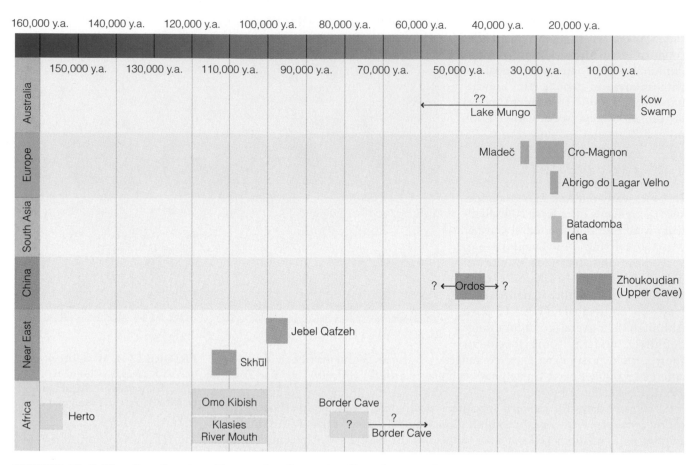

FIGURE 13–6 Time line of modern *Homo sapiens* discoveries. Note that most dates are approximations. Question marks indicate those estimates that are most tentative.

TABLE 13–1 Additional Techniques for Dating middle and Upper Pleistocene Sites

TECHNIQUE	PHYSICAL BASIS	EXAMPLES OF USE
Uranium series dating	Radioactive decay of short-lived uranium isotopes	To date limestone formations (e.g., stalagmites) and ancient ostrich eggshells; to estimate age of Jinniushan site in China and Ngandong site in Java, both corroborated by ESR dates
Thermoluminescence (TL) dating	Accumulation of trapped electrons within certain crystals released during heating	To date ancient flint tools (either deliberately or accidentally heated); to provide key dates for the Qafzeh site
Electron spin resonance (ESR) dating	Measurement (counting) of accumulated trapped electrons	To date dental enamel; to corroborate dating of Qafzeh, Skhūl, and Tabun sites in Israel, Ngandong site in Java, Klasies River Mouth and Border Cave in South Africa, and the Lake Mungo site in Australia

Source: Cook et al., 1984; Aiken et al., 1993.

CENTRAL EUROPE

Central Europe has been a source of many fossil finds, including numerous fairly early anatomically modern *H. sapiens*. At several sites, it appears that some fossils display both Neandertal and modern features, which supports some form of regional continuity (from Neandertal to modern). Such genetic continuity from earlier (Neandertal) to later (modern *Homo sapiens*) populations was perhaps the case at Vindija in Croatia, where typical Neandertals were found in earlier contexts (see p. 348).

Smith (1984) offers another example of local continuity from Mladeč, in the Czech Republic. Among the earlier European modern *H. sapiens* fossils, dated to about 33,000 y.a., the Mladeč crania display a great deal of variation, probably in part due to sexual dimorphism. Although each of the crania (except for one of the females) displays a prominent supraorbital torus, it is reduced from the typical Neandertal pattern. Even though there is some suggestion of continuity from Neandertals to modern humans, Smith is certain that, given certain anatomical features, the Mladeč remains are best classified as *H. sapiens sapiens*. Reduced midfacial projection, a higher forehead, and postcranial elements "are clearly modern *H. sapiens* in morphology and not specifically Neandertal-like in a single feature" (Smith, 1984, p. 174).

WESTERN EUROPE

This area of the world and its fossils have received the greatest attention for several reasons, one of which is probably serendipity. Over the last century and a half, many of the scholars interested in this kind of research happened to live in western Europe, and the southern region of France happened to be a fossil treasure trove. Also, early on, discovering and learning about human ancestors caught the curiosity and pride of the local population.

Because of this scholarly interest beginning back in the nineteenth century, a great deal of data accumulated, with little reliable comparative information available from elsewhere in the world. Consequently, theories of human evolution were based almost exclusively on the western European material. It has only been in recent years, with growing evidence from other areas of the world and with the application of new dating techniques, that recent human evolutionary dynamics have been seriously considered on a worldwide basis.

There are many anatomically modern human fossils from western Europe, possibly going back 35,000 years or more, but by far the best-known sample of western European *H. sapiens* is from the **Cro-Magnon** site. A total of eight individuals were discovered in 1868 in a rock shelter in the village of Les Eyzies, in the Dordogne region of southern France (Gambier, 1989).

Associated with an **Aurignacian** tool assemblage, an Upper Paleolithic industry, the Cro-Magnon materials, dated at 30,000 y.a., represent the earliest of France's anatomically modern humans. The so-called "Old Man" (Cro-Magnon I) became the archetype for what was once termed the Cro-Magnon, or Upper Paleolithic, "race" of Europe (Fig.13–7). Actually, of course, there is no such category, and Cro-Magnon I is not typical of Upper Paleolithic western Europeans and not even all that similar to the other two male skulls found at the site.

Considered together, the male crania reflect a mixture of modern and archaic traits. Cro-Magnon I is the most gracile of the three; the supraorbital tori of the other two males, for example, are more robust. The most modern-looking is the female cranium, the appearance of which may be a function of sexual dimorphism.

The question of whether continuous local evolution produced anatomically modern groups directly from Neandertals in some regions of Eurasia is far from settled. From central Europe, some variation indicates a combination of both Neandertal and modern characteristics and may suggest gene flow between the two different *H. sapiens* groups. However, tracing such relatively minor genetic changes—considering the ever-present problems of dating, lack of fossils, and fragmented fossil finds—has proved extremely difficult.

Cro-Magnon (crow man´yon)

Aurignacian Pertaining to an Upper Paleolithic stone tool industry in Europe beginning at about 40,000 y.a.

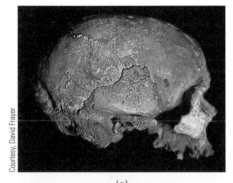

Courtesy, David Frayer

(a)

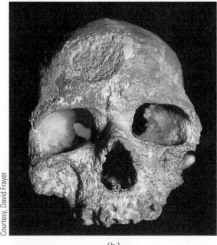

Courtesy, David Frayer

(b)

FIGURE 13–7 Cro-Magnon I (France). In this specimen, modern traits are quite clear. (a) Lateral view. (b) Frontal view.

See Virtual Lab 12, section I, for a discussion of the transformation in physical characteristics that accompanied the evolution of modern *Homo sapiens*.

However, a newly discovered child's skeleton from Portugal has provided some of the best evidence yet of possible hybridization between Neandertals and anatomically modern *H. sapiens*. This important new hominid discovery from the Abrigo do Lagar Velho site was excavated in late 1998 and is dated to 24,500 y.a. (i.e., at least 5,000 years *later* than the last clearly Neandertal find). Associated with an Upper Paleolithic industry (see p. 381) and interred with red ocher and pierced shell is a fairly complete skeleton of a four-year-old child (Duarte et al., 1999). Cidália Duarte, Erik Trinkaus, and colleagues, who have studied the remains, found a highly mixed set of anatomical features. Many characteristics (of the teeth, lower jaw, and pelvis) were like those seen in anatomically modern humans. Yet, several other features (lack of chin, limb proportions, muscle insertions) were more similar to Neandertals. The authors thus conclude, "The presence of such admixture suggests the hypothesis of variable admixture between early modern humans dispersing into Europe and local Neandertal populations" (Duarte et al., 1999, p. 7608). These researchers thus argue that this new evidence provides strong support for the partial replacement model while seriously weakening the complete replacement model. However, the evidence from one child's skeleton—while intriguing—is certainly not going to convince everyone!

ASIA

There are six early anatomically modern human localities in China, the most significant of which are Upper Cave at Zhoukoudian and Ordos in Mongolia. The fossils from these sites are all fully modern, and most are considered to be of quite late Upper Pleistocene age. Upper Cave at Zhoukoudian has been dated to between 18,000 and 10,000 y.a. The Ordos find may be the oldest anatomically modern material from China, perhaps dating to 50,000 y.a. or more (Etler, personal communication) (see Fig. 13–6).

In addition, the Jinniushan skeleton discussed in Chapter 12 (see p. 337) has been suggested by some researchers (Tiemel et al., 1994) as hinting at modern features in China as early as 200,000 y.a. If this date (as early as that proposed for direct antecedents of modern *H. sapiens* in Africa) should prove accurate, it would cast doubt on the complete replacement model. Indeed, quite opposed to the complete replacement model and more in support of regional continuity, many Chinese paleoanthropologists see a continuous evolution from Chinese *H. erectus* to premodern forms. to anatomically modern humans. This view is supported by Wolpoff, who mentions that materials from Upper Cave at Zhoukoudian "have a number of features that are characteristically regional" and that these features are definitely not African (1989, p. 83).*

In addition to the well-known finds from China, anatomically modern remains have also been discovered in southern Asia. At Batadomba Iena, in southern Sri Lanka, modern *Homo sapiens* finds have been dated to 25,500 y.a. (Kennedy and Deraniyagala, 1989).

AUSTRALIA

During glacial times, the Indonesian islands were joined to the Asian mainland, but Australia was not. It is likely that by 50,000 y.a., Sahul—the area including New Guinea and Australia—was inhabited by modern humans. Bamboo rafts may have been the means of crossing the sea between islands, which would not have been a simple exercise. Just where the future Australians

---

*Wolpoff's statement supports his regional continuity hypothesis. His reference to Africa is a criticism of the complete replacement hypothesis.

came from is unknown, but Borneo, Java, and New Guinea have all been suggested.

Human occupation of Australia appears to have occurred quite early, with some archaeological sites dating to 55,000 y.a. Dating of the earliest Australian human remains (which are all modern *H. sapiens*), however, is controversial. The earliest finds thus far discovered have come from Lake Mungo in southeastern Australia. In agreement with archaeological context and radiocarbon dates, the

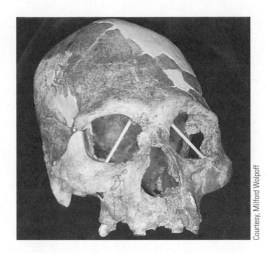

FIGURE 13–8 Kow Swamp (Australia). Note the considerable robusticity in this relatively late Australian *Homo sapiens sapiens* cranium.

hominids from this site have been dated at approximately 30,000–25,000 y.a. Newly determined age estimates, using ESR and uranium series dating (see Table 13–1) have dramatically extended the suggested time depth to about 60,000 y.a. (Thorne et al., 1999). The lack of correlation of these more ancient age estimates with other data, however, has provoked serious concerns among some researchers (Gillespie and Roberts, 2000).

Equally intriguing as these proposed early dates for the first Australians are recent reports of mitochondrial DNA sequences derived from the fossil remains from Lake Mungo (Adcock et al., 2001). While the primary researchers are confident that these samples are authentically ancient, the nagging possibility of contamination cannot be entirely ruled out. Indeed, other researchers remain unconvinced that the mtDNA from Lake Mungo is ancient at all (Cooper et al., 2001). Obviously, given the controversies, we will need further corroboration for both the dating and DNA findings before passing judgment.

Unlike the more gracile early Australian forms from Lake Mungo are the Kow Swamp people, who are thought to have lived between about 14,000 and 9,000 y.a. (Figs. 13–8 and 13–9). The presence of certain archaic traits, such as receding foreheads, heavy supraorbital tori, and thick bones, are difficult to explain, since these features contrast with the postcranial anatomy, which matches that of recent native Australians.

AT A GLANCE	Key Early Modern *Homo sapiens* Discoveries from Europe, Asia, and Australia	
Site	**Dates (y.a.)**	**Human Remains***
Abrigo do Lagar Velho (Portugal)	24,500	Four-year-old child's skeleton
Cro-Magnon (France)	30,000	8 individuals
Ordos (Mongolia, China)	50,000	1 individual
Kow Swamp (Australia)	14,000–9,000	Large sample (more than 40 individuals), including adults, juveniles, and infants
Lake Mungo (Australia)	?60,000–30,000	3 individuals, one a cremation

*Note: All fossils are classified as *H. sapiens sapiens*.

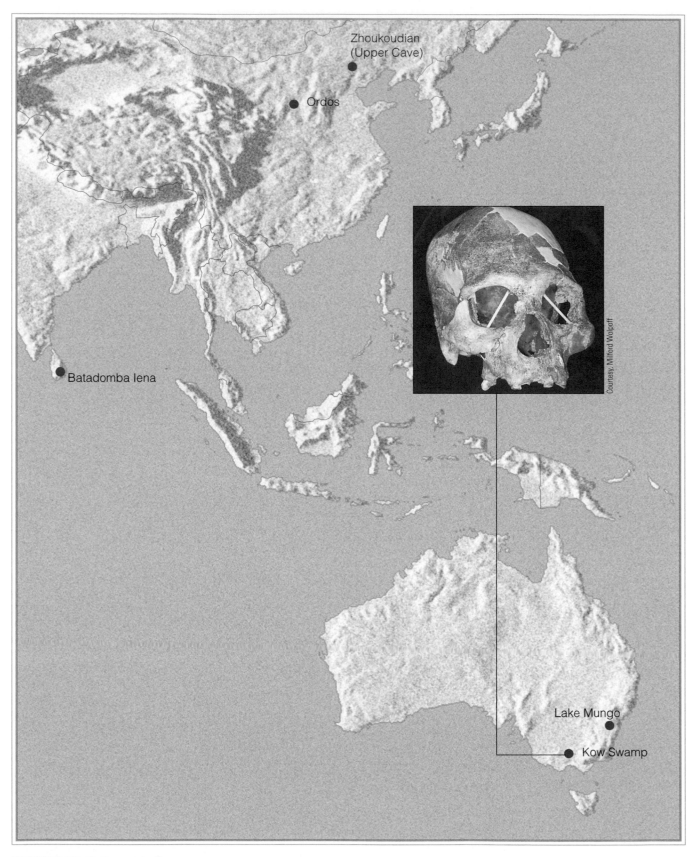

FIGURE 13–9 Anatomically modern *Homo sapiens* (Asia and Australia).

Technology and Art in the Upper Paleolithic

EUROPE

The cultural period known as the Upper Paleolithic began in western Europe approximately 40,000 years ago (Fig. 13–10). Upper Paleolithic cultures are usually divided into five different industries based on stone tool technologies: (1) Chatelperronian, (2) Aurignacian, (3) Gravettian, (4) Solutrean, and (5) Magdalenian. Major environmental shifts were also apparent during this period. During the last glacial period, at about 30,000 y.a., a warming trend lasting several thousand years partially melted the glacial ice. The result was that much of Eurasia was covered by tundra and steppe, a vast area of treeless country dotted with lakes and marshes. In many areas in the north, permafrost prevented the growth of trees but permitted the growth, in the short summers, of flowering plants, mosses, and other kinds of vegetation. This vegetation served as an enormous pasture for herbivorous animals, large and small, and carnivorous animals fed off the herbivores. It was a hunter's paradise, with millions of animals dispersed across expanses of tundra and grassland, from Spain through Europe and into the Russian steppes.

Large herds of reindeer roamed the tundra and steppes along with mammoths, bison, horses, and a host of smaller animals that served as a bountiful source of food. In addition, humans exploited fish and fowl systematically for the first time, especially along the southern tier of Europe. It was a time of relative affluence, and ultimately Upper Paleolithic people spread out over Europe, living in caves and open-air camps and building large shelters. Large dwellings with storage pits have been excavated in the former Soviet Union, with archaeological evidence of social status distinctions (Soffer, 1985). During this period, either western Europe or perhaps portions of Africa achieved the highest population density in human history up to that time.

In Eurasia, cultural innovations allowed humans for the first time to occupy easternmost Europe and northern Asia. In these areas, even during glacial warming stages, winters would have been long and harsh. Human groups were able to tolerate these environments probably because of better-constructed structures as well as warmer, better-fitting *sewn* clothing. The evidence for wide use of such tailored clothing comes from many sites and includes pointed stone tools such as awls and (by at least 19,000 y.a.) bone needles as well. Especially noteworthy is the clear evidence of the residues of clothing (including what has been interpreted as a cap, a shirt, a jacket, trousers, and moccasins) in graves at the 22,000-year-old Sungir site, located not far from Moscow (Klein, 1989).

Humans and other animals in the midlatitudes of Eurasia had to cope with shifts in climatic conditions, some of which were quite rapid. For example, at 20,000 y.a. another climatic "pulse" caused the weather to become noticeably colder in Europe and Asia as the continental glaciations reached their maximum extent for this entire glacial period (called the Würm in Eurasia).

As a variety of organisms attempted to adapt to these changing conditions, *Homo sapiens* had a major advantage: the elaboration of an increasingly sophisticated technology (and probably other components of culture as well). Indeed, probably one of the greatest challenges facing numerous late Pleistocene mammals was the ever more dangerously equipped humans—a trend that has continued to modern times.

The Upper Paleolithic was an age of technological innovation and can be compared to the past few hundred years in our recent history of amazing technological change after centuries of relative inertia. Anatomically modern humans of the Upper Paleolithic not only

FIGURE 13–10 Cultural periods of the European Upper Paleolithic and their approximate beginning dates.

GLACIAL	UPPER PALEOLITHIC (beginnings)	CULTURAL PERIODS
W Ü R M	17,000 –	Magdalenian
	21,000 –	Solutrean
	27,000 –	Gravettian
	40,000 –	Aurignacian Chatelperronian
Middle Paleolithic		Mousterian

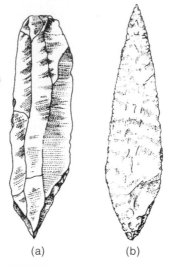

(a)   (b)

FIGURE 13–11 (a) Burin. A very common Upper Paleolithic tool. (b) Solutrean blade. This is the best-known work of the Solutrean tradition. Solutrean stonework is considered the most highly developed of any Upper Paleolithic industry.

Magdalenian Pertaining to the final phase of the Upper Paleolithic stone tool industry in Europe.

burins Small, chisel-like tools (with a pointed end) thought to have been used to engrave bone, antler, ivory, or wood.

FIGURE 13–12 Spear-thrower (atlatl). Note the carving.

invented new and specialized tools (Fig. 13–11), but, as we have seen, also greatly increased the use of (and probably experimented with) new materials, such as bone, ivory, and antler.

Solutrean tools are good examples of Upper Paleolithic skill and perhaps aesthetic appreciation as well (Fig. 13–11b). In this lithic (stone) tradition, stone-knapping developed to the finest degree ever known. Using specialized flaking techniques, the artist/technicians made beautiful parallel-flaked lance heads, expertly flaked on both surfaces, with such delicate points that they can be considered works of art that quite possibly never served, or were intended to serve, a utilitarian purpose.

The last stage of the Upper Paleolithic, known as the **Magdalenian,** saw even more advances in technology. The spear-thrower (Fig. 13–12), a wooden or bone hooked rod (called an *atlatl*), acted to extend the hunter's arm, thus enhancing the force and distance of a spear throw. For catching salmon and other fish, the barbed harpoon is a clever example of the craftsperson's skill. There is also evidence that the bow and arrow may have been used for the first time during this period. The introduction of the punch technique (Fig. 13–13) provided an abundance of standardized stone blades that could be fashioned into **burins** (see Fig. 13–11a) for working wood, bone, and antler; borers for drilling holes in skins, bones, and shells; and knives with serrated or notched edges for scraping wooden shafts into a variety of tools.

The elaboration of many more specialized tools by Upper Paleolithic peoples probably made more resources available to them and may also have had an impact on the biology of these populations. C. Loring Brace of the University of Michigan has suggested that with more efficient tools used for food processing, anatomically modern *H. sapiens* would not have required the large front teeth (incisors) seen in earlier populations. With relaxed selection pressures (no longer favoring large anterior teeth), incorporation of random mutations would through time lead to reduction of dental size and accompanying facial features. In particular, the lower face became less prognathic (as compared to premodern specimens) and thus produced the concavity of the cheekbones called *a canine fossa* (see Fig. 13–2). Moreover, as the dental-bearing portion of the lower jaw regressed, the buttressing below would have become modified into a *chin*, that distinctive feature seen in anatomically modern *H. sapiens*.

In addition to their reputation as hunters, western Europeans of the Upper Paleolithic are even better known for their symbolic representation, what has commonly been called "art." Certainly, in the famous caves of France and Spain (discussed shortly), we easily relate to an aesthetic property of the images—one that *may* have been intended by the people who created them. But here we cannot be certain. Our own cultural perspectives create labels (and categories) such as "art," which in itself *assumes* aesthetic intent. While such a cultural orientation is obviously a recognizable part of Western culture, many other contemporary peoples would not relate to this concept within their own cultural context. Furthermore, prehistoric peoples during the Upper Paleolithic did not necessarily create their symbols as true artistic representations. Rather, these representations may have served a variety of quite utilitarian and/or social functions—as do contemporary highway signs or logos on a company's letterhead. Would we call these symbols art?

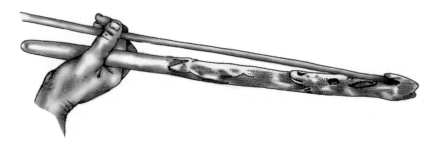

(a) A large core is selected and the top portion is removed by use of a hammerstone.

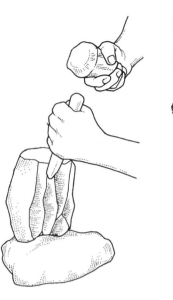

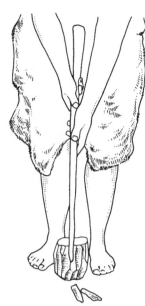

Striking platform

(b) The objective is to create a flat surface called a striking platform.

(c) Next, the core is struck by use of a hammer and punch (made of bone or antler) to remove the long narrow flakes (called blades).

(d) Or the blades can be removed by pressure flaking.

(e) The result is the production of highly consistent sharp blades, which can be used, as is, as knives; or they can be further modified (retouched) to make a variety of other tools (such as burins, scrapers, and awls).

Given these uncertainties, archaeologist Margaret Conkey of the University of California, Berkeley, refers to Upper Paleolithic cave paintings, sculptures, engravings, and so forth, as "visual and material imagery" (Conkey, 1987, p. 423). We will continue to use the term *art* to describe many of these prehistoric representations, but you should recognize that we do so mainly as a cultural convention—and perhaps a limiting one.

Moreover, the time depth for these prehistoric forms of symbolic imagery is quite long, encompassing the entire Upper Paleolithic (from at least 35,000 to 10,000 y.a.). Over this time span there is considerable variability in style, medium, content, and no doubt meaning as well. In addition, there is an extremely wide geographical distribution of symbolic images, best known from many parts of Europe, but now also well documented from Siberia, North Africa, South Africa, and Australia. Given the 25,000-year time depth of what we call "Paleolithic art" and its nearly worldwide distribution, there is indeed marked variability in expression.

In addition to cave art, there are numerous examples of small sculptures excavated from sites in western, central, and eastern Europe. Beyond these quite well-known figurines, there are numerous other examples of what is frequently termed "portable art," including elaborate engravings on tools and tool handles (Fig. 13–14). Such symbolism can be found in many parts of Europe and was already well established early in the Aurignacian (by 33,000 y.a.). Innovations in symbolic representations also benefited from, and probably further stimulated, technological advances. New methods of mixing pigments and applying them were important in rendering painted or drawn images. Bone and ivory carving and engraving were made easier with the use of special stone tools (see Fig. 13–11). At two sites in the Czech Republic, Dolni Vestonice and Predmosti (both

FIGURE 13–13 The punch blade technique.

See Virtual Lab 11, section IV, for a discussion of blade manufacture.

FIGURE 13–14 Magdalenian bone artifact. Note the realistic animal engraving on this object, the precise function of which is unknown.

FIGURE 13–15 Venus of Brassempouy. Upper Paleolithic artists were capable of portraying human realism (shown here) as well as symbolism (depicted in Fig. 13–16). (a) Frontal view. (b) Lateral view.

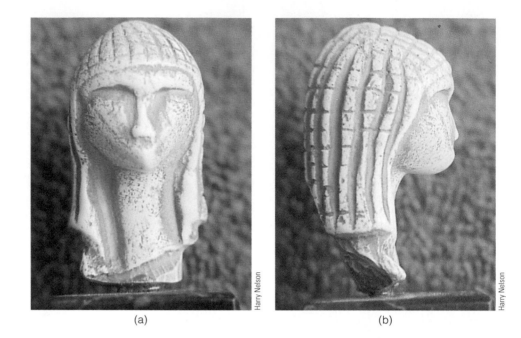

(a)   (b)

dated at 27,000 y.a.), small animal figures were fashioned from fired clay—the first documented use of ceramic technology anywhere (and preceding later pottery invention by more than 15,000 years!).

Female figurines, popularly known as "Venuses," were sculpted not only in western Europe, but in central and eastern Europe and Siberia as well. Some of these figures were realistically carved, and the faces appear to be modeled after actual women (Fig. 13–15). Other figurines may seem grotesque, with sexual characteristics exaggerated, perhaps for fertility or other ritual purposes (Fig. 13–16).

It is, however, during the final phases of the Upper Paleolithic, particularly during the Magdalenian, that European prehistoric art reached its climax. Cave art is now known from more than 150 separate sites, the vast majority from southwestern France and northern Spain. Apparently, in other areas the rendering of such images did not take place in deep caves. Peoples in central Europe, China, Africa, and elsewhere certainly may have painted or carved representations on rockfaces in the open, but these images long since would have eroded. Thus, it is fortuitous that the people of at least one of the many sophisticated cultures of the Upper Paleolithic chose to journey belowground to create their artwork, preserving it not just for their immediate descendants, but for us as well.

In Lascaux Cave of southern France, immense wild bulls dominate what is called the Great Hall of Bulls, and horses, deer, and other animals adorn the walls in black, red, and yellow, drawn with remarkable skill. In addition to the famous cave of Lascaux, there is equally exemplary art from Altamira Cave in Spain. Indeed, discovered in 1879, Altamira was the first example of advanced cave art recorded in Europe. Filling the walls and ceiling of the cave are superb portrayals of bison in red and black, the "artist" taking advantage of bulges to give a sense of relief to the paintings. The cave is a treasure of beautiful art whose meaning has never been satisfactorily explained. It could have been religious or magical, a form of visual communication, or art for the sake of beauty.

Yet another spectacular example of cave art from western Europe was discovered in late 1994. On December 24, a team of three French cave explorers chanced upon a fabulous discovery in the valley of the Ardèche at Combe d'Arc. Inside the cave, called the Grotte Chauvet after one of its discoverers, preserved unseen for perhaps 30,000 years are many hundreds of images, including stylized dots, stenciled human handprints, and, most dramatically, hundreds of animal representations (Fig. 13–17). Included are depictions of such typical Paleolithic

FIGURE 13–16 Venus of Willendorf, Austria. (*Note:* This figure is among the most exaggerated and should be compared with Fig. 13–15.)

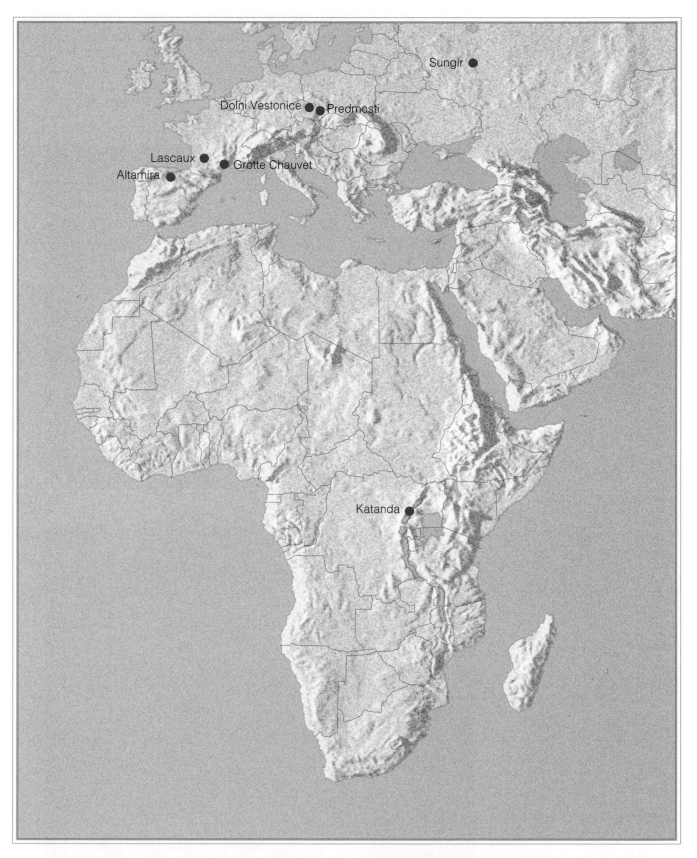

FIGURE 13–17 Upper Paleolithic archaeological sites. (Katanda, in the Democratic Republic of the Congo, may be considerably older than the European sites, perhaps dating to the Middle Stone Age.)

subjects as bison, horse, ibex, auroch, deer, and mammoth. But quite surprisingly, there are also numerous images of animals rarely portrayed elsewhere—such as rhino, lion, and bear (Fig. 13–18). Three animals seen at Grotte Chauvet—a panther, a hyena, and an owl—have never before been documented at cave sites. The artwork, at least after provisional study, seems to consistently repeat several stylistic conventions, causing French researchers to suggest that the images all may

FIGURE 13–18 Cave art from Grotte Chauvet, France. (a) Bear. (b) Aurochs and rhinoceros.

Jean Clottes/Document elaborated with the support of the French Ministry of Culture and Communication, Regional Direction for Cultural Affairs, Rhône-Alpes, Regional Department of Archaeology.

(a)

Jean-Marie Chauvet/Document elaborated with the support of the French Ministry of Culture and Communication, Regional Direction for Cultural Affairs, Rhône-Alpes, Regional Department of Archaeology.

(b)

have been produced by the same artist. Radiocarbon dating has placed the paintings during the Aurignacian (more than 30,000 y.a.), and thus Grotte Chauvet is considerably earlier than the Magdalenian sites of Lascaux and Altamira. The cave was found as Paleolithic peoples had left it, and the initial discoverers, as well as archaeologists, have been careful not to disturb the remains. Among the archaeological traces already noted are dozens of footprints on the cave floor, produced by bears as well as by humans. Further precise excavations are certain to reveal additional secrets from this extraordinary site.

A familiar motif seen at Grotte Chauvet and elsewhere is the representation of human hands, usually in the form of outlines. Apparently, the technique used was to liquefy the pigment and blow it onto a hand held flat against the cave wall. At one site in France, at least 159 such hand outlines were found (Leroi-Gourhan, 1986). Another stylistic innovation was the partial sculpting of a rock face—in what is called bas-relief (a technique used much later, for example, by the ancient Greeks at the Parthenon). Attaining depths of up to 6 inches, some of the Paleolithic sculptures are quite dramatic and were attempted on a fairly grand scale. In one rock shelter in southwest France, several animals (including mountain goats, bison, reindeer, and horses) and one human figure are depicted in bas-relief. Interestingly, these representations were carved in an area also used as a living site—quite distinct from the special-purpose contexts in the deep cave locations. These bas-reliefs were executed throughout the Magdalenian, always in areas immediately adjacent to those of human habitation.

Strikingly, subject matter seems to differ by location and type of art motif. In portable art, common themes are horses and reindeer as well as stylized human figures; rarely are bison represented. However, in cave contexts, bison and horses are frequently seen, but almost never do we see reindeer (although in Europe, reindeer were probably the most common meat source). Cave artists were thought heretofore to have depicted carnivores only rarely, but the new finds at Grotte Chauvet give us a further perspective on the richness *and* diversity of Paleolithic art.

Ever since ancient art was discovered, attempts have been made to interpret the sculptures, paintings, and other graphic material found in caves or on rocks and tools at open-air archaeological sites. One of the early explanations of Upper Paleolithic art emphasized the relationship of paintings to hunting. Hunting rituals were viewed as a kind of imitative magic that would increase prey animal populations or help hunters successfully find and kill their quarry. As new hypotheses were published, their applicability and deficiencies were discussed. When many of these new hypotheses faded, others were expounded, and the cycle of new hypotheses followed by critiques continued.

Among these hypotheses, the association of ritual and magic is still considered viable because of the importance of hunting in the Upper Paleolithic. Nevertheless, other ideas about these graphics have been widely discussed, including the viewing of Upper Paleolithic art from a male/female perspective and the consideration of a prevalent dots-and-lines motif as a notational system associated with language, writing, or a calendar (Marshack, 1972). Other perspectives and ongoing questions include why certain areas of caves were used for painting, but not other, similar areas; why certain animals were painted, but not others; why males were painted singly or in groups, but women only in groups; why males were painted near animals, but women never were; and why groups of animals were painted in the most acoustically resonant areas. (Were rituals perhaps performed in areas of the cave with the best acoustic properties?) It should be noted that given the time depth, different contexts, and variable styles of symbolic representations, no *single* explanation regarding their meaning is likely to prove adequate. As one expert has concluded, "It is clear that there can no longer be a single 'meaning' to account for the thousands of images, media, contexts, and uses of what we lump under the term 'paleolithic art'" (Conkey, 1987, p. 414).

A more recent explanation for the florescence of cave art in certain areas has been suggested by archaeologists Clive Gamble (1991) and Lawrence Straus (1993), who point to the severe climatic conditions during the maximum (coldest interval) of the last glacial, around 20,000–18,000 y.a. It was during this period in southwestern France and northern Spain that most of the cave art was created. Straus notes that wherever there are clusters of living sites, there are cave art sanctuaries and residential sites with abundant mobile art objects. The caves could have been meeting places for local bands of people and locations for group activities. Bands could share hunting techniques and knowledge, and paintings and engravings could serve as "encoded information" that could be passed on across generations. Such information, Straus argues, would have been crucial for dealing with the severe conditions of the last glacial period.

AFRICA

Early accomplishments in rock art, perhaps as early as in Europe, are seen in southern Africa (Namibia), where a site containing such art is dated between 28,000 and 19,000 y.a. In addition, evidence of portable personal adornment is seen as early as 38,000 y.a. in the form of beads fashioned from ostrich eggshells.

In terms of stone tool technology, microliths (thumbnail-sized stone flakes hafted to make knives, saws, etc.) and blades characterize Late Stone Age* African industries. There was also considerable use of bone and antler in central Africa, perhaps some of it quite early. Recent excavations in the Katanda area of the eastern portion of the Democratic Republic of the Congo have shown remarkable development of bone craftwork. In fact, preliminary reports by Alison Brooks of George Washington University and John Yellen of the National Science Foundation have demonstrated that these technological achievements rival those of the more renowned European Upper Paleolithic (Yellen et al., 1995).

The most important artifacts discovered at Katanda are a dozen intricately made bone tools excavated from three sites along the Semiliki River (not far from Lake Rutanzige—formerly, Lake Edward) (see Fig. 13–17). These tools, made from the ribs or long bone splinters of large mammals, apparently were first ground to flatten and sharpen them, and then some were precisely pressure-flaked to produce a row of barbs. In form these tools are similar to what have been called "harpoons" from the later Upper Paleolithic of Europe (Magdalenian, c. 15,000 y.a.). Their function in Africa, as well, is thought to have been for spearing fish, which archaeological remains indicate were quite large (catfish weighing up to 150 pounds!). In addition, a few carved bone rings with no barbs were also discovered, but their intended function (if indeed they were meant to have a utilitarian function at all) remains elusive.

The dating of the Katanda sites is crucial for drawing useful comparisons with the European Upper Paleolithic. However, the bone used for the tools

---

*The Late Stone Age in Africa is equivalent to the Upper Paleolithic in Eurasia.

retained no measurable nitrogen and thus proved unsuitable for radiocarbon dating (perhaps it was too old and beyond the range of this technique). As a result, the other techniques now used for this time range—thermoluminescence, electron spin resonance, and uranium series dating (see Table 13–1, p. 376)—were all applied. The results proved consistent, indicating dates between 180,000 and 75,000 y.a.*

However, there remain some difficulties in establishing the clear association of the bone implements with the materials that have supplied the chronometric age estimates. Indeed, Richard Klein, a coauthor of one of the initial reports (Brooks et al., 1995), does not accept the suggested great antiquity for these finds and believes they may be much younger. Nevertheless, if the early age estimates should hold up, we once again will look *first* to Africa as the crucial source area for human origins—not just for biological aspects, but for cultural aspects as well.

Summary of Upper Paleolithic Culture

As we look back at the Upper Paleolithic, we can see it as the culmination of 2 million years of cultural development. Change proceeded incredibly slowly for most of the Pleistocene, but as cultural traditions and materials accumulated and the brain (and, we assume, intelligence) expanded and reorganized, the rate of change quickened.

Cultural evolution continued with the appearance of early premodern humans and moved a bit faster with later premoderns. Neandertals in Eurasia and their contemporaries elsewhere added deliberate burials, technological innovations, and much more.

Building on existing cultures, late Pleistocene populations attained sophisticated cultural and material heights in a seemingly short (by previous standards) burst of exciting activity. In Europe and central Africa particularly, there seem to have been dramatic cultural innovations that saw big game hunting, potent new weapons (including harpoons, spear-throwers, and possibly the bow and arrow), body ornaments, needles, "tailored" clothing, and burials with elaborate grave goods (the latter perhaps indicating some sort of status hierarchy).

This dynamic age was doomed, or so it appears, by the climatic changes of about 10,000 y.a. As the temperature slowly rose and the glaciers retreated, animal and plant species were seriously impacted, and humans were thus affected as well. As traditional prey animals were depleted or disappeared altogether, other means of obtaining food were sought.

Grinding hard seeds or roots became important, and as familiarity with plant propagation increased, domestication of plants and animals developed. Dependence on domestication became critical, and with it came permanent settlements, new technology, and more complex social organization. The continuing story of human evolution and the ways we study contemporary population diversity will be the topics of the remainder of this text.

---

*If these dates prove accurate, Katanda would actually be earlier than Late Stone Age (and thus be considered Middle Stone Age).

Visual Summary

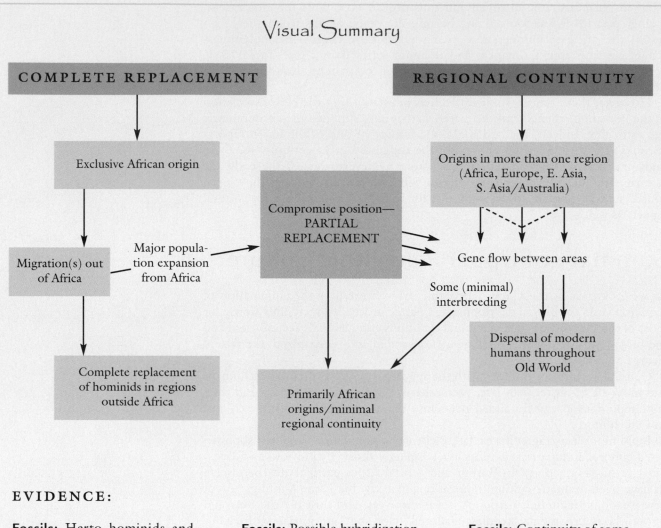

EVIDENCE:

Fossils: Herto hominids and other less well-dated and likely later remains

Fossils: Possible hybridization shown by Abrigo do Lagar Velho

Fossils: Continuity of some anatomical traits—especially in C. and W. Europe and Australia

Genetic: Ancient DNA (Neandertal compared to *H. sapiens sapiens*); contemporary human distribution of population variation (derived from mtDNA, automosomal nuclear DNA, Y chromosome, X chromosome)

Genetic: Likelihood of larger population size in Africa and migration to other regions with interbreeding; but mostly African genetic ancestry of all living humans

Genetic: Not a prime source of support for regional continuity

Archaeological: Rapid replacement in Europe of Mousterian (and Chatelperronian) by Aurignacian; major behavioral innovations correlated with Upper Paleolithic

Archaeological: Chatelperronian in Europe suggests tools were imitated or exchanged between Neandertals and modern humans

Archaeological: Overlap of Mousterian in Near East between Neandertal and modern human sites

Summary

The date and location of the origin of anatomically modern human beings have been the subjects of a fierce debate for the past decade, and the end is not in sight. One hypothesis (complete replacement) claims that anatomically modern forms first evolved in Africa more than 100,000 y.a. and then, migrating out of Africa, completely replaced premodern *H. sapiens* in the rest of the world. Another school (regional continuity) takes a diametrically different view and maintains that in various geographical regions of the world, local groups of premodern *H. sapiens* evolved directly to anatomically modern humans. A third hypothesis (partial replacement) takes a somewhat middle position, suggesting an African origin but also accepting some later hybridization outside of Africa.

Recent research coming from several sources is beginning to provide more clarity concerning the likely origins of modern humans. Data from sequenced ancient DNA, various patterns of contemporary human DNA, and the newest fossil finds from Ethiopia all suggest that a "strong" multiregional model is extremely unlikely. This more extreme form of multiregionalism posits that modern human populations in Asia and Europe evolved *mostly* from local premodern ancestors—with only minor influence coming from African population expansion. Given the breadth and consistency of the latest research, for practical purposes, this strong version of multiregionalism is falsified.

Morever, as various investigators integrate these new data, views are beginning to converge. Several researchers suggest an out-of Africa model that leads to virtually complete replacement elsewhere. At the moment, this complete replacement rendition cannot be falsified. Still, even devoted advocates of this strong replacement version recognize that *some* interbreeding was possible—although they believe it to have been very minor. In conclusion, then, during the latter Pleistocene, one or more major migrations from Africa fueled the worldwide dispersal of modern humans. However, the African migrants might well have interbred with resident populations outside Africa. In a sense, it is all the same, whether we see this process either as very minimal mulitregional continuity or as almost complete replacement.

Archaeological evidence of early modern humans also presents a fascinating picture of our most immediate ancestors. The Upper Paleolithic was an age of extraordinary innovation and achievement in technology and art. Many new and complex tools were introduced, and their production indicates fine skill in working wood, bone, and antler. Cave art in France and Spain displays the masterful ability of Upper Paleolithic painters, and beautiful sculptures have been found at many European sites. Sophisticated symbolic representations have also been found in Africa and elsewhere. Upper Paleolithic *Homo sapiens* displayed amazing development in a relatively short period of time. The culture produced during this period led the way to still newer and more complex cultural techniques and methods.

As a further study aid, the most significant fossil discoveries discussed in this chapter are presented in Table 13–2.

TABLE 13–2 Most Significant Modern *Homo sapiens* Discoveries Discussed in this Chapter

SITE	DATES (Y.A.)	HUMAN REMAINS	COMMENTS
Abrigo do Lagar Velho (Portugal)	24,500	Four-year-old child's skeleton	Possible evidence of hybridization between Neandertals and modern *H. sapiens*
Cro-Magnon (France)	30,000	8 individuals	Famous site of early modern *H. sapiens*, but there are dozens of other sites in Europe and elsewhere
Lake Mungo (Australia)	?60,000–30,000	3 individuals	Early dating estimate is surprising; if confirmed, would be earlier than established evidence in Europe or Asia
Qafzeh (Israel)	110,000	Minimum of 20 individuals	Quite early site; shows considerable variation
Skhūl (Israel)	115,000	Minimum of 10 individuals	Earliest well-dated modern *H. sapiens* outside of Africa; also perhaps contemporaneous with neighboring Tabun Neandertal site
Herto (Ethiopia)	160,000–154,000	3 individuals and other fragments	Earliest well-dated modern humans; placed in separate subspecies (*H. sapiens idaltu*); location (in Africa) is notable

For Further Thought

1. If all living humans evolved quite recently from a common (African) origin, what does that say about the relationships between all people? How different are people from each other?

Go to the book website at **http://www.anthropology.wadsworth.com** for resources to help you explore these questions further. Click on "For Further Thought" for this chapter.

Questions for Review

1. What anatomical characteristics define "modern" as compared to "premodern" humans? Assume that you are analyzing an incomplete skeleton of a possible early modern *H. sapiens*. Which portions of the skeleton would be most informative, and why?
2. What are the central aspects of the complete replacement model? How do they compare with the central aspects of the regional continuity model?
3. Go through the chapter and list all the forms of evidence that you think support the complete replacement model. Now, do the same for the regional continuity model. What evidence do you find most convincing, and why?
4. Why are the fossils recently discovered from Herto so important? How does this evidence influence your conclusions in question 3?
5. What is meant by "partial replacement"? What sorts of evidence support this hypothesis?
6. Why are models of "minimal regional continuity" and "mostly complete replacement" really the same thing?
7. What archaeological evidence shows that modern human behavior during the Upper Paleolithic was significantly different from that of earlier hominids? Do you think that early modern *H. sapiens* populations were behaviorally "superior" to the Neandertals? Be careful to define what you mean by "superior."
8. Why do you think some Upper Paleolithic people painted in caves? Why don't we find such evidence of cave painting from a wider geographical area?

Suggested Further Reading

Klein, Richard. 1999. *The Human Career: Human Biological and Cultural Origins.* 2nd ed. Chicago: University of Chicago Press.

Klein, Richard (with Blake Edgar). 2002. *The Dawn of Human Culture.* New York: Wiley

Lewin, Roger. 1998. *The Origin of Modern Humans.* New York: *Scientific American Origins.*

Relethford, John. 2001. *Genetics and the Search for Modern Human Origins.* New York: Wiley-Liss.

Stringer, Christopher, and Robin McKie. 1997. *African Exodus: The Origins of Modern Humanity.* New York: Holt.

Online Anthropology Resource Center

Go to the Anthropology Resource Center at **http://www.anthropology.wadsworth.com** for a wealth of online resources, including a companion website for your text that provides study aids such as self-quizzes for each chapter and a practice final exam, as well as links to anthropology websites and information on the latest theories and discoveries in the field. Also, check out InfoTrac College Edition®, your online library that offers full-length articles from thousands of scholarly and popular publications. Just click on the InfoTrac button at the companion website and use the passcode that came with your book.

The Evolution of Language

One of the most distinctive behavioral attributes of all modern humans is our advanced ability to use highly sophisticated symbolic language. Indeed, it would be impossible to imagine human social relationships or human culture without language.

When did language evolve? First, we should define what we mean by *full* human language. As we discussed in Chapter 8 (see pp. 207–212), nonhuman primates have shown some elements of language. For example, some chimpanzees, gorillas, and bonobos display abilities to manipulate symbols and a rudimentary understanding of grammar. Nevertheless, the full complement of skills displayed by humans includes the extensive use of arbitrary symbols, sophisticated grammar, and a complex *open* system of communication (see p. 208).

Most scholars are comfortable attributing such equivalent skills to early members of *H. sapiens sapiens*, as early as 200,000–100,000 years ago. In fact, several researchers hypothesize that the elaborate technology and artistic achievements, as well as the rapid dispersal of anatomically modern humans, were directly a result of behavioral advantages—particularly full language capabilities. This rapid expansion of presumably culturally sophisticated modern *H. sapiens* (and the consequent disappearance of other hominids) has sometimes been termed "the human revolution."

Of course, this hypothesis does not deny that earlier hominids had some form of complex communication; almost everyone agrees that even the earliest hominids did (at least as complex as that seen in living apes). What is not generally agreed upon is just when the full complement of human language capacity *first* emerged. Indeed, the controversy relating to this process will continue to ferment, since there is no clear answer to the question. The available evidence is not sufficient to establish clearly the language capabilities of any fossil hominid. We have discussed in Chapter 8 that there are neurological foundations for language and that these features relate more to brain reorganization than to simple increase in brain size. Moreover, as far as *spoken* language is concerned, during hominid evolution there were also physiological alterations of the vocal tract (in particular, a lower position of the larynx as compared to other primates).

Yet, we have no complete record of fossil hominid brains or their vocal tracts. We do have *endocasts* (see p. 281), which preserve a few external features of the brain. For example, there are several preserved endocasts of australopithecines from South Africa. However, the information is incomplete and thus subject to varying interpretations. (For example, did these hominids possess language? If not, what form of communication did they display?) Evidence from the vocal tract is even more elusive.

In such an atmosphere of fragmentary data, a variety of conflicting hypotheses have been proposed. Some paleoanthropologists argue that early australopithecines (3 m.y.a.) had language. Others think that such capabilities were first displayed by early *Homo* (perhaps 2 m.y.a.). Still others suggest that language did not emerge fully until the time of *Homo erectus* (2–1 m.y.a.), or perhaps it was premodern humans (such as the Neandertals) who first displayed such skills. And finally, a number of researchers assert that language first developed *only* with the appearance of *H. sapiens sapiens*.

Because the question of language evolution is so fundamental to understanding human evolution (indeed, what it *means* to be human), a variety of creative techniques have been applied to assess the (limited) evidence that is available. We have already mentioned the analysis of endocasts. Other researchers have suggested that the size of the vertebral canal in the thoracic region of the spine might be related to precise muscle control of breathing and thus an indicator of certain language skills. This conclusion was drawn from features of the *H. erectus* skeleton from Nariokotome (see p. 316). Lastly, and perhaps most informative of all, other paleoanthropologists have recently presented provisional data on the size of the hypoglossal canal at the base of the cranium (the size of the canal is thought to reflect the degree of neurological control of the tongue). Investigators have suggested that australopithecines and early *Homo* (with small canals) did not have full articulate language, but that premodern *H. sapiens* (Neandertals) and early *H. sapiens sapiens* probably did (these latter showing canals as large as those of contemporary people).

Subsequent to the initial suggestion that size of the hypoglossal canal might reflect speech capabilities (Kay et al., 1998), the hypothesis has been further tested using a much wider sample of nonhuman primates, fossil hominids, and modern humans (DeGusta et al., 1999). These new data do *not* confirm the hypothesis and in fact seriously question it. For example, many nonhuman primates have hypoglossal canals as large as humans; similarly, some early hominids (members of *Australopithecus*) also have canals as large as contemporary humans. Perhaps even more revealing, the size of the canal, as shown in dissections of human cadavers, does not appear correlated with the size of the (hypoglossal) nerve running through it. Further studies might help resolve some of these issues, but for the moment, the initial hypothesis concerning the utility of hypoglossal canal size for estimating speech abilities has been seriously weakened.

Also potentially informative are possible genetic differences between humans and apes in regard to language (see p. 211). As the human genome is fully mapped (especially

The Evolution of Language (continued)

identifying functional regions and their specific actions) and compared with ape DNA (the chimpanzee genome is currently being fully sequenced), we might at long last begin to find a key to solving this great mystery.

A final line of inquiry has focused on language (i.e., speech) by reconstructing in various fossil hominids the presumed position of the larynx within the vocal tract. As first proposed by Lieberman and Crelin (Lieberman and Crelin, 1971; Lieberman, 1992) and later by Laitman (Laitman et al., 1993), it is argued that Neandertals and other members of premodern *H. sapiens* could not articulate full speech, since the larynx would have been positioned higher in the throat than is seen in *H. sapiens sapiens*. This inference is based on indirect reconstruction of the vocal tract from the contours of the cranial base. Again, the evidence is far from unambiguous, and interpretations are often varied (and contentious; see, for example, Falk, 1975; Frayer, 1993). Given these uncertainties, most paleoanthropologists have been reluctant to conclude exactly what *speech* capabilities Neandertals had. The most *direct* evidence was discovered in 1983 and includes an adult Neandertal *hyoid bone* (from Kebara Cave in Israel; see p. 349). This important structure, which supports the larynx, is identical in this Neandertal to that seen in modern humans. Given this information, it would be most imprudent to argue that Neandertals could not articulate full human speech. Nevertheless, simply because Neandertals *could* speak in a fully articulate manner does not necessarily argue that they communicated with the entire array of contemporary human symbolic language. We have noted in Chapter 12 several probable behavioral contrasts of Neandertals with Upper Paleolithic *H. sapiens sapiens*. Was language ability among these contrasts and perhaps the most important difference? Do more advanced language capabilities help explain the rapid success of modern humans in displacing other hominids? Does language, then, mostly account for the human revolution? Surely, these are fascinating and important questions. Perhaps someday we will be able to answer them in a comprehensive, scientifically rigorous manner.

Critical Thinking Questions

1. What is meant by human language? How does it differ from communication seen in great apes?
2. What direct evidence (fossil and archaeological) is used to suggest that early hominids had language capabilities? How sufficient is this evidence?
3. What kind of evidence would convince you that an earlier hominid (Neandertals, for example) did or did not possess language?

Sources

DeGusta, D., W. H. Gilbert, and S. P. Turner. 1999. "Hypoglossal Canal Size and Hominid Speech." *Proceedings of the National Academy of Sciences* 96: 1800–1804.

Falk, Dean. 1975. "Comparative Anatomy of the Larynx in Man and the Chimpanzee: Implications for Language in Neandertal." *American Journal of Physical Anthropology* 43: 123–132.

Frayer, D. W. 1993. "On Neanderthal Crania and Speech: Response to Lieberman." *Current Anthropology* 34: 721.

Kay, R. F., M. Cartmill, and M. Balow. 1998. "The Hypoglossal Canal and the Origins of Human Vocal Behavior" (abstract). *American Journal of Physical Anthropology, Supplement* 26: 137.

Laitman, J. T., J. S. Reidenberg, D. R. Friedland, et al. 1993. "Neandertal Upper Respiratory Specializations and Their Effect upon Respiration and Speech" (abstract). *American Journal of Physical Anthropology* 16: 129.

Lieberman, Phillip. 1992. "On Neanderthal Speech and Neanderthal Extinction." *Current Anthropology* 33: 409–410.

Lieberman, P., and E. S. Crelin. 1971. "On the Speech of Neanderthal Man." *Linguistic Inquiries* 2: 203–222.

MacLarnon, Ann. 1993. "The Vertebral Canal of KNM-WT 15000 and the Evolution of the Spinal Cord and Other Canal Contents." In A. Walker and R. E. Leakey (eds.), *The Nariokotome* Homo erectus *Skeleton*. Cambridge: Harvard University Press, pp. 359–390.

Modern Human Biology: Patterns of Variation

14

Composite satellite image
Courtesy, Craig Mayhew and Robert Simmon, NASA

Introduction

See the following sections of the CD-ROM for topics covered in this chapter: Virtual Lab 2, sections I, II, and III.

At some time or other, you have probably been asked to specify your "race" or "ethnic identity" on an application form or census form. What do you think when you see this question? Do you think of your own "race" as separate from your "ethnic identity," or do you regard the two as essentially the same? How comfortable were you in answering the question in the first place? Usually, there is a variety of racial/ethnic categories to choose from. Was it easy to pick an appropriate category? What about your parents and grandparents? Where would they fit in?

Notions relating to human diversity have for centuries played a large role in human relations, and they still influence political and social perceptions. While it would be comforting to believe that informed views have become almost universal, the gruesome tally of genocidal/ethnic cleansing atrocities in recent years tell us tragically that worldwide, as a species, we have a long way to go before ethnic and cultural tolerance becomes the norm.

In Chapter 13, we discussed the origin and dispersal of modern humans. That was the last major episode in our lineage of what we have termed *macroevolution*. However, our species continues to evolve, and the ongoing process is referred to as *microevolution*. Physical anthropologists study human microevolution from an evolutionary perspective.

As noted, most people don't seem to understand the nature of human diversity—and worse yet, many seem quite unwilling to accept what science has to contribute on the subject. Many of the misconceptions are no doubt rooted in cultural history over the last few centuries, especially regarding how *race* is defined and categorized. Although many cultures have attempted to come to grips with these issues, for better or worse, the most influential of these perspectives developed in the Western world (i.e., Europe and North America). The way many individuals still view themselves and their relationship to other peoples is a legacy of the last four centuries of racial interpretations.

Historical Views of Human Variation

The first step toward understanding natural phenomena is the ordering of variation into categories that can then be named, discussed, and perhaps studied. Historically, when different groups of people came into contact, they tried to explain the phenotypic variations they saw. Because skin color was so noticeable, it was one of the more frequently described traits, and most systems of racial classification came to be based on it.

As early as 1350 B.C., the ancient Egyptians had classified humans on the basis of skin color: red for Egyptian, yellow for people to the east, white for those to the north, and black for Africans to the south (Gossett, 1963, p. 4). In the sixteenth century, after the discovery of the New World, Europeans embarked on a period of intense exploration and colonization in both the New and Old Worlds, and they became more aware of human diversity.

As you learned in Chapter 2, the discovery of the New World was of major importance in altering the views of Europeans, who had perceived the world as static and nonchanging. One of the most influential discoveries of the early European explorers was that the Americas were inhabited by people, some of whom were dark-skinned (compared to most Europeans). At first, Native Americans were thought to be Asian, and since Columbus believed that he had discovered a new route to India, he called them "Indians." But these people weren't Christian, and furthermore, Europeans didn't consider them "civilized." So as colonization of the New World proceeded, indigenous populations were slaughtered, exposed to European diseases, and driven off their land. This appalling pattern was repeated elsewhere, including South Africa and Australia.

Throughout the eighteenth and nineteenth centuries, European and American scientists concentrated primarily on describing and classifying biological diversity as observed in humans as well as in nonhuman species. The first scientific attempt to categorize the newly discovered variation among humans was Linnaeus' taxonomic classification, which placed humans into four separate groupings (Linnaeus, 1758). Linnaeus assigned behavioral and intellectual qualities to each group, with the least complimentary descriptions going to black Africans. This ranking was typical of the period and reflected the almost universal European view that they were superior to all other peoples. (To be fair, we should note that the Europeans were not—and are not—the only people guilty of *ethnocentrism*. Most, if not all, human societies participate in the belief that their own culture is superior to that of others.)

Johann Friedrich Blumenbach (1752–1840), a German anatomist, classified humans into five categories, or races. Although Blumenbach's categories came to be described simply as white, yellow, red, black, and brown, he also used criteria other than skin color. Moreover, he emphasized that divisions based on skin color were arbitrary and that many traits, including skin color, weren't discrete phenomena. Blumenbach pointed out that to attempt to classify all humans using such a system would be to omit completely all those who did not neatly fall into a specific category. Furthermore, he and other scientists recognized that traits such as skin color showed overlapping expression between groups.

In 1842, Anders Retzius, a Swedish anatomist, developed the *cephalic index* as a method of describing the shape of the head. The cephalic index, derived by dividing maximum head breadth by maximum length and multiplying by 100, gives the ratio of head breadth to length. (It is important to note that the cephalic index does not measure head size.) Compared to the statistical methods in use today, the cephalic index seems rather simplistic, but in the nineteenth century, it was viewed as a sophisticated scientific tool. Furthermore, because a single number could neatly categorize people, it provided an extremely efficient method for describing and ordering phenotypic variation. Individuals with an index of less than 75 had long, narrow heads and were termed **dolichocephalic. Brachycephalic** individuals, with broad heads, had an index of over 80. And those whose indices were between 75 and 80 were *mesocephalic*.

Northern Europeans tended to be dolichocephalic, while southern Europeans were brachycephalic. Not surprisingly, these results led to heated and nationalistic debate over whether one group was superior to the other. But when it was shown that northern Europeans shared their tendency to long, narrow heads with several African populations, the cephalic index ceased to be considered such a reliable indicator of race.

By the mid-nineteenth century, populations were ranked essentially on a scale based on skin color (along with size and shape of the head), with sub-Saharan Africans at the bottom. Additionally, Europeans themselves were ranked so that northern, light-skinned populations were considered superior to their southern, more olive-skinned neighbors.

dolichocephalic Having a long, narrow head in which the width measures less than 75 percent of the length.

brachycephalic Having a broad head in which the width measures more than 80 percent of the length.

biological determinism The concept that phenomena, including various aspects of behavior (e.g., intelligence, values, morals) are governed by biological (genetic) factors; the inaccurate association of various behavioral attributes with certain biological traits, such as skin color.

To many Europeans, the fact that non-Europeans were not Christian suggested to them that these "foreigners" were "uncivilized" and implied an even more basic inferiority of character and intellect. This view was rooted in a concept called **biological determinism**, which in part holds that there is an association between physical characteristics and such attributes as intelligence, morals, values, abilities, and even social and economic condition. In other words, cultural variations are *inherited* in the same manner as biological variations. It follows, then, that there are inherent behavioral and cognitive differences between groups and that some groups are *by nature* superior to others. Following this logic, it is a simple matter to justify the persecution and even enslavement of other peoples simply because their appearance differs from what is familiar.

After 1850, biological determinism was a constant theme underlying common thinking as well as scientific research in Europe and the United States. Deterministic (and what we today would call racist) views were held to some extent by most people, including such notable figures as Thomas Jefferson, Georges Cuvier, Benjamin Franklin, Charles Lyell, Abraham Lincoln, Charles Darwin, and Oliver Wendell Holmes. Commenting on this usually de-emphasized characteristic of notable historical figures, Stephen J. Gould (1981, p. 32) concluded that "all American culture heroes embraced racial attitudes that would embarrass public-school mythmakers."

Francis Galton (1822–1911), a cousin of Charles Darwin, shared the increasingly common fear among Europeans that "civilized society" was being weakened by the failure of natural selection to eliminate unfit and inferior individuals (Greene, 1981, p. 107). Galton wrote and lectured on the necessity of "race improvement" and suggested government regulation of marriage and family size, an approach he called **eugenics**.

eugenics The philosophy of "race improvement" through the forced sterilization of members of some groups and increased reproduction among others; an overly simplified, often racist view that is now discredited.

Although eugenics had its share of critics, its popularity flourished in the years following World War I and especially throughout the 1930s. The movement was widely supported in most of Europe and the United States, but nowhere was it more popular than in Germany, where the viewpoint took a horrifying turn. The idea of a "pure race" (see Issue, pp. 444–445) was increasingly extolled as a means of reestablishing a strong and prosperous state. Eugenics was seen as a scientific rationale for purging Germany of its "unfit," and many of Germany's scientists continued to support the policies of racial purity and eugenics during the Nazi period (Proctor, 1988, p. 143), when these policies served as justification for condemning millions of people to death.

But at the same time, many scientists were turning away from racial typologies and classification in favor of a more evolutionary approach. No doubt for some, this shift in direction was motivated by growing concerns over the goals of the eugenics movement. Probably more important, however, was the integration of Mendelian genetics and Darwin's theories of natural selection during the 1930s (see discussion of the Modern Synthesis, p. 92). This breakthrough influenced all the biological sciences, and many physical anthropologists began to apply evolutionary principles to the study of human variation.

The Concept of Race

polytypic Referring to species composed of populations that differ with regard to the expression of one or more traits.

All contemporary humans are members of the same **polytypic** species, *Homo sapiens*. A polytypic species is one composed of local populations that differ with regard to the expression of one or more traits. Moreover, *within* local populations, there is a great deal of genotypic and phenotypic variation between individuals.

In discussions of human variation, people have traditionally clumped together various attributes, such as skin color, shape of the face, shape of the nose, hair color, hair form (curly, straight), and eye color. People possessing particular combinations of these and other traits have been placed together into categories associated with specific geographical localities. Such categories are called *races*.

We all think we know what we mean by the word *race*, but in reality, the term has had a number of meanings since it gained common usage in English in the 1500s. It has been used synonymously with *species,* as in "the human race." Since the 1600s, race has also referred to various culturally defined groups, and this meaning still enjoys popular usage. For example, one hears "the English race" or "the Japanese race," where the reference is actually to nationality. Another often heard phrase is "the Jewish race," where the speaker is really talking about a particular ethnic and religious identity.

Thus, while *race* is usually a term with biological connotations, it is also one with enormous social significance. Moreover, there is still a widespread perception that there is an association between certain physical traits (skin color, in particular) and numerous cultural attributes (such as language, occupational preferences, or even morality). Therefore, in many cultural contexts, a person's social identity is strongly influenced by the manner in which he or she expresses those physical traits traditionally used to define "racial groups." Characteristics such as skin color are highly visible, and they facilitate an immediate and superficial designation of individuals into socially defined categories. However, so-called racial traits are not the only phenotypic expressions that contribute to social identity. Sex and age are also critically important. But aside from these two variables, an individual's biological and/or ethnic background is still inevitably a factor that influences how he or she is initially perceived and judged by others.

References to national origin (e.g., African, Asian) as substitutes for racial labels have become more common in recent years, both within and outside anthropology. Within anthropology, the term *ethnicity* was proposed in the early 1950s as a means of avoiding the more emotionally charged term *race*. Strictly speaking, ethnicity refers to cultural factors, but the fact that the words *ethnicity* and *race* are used interchangeably reflects the social importance of phenotypic expression and demonstrates once again how phenotype is mistakenly associated with culturally defined variables.

In its most common biological usage, the term *race* refers to geographically patterned phenotypic variation within a species. By the seventeenth century, naturalists had begun to describe races in plants and nonhuman animals, because they recognized that when populations of a species occupied different regions, they sometimes differed from one another in the expression of one or more traits. But even today, there are no established criteria by which races of plants and animals, including humans, are to be assessed.

Prior to World War II, most studies of human variation focused on visible phenotypic variation between large, geographically defined populations, and these studies were largely descriptive. Since World War II, the emphasis has shifted to the examination of differences in allele frequencies within and between populations, as well as the adaptive significance of phenotypic and genotypic variation. This shift in focus occurred partly as a result of the Modern Synthesis in biology and because of advances in genetics.

Hence, the application of evolutionary principles to the study of modern human variation has replaced the superficial nineteenth-century view of race *based solely on observed phenotype*. Additionally, the genetic emphasis has dispelled previously held misconceptions that races are fixed biological entities that do not change over time and that are composed of individuals who all conform to a particular *type*.

Clearly, there are phenotypic differences between humans, and some of these differences roughly correspond to particular geographical locations. But certain questions must be asked: Is there any adaptive significance attached to observed phenotypic variation? Is genetic drift a factor? What is the degree of underlying genetic variation that influences phenotypic variation? These questions place considerations of human variation within a contemporary evolutionary framework.

Although, in part, physical anthropology has its roots in attempts to explain human diversity, anthropologists have never been in complete agreement on the topic of race. Furthermore, no contemporary scholar subscribes to pre-Darwinian and pre–Modern Synthesis concepts of races (human or nonhuman) as fixed biological entities. Many who continue to use broad racial categories do not view them as particularly important, especially from a genetic perspective, because the amount of genetic variation accounted for by differences *between* groups is vastly exceeded by the variation that exists *within* groups. But given these considerations, there are anthropologists who continue to view variation in outwardly expressed phenotype as potentially informative of population adaptation, genetic drift, mutation, and gene flow (Brues, 1991).

Forensic anthropologists, in particular, find the phenotypic criteria associated with race to have practical applications because they are frequently called on by law enforcement agencies to assist in the identification of human skeletal remains. Inasmuch as unidentified human remains are often those of crime victims, identification must be as accurate as possible. The most important variables in such identification are the individual's sex, age, stature, and ancestry or "racial" and ethnic background. Using metric and nonmetric criteria, forensic anthropologists employ a number of techniques for establishing broad population affinity, and they are generally able to do so with about 80 percent accuracy.

On the other side of the issue, there are numerous physical anthropologists who argue that race is a meaningless concept when applied to humans. Race is seen as an outdated creation of the human mind that attempts to simplify biological complexity by organizing it into categories. Thus, human races are a product of the human tendency to superimpose order on complex natural phenomena. While classification may have been an acceptable approach some 150 years ago, it is no longer valid given the current state of genetic and evolutionary science.

Objections to racial taxonomies have also been raised because classification schemes are *typological* in nature, meaning that categories are discrete and based on stereotypes or ideals that comprise a specific set of traits. Thus, in general, typologies are inherently misleading, because there are always many individuals in any grouping who do not conform to all aspects of a particular type.

In any so-called racial group, there will be individuals who fall into the normal range of variation for another group with regard to one or several characteristics. For example, two people of different ancestry might vary with regard to skin color, but they could share any number of other traits, such as height, shape of head, hair color, eye color, or ABO blood type. In fact, they could easily share more similarities with each other than they do with many members of their own populations (Fig. 14–1).

Moreover, the characteristics that have traditionally been used to define races are *polygenic*; that is, they are influenced by several genes and therefore exhibit a continuous range of expression. It thus becomes difficult, if not impossible, to draw discrete boundaries between populations with regard to many traits. This limitation becomes clear if you ask yourself, "At what point is hair color no longer dark brown but medium brown, or no longer light brown but blond?"

The scientific controversy over race will diminish as we increase our understanding of the genetic diversity (and uniformity) of our species. Given the rapid changes in genome studies and the fact that very few genes contribute to outward expressions of phenotype, dividing the human species into racial categories is not a biologically meaningful way to look at human variation. Among the general public, however, variations on the theme of race will undoubtedly continue to be the most common view of human biological and cultural varia-

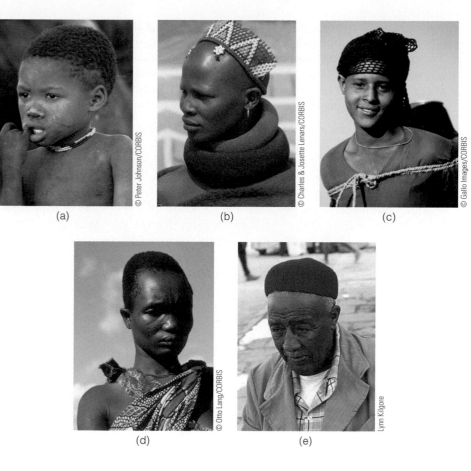

FIGURE 14–1 Some examples of phenotypic variation among Africans.
(a) San (South African)
(b) West African (Bantu)
(c) Ethiopian
(d) Ituri (Central African)
(e) North African (Tunisia)

tion. Given this fact, it falls to anthropologists and biologists to continue to explore the issue so that, to the best of our abilities, accurate information regarding human variation is available to anyone who seeks informed explanations of complex phenomena.

Racism

Racism is based on the false belief that intellect and various cultural attributes are inherited along with physical characteristics. Such beliefs also commonly rest on the assumption that one's own group is superior to other groups.

Because we have already alluded to certain aspects of racism, such as the eugenics movement and persecution of people based on racial or ethnic misconceptions, we will not belabor the point here. However, it is important to point out that racism is hardly a thing of the past, nor is it restricted to European and American whites. Racism is a cultural, not a biological, phenomenon, and it is found worldwide.

Ultimately, racism is one of the more dangerous aspects of human behavior. We continue to see manifestations of racism in the United States and elsewhere. Sadly, the twentieth century provided numerous examples of ethnic/racial conflict, and the twenty-first century has begun by following its example. But it is important to point out that virtually all these conflicts were due to cultural, not biological, differences between the participants. The unspeakable genocidal events of the Holocaust during World War II, in Cambodia in the 1970s, in Rwanda in 1994; the tragedies of Bosnia, Croatia, and Kosovo; the devastating terrorist attacks on the United States on September 11, 2001; and the ongoing conflicts in the Middle East fueled by the disastrous mistrust between Muslim and non-Muslim nations all bespeak the outcomes of intolerance of groups we call "others," however we define the term.

We end this brief discussion of racism with an excerpt from an article, "The Study of Race," by the late Sherwood Washburn, a well-known physical anthropologist at the University of California, Berkeley. Although written some years ago, the statement is as fresh and applicable today as it was when it was written:

> Races are products of the past. They are relics of times and conditions which have long ceased to exist.
>
> Racism is equally a relic supported by no phase of modern science. We may not know how to interpret the form of the Mongoloid face, or why Rh is of high incidence in Africa, but we do know the benefits of education and of economic progress. We . . . know that the roots of happiness lie in the biology of the whole species and that the potential of the species can only be realized in a culture, in a social system. It is knowledge and the social system which give life or take it away, and in so doing change the gene frequencies and continue the million-year-old interaction of culture and biology. Human biology finds its realization in a culturally determined way of life, and the infinite variety of genetic combinations can only express themselves efficiently in a free and open society. (Washburn, 1963, p. 531)

Intelligence

intelligence Mental capacity; ability to learn, reason, or comprehend and interpret information, facts, relationships, and meanings; the capacity to solve problems, whether through the application of previously acquired knowledge or through insight.

As we have shown, belief in the relationship between physical characteristics and specific behavioral attributes is popular even today, but there is no evidence that personality or any other behavioral trait differs genetically *between* human groups. Most scientists would agree with this last statement, but one question that has produced controversy both inside scientific circles and among laypeople is whether population affinity and **intelligence** are associated.

Both genetic and environmental factors contribute to intelligence, although it isn't yet possible to accurately measure the percentage each contributes. What can be said is that IQ scores and intelligence are *not* the same thing. IQ scores can change during a person's lifetime, and average IQ scores of different populations overlap. The differences in average IQ scores that do exist between groups are difficult to interpret, given the problems inherent in the design of the tests. Moreover, complex cognitive abilities, however measured, are influenced by multiple loci and are consequently polygenic.

As we said in Chapter 7, innate factors set limits and potentials for behavior and cognitive ability in any species. In humans, the limits are broad and the potentials aren't fully known. Individual abilities result from complex interactions between genetic and environmental factors. One product of this interaction is learning, and the ability to learn is influenced by genetic and other biological components.

Undeniably, there are differences between individuals regarding these biological components. However, elucidating what proportion of the variation in test scores is due to biological factors probably isn't possible. Moreover, innate differences in abilities reflect individual variation *within* populations, not inherent differences *between* groups. Comparing populations on the basis of IQ test results is a misuse of testing procedures, and there is no convincing evidence *whatsoever* that populations vary with regard to cognitive abilities, regardless of the assertions in some popular books. Unfortunately, despite the questionable validity of intelligence tests and the lack of evidence of mental inferiority of some populations and mental superiority of others, racist attitudes toward intelligence continue to flourish.

Contemporary Interpretations of Human Variation

Since the physical characteristics such as skin color, hair form, etc. used to define race are *polygenic*, precisely measuring the genetic influence on them has proven unattainable. So, physical anthropologists and other biologists who study modern human variation have largely abandoned the traditional perspective of describing superficial phenotypic characteristics in favor of *measuring* actual *genetic* characteristics.

Beginning in the 1950s, studies of modern human variation focused on the various components of blood as well as other body chemistry. Such traits as the ABO blood types are *phenotypes,* but they are *direct* products of the genotype. (Recall that many genes code for proteins, and the antigens on blood cells and many components of blood serum are partly composed of proteins; Fig. 14–2). During the twentieth century, this perspective met with a great deal of success, as eventually dozens of loci were identified and the frequency data of many specific alleles obtained from numerous human populations. Nevertheless, in all these cases, it was the phenotype that was observed, and information about the underlying genotype remained largely unobtainable. Beginning in the 1990s, however, with the development of genomic studies, a drastic shift in techniques has taken place.

As a result of precise DNA sequencing, genotypes can now be ascertained directly. Moreover, while a decade ago only a small portion of the human genome was accessible to physical anthropologists, we are now on the threshold of deciphering the entire genetic blueprint for our species. As specific DNA variability is explored within and between human populations, we will dramatically increase our knowledge of human variation.

HUMAN POLYMORPHISMS

Those traits that differ in expression among various populations and between individuals are most important in contemporary studies of human variation. Such characteristics with different phenotypic expressions are called **polymorphisms**.

polymorphisms Loci with more than one allele. Polymorphisms can be expressed in the phenotype as the result of gene action (as in ABO), or they can exist solely at the DNA level within noncoding regions.

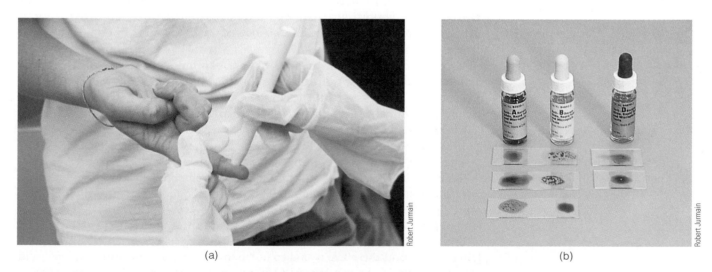

(a)   (b)

FIGURE 14–2 (a) A blood sample is drawn. (b) To determine an individual's blood type, a few drops of blood are treated with specific chemicals. Presence of A and B blood type, as well as Rh, can be detected by using commercially available chemicals. The glass slides below the blue- and yellow-labeled bottles show reactions for the ABO system. The blood on the top slide (at left) is type AB; the middle is type B; and the bottom is type A. The two samples to the right depict Rh-negative blood (top) and Rh-positive blood (bottom).

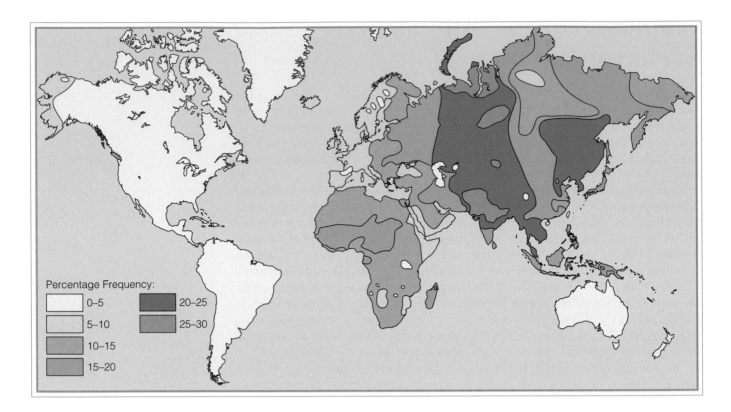

FIGURE 14–3 ABO blood group system. Distribution of the *B* allele in the indigenous populations of the world. (After Mourant et al., 1976.)

cline A gradual change in the frequency of genotypes and phenotypes from one geographical region to another.

See Virtual lab 2, section III, for an interactive exercise covering the ABO blood group.

A genetic trait is *polymorphic* if the locus that governs it has two or more alleles. (Refer back to p. 82 for a discussion of the ABO blood group system governed by three alleles at one locus.)

Understanding polymorphisms requires evolutionary explanations, and geneticists use polymorphisms as a principal tool to understand evolutionary processes in modern populations. Moreover, by using these polymorphisms to compare allele frequencies between different populations, we can begin to reconstruct the evolutionary events that link human populations with one another.

By the 1960s, the study of *clinal distributions* of individual polymorphisms had become a popular alternative to the racial approach to human diversity. A **cline** is a gradual change in the frequency of a trait or allele in populations dispersed over geographical space. In humans, the various expressions of polymorphic characteristics exhibit a more or less continuous distribution from one region to another; most traits that show a clinal distribution are Mendelian. The distribution of the *A* and *B* alleles in the Old World provides a good example of a clinal distribution (Fig. 14–3). Clinal distributions are generally thought to reflect microevolutionary influences of natural selection and/or gene flow. Consequently, clinal distributions are explained in evolutionary terms.

The ABO system is interesting from an anthropological perspective because the frequencies of the *A*, *B*, and *O* alleles vary tremendously among humans. In most groups, *A* and *B* are only rarely found in frequencies greater than 50 percent; usually, frequencies for these two alleles are considerably lower. Most human groups, however, are polymorphic for all three alleles.

But in some native South American Indians, frequencies of the *O* allele reach 100 percent, and this allele is said to be "fixed" in these populations. (You could say that in these groups, the ABO blood system is not a polymorphic trait.) Indeed, in most indigenous New World populations, the frequency of *O* is at least 80 percent. Uncommonly high frequencies of *O* are also found in northern Australia, and on some islands off the Australian coast, the frequency of *O*

Percentage Frequency:

0–5
5–10
10–15
15–20
20–25
25–30

exceeds 90 percent. In these populations, the high frequencies of the *O* allele are probably due to genetic drift (founder effect), although the influence of natural selection can't be entirely ruled out.

In addition to ABO, there are numerous other red blood cell phenotypes, each under the control of a different genetic locus. These include the well-known Rh blood group as well as the MN blood group (the latter has been widely used in population studies; e.g., see p. 411).

Important polymorphisms also occur for antigens on white blood cells. Called HLA in humans (human leukocyte antigen), these antigens are crucial to the immune response because they allow the body to recognize and resist potentially dangerous infections. What is quite interesting is that, unlike simple polymorphisms like ABO (one locus, three alleles) or MN (one locus, just two alleles), HLA is governed by six loci together possessing *hundreds* of alleles. In fact, HLA is by far the most polymorphic genetic system known in humans (Knapp, 2002).

Because HLA alleles are so numerous, they are useful in showing patterns of human population diversity. For example, Lapps, Sardinians, and Basques differ in allele frequencies from other European populations, and these data support allele frequency distributions for ABO, MN, and Rh (Fig. 14–4). Founder effect (i.e., genetic drift) most likely explains the distinctive genetic patterning in these smaller, traditionally more isolated groups. Likewise, the unusual HLA allele frequencies found in many populations in Australia and New Guinea also likely result from founder effect. Natural selection also has influenced the evolution of HLA alleles in humans, especially as related to infectious disease. For example, certain HLA antigens appear to be associated with resistance to malaria and hepatitis B and perhaps to HIV as well.

A final physiological and evolutionary influence of HLA concerns male fertility. Recent data suggest that some HLA antigens are found in higher frequency in males with severe infertility, suggesting that there may be some influence of two or more HLA loci on sperm production and function (van der Ven et al., 2000).

Another useful polymorphism is that for PTC tasting. PTC (phenylthiocarbamide) is an artificial substance. Interestingly, while some people are able to taste PTC (as a bitter substance), many others don't taste it at all. The mode of inheritance follows a Mendelian pattern, with two alleles (*T* and *t*); nontasting is largely a recessive trait, so that nontasters are homozygous (*tt*). The frequency of PTC tasting varies considerably in human populations, but the evolutionary explanation for the patterns of variation is not clear. It is possible, however, that various aspects of taste could under certain circumstances be selectively advantageous, especially in avoiding toxic plants (which are often bitter).

FIGURE 14–4 People in Sardinia, a large island off the west coast of Italy, differ in allele frequencies at some loci from other European populations.

PATTERNS OF POLYMORPHIC VARIATION

Examining single traits can be informative regarding potential influences of natural selection or gene flow. This approach, however, is limited when we try to sort out population relationships, since the study of single traits, by themselves, can yield confusing interpretations regarding likely population relationships. A more meaningful approach is to study several traits simultaneously.

An excellent and early example of this approach to human diversity was undertaken by Harvard population geneticist R. D. Lewontin (1972). Lewontin calculated population differences in allele frequency for 17 polymorphic characteristics. In his analysis, he divided his sample into seven geographical areas, and he included several population samples within each region (Table 14–1). Next he calculated how much of the total genetic variability within our species could be accounted for by these population subdivisions, and the results were surprising.

TABLE 14–1 Population Groupings Used by Lewontin in Population Genetics Study (1972)

GEOGRAPHICAL GROUP	EXAMPLES OF POPULATIONS INCLUDED
Caucasians	Arabs, Armenians, Tristan da Cunhans
Black Africans	Bantu, San, U.S. blacks
Asians	Ainu, Chinese, Turks
South Asians	Andamanese, Tamils
Amerinds	Aleuts, Navaho, Yanomama
Oceanians	Easter Islanders, Micronesians
Australians	All treated as a single group

Only 6.3 percent of the total genetic variation was explained by differences between major population groups (Lewontin's seven geographical units). In other words, close to 94 percent of human genetic diversity occurs *within* these groups. The larger population subdivisions within the geographical clusters (e.g., within Native Americans, the differences between subgroups such as Aleut and Yanomama) account for another 8.3 percent. Thus, geographical and local "races" together account for just 15 percent of all human genetic variation, leaving the remaining 85 percent unaccounted for. This means that the vast majority of genetic differences among human beings is explained in terms of differences from one village to another, one family to another, and, to a significant degree, one person to another, even within the same family.

Our visual perceptions tell us that human races exist. But as we mentioned previously, the visible traits most frequently used to make racial distinctions (skin color, hair form, nose shape, etc.) don't provide an accurate picture of the actual pattern of *genetic variation*. Simple polymorphic traits provide a more objective basis for accurate biological comparisons of human groups. Indeed, Lewontin concluded his analysis with a ringing condemnation of traditional studies: "Human racial classification is of no social value and is positively destructive of social and human relations. Since such racial classification is now seen to be of virtually no genetic or taxonomic significance either, no justification can be offered for its continuance" (Lewontin, 1972, p. 397).

In addition, there are even broader patterns of human diversity that we have discussed earlier in the text. At the species level, *Homo sapiens* is an unusually homogeneous species compared to most other animals. For example, within-species variation of mtDNA is three to four times greater in both chimpanzees and gorillas than in humans. Moreover, given that our species is overall not genetically variable, the differences that do exist reveal an interesting geographical pattern. Compared to all other areas, African populations show much more genetic variation. As emphasized in Chapter 13, this pattern of genetic diversity is thought to reflect a longer history of human occupation in Africa, with subsequent migrations to other parts of the world.

POLYMORPHISMS AT THE DNA LEVEL

The *Human Genome Project* has facilitated the direct study of both mitochondrial DNA and chromosomal (nuclear) DNA. Thus, considerable insight has been gained regarding human variation *directly at the DNA level*. Using techniques described in Chapter 3, researchers can directly compare DNA sequences from different individuals and between populations.

In addition, new molecular technologies have uncovered a host of other regions of DNA variability. As we discussed in Chapter 3, there are, scattered throughout the human genome, hundreds of sites where DNA segments are repeated. In some cases, there are only a few repeated segments, but in other cases, there can be hundreds. One type of DNA repeats, called *microsatellites*, are extraordinarily variable from person to person. In fact, as we discussed in Chapter 3, everyone is unique for his or her particular arrangement, and using current analytical approaches, the individual pattern produces a distinctive "DNA fingerprint" (see p. 68).

Another kind of DNA segment, called an *Alu*, can also occasionally be copied, but not over and over again (as in microsatellites). Instead, Alus are fairly short DNA segments that typically are copied once and then insert randomly, perhaps elsewhere on the same chromosome; or, just as easily, they can "jump" and insert on some other chromosome. Several hundred of these Alus have now been mapped in the human genome, and their patterns are quite informative concerning recent population history.

Finally, researchers are beginning to expand their approach and map patterns of variation at individual nucleotide sites. Of course, it has been recognized for some time that changes of individual DNA bases can occur within functional loci, producing what are called "point mutations." The sickle-cell allele at the hemoglobin beta locus is a good example of such a mutation in humans.

What has only been recently appreciated, however, is that such single nucleotide alterations also frequently occur in *noncoding* portions of DNA, and these sites, together with those in coding regions of DNA, are all referred to as *single nucleotide polymorphisms* (*SNPs*). Already, more than a million such sites have been recognized dispersed throughout the human genome (96 percent of which are in noncoding DNA), and these single nucleotide polymorphisms are extraordinarily variable (the International SNP Map Working Group, 2001). Thus, at the beginning of the twenty-first century, geneticists have gained access to a vast biological "library" documenting the genetic history of our species.

Population geneticists are just beginning to take advantage of these new opportunities. While traditional polymorphic traits, such as ABO, are still being investigated, more and more attention is being directed at the remarkably variable DNA polymorphisms. These molecular applications are now being widely used to evaluate contemporary variation at a microevolutionary level and this information provides far more accurate measures of within-group and between-group variation than was possible previously. Moreover, the vast amount of new data can now be used to more fully understand very recent events in human population history—including the varied roles of natural selection, genetic drift, gene flow, and mutation.

As an example of how far the study of human variation has moved towards a molecularly based approach, more than 95 percent of the papers presented at a recent anthropology conference on population variation used DNA polymorphisms. Populations evaluated using direct DNA ascertainment come from every corner of the inhabited world. The information is increasing at an incredibly rapid rate, as indicated in a new online database called ALFRED (ALlele FREquency Database).* Recently, in just a 12-month period, the information in this database almost doubled (Kidd et al., 2003)!

These genetic data, including the more traditional polymorphisms such as blood groups and the vast new DNA-based evidence, all point in the same direction: Genetically, humans differ individually within populations far more

population geneticists Geneticists who study the frequency of alleles, genotypes, and phenotypes in populations.

---

* See website: http://alfred.med.yale.edu.

than large geographical groups ("races") differ. Does this mean, as Richard Lewontin suggested more than 30 years ago (see p. 406), that there is no biological value in further study and scientific understanding of geographical races (ethic groups)? Even with all our new information, the answer is not entirely clear. Some of the newest genetic evidence from patterns of Alus (Bamshad et al., 2003) and microsatellites (Rosenberg et al., 2002) has found broad genetic correlations that quite consistently indicate accurately an individual's region of geographical ancestry. Some important cautions are needed, however. These geographically patterned genetic clusters are not "races" as traditionally defined—and so they aren't closely linked to simple patterns of phenotypic variation (such as skin color). Moreover, the correlations are broad, such that not all individuals can be easily classified, and many individuals, in fact, will likely be misclassified—even when using the best information incorporating dozens of loci.

This debate is not entirely academic, and it really never has been; just consider the destructive social impact caused over the last few centuries by misuse of the race concept. A contemporary continuation of the debate concerns the relationship of ancestry and disease. It has long been recognized that some disease-causing genes are more common in certain populations than in others (e.g., the allele causing sickle-cell anemia or that causing cystic fibrosis). The much more complete data on human DNA patterns have further expanded our knowledge,

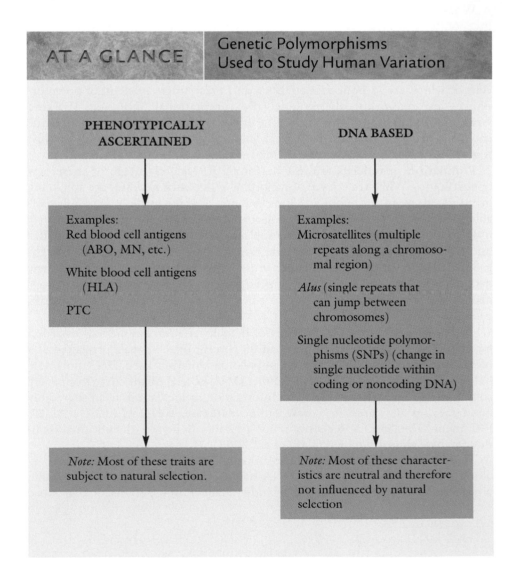

showing, for example, that some individuals are much more resistant than most people to HIV infection (see Chapter 15 for further discussion). Does this mean that a person's ancestry provides valuable medical information in screening or even treating certain diseases?

Some experts argue that such information is medically helpful (e.g., Rosenberg et al., 2002; Bamshad and Olson, 2003; Burchard et al., 2003). Moreover, official federal guidelines recently issued by the Food and Drug Administration recommend collection of ancestry ("race/ethnic identity") in all clinical trials testing new drugs. Other researchers, however, disagree and suggest that such information is, at best, tenuous (King and Motulsky, 2002) or not of any obvious medical use (e.g., Cooper et al., 2003).

Even the general public has weighed in on this issue, defeating in October 2003 a California ballot measure restricting the collection of "racial" or ethnic information on medical records. There is no easy answer to the questions we have raised, arguing all the more strongly for an informed public. The subject of race has been a contentious one, and anthropology and other disciplines have struggled to come to grips with it. Our new genetic tools have allowed us to expand our knowledge at a rate far beyond anything seen previously. But increased information alone does not permit us to fully address all human concerns. How we address diversity, individually and collectively, must balance the potential scientific benefits against a history of social costs.

Population Genetics

As we defined it in Chapter 4, a *population* is a group of interbreeding individuals. More precisely, a population is the group within which one is most likely to find a mate. As such, a population is marked by a degree of genetic relatedness and shares a common **gene pool**.

In theory, this is a straightforward concept. In every generation, the genes (alleles) are mixed by recombination and rejoined through mating. What emerges in the next generation is a direct product of the genes going into the pool, which in turn is a product of who is mating with whom.

In practice, however, defining and describing human populations is difficult. The largest population of *Homo sapiens* that could be described is the entire species. All members of a species are *potentially* capable of interbreeding, but are incapable of fertile breeding with members of other species. Our species is thus a *genetically closed system*. The problem arises not in describing who potentially can interbreed, but in isolating exactly the pattern of those individuals who are doing so.

Factors that determine mate choice are geographical, ecological, and social. If individuals are isolated on a remote island in the middle of the Pacific, there is not much chance of their finding a mate outside the immediate vicinity. Such **breeding isolates** are fairly easily defined and are a favorite target of microevolutionary studies. Geography plays a dominant role in producing these isolates by severely limiting the range of available mates. But even within these limits, cultural rules can easily play a deciding role by prescribing who is most appropriate among those who are potentially available.

Human population segments within the species are defined as groups with relative degrees of **endogamy** (marrying/mating within the group). These are, however, not totally closed systems. Gene flow often occurs between groups, and individuals may choose mates from distant localities. With the modern advent of rapid transportation, greatly accelerated rates of **exogamy** (marrying/mating outside the group) have emerged.

Most humans today are not so clearly defined as members of particular populations as they would be if they belonged to a breeding isolate. Inhabitants of

gene pool The total complement of genes shared by reproductive members of a population.

See Virtual Lab 2, sections I and II, for a discussion of populations and an example of the Hardy-Weinberg equilibrium.

breeding isolates Populations that are clearly isolated geographically and/or socially from other breeding groups.

endogamy Mating with individuals from the same group.

exogamy Mating pattern whereby individuals obtain mates from groups other than their own.

large cities may appear to be members of a single population, but within the city, social, ethnic, and religious boundaries crosscut in a complex fashion to form smaller population segments. In addition to being members of these highly open local population groupings, we are simultaneously members of overlapping gradations of larger populations—the immediate geographical region (a metropolitan area or perhaps an entire state), a section of the country, the whole nation, and, ultimately, the whole species.

Once specific human populations have been identified, the next step is to ascertain what evolutionary forces, if any, are operating on this group. To determine whether evolution is taking place at a given genetic locus, we measure allele frequencies for specific traits and compare these observed frequencies with a set predicted by a mathematical model called the **Hardy-Weinberg theory of genetic equilibrium**. This model provides us with a baseline set of evolutionary expectations under *known* conditions.

The Hardy-Weinberg theory of genetic equilibrium establishes a set of conditions in a population where *no* evolution occurs. In other words, none of the forces of evolution are acting, and all genes have an equal chance of recombining in each generation (i.e., there is random mating of individuals). More precisely, the hypothetical conditions that such a population would be *assumed* to meet are as follows:

1. The population is infinitely large. This condition eliminates the possibility of random genetic drift or changes in allele frequencies due to chance.
2. There is no mutation. Thus, no new alleles are being added by molecular changes in gametes.
3. There is no gene flow. There is no exchange of genes with other populations that can alter allele frequencies.
4. Natural selection is not operating. Specific alleles confer no advantage over others that might influence reproductive success.
5. Mating is random. There are no factors that influence who mates with whom. Thus, any female is assumed to have an equal chance of mating with any male.

If all these conditions are satisfied, allele frequencies won't change from one generation to the next (i.e., no evolution will take place), and a permanent equilibrium will be maintained as long as these conditions prevail. Using this equilibrium model, population geneticists have a standard against which they can compare actual circumstances. Note that the idealized conditions that define the Hardy-Weinberg equilibrium are just that: an idealized, *hypothetical* state. In the real world, no actual population would fully meet any of these conditions. But don't be confused by this distinction. By explicitly defining the genetic distribution that would be *expected* if *no* evolutionary change were occurring (i.e., in equilibrium), we can compare the *observed* genetic distribution obtained in real human populations.

If the observed frequencies differ from those of the expected model, we can then say that evolution is taking place at the locus in question. The alternative, of course, is that the observed and expected frequencies do not differ sufficiently to state with certainty that evolution is occurring at a locus in a population. Indeed, frequently this is the result that is obtained, and in such cases, population geneticists are unable to delineate evolutionary changes at the particular locus under study. Put another way, geneticists are unable to reject what statisticians call the *null hypothesis* (where *null* means "nothing," a statistical condition of randomness).

The simplest situation applicable to a microevolutionary study is a genetic trait that follows a simple Mendelian pattern and has only two alleles (*A, a*). As you recall from earlier discussions, there are then only three possible genotypes:

Hardy-Weinberg theory of genetic equilibrium The mathematical relationship expressing—under ideal conditions—the predicted distribution of alleles in populations; the central theorem of population genetics.

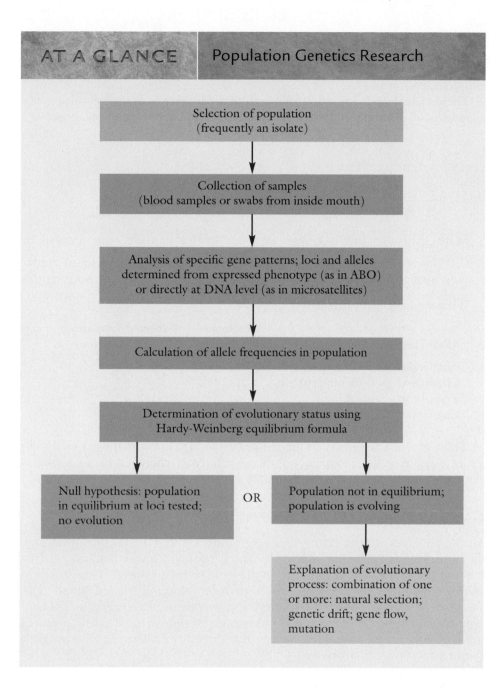

AA, Aa, aa. Proportions of these genotypes (*AA:Aa:aa*) are a function of the *allele frequencies* themselves (percentage of *A* and percentage of *a*). To provide uniformity for all genetic loci, a standard notation is employed to refer to these frequencies:

Frequency of dominant allele *(A)* = p
Frequency of recessive allele *(a)* = q

Since in this case there are only two alleles, their combined total frequency must represent all possibilities. In other words, the sum of their separate frequencies must be 1:

$$p \quad + \quad q \quad = 1 \text{ (100\% of alleles at the locus in question)}$$
(Frequency of *A* alleles) (Frequency of *a* alleles)

To ascertain the expected proportions of genotypes, we compute the chances of the alleles combining with one another into all possible combinations. Remember, they all have an equal chance of combining, and no new alleles are being added.

These probabilities are a direct function of the frequency of the two alleles. The chances of all possible combinations occurring randomly can be simply shown as

$$
\begin{array}{r}
p + q \\
\times \quad p + q \\
\hline
pq + q^2 \\
p^2 + pq \\
\hline
p^2 + 2pq + q^2
\end{array}
$$

Mathematically, this is known as a binomial expansion and can also be shown as

$$(p + q)(p + q) = p^2 + 2pq + q^2$$

What we have just calculated is simply:

Allele Combination	Genotype Produced	Expected Proportion in Population
Chances of A combining with A	AA	$p \times p = p^2$
Chances of A combining with a;	Aa	$p \times q$
a combining with A	aA	$p \times q$ = $2pq$
Chances of a combining with a	aa	$q \times q = q^2$

Thus, p^2 is the frequency of the AA genotype, $2pq$ is the frequency of the Aa genotype, and q^2 is the frequency of the aa genotype, where p is the frequency of the dominant allele and q is the frequency of the recessive allele in a population.

CALCULATING ALLELE FREQUENCIES

How geneticists use the Hardy-Weinberg formula is best demonstrated through an example. Let us assume that a population contains 200 individuals, and we will use the MN blood group locus as the gene to be measured. This gene produces a blood group antigen—similar to ABO—located on red blood cells. Because the M and N alleles are codominant, we can ascertain everyone's phenotype by taking blood samples and observing reactions with specially prepared antisera. From the phenotypes, we can then directly calculate the *observed* allele frequencies. So let us proceed.

All 200 individuals are tested, and the observed data for the three phenotypes are as follows:

Genotype	Number of individuals*	Percent	Number of Alleles M	N
MM	80	40	160	0
MN	80	40	80	80
NN	40	20	0	80
Totals	200	100	240 + 160	= 400
		Proportion	.6 + .4	= 1

---

* Each individual has two alleles. Thus, a person who is MM contributes two M alleles to the total gene pool. A person who is MN contributes one M and one N. Two hundred individuals, then, have 400 alleles for the MN locus.

From these observed results, we can count the number of *M* and *N* alleles and thus calculate the observed allele frequencies:

p = frequency of M = .6
q = frequency of N = .4

The total frequency of the two alleles combined should always equal 1. As you can see, they do.

Next, we need to calculate the expected genotypic proportions. This calculation comes directly from the Hardy-Weinberg equilibrium formula: $p^2 + 2pq + q^2$.

p^2 = (.6)(.6) = .36
$2pq$ = 2(.6)(.4) = 2(.24) = .48
q^2 = (.4)(.4) = .16

Total   1.00

There are only three possible genotypes: *MM, MN, NN*. The total of the relative proportions should equal 1. Again, as you can see, they do.

Finally, we need to compare the two sets of data—that is, the observed frequencies (what we actually found in the population) with the expected frequencies (those predicted by Hardy-Weinberg under conditions of genetic equilibrium). How do these two sets of data compare?

	Expected Frequency	Expected Number of Individuals	Observed Frequency	Actual Number of Individuals with Each Genotype
MM	.36	72	.40	80
MN	.48	96	.40	80
NN	.16	32	.20	40

We can see that although the match between observed and expected frequencies is not perfect, it is close enough statistically to satisfy equilibrium conditions. Since our population is not a large one, sampling may easily account for the small observed deviations. Our population is therefore probably in equilibrium (i.e., at this locus, it is not evolving). At the minimum, what we can say scientifically is that we cannot reject the null hypothesis.

Of course, sometimes the observed allele frequencies do vary sufficiently from equilibrium predictions to warrant rejection of the null hypothesis. For example, consider the locus influencing the tasting of PTC, an artificial chemical (see p. 81). What makes PTC tasting such a useful characteristic is its ease of ascertainment. Unlike blood antigens like ABO or MN, PTC tasting can be tested by simply having test subjects place a thin paper strip between their lips. This paper contains concentrated PTC, and individuals simply taste or do not taste its presence. Thus, testing is quick and inexpensive and does not expose anyone to the blood of others (a major concern, owing to the risks of HIV or hepatitis infection).

With such an efficient means of screening subjects, we now consider a sample population of 500 individuals. The results from observation of the phenotypes and calculations of expected genotypic proportions are shown in A Closer Look. Further examples of population genetics calculations can be found in Appendix C.

A CLOSER LOOK

Calculating Allele Frequencies: PTC Tasting in a Hypothetical Population

For the PTC tasting trait, it is assumed that there are two alleles, T and t. Moreover, while dominance is displayed, it is incomplete. Thus, it is theoretically possible to ascertain the phenotypes of heterozygotes. To simplify calculations for this example, we assume that *all* heterozygotes can be ascertained.

In our population of 500 individuals, the following observed phenotypic frequencies are found:

Genotype	Number of Individuals	Percent	Number of Alleles T	t
TT	125	25	250	0
Tt	325	65	325	325
tt	50	10	0	100
Totals	500	100	575	425

Thus, the observed allele frequencies are

$T(p) = .575$
$t(q) = .425$

The expected genotypic proportions are

$$p^2 = (.575)(.575) = .33$$
$$2pq = 2(.575)(.425) = .49$$
$$q^2 = (.425)(.425) = .18$$

Now we compare the observed and expected genotypic frequencies:

	Expected Frequency	Expected Number of Individuals	Observed Frequency	Actual Number of Individuals with Each Genotype
TT	.33	165	.25	125
Tt	.49	245	.65	325
tt	.18	90	.10	.50

These results show considerable departures of the observed genotypic proportions from those predicted under equilibrium conditions. Both types of homozygotes (*TT* and *tt*) are *less* commonly observed than expected, while the heterozygote (*Tt*) is *more* common than expected.

A statistical test (called a chi-square) can be performed to test the *statistical significance* of this difference. The results of this test are shown in Appendix C.

Evolution in Action: Modern Human Populations

Once a population has been defined, a population geneticist will ascertain whether allele frequencies are stable (i.e., in genetic equilibrium) or whether they are changing. As we have seen, the Hardy-Weinberg formula provides the tool to establish whether allele frequencies are indeed changing. What factors initiate changes in allele frequencies? There are a number of factors, including those that

1. Produce new variation (i.e., *mutation*)
2. Redistribute variation through *gene flow* or *genetic drift*
3. Select "advantageous" allele combinations that promote reproductive success (i.e., *natural selection*)

Note that factors 1 and 2 constitute the first stage of the evolutionary process, as first emphasized by the Modern Synthesis, while factor 3 is the second stage (see p. 92). There is yet another factor, as implied by the condition of genetic equilibrium that under idealized conditions all matings are random. Thus, the evolutionary alteration (i.e., deviation from equilibrium) is called **nonrandom mating**.

NONRANDOM MATING

Although sexual recombination does not itself alter *allele frequencies*, any consistent bias in mating patterns can alter the *genotypic proportions*. By affecting the frequencies of genotypes, nonrandom mating causes deviations from Hardy-Weinberg expectations of the proportions p^2, $2pq$, and q^2. It therefore sets the stage for the action of other evolutionary factors, particularly natural selection.

A variety of nonrandom mating, called assortative mating, occurs when individuals of either similar phenotypes (positive assortative mating) or dissimilar phenotypes (negative assortative mating) mate more often than expected by Hardy-Weinberg predictions. However, in the vast majority of human populations, neither factor appears to have much influence.

Inbreeding is a second type of nonrandom mating, and it can have both important medical and evolutionary consequences. Inbreeding occurs when relatives mate more often than expected. Such matings will increase the amount of homozygosity, since relatives who share close ancestors will more than likely also share more alleles than two unrelated people would. When relatives mate, their offspring have an increased probability of inheriting two copies of potentially harmful recessive alleles from a relative (perhaps a grandparent) that they share in common. Many potentially deleterious genes normally "masked" in heterozygous carriers may be expressed in offspring of consanguineous matings and thereby "exposed" to the action of natural selection. Among offspring of first-cousin matings in the United States, the risk of congenital disorders is 2.3 times greater than it is for the overall population. Matings between especially close relatives—incest—often lead to multiple genetic defects.

All societies have some sort of incest taboo banning matings between very close relatives, such as between parent and child or brother and sister. Therefore, these matings usually occur less frequently than predicted under random mating conditions.

Whether incest is strictly prohibited by social proscriptions or whether biological factors also interact to condition against such behavior has long been a topic of heated debate among anthropologists. For numerous social, economic, and ecological reasons, exogamy is an advantageous strategy for hunting and gathering bands. Moreover, selective pressures may also play a part, since highly inbred offspring have a greater chance of expressing a genetic disorder and thereby lowering their reproductive fitness. In addition, inbreeding reduces genetic variability among offspring, potentially reducing reproductive success (Murray, 1980). In this regard, it is interesting to note that incest avoidance is widespread among vertebrates. Moreover, detailed studies of free-ranging chimpanzees indicate that they usually avoid incestuous matings within their family group, although exceptions do occur (Constable et al., 2001). In fact, adults of at least one sex in most primate species consistently establish themselves and then mate within groups other than the one in which they were reared. Moreover, as we have seen, recognition of close kin apparently is an ability displayed by several (perhaps all) primates. Primatologists are currently investigating this fascinating aspect of our primate cousins (see p. 224). Apparently, both biological factors (in common with other primates) and uniquely human cultural factors have interacted during hominid evolution to produce this universal behavior pattern among contemporary societies.

nonrandom mating Patterns of mating in a population in which individuals choose mates preferentially.

inbreeding A type of nonrandom mating in which relatives mate more often than predicted under random mating conditions.

Human Biocultural Evolution

We have defined culture as the human strategy of adaptation. Human beings live in cultural environments that are continually modified by human activity; thus, evolutionary processes are understandable only within this *cultural* context. You will recall that natural selection pressures operate within specific environmental settings. For humans and many of our hominid ancestors, this means an environment dominated by culture. For example, the sickle-cell allele has not always been an important genetic factor in human populations. Before the development of agriculture, humans rarely, if ever, lived close to mosquito-breeding areas. With the spread in Africa of **slash-and-burn agriculture**, perhaps in just the last 2,000 years, penetration and clearing of tropical rain forests occurred. As a result of this deforestation, open, stagnant pools provided prime mosquito-breeding areas in close proximity to human settlements. DNA analyses have further confirmed such a recent origin and spread of the sickle-cell allele in West Africa. A recent study of a population from Senegal has estimated the origin of the Hb^S mutation in this group at between 1,250 and 2,100 y.a. (Currat et al., 2002).

Thus, quite recently, malaria, for the first time, struck human populations with its full impact, and as a selective force it was powerful indeed. No doubt, humans attempted to adjust culturally to these circumstances, and numerous biological adaptations also probably came into play. The sickle-cell trait is one of these biological adaptations. However, there is a definite cost involved with such an adaptation. Carriers have increased resistance to malaria and presumably higher reproductive success, but some of their offspring may be lost through the genetic disease sickle-cell anemia. So there is a counterbalancing of selective forces with an advantage for carriers *only* in malarial environments. The genetic patterns of recessive traits such as sickle-cell anemia are discussed in Chapter 4.

Following World War II, extensive DDT spraying by the World Health Organization began systematically to control mosquito-breeding areas in the tropics. Forty years of DDT spraying killed many mosquitoes, but natural selection, acting on these insect populations, produced several DDT-resistant strains (Fig. 14–5). Accordingly, malaria is again on the rise, with several hundred thousand new cases reported annually in India, Africa, and Central America.

A genetic trait (such as sickle-cell trait) that provides a reproductive advantage to the heterozygote in certain environments is a clear example of natural selection in action among human populations. The precise evolutionary mechanism in the sickle-cell example is termed a **balanced polymorphism**. A polymorphism, as we have defined it, is a trait with more than one allele at a locus in a population. But when a harmful allele (such as sickle-cell) has a higher frequency than can be accounted for by mutation alone, a fuller evolutionary explanation is required. In this case, the additional mechanism is natural selection.

This brings us back to the other part of the term *balanced polymorphism*. By "balanced," we are referring to the interaction of selective pressures operating in a malarial environment. Some individuals (mainly homozygous normals) will be removed by the infectious disease malaria and some (homozygous recessives) will die of the inherited disease sickle-cell anemia. Those with the highest reproductive success are the heterozygous carriers. But what alleles do they carry? Clearly, they are passing *both* the normal allele and the sickle-cell allele to offspring, thus maintaining both alleles at fairly high frequencies. Since one allele in this population will not significantly increase in frequency over the other allele, this situation will reach a balance and persist, at least as long as malaria continues to be a selective factor.

Another example of human biocultural evolution involves the ability to digest fresh milk. In all human populations, infants and young children have

slash-and-burn agriculture A traditional land-clearing practice whereby trees and vegetation are cut and burned. In many areas, fields are abandoned after a few years and clearing occurs elsewhere.

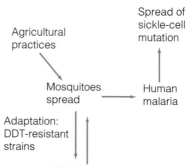

FIGURE 14–5 Evolutionary interactions affecting the frequency of the sickle-cell allele.

balanced polymorphism The maintenance of two or more alleles in a population due to the selective advantage of the heterozygote.

See Virtual Lab 2, section I, for a discussion of natural selection and variation.

this ability, an obvious necessity for any young mammal. One ingredient of milk is the sugar *lactose*, which is broken down in humans and other mammals by the enzyme *lactase*. In most mammals, including humans, the gene coding for lactase production "switches off" in adolescence. If too much milk is then ingested, the lactose ferments in the large intestine, leading to diarrhea and severe gastrointestinal upset. Among many African and Asian populations—a majority of humankind today—most adults are intolerant of milk (Table 14–2).

Evidence has suggested a simple dominant mode of inheritance for **lactose intolerance**. The environment also plays a role in expression of the trait—that is, whether a person will be lactose-intolerant—since intestinal bacteria can somewhat buffer the adverse effects. Because these bacteria will increase with previous exposure, some tolerance can be acquired, even in individuals who genetically have become lactase-deficient.

Why do we see variation in lactose tolerance among human populations? Throughout most of hominid evolution, milk was unavailable after weaning. Perhaps, in such circumstances, continued action of an unnecessary enzyme might inhibit digestion of other foods. Therefore, there *may* be a selective advantage for the gene coding for lactase production to switch off. So why can some adults (the majority in some populations) tolerate milk? The distribution of lactose-tolerant populations may provide an answer to this question, and it suggests a likely powerful cultural influence on this trait.

European groups, who are generally lactose-tolerant, are partially descended from groups of the Middle East. Often economically dependent on pastoralism, these groups raised cows and/or goats and no doubt drank considerable quantities of milk. In such a cultural environment, strong selection pressures would act to shift allele frequencies in the direction of more lactose tolerance. Modern European descendants of these populations apparently retain this ancient ability.

Even more informative is the distribution of lactose tolerance in Africa. For example, groups such as the Fulani and Tutsi, who have been pastoralists probably for thousands of years, have much higher rates of lactose tolerance than nonpastoralists. Within Africa, the population pattern has become somewhat complicated, however, perhaps as a result of recent gene flow (Powell et al., 2003).

As we have seen, the geographical distribution of lactose tolerance is related to a history of cultural dependence on fresh milk products. There are, however, some populations that rely on dairying but are not characterized by high rates of lactose tolerance (Fig. 14–6). It has been suggested that such populations traditionally have consumed their milk in the form of cheese and yogurt, in which the lactose has been broken down by bacterial action (Durham, 1981).

The interaction of human cultural environments and changes in lactose tolerance among human populations is another example of biocultural evolution. In the last few thousand years, cultural factors have initiated specific evolutionary changes in human groups. Such cultural factors have probably influenced the course of human evolution for at least 3 million years, and today they are of paramount importance.

TABLE 14–2 Frequencies of Lactose Intolerance

POPULATION GROUP	PERCENT
U.S. whites	2–19
Finnish	18
Swiss	12
Swedish	4
U.S. blacks	70–77
Ibos	99
Bantu	90
Fulani	22
Thais	99
Asian Americans	95–100
Native Australians	85

Source: Lerner and Libby, 1976, p. 327.

lactose intolerance The inability to digest fresh milk products, caused by the discontinued production of lactase, the enzyme that breaks down lactose, or milk sugar.

FIGURE 14–6 Natives of Mongolia rely heavily on milk products from goats and sheep, but mostly consume these foods in the form of cheese and yogurt.

© Michael S. Yamashita/CORBIS

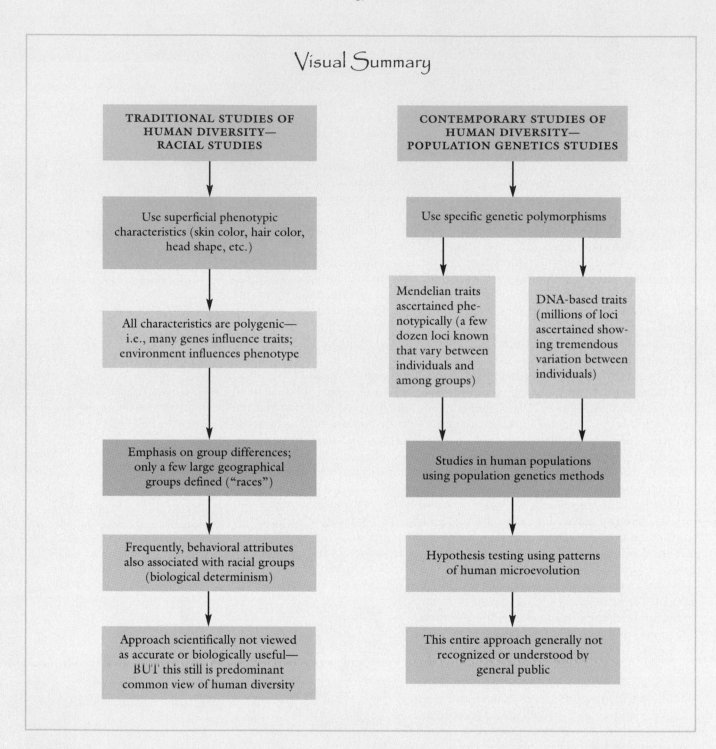

Visual Summary

TRADITIONAL STUDIES OF
HUMAN DIVERSITY—
RACIAL STUDIES

↓

Use superficial phenotypic
characteristics (skin color, hair color,
head shape, etc.)

↓

All characteristics are polygenic—
i.e., many genes influence traits;
environment influences phenotype

↓

Emphasis on group differences;
only a few large geographical
groups defined ("races")

↓

Frequently, behavioral attributes
also associated with racial groups
(biological determinism)

↓

Approach scientifically not viewed
as accurate or biologically useful—
BUT this still is predominant
common view of human diversity

CONTEMPORARY STUDIES OF
HUMAN DIVERSITY—
POPULATION GENETICS STUDIES

↓

Use specific genetic polymorphisms

↓

Mendelian traits
ascertained phe-
notypically (a few
dozen loci known
that vary between
individuals and
among groups)

DNA-based traits
(millions of loci
ascertained show-
ing tremendous
variation between
individuals)

↓

Studies in human populations
using population genetics methods

↓

Hypothesis testing using patterns
of human microevolution

↓

This entire approach generally not
recognized or understood by
general public

Summary

People obviously differ physically from each other, and some of this variation is superficially visible. Physically visible traits long used in attempts to classify humans into clearly defined groups ("races") have emphasized such features as skin color, hair color, hair form, head shape, and shape of the nose. However, all of these physical characteristics are influenced by numerous genetic loci and are also modified by the environment. As a result, these traditional markers of race are not reliable indicators of genetic relationships and are not biologically useful in depicting patterns of human diversity.

Since the middle of the twentieth century, more precise techniques have allowed far better understanding of actual patterns of *genetic* differences within our species. Initially, this genetic information was obtained from phenotypic expression of Mendelian traits such as blood groups.

For Further Thought

1. If biological race is, at best, a limited biological concept, why do the contemporary popular views of race/ethnicity have such a wide following? Do you think that these popular concepts contribute positively or negatively to human relationships?

Go to the book website at **http://www.anthropology.wadsworth.com** for resources to help you explore these questions further. Click on "For Further Thought" for this chapter.

Analysis of several of these genetic polymorphisms proved useful in showing broad patterns, such as the high degree of within-population variation and the relatively minor amount of beween-population variation.

Nevertheless, these phenotypically ascertained polymorphisms were limited in number and precision. Since the 1990s, the development and rapid application of genomics has drastically expanded genetic data. Armed with these powerful new tools, population geneticists now use an array of precisely defined DNA sequences to investigate human population variation. Such population studies are aimed at reconstructing the microevolutionary population history of *Homo sapiens* and understanding the varied roles of natural selection, genetic drift, gene flow, and mutation.

For humans, of course, culture also plays a crucial evolutionary role. Interacting with biological influences, these factors define the distinctive *biocultural* nature of human evolution. Two excellent examples of recent human biocultural evolution involve the sickle-cell allele and lactose tolerance.

Questions for Review

1. Imagine you are with a group of three friends discussing human diversity and the number of races. One friend asserts that there are three clearly defined races. A second disagrees, claiming there are five, while the third is positive that there are actually nine races. Would you agree with any of these views? Why or why not?
2. For the same group of friends mentioned in question 1 (none of whom have had a course in biological anthropology), how would you explain how scientific knowledge fits with their preconceived notions about human races?
3. Explain how the concept of race has developed in the Western world. What are the limitations of this approach?
4. In the twentieth century, how did the scientific study of human diversity change from the more traditional approach? Be sure to discuss *both* phenotypically ascertained polymorphisms and DNA-based polymorphisms.

5. Assume that you are a trained population geneticist, and you are about to begin a study of a human population. How will you select a population to study (one that can be defined fairly easily)? What kinds of characteristics will you measure in the group—and what kinds of methods/tools do you plan to use? Finally, what are you trying to learn about this population (in other words, what is your hypothesis)?

Suggested Further Reading

Bamstad, Michael J. and Steve E. Olson. 2003. "Does Race Exist?" *Scientific American* 289(Dec.):78–85.
Cavalli-Sforza, C.C. 2000. *Genes, People, and Languages.* New York: North Point Press.
Gould, Stephen Jay. 1981. *The Mismeasure of Man.* New York: Norton.
Olson, Steve. 2003. *Mapping Human History: Genes, Race, and Our Common Origins.* Boston: Mariner Books.
Relethford, John. 2003. *Reflections of Our Past. How Human History is Revealed in Our Genes.* Boulder, CO: Westview Press.

Online Anthropology Resource Center

Go to the Anthropology Resource Center at **http://www.anthropology.wadsworth.com** for a wealth of online resources, including a companion website for your text that provides study aids such as self-quizzes for each chapter and a practice final exam, as well as links to anthropology websites and information on the latest theories and discoveries in the field. Also, check out InfoTrac College Edition, your online library that offers full-length articles from thousands of scholarly and popular publications. Just click on the InfoTrac button at the companion website and use the passcode that came with your book.

Molecular Applications in Modern Human Biology

As you certainly have become aware, molecular data are immensely enhancing anthropological studies of modern human biology. For example, numerous researchers employing both mitochondrial and nuclear DNA are investigating population relationships spanning the last 100,000 years or so.

Anthropologists seeking to untangle more recent population relationships also make good use of these same techniques. Dozens of studies have been completed, and hundreds more are in progress. Here, it is feasible to review some recent and particularly fascinating examples of this research.

The Y chromosome, especially, has been a focus of innovative research. It provides a particularly useful genetic tool, since (like mtDNA) most of the loci on the Y chromosome do not recombine during sexual reproduction. Thus, excepting for mutation, gene sequences are passed intact over generations of related males. This general lack of recombination is only one feature of this often neglected and misunderstood chromosome. As two leading geneticists have put it, "Until recently, the Y chromosome seemed to fulfill the role of juvenile delinquent among human chromosomes—rich in junk, poor in useful attributes, reluctant to socialize with its neighbours and with an inescapable tendency to degenerate" (Jobling and Tyler-Smith, 2003, p. 598).

These same authors are quick to point out that in the last few years, great strides have been made in understanding the Y chromosome, including the identification of hundreds of SNPs, microsatellites, 27 coding loci (which produce proteins), and a small number of loci that can recombine (cross over) with homologous regions on the X chromosome. Remarking on these latest advances, geneticists Mark Jobling and Chris Tyler-Smith conclude, "Y-chromosome research is growing up" (2003, p. 598).

Indeed, it is no longer the "juvenile delinquent" of the human genome. In the last decade, along with tremendously enhanced information coming from mtDNA, the X chromosome, and autosomes, Y chromosome molecular sequences have helped elucidate modern human origins (Underhill et al., 2001; Jobling and Tyler-Smith, 2003). Moreover, numerous microevolutionary insights have also been recently gained, such as those showing (1) aspects of a Bantu expansion in Africa in the last 3,000

years; (2) the gradual occupation of Europe by early farmers (in the last 5,000 plus years); (3) the imprint of genetic drift in small northern Asian populations; and (4) a quite recent occupation (dating to 20,000–10,000 y.a.) of the New World by North Asians. It should be emphasized that in all these cases, genetic data are used in correlation with (and strongly corroborate) archaeological evidence.

The most fascinating new finding traces an expansion of Mongols from central Asia, probably sometime in the last 1,000 years (c. 1,300–700 y.a.). An unusual Y chromosome variant is found in about 8 percent of Asians today (i.e., a total of 1/200 of all males in the world). Furthermore, the geographical patterns of genotypes traces back to Mongolia—and likely spread from there to its present distribution stretching from northeast China to Uzbekistan.

This genetic pattern is most remarkable and can't be easily accounted for by natural selection. Alternatively, a team of international investigators has proposed a form of "social selection" in which only a few related males fathered a disproportionately large number of descendants (Zerjal et al., 2003). Presumably, these active and highly successful men began spreading their genes in earnest not long before A.D. 1300.

Assembling these clues, Tatiana Zerjal, Chris Tyler-Smith (both from Oxford University), and colleagues raise a tantalizing suggestion. Was it Genghis Kahn himself who happened to inherit this Y chromosome and who then passed it to potentially dozens of sons (with many, in turn, also producing large broods)?

The timing and geography support this interesting hypothesis. Genghis Kahn (1162–1227) lived almost 800 years ago, and, presumably one of his direct male ancestors first possessed this unique Y chromosome variant. Today, more than 15 million men have this same (or nearly identical) Y chromosome. How did it spread so quickly, and from where did it originate? Allele frequency distribution strongly points to Mongolia as the area of origin. Moreover, the broader geographical pattern of contemporary high frequency of this genotype nearly exactly coincides with the extent of the Mongol empire at the time of Genghis Kahn's death (Fig. 1).

So, was it the great Kahn who is responsible—and are all these 15 million living males his direct descendants?

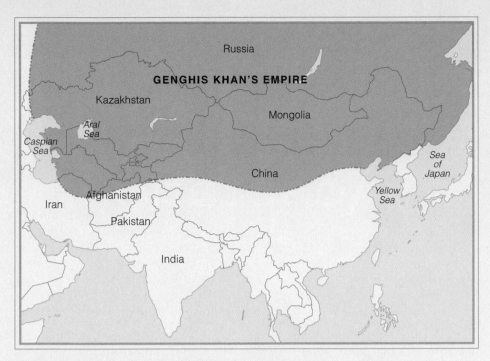

FIGURE 1 The extent of the empire of Genghis Kahn at the time of his death.

Source: Adapted from *Science News,* February 8, 2003, Vol. 163, No. 6, p. 91.

Perhaps. Certainly, some small group of Asian males who lived about 800 years ago is responsible. And most likely, the males were part of the Mongol empire, perhaps soldiers (who tend to get around widely and reproduce). It is not at all impossible that it was the greatest Mongol warrior of all (and his sons) who had the most mates and thus spread their genes very quickly indeed.

One last tantalizing avenue of investigation might just help seal the case. Currently, archaeologists are excavating a site in Mongolia that might be the location of Genghis Kahn's tomb (Travis, 2003). *If* it is, and *if* ancient DNA can be extracted and analyzed (including nuclear DNA), then just maybe we will get a final solution to this mystery!

Sources

Jobling, Mark A., and Chris Tyler-Smith. 2003. "The Human Y Chromosome: An Evolutionary Marker Comes of Age." *Nature Reviews Genetics* 4:598–612.

Travis, John. 2003. "Genghis Kahn's Legacy?" *Science News* 163:91.

Underhill, P.A., G. Passarino, A.A. Lin, et al. 2001. "The Paleogeography of the Y Chromosome Binary Haplotypes and the Origins of Modern Human Populations." *Annals of Human Genetics* 65:43–62.

Zerjel, Tatiana, Yali Xue, Giorgio Bertorelle, et al. 2003. "The Genetic Legacy of the Mongols." *American Journal of Human Genetics* 72:717–721.

15

Modern Human Biology: Patterns of Adaptation

Composite satellite image
Courtesy, Craig Mayhew and Robert Simmon, NASA

See the following sections of the CD-ROM for topics covered in this chapter: Virtual Lab 2, sections III and IV.

Key Questions

Can patterns of evolution in contemporary human populations be linked to the role of natural selection?

Are there particular environmental (selective) factors to which human populations have adapted?

Introduction

We've all heard it said: "No two people are alike." It's a time-worn expression, but it's true, and now that we're approaching the end of this book, you should know why. One exception to this old adage is identical twins, who are genetically the same, but even they have personality differences, and you should also know why this is true.

In previous chapters, we explored the genetic bases for biological variation within and between human populations. We also discussed how, as a species, humans are remarkably genetically uniform compared with our closest primate relatives. And we've placed these discussions within an evolutionary framework by emphasizing the roles of natural selection and genetic drift in human evolution.

Given this foundation, we can turn our attention to some of the factors that have challenged us through our evolutionary journey and consider how we've met these challenges as a species, as populations, and as individuals. With the exception of the oceans, the highest mountains, and Antarctica, we have managed to colonize the entire planet. But this hasn't been an easy task, and we've had to adapt biologically and culturally to ultraviolet (UV) radiation, altitude differences, temperature extremes, and infectious diseases.

The Adaptive Significance of Human Variation

Today, biological anthropologists view human variation as the result of such evolutionary factors as genetic drift, founder effect, gene flow, and adaptations to environmental conditions, both past and present. Cultural adaptations have certainly played a critical role in the evolution of *Homo sapiens,* and although in this discussion we are primarily concerned with biological issues, we must still consider the influence of cultural practices on human adaptive responses.

All organisms need to maintain the normal functions of internal organs, tissues, and cells in order to survive, and this task must be accomplished within the context of an ever-changing environment. Even during the course of a single, seemingly uneventful day, there are numerous fluctuations in temperature, wind, solar radiation, humidity, and so on. Physical activity also places **stress** on physiological mechanisms. The body must accommodate all these changes by compensating in some manner to maintain internal constancy, or **homeostasis,** and all life forms have evolved physiological mechanisms that, within limits, achieve this goal.

Physiological response to environmental change is influenced by genetic factors. We have already defined adaptation as a functional response to environmental conditions in populations and individuals. In a narrower sense, adaptation refers to *long-term* evolutionary (i.e., genetic) changes that characterize all individuals within a population or species.

stress In a physiological context, any factor that acts to disrupt homeostasis; more precisely, the body's response to any factor that threatens its ability to maintain homeostasis.

homeostasis A condition of balance, or stability, within a biological system, maintained by the interaction of physiological mechanisms that compensate for changes (both external and internal).

acclimatization Physiological responses to changes in the environment that occur during an individual's lifetime. Such responses may be temporary or permanent, depending on the duration of the environmental change and when in the individual's life it occurs. The *capacity* for acclimatization may typify an entire species or population, and because it is under genetic influence, it is subject to evolutionary factors such as natural selection or genetic drift.

See Virtual Lab 2, section IV, for an exercise on the adaptive significance of skin color.

Examples of long-term adaptations in *Homo sapiens* include some physiological responses to heat (sweating) or excessive levels of ultraviolet (UV) light (deeply pigmented skin near the equator). These characteristics are the results of evolutionary change in our species or in populations, and they don't vary as the result of short-term environmental change. For example, the ability to sweat isn't lost in people who spend their lives in predominantly cool areas. Likewise, individuals born with dark skin don't become pale, even if never exposed to intense sunlight.

Acclimatization is another type of physiological response to environmental conditions that can be short-term, long-term, or even permanent. The physiological responses to environmental stressors are at least partially influenced by genetic factors, but some can also be affected by duration and severity of the exposure, technological buffers (e.g., shelter, clothing), individual behavior, weight, and overall body size.

Hanna (1999) describes three main types of acclimatization. The simplest is a temporary and rapid adjustment to an environmental alteration. As we are about to discuss, tanning is an example of this type. Another example is one you may not know about, although you have probably experienced it, and that is the very rapid increase in hemoglobin production that occurs when people who live at lower elevations travel to higher ones (see p. 434). In both these examples, the physiological changes are temporary. Tans fade when exposure to sunlight is reduced, and hemoglobin production drops to original levels following a return to lower elevations.

A second type of acclimatization is permanent since, after exposure has ceased, the physical adjustments don't disappear. The third form, *developmental* acclimatization, results from exposure to an environmental challenge during growth and development. Because this kind of acclimatization is incorporated into an individual's physiology, it isn't reversible. An example of developmental acclimatization is the physiological responses we see in lifelong residents of high altitude (see p. 434).

In the following section, we present some of the many examples of how humans respond to environmental challenges. Some of these examples describe adaptations that characterize our entire species. Others are shared by most or all members of only certain populations. And a few illustrate the process of acclimatization in individuals.

SOLAR RADIATION AND SKIN COLOR

Skin color is commonly cited as an example of adaptation by natural selection in human populations. In general, pigmentation in indigenous populations prior to European contact (beginning around 1500) follows a particular geographical distribution, especially in the Old World. Figure 15–1 illustrates that populations with the most pigmentation are found in the tropics, while lighter skin color is associated with more northern latitudes, especially the long-term inhabitants of northwestern Europe.

There are three substances that influence skin color: hemoglobin, the protein carotene, and, most important, the pigment *melanin*. Melanin is a granular substance produced by specialized cells called melanocytes, located in the outer layer of the skin (see Fig. 15–3 on p. 426). All humans have approximately the same number of melanocytes, but they vary in the amount of melanin they produce and the size of the melanin granules.

Melanin is important because it acts as a built-in sunscreen by absorbing potentially dangerous ultraviolet (UV) rays that are present, but not visible, in sunlight. Therefore, melanin protects us from overexposure to UV radiation, which frequently causes genetic mutations in skin cells. These mutations can lead to skin cancer, which, if left untreated, can eventually spread to other organs and even result in death (see A Closer Look on p. 428).

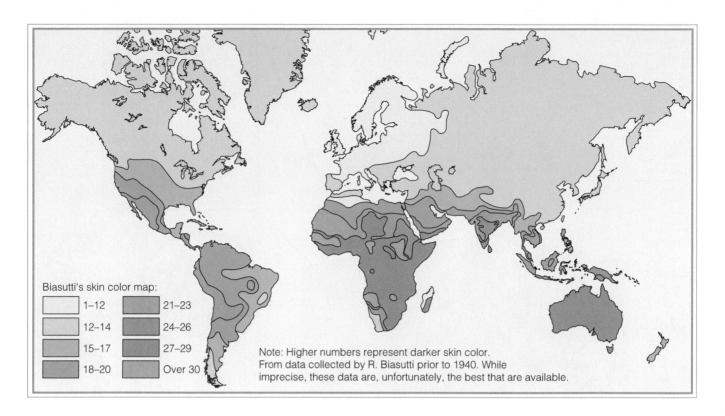

Biasutti's skin color map:

1–12		21–23	
12–14		24–26	
15–17		27–29	
18–20		Over 30	

Note: Higher numbers represent darker skin color. From data collected by R. Biasutti prior to 1940. While imprecise, these data are, unfortunately, the best that are available.

FIGURE 15–1 Geographical distribution of skin color in indigenous human populations. (After Biasutti, 1959.)

As we previously mentioned, exposure to sunlight triggers a protective mechanism in the form of tanning, the result of temporarily increased melanin production (acclimatization). This response occurs in all humans except albinos, who carry a genetic mutation that prevents their melanocytes from producing melanin (Fig. 15–2). But even humans who do produce melanin differ in their ability to tan. For instance, many people of northern European descent tend to have very fair skin, blue eyes, and light hair. Their cells obviously produce small amounts of melanin, but when exposed to sunlight, they have little ability to increase production. And, in all populations, women tend not to tan as deeply as men.

Natural selection has favored dark skin in areas nearest the equator, where the sun's rays are most direct and thus where exposure to UV light is most intense and constant. In considering the cancer-causing effects of UV radiation from an *evolutionary* perspective, three points must be kept in mind:

1. Early hominids lived in the tropics, where solar radiation is more intense than in temperate areas to the north and south.
2. Unlike modern city dwellers, early hominids spent their days outdoors.
3. Early hominids didn't wear clothing that would have protected them from the sun.

Given these conditions, UV radiation was probably a powerful agent selecting for optimum levels of melanin production in early humans, especially as they migrated out of the tropics.

However, there is an important objection to this theory. As we mentioned in Chapter 4, natural selection can act only on traits that affect reproduction. Because cancers tend to occur later in life, after the reproductive years, it should theoretically be difficult for selection to act effectively against any factor that might predispose people to cancer. But in one African study, it was shown that all albino individuals in dark-skinned populations of Nigeria and Tanzania had either precancerous lesions or skin cancer by the age of 20 (Robins, 1991). This evidence suggests that even in early humans of reproductive age, less pigmented skin could have reduced individual reproductive fitness in regions of intense sunlight.

FIGURE 15–2 An African albino. This young man has a greatly increased likelihood of developing skin cancer.

Norman Lightfoot/Photo Researchers

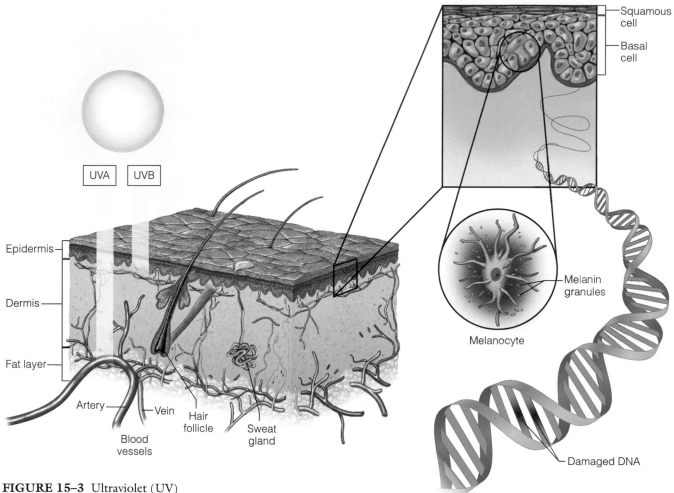

FIGURE 15–3 Ultraviolet (UV) rays penetrate the skin and can eventually damage DNA within skin cells. The three major types of cells that can be affected are squamous cells, basal cells, and melanocytes. (See also A Closer Look on p. 428.)

neural tube In early embryonic development, the anatomical structure that develops to form the brain and spinal cord.

spina bifida A condition in which the arch of one or more vertebrae fails to fuse and form a protective barrier around the spinal cord.

Jablonski (1992) and Jablonski and Chaplin (2000) have provided substantial evidence for an additional explanation for the distribution of skin color, one that proposes an even greater role for natural selection than skin cancer. This research concerns the degradation of folate by UV radiation. Folate is a B vitamin that is not stored in the body and must be replenished through dietary sources. Adequate levels of folate are required for many developmental processes, including DNA synthesis, red blood cell formation, and, in males, sperm production. In pregnant women, insufficient levels of folate are associated with numerous fetal developmental disorders, including **neural tube** defects such as **spina bifida.** The consequences of severe neural tube defects can include pain, infection, paralysis, and failure of the brain to develop. Given the importance of folate to many processes related to reproduction, it is clear that maintaining adequate levels of this vitamin contributes to indvidual reproductive fitness.

A number of studies have shown that UV radiation rapidly depletes folate serum levels both in laboratory experiments and in light-skinned individuals. These findings have implications for pregnant women, children, and for the evolution of dark skin in early hominids. Jablosnki (1992) proposed that the earliest hominids may have had light body skin covered with dark hair, as is seen in chimpanzees and gorillas (who have darker skin on exposed body parts, e.g., faces and hands). But as loss of body hair in occurred hominids, dark skin evolved as a protective response to the damaging effects of UV radiation on folate.

The folate hypothesis doesn't contradict the importance of the relationship between UV radiation and skin cancer. In fact, it reinforces the argument that UV radiation has been a major selective force in the geographical distribution of human skin color.

As hominids migrated out of Africa into Asia and Europe, they faced new selective pressures. In particular, those populations that eventually occupied northern Europe encountered cold temperatures and cloudy skies, sometimes during summer as well as in winter. Winter also meant fewer hours of daylight, and with the sun well to the south, solar radiation was indirect. Moreover, to survive the cold, these populations used fire and wore animal skins and other types of clothing. Brace and Montagu (1977) proposed that as a consequence of reduced exposure to sunlight, the advantages of deeply pigmented skin in the tropics no longer applied and selection for melanin production may have been relaxed.

However, relaxed selection for dark skin is probably not adequate to explain the very depigmented skin seen in some northern Europeans. In fact, the need for a physiological UV filter conflicted with another biological necessity as people moved into areas with less direct solar radiation. That necessity was probably the production of vitamin D, and the theory concerning the role of vitamin D is called the *vitamin D hypothesis.*

Vitamin D is essential for the mineralization and normal growth of bone during infancy and childhood because it enables the body to absorb calcium (the major source of bone mineral) from dietary sources. (Vitamin D is also required for the continued mineralization of skeletal tissue in adults.) Many foods, including fish oils, egg yolk, butter, cream, and liver, are good sources of vitamin D. But the body's primary source of vitamin D is its own ability to synthesize it through the interaction of UV light and a form of cholesterol found in skin cells. Therefore, if normal bone growth is to occur, adequate exposure to sunlight is essential. Insufficient amounts of vitamin D during childhood result in *rickets,* a condition that leads to bone deformities throughout the skeleton, especially the weight-bearing bones of the legs and pelvis. Thus, people with rickets frequently have bowed legs and pelvic deformities (Fig. 15–4). Pelvic deformities are of particular concern for women, since they can lead to a narrowing of the birth canal, which, in the absence of surgical intervention, frequently results in the death of both mother and infant during childbirth.

The vitamin D hypothesis hasn't gone unchallenged. Robins (1991) has argued that rickets in modern populations primarily affects people living in industrial cities who work indoors. Furthermore, in the past, people would have spent a great deal of time outdoors and would have had sufficient exposure to UV radiation during spring and summer to produce enough vitamin D to be stored in body tissues through the winter months.

But rickets, although very important, may not be the only factor involved in the development of less pigmented skin. A related factor is probably reflected in the fact that in all populations, the average skin color in females (as measured by the reflection of light from the skin's surface) is significantly lighter than that of males. This at least suggests that women require higher levels of vitamin D than men because of their increased demands for calcium during pregnancy and lactation.

Jablonski and Chaplin (2000), however, have looked at the *potential* for vitamin D synthesis in people of different skin color based on the yearly average UV radiation at various latitudes (Fig. 15–5 on p. 430). Their conclusions support the vitamin D hypothesis to the point of stating that the requirement of vitamin D synthesis in northern latitudes was as important to natural selection as the need for protection from UV radiation in tropical regions.

There is substantial evidence, both historically and in contemporary populations, to support the vitamin D hypothesis. During the latter decades of the nineteenth century, African Americans in northern cities suffered a higher incidence

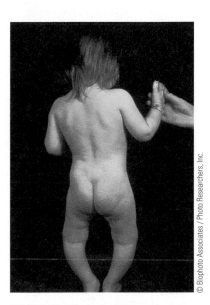

FIGURE 15–4 A child with rickets.

© Biophoto Associates / Photo Researchers, Inc.

A CLOSER LOOK

Skin Cancer and UV Radiation

Even though we know we can't live without it, most people tend to take their skin for granted. The many functions of this complex organ (and skin *is* an organ) are vital to life. Yet most of us thoughtlessly expose our skin to any number of environmental assaults and especially abuse it with overexposure to the sun, practically to the point of charbroil. Thus, we think it appropriate to examine a little more closely this watertight, evolutionary achievement that permits us to live on land, just as it allowed some vertebrates to leave the oceans several hundred million years ago.

Skin is composed of two layers, the epidermis and, just beneath it, the dermis (see Fig. 15–3). The upper portion of the epidermis is made up of flattened, somewhat overlapping *squamous* cells. Below these scale-like cells, near the base of the epidermis, lie several layers of round *basal* cells, and interspersed within them are still two other cell types: *melanocytes,* which produce melanin, and *keratinocytes,* which are involved in vitamin D synthesis.

Skin cells are continuously produced at the base of the epidermis through mitosis, and as they mature, they migrate to the surface, becoming flattened and avascular (i.e., they have no direct blood supply). Approximately one month after they have formed, they die in a process of genetically directed cellular suicide. The results of this suicidal act are the little white flakes people with dry skin are uncomfortably aware of. (Incidentally, a major constituent of common household dust is dead skin cells!)

The dermis is composed of connective tissue and many structures, including blood vessels, lymphatic vessels, sweat glands, oil glands, and hair follicles. Together, the epidermis and dermis allow the body to retain fluid, help regulate body temperature, synthesize a number of essential substances, and provide protection from ultraviolet (UV) radiation.

There are three main types of UV radiation, but we are concerned with only two: UVA and UVB. UVA has the longest wavelength and can penetrate through to the bottom of the dermis, while the medium-length UVB waves usually penetrate only to the basal layer of the epidermis (see Fig. 15–3).

The stimulation of vitamin D production by UVB waves is the only benefit we get from exposure to UV radiation. Following a sunburn, both UVB and UVA rays cause short-term suppression of the immune system. But because UVB is directly absorbed by the DNA within cells, potentially causing genetic damage, we face a much greater threat from skin cancer,

You know that cancers are tumorous growths that invade organs, a process that often results in death, even after treatment. But you may not know that a cell becomes cancerous when a carcinogenic agent, such as UV radiation, damages its DNA—and some DNA segments are more susceptible than others. The damage allows the affected cell to divide unchecked. Each subsequent generation of cells receives the mutant DNA, and with it, the potential to divide indefinitely. Eventually, cancer cells form a mass that invades other tissues. They can also break away from the original tumor and travel through the circulatory or lymphatic system to other parts of the body, where they establish themselves and continue to divide. For example, cells from lung tumors (frequently caused by carcinogenic agents in tobacco) can travel to the brain or parts of the skeleton and develop tumors in these new sites before the lung tumor is even detectable.

All three types of cells in the epidermis are susceptible to cancerous changes. The most common form of skin cancer is basal cell carcinoma (BCC), which affects about 800,000 people per year in the United States. Fortunately, BCCs are slow growing and, if detected early, can be successfully removed before they spread. They can appear as a raised lump and be uncolored, red-brown, or black (Fig.1a).

Squamous cell carcinomas (SCC) are the second most common skin cancer (Fig. 1b). They grow faster than BCCs, but they, too, are amenable to treatment if detected reasonably early. They usually appear as firm pinkish lesions and may spread rapidly on skin exposed to sunlight.

The third form is malignant melanoma, a cancer of the melanocytes. Melanoma is thought to be caused by UVA radiation, and it accounts for only about 4 percent of all skin cancers. But while it's the least common of the three, melanoma is the fastest growing and the deadliest,

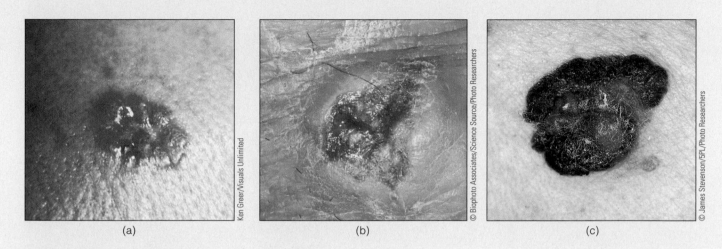

(a)   (b)   (c)

FIGURE 1 (a) Basal cell carcinoma. (b) Squamous cell carcinoma. (c) Malignant melanoma.

killing 30 to 40 percent of affected people. Melanoma looks like an irregularly shaped, very dark or black mole (Fig. 1c). In fact, it may be a mole that has changed because some of its cells have been damaged. It's extremely important to notice any changes in a mole or the appearance of a new dark, perhaps roughened spot on the skin and to have it examined as soon as possible. If a melanoma is less than a millimeter deep, it can be removed before it spreads. But if it has progressed into the dermis, the likelihood that it has already spread to other tissues is high.

Brash et al (1991) and Ziegler et al (1994) determined that the underlying genetic factor in a majority of nonmelanoma skin cancers is a mutation of a gene called *p53* located on chromosome 17. This gene produces a protein, also called p53, which prevents any cell (not just skin cells) with damaged DNA from dividing until the damage is repaired. In addition, if the damage to a cell's DNA is too severe to repair, the p53 protein can cause the cell to die. Hence, *p53* is what is known as a tumor suppressor gene (Vogelstein et al., 2000).

Unfortunately, the *p53* gene is itself susceptible to mutation, and when certain mutations occur, it can no longer prevent cancer cells from dividing. Luckily, there are other tumor suppressor genes. In fact, damaged *p53* genes don't appear to be involved in melanoma. Instead, a UV-induced mutation in another tumor suppressor gene on chromosome 9 appears to be the culprit (NCBI, 2003).

BCCs and SCCs tend to appear in middle age long after the underlying genetic damage occurred during childhood and adolescence. If you've had even one serious sunburn in your youth, your odds of developing one of the nonmelanoma skin cancers have increased dramatically. Malignant melanomas can occur at any age, although the DNA damage can precede the development of cancer by several years. The best advice is don't take the threat of skin cancer lightly, and don't overexpose your skin to the sun. Wear a hat and a broad-based sun block that will filter out both UVA and UVB rays. In other words, do your best to keep your tumor suppressor genes happy.

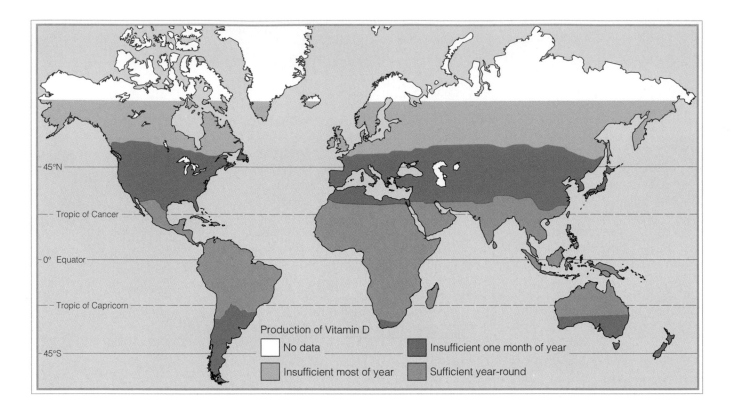

FIGURE 15–5 Populations indigenous to the tropics (blue band) receive sufficient UV radiation for vitamin D synthesis (year-round). The darker brown band represents areas where people with moderately melanized skin do not receive sufficient UV light for vitamin D synthesis for one month of the year. The lighter brown band represents an area where even light skin does not receive enough UV light for vitamin D synthesis on a yearly basis. (Adapted from Jablonski and Chaplin, 2000, 2002.)

Production of Vitamin D
- No data
- Insufficient most of year
- Insufficient one month of year
- Sufficient year-round

of rickets than African Americans who lived in the southern states, where exposure to sunlight is greater. (The supplementation of milk with vitamin D was initiated to correct this problem.) Another example is seen in Britain, where darker-skinned East Indians and Pakistanis show a higher incidence of rickets than whites (Molnar, 1983; Henderson et al., 1987).

Except for a person's sex (and consequently, gender) more social importance has been attached to skin color than to any other single human biological trait. Obviously, there is no reason this should be so. Aside from its probable adaptive significance relative to UV radiation, skin color is no more important physiologically than many other biological characteristics. But from an evolutionary perspective, skin color provides an outstanding example of how the forces of natural selection have produced geographically patterned variation as the consequence of two conflicting selective forces: the need for protection from overexposure to UV radiation, on the one hand, and the need for adequate UV exposure for vitamin D synthesis on the other.

THE THERMAL ENVIRONMENT

Mammals and birds have evolved complex mechanisms to maintain a constant internal body temperature. While reptiles must rely on exposure to external heat sources to raise body temperature and energy levels, mammals and birds possess physiological mechanisms that, within certain limits, increase or reduce the loss of body heat. The optimum body temperature for normal cellular functions is species-specific, and for humans it is approximately 98.6°F.

Homo sapiens is found in a wide variety of habitats, with thermal environments ranging from exceedingly hot (in excess of 120°F) to bitter cold (less than −60°F). In such extremes, particularly cold, human life would not be possible without cultural innovations. But even accounting for the artificial environments in which we live, such external conditions place the human body under enormous stress.

Response to Heat All available evidence suggests that the earliest hominids evolved in the warm-to-hot woodlands and savannas of East Africa. The fact that humans cope better with heat (especially dry heat) than they do with cold is testimony to the long-term adaptations to heat that evolved in our ancestors.

In humans, as well as certain other species, such as horses, sweat glands are distributed throughout the skin. This wide distribution of sweat glands makes it possible to lose heat at the body's surface through evaporative cooling, a mechanism that has evolved to the greatest degree in humans. In fact, perspiration is the most important factor in heat dissipation in humans.

The capacity to dissipate heat by sweating is seen in all human populations to an almost equal degree, with the average number of sweat glands per individual (approximately 1.6 million) being fairly constant. However, there is variation since people who aren't generally exposed to hot conditions do experience a period of acclimatization that initially involves significantly increased perspiration rates (Frisancho, 1993). An additional factor that enhances the cooling effects of sweating is increased exposure of the skin through reduced amounts of body hair. We do not know when in our evolutionary history loss of body hair occurred, but it represents a species-wide adaptation.

Heat reduction through evaporation can be expensive, and indeed dangerous, in terms of water and sodium loss. Up to 3 liters of water can be lost per hour by an average human engaged in heavy work in high heat. The importance of this fact can be appreciated if you consider that the loss of 1 liter of water is approximately equivalent to losing 1.5 percent of total body weight, and loss of 10 percent of body weight can be life threatening. Therefore, it is essential that water be continuously replaced during exercise in heat.

There are two basic types of heat, arid and humid. Arid environments, such as those of the southwestern United States, the Middle East, and much of Africa, are characterized by high temperatures, wind, and low water vapor. Humid heat is associated with increased water vapor and is found in regions with a great deal of vegetation and precipitation, typical of the eastern and southern United States, parts of Europe, and much of the tropics. Because the increased water vapor in humid climates inhibits the evaporation of sweat on the skin's surface, humans adjust much more readily to dry heat. In fact, people exercising in dry heat may be unaware that they are sweating because the perspiration evaporates as soon as it reaches the surface of the skin. While rapid evaporation increases comfort, it can lead to dehydration. Therefore, in dry heat it's important to continue to drink water, even if you aren't aware of how much you are actually losing.

Another mechanism for radiating body heat is **vasodilation,** whereby capillaries near the skin's surface widen to permit increased blood flow to the skin. The visible effect of vasodilation is flushing, or increased redness of the skin, particularly of the face, accompanied by warmth. But the physiological effect is to permit heat, carried by the blood from the interior of the body, to be emitted from the skin's surface to the surrounding air. (Some drugs, including alcohol, also produce vasodilation, which accounts for the increased redness and warmth of the face in some people after a couple of drinks.)

Body size and proportions are also important in regulating body temperature. In fact, there seems to be a general relationship between climate and body size and shape in birds and mammals. In general, within a species, body size (weight) increases as distance from the equator increases. In humans, this relationship holds up fairly well, but there are numerous exceptions.

Two rules that pertain to the relationship between body size, body proportions, and climate are *Bergmann's rule* and *Allen's rule.*

1. *Bergmann's rule (concerns the relationship of body mass or volume to surface area):* Among mammals, body size tends to be greater in populations that live in colder climates. This is because as mass increases, the relative amount

vasodilation Expansion of blood vessels, permitting increased blood flow to the skin. Vasodilation permits warming of the skin and also facilitates radiation of warmth as a means of cooling. Vasodilation is an involuntary response to warm temperatures, various drugs, and even emotional states (blushing).

of surface area decreases proportionately. Because heat is lost at the surface, it follows that increased mass allows for greater heat retention and reduced heat loss. (Remember our discussion of basal metabolic rate and body size in Chapter 7.)

2. *Allen's rule (concerns shape of body, especially appendages):* In colder climates, shorter appendages, with increased mass-to-surface ratios, are adaptive because they are more effective at preventing heat loss. Conversely, longer appendages, with increased surface area relative to mass, are more adaptive in warmer climates because they promote heat loss.

According to these rules, the most suitable body shape in hot climates is linear with long arms and legs. In a cold climate, a more suitable body type is stocky with shorter limbs. Considerable data gathered from several human populations generally conform to these principles. In colder climates, body mass tends, on average, to be greater and characterized by a larger trunk relative to arms and legs (Roberts, 1973). People living in the Arctic tend to be short and stocky, while many sub-Saharan Africans, especially the East African pastoralists, are tall and linear (Fig. 15–6). But there's a lot of human variability regarding body proportions, and not all populations conform so obviously to Bergmann's and Allen's rules.

Response to Cold Human physiological responses to cold increase heat production and enhance heat retention. Of the two, heat retention is more efficient because less energy is required. This is an important point because energy is derived from dietary sources. Unless food resources are abundant, and in winter they frequently aren't, any factor that conserves energy can have adaptive value.

Short-term responses to cold include increased metabolic rate and shivering, both of which generate body heat, at least for a short time. **Vasoconstriction,** another short-term response, restricts heat loss and conserves energy. In addition, humans possess a subcutaneous (beneath the skin) fat layer that serves as insulation throughout the body. Behavioral modifications include increased activity, increased food consumption, and even curling up into a ball.

Increases in metabolic rate (the rate at which cells break up nutrients into their components) release energy in the form of heat. Shivering also generates muscle heat, as does voluntary exercise. But these methods of heat production

vasoconstriction Narrowing of blood vessels to reduce blood flow to the skin. Vasoconstriction is an involuntary response to cold and reduces heat loss at the skin's surface.

FIGURE 15–6 (a) This African woman has the linear proportions characteristic of many inhabitants of sub-Saharan Africa. (b) By comparison, the Inuit woman is short and stocky. These two individuals serve as good examples of Bergmann's and Allen's rules.

(a)   (b)

are costly because they require an increased intake of nutrients to provide needed energy. (Perhaps this explains why we tend to have a heartier appetite during the winter and why we also tend to increase our intake of fats and carbohydrates, the very sources of energy we require.)

In general, people exposed to chronic cold (meaning much or most of the year) maintain higher metabolic rates than those living in warmer climates. The Inuit (Eskimo) people living in the Arctic maintain metabolic rates between 13 and 45 percent higher than observed in non-Inuit control subjects (Frisancho, 1993). Moreover, the highest metabolic rates are seen in inland Inuit, who are exposed to even greater cold stress than coastal populations. Traditionally, the Inuit had the highest animal protein and fat diet of any population in the world (i.e., the original Atkins diet). Such a diet was necessitated by the available resource base, and it served to maintain the high metabolic rates required by exposure to chronic cold.

Vasoconstriction restricts capillary blood flow to the surface of the skin, thus reducing heat loss at the body surface. Because retaining body heat is more economical than creating it, vasoconstriction is very efficient, provided temperatures don't drop below freezing. However, if temperatures do fall below freezing, continued vasoconstriction can allow the skin temperature to decrease to the point of frostbite or worse.

Long-term responses to cold vary among human groups. For example, in the past, desert-dwelling native Australian populations were subjected to wide temperature fluctuations from day to night. As they wore no clothing and didn't build shelters, their only protection from nighttime temperatures that hovered only a few degrees above freezing was provided by sleeping fires. They experienced continuous vasoconstriction throughout the night that permitted a degree of skin cooling most people would find extremely uncomfortable. But since there was no threat of frostbite, continued vasoconstriction helped prevent excessive internal heat loss.

By contrast, the Inuit experience intermittent periods of vasoconstriction and vasodilation. This compromise provides periodic warmth to the skin that helps prevent frostbite in below-freezing temperatures. At the same time, because vasodilation is intermittent, energy loss is restricted, with more heat retained at the body's core.

These examples illustrate two of the many ways in which human populations vary with regard to adaptation to cold. Although all humans respond physiologically to cold stress in much the same manner, there is variation in how adaptation and acclimatization are manifested. Obviously, winter conditions exceed our ability to adapt physiologically in many parts of the world. So, without cultural innovations, our ancestors would have remained in the tropics.

HIGH ALTITUDE

Studies of high-altitude residents have greatly contributed to our understanding of physiological adaptation. As you would expect, altitude studies have focused on inhabited mountainous regions, particularly in the Himalayas, Andes, and Rocky Mountains. Of these three areas, permanent human habitation probably has the longest history in the Himalayas (Moore et al., 1998). Today, perhaps as many as 25 million people live at altitudes above 10,000 feet. In Tibet, permanent settlements exist above 15,000 feet, and in the Andes, they can be found as high as 17,000 feet (Fig. 15–7).

Because the mechanisms that maintain homeostasis in humans evolved at lower altitudes, they are compromised by the conditions at higher elevations. At high altitudes, many factors produce stress on the human body. These include **hypoxia** (reduced available oxygen), more intense solar radiation, cold, low humidity, wind (which amplifies cold stress), a reduced nutritional base, and rough terrain. Of these, hypoxia exerts the greatest amount of stress on human physiological systems, especially the heart, lungs, and brain.

hypoxia Lack of oxygen. Hypoxia can refer to reduced amounts of available oxygen in the atmosphere (due to lowered barometric pressure) or to insufficient amounts of oxygen in the body.

(a)   (b)

FIGURE 15–7 (a) A household in northern Tibet, situated at an elevation of over 15,000 feet above sea level. (b) La Paz, Bolivia, at just over 12,000 feet above sea level, is home to more than 1 million people.

Hypoxia results from reduced barometric pressure. It's not that there is less oxygen in the atmosphere at high altitudes; rather, it's less concentrated. Therefore, to obtain the same amount of oxygen at 9,000 feet as at sea level, people must make certain physiological alterations aimed at increasing the body's ability to transport and efficiently utilize the oxygen that is available.

Reproduction, in particular, is affected through increased infant mortality rates, miscarriage, low birth weights, and premature birth. An early study (Moore and Regensteiner, 1983) reported that in Colorado, infant deaths are almost twice as common above 8,200 feet (2,500 m) as at lower elevations. One cause of fetal and maternal death is preeclampsia, a severe elevation of blood pressure in pregnant women after the twentieth gestational week. In another study of Colorado residents, Palmer et al. (1999) reported that among pregnant women living at elevations over 10,000 feet, the prevalence of preeclampsia was 16 percent, compared to 3 percent at around 4,000 feet. In general the problems related to childbearing are attributed to issues that compromise the vascular supply (and thus oxygen transport) to the fetus.

People born at lower altitudes and high-altitude natives differ somewhat in how they adapt to hypoxia. Acclimatization occurs upon exposure to high altitude in people born at low elevation. The responses may be short-term modifications, depending on duration of stay, but they begin within hours of the altitude change. These changes include an increase in respiration rate, heart rate, and production of red blood cells. (Red blood cells contain hemoglobin, the protein responsible for transporting oxygen to organs and tissues.)

Developmental acclimatization occurs in high-altitude natives during growth and development. This type of acclimatization is present only in people who grow up in high-altitude areas, not in those who moved there as adults. Compared to populations at lower elevations, lifelong residents of high altitude display slowed growth and maturation. Other differences include larger chest size, associated, in turn, with greater lung volume and larger heart. In addition to greater lung capacity, people born at high altitudes are more efficient than migrants at diffusing oxygen from blood to body tissues. Developmental acclimatization to high-altitude hypoxia serves as a good example of physiological plasticity by illustrating how, within the limits set by genetic factors, development can be influenced by environment.

There is evidence that entire *populations* have also genetically adapted to high altitudes. Indigenous peoples of Tibet who have inhabited regions higher than 12,000 feet for around 25,000 years may have made genetic (i.e., evolutionary) accommodations to hypoxia. Altitude doesn't appear to affect reproduction in these people to the degree it does in other populations. Infants have birth weights as high as those of lowland Tibetan groups and higher than those of recent (20 to 30 years) Chinese immigrants. This fact may be the result of alterations in maternal blood flow to the uterus during pregnancy (Moore et al., 1994; 1999).

Another line of evidence concerns how the body processes glucose (blood sugar). Glucose is critical because it's the only source of energy used by the brain, and it's also utilized, although not exclusively, by the heart. Both highland Tibetans and the Quechua (inhabitants of high-altitude regions of the Peruvian Andes) burn glucose in a way that permits more efficient use of oxygen. This implies the presence of genetic mutations in the mitochondrial DNA because mtDNA directs how cells use glucose. It also implies that natural selection has acted to increase the frequency of these advantageous mutations in these groups.

There is no certain evidence that Tibetans and Quechua have made evolutionary changes to accommodate high-altitude hypoxia. Moreover, the genetic mechanisms that underlie these populations' unique abilities have not been identified. But, the data strongly suggest that selection has operated to produce evolutionary change in these two groups. If further study supports these findings, we have an excellent example of evolution in action producing long-term adaptation at the population level.

See Virtual Lab 2, section III, for a discussion of the human adaptive response to malaria.

Infectious Disease

Infection, as opposed to other disease categories, such as degenerative or genetic disease, includes those pathological conditions caused by microorganisms (viruses, bacteria, and fungi). Throughout the course of human evolution, infectious disease has exerted enormous selective pressures on populations and thus has influenced the frequency of certain alleles that affect the immune response. Indeed, it would be difficult to overemphasize the importance of infectious disease as an agent of natural selection in human populations. But as important as infectious disease has been, its role in this regard is not very well documented.

The effects of infectious disease on humans are mediated culturally as well as biologically. Innumerable cultural factors, such as architectural styles, subsistence techniques, exposure to domesticated animals, even religious practices, all affect how infectious disease develops and persists within and between populations.

Until about 10,000 to 12,000 years ago, all humans lived in small nomadic hunting and gathering groups. As these groups rarely remained in one location more than a few days at a time, they had minimal contact with refuse heaps that house disease **vectors.** But with the domestication of plants and animals, people became more sedentary and began living in small villages. Gradually, villages became towns, and towns, in turn, developed into densely crowded, unsanitary cities.

As long as humans lived in small bands, there was little opportunity for infectious disease to have much impact on large numbers of people. Even if an entire local group or band were wiped out, the effect on the overall population in a given area would have been negligible. Moreover, for a disease to become **endemic** in a population, sufficient numbers of people must be present. Therefore, small bands of hunter-gatherers weren't faced with continuous exposure to endemic disease.

But with the advent of settled living and association with domesticated animals, opportunities for disease increased. As sedentary life permitted larger group size, it became possible for several diseases to become permanently established in

vectors Agents that serve to transmit disease from one carrier to another. Mosquitoes are vectors for malaria, just as fleas are vectors for bubonic plague.

endemic Continuously present in a population.

zoonotic (zoh-oh-no´-tic) Pertaining to a zoonosis (*pl.,* zoonoses), a disease that is transmitted to humans through contact with nonhuman animals.

some populations. Moreover, exposure to domestic animals, such as cattle and fowl, provided an opportune environment for the spread of several **zoonotic** diseases, such as tuberculosis. Close association with nonhuman animals has always been a source of disease for humans. But with the domestication of animals, humans greatly increased the spread of *zoonoses,* or infectious conditions that spread to humans through contact with nonhuman animals. The crowded, unsanitary conditions that characterized parts of all cities until the late nineteenth century and that persist in much of the world today further added to the disease burden borne by human inhabitants.

Malaria provides perhaps the best-documented example of how disease can act to change allele frequencies in human populations. In Chapter 4, you saw how malaria has operated in some African and Mediterranean populations to alter allele frequencies at the locus governing hemoglobin formation. In spite of extensive long-term eradication programs, malaria still poses a serious threat to human health. Indeed, the World Health Organization estimates the number of people currently infected with malaria to be between 300 and 500 million worldwide. Moreover, this number is increasing as drug-resistant strains of the disease-causing microorganism become more common (Olliaro et al., 1995).

Another example of the selective role of infectious disease is indirectly provided by AIDS (acquired immune deficiency syndrome). In the United States, the first cases of AIDS were reported in 1981. Since that time, perhaps as many as 1.5 million Americans have been infected by HIV (human immunodeficiency virus), the agent that causes AIDS. However, most of the burden of AIDS is borne by developing countries, where 95 percent of all HIV-infected people live. By the end of 2003, an estimated 42 million people worldwide were living with HIV infection, and at least 23 million had died.

HIV is transmitted from person to person through the exchange of bodily fluids, usually blood or semen. It is not spread through casual contact with an infected person. Within six months of infection, most infected people test positive for anti-HIV antibodies, meaning that their immune system has recognized the presence of foreign antigens and has responded by producing **antibodies.** However, serious HIV-related symptoms may not appear for years. HIV is a "slow virus" in that it may persist in a host's body for years before the onset of severe illness. This asymptomatic state is called a "latency period," and the average latency period in the United States is more than 11 years.

antibodies Proteins that are produced by some types of immune cells and that serve as major components of the immune system. Antibodies recognize and attach to foreign antigens on bacteria, viruses, and other pathogens. Then other immune cells destroy the invading organism.

Like all viruses, HIV must invade certain types of cells and alter the functions of those cells to produce more virus particles in a process that eventually leads to cell destruction. (The way HIV does this is different from that of many other viruses.) HIV can attack various types of cells, but it especially targets so-called T4 helper cells, which are major components of the immune system. As HIV infection spreads and T4 cells are destroyed, the patient's immune system begins to fail. Consequently, he or she begins to exhibit symptoms caused by various **pathogens** that are commonly present but usually kept in check by a normal immune response. When an HIV-infected person's T cell count drops to a level indicating that immunity has been suppressed, and when symptoms of "opportunistic" infections appear, the patient is said to have AIDS.

pathogens Substances or microorganisms, such as bacteria, fungi, or viruses, that cause disease.

By the early 1990s, scientists were aware of a number of patients who had been HIV positive for 10 to 15 years, but who continued to show few if any symptoms. Awareness of these patients led researchers to suspect that some individuals possess a natural immunity or resistance to HIV infection. This was shown to be true in late 1996 with the publication of two different studies (Dean et al., 1996; Samson et al., 1996) that demonstrated a mechanism for resistance to HIV.

These two reports describe a genetic mutation that concerns a major protein "receptor site" on the surface of certain immune cells, including T4 cells. (Receptor sites are protein molecules that enable HIV and other viruses to invade cells.) In this particular situation, the mutant allele results in a malfunctioning receptor site to which HIV is unable to bind, and current evidence strongly suggests that individuals who are homozygous for this allele may be completely resistant to many types of HIV infection. In heterozygotes, infection may still occur, but the course of HIV disease is markedly slowed.

Interestingly, and for unknown reasons, the mutant allele occurs mainly in people of European descent, among whom its frequency is about 10 percent. Samson and colleagues (1996) reported that in the Japanese and West African samples they studied, the mutation was absent, but Dean and colleagues (1996) reported an allele frequency of about 2 percent among African Americans. These researchers speculated that the presence of the allele in African Americans may be entirely due to genetic admixture (gene flow) with European Americans. Moreover, they suggest that this polymorphism exists in Europeans as a result of selective pressures favoring an allele that originally occurred as a rare mutation. But, it is critical to note, the original selective agent was *not* HIV. Instead, it was some other, as yet unidentified pathogen that requires the same receptor site as HIV. Researchers may be close to identifying which pathogen, or group of pathogens, it was. In December 1999, a group of scientists reported that the myxoma poxvirus, which is related to the virus that causes smallpox, can use the same receptor site as HIV. These authors (Lalani et al., 1999) suggested that the agent that had selected for the altered form of the receptor site may have been smallpox. While this conclusion hasn't yet been proved, or even really investigated, it offers an exciting avenue of research with the possibility of revealing how a mutation that has been favored by selection because it provides protection against one disease can increase resistance to another one (AIDS) as well.

Examples such as AIDS and the relationship between malaria and sickle-cell anemia are continuously revealing new insights into the complex interactions between disease organisms and their host populations. These insights in turn provide a growing basis for understanding the many variations between individuals and populations that have arisen as adaptive responses to infectious disease.

Smallpox, once a deadly viral disease, may provide a good example of how exposure to infectious agents can produce polymorphisms in host populations. During the eighteenth century, smallpox is estimated to have accounted for 10 to 15 percent of all deaths in parts of Europe. But today, this once devastating killer is the only condition to have been successfully eliminated by modern medical technology. By 1977, through massive vaccination programs, the World Health Organization was able to declare the smallpox virus extinct, except for a few colonies in research labs in the United States and Russia.*

Smallpox had a higher incidence in persons with either blood type A or AB than in type O individuals, a fact that has been explained by the presence of an antigen on the smallpox virus that is similar to the A antigen. It follows that when some type A individuals were exposed to smallpox, their immune systems failed to recognize the virus as foreign and didn't mount an adequate immune response. Consequently, in regions where smallpox was common in the past, it could have altered allele frequencies at the ABO locus by selecting against the *A* allele.

---

*Concern over the potential use of the smallpox virus by bioterrorists relates to these laboratory colonies. Although the virus is extinct outside these labs, some officials fear the possibility that samples of the virus could be stolen. Also, there are apparently some concerns that unknown colonies of the virus may exist in labs in countries other than Russia and the United States. The use of disease organisms against enemies is not new. In the Middle Ages, the corpses of smallpox and plague victims were catapulted into towns under siege, and during the U.S. colonial period, British soldiers knowingly gave Native Americans blankets used by smallpox victims.

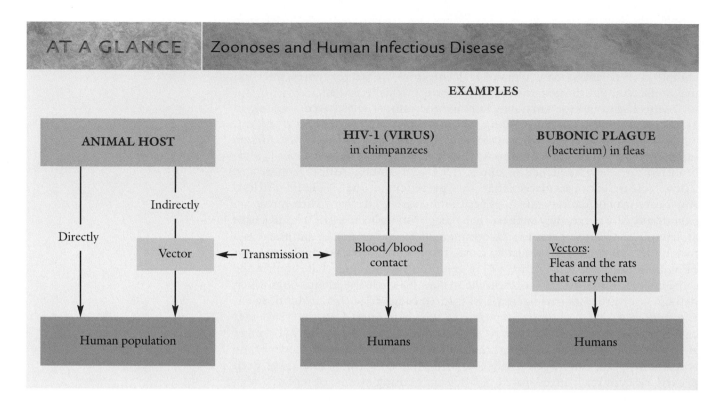

THE CONTINUING IMPACT OF INFECTIOUS DISEASE

It's important to understand that humans and pathogens exert selective pressures on each other, creating a dynamic relationship between disease organisms and their human (and nonhuman) hosts. Just as disease exerts selective pressures on host populations to adapt, microorganisms also evolve and adapt to various pressures exerted on them by their hosts.

Evolutionarily speaking, it's to the advantage of any pathogen not to be so virulent as to kill its host too quickly. If the host dies shortly after becoming infected, the viral or bacterial agent may not have time to reproduce and infect other hosts. Thus, selection sometimes acts to produce resistance in host populations and/or to reduce the virulence of disease organisms, to the benefit of both. However, members of populations exposed for the first time to a new disease frequently die in huge numbers. This type of exposure was a major factor in the decimation of indigenous New World populations after contact with Europeans introduced smallpox into Native American groups. And this has also been the case with the current worldwide spread of HIV.

Of the known disease-causing organisms, HIV provides the best-documented example of evolution and adaptation in a pathogen. It is also one of several examples of interspecies transfer of infection. For these reasons, we focus much of this discussion of evolutionary factors and infectious disease on HIV and AIDS.

HIV is the most mutable and genetically variable virus known. The type of HIV responsible for the AIDS epidemic is HIV-1, which in turn is divided into three major subtypes comprising at least 10 different varieties that vary genetically from one population to another (Hu et al., 1996; Gao, 1999). Another far less common type is HIV-2, which is present only in populations of West Africa. HIV-2 also exhibits a wide range of genetic diversity, and while some strains cause AIDS, others are far less virulent.

Since the late 1980s, researchers have been comparing the DNA sequences of HIV and a closely related retrovirus called *simian immunodeficiency virus (SIV)*. SIV is found in chimpanzees and several African monkey species. Like HIV, SIV is genetically variable, and each strain appears to be specific to a given species and even subspecies of primate. SIV produces no symptoms in the African monkeys and chimpanzees that are its traditional hosts, but when injected into Asian monkeys, it eventually causes immune suppression, AIDS-like symptoms, and death. These findings indicate that the various forms of SIV have shared a long evolutionary history (perhaps several hundred thousand years) with a number of African primate species and that the latter are able to accommodate this virus, which is deadly to their Asian relatives. Moreover, these results substantiate long-held hypotheses that SIV and HIV evolved in Africa.

Comparisons of the DNA sequences of HIV-2 and the form of SIV found in one monkey species (the sooty mangabey) revealed that, genetically, these two viruses are almost identical. These findings led to the generally accepted conclusion that HIV-2 evolved from sooty mangabey SIV. Moreover, sooty mangabeys are hunted for food and also kept as pets in western central Africa, and the transmission of SIV to humans probably occurred through bites and the butchering of monkey carcasses.

But although the origin of HIV-2 was established, there was continuing debate over which primate species had been the source of HIV-1. Recently, a group of medical researchers (Gao et al., 1999) compared DNA sequences of HIV-1 and the form of SIV found in chimpanzees indigenous to western central Africa. The results of this research demonstrated that HIV-1 almost certainly evolved from the strain of chimpanzee SIV that infects the subspecies *Pan troglodytes troglodytes,* which is indigenous to central Africa.

Unfortunately for both species, chimpanzees are routinely hunted by humans for food in parts of West Africa (see p. 134). Consequently, the most probable explanation for the transmission of SIV from chimpanzees to humans is, as with sooty mangabeys, the hunting and butchering of chimpanzees (Gao et al., 1999; Weiss and Wrangham, 1999) (Fig. 15–8). Hence, HIV/AIDS is a zoonotic disease. The DNA evidence further suggests that there were at least three separate human exposures to chimpanzee SIV, and at some point the virus was altered to the form we call HIV. When chimpanzee SIV was transmitted to humans is unknown. The oldest evidence of human infection is a frozen HIV-positive blood sample taken from a West African patient in 1959. There are also a few documented cases of AIDS infection by the late 1960s and early 1970s. Therefore, although human exposure to SIV/HIV probably occurred many times in the past, the virus didn't become firmly established in humans until the latter half of the twentieth century.

Severe Acute Respiratory Syndrome (SARS) is another contemporary example of zoonotic transmission of disease. In early 2003 an outbreak of SARS in southern China surprised the world health community by quickly spreading through much of Asia, then to North America (especially Canada), South America, and Europe.

When compared to diseases such as HIV/AIDS, tuberculosis, influenza, and malaria, the threat from SARS is relatively minor. Nevertheless, it can be fatal and is especially severe among the elderly. As of July 2003, the total number of SARS-related deaths was 812 out of around 8,500 cases. But there are fears that it may return and, as of this writing, the development of a SARS vaccine is a long way off.

Currently, scientists don't know the exact mode of SARS transmission in humans but, most believe that it's spread through close contact by means of infected droplets (i.e., when people cough or

FIGURE 15–8 These people, selling butchered chimpanzees, may not realize that by handling this meat they could be exposing themselves to HIV or the ebola virus.

Karl Ammann

sneeze). Many health officials believe it was initially transmitted to humans through contact either with domesticated animals or wild animals, such as civet cats, sold in Asian markets for food. Indeed, many of the influenza strains that frequently originate in China are believed to originate in pigs and fowl that live in very close contact with humans (Clarke, 2003).

The fact that SARS spread so quickly around the world, even though it has a fairly low transmission rate, is due to travel. If modern technology didn't exist, this infection would have been confined to one or a few villages, and perhaps a small number of people would have died. But it would have been a fairly unre-markable event and it certainly wouldn't have become widely known. In fact, this and many other similar scenarios have undoubtedly been repeated countless times throughout the course of human history.

From these SIV/HIV and SARS examples, you can appreciate how, through the adoption of various cultural practices, humans have radically altered patterns of infectious disease. The interaction of cultural and biological factors has influenced microevolutionary change in humans (as in the example of sickle-cell anemia) to accommodate altered relationships with disease organisms.

Until the twentieth century, infectious disease was the number one cause of death in all human populations. Even today, in many developing countries, as much as half of all mortality is due to infectious disease, compared to about 10 percent in the United States. For example, malaria is a disease of the poor in developing nations. Annually, there are an estimated 1 million deaths due to malaria. That figure computes to one malaria-related death every 30 seconds (Weiss, 2002)! Ninety percent of these deaths occur in sub-Saharan Africa, where 5 percent of children die of malaria before age 5 (Greenwood and Mutabingwa, 2002; Weiss, 2002). In the United States and other developed nations, with better living conditions and sanitation and especially with the widespread use of antibiotics and pesticides beginning in the late 1940s, infectious disease has given way to heart disease and cancer as the leading causes of death.

Optimistic predictions held that infectious disease would be a thing of the past in developed countries and, with the introduction of antibiotics and better living standards, in developing nations as well. But by the mid-1980s, such predictions were increasingly seen to be wrong. Between 1980 and 1992, the number of deaths in the United States in which infectious disease was the underlying cause rose from 41 to 65 per 100,000, an increase of 58 percent (Pinner et al., 1996). During that same period, there was a 25 percent increase in infectious disease mortality among people aged 65 and older, from 271 to 338 per 100,000. And deaths due to respiratory tract infections rose from 25 to 30 deaths per 100,000.

Additionally, AIDS contributed substantially to the increase in mortality due to infectious disease in the United States between 1980 and 1992. By 1992, AIDS was the leading cause of death in men aged 25 to 44 years. As of 1998, mortality due to AIDS had decreased significantly, but even when subtracting the effect of AIDS in mortality rates, there was still a 22 percent increase in mortality rates due to infectious disease between 1980 and 1992 (Pinner et al., 1996).

Increase in the prevalence of infectious disease may partly be due to the overuse of antibiotics. It is estimated that half of all antibiotics prescribed in the United States are used to treat viral conditions such as colds and flu. Because antibiotics are completely ineffective against viruses, such therapy not only is useless, but may also have dangerous long-term consequences. There is considerable concern in the biomedical community over the indiscriminate use of antibiotics and pesticides since the 1950s. Antibiotics have exerted selective pressures on bacterial species that have, over time, developed antibiotic-resistant strains (an excellent example of natural selection). Consequently, the past few years have seen the *reemergence* of many bacterial diseases, including influenza, pneumonia, tuberculosis, and cholera, in forms that are less responsive to treatment.

Tuberculosis is now listed as the world's leading killer of adults by the World Health Organization (Colwell, 1996). In fact, the number of tuberculosis cases has risen 28 percent since the mid-1980s worldwide, with an estimated 10 million infected in the United States alone. Although not all infected persons develop active disease, an estimated 30 million are believed to have died from TB in the 1990s worldwide. One very troubling aspect of the increase in tuberculosis infection is that newly developed strains of *Mycobacterium tuberculosis,* the bacterium that causes TB, are resistant to antibiotics and other treatments.

Cholera, a dangerous and often fatal gastrointestinal disease caused by a bacterium found in sewage-contaminated water, has periodically occurred in epidemic proportions throughout history, including outbreaks in the nineteenth century in New York, Philadelphia, and London. Currently, cholera claims about 100,000 lives annually in Asia alone, and an antibiotic-resistant strain, first identified in India in 1992, is spreading throughout Southeast Asia. Recent cholera outbreaks throughout much of South America, India, Bangladesh, China, and parts of Southeast Asia have been partly attributed to rising ocean temperatures, lack of sanitation, and overcrowding.

Various treatments for nonbacterial conditions have also become ineffective. One such example is the appearance of chloroquin-resistant malaria, which has rendered chloroquin (the traditional preventive medication) virtually useless in some parts of Africa. And many insect species have also developed resistance to commonly used pesticides.

In addition to threats posed by resistant strains of pathogens, there are other factors that may contribute to the emergence (or reemergence) of infectious disease. Scientists are becoming increasingly concerned over the potential for global warming to expand the geographical range of numerous tropical disease vectors, such as mosquitoes. And the destruction of natural environments not only contributes to global warming; it also has the potential of causing disease vectors formerly restricted to local areas to spread to new habitats.

One other factor associated with the rapid spread of disease and directly related to technological change is the mixing of people at an unprecedented rate. Indeed, an estimated 1 million people per day cross national borders by air (Lederberg, 1996)! In addition, new road construction and wider availability of motor-driven vehicles allow more people (armies, refugees, truck drivers, etc.) to travel farther and faster than ever before.

Fundamental to all these factors is human population size (see p. 462), which, as it continues to soar, causes more environmental disturbance and, through additional human activity, adds further to global warming. Moreover, in developing countries, where as much as 50 percent of mortality is due to infectious disease, overcrowding and unsanitary conditions increasingly contribute to increased rates of communicable illness. One could scarcely conceive of a better set of circumstances for the appearance and spread of communicable disease, and it remains to be seen if scientific innovation and medical technology are able to meet the challenge.

It's still unclear what the long-term consequences of twentieth-century antibiotic therapy, pesticide-based eradication programs, environmental change, and human population growth will be on disease patterns. But there are many scientists who fear that we may not be able to develop new antibiotics and treatments fast enough to keep pace with the appearance of potentially deadly new bacteria and other pathogens. Thus, we have radically altered the course of evolution in some microbial species, just as they have altered our own evolutionary course in the past and clearly continue to do so in the present.

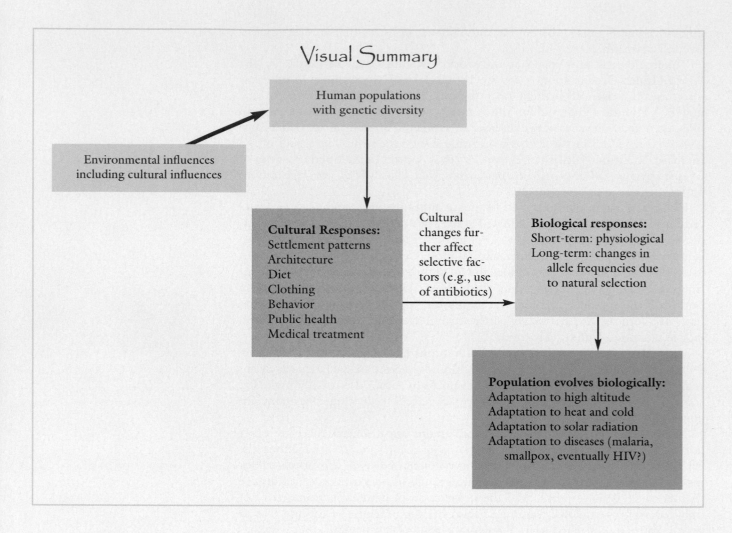

Visual Summary

Human populations with genetic diversity

Environmental influences including cultural influences

Cultural Responses:
Settlement patterns
Architecture
Diet
Clothing
Behavior
Public health
Medical treatment

Cultural changes further affect selective factors (e.g., use of antibiotics)

Biological responses:
Short-term: physiological
Long-term: changes in allele frequencies due to natural selection

Population evolves biologically:
Adaptation to high altitude
Adaptation to heat and cold
Adaptation to solar radiation
Adaptation to diseases (malaria, smallpox, eventually HIV?)

Summary

In this chapter, we have explored some of the numerous ways humans have adapted to environmental challenges as they evolved and migrated out of Africa to eventually inhabit most of the planet. We began with a brief discussion of acclimatization as a form of adaptation and the various ways it can occur.

We considered skin color and its adaptive value in response to conflicting selective pressures, all having to do with ultraviolet radiation. One reason we focused on skin color is because so much importance has been placed on it in the past, particularly in racial classification schemes. Also, skin color is an excellent example of how variations in a characteristic can develop rapidly in response to strong selective pressures. Heavily pigmented skin is adaptive in the tropics because of the protection it provides against ultraviolet radiation, which can cause skin cancer and degrade folate. But as populations moved away from the tropics, dark skin became disadvantageous, because a decrease in sunlight meant insufficient exposure to UV radiation for the adequate production of vitamin D.

We also dealt with the various forms of acclimatization that have evolved in humans to deal with environmental stressors like heat, cold, and high altitude. And we emphasized the role of infectious disease in human evolution. We are still coping with infectious disease as we alter the environment and as global climate change facilitates the spread of disease vectors. Moreover, cultural innovations have altered disease patterns and have increased the rate at which infections can spread. Examples of this type of spread are HIV/AIDS and SARS.

Certainly, without cultural adaptations, our species would have never left the tropics. But, as in the case of sickle-cell anemia, HIV, and many bacterial diseases, some of our cultural innovations themselves have become selective agents. Many of our practices have had a nasty way of turning on us, and they continue to do so—often with devastating consequences. More than ever, we need to examine our biocultural interactions if we want to explain our history and perhaps predict our future.

For Further Thought

1. Given the time required for natural selection to act and the speed at which humans are altering their environments, do you think we will be able to biologically change (i.e., adapt) to meet these new challenges?

Go to the book website at **http://www.anthropology.wadsworth.com** for resources to help you explore these questions further. Click on "For Further Thought" for this chapter.

Questions for Review

1. Why can we say that variations in human skin color are the result of natural selection in different environments? Why is less pigmented skin a result of conflicting selective factors?
2. What would you say was the major evolutionary factor in the development of lighter skin in human populations that eventually migrated to more northern latitudes?
3. Do you think that skin cancer has been an important factor in the evolution of skin color? What is an objection to this theory, and do you agree with this objection? Why or why not?
4. What are the major complications of living at high altitude? How have some populations that have a long history of high-altitude living adapted to their environments?
5. How would you explain the fact that humans adapt more readily to heat, especially dry heat, than they do to cold?
6. Do you think that infectious disease has played an important role in human evolution? Do you think it plays a *current* role in human adaptation?
7. How have human cultural practices influenced the patterns of infectious disease seen today? Provide as many examples as you can, including some not discussed in this chapter.

Suggested Further Reading

Discover. 1994. Special Issue: The Science of Race. 15 (November).

Frisancho, A. Roberto. 1993. *Human Adaptation and Accommodation*. Ann Arbor: University of Michigan Press.

Journal of the American Medical Association, 1996. Entire issue, 275 (January 17). (Numerous articles pertaining to climate change and reemergence of infectious diseases.)

Leffell, David J., and Douglas E. Brash. 1996. "Sunlight and Skin Cancer." *Scientific American* 275(1): 52–59.

Nesse, Randolph M., and George C. Williams. 1998. "Evolution and the Origins of Disease." *Scientific American* 279(5): 86–93.

O'Brien, Stephen J., and Michael Dean. 1997. "In Search of AIDS-Resistance Genes." *Scientific American* 277(3): 44–51.

⊕ Online Anthropology Resource Center

Go to the Anthropology Resource Center at **http://www.anthropology.wadsworth.com** for a wealth of online resources, including a companion website for your text that provides study aids such as self-quizzes for each chapter and a practice final exam, as well as links to anthropology websites and information on the latest theories and discoveries in the field. Also, check out InfoTrac College Edition®, your online library that offers full-length articles from thousands of scholarly and popular publications. Just click on the InfoTrac button at the companion website and use the passcode that came with your book.

Racial Purity: A False and Dangerous Ideology

During the late nineteenth and early twentieth centuries, a growing sense of nationalism was sweeping Europe and the United States. At the same time, an increased emphasis on racial purity had been coupled with the more dangerous aspects of what is termed *biological determinism* (see p. 398). The concept of pure races is based, in part, on the notion that in the past, races were composed of individuals who conformed to idealized types and who were similar in appearance and intellect. Over time, some variation had been introduced into these pure races through interbreeding with other groups, and increasingly, this type of "contamination" was viewed as a threat to be avoided.

In today's terminology, pure races would be said to be genetically homogenous, or to possess little genetic variation. Everyone would have the same alleles at most of their loci. Actually, we do see this situation in "pure breeds" of domesticated animals and plants, developed *deliberately* by humans through selective breeding. We also see many of the detrimental consequences of such genetic uniformity in various congenital abnormalities, such as hip dysplasia in some breeds of dogs.

With our current understanding of genetic principles, we are able to appreciate the potentially negative outcomes of matings between genetically similar individuals. For example, we know that inbreeding increases the likelihood of offspring who are homozygous for certain deleterious recessive alleles. We also know that decreased genetic variation in a species diminishes the potential for natural selection to act, thus compromising that species' ability to adapt to certain environmental fluctuations. Furthermore, in genetically uniform populations, individual fertility can be seriously reduced, potentially with disastrous consequences for the entire species. Thus, even if pure human races did exist at one time (and they didn't), theirs would not have been a desirable condition genetically, and they most certainly would have been at an evolutionary disadvantage.

During the latter half of the nineteenth century, many Americans and Europeans had come to believe that nations could be ranked according to technological achievement. It followed that the industrial societies of the United States and Europe were considered to be the most advanced and to have attained a "higher level of civilization" owing to the "biological superiority" of their northern European forebears. This concept arose in part from the writings of Herbert Spencer, a British philosopher who misapplied the principles of natural selection to societies in a doctrine termed *social Darwinism*. Spencer believed that societies evolved, and through competition, "less endowed" cultures and the "unfit" people in them would be weeded out. Indeed, it was Spencer who coined the almost always misused phrase "survival of the fittest," and his philosophy became widely accepted on both sides of the Atlantic, where its principles accorded well with notions of racial purity.

In northern Europe, particularly Germany, and in the United States, racial superiority was increasingly embodied in the so-called "Aryan race." *Aryan* is a term that is still widely used, albeit erroneously, with biological connotations. Actually, *Aryan* doesn't refer to a biological unit or Mendelian population, as the majority of people who use the term intend it. Rather, it's a linguistic term that refers to an ancient language group that was ancestral to the Indo-European family of languages.

By the early twentieth century, the "Aryans" had been transformed into a mythical super race of people whose noble traits were embodied in an extremely idealized "nordic type." The true Aryan was held to be tall, blond, blue-eyed, strong, industrious, and "pure in spirit." Nordics were extolled as the developers of all ancient "high" civilizations and as the founders of modern industrialized nations. In Europe, there was growing emphasis on the superiority of northwestern Europeans as the modern representatives of "true Nordic stock," while southern and eastern Europeans were viewed as inferior.

In the United States, there prevailed the strongly held opinion that America was originally settled by Christian Nordics. Prior to about 1890, the majority of newcomers to the United States had come from Germany, Scandinavia, Britain, and Ireland. But by the 1890s, the pattern of immigration had changed. The arrival of increasing numbers of Italians, Turks, Greeks, and Jews among the thousands of newcomers raised fears that society was being contaminated by immigration from southern and eastern Europe.

Moreover, in the United States, there were additional concerns about the large population of former slaves and their descendants. As African Americans left the South in increasing numbers to work in the factories of the North, many unskilled white workers felt economically threatened by new competition. It was no coincidence that the Ku Klux Klan, which had been inactive for a number of years, was revived in 1915 and by the 1920s was preaching vehement opposition to African Americans, Jews, and Catholics in support of the supremacy of the white, Protestant "Nordic race." These sentiments were widespread in the general population, although they didn't always take the extreme form extolled by the Klan. One result of these views was the Immigration Restriction Act of 1924, which was aimed at curtailing the immigration of non-Nordics, including Italians, Jews, and eastern Europeans, in order to preserve America's Nordic heritage.

To avoid the further "decline of the superior race," many states practiced policies of racial segregation until the mid-1950s. Particularly in the South, segregation laws resulted in an almost total separation of whites and blacks, except where blacks were employed as servants or laborers. Moreover, *antimiscegenation* laws prohibited marriage between whites and blacks in over half the states, and unions between whites and Asians were also frequently illegal. In several states, marriage between whites and blacks was punishable as either a misdemeanor or a felony, and astonishingly, some of these laws were not repealed until the late 1950s or early 1960s. Likewise, in Germany by 1935, the newly instituted Nuremberg Laws forbade marriage or sexual intercourse between so-called Aryan Germans and Jews.

The fact that belief in racial purity and superiority led ultimately to the Nazi death camps in World War II is undisputed (except for continuing efforts by certain white supremacist and neo-Nazi organizations). It is one of the great tragedies of the twentieth century that some of history's most glaring examples of discrimination and viciousness were perpetrated by people who believed that their actions were based in scientific principles. In reality, such beliefs constitute nothing more than myth. There is absolutely no evidence to suggest that "pure" human races ever existed. Indeed, such an idea flies in the face of everything we know about natural selection, recombination, and gene flow. The degree of genetic uniformity throughout our species (compared to some other species), as evidenced by mounting data from mitochondrial and nuclear DNA analysis, argues strongly that there has always been gene flow between human populations and that genetically homogenous races are nothing more than fabrication.

The numerous abuses committed in the name of racial purity in the twentieth century were, in part, outgrowths of the rise of nationalism in Europe and the United States during the late nineteenth century. Unfortunately, however, prejudice based on a belief in racial purity and superiority is alive and well. The dogma preached by such white supremacist groups as White Aryan Resistance is no different from that espoused by the Nazi leadership in pre-World War II Germany. The dangers of such thinking have been manifested in incalculable human suffering. Now, early in the twenty-first century, we can but wonder if the generations who will see it to its conclusion will have learned from the mistakes of their predecessors.

Critical Thinking Questions

1. Given what you know about evolutionary factors, discuss why the notion of "pure races" is inaccurate. Also discuss why you think the concept of racial purity has been (and remains) so prevalent.
2. What is the concept of an "Aryan race," and why is it incorrect? Is this concept dead today?

16

Legacies of Human Evolutionary History

Composite satellite image
Courtesy, Craig Mayhew and Robert Simmon, NASA

> ## Key Questions
>
> How are humans part of a biological continuum that includes all living things?
>
> Given that humans are part of a biological continuum, how does culture make us different from other species?

Introduction

By now, you've read 15 chapters that have emphasized human biological evolution and adaptation. You have followed along as we've talked about genetics, evolutionary factors, nonhuman primates, fossil hominids, and how humans vary from one another. But you have also learned that we are remarkably genetically uniform when compared to other primate species that have been studied.

You have accompanied us through geological time to the development of *Homo sapiens:* 225 million years of mammalian evolution, 65 million years of primate evolution, 6 million years of hominid evolution, and 2 million years of evolution of the genus *Homo.* So, what do you think now? Are we just another mammal—or just another primate? In most ways, of course, we *are* like other mammals and primates. But as we have emphasized throughout the text, modern human beings are the result of *biocultural evolution.* In other words, modern human biology and behavior have been shaped by the biological and cultural forces that operated on our ancestors. In fact, it would be fruitless to attempt an understanding of modern human biology and diversity without considering that humans have evolved in the context of culture. It would be like trying to understand the biology of fish without considering that they live in water.

In the two previous chapters, we have seen that modern human beings are a highly generalized species. This means that we can live in a great variety of climates, eat a wide variety of foods, and respond to most environmental challenges in myriad ways. For example, as human populations moved into cold northern climates, they were able to respond both physiologically and behaviorally to the environmental challenges they faced. As noted in Chapter 15, physiological adaptations to cold include vasoconstriction of the capillaries to conserve heat, increased metabolic rate, and shivering to warm the body. Thinking of these responses from an evolutionary perspective, we can assume that among the members of the earliest populations inhabiting cold regions of the world, those who had genotypes enabling them to respond physiologically had more surviving offspring to pass along these characteristics. Behavioral and cultural adaptations to cold climates probably included fire, house structures, warm clothing, and hunting for foods that provided energy to withstand the cold. In these examples we see evidence of human adaptations to cold that are both biological and cultural and that are rooted in evolution.

In this chapter, we will explore ways in which the legacies of human evolution have profound impact on our behavior throughout our lives and on our impact on the planet. We begin with a view of the legacies of human evolution that impact each person throughout the life course.

Evolution of Human Behavior and the Life Course

Examining human social behavior in an evolutionary framework is known as *behavioral ecology,* which we discussed in Chapter 7 in the context of primate behavior. Of course, humans are primates, and many biological anthropologists are interested in the extent to which evolution can explain contemporary human behaviors. Behavioral ecologists suggest that humans, like other animals, behave in ways that increase their fitness, or reproductive success. This includes behaviors affecting mating and parenting success. Finding mates and taking care of offspring require time and energy, and as we know all too well, both of these commodities exist in finite amounts. Thus, reproductive efforts require trade-offs in time, energy, and resources invested in mating and parenting. When we read about these concepts as they pertain to monkeys and apes, most of us probably find little to disagree with. But to suggest that evolutionary processes have an impact on human behavior today raises a lot of issues, some of which aren't so easily resolved.

For example, this view argues that natural selection is not limited to physical and physiological responses, but has had an effect on the way humans think—in other words, on human cognition, perception, and memory. The argument goes something like this: The ability to remember a dangerous event that may have resulted in loss of life would be favorably selected if it prevented a person from being caught in a similar situation. The ability to distinguish a wildebeest (food) from a lion (danger) would be selectively favored. Likewise, economic behaviors involved in the allocation of resources to increase survival and reproductive success would be favored.

The study of how natural selection has influenced how humans and other primates think is often called *evolutionary psychology.* Among the topics explored by evolutionary psychologists are mate attraction, sexuality, aggression, and violence. As you might guess, all of these are hot topics, and there is no end in sight to the controversy that surrounds them.

Many people are uncomfortable with such an explicit evolutionary perspective on contemporary human behavior and thought because it implies that there are constraints on our behavior that we may not be able to overcome. For example, it can be argued that individual males can increase their reproductive success by increasing the number of women with whom they mate. Women, meanwhile, are thought to best increase the health of their offspring (and thus their reproductive success) if they can find faithful mates who will supply resources to them and their children. At first glance, these two recipes for reproductive success seem to conflict. Further examination, however, reveals that the optimal route to reproductive success for males and females represents a compromise between what is argued to be the best strategy for each sex. Males who "love 'em and leave 'em" usually end up with fewer surviving offspring in comparison with males who take on the role of faithful providers.

Aggression and violence, particularly on the part of males, is the subject of a number of books and papers in evolutionary psychology, including the book *Demonic Males: Apes and the Origins of Human Violence,* by Richard Wrangham and Dale Peterson. These authors contrast the behaviors of our two closest living relatives, the chimpanzees and bonobos. Most striking is that chimpanzee society seems to be based on male-male competition and aggression leading occasionally to violence both within and between troops, whereas bonobo society is described as a female-dominated community based on cooperation and peaceful interaction (Fig. 16–1). To Wrangham and Peterson, these two behavior patterns represent the extremes of human societies and also show potentials for both violence and peace that may be rooted in human evolutionary history.

(a)   (b)

FIGURE 16–1 (a) These chimpanzees exhibit an aggressive reaction when confronted by others. (b) The bonobos show more relaxed expressions.

On the other hand, they clearly acknowledge the role of culture and society in fostering aggression and violence in males. Mirroring some of the discussions of terrorism today, *Demonic Males* points out that chimpanzee communities with abundant resources have far fewer incidents of violence than communities with limited resources; in general, bonobos live in areas of relative resource abundance. But whatever their roots, it appears to many observers that war, genocide, rape, rioting, and terrorism are unwelcome legacies of human evolutionary history. Unfortunately, because of recent events like the 2001 terrorist attacks and the wars in Afghanistan and Iraq, the arguments presented in *Demonic Males* resonate more profoundly and convincingly than they did when the first edition of this textbook was written. Perhaps by the next edition, the pendulum of thinking about world events will have swung toward the idea that peaceful cooperation is more fundamental to human behavior.

To suggest that some of our behaviors reflect our evolutionary history is not to say that there are "genes for" such behaviors (see p. 175). No matter how you cut it, behavior is an extremely complex phenomenon, and its expression depends on a combination of myriad genes, environmental context, and individual experience. There is really no way of predicting how an individual mother or father will allocate resources in the task of child rearing, but behavioral ecologists argue that patterns can be seen when populations (or even the entire species) are examined for allocation of parenting resources.

One aspect of behavioral ecology that may have less emotional baggage than reproductive and parenting strategies is how people make decisions about food acquisition. For example, when a behavioral ecologist examines the hunting strategy on a given day for a band of foragers, the prediction would be that the hunters would pursue a strategy that would maximize return and minimize time and energy invested (Fig. 16–2). In other words, it is predicted that the hunters would pursue an "optimal foraging strategy." But if the analysis considers only the calories in the prey obtained weighed against the calories expended in pursuit of the prey, the theory will always come up short, because other important factors are left out of the model. What dangers were between the hunters and the prey that may have led them to take an alternate route or avoid that target altogether? Does pursuit of a particular prey take them too far away from home when night falls? Does a smaller prey item provide additional resources such as a pelt that is useful for clothing? And have the people been eating this prey item for several days, and do they desire a bit of variety? All of these factors could explain why a band of hunters might choose to pursue a prey item of less caloric

FIGURE 16–2 When these G/wi hunters plan their hunting strategy, they consider many factors in addition to calories expended and acquired.

value and thus deviate from the prediction. To return to the idea of an optimal reproductive strategy, would not similar complicating factors apply? Certainly, contemporary humans choose mates based on many more factors than how many offspring they can produce or raise together.

Biocultural Evolution and the Life Cycle

Despite its limitations and challenges, examining human behavior as a product of evolution not only helps us explain and understand some aspects of our lives, but also allows predictions that can be examined and tested through field observations, demographic studies, and other methods. Examples from the human life cycle further illustrate how evolution has influenced human reproductive behavior and how reproduction is embedded in culture. In other words, we view the life cycle as a biocultural process. If we consider how a human develops from an embryo into an adult and examine the forces that operate on that process, then we will have a better perspective of how both biology and culture influence our own lives and how our evolutionary history creates opportunities and set limitations.

There is, of course, much variation in the extent to which cultural factors interact with genetically based biological characteristics; these variable interactions influence how characteristics are expressed in individuals. Some genetically based characteristics will be exhibited no matter what the cultural context of a person's life happens to be. If a person inherits two alleles for albinism, for example (see Chapter 4), he or she will be deficient in the production of the pigment melanin, resulting in lightly colored skin, hair, and eyes. This phenotype will emerge regardless of the cultural environment in which the person lives. Likewise, the sex-linked trait for hemophilia (also described in Chapter 4) will be exhibited by all males who inherit it, no matter where they live.

Other characteristics, such as intelligence, body shape, and growth reflect the interaction of environment and genes. We know, for example, that each of us is born with a genetic makeup that influences the maximum stature we can achieve in adulthood. But to reach that maximum stature, we must be properly nourished during growth, and we must avoid many childhood diseases and other stresses that inhibit growth. What factors determine whether we are well fed and receive good medical care? In the United States, socioeconomic status is probably the primary determinant of nutrition and health. Thus, socioeconomic status is an example of a cultural factor that affects growth. But in another culture, diet and health status might be influenced by whether the individual is male or female. In some cultures, males receive preferential care in childhood and are thus often larger and healthier as adults than are females (Fig. 16–3). And if a culture values slimness in women, young girls may try to restrict their food intake in ways that affect their growth; but if plumpness is valued, the effect on diet in adolescence will likely be different. These are all examples of how cultural values affect growth and development.

As noted in earlier chapters, primatologists and other physical anthropologists view primate and human growth and development from an evolutionary perspective, with an interest in how natural selection has operated on the life cycle from conception to death, a perspective known as *life history theory* (see pp. 179–180). Why, for example, do humans have longer periods of infancy and childhood compared with other primates? What accounts for differences seen in the life cycles of such closely related species as humans and chimpanzees? Life history research seeks to answer such questions (See Mace, 2000, for a review).

Life history theory begins with the premise that there is only a certain amount of energy available to an organism for growth, maintenance of life, and reproduction. Energy that is invested in one of these processes is not available to another. Thus, the entire life course represents a series of trade-offs among life history traits (see pp. 179–180), such as length of gestation, age at weaning, time spent in growth to adulthood, adult body size, and length of life span. For example, life history theory provides the basis for understanding how fast an organism will grow and to what size, how many offspring can be produced, how long gestation will last, and how long an individual will live. Crucial to

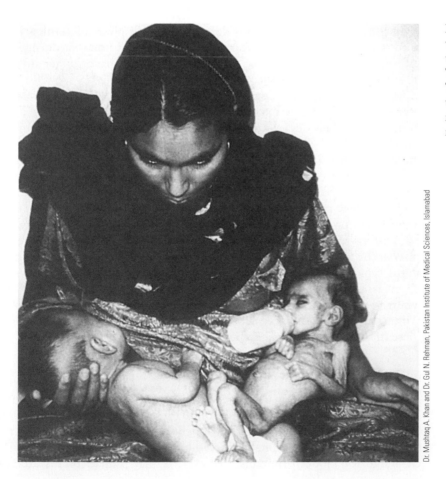

Dr. Mushtaq A. Khan and Dr. Gul N. Rehman, Pakistan Institute of Medical Sciences, Islamabad

FIGURE 16–3 This is a mother with her twin children. The one on the left is a boy and is breast-fed. The girl, on the right, is bottle-fed. This illustrates both differential treatment of boys and girls in many societies and the potential negative effects of bottle-feeding.

FIGURE 16–4 Life cycle stages for various animal species.

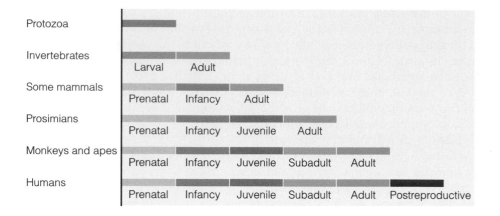

menopause The end of menstruation in women, usually occurring at around age 50.

understanding life history theory is its link to the evolutionary process: It is the action of natural selection that shapes life history traits, determining which ones will succeed or fail in a given environment. Although there is uncertainty about whether life history theory works in contemporary human populations (Strassman and Gillespie, 2002), it serves as a useful guide for examining the various life cycle phases from evolutionary and ecological perspectives.

Not all animals have clearly demarcated phases in their lives; moreover, among mammals, humans have more such phases than do other species (Fig. 16–4). Protozoa, among the simplest of animals, have only one phase; many invertebrates have two: larval and adult. Most primates have four phases: gestation, infancy, juvenile (usually called childhood in humans), and adult. Monkeys, apes, and humans add a phase between the juvenile phase and adulthood that is referred to as the subadult period (adolescence, or teenage years, in humans). Finally, for humans there is the addition of a sixth phase in women, the postreproductive years following **menopause.** One could argue that during the course of primate evolution, more recently evolved forms have longer life spans and more divisions of the life span into phases, or stages.

Most of these life cycle stages are well marked by biological transitions. The prenatal phase begins with conception and ends with birth; infancy is the period of nursing; childhood, or the juvenile phase, is the period from weaning to sexual maturity (puberty in humans); adolescence is the period from puberty to the end of growth; adulthood is marked by the birth of the first child and/or the completion of growth; and menopause is recognized as having occurred one full year after the last menstrual cycle. These biological markers are similar among higher primates, but for humans, there is an added complexity: They occur in cultural contexts that define and characterize them. Puberty, for example, has very different meanings in different cultures. A girl's first menstruation (**menarche**) is often marked with ritual and celebration, and a change in social status typically occurs with this biological transition. Likewise, menopause is often associated with a rise in status for women in non-Western societies, whereas it is commonly seen as a negative transition for women in many Western societies. As we shall see, collective and individual attitudes toward these life cycle transitions have an effect on growth and development.

menarche The first menstruation in girls, usually occurring in the early to mid teens.

GROWTH IN INFANCY AND CHILDHOOD

A characteristic that humans share with most other primates is a relatively large brain compared with body size (see p. 201). In fact, the delivery of a large newborn head through a somewhat small pelvis is a challenge that modern humans share with many other primates, including most monkeys (Fig. 16–5). A further challenge for modern humans, however, is that human brains are somewhat

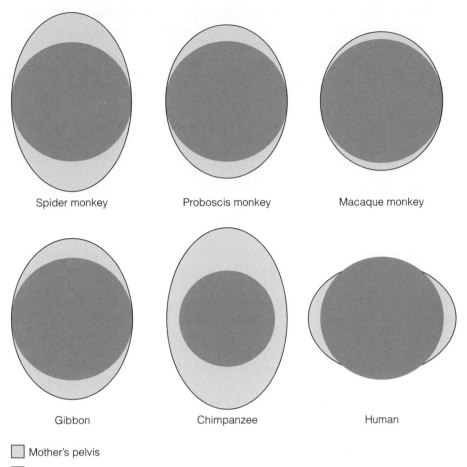

Spider monkey

Proboscis monkey

Macaque monkey

Gibbon

Chimpanzee

Human

Mother's pelvis

Newborn head

FIGURE 16–5 The relationship between the average diameter of the birth canal of adult females and average head length and breadth of newborns of the same species. (After Jolly, 1985.)

undeveloped at birth, so the babies are more helpless and dependent on their caretakers than are most monkey infants. The continued growth of the brain after birth occurs at a rate far greater than that of any other part of the body, with the exception of the eyeball. At birth, the human brain is about 25 percent of its adult size. By 6 months of age, the brain has doubled in size, reaching 50 percent of adult size. It reaches 75 percent of adult size at age 2½ years, 90 percent at age 5 years, and 95 percent by age 10 years. There is only a very small spurt at adolescence, making the brain an exception to the growth curves characteristic of most other parts of the body. This pattern of brain growth, including the relatively small amount of growth before birth, is unusual among primates and other mammals. By contrast, the typical picture for most mammalian species is that at least 50 percent of adult brain size has been achieved prior to birth. For humans, however, the narrow pelvis necessary for walking bipedally provides limits on the size of the fetal head that can be delivered through it. That limitation, in addition to the value of having most brain growth occur in the more stimulating environment outside the womb, has resulted in human infants being born with far less of their total adult brain size than most other mammals. (As we saw in Chapter 11, this pattern of delayed maturation was probably already established in hominid evolution by 1.5 m.y.a.)

Delayed brain growth may be particularly important for a species dependent on language. The language centers of the brain develop in the first three years of life, when the brain is undergoing its rapid expansion; these three years are considered a critical period for the development of language in the human child.

The narrow human pelvis adapted for bipedalism and the large newborn head offer another challenge in human development. Most primate infants are born head first, facing the front of the birth canal, making it easy for the mother to reach down and guide the infant out. Because of a number of modifications to the human pelvis, the infant is born facing the back of the birth canal. This means that the mother must reach behind her to pull the infant into the world. This added difficulty may explain why humans routinely seek assistance at birth, rather than deliver an infant alone as most mammals do. Although it is certainly possible for a woman to deliver an infant alone (Walrath, 2003), having someone else to guide the baby out, to wipe its face so it can breathe, and to prevent the umbilical cord from choking the infant, can significantly reduce mortality associated with birth (Rosenberg and Trevathan, 2001). In fact, a survey of world cultures reveals that it is unusual to give birth alone, particularly to a first child. Assistance at birth may also enhance the survival of the relatively helpless infant.

Infancy is defined as the period during which nursing takes place, typically lasting about four years in humans. When we consider how unusual it is for a mother to nurse her child for even a year in the United States or Canada, this figure may surprise us. But considering that four or five years of nursing is the norm for chimpanzees, gorillas, orangutans, and for women in foraging societies, most anthropologists conclude that four years was the norm for most humans in the evolutionary past (Stuart-Macadam and Dettwyler, 1995).

Humans have unusually long childhoods and a slowed growth process, reflecting the importance of learning for our species. Childhood is the time between weaning and puberty when growth in stature is occurring, the brain is completing its growth, and acquisition of technical and social skills is taking place.

Before continuing to examine the life cycle from the vantage point of life history theory, let's take a look at factors that affect growth and development throughout the growing years.

NUTRITIONAL EFFECTS ON GROWTH AND DEVELOPMENT

Nutrition has an impact on human growth at every stage of the life cycle. During pregnancy, for example, a woman's diet can have a profound effect on the development of her fetus and the eventual health of the child. Moreover, the effects are transgenerational, because a woman's own supply of eggs is developed while she herself is *in utero*. Thus, if a woman is malnourished during pregnancy, the eggs that develop in her female fetus may be damaged in a way that will impact the health of her future grandchildren.

Nutrients needed for growth, development, and body maintenance include proteins, carbohydrates, lipids (fats), vitamins, and minerals. The specific amount that we need of each of these nutrients coevolved with the types of foods that were available to human ancestors throughout our evolutionary history. For example, the specific pattern of amino acids required in human nutrition (the essential amino acids) reflects an ancestral diet high in animal protein. Unfortunately for modern humans, these coevolved nutritional requirements are often incompatible with the foods that are available and typically consumed today. To understand this mismatch of our nutritional needs and contemporary diets, we need to examine the impact of agriculture on human evolutionary history.

The preagricultural diet, while perhaps high in animal protein, was low in fats, particularly saturated fats. The diet was also high in complex carbohydrates (including fiber), low in salt, and high in calcium. We do not need to be reminded that the contemporary diet that typifies many industrialized societies has the opposite configuration of the one just described. It is high in saturated

TABLE 16–1 Preagricultural, Contemporary American, and Recently Recommended Dietary Composition

	PREAGRICULTURAL DIET	CONTEMPORARY DIET	RECENT RECOMMENDATIONS
Total dietary energy (%)			
Protein	33	12	12
Carbohydrate	46	46	58
Fat	21	42	30
Alcohol	~0	(7–10)	—
P:S ratio*	1.41	0.44	1
Cholesterol (mg)	520	300–500	300
Fiber (g)	100–150	19.7	30–60
Sodium (mg)	690	2,300–6,900	1,000–3,300
Calcium (mg)	1,500–2,000	740	800–1,500
Ascorbic acid (mg)	440	90	60

*Polyunsaturated: saturated fat ratio.

Source: From Eaton, Shostak, and Konner, 1988.

fats and salt and low in complex carbohydrates, fiber, and calcium (Table 16–1). There is very good evidence that many of today's diseases in industrialized countries are related to the lack of fit between our diet today and the one with which we evolved (Eaton, Shostak, and Konner, 1988).

Many of our biological and behavioral characteristics evolved because in the past they contributed to adaptation; but today these same characteristics may be maladaptive. An example is our ability to store fat. This capability was an advantage in the past, when food availability often alternated between abundance and scarcity. Those who could store fat during the times of abundance could draw on those stores during times of scarcity and remain healthy, resist disease, and, for women, maintain the ability to reproduce. Today, people with adequate economic resources spend much of their lives with a relative abundance of foods. Considering the number of disorders associated with obesity, the formerly positive ability to store extra fat has now turned into a liability. Our "feast or famine" biology is now incompatible with the constant feast many of us indulge in today.

Perhaps no disorder is as clearly linked with dietary and lifestyle behaviors as the form of diabetes mellitus that typically has its onset in later life, referred to variously as Type II diabetes or NIDDM (non–insulin dependent diabetes mellitus). In 1900, diabetes ranked twenty-seventh among the leading causes of death in the United States; today it ranks seventh. Moreover, the threat to world health from this disease is growing, with projections of an increase in incidence between 2000 and 2010 of 57 percent in Asia, 50 percent in Africa, 44 percent in South America, and 23 percent in North America (Zimmet, Alberti, and Shaw, 2001). Part of this projected increase will be due to decreases in other causes of death (e.g., infectious diseases), but much of it has to do with lifestyle and dietary changes associated with modernization and globalization, especially the decrease in levels of daily activity and increase in dietary intake of fats and refined carbohydrates.

Rates for obesity and diabetes in the United States have grown over the last decade, and there is fear that the increase is accelerating. In fact, obesity and diabetes have been referred to as "epidemics" in medical and popular news reports (Mokdad et al., 2001). Unlike many scourges that threaten our health, however, obesity and diabetes are easily preventable with modifications in diet and activity.

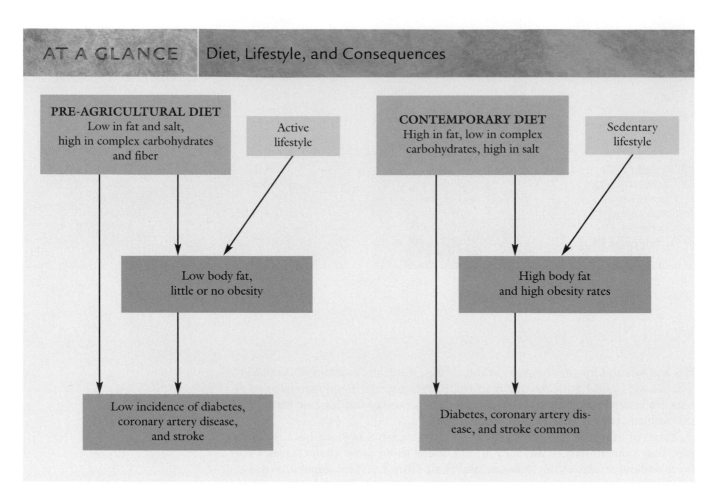

AT A GLANCE   Diet, Lifestyle, and Consequences

It is clear that both deficiencies and excesses of nutrients can cause health problems and interfere with childhood growth. Certainly, many people in all parts of the world, both industrialized and developing, suffer from inadequate supplies of food of any quality. We read daily of thousands dying from starvation due to drought, warfare, or political instability. The blame must be placed not only on the narrowed food base that resulted from the emergence of agriculture, but also on the increase in human population that occurred when people began to settle in permanent villages and have more children. Today, the crush of billions of humans almost completely dependent on cereal grains means that millions face undernutrition, malnutrition, and even starvation. Even with these huge populations, however, food scarcity may not be as big a problem as food inequality. In other words, there may be enough food produced for all people on earth, but economic and political forces keep it from reaching those who need it most.

In summary, our nutritional adaptations were shaped in an environment that included times of scarcity alternating with times of abundance. The variety of foods consumed was so great that nutritional deficiency diseases were rare. Small amounts of animal foods were probably an important part of the diet in many parts of the world. In northern latitudes, subsequent to approximately 1 million years ago, meat was an important part of the diet, but because such meat was low in fats, the negative effects of high meat intake that we see today did not occur. Our diet today is often incompatible with the adaptations that evolved in the millions of years preceding the development of agriculture. The consequences of that incompatibility include both starvation and obesity (Fig. 16–6).

(a)

(b)

ONSET OF REPRODUCTIVE FUNCTIONING IN HUMANS

Having reviewed nutritional factors that influence growth during childhood, let's return to the life cycle and follow it through until the end of life. If you take another look at Figure 16–4, you will see that for most animals, the juvenile, or childhood, stage ends when adulthood begins. For humans, some monkeys, and apes, however, there is an additional life cycle stage called subadulthood. This is the time following the onset of reproductive functioning, usually called adolescence in humans, when individuals may be mature in some ways, but immature in others. For example, an adolescent girl of 14 may be capable of bearing children, but she is not yet fully grown herself and she is usually immature socially.

The onset of menarche in girls is affected by several factors, including genetic patterns (girls tend to become mature at about the same age as their mothers), nutrition, stress, and disease. It also appears that a certain amount of body fat is necessary for menarche and the maintenance of ovulation (Frisch, 1988). Both diet and activity levels affect the accumulation of body fat. This may explain the trend toward the lower age of menarche that has been noted in human populations in the last hundred years and the tendency for girls who are very active and thin to mature later than those who are heavier and less active. High activity and low body fat also characterize many ballet dancers and marathon runners, who often cease to menstruate during periods of intense training. Since pregnancy and nursing require an increase in caloric consumption, body fat may serve as a signal to the body that there is enough caloric reserve to support a pregnancy. When the levels of body fat fall too low, ovulation may cease temporarily to prevent initiation of a pregnancy that is likely to fail.

Life history theory provides ways of predicting the timing of reproduction under favorable circumstances. For example, if early maturity results in higher numbers of surviving offspring, then it is predicted that natural selection would favor those members of a population who mature earlier. Until the advent of settled living, it is likely that females became pregnant as soon as they were biologically able to do so. This would be advantageous in view of the fact that individual life expectancy would have been low. Paleodemographic studies indicate a mortality rate of at least 50 percent in subadults in preindustrial populations; and of the half that survived to adulthood, most did not survive to age 50. Given the reality of short life spans combined with the long period of infant dependency, producing offspring as early as possible may have contributed to the reproductive success of females, particularly early hominid females. If we use chimpanzees as a model for this discussion, it is noteworthy that with one exception, no infant chimpanzee orphaned prior to the age of three has survived.

FIGURE 16–6 Some people suffer from an overabundance of food (a), while others suffer from tragically insufficient amounts (b).

Consequently, one could argue that a similar situation applied to early hominids, who, in addition to the numerous risk factors faced by chimpanzees, were subject to greater degrees of predation pressure. Hence, an early hominid female's chances of rearing even one offspring to the point it could survive without her were enhanced by giving birth as soon as she reached sexual maturity.

The high rates of adolescent pregnancy that typify so many cultures today reflect this ancient biological heritage. Today, however, there may be disadvantages to early maturity. If delayed maturity is associated with higher-quality care of the offspring, then offspring survival may improve, resulting in a net increase in fitness for those who mature a few years later. Unfortunately, all too frequently today in many parts of the world, young girls become reproductively mature long before they are socially mature. And if they are also sexually active, they may become pregnant before they have finished school or obtained the skills necessary for economic self-sufficiency. This means that the quality of care that they can provide their offspring will be compromised. It is known that the infant mortality rate in humans rises rapidly as mothers' age at first birth decreases (Stearns, 1992). In contemporary society, it's likely that those who delay reproducing until they are emotionally, socially, and economically mature will have more surviving offspring than those who begin their parenting careers before they themselves have matured. But if the young, maturing parents have sufficient help from their extended families, religious organizations, or government agencies, early childbearing may not compromise their reproductive fitness. Clearly, the road to reproductive success is more complicated than most early theories of behavioral ecology suggested, although they serve as useful models on which to base predictions about behavior.

What about the number of offspring produced at each birth? Primates such as monkeys, apes, and humans typically give birth to one infant at a time. Twins occur in apes and humans at about the same frequency, but the survival rate of twins (or triplets) is far lower than the survival rate of singletons. Thus, we can argue that humans are physiologically constrained in the number of offspring resulting from each conception. Because we are mammals, we are also physiologically constrained regarding the dependency of our offspring in the first few years of life, as discussed earlier in this chapter (Fig. 16–7). Apes (and, we assume, ancestral humans) nurse their infants for three to four years, resulting in an approximate four-year birth interval. That interval can be reduced with earlier weaning or, in the case of formula feeding, by not nursing at all. This means that contemporary humans can easily reduce the birth interval to fewer than two years, potentially doubling the number of offspring produced. But again, in most cases, the quality of parental care is compromised when there are too many dependent offspring. If the number of offspring reaching reproductive maturity is lower in individuals and families with two-year birth intervals than in those with four-year birth intervals, then natural selection will favor the latter.

While an evolutionary perspective can help us understand how natural selection has had an impact on offspring quantity, it can also help us understand parenting behaviors that may, at first glance, seem counter to the goal of increasing reproductive success. For example, in Chapter 7, we discussed infanticide in langurs and other species, noting that it seems counterproductive to the supposed goal of increasing reproductive success. The evolutionary perspective argues that when infanticide is perpetrated by a male against the offspring of another male, then it can be interpreted as increasing his own reproductive success at the expense of the other male. But what about situations in which a mother kills her own offspring? Can this contribute to her reproductive success in any way? Sara Hrdy tackles such challenging questions in her book *Mother Nature: A History of Mothers, Infants, and Natural Selection* (1999). She points out that there are many instances in which maternal behavior defies the claim that there is a natural "instinct" for mother love in mammals. But if the behaviors are placed in an evo-

FIGURE 16–7 Human infants require extensive parental care, especially in the first few years of life.

lutionary context, the discrepancies can often be resolved. For example, consider a mother who abandons her newborn infant when social and economic conditions are so dire that the chances of the child surviving very long are diminished. It may be better (in an evolutionary sense, *not* in a moral sense) to let that child die so that she can bear another as soon as conditions and chances for child survival are improved. This illustrates the concept that for most measures of reproductive success, quality of offspring produced is more important than quantity. This is not to say that all maternal behaviors are adaptive. But a behavior that at first glance seems maladaptive may actually serve to increase reproductive success for the mother in the long run.

Can behavioral ecology explain the long period of reproductive sterility in human females following menopause? If increasing reproductive success is what it is all about, then how could natural selection favor cessation of reproductive functioning relatively early in a woman's lifetime?

For women, menopause, or the end of menstruation, is a sign of entry into a new phase of the life cycle. Estrogen and progesterone production begin to decline toward the end of the reproductive years until ovulation (and thus menstruation) ceases altogether. This occurs at approximately age 50 in all parts of the world. Throughout human evolution, the majority of females (and males) did not survive to age 50; thus, few women lived much past menopause. But today, this event occurs when women have as much as one-third of their active and healthy lives ahead of them. Such a long postreproductive period is not found in other primates. Female chimpanzees and monkeys experience decreased fertility in their later years, but most continue to have reproductive cycles until their deaths. Occasional reports of menopause in apes and monkeys have been noted, but it is far from a routine and expected event.

Why do human females have such a long period during which they can no longer reproduce? One theory relates to parenting. Since it takes about 12 to 15 years before a child becomes independent, it has been argued that females are biologically "programmed" to live 12 to 15 years beyond the birth of their last child (Mayer, 1982). This suggests that the maximum human life span for pre-agricultural humans was about 65 years, a figure that corresponds to what is known for contemporary hunter-gatherers and for prehistoric populations. Another theory regarding menopause suggests that it was not itself favored by natural selection; rather, it is an artifact of the extension of the human life span. Some have suggested that the maximum life span of the mammalian egg is 50 years (you will recall that all the ova are already present before birth; see p. 454). Thus, although the human life span has increased in the last several hundred years, the reproductive life span has not.

One final explanation for the long postreproductive period in human females has been proposed by behavioral ecologists and is known as the "grandmother hypothesis." This proposal argues that natural selection may have favored this long period in women's lives because postmenopausal women could provide high-quality care for their grandchildren (Fig. 16–8). In other words, an older woman would be more likely to increase her lifetime fitness by enhancing the survival of her older grandchildren (who share one-quarter of her genes) through provisioning and direct child care than she would by having her own infants. Support of this hypothesis comes from field studies of the Hadza of Tanzania. The Hadza are food foragers who spend hours each day gathering roots, tubers, berries, honey, and other plant foods. Anthropologists Kristen Hawkes, James F. O'Connell, and Nicholas Blurton-Jones (1997) found that grandmothers with no dependent offspring spent more time per day and were more successful gathering foods than mothers or unmarried

FIGURE 16–8 Senior Hadza woman and grandchild.

girls. The contribution of grandmothers was particularly important when their daughters had recently given birth, resulting in constraints on their own ability to forage for food just when, owing to lactation, their caloric needs were high.

HUMAN LONGEVITY

Relative to most other animals, humans have a long life span (Table 16–2). The maximum life span potential, estimated to be about 120 years, has probably not changed in the last several thousand years, although life expectancy at birth (the average length of life) has increased significantly in the last 100 years, owing to advances in medical care. Probably the most important advance has been treatment and prevention of infectious diseases, which typically take their toll on the young (Crews and Harper, 1998).

To some extent, aging is something we do throughout our entire lives. But we usually think of aging as **senescence,** the process of physiological decline in all systems of the body that occurs toward the end of the life course. Actually, throughout adulthood, there is a gradual decline in our cells' ability to synthesize proteins, in immune system function, in muscle mass (with a corresponding increase in fat mass) and strength, and in bone mineral density (Lamberts et al., 1997). This decline is associated with an increase in risk for the chronic degenerative diseases that are usually listed as the causes of death in industrialized nations.

As you know, most causes of death that have their effects after the reproductive years will not be subjected to the forces of natural selection. Furthermore, in evolutionary terms, reproductive success isn't measured by how long we live. Rather, as we have emphasized throughout this textbook, it is measured by how many offspring we produce. Thus, organisms need to survive only long enough to produce offspring and rear them to maturity. Contrary to what most people probably think, the majority of wild animals (certainly small bodied ones) don't live out their potential lifespan. Most wild animals die young of infection, starvation, predation, injury, and cold. Obviously there are exceptions to this statement, especially in larger bodied animals. Elephants, for example, may live over 50 years and we know of several chimpanzees at Gombe that have survived into their forties.

One explanation for why humans age and are affected by chronic degenerative diseases like atherosclerosis, cancers, and hypertension is that genes that enhance reproductive success in earlier years (and thus were favored by natural selection) may have detrimental effects in later years. These are referred to as **pleiotropic genes,** meaning that they have multiple effects at different times in the life span or under different conditions (Williams, 1957). For example, genes that enhance the function of the immune system in the early years may also damage tissue so that cancer susceptibility increases in later life (Nesse and Williams, 1994). Alternatively, cancer-protecting genes may override genes for organ and tissue renewal in later life.

Pleiotropy may help us understand evolutionary reasons for aging, but what are the causes of senescence in the individual? Much attention has been focused recently on free radicals, highly reactive molecules that can damage cells. Protection against these by-products of normal metabolism is provided by antioxidants such as vitamins A, C, and E and by a number of enzymes (Kirkwood, 1997). Ultimately, damage to DNA can occur, which in turn contributes to the senescence of cells, the immune system, and other functional systems of the body. Additionally, there is evidence that programmed cell death is also a part of the normal processes of development that can obviously contribute to senescence.

Another hypothesis for senescence is known as the "telomere hypothesis." In this view, the DNA sequence at the end of each chromosome, known as the telomere, is shortened each time a cell divides (Fig. 16–9). Cells that have

TABLE 16–2 Maximal Life Spans for Selected Species

ORGANISM	APPROXIMATE MAXIMUM LIFE SPAN (IN YEARS)
Bristlecone pine	5,000
Tortoise	170
Rockfish	140
Human	120
Blue whale	80
Indian elephant	70
Gorilla	39
Domestic dog	34
Rabbit	13
Rat	5

Source: Stini, 1991.

senescence The process of physiological decline in body function that occurs with aging.

pleiotropic genes Genes that have more than one effect; genes that have different effects at different times in the life cycle.

divided many times throughout the life course have short telomeres, eventually reaching the point at which they can no longer divide and are unable to maintain healthy tissues and organs. Changes in telomere length have also been implicated in cancers. In the laboratory, the enzyme telomerase can lengthen telomeres, allowing the cell to continue to divide. For this reason, the gene for telomerase has been called the "immortalizing gene." But this may not be a good thing since the only cells that can divide indefinitely are cancer cells. Although this research isn't likely to lead to a lengthening of the life span, it may contribute to a better understanding of cellular functions and of cancer.

Far more important than genes in the aging process, however, are lifestyle factors, such as smoking, physical activity, diet, and medical care. Life expectancy at birth varies considerably from country to country and among socioeconomic classes within a country. Throughout the world, women have higher life expectancies than men. A Japanese girl born in 2003, for example, can expect to live to age 84, a boy to age 78. Girls and boys born in that same year in the United States have life expectancies of 80 and 73, respectively. In contrast to these children in industrialized nations, girls and boys in Mali have life expectancies of only 48 and 46, respectively. Many African nations have seen life expectancy drop below 40 owing to deaths from AIDS. For example, before the AIDS epidemic, Zimbabweans had a life expectancy of 65 years; today, life expectancy in Zimbabwe is 39.

FIGURE 16–9 Telomeres are repeated sequences of DNA at the ends of chromosomes and the sequences appear to be the same in all animals. They stabilize and protect the ends of chromosomes and, as they shorten with each cell division, the chromosomes eventually become unstable.

Human Impact on the Planet and Other Life Forms

The figures for life expectancy in various nations of the world remind us of the importance of diet, health care, and social environment for lifelong health and survival. Clearly, the data indicate that living conditions in Japan are more supportive of good health for the general population than those in Mali. At some level, the success of a nation can be measured by statistics measuring things like infant mortality rates and life expectancy. But how do we measure the success of a species?

By most standards, *Homo sapiens* is a successful species. There are currently more than 6 billion human beings living on this planet. Each one of these 6,300,000,000 individuals comprises upwards of 20 trillion cells. Nevertheless, we and all other multicellular organisms contribute but a small fraction of all the cells on the planet—the vast majority of which are bacteria. Thus, if we see life ultimately as a competition among reproducing organisms, bacteria are the winners, hands down.

Bacteria, then, could be viewed as the dominant life form on earth. However, even when only considering multicellular animals, there are additional lessons in evolutionary humility. As mammals, we are members of a group that includes about 4,000 species—a group of animals that has been on the decline over the last several million years. Looking even more specifically, as primates, we see ourselves belonging to a grouping that today numbers not even 200 species (and is also probably declining since its peak several million years ago). Compare these species numbers with those estimated for insects. Over 750,000 insect species have been identified, and estimates are as high as 30 million (Wilson, 1992)! Number of species (as an indicator of biological diversity) is as good a barometer of evolutionary success as any other. By this standard, humans (and our close relatives) could hardly be seen as the most successful of species.

Evolutionary success can also be gauged by species longevity. As we have seen, fossil evidence indicates that *Homo sapiens* has been on the scene for at least 200,000 years and perhaps as long as 400,000 years. Such time spans, seen through the perspective of a human lifetime, may seem enormous. But consider this: Our immediate predecessor, *Homo erectus,* had a species longevity of about 1.5 million years. In other words, we as a species would need to exist another million years simply to match *Homo erectus!* If such considerations as these are not humbling enough, remember that some sharks and turtles have thrived basically unchanged structurally for 400 million years (although many of these species are now seriously threatened).

OVERPOPULATION

No matter what criterion for success is used, there is no question that *Homo sapiens* has had an inordinate impact on the earth and all other forms of life. In the past, humans had to respond primarily to challenges in the natural world; today the greatest challenges for our species (and all others) are environments of our own making.

If we had to point to one single challenge facing humanity, a problem to which virtually all others are tied, it would have to be population growth. We currently are trapped in a destructive cycle of our own making. Population size has skyrocketed in our own species as we have increased our ability to produce food surpluses. As population size increases, more and more land is converted to crops, pasture, and construction, providing more opportunities for yet more humans. Additionally, through recent medical advances, we have reduced mortality at both ends of the life cycle. Thus, fewer people die in childhood, and having survived to adulthood, they live longer than ever before. Although these medical advances are unquestionably beneficial to individuals (who has not benefited from medical technology?), it is also clear that there are significant detrimental consequences to the species and to the planet.

Population size, if left unchecked, increases exponentially, that is, as a function of some percent, like compound interest in a bank account. Currently, human population increases worldwide at an annual rate of about 1.8 percent. Although this figure may not seem too startling at first, it deserves some examination. In addition, it is useful to discuss doubling time, or the amount of time it takes for a population to double in size.

Scientists estimate that around 10,000 years ago, only about 5 million people inhabited the earth (not even half as many as live in Los Angeles County or New York City today). By the year 1650, there were perhaps 500 million, and by 1800, around 1 billion (Fig. 16–10). In other words, between 10,000 years ago and 1650 (a period of 9,650 years), population size doubled seven and a half times. On average, then, the doubling time between 10,000 years ago and 1650 was about 1,287 years. But from 1650 to 1800 it doubled again, which means that doubling time had been reduced to 150 years (Ehrlich and Ehrlich, 1990). And in the 37 years between 1950 and 1987, world population doubled from 2 billion to 4 billion. To state this problem in terms we can appreciate, we add 1 billion people to the world's population approximately every 11 years. That comes out to 90 to 95 million every year and roughly a quarter of a million every day—or more than 10,000 an hour.

The rate of growth is not equally distributed among all nations. Although the world's rate of increase has ranged from 1.7 to 2.1 percent since the 1950s (Ehrlich and Ehrlich, 1990), it is the developing countries that share most of the burden (not to be interpreted as blame). During the 1980s, the population of Kenya grew at a rate of a little over 4 percent per year, while India added a million per month, and 36,000 babies were born every day in Latin America.

The most recent United Nations International Conference on Population and Development set as its goal the development of a plan to contain the world's population to about 7.3 billion by the year 2015 and to prevent future growth.

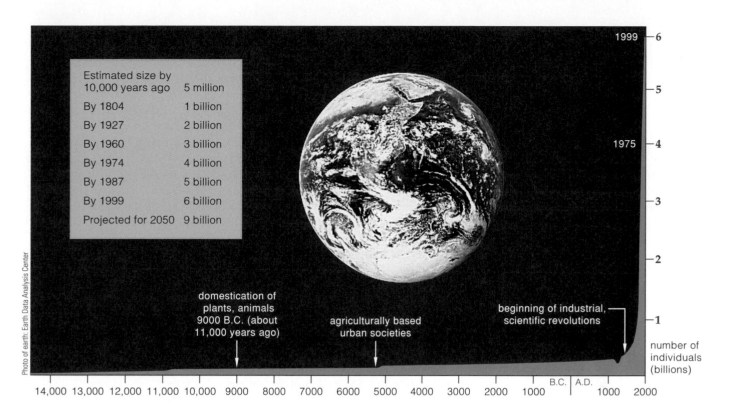

Estimated size by

10,000 years ago	5 million
By 1804	1 billion
By 1927	2 billion
By 1960	3 billion
By 1974	4 billion
By 1987	5 billion
By 1999	6 billion
Projected for 2050	9 billion

Photo of earth: Earth Data Analysis Center

domestication of
plants, animals
9000 B.C. (about
11,000 years ago)

agriculturally based
urban societies

beginning of industrial,
scientific revolutions

number of
individuals
(billions)

14,000 13,000 12,000 11,000 10,000 9000 8000 7000 6000 5000 4000 3000 2000 1000   B.C. | A.D.   1000 2000

Otherwise, by the year 2050, human numbers will approach 10 billion. The United Nations plan emphasizes women's education, health, and rights throughout the world, but has met with stiff resistance from religious groups opposed to abortion and contraception.

The United Nations goal is an admirable but ambitious one, and achieving it will be a formidable task. Although the average number of live births per woman declined in developing nations from 5 in 1955 to 3 by the 1990s, it will still be next to impossible to prevent huge population increases in this century. Bear in mind that *approximately half of all people currently living in the developing world are less than 15 years old.* These young people have not yet reproduced, but they will.

You might logically ask, Can we not make technological changes sufficient to feed all these people? Certainly this and similar questions are being asked more frequently today than in the past. There surely are methods that would more efficiently utilize agricultural lands already available. Clearly, there are better ways to distribute the food surpluses already produced (in the United States in particular). But can we continue forever to make technological changes sufficient to feed ever-growing numbers of humans? Is there enough land to support an endless demand for housing, crop cultivation, and grazing? Is there enough water? We probably can develop technologies to meet our species' increasing needs for a while. But can we do so and still meet the requirements of thousands of undomesticated species? The answer for the immediate future is: Probably not. For the long term, without major changes in human population growth, the answer is: Certainly not.

FIGURE 16–10 The growth curve (orange), depicting the exponential growth of the human population. The vertical axis shows the world population in billions. Note that it wasn't until 1804 that the population reached 1 billion, but the numbers went from 5 billion to 6 billion in 12 short years (see blue box). Population increase occurs as a function of some percent (in developing countries, the annual rate is over 3 percent). With advances in food production and medical technologies, humans are undergoing a population explosion, as this figure illustrates.

IMPACT ON BIODIVERSITY

Another legacy of the human evolutionary process is expressed in the proposal recently put forth by biologist Stephen Palumbi (2001) that humans are the "world's greatest evolutionary force." What Palumbi means is that we humans, like no other species before us, have profound effects on the evolutionary histories of almost all forms of life, including the ability to alter global ecology and the potential to destroy ourselves and virtually all life on earth. Clearly, such wide and sudden impacts have no precedents in the fossil record. Even massive evolutionary catastrophes and mass extinctions did not wreak the havoc that may result from modern human technology.

As we mentioned earlier (see p. 134), two major extinction events have occurred in the last 250 million years. A third major extinction event, perhaps of the same magnitude, is occurring now and, according to some scientists, may have begun in the late Pleistocene or early **Holocene** (Ward, 1994). Unlike all other mass extinctions, the current one has not been caused by continental drift, climate change (so far), or collisions with asteroids. Rather, these recent and ongoing extinctions are due to the activities of a single species—*Homo sapiens.*

Many scientists, in fact, believe that several large mammalian species were pushed toward extinction due to overhunting by earlier human populations, particularly near the end of the Pleistocene, some 10,000 years ago. In North America, at least 57 mammalian species became extinct, including the mammoth, mastodon, giant ground sloth, saber-toothed cat, several large rodents, and numerous ungulates (hooved mammals) or grazing animals (Lewin, 1986; Simmons, 1989). Although climate change (warming) was undoubtedly a factor in these Pleistocene extinctions, hunting and other human activities may also have been important. Although there is some dispute as to when humans first entered North America from Asia, it is certain that they were firmly established by at least 12,000 years ago (and probably earlier).

We have no direct evidence that early American big game hunters contributed to extinctions; but we do have evidence of what can happen to indigenous species when new areas are colonized by humans for the first time. Within just a few decades of human occupation of New Zealand, the moa, a large flightless bird, was exterminated. Madagascar serves as a similar example. In the last one thousand years, after the arrival of permanent human settlement, 14 species of lemurs, in addition to other mammalian and bird species, have become extinct (Jolly, 1985; Napier and Napier, 1985). One such species was *Megaladapis,* a lemur that weighed an estimated 300 pounds (Fleagle, 1999)! Lastly, scientists have debated for years whether the extinction of all large-bodied animals (some 60 species) in Australia during the late Pleistocene was due to human hunting and other activities or to climate change.

Since the end of the Pleistocene, human activities have continued to take their toll on nonhuman species. Today, however, species are disappearing at an unprecedented rate. Hunting, which occurs for a number of reasons other than acquisition of food, continues to be a major factor (see Issue, pp. 134–136). Competition with introduced nonnative species, such as pigs, goats, and rats, has also contributed to the problem. But in many cases, the most important single cause of extinction is habitat reduction.

Habitat reduction is a direct result of the burgeoning human population and the resulting need for building materials, grazing and agricultural land, and living areas. We are all aware of the risk to such visible species as the elephant, panda, rhinoceros, tiger, and mountain gorilla, to name a few. These risks are real, and within your lifetime some of these will certainly become extinct, at least in the wild. But the greatest threat to biodiversity is to the countless unknown species that live in the world's rain forests (Fig. 16–11).

It is estimated that over half of all plants and animals on earth live in rain forests. By 1989, these habitats had been reduced to a little less than half their original size—that is, down to about 3 million square miles. The annual net loss between 1980 and 1995 was almost 67,000 square miles. As Harvard biologist E. O. Wilson puts it: "The loss is equal to the area of a football field every second. Put another way, in 1989 the surviving rain forests occupied an area about that of the continuous forty-eight states of the United States, and they were

Holocene The most recent epoch of the Cenozoic. Following the Pleistocene, it is estimated to have begun 10,000 years ago.

being reduced by an amount equivalent to the size of Florida every year" (Wilson, 1992, p. 275). By the year 2022, half the world's remaining rain forests will be gone if destruction continues at its present rate. This will result in a loss of between 10 and 22 percent of all rain forest species, or 5 to 10 percent of all plant and animal species on earth (Wilson, 1992).

Should we care about the loss of biodiversity? If so, why? In fact, there are many people who do not show much concern. Moreover, reasons as to why we should care are usually stated in terms of the benefits (known and unknown) that humans may derive from rain forest species. An example of such a benefit is the chemical taxol (derived from the Pacific yew tree), which may be an effective treatment for ovarian and breast cancer.

It is undeniable that humans stand to benefit from continued research into potentially useful rain forest products. However, such anthropocentric reasons are not the sole justification for preserving the earth's biodiversity. Each species that is lost is the product of millions of years of evolution, and each fills a specific econiche. Quite simply, the destruction of so much of the planet's biota is within our power. But ethically, we must ask ourselves, Is it within our rights?

FIGURE 16–11 Stumps of recently felled forest trees are still visible in this newly cleared field in Rwanda. The haze is wood smoke from household fires.

ACCELERATION OF EVOLUTIONARY PROCESSES

Another of the major impacts that human activities have had is on the acceleration of the evolutionary process for hundreds of life forms. Many of these changes have occurred over one human generation, rather than the millions of years that have been familiar in our discussions of evolution in this text. For example, as noted in Chapter 15, our use of antibiotics has directed the course of evolution of several infectious diseases to the point that many have become resistant to our antibiotics. The analogy often used is that of an arms race: We use slingshots, they come back with spears; we use swords, they come back with guns; we use bigger guns, they come back with bombs; then we come back with weapons of mass destruction. Finally we reach a point where our armaments are matched and no longer work as deterrents to war. Similarly, our antibiotics reach a point where they are no longer effective on strains of infectious diseases that were once relatively mild. Human-invented antibiotics have become the agents of natural selection directing the course of evolution of many bacteria to a more virulent state.

It is even likely that human technology and lifestyles are responsible for the deadly nature of some of the so-called "new" diseases that have arisen in recent decades, such as HIV-AIDS (see p. 434), dengue hemorrhagic fever, Legionnaire's disease, Lyme disease, and resistant strains of tuberculosis, *Staphylococcus,* and *E coli.* A few years ago, the fear of anthrax drove thousands of people to use antibiotics such as ciprofloxacin in the extremely rare event that they would be exposed to the deadly bacterium. Certainly, we understand the desire for preventive action on the part of those at heightened risk. But if more harmful bacteria become resistant as a by-product of this practice, the risk to society from the overuse and improper use of this powerful class of antibiotics is potentially far greater. We could reach a point where we have no antibiotics strong enough to overpower dangerous bacteria that live in our midst.

A similar phenomenon has occurred with the overuse and misuse of insecticides and pesticides on agricultural crops (Palumbi, 2001). Insects evolve resistance to each new generation of toxic agents, eventually reaching a point where they are no longer affected by most of the insecticides used on the fields. Bt toxin *(Bacillus thuringiensis)* has been highly touted as an "organic" and environmentally friendly agent because it is naturally produced (often by the crops it protects), targets specific insect larvae, and is not toxic to humans. Genes for producing Bt toxin have been engineered into millions of acres of plants, but unfortunately, recent evidence suggests that some insects are evolving resistance to it.

As mentioned in Chapter 14, perhaps the best-known insecticide to have altered the course of evolution of a species is DDT. When this insecticide was first developed, it was hailed as the best way to reduce malaria, eliminating the mosquitoes that transmit the disease. DDT was highly effective when it was first applied to mosquito-ridden areas, but soon, mosquitoes had evolved resistance to the powerful agent, rendering it almost useless in the fight against malaria. Moreover, the use of DDT proved disastrous to many bird species, including the bald eagle.

From these examples, it is clear that the process of evolution is something that can result in great harm for our species and planet. Certainly, none of the scientists working to develop antibiotics, insecticides, pesticides, and other biological tools intend to cause harm (with the obvious exceptions of those working for bioterrorists), but often those working in these areas lack the understanding of the evolutionary process necessary to foresee long-term consequences of their work. As the great geneticist Theodosius Dobzhansky said, "Nothing in biology makes sense except in the light of evolution." Indeed, we cannot afford even a single generation of scientists who lack knowledge about the process of evolution, which is responsible for the life forms around us, both helpful and harmful. If human actions can cause an organism to evolve from a relatively benign state to a dangerously virulent state, then there is no reason why that process cannot be "turned around." In other words, it is theoretically possible to direct the course of evolution of a dangerous organism like HIV to a more benign, less harmful state (Ewald, 1999). But this requires a very sophisticated understanding of evolution.

Is There Any Good News?

Now that you are thoroughly depressed about the potentially gloomy future of the earth and our species, is there any good news? In 2000, heads of state from almost 150 countries agreed to support a set of Millennium Development Goals that would help to reduce human misery throughout the world. Here are the eight goals:

1. Eradicate extreme poverty and hunger.
2. Achieve universal primary education.
3. Promote gender equity and empower women.
4. Reduce child mortality.
5. Improve maternal health.
6. Combat HIV/AIDS, malaria, and other diseases.
7. Ensure environmental sustainability.
8. Build a global partnership for development.

These goals set measurable targets that can be examined year after year to see how close we come to meeting them. Although there will be immense and expensive challenges, this international agreement seems a good start toward concerted cooperative efforts to solve the major problems of the world today, and it goes a long way toward encouraging partnerships between rich and poor nations.

Although world population growth continues, it appears that the rate of growth has slowed somewhat. It is common knowledge among economists that as income and education increase, family size decreases, and as infant and child mortality rates decrease, families are having fewer children. In fact, it has frequently been argued that one of the best strategies for reducing family size and thus world population is to educate girls and women. Educated woman are more likely to be in the labor force and are better able to provide food for their families, seek health care for themselves and their children, delay marriage, and use family planning. In 1990, the international community adopted the World Declaration on Education for All. Since that time, there have been steady increases in efforts to educate all segments of society. In fact, in some parts of the world, there have been so many efforts to improve education for girls that they are now favored by the gender gap in education.

With decreases in family size and improvements in education and employment opportunities for both men and women throughout the world, we are also likely to see improvements in environmental conservation and habitat preservation. A generally recognized phenomenon is that habitat destruction and poverty often go hand in hand. Although successes in Costa Rica cannot be replicated everywhere, this small nation has been a model for making environmental concerns integral to social and economic development. Ecotourism, built on preservation of abundant and beautiful natural resources, has now become the nation's primary industry, and poverty levels are the lowest in Central America.

Recently, there have been several international agreements designed to preserve endangered species and habitats. These often mean the development of national parks and preserves. Figure 16–12 shows the increase in protected sites during the past 30 years.

There are also a number of international efforts to preserve primates, most notably the United Nation's Great Apes Survival Project (GRASP). This project brings together great ape research and conservation organizations that have struggled to save the animals they care about with varying degrees of success and failure. Three UN Special Envoys have been appointed: Russell Mittermeier (Director of Conservation International), Jane Goodall (see p. 174), and Toshisada Nishida (see p. 215). Their hope is that by combining efforts and targeting resources, they will be able to have the political and financial clout to halt the decline of great ape species (see also p. 135).

FIGURE 16–12 There has been a steady increase in the number and total area of protected sites in the world in the past few decades.

Finally, in March 2002, leaders from both developing and developed countries came together in Monterrey, Mexico, to discuss new ways of reducing global poverty. The developed countries, including the European Union, the United States, Canada, and Australia, made commitments to increase development assistance by about $16 billion a year by 2006. Countries in Latin America and the Caribbean have made significant progress in meeting some of the goals, but countries in sub-Saharan Africa have fallen further behind than when agreements were made.

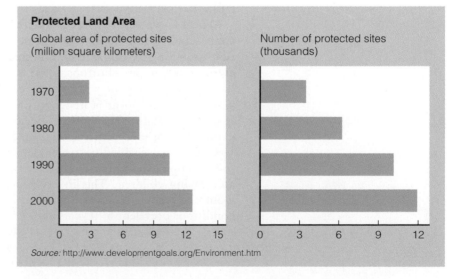

Protected Land Area

Global area of protected sites (million square kilometers)

Number of protected sites (thousands)

Source: http://www.developmentgoals.org/Environment.htm

What should be obvious from these examples is that only by working together can nations of the world hope to bring about solutions to the world's problems. As we argued earlier in this chapter and in Chapter 8, despite occasional evidence to the contrary, cooperation may have been more important in human evolution than conflict. These international efforts illustrate the extent to which we believe that to be the case. The question now is whether or not we have the collective will to see that our admirable goals are met. Many people believe that it is our only hope.

Are We Still Evolving?

In many ways, it seems that culture has enabled us to transcend most of the limitations imposed on us by our biology. But that biology was shaped during millions of years of evolution in environments very different from those in which most of us live today. There is, to a great extent, a lack of fit between our biology and our twenty-first-century cultural environment. Our expectations that scientists can easily and quickly discover a "magic bullet" to enable us to resist any disease that arises have been painfully dashed with death tolls from AIDS reaching catastrophic levels in many parts of the world.

Socioeconomic and political concerns also have powerful effects on our species today. Whether you die of starvation or succumb to disorders associated with overconsumption depends a great deal on where you live, what your socioeconomic status is, and how much power and control you have over your life, factors not likely to be related to biology. These factors also have an effect on whether or not you are killed in a war or spend most of your life in a safe, comfortable community. Whether or not you are exposed to one of the "new" pathogens such as HIV, SARS, or tuberculosis has a lot to do with your lifestyle and other cultural factors, but whether or not you die from it or fail to reproduce because of it still has a lot to do with your biology. The 4.3 million children dying annually from respiratory infections are primarily those in the developing world, with limited access to adequate medical care, clearly a cultural factor. But in those same areas, lacking that same medical care, are millions of other children who are not getting the infections or are not dying from them. Presumably, among the factors affecting this difference is resistance afforded by genes. By considering this simple example, we can see that human gene frequencies are still changing from one generation to the next in response to selective agents such as disease; thus, our species is still evolving.

Whether we will become a different species or become extinct as a species (remember, that is the fate of almost everything that has ever lived on earth) is not something we can answer. Whether our brains will get larger, our hands will evolve solely to push buttons, or we will change genetically so that we no longer have to eat food is the stuff of science fiction, not anthropology. But as long as new pathogens appear or new environments are introduced by technology, there is little doubt that the human species will continue to evolve or will become extinct, just as every other species on earth has done.

Culture has enabled us to transcend many limits imposed by our biology, and today people who never would have been able to do so in the past are surviving and having children. This in itself means we are evolving. How many of you would be reading this text if you had been born under the health and economic conditions prevalent 500 years ago?

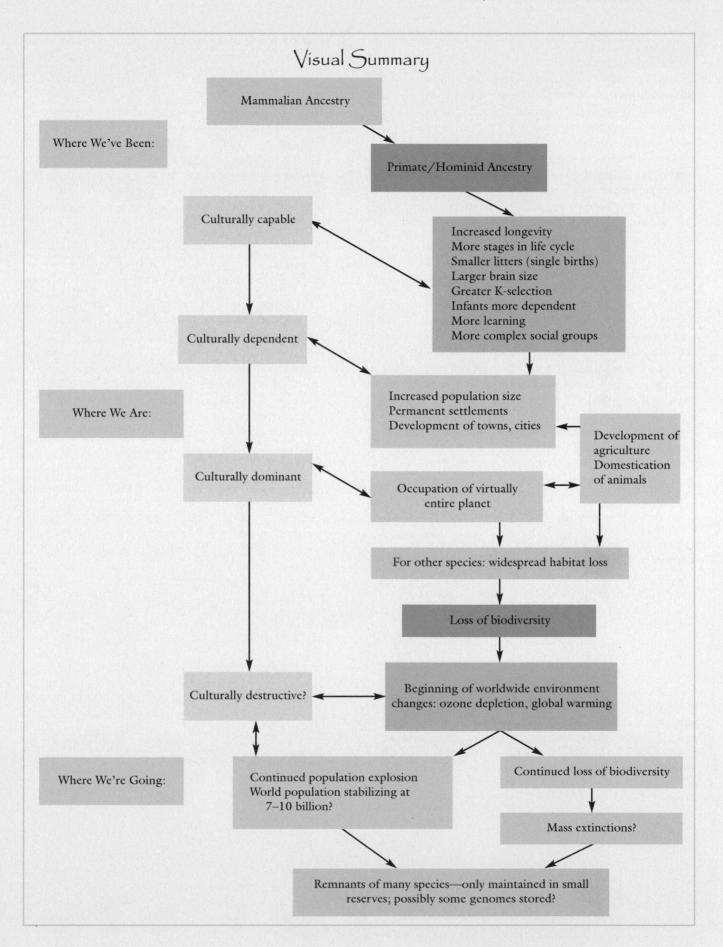

Visual Summary

Mammalian Ancestry

Where We've Been:

Primate/Hominid Ancestry

Culturally capable

Increased longevity
More stages in life cycle
Smaller litters (single births)
Larger brain size
Greater K-selection
Infants more dependent
More learning
More complex social groups

Culturally dependent

Where We Are:

Increased population size
Permanent settlements
Development of towns, cities

Development of
agriculture
Domestication
of animals

Culturally dominant

Occupation of virtually
entire planet

For other species: widespread habitat loss

Loss of biodiversity

Culturally destructive?

Beginning of worldwide environment
changes: ozone depletion, global warming

Where We're Going:

Continued population explosion
World population stabilizing at
7–10 billion?

Continued loss of biodiversity

Mass extinctions?

Remnants of many species—only maintained in small
reserves; possibly some genomes stored?

Summary

In this chapter, we have discussed legacies of human evolutionary history that leave their marks on us today. For the individual, these legacies include patterns of growth and nutritional requirements that result from millions of years of biological evolution and thousands of years of cultural evolution. Our evolutionary history also means that human infants are relatively undeveloped at birth, especially in brain size, and require intense parental investment to reach adulthood and independence. For humans in society, legacies from evolutionary history include thought processes and behaviors that reflect natural selection operating on individuals to increase reproductive success, or fitness. A review of behavioral ecology summarizes the ways in which genes, environment, and culture have interacted to produce complex adaptations to equally complex challenges. Critical review of hypotheses for such human behaviors as aggression, violence, nurturance, and reproduction reveals the complexity of this interrelationship. The final set of legacies reviewed in this chapter concerns the impact of the human species on the planet and other life forms. Through amazing reproductive "success," the human population has reached more than 6 billion from an estimated base of about 5 million people 10,000 years ago. These numbers, coupled with technological developments, have turned humans into what Stephen Palumbi has called "the world's greatest evolutionary force." *Homo sapiens* has become a powerful agent of natural selection, influencing virtually every life form on earth, causing the extinction of many species, and accelerating evolutionary change in others.

Studies of human evolution have much to contribute to our understanding of how we, as a single species, came to exert such control over the destiny of our planet. It is a truly phenomenal story of how a small apelike creature walking on two feet across the African savanna challenged nature by learning to make stone tools. From these humble beginnings came large-brained humans who, instead of stone tools, have telecommunications satellites, computers, and nuclear arsenals at their fingertips. The human story is indeed unique and wonderful. Our two feet have carried us not only across the plains of Africa, but onto the polar caps, the ocean floor, and even across the surface of the moon! Surely, if we can accomplish so much in so short a time, we can act responsibly to preserve our home and the wondrous creatures who share it with us.

Questions For Review

1. What is meant by the analogy, "Water is to fish as culture is to humans"?
2. Give two examples of how culture and biology interact in meeting human nutritional requirements.
3. Compare and contrast the human preagricultural diet with that seen today (in places like the United States). Discuss at least one major health consequence of what has been termed the "lack of fit" between the diet to which humans have evolved and the one many people now consume.
4. Is aging inevitable? Why do humans age?
5. How natural selection might act on such behaviors as mate selection, parenting, and aggression is controversial. Choose one of these and first argue how natural selection *could* have shaped the way the behavior is expressed in humans. Then, critique your first argument, suggesting, instead, some alternatives.
6. Describe circumstances under which adolescent pregnancy might be advantageous, in an evolutionary sense. What are some of the disadvantages of adolescent pregnancy for reproductive success?
7. Under what circumstances might natural selection favor infanticide in humans?
8. What are some of the proposed explanations for menopause in human females? Do other primates experience menopause?
9. Why do the authors of this text claim that human overpopulation is one of the greatest challenges facing our planet today? Do you agree or disagree? Why?
10. How have humans contributed to the decrease of biodiversity on our planet?
11. Provide two examples of how human activities have had an impact on the pace of evolution of other life forms.
12. Are we still evolving? What evidence is there that we are still subject to the forces of evolution?

For Further Thought

1. Does an understanding of the human species within a broad, evolutionary framework help us to predict (even to determine, if we so choose) the future of our species?

Go to the book website at **http://www.anthropology.wadsworth.com** for resources to help you explore these questions further. Click on "For Further Thought" for this chapter.

Suggested Further Reading

Eaton, S. Boyd, Marjorie Shostak, and Melvin Konner. 1988. *The Paleolithic Prescription*. New York: Harper & Row.

Ellison, Peter T. 2001. *On Fertile Ground: A Natural History of Human Reproduction*. Cambridge, MA: Harvard University Press.

Farmer, Paul. 2003. *Pathologies of Power: Health, Human Rights, and the New War on the Poor*. Berkeley: University of California Press.

Hrdy, Sarah Blaffer. 1999. *Mother Nature: A History of Mothers, Infants, and Natural Selection*. New York: Pantheon Books.

Palumbi, Stephen R. 2001. *The Evolution Explosion: How Humans Cause Rapid Evolutionary Change*. New York: Norton.

Potts, M., and R. Short. 1999. *Ever Since Adam and Eve: The Evolution of Human Sexuality*. Cambridge, England: Cambridge University Press.

Wilson, Edward O. 1992. *The Future of Life*. New York: Knopf.

Wrangham, Richard, and Dale Peterson. 1996. *Demonic Males: Apes and the Origins of Human Violence*. Boston: Houghton Mifflin.

Online Anthropology Resource Center

Go to the Anthropology Resource Center at **http://www.anthropology.wadsworth.com** for a wealth of online resources, including a companion website for your text that provides study aids such as self-quizzes for each chapter and a practice final exam, as well as links to anthropology websites and information on the latest theories and discoveries in the field. Also, check out InfoTrac College Edition®, your online library that offers full-length articles from thousands of scholarly and popular publications. Just click on the InfoTrac button at the companion website and use the passcode that came with your book.

Atlas of Primate Skeletal Anatomy

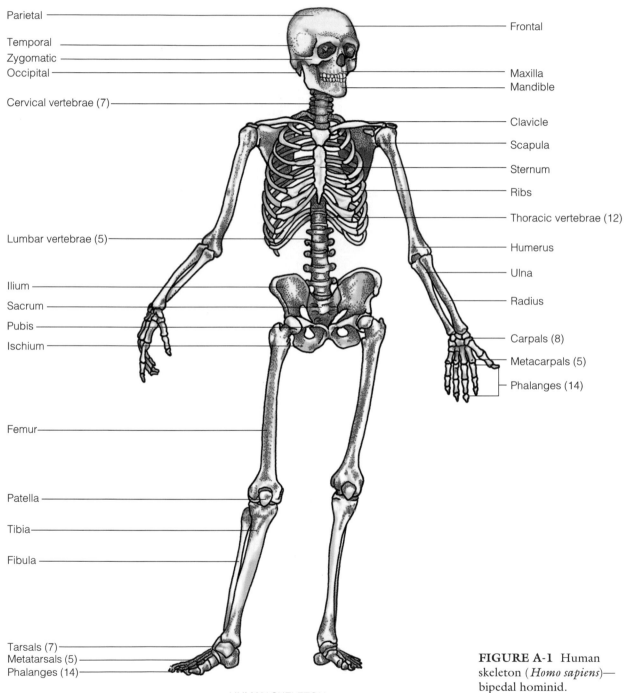

Parietal

Temporal

Zygomatic

Occipital

Cervical vertebrae (7)

Lumbar vertebrae (5)

Ilium

Sacrum

Pubis

Ischium

Femur

Patella

Tibia

Fibula

Tarsals (7)
Metatarsals (5)
Phalanges (14)

Frontal

Maxilla
Mandible

Clavicle

Scapula

Sternum

Ribs

Thoracic vertebrae (12)

Humerus

Ulna

Radius

Carpals (8)

Metacarpals (5)

Phalanges (14)

HUMAN SKELETON

FIGURE A-1 Human skeleton (*Homo sapiens*)—bipedal hominid.

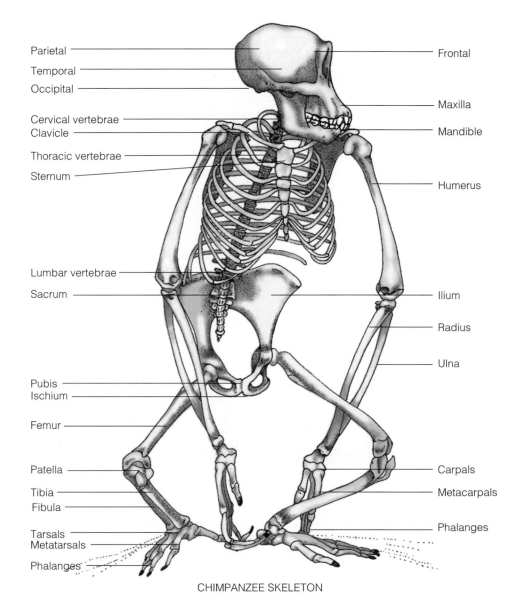

Parietal

Temporal

Occipital

Cervical vertebrae

Clavicle

Thoracic vertebrae

Sternum

Lumbar vertebrae

Sacrum

Pubis

Ischium

Femur

Patella

Tibia

Fibula

Tarsals

Metatarsals

Phalanges

Frontal

Maxilla

Mandible

Humerus

Ilium

Radius

Ulna

Carpals

Metacarpals

Phalanges

CHIMPANZEE SKELETON

FIGURE A-2 Chimpanzee skelton (*Pan troglodytes*)—knuckle-walking pongid.

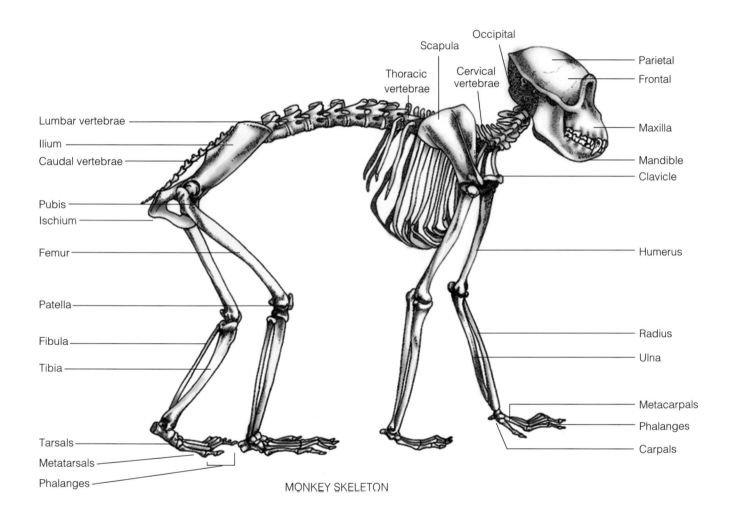

Occipital

Scapula

Thoracic vertebrae

Cervical vertebrae

Parietal

Frontal

Maxilla

Mandible

Clavicle

Lumbar vertebrae

Ilium

Caudal vertebrae

Pubis

Ischium

Femur

Humerus

Patella

Fibula

Tibia

Radius

Ulna

Metacarpals

Phalanges

Carpals

Tarsals

Metatarsals

Phalanges

MONKEY SKELETON

FIGURE A–3 Monkey skeleton (rhesus macaque; *Macaca mulatta*)— a typical quadrupedal primate.

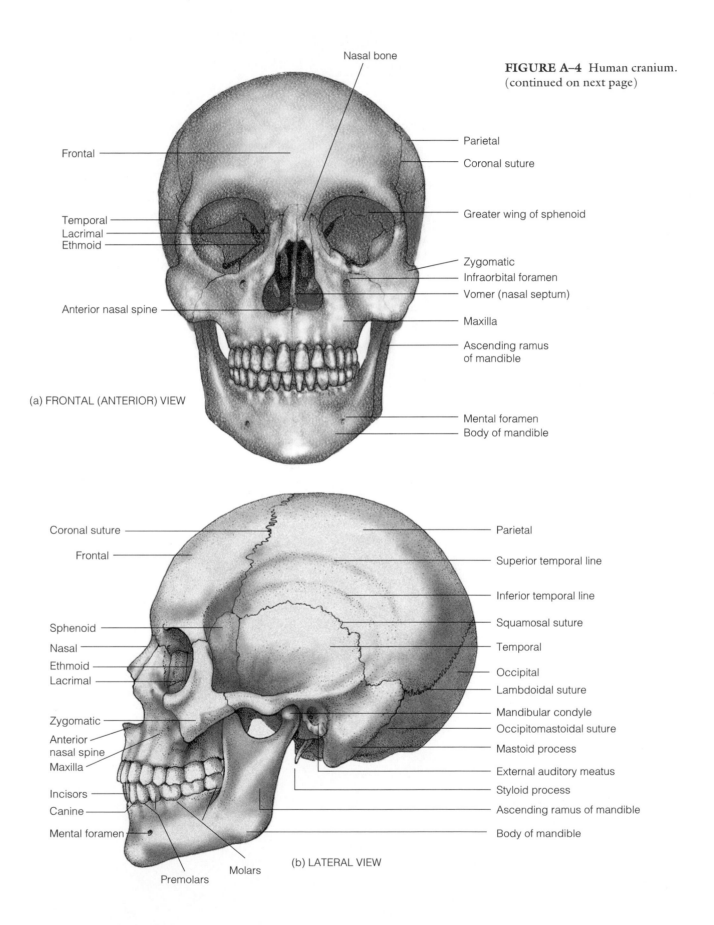

Nasal bone

FIGURE A–4 Human cranium.
(continued on next page)

Frontal

Parietal
Coronal suture

Greater wing of sphenoid

Temporal
Lacrimal
Ethmoid

Zygomatic
Infraorbital foramen
Vomer (nasal septum)

Anterior nasal spine

Maxilla
Ascending ramus
of mandible

Mental foramen
Body of mandible

(a) FRONTAL (ANTERIOR) VIEW

Coronal suture

Parietal

Frontal

Superior temporal line

Inferior temporal line

Sphenoid

Squamosal suture

Nasal

Temporal

Ethmoid
Lacrimal

Occipital
Lambdoidal suture

Zygomatic

Mandibular condyle
Occipitomastoidal suture

Anterior
nasal spine
Maxilla

Mastoid process

External auditory meatus

Incisors

Styloid process

Canine

Ascending ramus of mandible

Mental foramen

Body of mandible

Premolars   Molars   (b) LATERAL VIEW

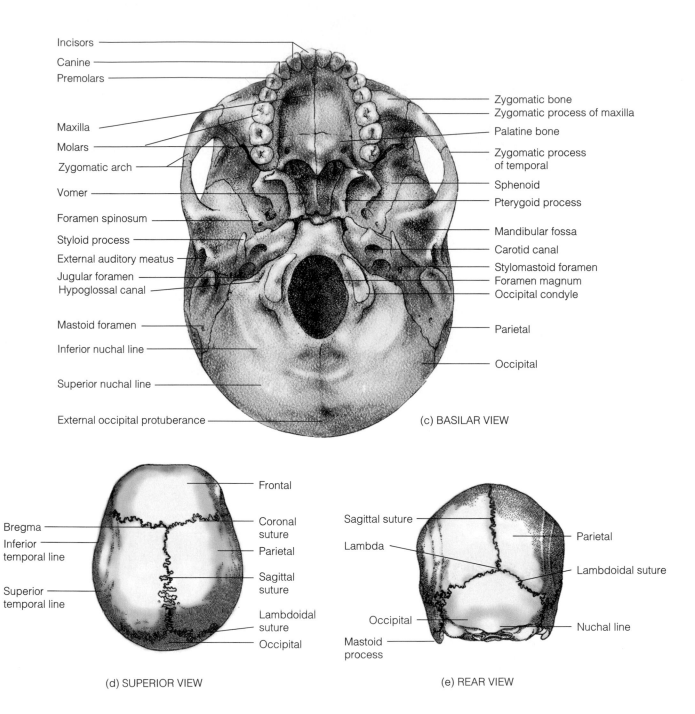

Incisors

Canine

Premolars

Maxilla

Molars

Zygomatic arch

Vomer

Foramen spinosum

Styloid process

External auditory meatus

Jugular foramen

Hypoglossal canal

Mastoid foramen

Inferior nuchal line

Superior nuchal line

External occipital protuberance

Zygomatic bone

Zygomatic process of maxilla

Palatine bone

Zygomatic process of temporal

Sphenoid

Pterygoid process

Mandibular fossa

Carotid canal

Stylomastoid foramen

Foramen magnum

Occipital condyle

Parietal

Occipital

(c) BASILAR VIEW

Bregma

Inferior temporal line

Superior temporal line

Frontal

Coronal suture

Parietal

Sagittal suture

Lambdoidal suture

Occipital

(d) SUPERIOR VIEW

Sagittal suture

Lambda

Occipital

Mastoid process

Parietal

Lambdoidal suture

Nuchal line

(e) REAR VIEW

FIGURE A–4 Human cranium. (continued)

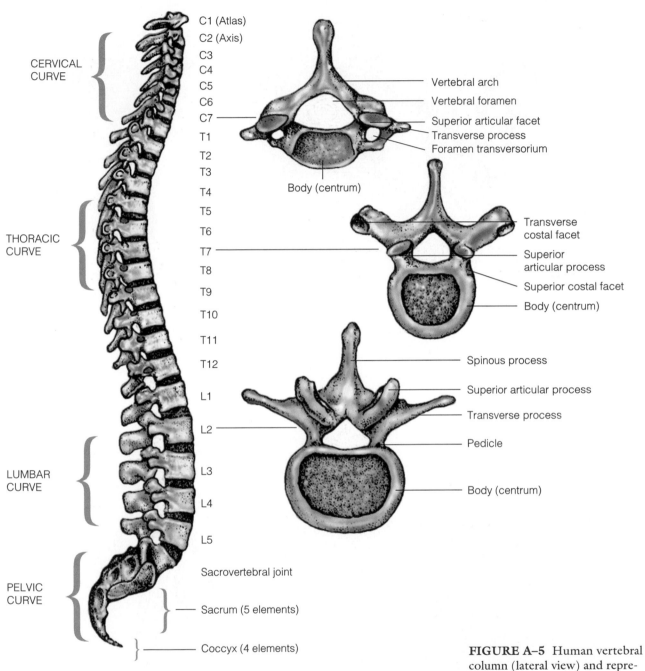

CERVICAL
CURVE

THORACIC
CURVE

LUMBAR
CURVE

PELVIC
CURVE

C1 (Atlas)
C2 (Axis)
C3
C4
C5
C6
C7
T1
T2
T3
T4
T5
T6
T7
T8
T9
T10
T11
T12
L1
L2
L3
L4
L5

Sacrovertebral joint

Sacrum (5 elements)

Coccyx (4 elements)

Vertebral arch
Vertebral foramen
Superior articular facet
Transverse process
Foramen transversorium

Body (centrum)

Transverse costal facet

Superior articular process

Superior costal facet

Body (centrum)

Spinous process

Superior articular process

Transverse process

Pedicle

Body (centrum)

FIGURE A–5 Human vertebral column (lateral view) and representative cervical, thoracic, and lumbar vertebrae (superior views).

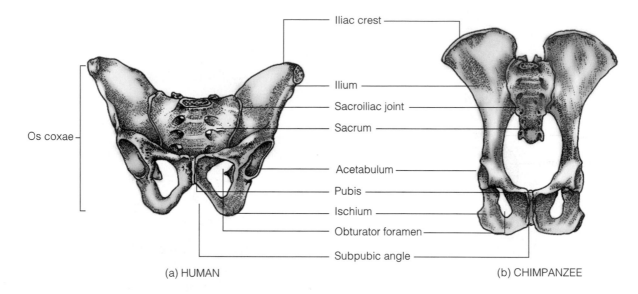

Iliac crest

Ilium

Sacroiliac joint

Sacrum

Acetabulum

Pubis

Ischium

Obturator foramen

Subpubic angle

Os coxae

(a) HUMAN

(b) CHIMPANZEE

FIGURE A–6 Pelvic girdles.

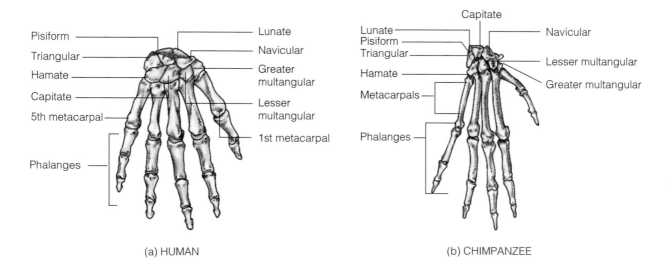

Pisiform

Triangular

Hamate

Capitate

5th metacarpal

Phalanges

Lunate

Navicular

Greater
multangular

Lesser
multangular

1st metacarpal

Capitate

Lunate

Pisiform

Triangular

Hamate

Metacarpals

Phalanges

Navicular

Lesser multangular

Greater multangular

(a) HUMAN

(b) CHIMPANZEE

FIGURE A–7 Hand anatomy.

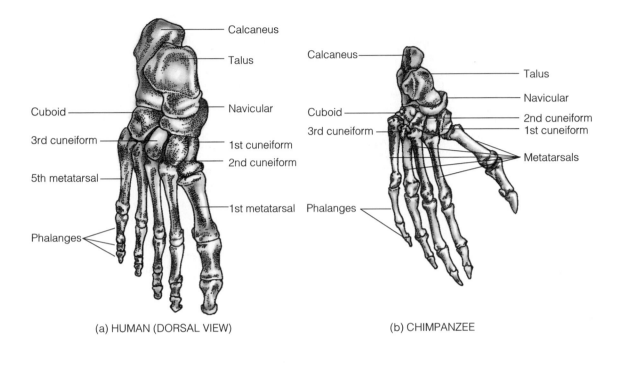

Calcaneus

Talus

Cuboid

Navicular

3rd cuneiform

1st cuneiform

5th metatarsal

2nd cuneiform

1st metatarsal

Phalanges

(a) HUMAN (DORSAL VIEW)

Calcaneus

Talus

Navicular

Cuboid

2nd cuneiform

3rd cuneiform

1st cuneiform

Metatarsals

Phalanges

(b) CHIMPANZEE

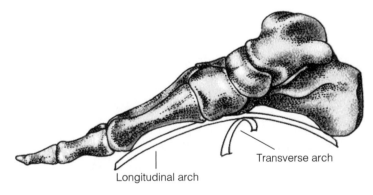

Transverse arch

Longitudinal arch

(c) HUMAN (MEDIAL VIEW)

FIGURE A–8 Foot (pedal) anatomy.

Summary of Early Hominid Fossil Finds from Africa

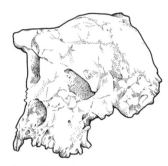

Sahelanthropus

Taxonomic designation:
Sahelanthropus tchadensis
Year of first discovery: 2001
Dating: ~7 m.y.a.
Fossil material: Nearly complete cranium, 2 jaw fragments, 3 isolated teeth

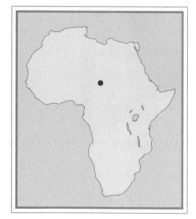

Location of finds: Toros Menalla, Chad, central Africa

Ardipithecus

Taxonomic designation:
Ardipithecus ramidus
Year of first discovery: 1992
Dating: Earlier sites, 5.8–5.6 m.y.a.; Aramis, 4.4 m.y.a.
Fossil material: Earlier materials: 1 jaw fragment, 4 isolated teeth, postcranial remains (foot phalanx, 2 hand phalanges, 2 humerus fragments, ulna). Later sample (Aramis) represented by many fossils, including up to 50 individuals (many postcranial elements, including at least 1 partial skeleton). Considerable fossil material retrieved from Aramis but not yet published; no reasonably complete cranial remains yet published.

Location of finds: Middle Awash region, including Aramis (as well as earlier localities), Ethiopia, East Africa

Orrorin

Taxonomic designation:
Orrorin tugenensis
Year of first discovery: 2000
Dating: ~6 m.y.a.
Fossil material: 2 jaw fragments, 6 isolated teeth, postcranial remains (femoral pieces, partial humerus, hand phalanx). No reasonably complete cranial remains yet discovered.

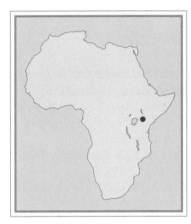

Location of finds: Lukeino Formation, Tugen Hills, Baringo District, Kenya, East Africa

Australopithecus anamensis

Taxonomic designation:
Australopithecus anamensis
Year of first discovery: 1965 (but not recognized as separate species at that time); more remains found in 1994 and 1995
Dating: 4.2–3.9 m.y.a.
Fossil material: Total of 22 specimens, including cranial fragments, jaw fragments, and postcranial pieces (humerus, tibia, radius). No reasonably complete cranial remains yet discovered.

Location of finds: Kanapoi, Allia Bay, Kenya, East Africa

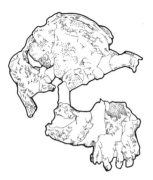

Australopithecus afarensis

Taxonomic designation:
Australopithecus afarensis
Year of first discovery: 1973
Dating: 3.7–3.0 m.y.a.
Fossil material: Large sample, with up to 65 individuals represented: 1 partial cranium, numerous cranial pieces and jaws, many teeth, numerous postcranial remains, including partial skeleton. Fossil finds from Laetoli also include dozens of fossilized footprints.

Location of finds: Laetoli (Tanzania), Hadar (Ethiopia), also likely found at East Turkana (Kenya) and Omo (Ethiopia), East Africa

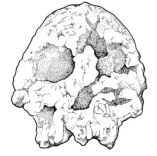

Kenyanthropus

Taxonomic designation:
Kenyanthropus platyops
Year of first discovery: 1999
Dating: 3.5 m.y.a.
Fossil material: Partial cranium, temporal fragment, partial maxilla, 2 partial mandibles

Location of finds: Lomekwi, West Lake Turkana, Kenya, East Africa

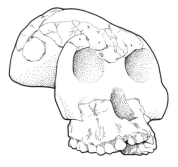

Australopithecus garhi

Taxonomic designation:
Australopithecus garhi
Year of first discovery: 1997
Dating: 2.5 m.y.a.
Fossil material: Partial cranium, numerous limb bones

Location of finds: Bouri, Middle Awash, Ethiopia, East Africa

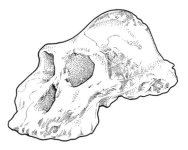

Australopithecus aethiopicus

Taxonomic designation:
Australopithecus aethiopicus (also called *Parantropus aethiopicus*)
Year of first discovery: 1985
Dating: 2.4 m.y.a.
Fossil material: Nearly complete cranium

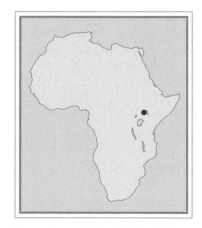

Location of finds: West Lake Turkana, Kenya

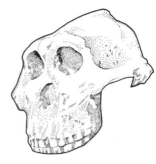

Australopithecus boisei

Taxonomic designation:
Australopithecus boisei (also called *Paranthropus boisei*)
Year of first discovery: 1959
Dating: 2.4–1.2 m.y.a.
Fossil material: 2 nearly complete crania, several partial crania, many jaw fragments, dozens of teeth. Postcrania less represented, but parts of several long bones recovered.

Location of finds: Olduvai Gorge and Peninj (Tanzania), East Lake Turkana (Koobi Fora), Chesowanja (Kenya), Omo (Ethiopia)

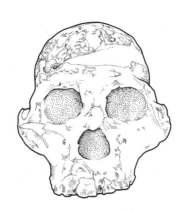

Australopithecus africanus

Taxonomic designation:
Australopithecus africanus
Year of first discovery: 1924
Dating: ~3.3–1.0 m.y.a.
Fossil material: 1 mostly complete cranium, several partial crania, dozens of jaws/partial jaws, hundreds of teeth, 4 partial skeletons representing significant parts of the postcranium

Location of finds: Taung, Sterkfontein, Makapansgat, Gladysvale (all from South Africa)

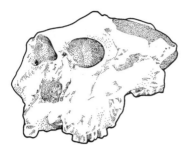

Australopithecus robustus

Taxonomic designation:
Australopithecus robustus (also called *Paranthropus robustus*)
Year of first discovery: 1938
Dating: ~2–1 m.y.a.
Fossil material: 1 complete cranium, several partial crania, many jaw fragments, hundreds of teeth, numerous postcranial elements

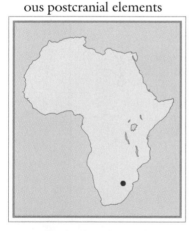

Location of finds: Kromdraai, Swartkrans, Drimolen, Cooper's Cave, possibly Gondolin (all from South Africa)

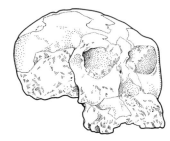

Early *Homo*
Taxonomic designation:
Homo habilis
Year of first discovery:
1959/1960
Dating: 2.4–1.8 m.y.a.
Fossil material: 2 partial crania, other cranial pieces, jaw fragments, several limb bones, partial hand, partial foot, partial skeleton

Location of finds: Olduvai Gorge (Tanzania), Lake Baringo (Kenya), Omo (Ethiopia), Sterkfontein (?) (South Africa)

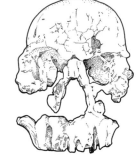

Early *Homo*
Taxonomic designation:
Homo rudolfensis
Year of first discovery: 1972
Dating: ~1.8 m.y.a.
Fossil material: 4 partial crania, 1 mostly complete mandible, other jaw pieces, numerous teeth, a few post-cranial elements (none directly associated with crania)

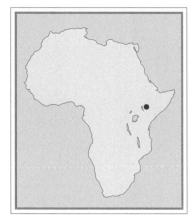

Location of finds: East Lake Turkana (Koobi Fora), Kenya, East Africa

APPENDIX C

Population Genetics: The Math of Microevolution

Part A. Further Examples Using the Hardy-Weinberg Equilibrium Formula

EXAMPLE 1. HEMOGLOBIN BETA LOCUS IN WEST AFRICA

As discussed in Chapter 14, there is a high frequency of the Hb^S allele in parts of West Africa. One study (see p. 416) in a Senegalese group found a frequency of the Hb^S allele at 12 percent.

What follows is a hypothetical example for a Senegalese population of 4,000 individuals. Ascertainment is done on all individuals at 6 months of age. Because of incomplete dominance, all three phenotypes (and therefore all three genotypes) can be determined.

Observed frequencies:

	Number of Individuals	Hb^A Alleles	Hb^S Alleles
$Hb^A Hb^A$	3,070	6,140	——
$Hb^A Hb^S$	905	905	905
$Hb^S Hb^S$	25	——	50
Totals	4,000	7,045	955

Allele frequencies:

$$Hb^A = p = 7,045/8,000 = .881$$
$$Hb^S = q = 955/8,000 = .119$$

Expected genotypic frequencies:

$$Hb^A Hb^A = p^2 = (.881)(.881) = .776$$
$$Hb^A Hb^S = 2pq = 2(.881)(.119) = .210$$
$$Hb^S Hb^S = q^2 = (.119)(.119) = .014$$

Comparison of expected and observed frequencies:

	Expected Frequency	Expected No. Individuals	Observed Frequency	Observed No. Individuals
$Hb^A Hb^A$	.776	3,105	.767	3,070
$Hb^A Hb^S$	.210	839	.227	905
$Hb^S Hb^S$	.014	57	.006	25

As you can see, there is a noticeable difference between the expected and observed frequencies. There are fewer actual (observed) individuals of both homozygotes than expected and more heterozygotes than expected. Indeed, when performing a statistical test (see Part 2 of this appendix), the difference is statistically significant.

We can extend the example further. Let us assume that we again ascertain allele frequencies in this same population 30 years later, at which point there are 3,000 survivors.

Observed phenotypic frequencies:

	Number of Individuals	Hb^A Alleles	Hb^S Alleles
$Hb^A Hb^A$	2,123	4,246	——
$Hb^A Hb^S$	875	875	875
$Hb^S Hb^S$	2	——	4
Totals	3,000	5,121	879

Allele frequencies:

$$Hb^A = p = 5,121/6,000 = .854$$
$$Hb^S = q = 879/6,000 = .146$$

Expected genotypic frequencies:

$$Hb^A Hb^A = p^2 = (.854)(.854) = .729$$
$$Hb^A Hb^S = 2pq = 2(.854)(.146) = .249$$
$$Hb^S Hb^S = q^2 = (.146)(.146) = .021$$

Comparison of expected and observed frequencies:

	Expected Frequency	Expected No. Individuals	Observed Frequency	Observed No. Individuals
$Hb^A Hb^A$	.729	2,188	.708	2,123
$Hb^A Hb^S$	.249	748	.292	875
$Hb^S Hb^S$	.021	64	.001	2

In this adult sample, the differences between the expected and observed frequencies are even greater than they were for the infant sample (and are even more highly statistically significant; see Part 2). Moreover, these differences are in the same direction as before: There are fewer homozygotes and more heterozygotes than expected under equilibrium conditions. A likely explanation for this pattern of allele frequencies would focus on natural selection. At age 6 months, there are slightly fewer $Hb^A Hb^A$ homozygotes than expected and considerably fewer $Hb^S Hb^S$ homozygotes than expected. Correspondingly, there are many more heterozygotes ($Hb^A Hb^S$) than expected. These differences could arise from differential mortality of $Hb^A Hb^A$ individuals due to malaria (likely in early infancy) and $Hb^S Hb^S$ individuals due to sickle-cell anemia occurring both *in utero* and during early infancy.

These same factors would continue throughout childhood and early adulthood, so that by age 30, the effects of differential mortality due to both malaria and sickle-cell anemia are even more dramatic. While hypothetical, these figures represent a good example of how natural selection could operate on this population.

EXAMPLE 2. ADENOSINE DEAMINASE (ADA) IN A SRI LANKAN POPULATION

ADA is an enzyme present in many types of cells. The locus producing this enzyme has two common codominant alleles, A^1 and A^2. There are also very rare mutant alleles that can cause a fatal form of inherited immune deficiency.

From actual data derived from a polymorphic population in Sri Lanka,* the following observed frequencies were found. (*Note:* Because the alleles are codominant, the three phenotypes correspond directly to the three genotypes.)

	Number of Individuals	A^1 Alleles	A^2 Alleles
A^1A^1	113	226	——
A^1A^2	38	38	38
A^2A^2	3	——	6
Totals	154	264	44

Allele frequencies:

$A^1 = p = 264/308 = .857$

$A^2 = q = 44/308 = .143$

Expected genotypic frequencies:

$A^1A^1 = p^2 = (.857)(.857) = .734$

$A^1A^2 = 2pq = 2(.857)(.143) = .249$

$A^2A^2 = q^2 = (.143)(.143) = .020$

Comparison of expected and observed frequencies:

	Expected Frequency	Expected No. Individuals	Observed Frequency	Observed No. Individuals
A^1A^1	.734	113	.734	113
A^1A^2	.245	38	.247	38
A^2A^2	.020	3	.019	3

As you can clearly see, the expected and observed frequencies are nearly identical (in fact, the raw frequencies are identical). There is thus a probability of 1.0 that the null hypothesis is correct and a 0 percent confidence limit in rejecting the null hypothesis. This population at this locus thus appears to be in equilibrium. Such is often the case in actual population genetics studies, especially when the sample size is small.

---

*Data from Bodmer and Cavalli-Sforza, 1976.

EXAMPLE 3. DETERMINING THE NUMBER OF HETEROZYGOUS CARRIERS FOR PKU IN A HYPOTHETICAL POPULATION

Another way to apply the Hardy-Weinberg formula is to first *assume* equilibrium and then work the formula in reverse. For example, for many recessive traits where there is complete dominance (or nearly complete dominance), traditionally it has been impossible to ascertain the heterozygotes directly. However, if we make certain assumptions, we can use the formula to estimate the number of heterozygotes (i.e., carriers) in a population.

Let us assume that we are studying PKU in a group of 20,000 students at a university. PKU is an autosomal recessive disorder with an overall frequency in the United States of approximately 1/10,000 (see p. 81). In some subgroups (e.g., individuals of European descent), the frequency of PKU is higher.

In our hypothetical student population, we find two individuals with PKU (which was treated when the individuals were children). Because PKU is an autosomal recessive, the number of PKU homozygotes (2/20,000, or .0001) is equal to q^2.

If $q^2 = .0001$, then

$q = .01$ and $p = .99$

The frequency of the heterozygote is $2pq$:

$2(.99)(.01) = .0198$

The estimated number of carriers for PKU in the university student sample is

$(.0198)(20,000) = 198$

An interesting pattern is evident here. In the entire population, there is a total of 200 individuals who possess at least one PKU allele. Of these, the vast majority (99 percent) are carriers.

EXAMPLE 4. APPLYING THE HARDY-WEINBERG FORMULA TO ABO, A MORE COMPLEX GENETIC SYSTEM

In Chapter 14 and in the three examples given so far in this appendix, we have used examples of loci with only two alleles (and therefore just three possible genotypes). However, many loci are more complex, having three or more alleles. For example, ABO has three alleles and six genotypes (see Table 4–2, p. 82)

How do we utilize the Hardy-Weinberg equilibrium formula for a locus like ABO? First, there are three alleles, so the allele frequencies are designated as:

Frequency of $A = p$
Frequency of $B = q$
Frequency of $O = r$

Under equilibrium conditions, the genotypic frequencies would be calculated as follows:

$$(p + q + r)^2 = 1$$

This is an expansion of a trinomial (rather than the binomial used in a two-allele system). With a three-allele system like ABO, the genotypic frequency formula is

$$p^2 + 2pq + 2pr + 2qr + q^2 = r^2 = 1$$

There are six terms in this formula, each one representing a different genotype:

Term	Genotype Represented
p^2	AA
$2pq$	AB
$2pr$	AO
$2qr$	BO
q^2	BB
r^2	OO

We will not include actual numbers here. We simply wish to illustrate that population genetics calculations can be considerably more complex than implied by our earlier examples.

Part B. Statistical Evaluation: Testing Hardy-Weinberg Results

Following are the results using statistical tests comparing the expected and observed frequencies for the relevant examples shown in Chapter 14 as well as those discussed in this appendix. The test used is the chi-square (χ^2), which assumes that two variables are independent. In our examples, this independence is tested against a null hypothesis stating that there is equilibrium (in other words, the expected and observed frequencies do not differ any more than would be the case strictly as a result of chance). Further details concerning statistical approaches can be found in any introductory statistics text.

In the data tables that follow, all figures are shown as *raw* frequencies.

MN Data (from Chapter 14, p. 413) Contingency Table:

Observed frequencies	80	80	40
Expected frequencies	72	96	32

$\chi^2 = 2.76, p = .251$

The generally accepted confidence limit for rejection of the null hypothesis is less than or equal to .05. Thus, in this case, we cannot confidently reject the null hypothesis.

PTC Tasting Data (from Chapter 14, p. 414) Contingency Table:

Observed frequencies	125	325	50
Expected frequencies	165	245	90

$\chi^2 = 28.17$, $p < .0000$

This result is highly significant and allows us to reject the null hypothesis with a great deal of confidence. We are able to say there is less than one chance in 10,000 that the null hypothesis applies to these data.

Hemoglobin Beta Locus (Example 1, this appendix) Contingency Tables:

At 6 months:

Observed frequencies	3,070	905	25
Expected frequencies	3,105	839	57

$\chi^2 = 15.18$, $p = .0005$

This is a highly significant result that allows us to reject the null hypothesis with high confidence.

At Age 30:

Observed frequencies	2,123	875	2
Expected frequencies	2,188	748	64

$\chi^2 = 69.16$, $p < .0000$

This result is even more highly significant than at age 6 months, as there has been further disruption of equilibrium expectations (i.e., greater evidence of evolutionary shifts in allele frequencies).

Glossary

acclimatization Physiological responses to changes in the environment that occur during an individual's lifetime. Such responses may be temporary or permanent, depending on the duration of the environmental change and when in the individual's life it occurs. The *capacity* for acclimatization may typify an entire species or population, and because it is under genetic influence, it is subject to evolutionary factors such as natural selection or genetic drift.

Acheulian (ash´-oo-lay-en) Pertaining to a stone tool industry of the Lower and Middle Pleistocene characterized by a large proportion of bifacial tools (flaked on both sides). Acheulian tool kits are very common in Africa, Southwest Asia, and western Europe, but are less common elsewhere. (Also spelled "Acheulean.")

adaptation Functional response of organisms or populations to the environment. Adaptation results from evolutionary change (specifically, as a result of natural selection).

adaptive niche The entire way of life of an organism: where it lives, what it eats, how it gets food, how it avoids predators, etc.

adaptive radiation The relatively rapid expansion and diversification of life forms into new ecological niches.

affiliative Pertaining to amicable associations between individuals. Affiliative behaviors, such as grooming, reinforce social bonds and promote group cohesion.

allele frequency In a population, the percentage of all the alleles at a locus accounted for by one specific allele.

alleles Alternate forms of a gene. Alleles occur at the same locus on homologous chromosomes and thus govern the same trait. However, because they are different, their action may result in different expressions of that trait. The term is sometimes used synonymously with *gene*.

allometry Also called "scaling," the differential proportion among various anatomical structures. For example, the size of the brain in proportion to overall body size changes during the development of an individual. Moreover, scaling effects must also be considered when comparing species.

alloparenting A common behavior in many primate species whereby individuals other than the parent(s) hold, carry, and in general interact with infants.

allopatric Living in different areas; important in the divergence of closely related species from each other and from

their shared ancestral species because it leads to reproductive isolation.

altruism Behavior that benefits another individual but at some potential risk or cost to oneself.

amino acids Small molecules that are the components of proteins.

analogies Similarities between organisms based strictly on common function with no assumed common evolutionary descent.

ancestral (primitive) Referring to characters inherited by a group of organisms from a remote ancestor and thus not diagnostic of groups (lineages) that diverged after the character first appeared.

antigens Large molecules found on the surface of cells. Several different loci govern various antigens on red and white blood cells. (Foreign antigens provoke an immune response.)

anthropocentric Viewing nonhuman organisms in terms of human experience and capabilities; emphasizing the importance of humans over everything else.

anthropoids Members of a suborder of Primates, the *Anthropoidea* (pronounced "ann-throw-poid´-ee-uh"). Traditionally, the suborder includes monkeys, apes, and humans.

anthropology The field of inquiry that studies human culture and evolutionary aspects of human biology; includes cultural anthropology, archaeology, linguistics, and physical, or biological, anthropology.

anthropometry Measurement of human body parts. When osteologists measure skeletal elements, the term *osteometry* is often used.

antibodies Proteins that are produced by some types of immune cells and that serve as major components of the immune system. Antibodies recognize and attach to foreign antigens on bacteria, viruses, and other pathogens. Then other immune cells destroy the invading organism.

arboreal Tree-living: adapted to life in the trees.

arboreal hypothesis The traditional view that primate characteristics can be explained as a consequence of primate diversification into arboreal habitats.

artifacts Objects or materials made or modified for use by hominids. The earliest artifacts tend to be tools made of stone or, occasionally, bone.

association Relationships between components of an archaeological site. All the things artifacts are found with.

Aurignacian Pertaining to an Upper Paleolithic stone tool industry in Europe beginning at about 40,000 y.a.

australopithecine (os-tra-loh-pith´-e-seen) The colloquial name for members of the genus *Australopithecus*. The term was first used as a subfamily designation, but it is now most commonly used informally.

Australopithecus An early hominid genus, known from the Plio-Pleistocene of Africa, characterized by bipedal locomotion, a relatively small brain, and large back teeth.

autonomic Pertaining to physiological responses not under voluntary control. An example in chimpanzees would be the erection of body hair during excitement. An example in humans is blushing. Both convey information regarding emotional states, but neither is a deliberate behavior, and communication is not intended.

autosomes All chromosomes except the sex chromosomes.

balanced polymorphism The maintenance of two or more alleles in a population due to the selective advantage of the heterozygote.

behavior Anything organisms do that involves action in response to internal or external stimuli. The response of an individual, group, or species to its environment. Such responses may or may not be deliberate and they aren't necessarily the results of conscious decision making, as in one-celled organisms, insects, and many other species.

behavioral ecology The study of the evolution of behavior, emphasizing the role of ecological factors as agents of natural selection. Behaviors and behavioral patterns have been selected for because they increase the reproductive fitness of individuals (i.e., they are adaptive) in specific environmental contexts.

binomial nomenclature (*binomial,* meaning "two names") In taxonomy, the convention established by Carolus Linnaeus whereby genus and species names are used to refer to species. For example, *Homo sapiens* refers to human beings.

biocultural evolution The mutual, interactive evolution of human biology and culture; the concept that biology makes culture possible and that developing culture further influences the direction of biological evolution; a basic concept in understanding the unique components of human evolution.

biological continuum Refers to the fact that organisms are related through common ancestry and that behaviors and traits seen in one species are also seen in others to varying degrees. (When expressions of a phenomenon continuously grade into one another so that there are no discrete categories, they are said to exist on a continuum. Color is such a phenomenon.)

biological determinism The concept that phenomena, including various aspects of behavior (e.g., intelligence, val-

ues, morals) are governed by biological (genetic) factors; the inaccurate association of various behavioral attributes with certain biological traits, such as skin color.

biological species concept A depiction of species as groups of individuals capable of fertile interbreeding, but reproductively isolated from other such groups.

biostratigraphy Dating method based on evolutionary changes within an evolving lineage.

bipedally On two feet. Walking habitually on two legs is the single most distinctive feature of the family Hominidae.

brachiation A form of locomotion in which the body is suspended beneath the hands and support is alternated from one forelimb to the other; arm swinging.

brachycephalic Having a broad head in which the width measures more than 80 percent of the length.

breeding isolates Populations that are clearly isolated geographically and/or socially from other breeding groups.

burins Small, chisel-like tools (with a pointed end) thought to have been used to engrave bone, antler, ivory, or wood.

catastrophism The view that the earth's geological landscape is the result of violent cataclysmic events. This view was promoted by Cuvier, especially in opposition to Lamarck.

centromere The constricted portion of a chromosome. After replication, the two strands of a double-stranded chromosome are joined at the centromere.

cercopithecines (serk-oh-pith´-eh-seens) The subfamily of Old World monkeys that includes baboons, macaques, and guenons.

Chatelperronian Pertaining to an Upper Paleolithic industry found in France and Spain, containing blade tools and associated with Neandertals.

Chordata The phylum of the animal kingdom that includes vertebrates.

chromatin The loose, diffuse form of DNA seen during interphase. When it condenses, chromatin forms into chromosomes.

chromosomes Discrete structures composed of DNA and protein found only in the nuclei of cells. Chromosomes are only visible under magnification during certain phases of cell division.

chronometric dating (*chrono,* meaning "time," and *metric,* meaning "measure") A dating technique that gives an estimate in actual numbers of years.

clade A group of organisms sharing a common ancestor. The group includes the common ancestor and all descendants.

cladistics An approach to classification that attempts to make rigorous evolutionary interpretations based solely on analysis of certain types of homologous characters (those considered to be derived characters).

cladogram A chart showing evolutionary relationships as determined by cladistic analysis. It is based solely on interpretation of shared derived characters. No time component is indicated, and ancestor-descendant relationships are *not* implied.

classification In biology, the ordering of organisms into categories, such as orders, families, and genera, to show evolutionary relationships.

cline A gradual change in the frequency of genotypes and phenotypes from one geographical region to another.

clone An organism that is genetically identical to another organism. The term may also be used to refer to genetically identical DNA segments, molecules, and cells.

codominance The expression of two alleles in heterozygotes. In this situation, neither allele is dominant or recessive; thus, both influence the phenotype.

codon A triplet of messenger RNA bases that refers to a specific amino acid during protein synthesis.

colobines (kole´-uh-beans) The subfamily of Old World monkeys that includes the African colobus monkeys and Asian langurs.

communication Any act that conveys information, in the form of a message, to another individual. Frequently, the result of communication is a change in the behavior of the recipient. Communication may not be deliberate but may instead be the result of involuntary processes or a secondary consequence of an intentional action.

complementary Referring to the fact that DNA bases form base pairs in a precise manner. For example, adenine can bond only to thymine. These two bases are said to be *complementary* because one requires the other to form a complete DNA base pair.

conspecifics members of the same species.

context The environmental setting where artifacts are found. A *primary* context is a setting in which archaeological material was originally deposited. A *secondary* context is one to which it has been moved (e.g., by the action of a stream).

continental drift The movement of continents on sliding plates of the earth's surface. As a result, the positions of large landmasses have shifted dramatically during the earth's history.

continuum A set of relationships in which all components fall along a single integrated spectrum. All life reflects a single biological continuum.

core Stone reduced by flake removal; a core may or may not be used as a tool itself.

core area The portion of a home range containing the highest concentration and most reliable supplies of food and water. The core area is frequently the area that will be defended.

cortex Layer. In the brain, the cortex is the layer that covers the cerebral hemispheres which, in turn, cover more primitive or older structures related to bodily functions and the sense of smell. It is composed of nerve cells called neurons, which communicate with each other and also send and receive messages to and from all parts of the body.

culture All aspects of human adaptation, including technology, traditions, language, religion, marriage patterns, and social roles. Culture is a set of *learned* behaviors that is transmitted from one generation to the next by nonbiological (i.e., nongenetic) means.

cusps The elevated portions (bumps) on the chewing surfaces of premolar and molar teeth.

cytoplasm The portion of the cell contained within the cell membrane, excluding the nucleus. The cytoplasm consists of a semifluid material and contains numerous structures involved with cell function.

data (*sing.*, datum) Facts from which conclusions can be drawn; scientific information.

deoxyribonucleic acid (DNA) The double-stranded molecule that contains the genetic code. DNA is a main component of chromosomes.

derived (modified) Referring to characters that are modified from the ancestral condition and thus *are* diagnostic of particular evolutionary lineages.

diploid Referring to the full complement of chromosomes in a somatic cell—both members of each pair.

direct percussion Striking a core or flake with a hammerstone.

displays Sequences of repetitious behaviors that serve to communicate emotional states. Nonhuman primate displays are most frequently associated with reproductive or agonistic behavior.

diurnal Active during the day.

dolichocephalic Having a long, narrow head in which the width measures less than 75 percent of the length.

dominance hierarchies Systems of social organization wherein individuals within a group are ranked relative to one another. Higher-ranking individuals have greater access to preferred food items, and mating partners than lower-ranking individuals. Dominance hierarchies are sometimes referred to as "pecking orders."

dominant Describing a trait governed by an allele that can be expressed in the presence of another, different allele (i.e., in heterozygotes). Dominant alleles prevent the expression of recessive alleles in heterozygotes. (This is the definition of *complete* dominance.)

ecological Pertaining to the relationships between organisms and all aspects of their environment (temperature, predators, nonpredators, vegetation, availability of food and water, types of food, disease organisms, parasites, etc.).

ecological niches The positions of species within their physical and biological environments, together making up the *ecosystem*. A species' ecological niche is defined by such components as diet, terrain, vegetation, type of predators, relationships with other species, and activity patterns, and each niche is unique to a given species.

ecological species concept The concept that a species is a group of organisms exploiting a single niche. This view emphasizes the role of natural selection in separating species from one another.

empirical Relying on experiment or observation; from the Latin *empiricus*, meaning "experienced."

encephalization The proportional size of the brain relative to some other measure, usually some estimate of overall body size, such as weight. More precisely, the term refers to increases in brain size beyond that which would be expected given the body size of a particular species.

endemic Continuously present in a population.

endocast A solid impression of the inside of the skull, often preserving details relating to the size and surface features of the brain.

endogamy Mating with individuals from the same group.

endothermic (*endo,* meaning "within" or "internal") Able to maintain internal body temperature through the production of energy by means of metabolic processes within cells; characteristic of mammals, birds, and perhaps some dinosaurs.

environmental determinism An interpretation that links simple environmental changes directly to a major evolutionary shift in an organism. Such explanations tend to be extreme oversimplifications of the evolutionary process.

enzymes Specialized proteins that initiate and direct chemical reactions in the body.

epochs Categories of the geological time scale; subdivisions of periods. In the Cenozoic, epochs include the Paleocene, Eocene, Oligocene, Miocene, and Pliocene (from the Tertiary) and the Pleistocene and Holocene (from the Quaternary).

estrus (ess´-truss) Period of sexual receptivity in female mammals (except humans), correlated with ovulation. When used as an adjective, the word is spelled "estrous."

ethnocentric Viewing other cultures from the inherently biased perspective of one's own culture. Ethnocentrism often results in other cultures being seen as inferior to one's own.

ethnographies Detailed descriptive studies of human societies. In cultural anthropology, an ethnography is traditionally the study of a non-Western society.

eugenics The philosophy of "race improvement" through the forced sterilization of members of some groups and increased reproduction among others; an overly simplified, often racist view that is now discredited.

evolution A change in the genetic structure of a population. The term is also frequently used to refer to the appearance of a new species.

evolution (modern genetic definition) A change in the frequency of alleles from one generation to the next.

evolutionary systematics A traditional approach to classification (and evolutionary interpretation) in which presumed ancestors and descendants are traced in time by analysis of homologous characters.

exogamy Mating pattern whereby individuals obtain mates from groups other than their own.

fitness Pertaining to natural selection, a measure of *relative* reproductive success of individuals. Fitness can be measured by an individual's genetic contribution to the next generation compared to that of other individuals. The terms *genetic fitness, reproductive fitness,* and *differential reproductive success* are also used.

fixity of species The notion that species, once created, can never change; an idea diametrically opposed to theories of biological evolution.

flake Thin-edged fragment removed from a core.

flexed The position of the body in a bent orientation, with arms and legs drawn up to the chest.

foramen magnum The opening at the base of the skull through which the spinal cord passes as it enters the body to descend through the vertebral column. In quadrupeds, it is located more to the rear of the skull, while in bipeds, it is located farther beneath the skull.

forensic anthropology An applied anthropological approach dealing with legal matters. Physical anthropologists work with coroners and others in the identification and analysis of human remains.

founder effect A type of genetic drift in which allele frequencies are altered in small populations that are taken from, or are remnants of, larger populations.

free-ranging Pertaining to non-captive animals living in their natural habitat. Ideally, the behavior of wild study groups would be free of human influence.

frugivorous (fru-give´-or-us) Having a diet composed primarily of fruit.

gametes Reproductive cells (eggs and sperm in animals) developed from precursor cells in ovaries and testes.

gene A sequence of DNA bases that specifies the order of amino acids in an entire protein, a portion of a protein, or any functional product. A gene may be made up of hundreds or thousands of DNA bases organized into coding and noncoding segments.

gene flow Exchange of genes between populations.

gene pool The total complement of genes shared by the reproductive members of a population.

genetic drift Evolutionary changes—that is, changes in allele frequencies—produced by random factors. Genetic drift is a result of small population size.

genetics The study of gene structure and action and the patterns of inheritance of traits from parent to offspring. Genetic mechanisms are the underlying foundation for evolutionary change.

genome The entire genetic makeup of an individual or species. In humans, it is estimated that each individual possesses approximately 3 billion DNA nucleotides.

genotype The genetic makeup of an individual. Genotype can refer to an organism's entire genetic makeup or to the alleles at a particular locus.

genus A group of closely related species.

geological time scale The organization of earth history into eras, periods, and epochs; commonly used by geologists and paleoanthropologists.

glaciations Climatic intervals when continental ice sheets cover much of the northern continents. Glaciations are associated with colder temperatures in northern latitudes and more arid conditions in southern latitudes (most notably in Africa).

grade A grouping of organisms sharing a similar adaptive pattern. It is not necessarily based on closeness of evolutionary relationship, but does contrast organisms in a useful way (e.g., *H. erectus* with *H. sapiens*).

grooming Picking through fur to remove dirt, parasites, and other materials that may be present. Social grooming is common among primates and reinforces social relationships.

half-life The time period in which a radioactive isotope is converted chemically (into a daughter product). For example, after 1.25 billion years half the ^{40}K remains; after 2.5 billion years one-fourth remains.

haploid Referring to a half set of chromosomes, one member of each pair. Haploid sets are found in gametes.

Hardy-Weinberg theory of genetic equilibrium The mathematical relationship expressing—under ideal conditions—the predicted distribution of alleles in populations; the central theorem of population genetics.

hemispheres Two halves of the cerebrum that are connected by a dense mass of fibers. (The cerebrum is the large rounded outer portion of the brain.)

hemizygous (*hemi,* meaning "half") Having only one member of a pair of alleles. Because males have only one X chromosome, all their X-linked alleles are hemizygous. All recessive alleles on a male's X chromosome are expressed in the phenotype.

hemoglobin A protein molecule that occurs in red blood cells and binds to oxygen molecules.

heterodont Having different kinds of teeth; characteristic of mammals, whose teeth consist of incisors, canines, premolars, and molars.

heterozygous Having different alleles at the same locus on members of a chromosome pair.

Holocene The most recent epoch of the Cenozoic. Following the Pleistocene, it is estimated to have begun 10,000 years ago.

home range The total area exploited by an animal or social group; usually given for one year—or for the entire lifetime—of an animal.

homeostasis A condition of balance, or stability, within a biological system, maintained by the interaction of physiological mechanisms that compensate for changes (both external and internal).

homeotic genes An evolutionarily ancient family of regulatory genes that directs the development of the overall body plan and the segmentation of body tissues; also called homeobox or *Hox* genes.

Hominidae The taxonomic family to which humans belong; also includes other, now extinct, bipedal relatives.

hominids Colloquial term for members of the family Hominidae, which includes all bipedal hominoids back to the divergence from African great apes.

Hominoidea The formal designation for the superfamily of anthropoids that includes apes and humans.

Homo habilis (hab´-ih-liss) A species of early *Homo,* well known from East Africa but perhaps also found in other regions.

homologies Similarities between organisms based on descent from a common ancestor.

homologous Referring to members of chromosome pairs. Homologous chromosomes carry loci that govern the same traits. During meiosis, homologous chromosomes pair and exchange segments of DNA. They are alike with regard to size, position of centromere, and banding patterns.

homoplasy (*homo,* meaning "same," and *plasy,* meaning "growth") The separate evolutionary development of similar characteristics in different groups of organisms.

homozygous Having the same allele at the same locus on both members of a chromosome pair.

hormones Substances (usually proteins) that are produced by specialized cells and that travel to other parts of the body, where they influence chemical reactions and regulate various cellular functions.

Human Genome Project An international effort aimed at sequencing and mapping the entire human genome.

hypothesis (*pl.,* hypotheses) A provisional explanation of a phenomenon. Hypotheses require verification or falsification through testing.

hypoxia Lack of oxygen. Hypoxia can refer to reduced amounts of available oxygen in the atmosphere (due to lowered barometric pressure) or to insufficient amounts of oxygen in the body.

inbreeding A type of nonrandom mating in which relatives mate more often than predicted under random mating conditions.

intelligence Mental capacity; ability to learn, reason, or comprehend and interpret information, facts, relationships, and meanings; the capacity to solve problems, whether through the application of previously acquired knowledge or through insight.

interglacials Climatic intervals when continental ice sheets are retreating, eventually becoming much reduced in size. Interglacials in northern latitudes are associated with warmer temperatures, while in southern latitudes the climate becomes wetter.

interphase The portion of a cell's cycle during which metabolic processes and other cellular activities occur.

Chromosomes are not visible as discrete structures at this time. DNA replication occurs during interphase.

interspecific Between species; refers to variation beyond that seen within the same species to include additional aspects seen between two different species.

intraspecific Within species; refers to variation seen within the same species.

ischial callosities Patches of tough, hard skin on the buttocks of Old World monkeys and chimpanzees.

K-selected Pertaining to an adaptive strategy whereby individuals produce relatively few offspring, in whom they invest increased parental care. Although only a few infants are born, chances of survival are increased for each individual because of parental investments in time and energy. Examples of nonprimate K-selected species are birds and canids (e.g., wolves, coyotes, and dogs).

karyotype The chromosomal complement of an individual or that which is typical for a species. Usually displayed in a photomicrograph, the chromosomes are arranged in pairs and according to size and position of the centromere.

knappers People (frequently archaeologists) who make stone tools.

lactose intolerance The inability to digest fresh milk products, caused by the discontinued production of lactase, the enzyme that breaks down lactose, or milk sugar.

large-bodied hominoids Those hominoids including the great apes (orangutans, chimpanzees, gorillas) and hominids, as well as all ancestral forms back to the time of divergence from small-bodied hominoids (i.e., the gibbon lineage).

lateralized Pertaining to lateralization, the functional specialization of the hemispheres of the brain for specific activities.

life history traits Also called *life history strategies;* characteristics and developmental stages that influence rates of reproduction.

linked Describing genetic loci or genes located on the same chromosome.

lithic (*lith,* meaning "stone") Referring to stone tools.

locus (*pl.,* loci) (lo´-kus, lo-sigh´) The position on a chromosome where a given gene occurs. The term is sometimes used interchangeably with *gene,* but this usage is technically incorrect.

macaques (muh-kaks´) Group of Old World monkeys comprising several species, including rhesus monkeys.

macroevolution Changes produced only after many generations, such as the appearance of a new species.

Magdalenian Pertaining to the final phase of the Upper Paleolithic stone tool industry in Europe.

material culture The physical manifestations of human activities; includes tools, campsites, art, and structures. As the most durable aspects of culture, material remains make up the majority of archaeological evidence of past societies.

meiosis Cell division in specialized cells in ovaries and testes. Meiosis involves two divisions and results in four daughter cells, each containing only half the original number of chromosomes. These cells can develop into gametes.

menarche The first menstruation in girls, usually occurring in the early to mid teens.

Mendelian traits Characteristics that are influenced by alleles at only one genetic locus. Examples include many blood types, such as ABO. Many genetic disorders, including sickle-cell anemia and Tay-Sachs disease, are also Mendelian traits.

menopause The end of menstruation in women, usually occurring at around age 50.

messenger RNA (mRNA) A form of RNA that is assembled on a sequence of DNA bases. It carries the DNA code to the ribosome during protein synthesis.

metabolism The chemical processes within cells that break-down nutrients and release energy for the body to use. (When nutrients are broken down into their component parts, such as amino acids, energy is released and made available for the cell to use.)

Metazoa Multicellular animals; a major division of the animal kingdom.

microevolution Small changes occurring within species, such as a change in allele frequencies.

microliths (*micro,* meaning "small," and *lith,* meaning "stone") Small stone tools usually produced from narrow blades punched from a core; found especially in Africa during the latter part of the Pleistocene.

microwear Polishes, striations, and other diagnostic microscopic changes on the edges of stone tools.

Middle Pleistocene The portion of the Pleistocene epoch beginning 780,000 y.a. and ending 125,000 y.a.

midline An anatomical term referring to a hypothetical line that divides the body into right and left halves.

mitochondria (*sing.,* mitochondrion) Structures contained within the cytoplasm of eukaryotic cells that convert energy, derived from nutrients, into a form that is used by the cell.

mitochondrial DNA (mtDNA) DNA found in the mitochondria; mtDNA is inherited only from the mother.

mitosis Simple cell division; the process by which somatic cells divide to produce two identical daughter cells.

molecules Structures made up of two or more atoms. Molecules can combine with other molecules to form more complex structures.

morphological Pertaining to the form and structure of organisms.

morphology The form (shape, size) of anatomical structures; can also refer to the entire organism.

mosaic evolution A pattern of evolution in which the rate of evolution in one functional system varies from that in other systems. For example, in hominid evolution, the dental system, locomotor system, and neurological system (especially the brain) all evolved at markedly different rates.

motor cortex That portion of the cortex involved in sending outgoing signals involved in muscle use. The motor cotex is located at the back of the frontal lobe.

Mousterian Pertaining to the stone tool industry associated with Neandertals and some modern *H. sapiens* groups; also called Middle Paleolithic. This industry is characterized by a larger proportion of flake tools than is found in Acheulian tool kits.

mutation A change in DNA. *Mutation* refers to changes in DNA bases (specifically called point mutations) and also to changes in chromosome number and/or structure.

natal group The group in which animals are born and raised. (*Natal* pertains to birth.)

natural selection The mechanism of evolutionary change first articulated by Charles Darwin; refers to genetic change or changes in the frequencies of certain traits in populations due to differential reproductive success between individuals.

neocortex The more recently evolved portions of the cortex of the brain that are involved with higher mental functions and composed of areas that integrate incoming information from different sensory organs.

neural tube In early embryonic development, the anatomical structure that develops to form the brain and spinal cord.

nocturnal Active during the night.

nondisjunction The failure of homologous chromosomes or chromosome strands to separate during cell division.

nonrandom mating Patterns of mating in a population in which individuals choose mates preferentially.

nuchal torus (nuke´-ul, pertaining to the neck) A ridge or elevated line of bone in the back of the cranium to which the muscles of the back of the neck are attached. These muscles hold the head upright.

nucleotides Basic units of the DNA molecule, composed of a sugar, a phosphate, and one of four DNA bases.

nucleus A structure (organelle) found in all eukaryotic cells. The nucleus contains chromosomes (nuclear DNA).

omnivorous Having a diet consisting of many food types (i.e., plant materials, meat, and insects).

organelles Structures contained within cells, surrounded by a membrane. There are many different types, and each performs specific functions.

osteodontokeratic (*osteo,* meaning "bone," *donto,* meaning "tooth," and *keratic,* meaning "horn")

osteology The study of skeletal material. Human osteology focuses on the interpretation of the skeletal remains of past groups. Some of the same techniques are used in paleoanthropology to study early hominids.

paleoanthropology The interdisciplinary approach to the study of earlier hominids—their chronology, physical structure, archaeological remains, habitats, etc.

paleoecologists (*paleo,* meaning "old," and *ecology,* meaning "environmental setting") Scientists who study ancient environments.

paleomagnetism Dating method based on shifts in the positions of the magnetic poles.

paleopathology The branch of osteology that studies the evidence of disease and injury in human skeletal (or, occasionally, mummified) remains.

paleospecies Species defined from fossil evidence, often covering a long time span.

pathogens Substances or microorganisms, such as bacteria, fungi, or viruses, that cause disease.

pedigree chart A diagram showing family relationships in order to trace the hereditary pattern of particular genetic (usually Mendelian) traits.

phenotypes The observable or detectable physical characteristics of an organism; the detectable expressions of genotypes.

phenotypic ratio The proportion of one phenotype to other phenotypes in a group of organisms. For example, Mendel observed that there were approximately three tall plants for every short plant in the F_2 generation. This is expressed as a phenotypic ratio of 3:1.

philopatric Remaining in one's natal group or home range as an adult. In most species, members of one sex disperse from their natal group as young adults, and members of the philopatric sex remain. In the majority of nonhuman primate species, the philopatric sex is female.

phylogenetic tree A chart showing evolutionary relationships as determined by phylogenetic systematics. It contains a time component and implies ancestor-descendant relationships.

phytoliths (*phyto,* meaning "hidden," and *lith,* meaning "stone") Microscopic silica structures formed in the cells of many plants, particularly grasses.

plasticity The capacity to change. In a behavioral context, the ability of animals to modify behaviors in response to differing circumstances.

pleiotropic genes Genes that have more than one effect; genes that have different effects at different times in the life cycle.

pleiotropy A situation whereby several seemingly unrelated phenotypic effects are influenced by the action of a single gene.

Pleistocene The epoch of the Cenozoic from 1.8 m.y.a. until 10,000 y.a. Frequently referred to as the Ice Age, this epoch is associated with continental glaciations in northern latitudes.

Plio-Pleistocene Pertaining to the Pliocene and first half of the Pleistocene, a time range of 5–1 m.y.a. For this time period, numerous fossil hominids have been found in Africa.

point mutation A chemical change in a single base of a DNA sequence.

polyandry A mating system wherein a female continuously associates with more than one male (usually two or three) with whom she mates. Among nonhuman primates, this pattern is seen only in marmosets and tamarins.

polygenic Referring to traits that are influenced by genes at two or more loci. Examples of such traits are stature, skin color, and eye color. Many polygenic traits are also influenced by environmental factors.

polymerase chain reaction (PCR) A method of producing thousands of copies of a DNA segment using the enzyme DNA polymerase.

polymorphisms Loci with more than one allele. Polymorphisms can be expressed in the phenotype as the result of gene action (as in ABO), or they can exist solely at the DNA level within noncoding regions.

polypeptide chain A sequence of amino acids that may act alone or in combination with others as a functional protein.

polytypic Referring to species composed of populations that differ with regard to the expression of one or more traits.

population Within a species, a community of individuals where mates are usually found.

population geneticists Geneticists who study the frequency of alleles, genotypes, and phenotypes in populations.

postcranial (*post*, meaning "after") In a quadruped, referring to that portion of the body behind the head; in a biped, referring to all parts of the body *beneath* the head (i.e., the neck down).

prehensility Grasping, as by the hands and feet of primates.

pressure flaking A method of removing flakes from a core by pressing a pointed implement (e.g., bone or antler) against the stone.

primates Members of the order of mammals *Primates* (pronounced "pry-may´-tees"), which includes prosimians, monkeys, apes, and humans.

primatologists Scientists who study the evolution, anatomy, and behavior of nonhuman primates. Those who study behavior in noncaptive animals are usually trained as physical anthropologists.

primatology The study of the biology and behavior of nonhuman primates (prosimians, monkeys, and apes).

principle of independent assortment The distribution of one pair of alleles into gametes does not influence the distribution of another pair. The genes controlling different traits are inherited independently of one another.

principle of segregation Genes (alleles) occur in pairs (because chromosomes occur in pairs). During gamete production, the members of each gene pair separate, so that each gamete contains one member of each pair. During fertilization, the full number of chromosomes is restored, and members of gene or allele pairs are reunited.

prosimians Members of a suborder of Primates, the *Prosimii* (pronounced "pro-sim´-ee-eye"). Traditionally, the suborder includes lemurs, lorises, and tarsiers.

protein synthesis The assembly of chains of amino acids into functional protein molecules. The process is directed by DNA.

proteins Three-dimensional molecules that serve a wide variety of functions through their ability to bind to other molecules.

protohominids The earliest members of the hominid lineage, as yet only poorly represented in the fossil record; thus, their structure and behavior are reconstructed mostly hypothetically.

punctuated equilibrium The concept that evolutionary change proceeds through long periods of stasis punctuated by rapid periods of change.

quadrupedal Using all four limbs to support the body during locomotion; the basic mammalian (and primate) form of locomotion.

quantitatively In a manner involving measurements of quantity and including such properties as size, number, and capacity. When data are quantified, they are expressed numerically and are capable of being tested statistically.

r-selected Pertaining to an adaptive strategy that emphasizes relatively large numbers of offspring and reduced parental care (compared to K-selected species). *K-selection* and *r-selection* are relative terms; e.g., mice are r-selected compared to primates but K-selected compared to many fish species.

random assortment The chance distribution of chromosomes to daughter cells during meiosis; along with recombination, the source of variation resulting from meiosis.

recessive Describing a trait that is not expressed in heterozygotes; also refers to the allele that governs the trait. For a recessive allele to be expressed, there must be two copies of the allele (i.e., the individual must be homozygous).

recognition species concept A depiction of species in which the key aspect is the ability of individuals to identify members of their own species for purposes of mating (and to avoid mating with members of other species). In theory, this type of selective mating is a component of a species concept emphasizing mating and is therefore compatible with the biological species concept.

recombinant DNA technology A process in which genes from the cell of one species are transferred to somatic cells or gametes of another species.

recombination (crossing over) The exchange of genetic material between homologous chromosomes during meiosis.

relativistic Pertaining to relativism. Viewing entities as they relate to something else. Cultural relativism is the view that cultures have merits within their own historical and environmental contexts and that they should not be judged through comparisons with one's own culture.

replicate To duplicate. The DNA molecule is able to make copies of itself.

reproductive strategies The complex of behavioral patterns that contributes to individual reproductive success. The behaviors need not be deliberate, and they often vary considerably between males and females.

reproductive success The number of offspring an individual produces and rears to reproductive age; an individual's genetic contribution to the next generation.

rhinarium (rine-air´-ee-um) The moist, hairless pad at the end of the nose seen in most mammalian species. The rhinarium enhances an animal's ability to smell.

ribonucleic acid (RNA) A single-stranded molecule, similar in structure to DNA. Three forms of RNA are essential to protein synthesis. They are messenger RNA (mRNA), transfer RNA (tRNA), and ribosomal RNA (rRNA).

ribosomes Structures composed of a form of RNA called ribosomal RNA (rRNA) and protein. Ribosomes are found in the cell's cytoplasm and are essential to the manufacture of proteins.

ritualized behaviors Behaviors removed from their original context and sometimes exaggerated to convey information.

scenarios General, speculative reconstructions derived from various scientific data. In paleoanthropology, scenarios are usually presented as imaginative reconstructions of early hominid behavior. Such interpretations are broader than typical scientific hypotheses and theories and are not as rigorously amenable to verification.

science A body of knowledge gained through observation and experimentation; from the Latin *scientia*, meaning "knowledge."

scientific method A research method whereby a problem is identified, a hypothesis (or hypothetical explanation) is stated, and that hypothesis is tested through the collection and analysis of data. If the hypothesis is verified, it becomes a theory.

scientific testing The precise repetition of an experiment or expansion of observed data to provide verification; the procedure by which hypotheses and theories are verified, modified, or discarded.

sectorial Adapted for cutting or shearing; among primates, refers to the compressed (side-to-side) first lower premolar, which functions as a shearing surface with the upper canine.

selective pressures Forces in the environment that influence reproductive success in individuals.

senescence The process of physiological decline in body function that occurs with aging.

sensory modalities Different forms of sensation (e.g., touch, pain, pressure, heat, cold, vision, taste, hearing, and smell).

sex chromosomes In mammals, the X and Y chromosomes.

sexual dimorphism Differences in physical characteristics between males and females of the same species. For example, humans are slightly sexually dimorphic for body size, with males being taller, on average, than females of the same population.

sexual selection A type of natural selection that operates on only one sex within a species. It is the result of competition for mates, and it can lead to sexual dimorphism with regard to one or more traits.

sickle-cell anemia A severe inherited hemoglobin disorder that results from inheriting two copies of a mutant allele. This allele results from a single base substitution in the DNA.

slash-and-burn agriculture A traditional land-clearing practice whereby trees and vegetation are cut and burned. In many areas, fields are abandoned after a few years and clearing occurs elsewhere.

social structure The composition, size, and sex ratio of a group of animals. Social structures are the results of natural selection in specific habitats, and they influence individual interactions and social relationships. In many species, social structure varies, depending on different environmental factors. Therefore, in most primate species, social structure should be viewed as flexible, not fixed.

somatic cells Basically, all the cells in the body except those involved with reproduction.

specialized Evolved for a particular function; usually refers to a specific trait (e.g., incisor teeth), but may also refer to the entire way of life of an organism.

speciation The process by which a new species evolves from a prior species. Speciation is the most basic process in macroevolution.

species A group of organisms that can interbreed to produce fertile offspring. Members of one species are reproductively isolated from members of all other species (i.e., they cannot mate with them to produce fertile offspring).

spina bifida A condition in which the arch of one or more vertebrae fails to fuse and form a protective barrier around the spinal cord.

stable carbon isotopes Isotopes of carbon that are produced in plants in differing proportions, depending on environmental conditions. Through analyzing the proportions of the isotopes contained in fossil remains of animals (who ate the plants), it is possible to reconstruct aspects of ancient environments (particularly temperature and aridity).

stereoscopic vision The condition whereby visual images are, to varying degrees, superimposed on one another. This provides for depth perception, or the perception of the external environment in three dimensions. Stereoscopic vision is partly a function of structures in the brain.

strategies Behaviors or behavioral complexes that have been favored by natural selection to increase individual reproductive fitness.

stratigraphy Study of the sequential layering of deposits.

stress In a physiological context, any factor that acts to disrupt homeostasis; more precisely, the body's response to any factor that threatens its ability to maintain homeostasis.

sympatric Living in the same area; pertaining to two or more species whose habitats partly or largely overlap.

taphonomy (*taphos,* meaning "dead") The study of how bones and other materials came to be buried in the earth and preserved as fossils. A taphonomist studies the processes of sedimentation, the action of streams, preservation properties of bone, and carnivore disturbance factors.

taxonomy The branch of science concerned with the rules of classifying organisms on the basis of evolutionary relationships.

territories Portions of an individual's or group's home range actively defended against intrusion, particularly by conspecifics.

theory A broad statement of scientific relationships or underlying principles that has been at least partially verified.

theropods Small- to medium-sized ground-living dinosaurs, dated to approximately 150 m.y.a. and thought to be related to birds.

transfer RNA (tRNA) The type of RNA that binds to specific amino acids and transports them to the ribosome during protein synthesis.

transmutation The change of one species to another. The term *evolution* did not assume its current meaning until the late nineteenth century.

uniformitarianism The theory that the earth's features are the result of long-term processes that continue to operate in the present as they did in the past. Elaborated on by Lyell, this theory opposed catastrophism and provided for immense geological time.

Upper Paleolithic A cultural period usually associated with modern humans (but also found with some Neandertals) and distinguished by technological innovation in various stone tool industries. Best known from western Europe, similar industries are also known from central and eastern Europe and Africa.

Upper Pleistocene The portion of the Pleistocene epoch beginning 125,000 y.a. and ending approximately 10,000 y.a.

variation (genetic) Inherited differences between individuals; the basis of all evolutionary change.

vasodilation Expansion of blood vessels, permitting increased blood flow to the skin. Vasodilation permits warming of the skin and also facilitates radiation of warmth as a means of cooling. Vasodilation is an involuntary response to warm temperatures, various drugs, and even emotional states (blushing).

vasoconstriction Narrowing of blood vessels to reduce blood flow to the skin. Vasoconstriction is an involuntary response to cold and reduces heat loss at the skin's surface.

vertebrates Animals with segmented bony spinal columns; includes fishes, amphibians, reptiles, birds, and mammals.

vectors Agents that serve to transmit disease from one carrier to another. Mosquitoes are vectors for malaria, just as fleas are vectors for bubonic plague.

viviparous Giving birth to live young.

world view General cultural orientation or perspective shared by members of a society.

zoonotic (zoh-oh-no´-tic) Pertaining to a zoonosis (*pl.,* zoonoses), a disease that is transmitted to humans through contact with nonhuman animals.

zygote A cell formed by the union of an egg and a sperm cell. It contains the full complement of chromosomes (in humans, 46) and has the potential of developing into an entire organism.

Bibliography

Adcock, Gregory J., Elizabeth S. Dennis, Simon Easteal, et al.
2001 "Mitochondrial DNA Sequences in Ancient Australians: Implications for Modern Human Origins." *Proceedings of the National Academy of Sciences,* 98:537–542.

Aiello, L. C.
1992 "Body Size and Energy Requirements." *In: The Cambridge Encyclopedia of Human Evolution,* J. Jones, R. Martin, and D. Pilbeam (eds.), Cambridge, England: Cambridge University Press, pp. 41–45.

Aiello, L. C. and J. C. K. Wells
2002 "Energetics and the Evolution of the Genus *Homo. Annual Review of Anthropology,* 31:323–338.

Aiello, L. C. and B. A. Wood
1994 Cranial Variables as Predictors of Hominine Body Mass. *American Journal of Physical Anthropology,* 95:409–426.

Aitken, M. J., C. B. Stringer, and P. A. Mellars (eds.)
1993 *The Origin of Modern Humans and the Impact of Chronometric Dating.* Princeton, N.J.: Princeton University Press.

Alexander, R. D.
1974 "The Evolution of Social Behavior." *Ann. Rev. Ecol. Syst.,* 5:325–383.

Alland Jr., Alexander
1971 *Human Diversity.* New York: Anchor Press/Doubleday.

Altmann, Jeanne
1981 *Baboon Mothers and Infants.* Cambridge: Harvard University Press.

Altmann, Stuart A. and Jeanne Altmann
1970 *Baboon Ecology.* Chicago: University of Chicago Press.

Anderson, J. Gunnar
1934 *Children of the Yellow Earth.* New York: Macmillan.

Andrews, Peter
1984 "An Alternative Interpretation of the Characters Used to Define *Homo erectus.*" *Cour Forschungist Senekenb,* 69:167–175.

———
1985 "Family Group Systematics and Evolution among Catarrhine Primates." *In: Ancestors: The Hard Evidence,* E. Delson (ed.), New York: Alan R. Liss, pp. 14–22.

———
1992 "Evolution and Environment in Miocene Hominoids." *Nature,* 360:641–646.

Andrews, Peter and Jens Lorenz Franzen (eds.)
1984 *The Early Evolution of Man.* Frankfurt: Cour. Forsch. Inst. Seckenberg.

Andrews, Peter and David Pilbeam
1996 "The Nature of the Evidence," News and Views. *Nature,* 379:123–124.

Ardrey, Robert
1976 *The Hunting Hypothesis.* New York: Atheneum.

Arensburg, B., L. A. Schepartz, et al.
1990 "A Reappraisal of the Anatomical Basis for Speech in Middle Paleolithic Hominids." *American Journal of Physical Anthropology,* 83(2):137–146.

Arensburg, B., A. M. Tillier, et al.
1989 "A Middle Paleolithic Human Hyoid Bone." *Nature,* 338:758–760.

Aronson, J. L., R. C. Walter, and M. Taieb
1983 "Correlation of Tulu Bor Tuff at Koobi Fora with the Sidi Hakoma Tuff at Hadar." *Nature,* 306:209–210.

Arsuaga, Juan-Luis et al.
1993 "Three New Human Skulls from the Sima de los Huesos Middle Pleistocene Site in Sierra de Atapuerca, Spain." *Nature,* 362:534–537.

Arsuaga, Juan-Luis, Carlos Lorenzon, and Ana Garcia
1999 "The Human Cranial Remains from Gran Dolina Lower Pleistocene Site (Sierra de Atapuerca, Spain)." *Journal of Human Evolution,* 37:431–457.

Arsuaga, J. L., I. Martinez, A. Garcia, et al.
1997 "Sima de los Huesos (Sierra de Atapuerca, Spain). The Site." *Journal of Human Evolution,* 33:109–127.

Ascenzi, A. I. Bidditu, P. F. Cassoli, et al.
1996 "A Calvarium of Late *Homo erectus* from Ceprano, Italy." *Journal of Human Evolution,* 31:409–423.

Asfaw, Berhane
1992 "New Fossil Hominids from the Ethiopian Rift Valley and the Afar." Paper presented at the Annual Meeting, American Association of Physical Anthropologists.

Asfaw, Berhane et al.
1992 "The Earliest Acheulian from Konso-Gardula." *Nature,* 360:732–735.

———
1995 Three Seasons of Hominid Paleontology at Aramis, Ethiopia. Paper presented at Paleoanthropology Society meetings, Oakland, Ca., March 1995.

Asfaw, Berhane, W. Henry Gilbert, Yonas Beyene, et al.
2002 "Remains of *Homo erectus* from Bouri, Middle Awash, Ethiopia. *Nature,* 416:317–320.

Asfaw, Berhane, Tim White, Owen Lovejoy, et al.
1999 "*Australopithecus garhi:* A New Species of Early Hominid from Ethiopia." *Science,* 284: 629–635.

Avery, O. T., C. M. MacLeod, and M. McCarty
1944 "Studies on the Chemical Nature of the Substances Inducing Transformation in Pneumoccal Types." *Journal of Experimental Medicine*, 79:137–158.

Ayala, Francisco
1995 "The Myth of Eve: Molecular Biology and Human Origins." *Science*, 270:1930–1936.

Badrian, Alison and Noel Badrian
1984 "Social Organization of *Pan paniscus* in the Lomako Forest, Zaire." *In: The Pygmy Chimpanzee*, Randall L. Susman (ed.), New York: Plenum Press, pp. 325–346.

Badrian, Noel and Richard K. Malenky
1984 "Feeding Ecology of *Pan paniscus* in the Lomako Forest, Zaire." *In: The Pygmy Chimpanzee*, Randall L. Susman (ed.), New York: Plenum Press, pp. 275–299.

Baker, Paul T. and Michael A. Little
1976 "The Environmental Adaptations and Perspectives." *In: Man in the Andes*, P. T. Baker and M. A. Little (eds.), Stroudsburg, Penn.: Dowden, Hutchinson, and Ross, pp. 405–428.

Baltimore, David
2001 "Our Genome Unveiled." *Nature*, 409:814–816.

Bamshad, Micahel J.
2003 "Human Population Genetic Structure and Inference of Group Membership." *American Journal of Human Genetics*, 72:578–589.

Bamshad, Michael J. and Steve E. Olson
2003 "Does Race Exist?" *Scientific American*, 289: (Dec):78–85.

Barash, David
1982 *Sociobiology and Behavior.* (2nd Ed.) New York: Elsevier.

Bartholomew, C. A. and J. B. Birdsell
1953 "Ecology and the Protohominids." *American Anthropologist*, 55:481–498.

Bartlett, Thad.Q., Robert W. Sussman, James M. Cheverud
1993 "Infant Killing in Primates: A Review of Observed Cases with Specific References to the Sexual Selection Hypothesis." *American Anthropologist*, 95(4):958–990.

Bartstra, Gert-Jan
1982 "*Homo erectus erectus:* The Search for Artifacts." *Current Anthropology*, 23(3):318–320.

Bar-Yosef, Ofer
1993 "The Role of Western Asia in Modern Human Origins." *In: M. J. Aitken et al. (eds.), q.v., pp. 132–147.

_____
1994 "The Contributions of Southwest Asia to the Study of the Origin of Modern Humans." *In: Origins of Anatomically Modern Humans*, M. H. Nitecki and D. V. Nitecki (eds.), New York: Plenum Press, pp. 23–66.

Barzun, Jacques
1965 *Race: A Study in Superstition.* New York: Harper & Row.

Bass, W. M.
1987 *Human Osteology: A Laboratory and Field Manual* (3rd Ed.). Columbia, Mo.: Missouri Archaeological Society Special Publication No. 2.

Beard, K. Christopher, Yong Shenj Tong, Mary R. Dawson, et al.
1996 "Earliest Complete Dentition of an Anthropoid Primate from the Late Middle Eocene of Shanxi Province, China." *Science*, 272:82–85.

Bearder, Simon K.
1987 "Lorises, Bushbabies and Tarsiers: Diverse Societies in Solitary Foragers." *In:* Smuts et al., q.v., pp. 11–24.

Begun, David R.
1992 "Phyletic Diversity and Locomotion in Primitive European Hominoids." *American Journal of Physical Anthropology*, 87:311–340.

_____
1994 "Relations Among the Great Apes and Humans: New Interpretations Based on the Fossil Great Ape *Dryopithecus*." *Yearbook of Physical Anthropology*, 37:11–63.

_____
2003 "Planet of the Apes." *Scientific American*, 289:74–83.

Begun, D. and A. Walker
1993 "The Endocast." *In:* A. Walker and R. E. Leakey (eds.), q.v., pp. 326–358.

Behrensmeyer, Anna K. and Andrew P. Hill
1980 *Fossils in the Making: Vertebrate Taphonomy and Paleoecology.* Chicago: University of Chicago Press.

Behrensmeyer, A. K., D. Western, and D. E. Dechant Boaz
1979 "New Perspectives in Vertebrate Paleoecology from a Recent Bone Assemblage." *Paleobiology*, 5(1):12–21.

Berger, Thomas and Erik Trinkaus
1995 "Patterns of Trauma Among the Neandertals." *Journal of Archaeological Science*, 22:841–852.

Bergman, T. L., J. C. Beehner, D. L. Cheney, and R. M. Seyfarth
2003 "Hierarchical Classification by Rank and Kinship in Baboons." *Science*, 302:1234–1236.

Bermudez de Castro, J. M., J. L. Arsuaga, E. Carbonell, et al.
1997 "A Hominid from the Lower Pleistocene of Atapuerca, Spain. Possible Ancestor to Neandertals and Modern Humans." *Science*, 276:1392–1395.

Bermudez de Castro, J. M., M. Martinon-Torres, E. Carbonell, et al.
2004 "The Atapuerca Sites and their Contribution to the Knowledge of Human Evolution in Europe." *Evolutionary Anthropology*, 13:25–41.

Bernor, R. L.
1983 "Geochronology and Zoogeographic Relationships of Miocene Hominoidea." *In:* R. L. Ciochon and R. S. Corruccini (eds.), q.v., pp. 21–66.

Biasutti, R.
1951 *Rassa e Popoli della Terra.* Torino: Unione Tipografico Editria Torinese.

Binford, Lewis R.
1981 *Bones. Ancient Men and Modern Myths.* New York: Academic Press.

_____
1983 *In Pursuit of the Past.* New York: Thames and Hudson.

_____
1985 "Ancestral Lifeways: The Faunal Record." AnthroQuest, 32, Summer 1985.

Binford, Lewis R. and Chuan Kun Ho
1985 "Taphonomy at a Distance: Zhoukoudian, 'The Cave Home of Beijing Man'?" *Current Anthropology*, 26:413–442.

Binford, Lewis R. and Nancy M. Stone
1986a "The Chinese Paleolithic: An Outsider's View." *AnthroQuest*, Fall 1986(1):14–20.

_____
1986b "Zhoukoudian: A Closer Look." *Current Anthropology*, 27(5):453–475.

Birdsell, Joseph B.
1981   *Human Evolution*. (3rd Ed.). Boston: Houghton Mifflin.

Blangero, John, Jeff T. Williams and Laura Almasy
2000   "Quantitative Trait Locus Mapping Using Human Pedigrees." *Human Biology*, 72:35–62.

Blumenschine, Robert J.
1986   *Early Hominid Scavenging Opportunities*. Oxford: Bar International Series 283.

——
1995   "Percussion Marks, Tooth Marks, and Experimental Determinants of the Timing of Hominid and Carnivore Access to Long Bones at FLK *Zinjanthropus*, Olduvai Gorge, Tanzania." *Journal of Human Evolution* 29: 21–51.

Blumenschine, Robert J., and John A. Cavallo
1992   "Scavenging and Human Evolution." *Scientific American* (Oct.): 90–96.

Blumenschine, Robert J., and Charles R. Peters
1998   "Archaeological Predictions for Hominid Land Use in the Paleo-Olduvai Basin, Tanzania, During Lowermost Bed II Times." *Journal of Human Evolution* 34: 565–607.

Boas, F.
1910   "Changes in the Bodily Form of Descendants of Immigrants." *American Anthropologist*, 14:530–562.

Boaz, N. T. and A. K. Behrensmeyer
1976   "Hominid Taphonomy: Transport of Human Skeletal Parts in an Artificial Fluviatile Environment." *American Journal of Physical Anthropology*, 45:56–60.

Boaz, N. T. and Russell L. Ciochon
2001   "The Scavenging of *Homo erectus pekinensis*." *Natural History*, 110(2):46–51.

Boaz, N. T., F. C. Howell, and M. L. McCrossin
1982   "Faunal Age of the Usno, Shungura B and Hadar Formation, Ethiopia." *Nature*, 300:633–635.

Bodmer, W. F.
1995   "Evolution and Function of the HLA Region." *Clinical Surveys*, 22:5–16.

Bodmer, W. F. and L. L. Cavalli-Sforza
1976   *Genetics, Evolution, and Man*. San Francisco: W. H. Freeman and Company.

Boesch, C.
1994   "Hunting Strategies of Gombe and Tai Chimpanzees." *In:* Wrangham, R. W., C. MGrew, Frans B. M. de Waal, and Paul G. Heltne (eds.). *Chimpanzee Cultures*. Cambridge: Harvard University Press, pp. 77–91

Boesch, C. and H. Boesch
1989   "Hunting Behavior of Wild Chimpanzees in the Tai National Park." *American Journal of Physical Anthropology*, 78(4):547–573

——
1990   "Tool Use and Tool Making in Wild Chimpanzees." *Folia Primatologica*, 54:86–99.

Boesch, Christophe, Paul Marchesi, Nathalie Marchesi, et al.
1994   "Is Nut Cracking in Wild Chimpanzees a Cultural Behaviour?" *Journal of Human Evolution*, 26:325–338.

Boggess, Jane
1984   "Infant Killing and Male Reproductive Strategies in Langurs (*Presbytis entellus*)." *In:* G. Hausfater and S. B. Hrdy (eds.), q.v., pp. 280–310.

Bogin, Barry
1988   *Patterns of Human Growth*. Cambridge: Cambridge University Press.

——
1998   "Social and Economic Class." *In: The Cambridge Encyclopedia of Human Growth and Development*, S. J. Ulijaszek, F. E. Johnston, and M. A. Preece (eds.). Cambridge, UK: Cambridge University Press, pp. 399–401.

Bongaarts, John
1980   Does Malnutrition Affect Fecundity? A Summary of Evidence. *Science*, 208:564–569.

Bordes, François
1968   *The Old Stone Age*. New York: McGraw-Hill.

Borries, C., et al.
1999   "DNA Analyses Support the Hypothesis that Infanticide is Adaptive in Langur Monkeys." *Proc. R. Soc. Lond.*, 266:901–904.

Bottini, N., G. F. Meloni, A. Finocchi, et al.
2001   "Maternal-Fetal Interaction in the ABO System: A Comparative Analysis of Healthy Mothers and Couples with Recurrent Spontaneous Abortion Suggests a Protective Effect of B Incompatability." *Human Biology*, 73:167–174.

Bower, Bruce
2003   "The Ultimate Colonists." *Science News*, 164:10–12.

Bowler, Peter J.
1983, 1989   *Evolution: The History of an Idea*. Berkeley: University of California Press.

——
1988   The *Non-Darwinian Evolution: Reinterpreting a Historical Myth*. Baltimore: Johns Hopkins University Press.

Brace, C. L. and Ashley Montagu
1977   *Human Evolution* (2nd Ed.). New York: Macmillan.

Brace, C. Loring, H. Nelson, and N. Korn
1979   *Atlas of Human Evolution* (2nd Ed.). New York: Holt, Rinehart & Winston.

Brain, C. K.
1970   "New Finds at the Swartkrans Australopithecine Site." *Nature*, 225:1112–1119.

——
1981   *The Hunters or the Hunted? An Introduction to African Cave Taphonomy*. Chicago: University of Chicago Press.

Bramblett, Claud A.
1994   *Patterns of Primate Behavior* (2nd Ed.). Prospect Heights, Ill.: Waveland Press.

Brash, D. E, J. A. Rudolph, J. A. Simon, et al.
1991   "A Role for Sunlight in Skin Cancer: UV-Induced p53 Mutations in Squamous Cell Carcinoma." *Proc. Nat. Acad. Sci.*, 88(22):10124–10128.

Bräuer, Günter
1984   "A Craniological Approach to the Origin of Anatomically Modern *Homo sapiens* in Africa and Implications for the Appearance of Modern Europeans." *In:* F. H. Smith and F. Spencer (eds.), q.v., pp. 327–410.

——
1989   "The Evolution of Modern Humans: A Comparison of the African and Non-African Evidence." *In:* Mellars and Stringer (eds.), q.v.

Brock, A., P. L. McFadden, and T. C. Partridge
1977 "Preliminary Paleomagnetic Results from Makapansgat and Swartkrans." *Nature,* 266:249–250.

Bromage, Timothy G. and Christopher Dean
1985 "Re-evaluation of the Age at Death of Immature Fossil Hominids." *Nature,* 317:525–527.

Brooks, Alison et al.
1995 "Dating and Context of Three Middle Stone Age Sites with Bone Points in the Upper Semliki Valley, Zaire." *Science,* 268:548–553.

Brose, David and Milford H. Wolpoff
1971 "Early Upper Paleolithic Man and Late Middle Paleolithic Tools." *American Anthropologist,* 73:1156–1194.

Brown, B, A. Walker, C. V. Ward, and R. E. Leakey
1993 "New *Australopithecus boisei*: Calvaria from East Lake Turkana, Kenya." *American Journal of Physical Anthropology,* 91:137–159.

Brown, F. H.
1982 "Tulu Bor Tuff at Koobi Fora Correlated with the Sidi Hakoma Tuff at Hadar." *Nature,* 300:631–632.

Brown, Lester R.
2001 *Eco-economy: Building an Economy for the Earth.* New York: W. W. Horton.

Brown, T. M. and K. D. Rose
1987 "Patterns of Dental Evolution in Early Eocene Anaptomorphine Primates Comomyidael from the Bighorn Basin, Wyoming." *Journal of Paleontology,* 61:1–62.

Brues, Alice M.
1959 "The Spearman and the Archer." *American Anthropologist,* 61:457–469.

———
1990 *People and Races* (2nd Ed.). Prospect Heights, Ill.: Waveland Press.

———
1991 "The Objective View of Race." Paper presented at American Anthropological Association 90th Annual Meeting, Chicago, Nov.

Brunet, Michel et al.
1995 "The First Australopithecine 2,500 Kilometers West of the Rift Valley (Chad)." *Nature,* 378:273–274.

Bshary, R. and R. Noe
1997 "Red Colobus and Diana Monkeys Provide Mutual Protection Against Predators." *Animal Behavior,* 54:1461–1474.

Buchan, J. C., S. C. Alberts, J. B. Silk, and J. Altmann
2003 "True Paternal Care in a Multi-male Primate Society." *Nature,* 425:179–180.

Buffon, George Louis Leclerc, Compte de
1860 "*Histoire Naturelle Generale et Particuliere.*" Translated by Wm. Smellie. *In: The Idea of Racism,* Louis L. Snyder, New York: Van Nostrand Reinhold, 1962.

Bunn, Henry T.
1981 "Archaeological Evidence for Meat-eating by Plio-Pleistocene Hominids from Koobi Fora and Olduvai Gorge." *Nature,* 291:574–577.

Burchard, E. G., E. Ziv, N. Coyle, et al.
2003 "The Importance of Race and Ethnic Background in Biomedical Research and Clinical Practice." *New England Journal of Medicine,* 348:1170–1175.

Burkhardt, Richard W., Jr.
1984 "The Zoological Philosophy of J. B. Lamarck." (Introduction) *In:* Lamarck, q.v.

Butzer, Karl W.
1974 "Paleoecology of South African Australopithecines: Taung Revisited." *Current Anthropology,* 15:367–382.

Cadbury, D.
2001 *Terrible Lizard: The First Dinosaur Hunters and the Birth of a New Science.* New York: Henry Holt and Co.

Cann, R. L., M. Stoneking, and A. C. Wilson
1987 "Mitochondrial DNA and Human Evolution." *Nature,* 325:31–36.

Cann, Rebecca L., Olga Rickards, and J. Koji Lum
1994 "Mitochondrial DNA and Human Evolution: Our One Lucky Mother." *In:* M H. Nitecki and D. V. Nitecki (eds.), q.v., pp. 135–148.

Cantalupo, Claudio and William D. Hopkins
2001 "Asymmetric Broca's Area in Great Apes." *Nature,* 414:505.

Caramelli, David, Carlos Lalueza-Fox, Cristiano Vernesi, et al.
2003 "Evidence for Genetic Discontinuity Between Neandertals and 24,000-year-old Anatomically Modern Humans." *Proceedings of the National Academy of Sciences,* 100:6593–6597.

Carbonell, E. et al.
1995 Lower Pleistocene Hominids and Artifacts from Atapuerca-TDG (Spain)." *Science,* 269:826–830.

Carrol, Robert L.
1988 *Vertebrate Paleontology and Evolution.* New York: W. H. Freeman and Co.

Carroll, Sean B.
2003 "Genetics and the Making of *Homo sapiens.*" *Nature,* 422:849–857.

Cartmill, Matt
1972 "Arboreal Adaptations and the Origin of the Order Primates." *In: The Functional and Evolutionary Biology of Primates,* R. H. Tuttle (ed.), Chicago: Aldine-Atherton, pp. 97–122.

———
1990 "Human Uniqueness and Theoretical Content in Paleoanthropology." *International Journal of Primatology,* 11(3):173–192.

———
1992 "New Views on Primate Origins." *Evolutionary Anthropology,* 1:105–111.

Cavalli-Sforza, L. L., A. Piazza, P. Menozzi, and J. Mountain
1988 "Reconstruction of Human Evolution: Bringing Together Genetic, Archaeological, and Linguistic Data." *Proceedings of the National Academy of Sciences,* 85:6002–6006.

Cela-Conde, Camillo J. and Francisco J. Ayala
2003 "Genera of the Human Lineage." *Proceedings of the National Academy of Sciences,* 100:7684–7689.

Censky, E. J., K. Hodge and J. Dudley
1998 "Over-Water Dispersal of Lizards Due to Hurricanes." *Nature,* 395 (6702):556.

Chagnon, N. A.
1979 "Mate Competition Favoring Close Kin and Village Fissioning among the Yanomamo Indians." *In: Evolutionary Biology and Human Social Behavior: An Anthropological Perspective,* N. Chagnon and W. Irons (eds.), North Scituak, Mass.: Duxbury Press, pp. 86–132.

1988 "Life Histories, Blood Revenge, and Warfare in a Tribal Population." *Science,* 239:985–992.

Charteris, J., J. C. Wali, and J. W. Nottrodt
1981 "Functional Reconstruction of Gait from Pliocene Hominid Footprints at Laetoli, Northern Tanzania." *Nature,* 290:496–498.

Chen, F-C., and Li, W-H.
2001 "Genomic Divergences Between Humans and Other Hominoids and the Effective Population Size of the Common Ancestor of Humans and Chimpanzees." *American Journal of Human Genetics,* 68:444–456.

Cheney, Dorothy L.
1987 "Interaction and Relationships between Groups." *In:* B. Smuts et al. (eds.), q.v., pp. 267–281.

Cheney, D. L. and R. M. Seyfarth
1990 *How Monkeys See the World.* Chicago: Chicago University Press.

Cheney, D. L., R. M. Seyfarth, S. J. Andelman, and P. C. Lee
1988 "Reproductive Success in Vervet Monkeys." In: Clutton-Brock, T.H. (ed.), *Reproductive Success.* Chicago: University of Chicago Press. pp.384–402.

Ciochon, R. L. and A. B. Chiarelli (eds.)
1980 *Evolutionary Biology of the New World Monkeys and Continental Drift.* New York: Plenum Press.

Ciochon, Russel L. and Robert S. Corruccini (eds.)
1983 *New Interpretations of Ape and Human Ancestry.* New York: Plenum Press.

Clark, A. G., S. Glanowski, R. Nielsen, et al.
2003 "Inferring Nonneutral Evolution from Human-Chimp-Mouse Orthologous Gene Trios." *Nature,* 302:1960–1963.

Clark, J. Desmond, Yonas Beyene, Gidoy Wold Gabriel, et al.
2003 "Stratigraphic, Chronological, and Behavioral Contexts of Pleistocene *Homo sapiens* from Middle Awash, Ethiopia." *Nature,* 423:747–752.

Clark, W. E. LeGros
1967 *Man-apes or Ape-men?* New York: Holt, Rinehart & Winston.
1971 New York Times Books (3rd Ed.).

Clarke, R. J.
1985 "*Australopithecus* and Early *Homo* in Southern Africa." *In: Ancestors: The Hard Evidence,* E. Delson (ed.), New York: Alan R. Liss, pp. 171–177.

Clarke, Ronald J. and Phillip V. Tobias
1995 "Sterkfontein Member 2 Foot Bones of the Oldest South African Hominid." *Science,* 269:521–524.

Cleveland, J. and C. T. Snowdon
1982 "The Complex Vocal Repertoire of the Adult Cotton-top Tamarin (*Saguinus oedipus oedipus*)." *Zeitschrift Tierpsychologie,* 58:231–270.

Clutton-Brock, T. H. and Paul H. Harvey
1977 "Primate Ecology and Social Organization." *Journal of Zoological Society of London,* 183:1–39.

Colwell, Rita R.
1996 Global Climate and Infectious Disease: The Cholera Paradigm. *Science,* 274 (5295):2025–2031.

Conkey, M.
1987 New Approaches in the Search for Meaning? A Review of the Research in "Paleolithic Art." *Journal of Field Archaeology,* 14:413–430.

Conroy, Glenn C.
1997 *Reconstructing Human Origins. A Modern Synthesis.* New York: Norton.

Conroy, G., C. J. Jolly, D. Cramer, and J. E. Kalb
1978 "Newly Discovered Fossil Hominid Skull from the Afar Depression." *Nature,* 272:67–70.

Conroy, G. C., M. Pickford, B. Senut, J. van Couvering, and P. Mein
1992 "*Otavipithecus namibiensis,* First Miocene Hominoid from Southern Africa." *Nature,* 356:144–148.

Conroy, Glenn C., Jeff W. Lichtman, and Lawrence B. Martin
1995 "Brief Communication: Some Observations on Enamel Thickness and Enamel Prism Packing in Miocene Hominoid *Otavipithecus namibiensis.*" *American Journal of Physical Anthropology,* 98:595–600.

Conroy, Glenn C., G. W. Weber, H. Seidler, et al.
1998 "Endocranial Capacity in an Early Hominid Cranium from Sterkfontein, South Africa." *Science,* 280:1730–1731.

Coon, C. S., S. M. Garn, and J. B. Birdsell
1950 *Races—A Study of the Problems of Race Formation in Man.* Springfield, Ill.: Charles C. Thomas.

Cooper, Alan, Andrew Rambaut, Vincent Macaulay, et al.
2001 "Human Origins and Ancient DNA." Letter to *Science,* 292:1655–1656.

Cooper, Richard S., S. Kaufman, and Ryk Ward
2003 "Race and Genomics." *New England Journal of Medicine.* 348:1166–1170.

Corruccini, R. S., M. Baba, M. Goodman, et al.
1980 "Non-Linear Macromolecular Evolution and the Moleculer Clock." *Evolution,* 34:1216–1219.

Corruccini, R. S. and H. M. McHenry
1980 "Cladometric Analysis of Pliocene Hominids." *Journal of Human Evolution,* 9:209–221.

Corruccini, Robert S.
1994 "Reaganomics and the Fate of the Progressive Neandertals." *In:* R. S. Corruccini and R. I. Ciochon (eds.), q.v., pp. 697–708.

Crapo, Lawrence
1985 *Hormones: The Messengers of Life.* New York: W. H. Freeman and Company.

Crews, D. E. and G. J. Harper
1998 "Ageing as Part of the Developmental Process." *In: The Cambridge Encyclopedia of Human Growth and Development,* S. J. Ulijaszek, F. E. Johnston, and M. A. Preece (eds.). Cambridge, UK: Cambridge University Press, pp. 425–427.

Cronin, J. E.
1983 "Apes, Humans, and Molecular Clocks. A Reappraisal." *In:* R. L. Ciochon and R. S. Corruccini (eds.), q.v., pp. 115–150.

Crook, J. H.
1970 "Social Organization and Environment: Aspects of Contemporary Social Ethology." *Animal Behavior,* 18:197–209.

Crook, J. H. and J. S. Gartlan
1966 "Evolution of Primate Societies." *Nature,* 210:1200–1203.

Culotta, Elizabeth
1995 "Asian Anthropoids Strike Back." *Science,* 270:918.

Cummings, Michael
2000 *Human Heredity. Principles and Issues* (5th Ed.). Pacific Grove: Brooks/Cole.

1997   *Human Heredity. Principles and Issues.* 4th ed. Belmont, CA: West/Wadsworth.

Current, M., G. Trabuchet, D. Rees, et al.
2002   "Molecular Analysis of the Beta-Globin Gene Cluster in the Niokholo Mandenka Population Reveals a Recent Origin of the Beta S Senegal Mutation." *American Journal of Human Genetics,* 70:207–223.

Curtin, R. and P. Dolhinow
1978   "Primate Social Behavior in a Changing World." *American Scientist,* 66:468–475.

Curtis, Garniss
1981   "A Matter of Time: Dating Techniques and Geology of Hominid Sites." Symposium Paper, Davis, Ca., May 10, 1981.

Cyranoski, D.
2003   "Why China?" *Nature,* 424:124–125.

Dalrymple, G. B.
1972   "Geomagnetic Reversals and North American Glaciations." *In: Calibration of Hominoid Evolution,* W. W. Bishop and J. A. Miller (eds.), Edinburgh: Scottish Academic Press, pp. 303–329.

Dart, Raymond
1959   *Adventures with the Missing Link.* New York: Harper & Brothers.

Darwin, Charles
1859   *On the Origin of Species.* A Facsimile of the First Edition, Cambridge, Mass.: Harvard University Press (1964).

Darwin, Charles
1871   *The Descent of Man and Selection in Relation to Sex.* Republished, 1981, Princeton: Princeton University Press.

Darwin, Francis (ed.)
1950   *The Life and Letters of Charles Darwin.* New York: Henry Schuman.

Day, M. H. and E. H. Wickens
1980   "Laetoli Pliocene Hominid Footprints and Bipedalism." *Nature,* 286:385–387.

Day, Michael
1986   *Guide to Fossil Man* (4th Ed.), Chicago: University of Chicago Press.

Deacon, T. W.
1992   "The Human Brain." *In: The Cambridge Encyclopedia of Human Evolution,* S. Jones, R. Martin, and D. Pilbeam (eds.), Cambridge, England: Cambridge University Press, pp. 115–123.

Dean, Christopher, Meave G. Leakey, Donald Reid, et al.
2001   "Growth Processes in Teeth Distinguishing Modern Humans from *Homo erectus* and Earlier Hominins." *Nature,* 414:628–631.

Dean, M., M. Carring, C. Winkler, et al.
1996   "Genetic Restriction of HIV-1 Infection and Progression to AIDS by a Deletion Allele of the CKR5 Structural Gene." *Science,* 273:1856–1862.

de Bonis, Louis and George D. Koufos
1994   "Our Ancestors' Ancestor: *Ouranopithecus* Is a Greek Link in Human Ancestry." *Evolutionary Anthropology,* 3:75–83.

Defleur, A., T. White, P. Valensi, et al.
1999   "Neanderthal Cannibalism at Moula-Guercy, Ardèche, France." *Science,* 286:128–131.

DeGusta, D., W. H. Gilbert, and S. P. Turner
1999   "Hypoglossal Canal Size and Hominid Speech." *Proceedings of the National Academy of Sciences,* 96:1800–1804.

de Heinzelin, Jean, J. Desmond Clark, Tim White, et al.
1999   "Environment and Behavior of 2.5-Million-Year-Old Bouri Hominids." *Science,* 284:625–629.

Deino, Alan L., Paul R. Renne, and Carl C. Swisher
1998   "^{40}Ar/^{39}Ar Dating in Paleoanthropology and Archeology." *Evolutionary Anthropology,* 6:63–75.

de Lumley, Henry and M. de Lumley
1973   "Pre-Neanderthal Human Remains from Arago Cave in Southeastern France." *Yearbook of Physical Anthropology,* 16:162–168.

Delson, Eric (ed.)
1985   *Ancestors: The Hard Evidence.* New York: Alan R. Liss.

———
1987   "Evolution and Paleobiology of Robust Australopithecus." *Nature,* 327:654–655.

Dene, H. T., M. Goodman, and W. Prychodko
1976   "Immunodiffusion Evidence on the Phylogeny of the Primates." *In: Molecular Anthropology,* M. Goodman, R. E. Tashian, and J. H. Tashian (eds.), New York: Plenum Press, pp. 171–195.

Deragon, J. M. and P. Capy
2000   "Impact of Transposable Elements on the Human Genome." *Annals of Medicine,* 32:264–273.

deReuter, J. R.
1986   "The Influence of Group Size on Predator Scanning and Foraging Behavior of Wedge-Capped Capuchin Monkeys (*Cebus olivaceus*)." *Behaviour,* 98:240–258.

Desmond, Adrian and James Moore
1991   *Darwin.* New York: Warner Books.

Dettwyler, K. A.
1991   "Can Paleopathology Provide Evidence for Compassion?" *American Journal of Physical Anthropology,* 84:375–384.

DeVore, I. and S. L. Washburn
1963   "Baboon Ecology and Human Evolution." *In: African Ecology and Human Evolution,* F. C. Howell and F. Bourlière (eds.), New York: Viking Fund Publication, No. 36, pp. 335–367.

De Vos, J.
1985   "Faunal Stratigraphy and Correlation of the Indonesian Hominid Sites." *In: Ancestors: The Hard Evidence,* E. Delson (ed.), New York: Alan R. Liss, pp. 215–220.

de Waal, Frans
1982   *Chimpanzee Politics.* London: Jonathan Cape.

———
1987   "Tension Regulation and Nonreproductive Functions of Sex in Captive Bonobos (*Pan paniscus*)." *National Geographic Research,* 3:318–335.

———
1989   *Peacemaking among Primates.* Cambridge: Harvard University Press.

———
1996   *Good Natured. The Origins of Right and Wrong in Humans and Other Animals,* Cambridge, Mass.: Harvard University Press.

1999 "Cultural Primatology Comes of Age." *Nature*, 399:635–636.

Dolhinow, P.
1978 "A Behavior Repertoire for the Indian Langur Monkey (*Presbytis entellus*)." *Primates*, 19:449–472.

Doran, Diane M. and Alastair McNeilage
1998 "Gorilla Ecology and Behavior." *Evolutionary Anthropology*, 6(4):120–131.

Dorit, R. L., H. Akashi, and W. Gilbert
1995 Absence of Polymorphism at the Zfy Locus on the Human Y Chromosome. *Science*, 268:1183–1185.

Duarte, C., J. Maurício, P. B. Pettitt, et al.
1999 "The Early Upper Paleolithic Human Skeleton from the Abrigo do Lagar Velho (Portugal) and Modern Human Emergence in Iberia." *Proceedings of the National Academy of Sciences*, 96:7604–7609.

Duchin, Linda E.
1990 "The Evolution of Articulate Speech." *Journal of Human Evolution*, 19:687–697.

Dumont, R. and B. Rosier
1969 *The Hungry Future*. New York: Praeger.

Dunbar, I. M.
1988 *Primate Social Systems*. Ithaca: Cornell University Press.

Dunbar, Robin
1998 "The Social Brain Hypothesis." *Evolutionary Anthropology*, 6(5):178–190.

2001 "Brains on Two Legs: Group Size and the Evolution of Intelligence." *In:* de Waal, Frans B. M. *Tree of Origin: What Primate Behavior Can Tell Us about Human Social Evolution*. Cambridge: Harvard University Press, pp. 173–191.

Durham, William
1981 Paper presented to the Annual Meeting of the American Anthropological Association, Washington, D.C., Dec. 1980. Reported in *Science*, 211:40.

Eaton, S. Boyd, Marjorie Shostak, and Melvin Konner.
1988 *The Paleolithic Prescription*. New York: Harper and Row.

Eaton, S. Boyd and Melvin Konner
1985 Paleolithic Nutrition: A Consideration of Its Nature and Current Implications. *New England Journal of Medicine*, 312:283–289.

Eaton, S. Boyd, Malcolm C. Pike, Roger V. Short, et al.
1994 Women's Reproductive Cancers in Evolutionary Context. *The Quarterly Review of Biology*, 69:353–367.

Ehret, G.
1987 "Left Hemisphere Advantage in the Mouse Brain for Recognizing Ultrasonic Communication Calls." *Nature*, 325: 249–251.

Ehrlich, Paul R. and Anne H. Ehrlich
1990 *The Population Explosion*. New York: Simon and Schuster.

Eiseley, Loren
1961 *Darwin's Century*. New York: Anchor Books.

Eisenberg, J. F., N. A. Muckenhirn, and R. Rudran
1972 "The Relation Between Ecology and Social Structure in Primates." *Science*, 176:863–874.

Eldredge, Niles and Joel Cracraft
1980 *Phylogenetic Patterns and the Evolutionary Process*. New York: Columbia University Press.

Enard, W., et al.,
2002 "Molecular Evolution of FOXP2, a Gene Involved in Speech and Language." *Nature*, 418:869–872.

Erickson, Clark
1998 "Applied Archaeology and Rural Development: Archaeology's Potential Contribution to the Future." *In:* M. Whiteford and S. Whiteford (eds.), *Crossing Currents: Continuity and Change in Latin America*. Upper Saddle, NJ: Prentice-Hall, pp. 34–45.

Etler, Denis
1992 Personal communication.

Etler, Denis A. and Li-Tianyuan
1994 "New Archaic Human Fossil Discoveries in China and Their Bearing on Hominid Species Definition During the Middle Pleistocene." *In:* R. Corruccini and R. Ciochon (eds.), q.v., pp. 639–675.

European Union GIS/Remote Sensing Expert Group
1997 Fires in Indonesia, September 1997, a Report to the European Union. Brussels, European Union.

Ewald, Paul
1999 "Evolutionary Control of HIV and Other Sexually Transmitted Viruses," *In: Evolutionary Medicine*, W. R. Trevathan, E. O. Smith, and J. J. McKenna, (eds.), New York: Oxford University Press.

Falgeres, Christophe, Jean-Jacques Bahain, Yugi Yokoyama, et al.
1999 "Earliest Humans in Europe: The Age of TD6 Gran Dolina, Atapuerca, Spain. *Journal of Human Evolution*, 37:345–352.

Falk, Dean
1980 "A Reanalysis of the South African Australopithecine Natural Endocasts." *American Journal of Physical Anthropology*, 53:525–539.

1983 "The Taung Endocast: A Reply to Holloway." *American Journal of Physical Anthropology*, 60:479–489.

1987 "Brain Lateralization in Primates and Its Evolution in Hominids." *Yearbook of Physical Anthropology*, 30:107–125.

1989 "Comments." *Current Anthropology*, 30:141.

Fedigan, Linda M.
1982 *Primate Paradigms*. Montreal: Eden Press.

1983 "Dominance and Reproductive Success in Primates." *Yearbook of Physical Anthropology*, 26:91–129.

1986 "The Changing Role of Women in Models of Human Evolution." *Annual Review of Anthropology*, 15:25–66.

Fisher, R. A.
1930 *The Genetical Theory of Natural Selection*. Oxford: Clarendon.

Fleagle, John
1983 "Locomotor Adaptations of Oligocene and Miocene Hominoids and their Phyletic Implications." *In:* R. L. Ciochon and R. S. Corruccini (eds.), q.v., pp. 301–324.

1988 *Primate Adaptation and Evolution*. New York: Academic Press. 2nd ed., 1999.

Fleagle, J. G. and R. F. Kay

1983 "New Interpretations of the Phyletic Position of Oligocene Hominoids." *In:* R. L. Ciochon and R. S. Corruccini (eds.), q.v., pp. 181–210.

Fleischer, R. F. and H. R. Hart, Jr.

1972 "Fission Track Dating Techniques and Problems." *In: Calibration of Hominid Evolution,* W. W. Bishop and J. A. Miller (eds.). Edinburgh: Scottish Academic Press, pp. 135–170.

Foley, R. A.

1991 "How Many Species of Hominid Should There Be?" *Journal of Human Evolution,* 30:413–427.

_____

2002 "Adaptive Radiations and Dispersals in Hominin Evolutionary Ecology." *Evolutionary Anthropology,* 11(Supplement 1):32–37.

Foley, R. A. and M. M. Lahr

1992 "Beyond 'Out of Africa.'" *Journal of Human Evolution,* 22:523–529.

_____

1997 "Mode 3 Technologies and the Evolution of Modern Humans." *Cambridge Archaeological Journal,* 7:3–36.

Fossey, Dian

1983 *Gorillas in the Mist.* Boston: Houghton Mifflin.

Fouts, Roger S., D. H. Fouts, and T. T. van Cantfort

1989 "The Infant Loulis Learns Signs from Cross-Fostered Chimpanzees." *In:* R. A. Gardner et al., q.v., pp. 280–292.

Francoeuer, Robert T.

1965 *Perspectives in Evolution.* Baltimore: Helicon.

Frayer, David

1980 "Sexual Dimorphism and Cultural Evolution in the Late Pleistocene and Holocene of Europe." *Journal of Human Evolution,* 9:399–415.

_____

1992 "Evolution at the European Edge: Neanderthal and Upper Paleolithic Relationships." *Préhistoire Européenne,* 2:9–69.

_____

n.d. "Language Capacity in European Neanderthals."

Frazer, K. L., X. Chen, A. Hinds, et al.

2003 "Genomic DNA Insertions and Deletions Occur Frequently Between Humans and Nonhuman Primates." *Genome Research,* 3:341–346.

Friedman, Milton J. and William Trager

1981 "The Biochemistry of Resistance to Malaria." *Scientific American,* 244:154–164.

Frisancho, A. Roberto

1978 "Nutritional Influences on Human Growth and Maturation." *Yearbook of Physical Anthropology,* 21:174–191.

_____

1993 *Human Adaptation and Accommodation.* Ann Arbor: University of Michigan Press.

Frisch, Rose E.

1988 Fatness and Fertility. *Scientific American,* 258:88–95.

Froelich, J. W.

1970 "Migration and Plasticity Physique in the Japanese-Americans of Hawaii." *American Journal of Physical Anthropology,* 32:429.

Gabrunia, Leo, Abesalom Vekua, David Lordkipanidze, et al.

2000 "Earliest Pleistocene Hominid Cranial Remains from Dmanisi, Republic of Georgia: Taxonomy, Geological Setting, and Age." *Science,* 288:1019–1025.

Galdikas, Biruté M.

1979 "Orangutan Adaptation at Tanjung Puting Reserve: Mating and Ecology." *In: The Great Apes,* D. A. Hamburg and E. R. McCown (eds.), Menlo Park, Ca.: Benjamin/Cummings Publishing Co., pp. 195–233.

Galli, C., I. Lagutina, G. Crotti, et al.

2003 "A Cloned Horse Is Born to Its Dam Twin." *Nature,* 424:635.

Gambier, Dominique

1989 "Fossil Hominids from the Early Upper Palaeolithic (Aurignacian) of France." *In:* Mellars and Stringer (eds.), q.v., pp. 194–211.

Gamble, C.

1991 "The Social Context for European Palaeolithic Art." *Proceedings of the Prehistoric Society,* 57:3–15.

Gao, Feng, Elizabeth Bailes, David L. Robertson, et al.

1999 "Origin of HIV-1 in the Chimpanzee *Pan troglodytes troglodytes.*" *Nature,* 397:436–441.

Gardner, R. Allen, B. T. Gardner, and T. T. van Cantfort (eds.)

1989 *Teaching Sign Language to Chimpanzees.* Albany: State University of New York Press.

Garn, Stanley M.

1965, 1969 *Human Races.* Springfield, Ill.: Charles C. Thomas.

Garner, K. J. and O. A. Ryder

1996 "Mitochondrial DNA diversity in gorillas." *Mol. Phylogenet. Evol.,* 6:39–48.

Gates, R. R.

1948 *Human Ancestry.* Cambridge: Harvard University Press.

Gavan, James

1977 *Paleoanthropology and Primate Evolution.* Dubuque, Ia.: Wm. C. Brown Co.

Gao, Feng, Elizabeth Bailes, David L. Robertson, et al.

1999 "Origin of HIV-1 in the Chimpanzee *Pan troglodytes troglodytes.*" *Nature,* 397:436–441

Gebo, Daniel L., Marian Dagosto, K. Christopher Beard, and Tao Qi

2000 "The Smallest Primates." *Journal of Human Evolution,* 38:585–594.

Gee, Henry

1996 "Box of Bones 'Clinches' Identity of Piltdown Paleontology Hoaxer." *Nature,* 381:261–262.

George, I., H. Cousillas, H. Richard, et al.

2002 "Song Perception in the European Starling: Hemispheric Specialization and Individual Variations." *C.R. Biol.,* 325:197–204.

Ghiglieri, Michael P.

1984 *The Chimpanzees of Kibale Forest.* New York: Columbia University Press.

Ghiselin, Michael T.

1969 *The Triumph of the Darwinian Method.* Chicago: University of Chicago Press.

Gibbons, Anne

1992 "Mitochondrial Eve, Wounded but Not Dead Yet." *Science,* 257:873–875.

_____

1998 "Ancient Tools Suggest *Homo erectus* was a Seafarer." Research News, *Science,* 279:1635–1637.

Giles, J. and J. Knight
2003 "Dolly's Death Leaves Researchers Woolly on Clone Ageing Issue." *Nature,* 421:776.

Gillespie, B. and R. G. Roberts
2000 "On the Reliability of Age Estimates for Human Remains from Lake Mungo." *Journal of Human Evolution,* 38:727–732.

Gingerich, Phillip D.
1985 "Species in the Fossil Record: Concepts, Trends, and Transitions." *Paleobiology,* 11:27–41.

Glantz, M. M. and T. B. Ritzman
2004 "A Re-Analysis of the Neandertal Status of the Teshik-Tash Child." *American Journal of Physical Anthropology, Supplement* 38:100–101 (Abstract).

Goldizen, Anne Wilson
1987 "Tamarins and Marmosets: Communal Care of Offspring." *In:* Smuts et al. (eds.), q.v., pp. 34–43.

Goldstein, M., P. Tsarong, and C. M. Beall
1983 "High Altitude Hypoxia, Culture, and Human Fecundity/Fertility: A Comparative Study." *American Anthropologist,* 85:28–49.

Goodall, A. G.
1977 "Feeding and Ranging Behaviour of a Mountain Gorilla Group, *Gorilla gorilla beringei* in the Tshibinda-Kahuze Region (Zaire)." *In: Primate Ecology.* T. H. Clutton-Brock (ed.). London: Academic Press, pp. 450–479.

Goodall, Jane
1968 "The Behavior of Free Living Chimpanzees in the Gombe Stream Reserve." *Animal Behavior Monographs,* 1:(3).

———
1986 *The Chimpanzees of Gombe.* Cambridge, Mass.: Harvard University Press.

———
1990 *Through a Window.* Boston: Houghton Mifflin.

Goodman, M., M. L. Baba, and L. L. Darga
1983 "The Bearing of Molecular Data on the Cladogenesis and Times of Divergence of Hominoid Lineages." *In:* R. L. Ciochon and R. S. Corruccini (eds.), q.v., pp. 67–86.

Goodman, M., C. A. Porter, J. Czelusniak, et al.
1998 "Toward a Phylogenetic Classification of Primates Based on DNA Evidence Complemented by Fossil Evidence." *Molecular Phylogenetics and Evolution,* 9:585–598.

Gossett, Thomas F.
1963 *Race, the History of an Idea in America.* Dallas: Southern Methodist University Press.

Gould, Stephen Jay
1977 *Ontogeny and Phylogeny.* Cambridge, Mass.: Harvard University Press.

———
1981 *The Mismeasures of Man.* New York: W. W. Norton.

———
1985 "Darwin at Sea—and the Virtues of Port." *In:* Stephen Jay Gould, *The Flamingo's Smile. Reflections in Natural History.* New York: W. W. Norton, pp. 347–359.

———
1987 *Time's Arrow Time's Cycle.* Cambridge: Harvard University Press.

Gould, S. J. and N. Eldedge
1977 "Punctuated Equilibria: The Tempo and Mode of Evolution Reconsidered." *Paleobiology,* 3:115–151.

Gould, S. J. and R. Lewontin
1979 "The Spandrels of San Marco and the Panglossian Paradigm: A Critique of the Adaptionist Programme." *Proceedings of the Royal Society of London,* 205:581–598.

Gowlett, John
1984 *Ascent to Civilization.* New York: Alfred A. Knopf.

Grant, B. S., and L. L. Wiseman
2002 "Recent History of Melanism in American Peppered Moths." *The Journal of Heredity,* 93(2):86–90.

Grant, P. R.
1986 *Ecology and Evolution of Darwin's Finches.* Princeton: Princeton University Press.

Grant, Peter R. and B. Rosemary Grant
2002 "Unpredictable Evolution in a 30-year Study of Darwin's Finches. *Science,* 296:707–711.

Greenberg, Joel
1977 "Who Loves You?" *Science News,* 112 (August 27):139–141.

Greene, John C.
1981 *Science, Ideology, and World View.* Berkeley: University of California Press.

Greenfield, L. O.
1979 "On the Adaptive Pattern of *Ramapithecus.*" *American Journal of Physical Anthropology,* 50:527–548.

Greenleaf, J. E.
1992 "Problem: Thirst, Drinking Behavior, and Involuntary Dehydration." *Med. Sci. Sports Exercise.* 24:645–656.

Greenwood, B. and T. Mutabingwa
2002 "Malaria in 2000." *Nature,* 415:670–672.

Grine, F. E.
1993 "Australopithecine Taxonomy and Phylogeny: Historical Background and Recent Interpretation." *In: The Human Evolution Source Book,* R. L. Ciochon and J. G. Fleagle (eds.), Englewood Cliffs, N.J.: Prentice Hall, pp. 198–210.

Grine, Frederick E. (ed.)
1988a *Evolutionary History of the "Robust" Australopithecines.* New York: Aldine de Gruyter.

1988b "New Craniodental Fossils of *Paranthropus* from the Swartkrans Formation and Their Significance in "Robust" Australopithecine Evolution." *In:* F. E. Grine (ed.), q.v., pp. 223–243.

Groves, Colin P.
2001 *Primate Taxonomy.* Washington DC: Smithsonian Institution Press.

———
2001b "Why Taxonomic Stability Is a Bad Idea, or Why Are There So Few Species of Primates (or Are There?)." *Evolutionary Anthropology,* 10:192–198.

Gursky, Sharon
2002 "The Behavioral Ecology of the Spectral Tarsier, *Tarsius Spectrum.*" *Evolutionary Anthropology,* 11(6):226–234.

Haile-Selassie, Yohannes
2001 "Late Miocene Hominids from the Middle Awash, Ethiopia." *Nature,* 412:178–181.

Haile-Selassie, Yohannes Gen Suwa, and Tim D. White
2004 "Late Miocene Teeth from Middle Awash, Ethiopia, and Early Hominid Dental Evolution." *Science,* 303:1503–1505.

Haldane, J.B.S.
1932 *The Causes of Evolution.* London: Longmans, Green (reprinted as paperback, Cornell University Press, 1966).

Hamilton, W. D.
1964 "The Genetical Theory of Social Behavior. I and II." *Journal of Theoretical Biology,* 7:1–52.

Handoko, Helina Y., J. Koji Lum, Gustiani, et al.
2001 "Length Variations in the COII-tRNA^{Lys} Intergenic Region of Mitochondrial DNA in Indonesian Populations." *Human Biology,* 73:205–223.

Hanna, J. M.
1999 "Climate, Altitude, and Blood Pressure." *Human Biology,* 71(4):553–582.

Hanna, Joel M. and Daniel A. Brown
1979 "Human Heat Tolerance: Biological and Cultural Adaptations." *Yearbook of Physical Anthropology,* 1979, 22:163–186.

Harlow, Harry F.
1959 "Love in Infant Monkeys." *Scientific American,* 200:68–74.

Harlow, Harry F. and Margaret K. Harlow
1961 "A Study of Animal Affection." *Natural History,* 70:48–55.

Harpending, Henry C., Mark A. Batzer, Michael Gurven, et al.
1998 "Genetic Traces of Ancient Demography." *Proceedings of the National Academy of Sciences,* 95:1961–1967.

Harris, E. E. and J. Hay
1999 "X Chromosome Evidence for Ancient Human Histories." *Proceedings of the National Academy of Sciences,* 96:3320–3324.

Harrold, Francis R.
1989 "Mousterian, Chatelperronian and Early Aurignacian in Western Europe: Continuity or Discontinuity." *In: The Human Revolution,* P. Mellars and C. Stringer (eds.), Princeton, N.J.: Princeton University Press, pp. 212–231.

Hartl, Daniel
1983 *Human Genetics.* New York: Harper & Row.

Harvey, Paul H., R. D. Martin, and T. H. Clutton-Brock
1987 "Life Histories in Comparative Perspective." *In:* Smuts et al. (eds.), q.v., pp. 181–196.

Hass, J. D., E. A. Frongillo, Jr., C. D. Stepick, J. L. Beard, and G. Hurtado
1980 Altitude, Ethnic and Sex Difference in Birth Weight and Length in Bolivia. *Human Biology,* 52:459–477.

Hausfater, Glenn
1984 "Infanticide in Langurs: Strategies, Counter Strategies, and Parameter Values." *In:* G. Hausfater and S. B. Hrdy, (eds.), q.v., pp. 257–281.

Hausfater, Glenn and Sarah Blaffer Hrdy (eds.)
1984 *Infanticide. Comparative and Evolutionary Perspectives.* Hawthorne, New York: Aldine de Gruyter.

Hawkes, K., J. F. O'Connell, and N. G. Blurton Jones
1997 Hadza Women's Time Allocation, Offspring Provisioning, and the Evolution of Long Postmenopausal Life Spans. *Current Anthropology,* 38:551–577.

Hayden, Brian
1993 "The Cultural Capacities of Neandertals: A Review and Reevaluation." *Journal of Human Evolution,* 24:113–146.

Henahan, Sean
1995 Men haven't changed in 270,000 years. Access Excellence, Genentech Inc., Worldwide Web Source.

Henzi, P. and L. Barrett
2003 "Evolutionary Ecology, Sexual Conflict, and Behavioral Differentiation Among Baboon Populations." *Evolutionary Anthropology,* 12(5):217–230.

Heyer, E.
1999 "One Founder/One Gene Hypothesis in a New Expanding Population: Saguenay (Quebec, Canada)." *Human Biology,* 71:99–109.

Hiernaux, Jean
1968 *La Diversité Humaine en Afrique subsahariénne.* Bruxelles: L'Institut de Sociologie, Université Libre de Bruxelles.

Hill, A., S. Ward, A. Deino, G. Curtis, and R. Drake
1992 "Earliest *Homo.*" *Nature,* 355:719–722.

Hill, Andrew and Steven Ward
1988 "Origin of the Hominidae: The Record of African Large Hominoid Evolution Between 14 my and 4 my." *Yearbook of Physical Anthropology,* 1988, 31:49–83.

Hillier, LaDeana, Robert S. Fulton, Lucinda A. Fulton, et al.
2003 "The DNA Sequence of Human Chromosome 7." *Nature,* 424:157–164.

Hinde, Robert A.
1987 "Can Nonhuman Primates Help Us Understand Human Behavior?" *In:* B. Smuts et al. (eds.), q.v., pp. 413–420.

Hirsch, V. M., R. A. Olmsted, M. Murphey-Corb, R. H. Purcell, and P. R. Johnson
1989 "An African Primate Lentivirus (SIVsm) Closely Related to HIV-2." *Nature,* 339: 389–392.

Hoffstetter, R.
1972 "Relationships, Origins, and History of the Ceboid Monkeys and the Caviomorph Rodents: A Modern Reinterpretation." *In: Evolutionary Biology* (Vol. 6), T. Dobzhansky, T. M. K. Hecht, and W. C. Steere (eds.), New York: Appleton-Century-Crofts, pp. 323–347.

Holloway, Ralph L.
1969 "Culture: A Human Domain." *Current Anthropology,* 10:395–407.

_____
1981 "Revisiting the South African Taung Australo-pithecine Endocast: The Position of the Lunate Sulcus as Determined by the Stereoplotting Technique." *American Journal of Physical Anthropology,* 56:43–58.

_____
1983 "Cerebral Brain Endocast Pattern of *Australopithecus afarensis* Hominid." *Nature,* 303:420–422.

_____
1985 "The Poor Brain of *Homo sapiens neanderthalensis.*" *In: Ancestors, The Hard Evidence,* E. Delson (ed.). New York: Alan R. Liss, pp. 319–324.

Horr, D. A.
1975 "The Bornean Orangutan: Population Structure and Dynamics in Relationship to Ecology and Reproductive Strategy." *In: Primate Behavior: Developments in Field*

and Laboratory Research, vol. 4, L. A. Rosenblum (ed.), New York: Academic Press.

Howell, F. Clark
1978   "Hominidae." *In: Evolution of African Mammals,* V. J. Maglio and H.B.S. Cooke (eds.), Cambridge: Harvard University Press, pp. 154–248.

————   1988   "Foreword." *In:* Grine (ed.), q.v., pp. xi–xv.

Howells, W. W.
1973   *Evolution of the Genus* Homo. Reading, Mass.: Addison-Wesley.

————   1980   "*Homo erectus*—Who, When, Where: A Survey. *Yearbook of Physical Anthropology,* 23:1–23.

Hrdy, Sarah Blaffer
1977   *The Langurs of Abu.* Cambridge, Mass.: Harvard University Press.

————   1984a   "Assumptions and Evidence Regarding the Sexual Selection Hypothesis: A Reply to Boggess." *In:* G. Hausfater and S. B. Hrdy (eds.), q.v., pp. 315–319.

————   1984b   "Female Reproductive Strategies." *In:* M. Small (ed.), q.v., pp. 103–109.

————   1999   *Mother Nature: A History of Mothers, Infants, and Natural Selection.* New York: Pantheon Books.

Hrdy, Sarah Blaffer, Charles Janson, and Carel van Schaik
1995   Infanticide: Let's not throw out the baby with the bath water." *Evolutionary Anthropology,* 3(5):151–154.

Hu, Dale J., Timothy J. Dondero, Mark A. Rayfield, et al.
1996   "The Emerging Genetic Diversity of HIV. The Importance of Global Surveillance, for Diagnostics, Research, and Prevention." *Journal of the American Medical Association,* 275(3):210–216.

Hublin, Jean-Jacques, F. Spoor, M. Braun, F. Zonneveld, and S. Condemi
1996   A Late Neanderthal Associated with Upper Palaeolithic Artifacts. *Nature,* 38:224–226.

Hull, David L.
1973   *Darwin and His Critics.* Chicago: University of Chicago Press.

Ingman, Max, Henrik Kaessmann, Svante Paabo, and Ulf Gyllensten
2000   "Mitochondrial Genome Variation and the Origin of Modern Humans." *Nature,* 408:708–713.

The Institute of Vertebrate Paleontology and Paleoanthropology, Chinese Academy of Sciences
1980   *Atlas of Primitive Man in China.* Beijing: Science Press (Distributed by Van Nostrand, New York).

The International SNP Map Working Group
2001   "A Map of Human Genome Sequence Variation Containing 1.42 Million Single Nucleotide Polymorphisms." *Nature,* 409:928–933.

Isaac, G. L.
1971   "The Diet of Early Man." *World Archaeology,* 2:278–299.

————   1975   "Stratigraphy and Cultural Patterns in East Africa During the Middle Ranges of Pleistocene Time." *In: After the Australopithecines,* K. W. Butzer and G. L.

Isaac (eds.), Chicago: Aldine Publishing Co., pp. 495–542.

————   1976   "Early Hominids in Action: A Commentary on the Contribution of Archeology to Understanding the Fossil Record in East Africa." *Yearbook of Physical Anthropology,* 1975, 19:19–35.

Isbell, L. A.
1994   "Predation on Primates: Ecological Patterns and Evolutionary Consequences." *Evolutionary Anthropology,* 3(2):61–71.

Isbell, L. A. and T. P. Young.
1993   "Social and Ecological Influences on Activity Budgets of Vervet Monkeys and Their Implications for Group Living." *Behav. Ecol. Sociobiol.,* 32:377–385.

Izawa, K. and A. Mizuno
1977   "Palm-Fruit Cracking Behaviour of Wild Black-Capped Capuchin (*Cebus apella*)." *Primates,* 18:773–793.

Jablonksi, Nina
1992   "Sun, Skin Colour and Spina Bifida: An Exploration of the Relationship between Ultraviolet Light and Neural Tube Defects." *Proceedings of the Australasian Society of Human Biology,* 5:455–462.

Jablonski, Nina G. and George Chaplin
2000   "The Evolution of Skin Coloration." *Journal of Human Evolution,* 39:57–106.

Janson, C. H.
1990   "Ecological Consequences of Individual Spatial Choice in Foraging Groups of Brown Capuchin Monkeys *Cebus apella.*" *Animal Behavior,* 40:922–934.

————   2000   "Primate Socio-ecology: The End of a Golden Age." *Evolutionary Anthropology,* 9(2):73–86.

Jensen, Arthur
1969   *Environment, Heredity, and Intelligence.* Cambridge, Mass.: Harvard Educational Review.

Jerison, H. J.
1973   *Evolution of the Brain and Behavior.* New York: Academic Press.

Jia, L. and Huang Weiwen
1990   *The Story of Peking Man.* New York: Oxford University Press.

Jia, Lan-po
1975   *The Cave Home of Peking Man.* Peking: Foreign Language Press.

Jobing, Mark A. and Chris Tyler-Smith
2003   "The Human Y Chromosome: An Evolutionary Marker Comes of Age." *Nature Review Genetics,* 4:598–612.

Johanson, D. C. and T. D. White
1979   "A Systematic Assessment of Early African Hominids." *Science,* 203:321–330.

Johanson, Donald and Maitland Edey
1981   *Lucy: The Beginnings of Humankind.* New York: Simon & Schuster.

Johanson, Donald, F. T. Masao, et al.
1987   "New Partial Skeleton of *Homo habilis* from Olduvai Gorge, Tanzania." *Nature,* 327:205–209.

Johanson, Donald C. and Maurice Taieb
1976   "Plio-Pleistocene Hominid Discoveries in Hadar, Ethiopia." *Nature,* 260:293–297.

1980 "New Discoveries of Pliocene Hominids and Artifacts in Hadar." International Afar Research Expedition to Ethiopia (Fourth and Fifth Field Seasons, 1975–77). *Journal of Human Evolution,* 9:582.

Jolly, Alison
1984 "The Puzzle of Female Feeding Priority." *In:* M. F. Small (ed.), q.v., pp. 197–215.

1985 *The Evolution of Primate Behavior* (2nd Ed.), New York: Macmillan.

Jolly, Clifford J.
1993 "Species, Subspecies, and Baboon Systematics." *In:* W. H. Kimbel and L. B. Martin (eds.), *Species, Species Concepts, and Primate Evolution.* New York: Plenum Press, pp. 67–107.

Jones, Rhys
1990 East of Wallace's Line: Issues and Problems in the Colonization of the Australian Continent." *In: The Human Revolution,* P. Mellars and C. Stringer (eds.), Princeton, N.J.: Princeton University Press, pp. 743–782.

Jungers, W. L.
1982 "Lucy's Limbs: Skeletal Allometry and Locomotion in *Australopithecus afarensis.*" *Nature,* 297:676–678.

1988 "New Estimates of Body Size in Australopithecines." *In:* F. E. Grine (ed.), q.v., pp. 115–125.

Kano, T.
1980 The Social Behavior of Wild Pygmy Chimpanzees (*Pan Paniscus*) of Wamba: A Preliminary Report. *Journal of Human Evolution,* 9:243–260.

1992 *The Last Ape. Pygmy Chimpanzee Behavior and Ecology.* Stanford: Stanford University Press.

Kappleman, John
1996 The Evolution of Body Mass and Relative Brain Size in Fossil Hominids. *Journal of Human Evolution,* 30:243–276.

Katz, D. and J. M. Suchey
1986 "Age Determination of the Male *Os Pubis.*" *American Journal of Physical Anthropology,* 69:427–435.

Katz, S. H., M. L. Hediger, and L. A. Valleroy
1974 Traditional Maize Processing Techniques in the New World. *Science,* 184:765–773.

Kay, R., M. Cartmill, and M. Balow
1998 "The Hypoglossal Canal and the Origins of Human Vocal Behavior (abstract)." *American Journal of Physical Anthropology, Supplement,* 26:137.

Kay, R. F., J. G. Fleagle, and E. L. Simons
1981 "A Revision of the Oligocene Apes of the Fayum Province, Egypt." *American Journal of Physical Anthropology,* 55:293–322.

Kay, Richard and Frederick E. Grine
1988 "Tooth Morphology, Wear and Diet in *Australopithecus* and *Paranthropus, In:* F. Grine (ed.), q.v., pp. 427–447.

Kelly, Mark and David Pilbeam
1986 "The Dryopithecines: Taxonomy, Comparative Anatomy, and Phylogeny of Miocene Large Hominoids." *In: Comparative Primate Biology.* Vol. 1, *Systematics, Evolution, and Anatomy,* D. R. Swindler and J. Erwin (eds.), New York: Alan R. Liss, pp. 361–411.

Kelley, R. I., D. Robinson, E. G. Puffenberger, et. al.
2002 "Amish Lethal Microcephaly: A New Metabolic Disorder with Severe Congenital Microcephaly and 2-Ketoglutaric Aciduria." *American Journal of Medical Genetics,* 112(4):318–326.

Kennedy, G. E.
1983 "A Morphometric and Taxonomic Assessment of a Hominid Femur from the Lower Member, Koobi Fora, Lake Turkana." *American Journal of Physical Anthropology,* 61:429–436.

Kennedy, K. A. R.
1991 "Is the Narmada Hominid an Indian *Homo erectus?*" *American Journal of Physical Anthropology,* 86:475–496.

Kennedy, Kenneth A. R. and S. U. Deraniyagala
1989 "Fossil Remains of 28,000-Year-Old Hominids from Sri Lanka." *Current Anthropology,* 30:397–399.

Kettlewell, H. B. D.
1956 "Further Selection Experiments on Industrial Melanism in the Lepidoptera. *Heredity,* 10:287–301.

Keynes, Randal
2002 *Darwin, His Daughter and Human Evolution.* New York: Riverhead Books.

Keyser, André W.
2000 "New Finds in South Africa." *National Geographic,* (May), pp. 76–83.

Kidd, K. H. Rajeevan, M. V. Osier, et al.
2003 "ALFRED—the Allele FREquency Database—an Update." *American Journal of Physical Anthropology,* Supplement 36:128 (Abstract).

Kimbel, William H.
1988 "Identification of a Partial Cranium of *Australopithecus afarensis* from the Koobi Fora Formation, Kenya." *Journal of Human Evolution,* 17:647–656.

Kimbel, William H., Donald C. Johanson, and Yoel Rak
1994 "The First Skull and Other New Discoveries of *Australopithecus afarensis* at Hadar, Ethiopia." *Nature,* 368:449–451.

Kimbel, W. H., R. C. Walter, D. C. Johanson, et al.
1996 Late Pliocene *Homo* and Oldowan Tools from the Hadar Formation (Kada Hadar Member), Ethiopia. *Journal of Human Evolution,* 31:549–561.

Kimbel, William H., Tim D. White, and Donald C. Johanson
1988 "Implications of KNM-WT-17000 for the Evolution of 'Robust' *Australopithecus.*" *In:* F. E. Grine (ed.), q.v., pp. 259–268.

King, Barbara J.
1994 *The Information Continuum.* Santa Fe: School of American Research.

King-Hele, D.
1999 *Erasmus Darwin. A Life of Unequalled Achievement.* London: Giles de la Mare Publishers Ltd.

King, Marie-Claire and Arno G. Motulaky
2002 "Mapping Human History." *Science,* 298:2342–2343.

Kiple, Kenneth F.
1993 *The Cambridge World History of Human Disease.* Cambridge: Cambridge University Press.

Kirkwood, T. B. L.
1997 "The Origins of Human Ageing." *Philosophical Transactions of the Royal Society of London B,* 352:1765–1772.

2002 "Evolution of Ageing." *Mechanisms of Ageing and Development,* 123:737–745.

Klein, R. G.
1989 *The Human Career. Human Biological and Cultural Origins.* Chicago: University of Chicago Press.

———
1992 "The Archeology of Modern Human Origins." *Evolutionary Anthropology,* 1:5–14.

Knapp, Leslie A.
2002 "Evolution and Immunology." *Evolutionary Anthropology,* 11 (Supplement 1):140–144.

Konner, Melvin and Carol Worthman
1980 Nursing Frequency, Gonadal Function, and Birth Spacing among !Kung Hunter-Gatherers. *Science,* 207:788–791.

Kramer, Andrew
1986 "Hominid-Pongid Distinctiveness in the Miocene-Pliocene Fossil Record: The Lothagam Mandible." *American Journal of Physical Anthropology,* 70:457–473.

———
1993 "Human Taxonomic Diversity in the Pleistocene: Does *Homo erectus* Represent Multiple Hominid Species?" *American Journal of Physical Anthropology,* 91:161–171.

Krings, Matthias, Cristian Capelli, Frank Tschentscher, et al.
2000 "A View of Neandertal Genetic Diversity." *Nature Genetics* 26:144–146.

Krings, Matthias, Anne Stone, Ralf W. Schmitz, et al.
1997 "Neandertal DNA Sequences and the Origin of Modern Humans." *Cell,* 90:19–30.

Kroeber, A. L.
1928 "Sub-human Cultural Beginning." *Quarterly Review of Biology,* 3:325–342.

Krogman, W. M.
1962 *The Human Skeleton in Forensic Medicine.* Springfield: C. C. Thomas.

Krummer, Hans
1971 *Primate Societies.* Chicago: Aldine-Atherton, Inc.

Kummer, H.
1968 *Social Organization of Hamadryas Baboons.* Chicago: University of Chicago Press.

Kunzig, Robert
1997 "Atapuerca. The Face of an Ancestral Child." *Discover,* 18:88–101.

Lack, David
1966 *Population Studies of Birds.* Oxford: Clarendon.

Lahr, Marta Mirazon and Robert Foley
1998 "Towards a Theory of Human Origins: Geography, Demography, and Diversity in Recent Human Evolution." *Yearbook of Physical Anthropology,* 41:137–176.

Lai, C., S. Fisher, J. Hurst, et al.
2001 "A Forkhead-domain Gene is Mutated in a Severe Speech and Language Disorder." *Nature,* 413:519–523.

Lalani, A. S., J. Masters, W. Zeng, et al.
1999 "Use of Chemokine Receptors by Poxviruses." *Science,* 286:1968–71.

Lamarck, Jean-Baptiste
1809, 1984 *Zoological Philosophy.* Chicago: University of Chicago Press.

Lamberts, S. W. J., A. W. van den Beld, and A-J van der Lely
1997 "The Endocrinology of Aging." *Science,* 278:419–424.

Lancaster, Jane B.
1975 *Primate Behavior and the Emergence of Human Culture.* New York: Holt, Rinehart & Winston.

Lancaster, Jane B. and C. S. Lancaster
1983 "Parental Investment: The Hominid Adaptation." *In:* Ortner, D. J. (ed.), *How Humans Adapt: A Biocultural Odyssey.* Washington, DC: Smithsonian Institution Press.

Landau, M.
1984 "Human Evolution as Narrative." *American Scientist,* 72:262–268.

Larick, Roy and Russell L. Ciochon
1996 "The African Emergence and Early Asian Dispersals of the Genus, *Homo.*" *American Scientist,* 84:538–551.

Larick, Roy, Russell L. Ciochon, Yahdi Zaim, et al.
2001 "Early Pleistocene ^{40}Ar/^{39}Ar Ages for Bapang Formation Hominins, Central Java, Indonesia." *Proceedings of the National Academy of Sciences,* 98:4866–4871.

Lasker, Gabriel W.
1969 "Human Biological Adaptability: The Ecological Approach in Physical Anthropology." *Science,* 166:1480–1486.

Latimer, Bruce
1984 "The Pedal Skeleton of *Australopithecus afarensis.*" *American Journal of Physical Anthropology,* 63:182.

Leakey, L. S. B., J. F. Everden, and G. H. Curtis
1961 "Age of Bed I, Olduvai Gorge, Tanganyika." *Nature,* 191:478–479.

Leakey, L. S. B., P. V. Tobias, and J. R. Napier
1964 "A New Species of the Genus *Homo* from Olduvai Gorge." *Nature,* 202:7–10.

Leakey, M. D.
1971 "Remains of *Homo erectus* and Associated Artifacts in Bed IV at Olduvai Gorge, Tanzania." *Nature,* 232:380–383.

Leakey, M. D. and R. L. Hay
1979 "Pliocene Footprints in Laetoli Beds at Laetoli, Northern Tanzania." *Nature,* 278:317–323.

Leakey, Meave G. et al.
1995 "New Four-Million-Year-Old Hominid Species from Kanapoi: and Allia Bay, Kenya." *Nature,* 376:565–571.

Leakey, R. E. F. and M. D. Leakey
1986 "A New Miocene Hominoid from Kenya." *Nature,* 324:143–146.

Lederberg, J.
1996 "Infection Emergent" (editorial). *Journal of the American Medical Association,* 275(3):243–245.

Lerner, I. M. and W. J. Libby
1976 *Heredity, Evolution, and Society.* San Francisco: W. H. Freeman and Company.

Leroi-Gourhan, André
1986 "The Hands of Gargas." *October* 37:18–34.

Lewontin, R. C.
1972 "The Apportionment of Human Diversity." *In:* *Evolutionary Biology* (Vol. 6), T. Dobzhansky et al. (eds.), New York: Plenum, pp. 381–398.

Li, Wen-Hsiung and Masako Tanimura
1987 "The Molecular Clock Runs More Slowly in Man than in Apes and Monkeys." *Nature,* 326:93–96.

Lieberman, Daniel, David R. Pilbeam, and Bernard A. Wood
1988 "A Probalistic Approach to the Problem of Sexual Dimorphism in *Homo habilis*: A Comparison of KNM-ER-1470 and KNM-ER-1813." *Journal of Human Evolution,* 17:503–511.

Linnaeus, C.
1758 *Systema Naturae.*

Lisowski, F. P.
1984 "Introduction." *In: The Evolution of the East African Environment.* Centre of Asian Studies Occasional Papers and Monographs, No. 59, R. O. Whyte (ed.), Hong Kong: University of Hong Kong, pp. 777–786.

Livingstone, Frank B.
1964 "On the Nonexistence of Human Races." *In: Concept of Race,* A. Montagu (ed.), New York: The Free Press, pp. 46–60.

_____
1969 "Polygenic Models for the Evolution of Human Skin Color Differences." *Human Biology,* 41:480–493.

_____
1980 "Natural Selection and the Origin and Maintenance of Standard Genetic Marker Systems." *Yearbook of Physical Anthropology,* 1980, 23:25–42.

Lovejoy, C. O.
1988 "Evolution of Human Walking." *Scientific American,* 259(Nov.):118–125.

Lovejoy, C. O., G. Kingsbury, G. Heiple, and A. H. Burstein
1973 "The Gait of *Australopithecus.*" *American Journal of Physical Anthropology,* 38:757–780.

Lovejoy, Thomas E.
1982 "The Tropical Forest—Greatest Expression of Life on Earth." *In: Primates and the Tropical Forest,* Proceedings, California Institute of Technology and World Wildlife Fund—U.S., pp. 45–48.

Lundelius, Ernest L., Jr., and Russell Graham
1999 "The Weather Changed." *Discovering Archaeology,* 1(5):48–53.

Mace, R.
2000 "Evolutionary Ecology of Human Life History: A Review." *Animal Behaviour* 59:1–10.

MacKinnon, J. and K. MacKinnon
1980 "The Behavior of Wild Spectral Tarsiers." *International Journal of Primatology,* 1:361–379.

MacLarnon, Ann
1993 "The Vertebral Canal of KNM-WT 1500 and the Evolution of the Spinal Cord and Other Canal Contents." *In:* A. Walker and R. E. Leakey (eds.), q.v., pp. 359–390.

Mai, L. L.
1983 "A Model of Chromosome Evolution and Its Bearing on Cladogenesis in the Hominoidea." *In:* R. Ciochon and R. Corruccini (eds.), q.v., pp. 87–114.

Makalowski, W.
2000 "Genomic Scrap Yard: How Genomes Utilize All That Junk." *Gene,* 259(1–2):61–67.

Manson, J. H. and R. Wrangham
1991 "Intergroup Aggression in Chimpanzees and Humans." *Current Anthropology,* 32:369–390.

Manzi, G. F. Mallegni, and A. Ascenzi
2001 "A Cranium for the Earliest Europeans: Phylogenetic Position of the Hominid from Ceprano, Italy. *Proceedings of the National Academy of Sciences,* 98:1011–1016.

Marshack, A.
1972 *The Roots of Civilization.* New York: McGraw-Hill Publishing Co.

_____
1989 "Evolution of the Human Capacity: The Symbolic Evidence." *Yearbook of Physical Anthropology,* 1989, 32:1–34.

Marth, Gabor, Greg Schuler, Raymond Yeh, et al.
2003 "Sequence Variations in the Public Human Genome Data Reflect a Bottlenecked Population History." *Proceedings of the National Academy of Sciences,* 100:376–381.

Masserman, J., S. Wechkin, and W. Terris
1964 "'Altruistic' Behavior in Rhesus Monkeys." *American Journal of Physical Anthropology,* 121:584–585.

Mayer, Peter J.
1982 Evolutionary Advantages of Menopause. *Human Ecology,* 10:477–494.

Mayr, Ernst
1962 "Taxonomic Categories in Fossil Hominids." *In: Ideas on Human Evolution,* W. W. Howells (ed.), New York: Atheneum, pp. 242–256.

_____
1970 *Population, Species, and Evolution.* Cambridge: Harvard University Press.

_____
1991 *One Long Argument.* Cambridge: Harvard University Press.

McConkey, Edwin H. and Ajit Varki
2000 "A primate genome project deserves high priority." Letters. *Science,* 289:1295.

McGraw, W. Scott and Redouan Bshary
2002 "Association of Terrestrial Monkeys (*Cercobus atys*) with Arboreal Monkeys: Experimental Evidence for the Effects of Reduced Ground Predator Pressure on Habitat Use." *International Journal of Primatology,* 23(2):311–325.

McGrew, W. C.
1992 *Chimpanzee Material Culture. Implications for Human Evolution.* Cambridge: Cambridge University Press.

_____
1998 "Culture in Nonhuman Primates?" *Annual Reviews of Anthropology,.* 27:301–328.

McGrew, W. C. and E. G. Tutin
1978 "Evidence for a Social Custom in Wild Chimpanzees?" *Man,* 13:234–251.

McHenry, Henry
1983 "The Capitate of *Australopithecus afarensis* and *A. africanus.*" *American Journal of Physical Anthropology,* 62:187–198.

_____
1988 "New Estimates of Body Weight in Early Hominids and Their Significance to Encephalization and Megadontia in 'Robust' Australopithecines." *In:* F. E. Grine (ed.), q.v., pp. 133–148.

_____
1992 "Body Size and Proportions in Early Hominids." *American Journal of Physical Anthropology,* 87:407–431.

McKenna, James J.
1982a "Primate Field Studies: The Evolution of Behavior and Its Socioecology." *In: Primate Behavior.* James L.

Fobes and James E. King (eds.). New York: Academic Press, pp. 53–83.

—— 1982b "The Evolution of Primate Societies, Reproduction, and Parenting." *In: Primate Behavior.* James L. Fobes and James E. King (eds.). New York: Academic Press, pp. 87–133.

McKern, T. W. and T. D. Stewart
1957 "Age Changes in Young American Males, Technical Report EP-45." Natick, MA: U.S. Army Quartermaster Research and Development Center.

McKusick, Victor
1998 *Mendelian Inheritance in Man.* (12th Ed.) Baltimore: Johns Hopkins Press.

McRae, M. and K. Ammann
1997 "Road kill in Cameroon." *Natural History* 106:36–47.

Mellars, P. and C. Stringer (eds.)
1989 *The Human Revolution.* Princeton, N.J.: Princeton University Press.

Mitchell, R. J., S. Howlett, N. G. White, et al.
1999 "Deletion Polymorphism in the Human COL1AZ Gene: Genetic Evidence of a Non-African Population Whose Descendants Spread to All Continents." *Human Biology,* 71:901–914.

Mittermeir, R. A.
1982 "The World's Endangered Primates: An Introduction and a Case Study—The Monkeys of Brazil's Atlantic Forests." *In: Primates and the Tropical Rain Forest,* Proceedings, California Institute of Technology, and World Wildlife Fund—U.S., pp. 11–22.

Mittermeir, R. A. and D. Cheney
1987 "Conservation of Primates in Their Habitats." *In:* B. B. Smuts et al., q.v., pp. 477–496.

Mokdad, A. H., B. A. Bowman, and E. S. Ford
2001 "The Continuing Epidemics of Obesity and Diabetes in the United States." *Journal of the American Medical Association* 286: 1195–1200.

Montagu, A.
1961 Neonatal and Infant Immaturity in Man. *Journal of the American Medical Association,* 178:56–57.

Molnar, Stephen
1983 *Human Variation. Races, Types, and Ethnic Groups* (2nd Ed.). Englewood Cliffs: Prentice Hall.

Moore, Lorna G. et al.
1994 Genetic Adaptation to High Altitude. *In: Sports and Exercise Medicine,* Stephen C. Wood and Robert C. Roach (eds.), New York: Marcel Dekker, Inc., pp. 225–262.

Moore, Lorna G. and Judith G. Regensteiner
1983 "Adaptation to High Altitude." *Annual Reviews of Anthropology,* 12:285–304.

Moore, L. G., S. Niermeyer, and S. Zamudio
1998 "Human Adaptation to High Altitude: Regional and Life-Cycle Perspectives." *American Journal of Physical Anthropology,* Suppl. 27:25–64.

Moore, L. G., S. Zamudio, J. Zhuang, et al.
1999 "Oxygen Transport in Tibetan Women During Pregnancy at 3,658 M." *American Journal of Physical Anthropology,* 114:42–53.

Morbeck, M. E.
1975 "*Dryopithecus africanus* Forelimb." *Journal of Human Evolution,* 4:39–46.

—— 1983 "Miocene Hominoid Discoveries from Rudabánya. Implications from the Postcranial Skeleton." *In:* R. L. Ciochon and R. S. Corruccini (eds.), q.v., pp. 369–404.

Morgan, Elaine
1972 *The Descent of Women.* New York: Stein and Day.

Morin, Phillip A., James J. Moore, Ranajit Chakraborty, et al.
1994 "In Selection, Social Structure, Gene Flow, and the Evolution of Chimpanzees." *Science,* 265:1145–1332.

Morris, Desmond
1967 *The Naked Ape.* New York: McGraw-Hill.

Mountain, Joanna L., Alice A. Lin, Anne M. Bowcock, and L. L. Cavalli-Sforza
1993 "Evolution of Modern Humans: Evidence from Nuclear DNA Polymorphisms." *In:* M. J. Aitken et al. (eds.), q.v., pp. 69–83.

Mourant, A. E., A. C. Kopec, and K. Sobczak
1976 *The Distribution of the Human Blood Groups.* Oxford: Oxford University Press.

Moxon, E. R. and C. Wills
1999 "DNA Microsatellites: Agents of Evolution?" *Scientific American,* 280:94-99.

Moyá-Solà, Salvador and Meike Köhler
1996 "A *Dryopithecus* Skeleton and the Origins of Great-ape Locomotion. *Nature,* 379:156–159.

Mueller, William H. et al.
1979 "A Multinational Andean Genetic and Health Program. VIII. Lung Function Changes with Migration between Altitudes." *American Journal of Physical Anthropology,* 51:183–196.

Murray, R. D.
1980 "The Evolution and Functional Significance of Incest Avoidance." *Journal of Human Evolution,* 9:173–178.

Nabhan, G. P.
1991 Desert Legumes as a Nutritional Intervention for Diabetic Indigenous Dwellers of Arid Lands. *Arid Lands Newsletter,* 31:11–13.

Napier, J. R. and P. H. Napier
1967 *A Handbook of Living Primates.* New York: Academic Press.

—— 1985 *The Natural History of the Primates.* Cambridge, Mass.: The MIT Press.

Napier, John
1967 "The Antiquity of Human Walking." *Scientific American,* 216:56–66.

Nature
1986 "Chernobyl Report." *Nature,* 323:26–30.

NCBI (National Center for Biological Information).
2003 Bookshelf: Genes and Disease. www.ncbi.nlm.nih.gov/books/bv.fcgi?rid=gnd.section.104

Neel, J. V.
1962 Diabetes Mellitus: A "Thrifty" Genotype Rendered Detrimental by "Progress"? *American Journal of Human Genetics,* 61:1099–1102.

Nesse, R. M., and G. C. Williams
1994 "Why We Get Sick." New York: Times Books.

Neu, H. C.
1992 "The Crisis in Antibiotic Resistance." *Science,* 257:1064–1073.

Newman, Marshall T.
1975 "Nutritional Adaptation in Man." *In: Physiological Anthropology,* Albert Damon (ed.), New York: Oxford University Press, pp. 210–259.

Newman, Russell W.
1970 "Why Man Is Such a Sweaty and Thirsty Naked Animal: A Speculative Review." *Human Biology,* 42:12–27.

Newman, Russell W. and Ella H. Munro
1955 "The Relation of Climate and Body Size in U.S. Males." *American Journal of Physical Anthropology,* 13:1–17.

Ni, Xijun, Yuanqing Wang, Yaoming Hu, and Chuankui Li
2004 "A Euprimate Skull from the Early Eocene of China." *Nature,* 427:65–68.

Nishida, T.
1968 "The Social Group of Wild Chimpanzees in the Mahale Mountains." *Primates,* 9:167–224.

———
1979 "The Social Structure of Chimpanzees of the Mahale Mountains." *In: The Great Apes,* D. A. Hamburg and E. R. McCown (eds.), Menlo Park: Benjamin Cummings, pp. 73–122.

———
1991 Comments. *In:* J. H. Manson and R. Wrangham, q.v., pp. 381–382.

Nishida, T., M. Hiraiwa-Hasegawa, T. Hasegawa, and Y. Takahata
1985 "Group Extinction and Female Transfer in Wild Chimpanzees in the Mahale National Park, Tanzania." *Zeitschrift Tierpsychologie,* 67:284–301.

Nishida, T., H. Takasaki, and Y. Takahata
1990 "Demography and Reproductive Profiles." *In: The Chimpanzees of the Mahale Mountains,* T. Nishida (ed.), Tokyo: University of Tokyo Press, pp. 63–97.

Nishida, T., R. W. Wrangham, J. Goodall, and S. Uehara
1983 "Local Differences in Plant-feeding Habits of Chimpanzees between the Mahale Mountains and Gombe National Park, Tanzania." *Journal of Human Evolution,* 12:467–480.

Noe, R. and R. Bshary
1997 "The Formation of Red Colobus-Diana Monkey Associations Under Predation Pressure from Chimpanzees. *Proceedings of the Royal Society of London, (B) Biological Science,* 264(1379):253–259.

Novitski, Edward
1977 *Human Genetics.* New York: Macmillan.

Nowak, Ronald M.
1999 *Walker's Primates of the World.* Baltimore: Johns Hopkins University Press.

Oakley, Kenneth
1963 "Analytical Methods of Dating Bones." *In: Science in Archaeology,* D. Brothwell and E. Higgs (eds.), New York: Basic Books, Inc.

Oates, John F., Michael Abedi-Lartey, W. Scott McGraw, et al.
2000 "Extinction of a West African Red Colobus Monkey." *Conservation Biology,* 14(5):1526–1532.

O'Brien, S. J., et al.
2002 "The Promise of Comparative Genomics in Mammals." *Science,* 286(5439):458–481.

Olliaro, Piero
1996 "Malaria, the Submerged Disease." *Journal of the American Medical Association,* 275(3):230–233.

Olson, John W. and R. Ciochon
1990 "A Review of the Evidence for Postulated Middle Pleistocene Occupation in Viet Nam." *Journal of Human Evolution,* 19:761–788.

OMIM (Online Mendelian Inheritance in Man).
2003 Johns Hopkins University. http://www.ncbi.nlm.nih.gov/omim/

O'Rourke, D. H., M. G. Hayes, and S. W. Carlyle
2000 "Spatial and Temporal Stability of mtDNA Haplogroup Frequencies in Native North America." *Human Biology,* 72:15–34.

Ortner, Donald J.
1981 "Biocultural Interaction in Human Adaptation." *In: How Humans Adapt.* Donald J. Ortner (ed.), Washington, D.C.: Smithsonian Institution Press.

Ovchinnikov, Igor V., Anders Götherström, Galina P. Romanova, et al.
2000 "Molecular Analysis of Neanderthal DNA from the Northern Caucasus." *Nature,* 404:490–493.

Padian, Kevin and Luis M. Chiappe
1998 "The Origin of Birds and Their Flight." *Scientific American,* 278:38–47.

Page, Susan E., et al.
2002 "The Amount of Carbon Released from Peat and Forest Fires in Indonesia During 1997. *Nature,* 420:61–65.

Palmer, S. K., L. G. Moore, D. Young, et al.
1999 "Altered Blood Pressure Course During Normal Pregnancy and Increased Preeclampsia at High Altitude (3100 meters) in Colorado." *Am. J. Obstet. Gynecol.,* 189 (5):1161–1168.

Palombit, R.
1994 "Dynamic Pair Bonds in Hylobatids: Implications Regarding Monogamous Social Systems. *Behavior,* 128:65–101.

Palumbi, Stephen R.
2001 *The Evolution Explosion: How Humans Cause Rapid Evolutionary Change.* New York: W. W. Norton

Parés, Josef M. and Alfredo Pérez-González
1995 "Paleomagnetic Age for Hominid Fossils at Atapuerca Archaeological Site, Spain." *Science,* 269:830–832.

Parker, Seymour
1976 "The Precultural Basis of the Incest Taboo: Toward a Biosocial Theory." *American Anthropologist,* 78:285–305.

Pennisi, Elizabeth
2001 "The Human Genome." *Science,* 291:1177–1180.

Penny, D.
2004 "Our Relative Genetics." *Nature,* 427:208–209.

Peres, C.A.
1990 "Effects of hunting on Western Amazonian primate communities." *Biological Conservation* 54: 47–59.

Perkins, Sid
2003 "Learning from the Present." *Science News,* 164:42–44.

Phillips, K.A.
1998 "Tool Use in Wild Capuchin Monkeys." *American Journal of Primatology,* 46(3):259–261.

Phillips-Conroy, J. E., C. J. Jolly, P. Nystrom, and H. A. Hemmalin
1992 "Migration of Male Hamadryas Baboons into Annubis Groups in the Awash National Park, Ethiopia." *International Journal of Primatology,* 13:455–476.

Pickford, M.
1983 "Sequence and Environments of the Lower and Middle Miocene Hominoids of Western Kenya." *In:* R. L. Ciochon and R. S. Corruccini (eds.), q.v., pp. 421–439.

Pickford, Martin and Brigitte Senut
2001 "The Geological and Faunal Context of Late Miocene Hominid Remains from Lukeino, Kenya." *C. R. Acad. Sci. Paris, Sciences de la Terre et des Planètes*, 332:145–152.

Pilbeam, David
1972 *The Ascent of Man.* New York: Macmillan.

_____
1977 "Beyond the Apes: Pre-*Homo* Hominids: The Ramapithecines of Africa, Asia, and Europe." Symposium Lecture, March 5, 1977, Davis, Ca.

_____
1982 "New Hominoid Skull Material from the Miocene of Pakistan." *Nature*, 295:232–234.

_____
1986 "Distinguished Lecture: Hominoid Evolution and Hominoid Origins." *American Anthropologist*, 88:295–312.

_____
1988 "Primate Evolution." *In: Human Biology*, G. A. Harrison et al., (eds.), New York: Oxford University Press, pp. 76–103.

Pinner, Robert W., Steven M. Teutsch, Lone Simonson, et al.
1996 "Trends in Infectious Diseases Mortality in the United States." *Journal of the American Medical Association*, 275(3):189–193.

Pope, G. G.
1984 "The Antiquity and Paleoenvironment of the Asian Hominidae." *In: The Evolution of the East Asian Environment.* Center of Asian Studies Occasional Papers and Monographs, No. 59, R. O. Whyte (ed.), Hong Kong: University of Hong Kong, pp. 822–847.

_____
1992 "Craniofacial Evidence for the Origin of Modern Humans in China." *Yearbook of Physical Anthropology*, 1992, 35:243–298.

Popp, Joseph L. and Irven DeVore
1979 "Aggressive Competition and Social Dominance Theory." *In: The Great Apes,* D. A. Hamburg and E. R. McCown (eds.), Menlo Park, Ca.: Benjamin/ Cummings Publishing Co., pp. 317–318.

Poremba, A., M. Malloy, R. C. Saunders, et al.
2004 "Species-specific Calls Evoke Asymmetric Activity in the Monkey's Temporal Poles." *Nature*, 427:448–451.

Post, Peter W., Farrington Daniels, Jr., and Robert T. Binford, Jr.
1975 "Cold Injury and the Evolution of 'White' Skin." *Human Biology*, 47:65–80.

Potts, Richard
1984 "Home Bases and Early Hominids." *American Scientist*, 72:338–347.

_____
1991 "Why the Oldowan? Plio-Pleistocene Toolmaking and the Transport of Resources." *Journal of Anthropological Research*, 47:153–176.

_____
1993 "Archeological Interpretations of Early Hominid Behavior and Ecology." *In:* D. T. Rasmussen (ed.), *The Origin and Evolution of Humans and Humanness,* Boston: Jones and Bartlett, pp. 49–74.

_____
1998 "Environmental Hypotheses of Hominin Evolution." *Yearbook of Physical Anthropology*, 41:93–136.

_____
2003 Paper presented at the Paleoanthropology Association Annual Meetings, Tempe, AZ, April 2003.

Potts, Richard and Pat Shipman
1981 "Cutmarks Made by Stone Tools from Olduvai Gorge, Tanzania." *Nature*, 291:577–580.

Powell, K. B., H. Mortensen, and S. A. Tishkoff
2003 "The Evolution of Lactase Persistence in African Populations." *American Journal of Physical Anthropology*, Supplement 36:170 (Abstract).

Proctor, Robert
1988 "From Anthropologie to Rassenkunde." *In: Bones, Bodies, Behavior. History of Anthropology* (Vol. 5), 6. W. Stocking, Jr. (ed.), Madison: University of Wisconsin Press, pp. 138–179.

Profet, M.
1988 The Evolution of Pregnancy Sickness as a Protection to the Embryo Against Pleistocene Teratogens. *Evolutionary Theory*, 8:177–190.

Pulliam, H. R. and T. Caraco
1984 "Living in groups: Is There an Optimal Size?" *In: Behavioral Ecology: An Evolutionary Approach* (2nd ed.), J. R. Krebs and N. B. Davies (eds.), Sunderland, Mass.: Sinauer Associates.

Pusey, Anne E. and Craig Packer
1987 "Dispersal and Philopatry." *In:* B. B. Smuts et al. (eds.), q.v., pp. 250–266.

Pusey, A., J. Williams, and J. Goodall
1997 "The Influence of Dominance Rank on the Reproductive Success of Female Chimpanzees." *Science*, 277:828–831.

Radinsky, Leonard
1973 "*Aegyptopithecus* Endocasts: Oldest Record of a Pongid Brain." *American Journal of Physical Anthropology*, 39:239–248.

Rafferty, Katherine L. et al.
1995 "Postcranial Estimates of Body Weight, with a Note on a Distal Tibia of *P. major* from Napak, Uganda. *American Journal of Physical Anthropology*, 97:391–402.

Rak, Y.
1983 *The Australopithecine Face.* New York: Academic Press.

Reddy, B. M., Guangyun Sun, Javier Rodriguez Luis, et al.
2001 "Genomic Diversity of Thirteen Short Tandem Repeat Loci in a Substructured Caste Population, Golla, of Southern Andhra Pradesh, India." *Human Biology*, 73:175–190.

Reithman, H. C., et al.
2001 "Integration of Telomere Sequences with the Draft Human Genome Sequence." *Nature*, 409:948–951.

Relethford, John H.
2001 *Genetics and the Search for Modern Human Origins."* New York: Wiley-Liss.

Relethford, John H. and Henry C. Harpending
1994 "Craniometric Variation, Genetic Theory, and Modern Human Origins." *American Journal of Physical Anthropology*, 95:249–270.

Reno, Phillip L., Richard S. Meindl, Melanie A. McCollum, and C. Owen Lovejoy

2003 "Sexual Dimorphism in *Australopithecus afarensis* Was Similar to that of Modern Humans." *Proceedings of the National Academy of Sciences,* 100:9404–9409.

Richard, A. F.

1985 *Primates in Nature.* New York: W. H. Freeman and Co.

Richard, A. F. and S. R. Schulman

1982 "Sociobiology: Primate Field Studies." *Annual Reviews of Anthropology,* 11:231–255.

Riddle, Robert D. and Clifford J. Tabin

1999 "How Limbs Develop." *Scientific American,* 280(2):74–79.

Ridley, Mark

1993 *Evolution.* Boston: Blackwell Scientific Publications.

Rightmire, G. P.

1981 "Patterns in the Evolution of *Homo erectus.*" *Paleobiology,* 7:241–246.

—— 1990 *The Evolution of* Homo erectus. New York: Cambridge University Press.

—— 1998 "Human Evolution in the Middle Pleistocene: The Role of *Homo heidelbergensis.*" *Evolutionary Anthropology,* 6:218–227.

—— 2004 "Affinities of the Middle Pleistocene Cranium from Dali and Jinniushan." *American Journal of Physical Anthropology, Supplement 38*:167 (Abstract).

Roberts, Charlotte, with Keith Manchester

1997 *The Archaeology of Disease.* 2nd ed. Ithaca, NY: Cornell University Press.

Roberts, D. F.

1973 *Climate and Human Variability.* An Addison-Wesley Module in Anthropology, No. 34. Reading, Mass.: Addison-Wesley.

Roberts, Richard, Rhys Jones, and M. A. Smith

1990 "Thermoluminescence Dating of a 50,000-Year-Old Human Occupation Site in Northern Australia," *Nature,* 345:153–156.

Robins, A. H.

1991 *Biological Perspectives on Human Pigmentation.* Cambridge: Cambridge University Press.

Robinson, J. T.

1972 *Early Hominid Posture and Locomotion.* Chicago: University of Chicago Press.

Rodman, P. S.

1973 "Population Composition and Adaptive Organisation among Orangutans of the Kutai Reserve." *In: Comparative Ecology and Behaviour of Primates,* R. P. Michael and J. H. Crook (eds.), London: Academic Press, pp. 171–209.

Romer, Alfred S.

1959 *The Vertebrate Story.* Chicago: University of Chicago Press.

Rose, M. D.

1991 "Species Recognition in Eocene Primates." *American Journal of Physical Anthropology,* Supplement 12, p. 153.

Rosenberg, K. and W. Trevathan

2001 "The Evolution of Human Birth." *Scientific American,* 285(5):72–77.

Rosenberg, M. J., R. Agarwala, G. Bouffard, et al.

2002 "Mutant Deoxynucleotide Carrier Is Associated with Congenital Microcephaly." *Nature Genetics,* 32(1):175–179.

Rosenberg, Noah A., Jonathan K. Prichard, James L. Weber, et al.

2002 "Genetic Structure of Human Populations." *Science,* 298:2381–2385

Ross, Caroline

1998 "Primate Life Histories." *Evolutionary Anthropology,* 6:54–63.

Rovner, Irwin

1983 "Plant Opal Pytolith Analysis." *Advances in Archaeological Method and Theory,* 6:225–266.

Roychoudhury, S., S. Roy, A. Basu, et al.

2001 Genomic Structures and Population Histories of Linguistically Distinct Tribal Groups of India." *Human Genetics,* 109:339–350.

Ruben, John A., Christiano Dal Sasso, Nicholas Geist, et al.

1999 "Pulmonary Function and Metabolic Physiology of Theropod Dinosaurs." *Science,* 283:514–516.

Rudran, R.

1973 Adult Male Replacement in One-Male Troops of Purple-Faced Langurs (*Presbytis senex senex*) and Its Effect on Population Structure. *Folia Primatologica,* 19:166–192.

Ruff, C. B. and Alan Walker

1993 "The Body Size and Shape of KNM-WT 15000." *In:* A. Walker and R. Leakey (eds.), q.v., pp. 234–265.

Rumbaugh, D. M.

1977 *Language Learning by a Chimpanzee: The Lana Project.* New York: Academic Press.

Ruvolo, M., D. Pan, S. Zehr, T. Goldberg, et al.

1994 "Gene Trees and Hominoid Phylogeny." *Proceedings of the National Academy of Sciences,* 91:8900–8904.

Sachick, Kathy B. and Dong Zhuan

1991 "Early Paleolithic of China and Eastern Asia." *Evolutionary Anthropology,* 2(1):22–35.

Samson, M., F. Libert, B. J. Doranz, et al.

1996 Resistance to HIV-1 Infection in Caucasian Individuals Bearing Mutant Alleles of the CCR-5 Chemokine Receptor Gene. *Nature* 382(22): 722–725.

Sarich, V. M. and A. C. Wilson

1967 "Rules of Albumen Evolution in Primates." *Proceedings, National Academy of Science,* 58:142–148.

Sarich, Vincent

1971 "A Molecular Approach to the Question of Human Origins." *In: Background for Man,* P. Dolhinow and V. Sarich (eds.), Boston: Little, Brown & Co., pp. 60–81.

Savage-Rumbaugh, E. S.

1986 *Ape Language: From Conditioned Responses to Symbols.* New York: Columbia University Press.

Savage-Rumbaugh, S., K. McDonald, R. A. Sevic, W. D. Hopkins, and E. Rupert

1986 "Spontaneous Symbol Acquisition and Communicative Use by Pygmy Chimpanzees (*Pan paniscus*)." *Journal of Experimental Psychology: General,* 115(3):211–235.

Savage-Rumbaugh, S. and R. Lewin

1994 *Kanzi. The Ape at the Brink of the Human Mind.* New York: John Wiley and Sons.

Schaller, George B.

1963 *The Mountain Gorilla.* Chicago: University of Chicago Press.

Scheller, Richard H. and Richard Axel
1984   "How Genes Control Innate Behavior." *Scientific American,* 250:54–63.

Schmitz, Ralf W., David Serre, Georges Bonani, et al.
2002   "The Neandertal Type Site Revisited: Interdisciplinary Investigations of Skeletal Remains from the Neander Valley, Germany. *Proceedings of the National Academy of Sciences,* 99:13342–13347.

Schwartzman, Stephen
1997   "Fires in the Amazon: An Analysis of NOAA-12 Satellite Data, 1996–1997." Washington D.C.: Environmental Defense Fund.

Scott, K.
1980   "Two Hunting Episodes of Middle Paleolithic Age at La Cotte Sainte-Brelade, Jersey (Channel Islands)." *World Archaeology,* 12:137–152.

Scozzari, R., F. Cruciani, A. Pangrazio, et al.
2001   "Human Y-Chromosome Variation in the Western Mediterranean Area: Implications for Peopling of the Area." *Human Immunology,* 62:871–874.

Scriver, Charles R.
2001   "Human Genetics" Lessons from Quebec Populations." *Annual Review of Genomics and Human Genetics,* 2:69–101.

Seehausen, O.
2002   "Patterns of Fish Radiation Are Compatible with Pliestocene Dessication of Lake Victoria and 14,600 Year History for Its Cichlid Species Flock." *Proceedings of the Royal Society of London (Biological Science),* 269:491–497.

Semaw, S., P. Renne, W. K. Harris, et al.
1997   2.5-million-year-old Stone Tools from Gona, Ethiopia. *Nature,* 385:333–336

Senut, Brigitte, Martin Pickford, Dominique Grommercy, et al.
2001   First Hominid from the Miocene (Lukeino Formation, Kenya). *C.R. Acad. Sci. Paris, Sciences de la Terre er des Planètes,* 332:137–144.

Senut, Brigitte and Christine Tardieu
1985   "Functional Aspects of Plio-Pleistocene Hominid Limb Bones: Implications for Taxonomy and Phylogeny." *In: Ancestors: The Hard Evidence,* E. Delson (ed.), New York: Alan R. Liss, pp. 193–201.

Seyfarth, Robert M.
1987   "Vocal Communication and its Relation to Language." *In:* Smuts et al., *Primate Societies.* Chicago: University of Chicago Press, pp. 440–451.

Seyfarth, Robert M., Dorothy L. Cheney, and Peter Marler
1980a   "Monkey Responses to Three Different Alarm Calls." *Science,* 210:801–803.

——   1980b   "Ververt Monkey Alarm Calls." *Animal Behavior,* 28:1070–1094.

Shea, John J.
1998   "Neandertal and Early Modern Human Behavioral Variability." *Current Anthropology,* 39 (Supplement):45–78.

Shipman, P. L.
1983   "Early Hominid Lifestyle. Hunting and Gathering or Foraging and Scavenging?" Paper presented at 52nd Annual Meeting, American Association of Physical Anthropologists, Indianapolis, April.

1987   "An Age-Old Question: Why Did the Human Lineage Survive?" *Discover,* 8:60–64.

Shipman, Pat
1983   "Early Hominid Lifestyle. Hunting and Gathering or Foraging and Scavenging?" Paper presented at 52nd Annual Meeting, American Association of Physical Anthropologists, Indianapolis.

Shuben, Nell, Cliff Tabin, and Sean Carroll
1997   "Fossils, Genes, and the Evolution of Animal Limbs." *Nature,* 388:639–648.

Sibley, Charles and Jon E. Ahlquist
1984   "The Phylogeny of the Hominoid Primates as Indicated by DNA-DNA Hybridization." *Journal of Molecular Evolution,* 20:2–15.

Silk, J. B., S. C. Alberts, and J. Altmann
2003   "Social Bonds of Female Baboons Enhance Infant Survival." *Science,* 302:1231–1234.

Simerly, C., et al.,
2003   "Molecular Correlates of Primate Nuclear Transfer Failures." *Science,* 300:297.

Simons, E. L.
1969   "The Origin and Radiation of the Primates." *Annals of the New York Academy of Sciences,* 167:319–331.

——   1972   *Primate Evolution.* New York: Macmillan.

——   1985   "African Origin, Characteristics and Context of Earliest Higher Primates." *In: Hominid Evolution: Past, Present, and Future.* P. Tobias (ed.), New York: Alan R. Liss, pp. 101–106.

——   1995   "Egyptian Oligocene Primates: A Review." *Yearbook of Physical Anthropology,* 38:199–238.

Simons, Elwyn L. and Tab Rasmussen
1994   "A Whole New World of Ancestors: Eocene Anthropoideans from Africa." *Evolutionary Anthropology,* 3:128–139.

Simpson, G. G.
1945   "The Principles of Classification and a Classification of Mammals." *Bulletin of the American Museum of Natural History,* 85:1–350.

Simpson, G. G., C. S. Pittendright, and L H. Tiffany
1957   *Life.* New York: Harcourt, Brace and Co., Inc.

Skaletsky, H., et al,
2003   "The Male-specific Region of the Human Y Chromosome is a Mosaic of Discrete Sequence Classes." *Nature,* 423:825–837.

Skelton, R. R., H. M. McHenry, and G. M. Drawhorn
1986   "Phylogenetic Analysis of Early Hominids." *Current Anthropology,* 27:1–43; 361–365.

Skelton, Randall R. and Henry M. McHenry
1992   "Evolutionary Relationships among Early Hominids." *Journal of Human Evolution,* 23:309–349.

Skirboll, Lana, et al.
2001   "Stem Cells: Scientific Progress and Future Research Directions." Report from the National Institutes of Health to the Secretary of Health and Human Services, Tommy G. Thompson. Internet version at: *www.nih.gov/news./stemcell/scireport.htm*

Small, Meredith F. (ed.)
1984   *Female Primates. Studies by Women Primatologists.* Monographs in Primatology, Vol. 4. New York: Alan R. Liss.

Smith, Fred H.
1984   "Fossil Hominids from the Upper Pleistocene of Central Europe and the Origin of Modern Europeans." *In:* F. H. Smith and F. Spencer (eds.), q.v., pp. 187–209.

Smith, Fred H., A. B. Falsetti, and S. M. Donnelly
1989   "Modern Human Origins." *Yearbook of Physical Anthropology,* 32:35–68.

Smith, Fred H. and Frank, Spencer (eds.)
1984   *The Origins of Modern Humans.* New York: Alan R. Liss, Inc.

Smith, Fred H., Erik Trinkaus, Paul B. Pettitt, et al.
1999   "Direct Radiocarbon Dates for Vindija G$_1$ and Velika Pécina Late Pleistocene Hominid Remains." *Proceedings of the National Academy of Sciences,* 96:12281–12286.

Smuts, Barbara
1985   *Sex and Friendship in Baboons.* Hawthorne, N.Y.: Aldine de Gruyter.

Smuts, Barbara B. et al. (eds.)
1987   *Primate Societies.* Chicago: University of Chicago Press.

Snowdon, Charles T.
1990   "Language Capacities of 'Nonhuman Animals.'" *Yearbook of Physical Anthropology,* 33:215–243.

Snyder, M. and M. Gerstein
2003   "Genomics. Defining Genes in the Genomics Era." *Science,* 300(5617):258–260.

Soffer, Olga
1985   *The Upper Paleolithic of the Central Russian Plain.* New York: Academic Press.

Solecki, Ralph
1971   *Shanidar, The First Flower People.* New York: Alfred A. Knopf.

Sponheimer, Matt and Julia A. Lee-Thorp
1999   "Isotopic Evidence for the Diet of an Early Hominid, *Australopithecus africanus.*" *Science,* 283:368–370.

Stanford, Craig
1998   *Chimpanzee and Red Colobus. The Ecology of Predator and Prey.* Cambridge: Harvard University Press.

——   1999   *The Hunting Apes. Meat Eating and the Origins of Human Behavior.* Princeton: Princeton University Press.

——   2001a   "The Ape's Gift: Meat-eating, Meat-sharing, and Human Evolution." *In:* de Waal, F. B. M. (ed.) *Tree of Origin.* Cambridge: Harvard University Press. pp. 95–117.

——   2001b   *Significant Others. The Ape-Human Continuum and the Quest for Human Nature.* New York: Basic Books.

Stanford, C. B., J. Wallis, H. Matama, and J. Goodall
1994   "Patterns of Predation by Chimpanzees on Red Colobus Monkeys in Gombe National Park." *American Journal of Physical Anthropology,* 94(2):213–228.

Stanyon, Roscoe and Brunetto Chiarelli
1982   "Phylogeny of the Hominoidea: The Chromosome Evidence." *Journal of Human Evolution,* 11:493–504.

Steegman, A. T., Jr.
1970   "Cold Adaptation and the Human Face." *American Journal of Physical Anthropology,* 32:243–250.

——   1975   "Human Adaptation to Cold." *In: Physiological Anthropology,* A. Damon (ed.), New York: Oxford University Press, pp. 130–166.

Steklis, Horst D.
1985   "Primate Communication, Comparative Neurology, and the Origin of Language Re-examined." *Journal of Human Evolution,* 14:157–173.

Stelzner, J. and K. Strier
1981   "Hyena Predation on an Adult Male Baboon." *Mammalia,* 45:106–107.

Stern, Curt
1973   *Principles of Human Genetics,* 3rd ed. San Francisco: W. H. Freeman.

Stern, Jack T. and Randall L. Susman
1983   "The Locomotor Anatomy of *Australopithecus afarensis.*" *American Journal of Physical Anthropology,* 60:279–317.

Sterns, S. C.
1992   *The Evolution of Life Histories.* New York: Oxford University Press.

Stewart, T. D.
1979   *Essentials of Forensic Anthropology: Especially as Developed in the United States.* Springfield: C. C. Thomas.

Stiner, Mary C.
1991   "The Faunal Remains from Grotta Guatari." *Current Anthropology,* 32(2)April:103–117.

Stoneking, Mark
1993   "DNA and Recent Human Evolution." *Evolutionary Anthropology,* 2:60–73.

Strassman, B. I. and B. Gillespie
2002   "Life-history Theory, Fertility, and Reproductive Success in Humans." *Proceedings of the Royal Society of London B,* 269:553–562.

Straus, Lawrence Guy
1993   "Southwestern Europe at the Last Glacial Maximum." *Current Anthropology,* 32:189–199.

——   1995   "The Upper Paleolithic of Europe: An Overview." *Evolutionary Anthropology,* 4:4–16.

Strier, Karen B.
2003   *Primate Behavioral Ecology,* 2nd Ed. Boston: Allyn and Bacon.

Stringer, C. B. (ed.).
1985   "Middle Pleistocene Hominid Variability and the Origin of Late Pleistocene Humans." *In: Ancestors: The Hard Evidence,* E. Delson (ed.), New York: Alan R. Liss, pp. 289–295.

——   1993   "Secrets of the Pit of the Bones." *Nature,* 362:501–502.

——   1995   "The Evolution and Distribution of Later Pleistocene Human Populations." *In:* E. Vrba et al. (eds.), op cit., pp. 524–531.

Stringer, C. B. and P. Andrews
1988   "Genetic and Fossil Evidence for the Origin of Modern Humans." *Science,* 239:1263–1268.

Struhsaker, T. T.
1967 "Auditory Communication among Vervet Monkeys (*Cercopithecus aethiops*)." *In: Social Communication Among Primates*, S. A. Altmann (ed.), Chicago: University of Chicago Press.

———
1975 *The Red Colobus Monkey.* Chicago: University of Chicago Press.

Struhsaker, Thomas T. and Lysa Leland
1979 "Socioecology of Five Sympatric Monkey Species in the Kibale Forest, Uganda." *Advances in the Study of Behavior,* Vol. 9, New York: Academic Press, pp. 159–229.

———
1987 "Colobines: Infanticide by Adult Males." *In:* B. B. Smuts et al. (eds.), q.v., pp. 83–97.

Strum, S. C.
1987 *Almost Human. A Journey into the World of Baboons.* New York: W. W. Norton.

Stuart-Macadam, P. and K. A. Dettwyler
1995 *Breastfeeding: Biocultural Perspectives.* Hawthorne, NY: Aldine de Gruyter.

Sugiyama, Y.
1965 "Short History of the Ecological and Sociological Studies on Non-Human Primates in Japan." *Primates,* 6:457–460.

Sugiyama, Y. and J. Koman
1979 "Tool-using and -making Behavior in Wild Chimpanzees at Bossou, Guinea." *Primates,* 20:513–524.

Sumner, D. R., M. E. Morbeck, and J. Lobick
1989 "Age-Related Bone Loss in Female Gombe Chimpanzees." *American Journal of Physical Anthropology,* 72:259.

Suomi, Stephen J., Susan Mineka, and Roberta D. DeLizio
1983 "Short- and Long-Term Effects of Repetitive Mother-Infant Separation on Social Development in Rhesus Monkeys." *Developmental Psychology,* 19(5):710–786.

Susman, Randall L. (ed.)
1984 *The Pygmy Chimpanzee: Evolutionary Biology and Behavior.* New York: Plenum Press.

Susman, Randall L.
1988 "New Postcranial Remains from Swartkrans and Their Bearing on the Functional Morphology and Behavior of *Paranthropus robustus*." *In:* F. E. Grine (ed.), q.v., pp. 149–172.

Susman, Randall L., Jack T. Stern, and William L. Jungers
1985 "Locomotor Adaptations in the Hadar Hominids." *In: Ancestors: The Hard Evidence,* E. Delson (ed.), New York: Alan R. Liss, pp. 184–192.

Sussman, Robert W.
1991 "Primate Origins and the Evolution of Angiosperms." *American Journal of Primatology,* 23:209–223.

Sussman, Robert W., James M. Cheverud and Thad Q. Bartlett
1995 Infant Killing as an Evolutionary Strategy: Reality or Myth? *Evolutionary Anthropology,* 3(5):149–151.

Suzman, I. M.
1982 "A Comparative Study of the Hadar and Sterkfontein Australopithecine Innominates." *American Journal of Physical Anthropology,* 57:235.

Swisher, C. C. III, G. H. Curtis, T. Jacob, et al.
1994 "Age of the Earliest Known Hominids in Java, Indonesia." *Science,* 263:1118–1121.

Swisher, C. C., W. J. Rink, S. C. Anton, et al.
1996 Latest *Homo erectus* of Java: Potential Contemporaneity with *Homo sapiens* in Southwest Java. *Science,* 274:1870–1874.

Szalay, Frederick S. and Eric Delson
1979 *Evolutionary History of the Primates.* New York: Academic Press.

Tattersal, Ian, Eric Delson, and John Van Couvering
1988 *Encyclopedia of Human Evolution and Prehistory.* New York: Garland Publishing.

Teleki, G.
1986 "Chimpanzee Conservation in Sierra Leone—A Case Study of a Continent-wide Problem." Paper presented at Understanding Chimpanzees Symposium, Chicago Academy of Sciences, Chicago, Nov. 7–10, 1987.

Templeton, Alan R.
1996 "Gene Lineages and Human Evolution." *Science,* 272:1363–1364.

———
2002 "Out of Africa Again and Again." *Nature,* 416:45–51.

Tenaza, R. and R. Tilson
1977 "Evolution of Long-Distance Alarm Calls in Kloss' Gibbon." *Nature,* 268:233–235.

Teresi, Dick
2002 *Lost Discoveries. The Ancient Roots of Modern Science—from the Babylonians to the Maya.* New York: Simon and Schuster.

Terwilliger, Joseph D. and Harold H.H. Göring
2000 "Gene Mapping in the 20th and 21st Centuries: Statistical Methods, Data Analysis, and Experimental Design." *Human Biology,* 72:63–132.

Thieme, Hartmut
1997 Lower Paleolithic Hunting Spears from Germany. *Nature,* 385:807–810.

Thorne, A., R. Grün, G. Mortimer, et al.
1999 "Australia's Oldest Human Remains: Age of the Lake Mungo 3 Skeleton." *Journal of Human Evolution,* 36:591–612.

Thorne, A. G. and M. H. Wolpoff
1992 "The Multiregional Evolution of Humans." *Scientific American,* 266:76–83.

Thorsby, Erik
1997 "Invited Anniversary Review: HLA Associated Diseases." *Human Immunology,* 53:1–11.

Tiemel, Chen, Yang Quan, and Wu En
1994 "Antiquity of *Homo sapiens* in China." *Nature,* 368:55–56.

Tishkoft, S. A., E. Dietzsch, W. Speed, et al.
1996 "Global Patterns of Linkage Disequilibrium at the CD4 Locus and Modern Human Origins." *Science,* 271:1380–1387.

Tobias, Phillip
1971 *The Brain in Hominid Evolution.* New York: Columbia University Press.

———
1983 "Recent Advances in the Evolution of the Hominids with Especial Reference to Brain and Speech." Pontifical Academy of Sciences, *Scrita Varia,* 50:85–140.

———
1991 *Olduvai Gorge, Volume IV. The Skulls, Endocasts and Teeth of Homo habilis.* Cambridge: Cambridge University Press.

Todd, T.W.
1920, "Age Changes in the Pubic Bone." *American*
1921 *Journal of Physical Anthropology*, 3:285–334; 4:1–70.

Trevathan, Wenda R.
1987 *Human Birth: An Evolutionary Perspective.*
Hawthorne, NY: Aldine de Gruyter.

Travis, John
2003 "Genghis Khan's Legacy?" *Science News*, 163:91.

Trinkaus, E.
1983 *The Shanidar Neandertals.* New York: Academic Press.

——— 1984 "Western Asia." *In:* F. H. Smith and F. Spencer (eds.),
q.v., pp. 251–293.

Trinkaus, E. and W. W. Howells
1979 "The Neandertals." *Scientific American*,
241(6):118–133.

Trinkaus, Erik and Pat Shipman
1992 *The Neandertals.* New York: Alfred A. Knopf.

Trivers, R. L.
1971 "The Evolution of Reciprocal Altruism." *Quarterly
Review of Biology*, 46:35–57.

——— 1972 "Parental Investment and Sexual Selection." *In: Sexual
Selection and the Descent of Man*, B. Campbell (ed.),
Chicago: Aldine, pp. 136–179.

Tuttle, Russell H.
1990 "Apes of the World." *American Scientist*, 78:115–125.

Twain, Mark
1870 *Innocents Abroad.* New York: New American Library.

Udvardy, Miklos
1977 *The Audubon Society of North American Birds.* New
York: Alfred A/ Knopf

Ulijaszek, S.
1998 "The Genetics of Growth." *In: The Cambridge
Encyclopedia of Human Growth and Development*, S. J.
Ulijaszek, F. E. Johnston, and M. A. Preece (eds.).
Cambridge, UK: Cambridge University Press, pp.
121–123.

van der Ven, K., R. Fimmers, G. Engels, et al.
2000 "Evidence for Major Histocompatability Complex-
Mediated Effects on Spermatogenesis in Humans."
Human Reproduction, 15:189–196.

Van Couvering, A. H. and J. A. Van Covering
1976 "Early Miocene Mammal Fossils From East Africa." *In:
Human Origins*, G. Isaac and E. R. McCown (eds.),
Menlo Park, CA.: Benjamin/Cummings, pp. 155–207.

van Schaik, C. P., M. Ancrenaz, G. Borgen, et al.
2003 "Orangutan Cultures and the Evolution of Material
Culture." *Science*, 299:102–105.

van Schaik, C. P. and P. M. Kappeler
1996 "The Social Systems of Gregarious Lemurs: Lack of
Convergence with Anthropoids Due to Evolutionary
Disequilibrium." *Ethology*, 102:915–941.

Varki, A.
2000 "A chimpanzee genome project is a biomedical impera-
tive." *Genome Research*, 8:1065–1070.

Villa, Paola
1983 *Terra Amata and the Middle Pleistocene Archaeological
Record of Southern France.* University of California
Publications in Anthropology, Vol. 13. Berkeley:
University of California Press.

Visalberghi, E.
1990 "Tool Use in Cebus." *Folia Primatologica*,
54:146–154.

Vogel, F.
1970 "ABO Blood Groups and Disease." *American Journal
of Human Genetics*, 22:464–475.

Vogel, F., M. Kopun, and R. Rathenberg
1976 "Mutation and Molecular Evolution." *In: Molecular
Anthropology*, M. Goodman et al. (eds.), New York:
Plenum Press, pp. 13–33.

Vogel, Gretchen
2001 "Objection #2: Why Sequence the Junk? *Science*,
291:1184.

Vogelstein, B., D. Lane, and A. J. Levine
2000 "Surfing the p53 Network." *Nature*, 408:307–310.

Von Koenigswald, G. H. R.
1956 *Meeting Prehistoric Man.* New York: Harper &
Brothers.

Vrba, E. S.
1985 "Ecological and Adaptive Changes Associated with
Early Hominid Evolution." *In: Ancestors: The Hard
Evidence*, E. Delson (ed.), New York: Alan R. Liss, pp.
63–71.

——— 1988 "Late Pliocene Climatic Events and Hominid
Evolution." *In:* F. Grine (ed.), q.v., pp. 405–426.

——— 1995 "The Fossil Record of African Antelopes (Mammalia,
Bovidae) in Relation to Human Evolution and
Paleoclimate." *In: Paleoclimate and Evolution with
Emphasis on Human Origins*, E. Vrba et al. (eds.). New
Haven: Yale University Press, pp. 385–424.

Wagner, Gunter A.
1996 "Fission-Track Dating in Paleoanthropology."
Evolutionary Anthropology, 5:165–171.

Wakayama, T., A. C. F. Perry, M. Zucotti, K. R. Johnson, and
R. Yanagimachi
1998 "Full-term Development of Mice from Enucleated
Oocytes Injected with Cumulus Cell Nuclei. *Nature*,
394:369–374.

Walker, A.
1976 "Remains Attributable to *Australopithecus* from East
Rudolf." *In: Earliest Man and Environments in the
Lake Rudolf Basin*, Y. Coppens et al. (eds.), Chicago:
University of Chicago Press, pp. 484–489.

——— 1991 "The Origin of the Genus *Homo*." *In:* S. Osawa and T.
Honjo (eds.), *Evolution of Life*. Tokyo: Springer-Verlag,
pp. 379–389.

——— 1993 "The Origin of the Genus *Homo*" *In:* D. T. Rasmussen
(ed.), *The Origin and Evolution of Humans and
Humanness.* Boston: Jones and Bartlett, pp. 29–47.

——— 2002 "New Perspectives on the Hominids of the Turkana
Basin, Kenya." *Evolutionary Anthropology*, 11
(Supplement):38–41.

Walker, A., D. Pilbeam, and M. Cartmill
1981 "Changing Views and Interpretations of Primate
Evolution." Paper presented to the Annual Meetings,
American Association of Physical Anthropologists.
Detroit, Mich.

Walker, Alan and R. E. Leakey (eds.)
1993   *The Nariokotome* Homo erectus *Skeleton.* Cambridge: Harvard University Press.

Walker, Alan and Mark Teaford
1989   "The Hunt for *Proconsul.*" *Scientific American,* 260(Jan):76–82.

Walsh, P. D., K. A. Abernathy, M. Bermejo, et al.
2003   "Catastrophic Ape Decline in Western Equatorial Africa." *Nature,* 422:611–614.

Walrath, D.
2003   "Rethinking Pelvic Typologies and the Human Birth Mechanism." *Current Anthropology* 44: 5–31.

Walters, Jeffrey and Robert Seyfarth
1987   "Conflict and Cooperation." *In:* B. B. Smuts et al. (eds.), q.v., pp. 306–317.

Wanpo, Huang, Russell Ciochon, et al.
1995   "Early *Homo* and Associated Artifacts from Asia." *Nature,* 378:275–278.

Ward, Peter
1994   *The End of Evolution.* New York: Bantam.

Ward, S. C. and D. R. Pilbeam
1983   Maxillofacial Morphology of Miocene Hominoids from Africa and Indo-Pakistan." *In:* R. L. Ciochon and R. S. Corruccini (eds.), q.v., pp. 211–238.

Ward, Steven and William H. Kimbel
1983   "Subnasal Alveolar Morphology and the Systematic Position of *Sivapithecus.*" *American Journal of Physical Anthropology,* 61:157–171.

Waser, Peter M.
1987   "Interactions among Primate Species." *In:* B. B. Smuts et al. (eds.), q.v., pp. 210–226.

Washburn, S. L.
1963   "The Study of Race." *American Anthropologist,* 65:521–531.

_____
1971   "The Study of Human Evolution." *In:* P. Dolhinow and V. Sarich (eds.), *Background for Man: Readings in Physical Anthropology,* Boston: Little, Brown, pp. 82–121.

Washburn, S. L. and C. S. Lancaster
1968   "The Evolution of Hunting." *In:* Lee, R. B. and I. DeVore (eds.), *Man the Hunter.* Chicago: Aldine de Gruyter: pp. 293–303.

Waterston, R. H., K. Lindblad-Toh, E. Birney, et al., (Mouse Genome Sequencing Consortium)
2002   Initial Sequencing and Comparative Analysis of the Mouse Genome. *Nature,* 421:520–562.

Watson, J. B. and F. H. C. Crick
1953a   "Genetical Implications of the Structure of the Deoxyribonucleic Acid." *Nature,* 171:964–967.

_____
1953b   "A Structure for Deoxyribonucleic Acid." *Nature,* 171:737–738.

Weiner, J. S.
1955   *The Piltdown Forgery.* London: Oxford University Press.

Weiner, Steve, Qinqi Xu, Paul Goldberg, Jinyi Liu, and Ofer Bar-Yosef
1998   "Evidence for the Use of Fire at Zhoukoudian, China." *Science,* 281:251–253.

Weiss, Kenneth
2003   "Come to Me My Melancholic Baby!" *Evolutionary Anthropology,* 12:3–6.

Weiss, K. M., K. K. Kidd, and J. R. Kidd
1992   "A Human Genome Diversity Project." *Evolutionary Anthropology,* 1:80–82.

Weiss, Mark L. and Alan E. Mann
1981   *Human Biology and Behavior,* 3rd ed. Boston: Little Brown.

Weiss, K. M., D. W. Stock, and Z. Zhao
1998   "Homeobox Genes." *In: The Cambridge Encyclopedia of Human Growth and Development,* S. J. Ulijaszek, F. E. Johnston, and M. A. Preece (eds.). Cambridge, UK: Cambridge University Press, pp. 137–139.

Weiss, Robin A. and Richard W. Wrangham
1999   "From *Pan* to Pandemic." *Nature,* 397:385–386.

Weiss, U.
2002   "Nature Insight: Malaria." *Nature,* 415:669.

Wheeler, P. E.
1991   "The Thermoregulatory Advantages of Hominid Bipedalism in Open Equatorial Environments: The Contribution of Increased Convective Heat Loss and Cutaneous Evaporative Cooling." *Journal of Human Evolution,* 21:107–115.

White, T. D.
1980   "Evolutionary Implications of Pliocene Hominid Footprints." *Science,* 208:175–176.

_____
1983   Comment Made at Institute of Human Origins Conference on the Evolution of Human Locomotion (Berkeley, Ca.).

_____
1986   "Cut Marks on the Bodo Cranium: A Case of Prehistoric Defleshing." *American Journal of Physical Anthropology,* 69:503–509.

White, T. D., Berhane Asfaw, David DeGusta, et al.
2003   "Pleistocene *Homo sapiens* from Middle Awash Ethiopia." *Nature,* 433:742–747.

White, T. D. and J. M. Harris
1977   "Suid Evolution and Correlation of African Hominid Localities." *Science,* 198:13–21.

White, T. D., D. C. Johanson, and W. H. Kimbel
1981   "*Australopithecus africanus:* Its Phyletic Position Reconsidered." *South African Journal of Science,* 77:445–470.

White, Tim D. and Donald C. Johanson
1989   "The Hominid Composition of Afar Locality 333: Some Preliminary Observations." *Hominidae,* Proceedings of the 2nd International Congress of Human Paleontology, Milan: Editoriale Jaca Book, pp. 97–101.

White, Tim D., Gen Suwa, and Berhane Asfaw
1994   *Australopithecus ramidus,* A New Species of Early Hominid from Aramis, Ethiopia. *Nature,* 371:306–312.

_____
1995   Corrigendum (White et al., 1994). *Nature,* 375:88.

Whiten, A., J. Goodall, W. C. McGrew, et al.
1999   "Cultures in Chimpanzees." *Nature,* 399:682–685.

Whyte, Robert Orr (ed.)
1984   "The Evolution of the East Asian Environment." Centre of Asian Studies Occasional Papers and Monographs, No. 59. Hong Kong: University of Hong Kong.

Wildman, Derek E., Monica Uddin, Guozhen Liu, et al.
2003   "Implications of Natural Selection in Shaping 99.4%
          Nonsynonymous DNA Identity Between Humans and
          Chimpanzees: Enlarging Genus *Homo*." *Proceedings of
          the National Academy of Sciences*, 100:7181–7188.
Williams, George C.
1957   "Pleiotropy, Natural Selection and the Evolution of
          Senescence." *Evolution*, 11:398–411.

_____

1966   *Adaptation and Natural Selection: A Critique of Some
          Current Evolutionary Thought.* Princeton: Princeton
          University Press.
Williams, George C. and Randolph M. Nesse
1991   The Dawn of Darwinian Medicine. *The Quarterly
          Review of Biology*, 66:1–22.
Williams, Robert C.
1985   "HLA II: The Emergence of the Molecular Model for
          the Major Histocompatibility Complex." *Yearbook of
          Physical Anthropology*, 1985, 28:79–95.
Wilson, E. O.
1975   *Sociobiology. The New Synthesis.* Cambridge: Harvard
          University Press.

_____

1992   *The Diversity of Life.* Cambridge, MA: The Belknap
          Press of Harvard University Press.

_____

2002   *The Future of Life.* New York: Alfred A. Knopf.
Wolf, Katherine and Steven Robert Schulman
1984   "Male Response to 'Stranger' Females as a Function of
          Female Reproduction Value among Chimpanzees." *The
          American Naturalist*, 123:163–174.
Wolpoff, Milford H.
1983a "Lucy's Little Legs." *Journal of Human Evolution*,
          12:443–453.

_____

1983b "*Ramapithecus* and Human Origins. An
          Anthropologist's Perspective of Changing
          Interpretations." *In:* R. L. Ciochon and R. S.
          Corruccini (eds.), q.v., pp. 651–676.

_____

1984   "Evolution in *Homo erectus:* The Question of Stasis."
          Paleobiology, 10:389–406.

_____

1989   "Multiregional Evolution: The Fossil Alternative to
          Eden." *In:* P. Mellars and C. Stringer, q.v., pp. 62–108.

_____

1995   *Human Evolution* 1996 Edition. New York: McGraw-
          Hill Inc, College Custom Series.

_____

1999   *Paleoanthropology.* 2nd ed. New York: McGraw-Hill.
Wolpoff, Milford H. et al.
1981   "Upper Pleistocene Human Remains from Vindija
          Cave, Croatia, Yugoslavia." *American Journal of
          Physical Anthropology*, 54:499–545.

_____

1994   "Multiregional Evolutions: A World-Wide Source for
          Modern Human Population." *In:* M. H. Nitecki and
          D. V. Nitecki (eds.), q.v., pp. 175–199.
Wolpoff, M., Wu Xin Chi, and Alan G. Thorne
1984   "Modern *Homo sapiens* Origins." *In:* Smith and
          Spencer (eds.), q.v., pp. 411–483.

Wolpoff, M. H., J. Hawks, D. Frayer, and K. Hunley
2001   "Modern Human Ancestry at the Peripheries: A Test of
          the Replacement Theory." *Science*, 291:293–297.
Wolpoff, Milford H., Brigitte Senut, Martin Pickford, and John
          Hawks
2002   "Palaeoanthropology (Communication Arising):
          Sahelanthropus or '*Salelpithecus*'"? *Nature*,
          419:581–582.
Wood, Bernard
1991   *Koobi Fora Research Project IV: Hominid Cranial
          Remains from Koobi Fora.* Oxford: Clarendon Press.

_____

1992a "Origin and Evolution of the Genus *Homo*." *Nature*,
          355:783–790.

_____

1992b "A Remote Sense for Fossils." *Nature*, 355:397–398.

_____

2002   "Hominid Revelations from Chad." News and Views.
          Nature, 418:133–135.
Wood Bernard and Mark Collard
1999(a) "The Human Genus." *Science*, 284:65–71.

_____

1999(b) "The Changing Face of Genus *Homo*." *Evolutionary
          Anthropology*, 8:195–207
Wood, B. C. Wood, and L. Konigsberg
1994   "*Paranthropus boisei:* An Example of Evolutionary
          Stasis?" *American Journal of Physical Anthropology*,
          95:117–136.
Wood, B. and B. G. Richmond
2000   "Human Evolution: Taxonomy and Paleobiology."
          Journal of Anatomy, 197:19–60.
Wood, C. S., G. A. Harrison, C. Dove, and J. S. Weiner
1972   "Selection Feeding of *Anopheles gambiae* According to
          ABO Blood Group Status." *Nature*, 239:165.
Wrangham, R. W.
1977   "Feeding Behaviour of Chimpanzees in Gombe
          National Park, Tanzania." *In: Primate Ecology*, T. H.
          Clutton-Brock (ed.). New York: Academic Press,
          pp. 503–538.

_____

1980   "An Ecological Model of Female-Bonded Primate
          Groups." *Behaviour*, 75:262–300.

_____

1986   "Ecology and Social Relationships in Two Species of
          Chimpanzees." *In: Ecology and Social Evolution: Birds
          and Mammals*, D. I. Rubenstein and R. W. Wrangham
          (eds.), Princeton: Princeton University Press, pp.
          352–378.

_____

1990   "An Ecological Model of Female-Bonded Primate
          Groups." *Behaviour*, 75:262-300.
Wrangham, Richard and Dale Peterson
1996   *Demonic Males: Apes and the Origins of Human
          Violence.* New York: Houghton Mifflin Co.
Wu, Rukang and S. Lin
1983   "Peking Man." *Scientific American*, 248(6):86–94.
Wu, Rukang and C. E. Oxnard
1983   "Ramapithecines from China: Evidence from Tooth
          Dimensions." *Nature*, 306:258–260.
Wu, Rukang and John W. Olsen (eds.)
1985   *Palaeoanthropology and Palaeolithic Archaeology in the
          People's Republic of China.* New York: Academic Press.

Wu, Rukang and Xingren Dong
  1985 "*Homo erectus* in China." *In: Palaeoanthropology and Palaeolithic Archaeology in the People's Republic of China,* R. Wu and J. W. Olsen (eds.), New York: Academic Press, pp. 79–89.

Wuehrich, Bernice
  1998 "Geological Analysis Damps Ancient Chinese Fires." *Science,* 28:165–166.

Yamei, Hon, Richard Potts, Yaun Baoyin, et al.
  2000 "Mid-Pleistocene Acheulean-like Stone Technology of the Bose Basin, South China." *Science,* 287:1622–1626.

Yanagimachi
  1998 "Full-term Development of Mice from Enucleated Oocytes Injected with Cumulus Cell Nuclei. *Nature,* 394:369–374.

Yellen, John E. et al.
  1995 "A Middle Stone Age Worked Bone Industry from Katanda, Upper Semliki Valley, Zaire." *Science,* 268:553–556.

Yi, Seonbok and G. A. Clark
  1983 "Observations on the Lower Palaeolithic of Northeast Asia." *Current Anthropology,* 24:181–202.

Young, David.
  1992 *The Discovery of Evolution.* Cambridge: Natural History Museum Publications, Cambridge University Press.

Yunis, Jorge J. and Om Prakesh
  1982 "The Origin of Man: A Chromosomal Pictorial Legacy." *Science,* 215:1525–1530.

Zhang, J., Y. Zhang, and H. E. Rosenberg
  2002 "Adaptive Evolution of a Duplicated Pancreatic Ribonuclease Gene in a Leaf-eating Monkey." *Nature Genetics,* 30:411–415.

Zhivotovsky, Lev A., Noah A. Rosenberg, and Marcus W. Feldman
  2003 "Features of Evolution and Expansion of Modern Humans, Inferred from Genomewide Microsatellite Markers." *American Journal of Human Genetics,* 72:1171–1186.

Zhou Min Zhen and Wang Yuan Quing
  1989 "Paleoenvironmental Contexts of Hominid Evolution in China." *Circum-Pacific Prehistory Conference,* Seattle: University of Washington Press.

Ziegler, A., A. S. Jonason, D. J. Leffellt, et al.
  1994 "Sunburn and p53 in the Onset of Skin Cancer." *Nature,* 372:773–776.

Zimmet, P., K. G. M. M. Alberti and Jonathan Shaw
  2001 "Global and Societal Implications of the Diabetes Epidemic." *Nature,* 414:782–787.

Zubrow, Ezra
  1989 "The Demographic Modeling of Neanderthal Extinction." *In: The Human Revolution,* P. Mellars and C. Stringer, Princeton, N.J.: Princeton University Press, pp. 212–231.

Photo Credits

This constitutes an extension of the copyright page. We have made every effort to trace the ownership of all copyrighted material and to secure permission from copyright holders. In the event of any question arising as to the use of any material, we will be pleased to make the necessary corrections in future printings. Thanks are due to the following authors, publishers, and agents for permission to use the material indicated.

1, Chapter opener, © Biophoto Associates/Photo Researchers, Inc.; 2, Fig. 1–1, Courtesy, Peter Jones; 3, Fig. 1–2, © Bettmann/CORBIS; 5, Fig. 1–3a–c, Lynn Kilgore; Fig. 1–3d, Robert Jurmain; 9, Fig. 1–4, © Kenneth Garrett/NGS Image Collection; Fig. 1–5, Lynn Kilgore; 10, Fig. 1–6a, Courtesy, L. G. Moore; Fig. 1–6b, Courtesy, Judith Regensteiner; Fig. 1–7, Courtesy, Kathleen Galvin; 11, Fig. 1–8, Robert Jurmain; Fig. 1–9, Courtesy, Bonnie Pedersen/Arlene Kruse; 12, Fig. 1–10a, Lynn Kilgore; Fig. 1–10b, Robert Jurmain; 13, Fig. 1–11a, Courtesy, Lorna Pierce/Judy Suchey; Fig. 1–11b, Provided by D. France; 14, Fig. 1–12, Courtesy, Linda Levitch; 26, Fig. 2–1, Courtesy, Dept. of Library Services, American Museum of Natural History; 22, Chapter opener, © Biophoto Associates/Photo Researchers, Inc.; 27, Fig. 2–2, Courtesy, Dept. of Library Services, American Museum of Natural History; Fig. 2–3, © Michael Nicholson/CORBIS; 28, Fig. 2–4, © Bettmann/CORBIS; 29, Fig. 2–6, Courtesy, Dept. of Library Services, American Museum of Natural History ; Fig. 2–7, Courtesy, Dept. of Library Services, American Museum of Natural History; 30, Fig. 2–8, Courtesy, Dept. of Library Services, American Museum of Natural History; Fig. 2–9, The Natural History Museum, London; 31, Fig. 2–10, © Bettmann/CORBIS; 32, Fig. 2–13, Lynn Kilgore; 33, Fig. 2–14, Wolf: John Giustina/Getty Images; Dogs surrounding wolf: Lynn Kilgore and Lin Marshall; 34, Fig. 2–15, Courtesy of Down House and The Royal College of Surgeons of England; 36, Fig. 2–16a, Michael Tweedie/Photo Researchers; Fig. 2–16b, Breck P. Kent/Animals Animals; 44, Chapter opener, © Biophoto Associates/Photo Researchers, Inc.; 47, Fig. 3–2, A. Barrington Brown,/Photo Researchers, Inc.; 50, Fig. 1, The Novartis Foundation; 57, Fig. 3–7a, b, © Dr. Stanley Flegler/Visuals Unlimited; 59, Fig. 3–10, Biophoto Associates/Science Source/Photo Researchers; 61, Fig. 3–12, Ifti Ahmed; 68, Fig. 3–16, Cellmark Diagnostics, Abingdon, UK; Fig. 3–17, Roslind Institute/PA Photos Limited; 69, Fig. 3–18, Courtesy of Advanced Cell Technology, Inc., Worcester, Massachusetts; 74, Chapter opener, © Biophoto Associates/Photo Researchers, Inc.; 75, Fig. 4–1, Raychel Ciemma and Precision Graphics; 89, Fig. 4–13c, Courtesy, Ray Carson, University of Florida News and Public Affairs; 89, Fig. 4–14a, Corbis; Fig. 4–14b, Lynn Kilgore; Fig. 4–14c, Corbis; Fig. 4–14d; Lynn Kilgore; Fig. 4–14e, Lynn Kilgore; Fig. 4–14f, Lynn Kilgore; Fig. 4–14g, Robert Jurmain; 93, Reprinted, with permission, from the *Annual Review of Genetics,* Volume 10 ©1976 by Annual Reviews, www.annualreviews.org; 104, Fig. 1, Courtesy, Margaret Maples; inset, ©Bettmann/CORBIS; 106, Fig. 2, Craig King, Armed Forces DNA Identification Laboratory; 107, Chapter opener, © Biophoto Associates/Photo Researchers, Inc.; 128, Fig. 5–12, Hansejudy Beste/Animals Animals; Fig. 5–13, J. C. Stevenson/Animals Animals; 135, Fig. 1, Courtesy, John Oates; Fig. 2, Karl Ammann; 139, Fig. 6–1a–e,Lynn Kilgore; 137, Chapter opener, Ryan McVay/Getty Images; 142, Fig. 1, Lynn Kilgore; 143, Fig. 2, 3a, b, Lynn Kilgore; 146, Fig. 6–4 (Howler species), Raymond Mendez/Animals Animals; (Spider and woolly monkeys), Robert L. Lubeck/Animals Animals; (Prince Bernhard's titi), Marc van Roosmalen; (Marmosets and tamarins), © Zoological Society of San Diego, photo by Ron Garrison; (Muriqui), Andrew Young; (White-faced capuchins), © Jay Dickman/CORBIS; (Squirrel monkeys), © Kevin Schafer/CORBIS; (Uakari), R. A. Mittermeier/Conservation International; 147, Fig. 6–4 (Baboon species), Courtesy, Bonnie Pedersen/Arlene Kruse; (Macaque species), Courtesy, Jean De Rousseau; (Gibbons and siamangs), Lynn Kilgore; (Tarsier species), David Haring, Duke University Primate Zoo; (Orangutans), © Tom McHugh/Photo Researchers, Inc.; (Colobus species) Robert Jurmain; (Galagos), Courtesy, Bonnie Pedersen/Arlene Kruse; (Chimpanzees and bonobos), Courtesy, Arlene Kruse/Bonnie Pedersen; (Mountain and lowland gorillas), Lynn Kilgore; (*Cercopithecus* species), Robert Jurmain; (Loris species), Courtesy, San Francisco Zoo; (Langur species), Joe MacDonald/Animals Animals; (Lemurs), Courtesy, Fred Jacobs; 149, Fig. 6–5a–d, Stephen D. Nash; 154, Fig. 6–11, Courtesy, Fred Jacobs; Fig. 6–12, Courtesy, Fred Jacobs; 155, Fig. 6–13, Courtesy, San Francisco Zoo; Fig. 6–14, Courtesy, Bonnie Pedersen/Arlene Kruse; Fig. 6–15, David Haring, Duke University Primate Zoo; 156, Fig. 6–17, (Squirrel monkeys), © Kevin Schafer/CORBIS; (Prince Bernhard's titi), Marc van Roosmalen; (Uakari), R. A. Mittermeier/Conservation International; (Muriqui), Andrew Young; (White-faced capuchins), © Jay Dickman/CORBIS; 157, Fig. 6–18, © Zoological Society of San Diego, photo by Ron Garrison; Fig. 6–19, Raymond Mendez/Animals Animals; 158, Fig. 6–21, Robert L. Lubeck/Animals Animals; 159, Fig. 6–23, Robert Jurmain; Fig. 6–24a, Courtesy, Bonnie Pedersen/Arlene Kruse; Fig. 6–24b, Courtesy, Bonnie Pedersen/Arlene Kruse; Fig. 6–25, Lynn Kilgore; 161, Fig. 6–27, Lynn Kilgore; 162, Fig. 6–28, Robert Jurmain, photo by Jill Matsumoto/Jim Anderson; 162, Fig. 6–30a, b, Lynn Kilgore; 163, Fig. 6–31a, b, Lynn Kilgore; 164, Fig. 6–32a, b, Robert Jurmain, photo by Jill Matsumoto/Jim Anderson; 165, Fig. 6–33, Courtesy, Ellen Ingmanson; 172, Chapter opener, Ryan McVay/Getty Images; 174, Fig. 7–1a, Courtesy, Jean De Rousseau; Fig. 7–1b, Courtesy, John Oates; 176, Fig. 7–2, Russ Mittermeir; 178, Fig. 7–3, Lynn Kilgore; 181, Fig. 7–4, Courtesy, John Oates; 182, Fig. 7–5, Time Life Pictures/Getty Images; 184, Fig. 7–6a, © Chris Hellier/CORBIS; Fig. 7–6b, © Theo Allofs/CORBIS; 186, Fig. 7–7, Lynn Kilgore; Fig. 7–8, Lynn Kilgore; 189, Fig. 7–10a, Robert Jurmain; Fig. 7–10b, Courtesy, Meredith Small; Fig. 7–10c, Courtesy, Arlene Kruse/Bonnie Pedersen; Fig. 7–10d, Courtesy, Arlene Kruse/Bonnie Pedersen; 190, Fig. 7–11, Lynn Kilgore; 191, Fig. 7–12, Joe MacDonald/Animals Animals; 192, Fig. 7–13, © Peter Henzi; 194, Fig. 7–14a, Courtesy, David Haring, Duke University Primate Center; Fig. 7–14b, Courtesy, Arlene Kruse/Bonnie Pedersen; Fig. 7–14c, Robert Jurmain; Fig. 7–14d, © Tom McHugh/Photo Researchers, Inc.; Fig. 7–14e, Robert Jurmain; 195, Fig. 7–15, Harlow Primate Laboratory, University of Wisconsin; Fig. 7–16, Lynn Kilgore; 200, Chapter

Index

World Political Map